BETWEEN TWO FIRES

OTHER BOOKS BY DAVID C. LARGE

WAGNERISM IN EUROPEAN CULTURE AND POLITICS
(COEDITOR)

THE POLITICS OF LAW AND ORDER:
A HISTORY OF THE BAVARIAN *"EINWOHNERWEHR,"* 1918–1921

BETWEEN TWO FIRES

Europe's Path in the 1930s

DAVID CLAY LARGE

W·W·NORTON & COMPANY
New York · London

Excerpt from the *London Times*, "Guernica,"
by George L. Steer, April 28, 1937.
© Times Newspapers Limited

First published as a Norton paperback 1991

The text of this book is composed in Avanta, with display type set in Novarese.
Composition and manufacturing by the Haddon Craftsmen, Inc.
Book design by Jacques Chazaud.

Library of Congress Cataloging-in-Publication Data
Large, David Clay.
Between two fires: Europe's path in the 1930s / by
David Clay Large.—1st ed.
p. cm.
Includes index.
1. Europe—History—1918–1945. I. Title.
D720.L34 1990
940.5—dc19   89–3125

ISBN 0-393-30757-3

W. W. Norton & Company, Inc., 500 Fifth Avenue, New York, N.Y. 10110
W. W. Norton & Company Ltd, 10 Coptic Street, London WC1A 1PU

7 8 9 0

To Margaret

Contents

Maps

Photographs appear following pages 33, 69, 113, 149, 191, 235, 277, 329

Acknowledgments

For their generous assistance with the research for this book, I would like to thank the staffs of the following institutions: Bayerische Staatsbibliothek, Munich; Bibliothèque Nationale, Paris; British Library, London; University of California Library, Berkeley; Central Library, South Shields, England; Österreichische Nationalbibliothek, Vienna; Sterling Library, Yale University; Widener Library, Harvard University; Interlibrary Loan Department, Montana State University.

I am grateful to Dr. John Jutila, vice-president for research at Montana State University, for assistance in defraying the costs of securing photographs.

My thanks, too, to the friends and colleagues who read parts of the original manuscript and made useful suggestions for improvement. They include Edward Barry, George Behlmer, Don Clark, Felix Gilbert, Klemens von Klemperer, Michelle Maskiell, John Merriman, Carol Payne, Billy G. Smith, and Henry A. Turner.

My editor at W. W. Norton, Steven Forman, encouraged this project at the outset and deftly guided it to its conclusion.

Finally, I owe more than I can say to my wife, Margaret, who assisted me in my research, read all the chapters and improved my prose, helped me lug trunks of books and papers around Europe, and put up with my cantankerous moods during the long gestation of this project.

Introduction

In *Les Misérables* (1862), Victor Hugo confidently predicts that the "twentieth century shall be happy," since the European peoples, having "perfected" themselves in the author's own time, will in the next century eat fully of the fruits of historical progress. From our own vantage point near the end of the twentieth century, we know that Hugo's prediction was rather off the mark. Europe in this century, for all its material and scientific advances, has not been on the whole a "happy" place. Its peoples have suffered through two protracted wars of unprecedented destructive power, the second accompanied by a genocidal terror rendered all the more thorough by the industrial progress Hugo thought would yield only increasing happiness.

Yet if the two great wars brought misery and devastation to much of Europe, the period between the cataclysms was certainly no oasis of tranquillity. This was especially true of the second interwar decade, the 1930s, which began with the onset of the Great Depression, witnessed the maturation of two aggressive dictatorships—Mussolini's Italy and Stalin's Russia—and the rise of another, Hitler's Germany. In the mid-thirties Europe's surviving democracies struggled with only partial success to control political turmoil at home and with virtually no success to contain the ambitions of the rising dictatorships abroad. All in all, this was an era of parliamentary impotence and corruption, civil war, colonial war, purges, and putsches—a period when the reek of blood competed with the stink of poverty and when much of Europe engaged in a kind of dress rehearsal for the greater cataclysm to come. No wonder W. H. Auden called the 1930s the "low dishonest decade" and the "rotten decade," while others spoke of the Devil's Decade, the

Pink Decade, the Decade of the Dictators, the Hungry Thirties, the Threadbare Thirties. In retrospect it seems entirely appropriate that Sigmund Freud wrote his most pessimistic book, *Civilization and Its Discontents,* on the eve of that unhappy era.

Between Two Fires illuminates this chaotic period by examining eight episodes of key significance for the history of Europe in the twentieth century. Its guiding premise is that this era, like other momentous periods, is most clearly and vividly brought to life by intimate "portraits" of exemplary events that occurred within it. Each of the chapters, with the exception of those on Italy's invasion of Ethiopia and the Munich conference, focuses on a single country. The episodes in question, however, were significant not only for the countries in which they took place but also in their broader implications beyond national boundaries. Of course, they do not, even when taken together, tell the whole story of the 1930s, and another historian might have chosen different events to get at the essence of that troubled decade. I selected these topics not only because of their seeming centrality to the period but because of their inherent interest. They afforded the stuff of a good story, and putting the "story" back into history has been one of my main concerns in writing this book.

The opening chapter explores the Stavisky affair in France. Serge Stavisky was a Parisian confidence man of Russian-Jewish origins who enjoyed the protection of high government officials. When his fraudulent financial empire collapsed, in late 1933, the ensuing scandal provoked bloody rioting by Communists and royalist-Fascist groups who maintained that the affair revealed the rottenness of France's parliamentary system. Like the Dreyfus affair some forty years earlier, when Frenchmen fought duels over the fate of a Jewish army officer accused of spying for the Germans, the Stavisky scandal generated widespread outbreaks of racism and social strife. Once again, self-professed "patriots" and defenders of "ancient French civilization" claimed that their nation was under attack by "parasitic aliens" bent upon sucking the country dry. Though the Third Republic weathered this crisis, France remained deeply divided against itself for the rest of the decade. The nation's latent civil war undermined its capacity to deal resolutely or efficiently with its foreign challengers, particularly Nazi Germany. The result was France's "strange defeat" in 1940, the installation of the collaborationist Vichy regime in the unoccupied part of the country, and a new—this time less latent—civil war between Vichy loyalists and members of the resistance.

The Stavisky affair is a very French story, but the political weaknesses it exposed and exacerbated were not confined to France. Corruption in high places, parliamentary ineptitude and irresponsibility, extremist attacks on the center— these were afflictions that plagued most European democracies in the twenties and thirties. The Stavisky affair was emblematic of a broader erosion of democratic values and institutions in post–World War I Europe.

Among the prominent victims of this corrosive process was Austria, whose authoritarian leader in the early thirties, Chancellor Engelbert Dollfuss, suspended constitutional government in 1933 and a year later waged a brief war against his socialist rivals that ended all chances for a return to parliamentary rule. My second chapter chronicles the bloody progress of this conflict and shows how it left the Austrian republic—as the Stavisky affair left France—internally weakened in the face of monumental pressures from abroad. The Austrian civil war and its aftermath pointed up a cluster of sociopolitical problems with implications reaching far beyond the borders of this small republic: it illustrated the precariousness of the new "successor states" created in the wake of the First World War; the tendency for old hostilities—class, regional, and religious—to assume new virulence in the face of severe economic distress and international pressure; the militarization of politics and the displacement of parties by party armies; and, finally, the inability or unwillingness of the strongest European democracies, Great Britain and France, to uphold the postwar treaty system and maintain the political balance of power.

Nazi Germany, which annexed Austria in 1938, had from the moment Adolf Hitler assumed power in 1933 shown little regard for established political conventions or the rule of law. Nowhere was the Nazis' contempt for these principles more sharply revealed than in the "Blood Purge" of June 1934, when Hitler and his top henchmen ordered black-shirted SS units to liquidate dozens of allegedly rebellious leaders of the brown-shirted SA, along with a number of conservatives who had fallen afoul of the Nazi regime. Hitler used this purge to ingratiate himself with the army leadership, which had long regarded the radical, rabble-rousing SA as a dangerous rival. He was thus able to consolidate his power within Germany in preparation for his campaign to overthrow the postwar treaty system, expand the Reich's "living space," and solve once and for all the "Jewish problem." Western diplomats and statesmen were generally shocked by Hitler's brutal action but could not or would not see its true implications. Rather, they hoped that Hitler would become more "reasonable" now that he had "disciplined" his unruly movement. Misperceptions like this helped justify the Western powers' infamous "appeasement" policy, by which Britain and France sought to prevent a new war with Germany. On the other hand, Hitler's Russian counterpart, Joseph Stalin, understood full well what Hitler had done in 1934 and sought to emulate—and outdo—the führer with his own Great Purge of the mid-1930s.

Like Stalin, Benito Mussolini drew inspiration from Hitler's example, though he took this lesson in a different direction. Plagued since his "March on Rome" in 1922 by chronic dissension among his followers and a disconcerting lack of Fascist zeal among the Italian people, he sought to consolidate his power, toughen his nation, and demonstrate Italian greatness through colonial conquest and the establishment of a new Roman empire. His primary target in this enterprise was another empire, the Ethiopian empire of Negus Haile Selassie in the Horn of Africa. In October 1935 Italy invaded Ethiopia in the expectation of a quick victory over this "primitive" tribal state. Yet it took the Italian forces ten months to overcome Ethiopian resistance, during which time Italy resorted to massive terror bombing and the employment of poison gas. Before Mussolini could complete his "civilizing mission" in Africa, Emperor Haile Selassie formally requested the League of Nations in Geneva to intercede in the conflict on Ethiopia's behalf. But the League, under the domination of the western European democracies, agreed only to impose limited sanctions against Italy. This half measure did not deter Mussolini; it only angered him. In his indignation he abandoned his earlier commitment to help the Western powers contain Germany and instead began to court Hitler. Soon Italy would cooperate with Germany in the Spanish civil war, then join the Reich in trying to conquer all of Europe in World War II. My discussion of Italy's Ethiopian venture will illustrate how Mussolini's campaign to find "a place in the sun" helped make Europe the true Dark Continent of the 1930s and early 1940s: it emboldened both Fascist dictators, exposed the impotence of the League of Nations, and demonstrated the kind of terror warfare that Europeans themselves would soon experience in their major cities.

The Western democracy that both Mussolini and Hitler most feared, most expected to oppose their expansionist ambitions, was Great Britain. In reality Britain was quite unprepared to keep the Fascist powers in their place. Of the many reasons for this, one of the most important was economic stringency. Economically weakened by the First World War, then further crippled by the Great Depression of the early thirties, Britain believed that it had to choose between a balanced economy maintained through reduced military outlays, on the one hand, and larger armaments and a bankrupt economy, on the other. Electing to avoid bankruptcy, Britain pursued a foreign policy designed to obviate the need for greater arms expenditures.

The depression that prompted this choice hit hardest in the old industrial sectors of mining, steelmaking, and shipbuilding. Dozens of steel plants and shipbuilding yards were forced to close; unemployment levels soared. My chapter on Britain lends concrete meaning to the bleak statistics of Britain's decline in these sectors by focusing on unemployment in the industrial northeast, and more precisely on the town of Jarrow, whose once-thriving shipbuilding yards were shut down in the early thirties. In October 1936 two hundred men from Jarrow embarked on a march to London to protest the closing of their shipyard and to demand government assistance in the resuscitation of industry in Jarrow. This "Jarrow crusade" generated a great deal of publicity partly because its leader, "Red Ellen" Wilkinson, the town's MP, was one of the most colorful and dynamic figures in British politics. She and her hardy constituents ensured that the Jarrow crusade would become a vivid symbol of Britain's economic malaise in the thirties—indeed, an abiding symbol of its long-term decline as an industrial power.

Although the Jarrow crusade's central focus was mass unemployment in Britain, its leaders, particularly Ellen Wilkinson, were also concerned about the latest political crisis on the foreign horizon, namely, the Spanish civil war. This war, the bloody culmination of long-standing class and regional antagonisms, was filled with atrocities as Spaniards massacred Spaniards and foreigners from all over the world descended on Spain to put their competing ideologies (and new weapons) to the test of war. For contemporaries and later generations alike, one atrocity in particular came to symbolize this horrifying war: the destruction of the Basque town of Guernica by German and Italian aircraft in April 1937. Though the bombing of this historic town, filled with civilians and lacking antiaircraft defenses, shocked public opinion around the world, it did not prompt the Western democracies to revise their policy of "nonintervention" in Spain. On the contrary, by demonstrating the destructive capacity of modern air warfare, this atrocity made western European leaders all the more determined to avoid any confrontation that might bring similar scenes to their countries.

For the Basque people the destruction of Guernica, site of their ancient parliament and symbol of their traditional autonomy, provided more evidence of Nationalist Spain's determination to crush their unique culture and regionalist aspirations. For the rest of the war, and indeed throughout the Franco period and beyond, Basque separatists made "Guernica" their battle cry in their campaign to create an independent Basque state. My discussion of the Guernica affair explores not just the bombing but also the ways in which this event was represented (and misrepresented) by contemporary commentators and politicians. It illustrates how the Spanish civil war, like most twentieth-century wars, was a war of words and images as well as of bullets and bombs.

The only foreign power that intervened directly in the Spanish civil war on the side of the Madrid government was Soviet Russia. But Russia's assistance fell far short of what was needed to defeat the Nationalist insurgents and their foreign supporters. One of the reasons for this was the preoccupation of the Soviet dictator, Joseph Stalin, with a pressing domestic concern: his Great Purge of allegedly traitorous elements in the Soviet Union. Although Stalin's purges of the middle to late 1930s may have been inspired partly by Hitler's "Blood Purge" of 1934, they were vastly more thorough and far-reaching. Indeed, they constitute the twentieth century's most horrifying example of a revolution's "eating its children." My discussion of this affair focuses on the Stalin regime's three public "show trials" of prominent Old Bolsheviks and its liquidation, after secret hearings, of much of the Red Army leadership. I examine Stalin's motives for launching the purges, the brutal process through which "confessions" were extracted from the defendants, the foreign response to the trials and executions, and, finally, the devastating effect of this internecine bloodletting on Russia's strength and coherence as a nation. We see that when it came to the Kafkaesque world of modern political terror—a central theme of European life in the 1930s—Stalin's purges were horrifying not only in their scope, but in their arbitrariness, their lack of apparent rhyme or reason.

One immediate effect of the Stalinist purges was Soviet Russia's increased estrangement from the Western democracies, which saw this internal butchery as further evidence of Russia's unreliability and dangerous volatility. Stalin was not invited to the Munich conference of 1938, where the British prime minister, Neville Chamberlain, bought "peace for our time" by ceding Hitler the ethnic-German Sudetenland, in Czechoslovakia. The Munich conference was the last major attempt by the West to keep the peace by "appeasing" the Fascist powers, particularly Nazi Germany. It provides a useful closing episode in this study because the issues confronting its four participating nations—Britain, France, Italy, and Germany—had been central to European politics for the past two decades. The Sudeten problem was a legacy of the postwar territorial settlement that established fragile successor states made up of mutually hostile ethnic groups. The Western powers' willingness to purchase peace at the expense of Czechoslovakia, which Chamberlain called "that faraway land," was also a legacy of the Great War: namely, of the West's determination not to let another "minor power" become the cause of a new world conflict. Another influence on the Munich agreement was the Western leaders' perennial fear of the Soviet Union, their conviction that another major war would benefit only Russia and leave "the Cossacks ruling Europe."

The chapters in this volume vary considerably in focus, but taken together they raise three broad issues central to European politics in the 1930s.

The first is the preeminence of domestic factors in shaping foreign policy. The leading western European democracies, France and Britain, were so afflicted with internal political and economic ailments that they were cautious and irresolute in foreign affairs. Austria's internecine battles contributed to its dependence on foreign "supporters" like Italy and Hungary and ultimately undermined whatever chances it might have had to remain independent from Germany. In the Spanish civil war both the Nationalists and the Republicans called upon outsiders to "save" Spain, but the foreign powers that answered this call turned the conflict into a devastating rehearsal for World War II. Stalin's great purge in the Soviet Union increased Russia's isolation from the West, paved the way for its deadly embrace with Nazi Germany in 1939, and finally ensured an almost fatally weak response to the German invasion two years later. In the two Fascist states, on the other hand, internal insecurities and turmoil helped inspire campaigns of external aggression designed to smooth over the fissures that rent these self-proclaimed "monolithic" powers.

Words like *turmoil* and *aggression* point up a second leitmotiv in European politics during the 1930s: the pervasive recourse to violence as a way of "solving" complex political and social problems. With the exception of the Jarrow crusade and the Munich conference, all of the episodes treated in this book were violent, sometimes breathtakingly so. The Jarrow case is instructive in this sense because it helps us understand why Britain, though hardly immune to violent confrontations, did not succumb to parliamentary collapse, civil war, or outright revolution during the terribly trying times of the Great Depression. As for the Munich conference, its participants may not have actually exchanged blows, but their agreement guaranteed the triumph of violence in Czechoslovakia and, ultimately, in Europe as a whole.

This pervasive recourse to violence in the thirties was partly a function of the disintegration of the moderate center in most European countries, England again being the prominent exception. As the center fell apart, the emboldened extremes often "touched"—perversely collaborated in devastating assaults on weakened "bourgeois-liberal" institutions and values. As early as 1920 William Butler Yeats had foreseen this trend: "Things fall apart; the center cannot hold," he wrote. And he asked, even more prophetically, "And what rough beast, its hour come round at last, / Slouches towards Bethlehem to be born?" A decade or so later, Europe would have the full answer.

Although the sociopolitical problems addressed in this book reached crisis proportions in the 1930s, they had their origins in earlier periods: in the twenties, the First World War, and the waning decades of the nineteenth century. Government corruption, parliamentary weakness, class and regional animosities, economic dislocations, racism, charismatic leadership, ideologically charged politics—these phenomena characterized the scene in many European countries in the late nineteenth and early twentieth centuries. They also persisted to varying degrees beyond the "rotten decade" and the war that emerged from it. William Faulkner once observed that the past is never dead, is never entirely "past" at all. Certainly this seems true of the 1930s, that "no man's land between two fires" whose ghosts remain to haunt us today.

BETWEEN TWO FIRES

Move then with new desires,
For where we used to build and love
Is no man's land, and only ghosts can live
Between two fires

—C. Day Lewis, "The Conflict"

I

"DOWN WITH
THE ROBBERS!"

The Stavisky Affair and the Twilight of
the Third Republic in France

> The citizen is free to do whatever he likes, but under police
> supervision.
>
> —Yves Guyot, *La Police* (1884)

"Stavisky Ends Life as Police Trap Him," ran a headline in the *New York Times* on January 9, 1934. The article went on to describe how Alexander Stavisky, a notorious Parisian confidence man on the lam from the law for some two weeks, had shot himself in the head at a lonely ski chalet in the French Alps just as the police were about to arrest him. The case was significant because Stavisky was not an ordinary con man. He had ties to some of the most powerful men in French politics and had worked as a police informer. He had been shielded from prosecution on many occasions by judicial officials. His most recent fraudulent dealings had implicated several parliamentary deputies and a cabinet minister. Could he have had even more highly placed accomplices? Why had it taken the police so long to find him? Why had he killed himself when he faced at most a prison term? "There are countless unanswered questions in this scandal," concluded the *Times*.

Indeed there were, and one of them was whether Stavisky had killed himself at all. Many Frenchmen immediately assumed that the police had murdered him because he either "knew too much" or was attempting to conduct his business without the traditional police supervision. The case quickly became a symbol of official corruption—a byword for the "rottenness" of the entire governmental and judicial system in republican France. The antirepublican Right, in particular, saw it as confirmation of its belief that the Third Republic was a "slut" who could regain her virtue only through the imposition of an authoritarian government.

As the affair took on momentum with more revelations, royalist and Fascist "leagues" took to the streets of Paris to protest against the government. The Left responded with its own violent demonstrations and a massive general strike. For a few days in February 1934 the French capital looked as it had during the revolution of 1848 or the commune of 1871: makeshift barricades blocked the streets; mobs threw stones and bricks at police and attacked government buildings. The question of the hour was whether France's parliamentary system would survive at all.

Survive it did, but as a deeply discredited and divided entity that was hardly in a position to address resolutely the many challenges that faced France in the middle to late thirties. The most pressing threat came from Nazi Germany, and France's failure to meet it either diplomatically or militarily was at least partly the result of its internal weaknesses. Given what one historian has called "the virtual French civil war of the mid-1930s," that nation's "strange defeat" in June 1940 was perhaps not so strange after all.

THE BAYONNE BOND FRAUD

The year 1933 was not a good one for France. It had begun with Hitler's appointment as chancellor in neighboring Germany, a development that signaled a new and much more ominous phase in Germany's campaign for the dissolution of the postwar treaty system designed to hold Germany in check. Most Frenchmen wished that the "shackles" of the Versailles treaty had bound the Germans more firmly than they did; Hitler's promise to cast them off altogether terrified a nation that had vivid memories of German armies sweeping across northeastern France, leaving desolation and misery in their wake.

The past year had also seen the widening world depression catch up with France, which because of its less industrialized economy had at first largely escaped the crippling repercussions of the great American crash. During the winter, prices of agricultural goods began to drop precipitously; then the program of government-subsidized rents collapsed, and people started withdrawing their savings from banks. The savings withdrawals were a result of growing unemployment: at the end of 1933 the *Official Journal* registered 350,000 without work, but one unofficial estimate put the figure at 1,700,000. Whatever the exact numbers, long lines of people now stood outside the gates of the barracks in Paris hoping to beg a scap of food from the soldiers.

Most Frenchmen hoped their government might take energetic measures to remedy the growing economic dislocation, but the French politicians of 1933 were no more energetic or capable than they had been at any other period since the war. Nor were the recent governments more stable. Premiers and cabinet ministers played their usual game of musical chairs, while parliament, that "talking shop," babbled away in a vacuum of political irresponsibility. No wonder a few Parisian bars began displaying signs saying, "No deputies served here!"

The Christmas holidays offered no respite from the gloom. The weather was even nastier than usual at this time of year: cold fogs descended on Paris, rendering the "City of Light" about as radiant as London. On one of these dark, foggy nights the Paris–Strasbourg *rapide* smashed into the Nancy express at Lagny, twenty-five miles east of Paris. First reports said that 80 people were killed in the grinding crash and subsequent fire that enveloped the trains. Within a couple of days the toll had climbed to 219 dead and about 300 injured, some of them so seriously that they would spend the rest of their lives like the ubiquitous war *mutilés* who propelled themselves along on little carts through the streets of Paris.

Newspaper accounts spoke of heroic deeds by some of the passengers, but more frequently (and more graphically) of twisted bodies, severed limbs, and pillagers rifling the pockets of the dead. The Parisian press demanded account-ability: Who were the negligent parties who had allowed such an accident to occur? Was it just a confused switchman, an inebriated engineer, or, more likely, some highly placed functionary who had scrimped on safety procedures, perhaps personally pocketing some of the funds designated for such purposes? The search for an elevated hook upon which to hang this tragedy exercised Parisians for the rest of the year; but predictably enough, it seemed to many, no major official was ever called to account. The Lagny disaster added greatly to the popular conviction that "something was rotten in the Republic of France."

Preoccupied with countless newspaper stories about the Lagny accident, Pari-sians understandably paid little attention to a news report on December 24 that the manager of the municipal pawnshop in provincial Bayonne apparently could not cover the value of some of the public bonds issued under the aegis of his institution.* If this was—as the monarchist paper *L'Action française*† insisted a few days later—"Another Republican Scandal," then it would have to be a major scandal indeed to arouse the interest, let alone the indignation, of a people who had more pressing concerns and to whom financial scandal was hardly new.

The French, claimed the British historian J. E. C. Bodley in 1897, oddly insisted on associating "purity of morals with the Republican form of govern-ment, for which history furnishes no justification." The history of the French Third Republic certainly furnished no such justification. Not long after the re-public was founded, in 1870, in the midst of military defeat and revolution, Daniel Wilson, a son-in-law of President Charles Grévy, was discovered to be selling national decorations, including the coveted Legion of Honor, to ambitious senators and generals. This aroused a great deal of patriotic breast-beating in a nation whose recent humiliation at the hands of the Germans made people very sensitive about national dignity. Despite threats of insurrection, President Grévy

---

*In France, city-run pawnshops were authorized to float short-term public bonds on the open market. The shops' pawned articles served as security for the bonds.

†*L'Action française* was published by a royalist political party of the same name. This organization initially gained prominence through its vitriolic campaign against Captain Alfred Dreyfus, the Jewish army officer accused unjustly of spying for the Germans. The Action Française, indeed, helped turn this case into a divisive "affair" that shook France to its foundations in the late nineteenth and early twentieth centuries.

refused to resign. He was finally forced out of office in favor of Sadi Carnot, said to have been chosen for his "perfect insignificance."*

Within five years of the Wilson imbroglio the so-called Panama Canal scandal (1891–92) revealed that a good portion of the nation's legislators were on the take, selling their votes and protection to shady businessmen who were bilking thousands of small investors out of their life savings. The financier responsible for raising funds for France's abortive Panama Canal project was a German Jew named Baron Jacques de Reinach. He was close to the dominant bourgeois party of the time, which appropriately enough called itself the Opportunist party. Reinach quickly became the target of a vicious anti-Semitic campaign, which broadened to include the republic itself when the baron suddenly died in mysterious circumstances. Although the official explanation of his death was "cerebral congestion," many suspected that he had been murdered by political accomplices who wanted him out of the way.

Of course, the Opportunist politicians involved in the Panama Canal scandal had no more been the first politicians to sell their protection than Daniel Wilson had been the first functionary to sell a medal. When one of the Panama culprits was accused of dishonesty, he replied, "What I have done all politicians worthy of the name have done before me." No doubt the note of injured pride was justified here, as was the contention, voiced recently by a historian of modern France, that most of these scandals occurred when the normal system of petty graft and kickbacks got out of hand because of "excessive zeal, righteousness or carelessness."

Financial misdealing involving highly placed politicians continued after World War I, whose victorious outcome had the effect of confirming France's previous political system with all its attendant abuses. Among these was the unwillingness of the wealthier citizens to tax themselves adequately to pay the nation's debts, which as a result of the war were enormous. France's hope was that the defeated Boche might be made to pay for the entire war, thus relieving the country of the need to make painful financial reforms or sacrifices. Failing in this ambition, the French government turned to the printing press, an expedient that soon undermined the value of the franc.

The country's financial dilemma was compounded by mismanagement of its significant resources. The first postwar minister of finance, Louis-Lucien Klotz, whom Georges Clemenceau called "the only Jew who knew nothing about money," was indeed spectacularly incompetent. He bungled first France's finances, then his own; in 1928 he was arrested for writing bad checks.

In the same year a lady by the name of Martha Hanau was accused of having swindled hundreds of investors through an array of shady schemes. With the help of some important political friends, however, Madame Hanau was able to delay her trial repeatedly. It took seven years to get her convicted, during which time

*France's great First World War leader Georges Clemenceau is alleged to have said, "We will vote for the most stupid!" on the occasion of Carnot's election.

she was in and out of investigative detention. When she was finally sent away for a long prison sentence, she cheated the system one last time by committing suicide in her cell.

Two years after Madame Hanau first made headlines, France was treated to its biggest financial-political scandal since the one involving the Panama Canal: the so-called Oustric affair. Oustric was a Parisian banker who had a reputation for sailing very close to the wind. His skills had attracted the attention of Premier Aristide Briand's minister of finance, Raoul Paret, who in 1926 authorized him to float some overvalued Italian stocks on the Paris bourse. In the following year Paret became Oustric's lawyer, while a former French ambassador to Rome, René Besnard, who had also assisted in the Italian stock transaction, found a comfortable position in an Oustric subsidiary. The addition of this governmental expertise did not prevent the Oustric bank from collapsing in 1930, taking with it another legion of small investors. A judicial inquiry was called for, but Paret, having since become minister of justice, promptly ordered a cover-up. Eventually the French senate conducted an internal disciplinary proceeding against Paret and Besnard. The men were found guilty of moral turpitude but not of any crime, a verdict that no doubt reflected some of the senators' understanding that a confusion of these two categories would put them all behind bars. The French public, however, was not attuned to these sophisticated nuances. Once again the cry went up that the republic was a "whore" and that her political procurers deserved at least a long stretch in prison, if not a shorter one from the nearest lamppost. Some segments of the Parisian public, on the other hand, had become so inured to financial corruption that they hardly bothered to protest. According to Simone de Beauvoir, the group of left-wing intellectuals around Jean-Paul Sartre was not terribly exercised about Oustric. "Vast financial scandals did not shake us," she wrote, "since for us capitalism and corruption were synonymous terms."

Coming so soon after the Hanau and Oustric affairs, the news about the Bayonne pawnshop's financial embarrassment hardly seemed the stuff of major scandal. To Beauvoir and her friends, it was "an unremarkable enough business at first," certainly not shocking enough to pull them away from their books and amorous intrigues. Even the Parisian press, which habitually made the most of every bit of muck it could rake from the republican gutter, gave the story only passing notice.

One paper, however, proved to be an exception. This was L'Action française, which, as we have seen, immediately pounced on the "republican scandal." In the last week of December 1933 L'Action française hammered away at the Bayonne incident while other papers still concentrated on the Lagny tragedy. The editors seemed to sense that there was more here than a bit of provincial skulduggery, that this might be as far-reaching a scandal as the Panama affair, a perfect political club with which to beat the republic.

Soon other, less militantly ideological, papers followed L'Action française's lead. On January 1, for example, Le Petit Parisien reported that the Bayonne pawnshop manager, a certain Tissier, had confessed to extensive fraudulence in the conduct of his agency's operations. He had issued millions of francs' worth of bonds on the security of pawned articles that either were greatly overvalued or had even disappeared. He had apparently hoped that by the time the bonds had matured he could redeem them from the profits he had earned by investing his ill-gotten millions. Unfortunately for him, an insurance company that held about eight million francs' worth of the Bayonne bonds had become belatedly suspicious about its holding and demanded an accounting. The accountants discovered that a number of large jewels that Tissier had listed as security were either inflated in value or missing, having been withdrawn by the man who had deposited them, one "Serge Alexander, called Staviski." Convinced that his arrest was imminent, Tissier went to the police and confessed his misdeeds, naming Stavisky as the mastermind behind the scheme.

This Serge-Alexander had to be hauled in for questioning as well, but he had disappeared from Paris on the very day Tissier had turned himself in, December 23. His whereabouts were unknown, though it was feared he had fled to Switzerland, ever a haven for shady financiers and their laundered fortunes. A full investigation, expected to take several months, had been launched by a Bayonne *juge d'instruction.* No doubt all would be revealed in due time. But for the moment *Le Petit Parisien* posed one pressing question that might carry broader implications: who had informed Stavisky of Tissier's confession, thus enabling him to avoid arrest?

FROM "BEAU SASHA" TO "MONSIEUR ALEXANDRE"

The new year brought all sorts of questions about this Serge or "Sasha" Stavisky, who, it soon became evident, was hardly unknown to the judicial authorities.

Serge-Alexander ("Sasha") Stavisky was born in 1886 in the Ukrainian village of Slobadka. Sasha's family name undoubtedly derived from that of a town called Staviski, in Bialystok, Poland, whence his ancestors had come. In 1890 the Stavisky family fled the pogroms of czarist Russia and settled in Paris. They thus added their small part to the rising tide of eastern European Jewish immigrants spilling into France, especially Paris, in the 1880s and 1890s. The arrival of these immigrants greatly exacerbated anti-Semitism in France, in part because it coincided with a period of economic depression and national anxiety. They met hostility not only among gentiles but also among assimilated French Jews who feared their presence would confirm traditional anti-Semitic stereotypes. Although it would be an exaggeration to say that these eastern European Jews had not improved their lot in France, their fate in the next half century was to show that if, as the historian Eugen Weber has recently reminded us, "anti-Semitism in nineteenth-century France was as French as croissants," it would remain so in the twentieth.

Four-year-old Sasha arrived in Paris with his father, mother, and grandfather Abraham. The father was a dentist who set up practice in the Marais district, where many eastern European Jewish doctors plied their trade without benefit of a license. Sasha's mother was a kind of eastern European Madame Bovary. She loathed being married to an impecunious dentist when, as she confided to her young son, she "could have married a count." Although Sasha tried to console her with the prospect that *he* would soon be rich and take care of her in aristocratic style, she simply disappeared one day. Before departing, however, she did a good job of spoiling her only child. When he stole a couple of gold ingots from his father, she would not allow him to be caned. "If he steals," she said sweetly, "it is only because he needs money." Sasha took this logic to heart for the rest of his life.

Sasha's next theft was not of money but of a name. As an adolescent this budding dandy much preferred attending theatrical performances than the Lycée Condorcet, where his father had sent him to prepare for a medical career. In order to secure better seats at his favorite performances, he usurped the name of a well-known theater critic, Alphonse Lemerre. Fortunately for Sasha, Lemerre was flattered by this piece of adolescent brashness and did not press charges. Sasha would not always be so lucky.

By this time Stavisky was already acquiring the physical features that would later help him advance his career with the assistance of women. Tall, fit, and supple, he had large dark eyes, wavy black hair, and a "mysterious" manner that reminded one of his friends of an "illusionist." Although moody and sometimes even violently melancholic, he was in essence a young man of great charm and natural generosity of spirit. He gave away money when he had little to give, expecting his friends to be equally forthcoming.

As he reached his early twenties, Sasha continued to spend most of his time in theaters and nightclubs. In this respect he was like many a young swell of the "Belle Epoque." This era, after all, was the heyday of bohemian Montmartre—of pleasure dens like the Chat Noir and the Moulin Rouge; of artist-intellectual coteries with self-mocking names like the Zutistes (Blow-offs), the Jemenfoutistes (I-don't-give-a-damns), the Hirsutes (Hairy ones), and the Hydropaths (Water haters), the last of whose battle cry was "The serious besots, gaiety regenerates." It was a time, in short, when a *"vent de folie* [crazy wind] blew over Paris."

Sasha must have been buffeted by this wind more than most, for he insisted on owning his own theater even before he could afford to attend one. He concluded that a particular theater on the Champs-Elysées that normally functioned only in winter might also open in the summer, and that he should be the man to open it. Lacking the necessary capital, he tried to raise money by selling various concessionary rights. Came summer, however, he still lacked sufficient funds to open, and the Folies-Marigny, as he called his theater, never mounted a play. This

did not deter Sasha from keeping the money paid him by his would-be concessionaires, who in 1909 took him to court. Defended by Albert Clemenceau,
brother of the famous politician, Stavisky managed to put off conviction for two
years. There were rumors that certain officials had been bribed. When the sentence was finally handed down, it was exceptionally light: a twenty-five-franc fine
and fifteen days in prison, suspended. Stavisky now had a file with the police, but
he had also gained a piece of Balzacian wisdom that would serve him well, at least
for a time: *"Tout le monde est à vendre, il suffit d'y mettre le prix"* ("All the world
is for sale; it's just necessary to name the price").

Sasha found his next major opportunity to test this wisdom during the First
World War—a time, indeed, when many an entrepreneur learned that great
killings were to be made in the business of killing. Overwhelmed for a moment by
the patriotic "spirit of 1914," he enlisted in the French army and served as a truck
driver for a few months. Soon, however, he concluded that his patriotic duty lay
elsewhere, and he arranged a fraudulent medical discharge by bribing some officials. His next move was to set himself up as a military supplier, participating in a
line of business with a rich history of corruption in France, as elsewhere. Somehow Stavisky and an accomplice were able to secure an order for twenty thousand
bombs from France's new ally, Italy. Displaying a precocious understanding of
the principles of defense contracting, the two young men vastly overcharged the
Italian government, underpaid their own subcontractors, and ultimately supplied
bombs that generally failed to explode. Toward the end of the war, as the first
American troops began to arrive in France, Stavisky saw to this new market
through the establishment of gambling dens and brothels, the whores for the
most part old war-horses brought out of provincial retirement to accommodate
the hordes of undiscriminating doughboys.

At the same time, Sasha hooked up with his own aging coquette, the ex–
cabaret singer Jeanne Darcy, alias Fanny Bloch. Jeanne now had a cabaret of her
own, the Cadet-Rouselle, which Stavisky gallantly helped her manage in the
boom years immediately following the war. He also operated the cabaret as an
informal apothecary, liberally dispensing such drugs as morphine and cocaine.
But the two partners soon quarreled, Jeanne charging Sasha with the theft of
fifteen thousand francs he was supposed to have used to get one of her jewels out
of hock. In the ensuing trial Stavisky was convicted and sentenced to a prison
term of thirteen months, which he managed to avoid serving because Jeanne
suddenly withdrew all charges. Sasha later blackmailed her and gained control of
the cabaret, which he reestablished under the name of his father. At the height of
their brief alliance Jeanne had called Sasha "Signor Pericoloso" ("Mr. Dangerous"). She had not known how apt this was.

In the early 1920s Stavisky expanded his operations to include check forging.
His modus operandi was quite elegant. He would hire an accomplice—he preferred impoverished Romanian medical students—to go to a nightclub, get drunk
(or pretend to get drunk), pay the check with a fifty-dollar bill, and then demand
change in the form of a check as a precaution against robbery. Once in possession

of this check, Stavisky would change its value from, say, 600 francs to 60,000. The scheme worked well enough until one of the medical students got caught by the police and promptly fingered Stavisky as the scheme's mastermind and chief profiteer. In deep trouble this time, Stavisky would undoubtedly have been sent up for a long stretch if the prime evidence against him—the forged checks—had not mysteriously disappeared from the police files.

This close call—and there were others—did not persuade Stavisky to take the advice of his father and settle down in a respectable profession. Instead, he moved on to other scams, including the establishment of trumped-up companies, the most intriguing of which was a patriotic enterprise called the Franco-American Cinematograph Corporation, whose announced purpose was to transfer the world's film capital from Hollywood to Paris, but whose actual purpose was to transfer large sums from other people's pockets to Stavisky's. The company soon failed, but its failure hurt its investors much more than its founder.

Although Stavisky remained essentially a small-time crook through the mid-1920s, he now began to live more like a leading Chicago mobster. "Handsome Sasha" wore expensive zoot suits, dined in the best restaurants, bought himself the finest lawyers, politicians, and policemen. But something was missing: he needed a flame to light his way to greater success. Thus far his search for an inspiring female companion had not been rewarding. In 1910 he had married a girl from a respectable family but abandoned her after going through her meager fortune. Nor did aging ex–cabaret singers suit a man used to stepping out on the town with chamber deputies and other rising businessmen. In 1926 he finally found his match in the very pleasing form of a young Chanel model named Arlette Simon. Although not entirely without a "past" of her own—she had been impregnated by one of her mother's lovers at seventeen, then kept by a rich Argentinian—she was both beautiful and intelligent. She also seemed eager to share the risk-filled life upon which she knew Sasha had embarked. Genuinely smitten with each other, they talked vaguely of marriage, then more seriously of it when Arlette discovered that she was carrying Stavisky's child.

This same year also brought Sasha a series of reverses. He tried to gain control of the radio transmitter in the Eiffel Tower so that he might advertise two new products he had patented: a powdered soup called P'ti' Pot and a liqueur for women. It turned out, however, that the man who sold him the "rights" to exploit the tower had no business doing so; for once, Sasha was bilked. Just as this scheme was collapsing, a prominent stockbroker whom Stavisky had swindled brought suit against him. Upon learning that his son was wanted by the police for fraud, Sasha's father shot himself in the head. The honest immigrant had not been able to bear the shame. Stavisky eluded capture until an accomplice denounced him to a Paris police inspector more intent on ending Sasha's life of crime than on sharing in it. The arrest occurred at a grand supper party Stavisky had thrown for his cronies at Marly-le-Roi. Vainly claiming special dispensation as a father-to-be, Stavisky was promptly locked away in the Santé prison in Paris.

He spent a total of seventeen months in the Santé while his lawyers worked on ways to get him out and Arlette gave birth to their son. Eventually Stavisky came up with his own getaway plan. Claiming to suffer from severe gastric disorders, he persuaded a prison doctor to recommend an operation. For this purpose he was given "provisional liberty." He never had the operation and never went back to prison. His trial was scheduled and then postponed some nineteen times; the Stavisky file moved from one police cubbyhole to the next in a kind of tour de force of calculated bureaucratic inertia. Stavisky had again managed to cheat the system, but the time in jail left its mark. Upon his "temporary" release he vowed he would kill himself before he would serve another prison term. It was one of the few promises in his life he would keep.

Following his release from the Santé in July 1927, Stavisky quickly built up an empire of crime. He did this primarily on the strength of the ruse that would eventually lead to his downfall: the issuance of overvalued bonds through municipal credit agencies in provincial towns. He (or his partners) used the following technique: they secured blank bonds that had already been signed by a municipal official, filled in small sums on the bonds' counterfoils and in the agency's books, and then sold purchasers bonds showing 500,000 or 1,000,000 francs. Stavisky hoped that, by the time the fraudulent bonds came due, he could cover them with funds garnered through other schemes. To cover his tracks further Stavisky managed his operations through a dummy holding company called first Les Etablissements Alex and then, more grandly, the Compagnie Foncière d'Entreprise et de Travaux Publics (Company for Real Estate Ventures and Public Works). An elderly retired general and a former South American diplomat served as figurehead executives in this firm.

In the summer of 1933 Stavisky cooked up a particularly audacious swindle. This involved the marketing of bonds based on as yet nonexistent reparations promised by the Allied powers to Hungarian aristocrats in compensation for lands they lost after the Great War. The French minister of finance saw through this ruse and urged the public not to purchase the bonds. Stavisky's failure to cash in on this scheme meant that he would be unable to pay off the Bayonne bonds, thus ensuring the collapse of his inverted financial pyramid.

Sasha's employment of executives to front for his schemes did not mean that he kept an entirely low profile. On the contrary, his social life in this period became grander than ever. Preferring now to be called Monsieur Alexander, he divided his time between an apartment on the Champs-Elysées and villas in the south of France. Accompanied by Arlette, whom he had married shortly after his release from prison, and a bevy of retainers (including two former boxing champions as bodyguards), he made the rounds of the casinos in Nice and Cannes. Soon he became known as the "king of the Côte d'Azur." He also played the horses and ran a stable of his own, though he was kept off the Paris turf by the vigilantly anti-Semitic aristocrats who controlled it. (Sasha tried to combat this prejudice by converting to Catholicism, but it did not help.) Indulging his taste for the stage, he bought a Parisian theater, the Olympia, which generally put on expensive flops. He also bought two newspapers, one of the Left and one of the

Right, and cultivated the journalist Albert Dubarry, a well-known blackmailer and Fascist sympathizer. His ventures into the world of publishing and entertainment bespoke a need to play the complete *homme du monde*. But in Paris—as in Vienna, Prague, Budapest, and Berlin—Jewish penetration of the arts and media fueled the fires of anti-Semitism.

Our best descriptions of Monsieur Alexander at his apogee come from the pen of his friend Joseph Kessel, the journalist and popular novelist. Kessel painted a picture of an enigmatic, grandly tragic figure, at once kind and mean-spirited, capable of both magnificent generosity and shocking vulgarity. Kessel claimed to see these dichotomies in Sasha's physiognomy: the upper half of his face, he said, was "energetic, firm and even beautiful," while the lower half, because of a "flabby chin and a downward turn of the mouth," seemed weak and ineffectual. Joining Stavisky and other cronies during many dinners at the opulent Poisson d'Or, Kessel was struck by Sasha's insistence on eating modestly, drinking hardly at all, and going home early to sleep with his wife. Surely if there was anything "un-French" about Stavisky, this was it!

By 1933 Stavisky apparently had at last achieved enough worldly success to convince himself that he had risen permanently above his immigrant origins and early career as gigolo and petty con man and that he could not be touched by the law. His elegance was still superficial, and, like Dr. Johnson, he was believed to have no passion for clean linen. Yet Kessel suggested that when Sasha looked in the mirror, he now saw *"le grand financier international"* and not the parvenu on the make. "There is some myth for every man," observed Yeats, "which if we but knew it, would make us understand all that he did and thought." Perhaps for Stavisky this private myth was most sharply revealed in those moments before the mirror. After all, just before the Bayonne crash sent him fleeing from Paris, he was apparently imagining ways that *he*, the financial genius par excellence, might help relieve the great depression that was choking the Western world's economies like a killer fog.

FLIGHT

On December 23 Stavisky received an alarming telephone call from the mistress of his man in Bayonne, Tissier. She said the pawnshop manager had panicked and gone to the police, presumably to exchange some information for his own skin. Knowing her paramour, the mistress thought it would be only a matter of time before he implicated Stavisky.

Sasha hastily consulted with his lawyers and other confederates. They all advised him to make himself scarce until this business blew over; they would hold things together in Paris until it was safe for their boss to return. Reluctantly Sasha agreed.

Rushing to the offices of his holding company, Stavisky scooped up a number of check stubs that implicated him in the Bayonne bond fraud. He also exchanged

Stavisky in 1924, already well established in his life of crime. *UPI/Bettmann Newsphotos*

Stavisky after he shot himself in the head at his rented hideout in Chamonix. He died hours later at a local hospital. *UPI/Bettmann Newsphotos*

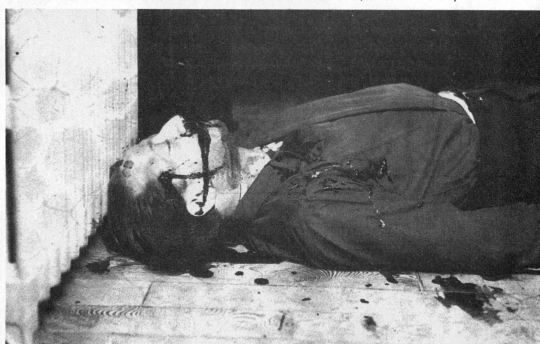

A wounded standard-bearer of the Croix de Feu veterans' association during the February 1934 rioting in Paris. *UPI/Bettmann Newsphotos*

a sack of jewels for travel money. And finally, he borrowed a revolver from one of his most trusted retainers, a certain Romagnino. In handing over the gun, Romagnino pleaded with Sasha not to use it: "Remember your wife and child!" he admonished. Thus equipped, Stavisky returned to his apartment and told Arlette to pack his bags. "I've got to take a little trip," he explained, as nonchalantly as possible. But his face betrayed his anxiety. All of a sudden he seemed to have lost his vaunted poise and confidence. Arlette feared the worst.

On the night of December 23, Stavisky left Paris by car accompanied by another loyal confederate, his boy Friday Pigalio. (The number of Italians in his retinue was not coincidental; in France, as in America, Italians played an important role in the underworld of the twenties and thirties.) Their destination was the town of Servos, in the French Alps, where Pigalio had recently rented a villa. This seemed a safe place to hide, for Stavisky was not known to frequent mountain resorts.

They planned to drive straight through to Servos (roughly seven hundred kilometers), but the same nasty weather that led to the Lagny rail disaster forced them to stop for the night in Fontainebleau, then to abandon the car altogether and take the train. Lagny may have figured in Stavisky's flight in another way. One memoirist of the period,* without offering any proof, insisted that Stavisky considered sending an accomplice (the former police inspector Bonny) to the disaster site to lift a passport from a mangled corpse; a little redesign of the document and Sasha would have a new identity!

During the flight Stavisky oscillated between maudlin self-pity and vindictive anger at the cowardly Tissier, who had panicked at the first sign of trouble. But he also tried to reassure himself that even if Tissier told all he knew, the authorities would have enough sense to keep a tight lid on the matter. After all, as he confided to Pigalio, there were plenty of "highly placed" persons with their fingers in this juicy pie. Another major financial-political scandal would only further erode popular confidence in the government.

The rest of the trip to the Alps was uneventful save for a potentially costly error near the Swiss border. Through inattention Pigalio had put them on a train headed for Geneva rather than Chamonix (near Servos), with the result that the two fugitives suddenly found themselves confronted by a Swiss frontier guard demanding passports. Caught by surprise, Stavisky showed his real identification rather than his spare one made out in the name of one of his bodyguards. Fortunately for him, however, the guard did not look carefully at the document, and the two were able to switch to a train traveling in the proper direction.

Arriving at their destination—Pigalio's rental villa—they discovered that all the pipes had burst, Pigalio having neglected to drain them after his last visit. There was nothing for them to do but look for lodgings in nearby Chamonix,

---

*Xavier Vallat, an extreme anti-Semite who later served as the Vichy government's first commissioner general for Jewish affairs.

which in those early days of the winter sports industry already boasted a number of rental chalets for visiting skiers.

As it happened, Pigalio knew a lady in town who owned a chalet she rented out for the season: called Les Argentières (The Silversmiths), it was comfortable enough to accommodate a man used to certain standards and apt to spend most of his time indoors. Having installed Stavisky in this chalet, Pigalio returned to Paris to check on the latest developments. He also hoped to assure Arlette that her husband was safe, but he was not so sure of this himself. Before leaving, he had tried to persuade Stavisky to give him his revolver, which the latter had placed conveniently on his night table. Like Romagnino, he reminded Sasha of his wife and child. "It is because of them that I've brought this weapon along," Stavisky replied. "I'd rather die than see them dishonored." Perhaps Sasha had something of his father in him after all.

To provide their chief with companionship, Stavisky's confederates arranged for another member of the band to go to Chamonix. They chose a minor gangster named Henri Voix, a man considered so unimportant that no one would miss him. It turned out that someone *would* miss him—namely, his girlfriend, one Lucette Almeras. When Henri told her he was going away on an important errand that "a woman wouldn't understand," she naturally assumed he was off to see another mistress. Voix eventually became convinced that Lucette would compromise him in every way if he left her alone in Paris, so he took her with him to the mountains. This meant that Stavisky would have another companion during the final few days of his life, and we would have a perhaps more reliable witness to his sad end.

Those last days in Chamonix, as Lucette recalled them, were filled with gloom and apprehension for the visiting Parisians, especially for the strange man who called himself Monsieur Maurice, and who Lucette was led to believe was an "overworked businessman" on holiday to recover his health. Monsieur Maurice spent almost all his time locked in his bedroom on the second floor. If he happened to be downstairs when anyone from the village came to the chalet, he fled to his room. Lucette soon concluded that this Maurice had more on his mind than his health; he was undoubtedly "on the lam."

Lucette's suspicions were hardened by her companions' secret conferences in the kitchen and by their sudden decision, on January 1, to decamp for a yet more secluded chalet, the Vieux Logis (Old House). Maurice himself waited until the dead of night to make this move, then resumed his hermetic ways, leaving his room only for the occasional game of belote. But if this "man enveloped in mystery" wanted to hide from the outside world, he also craved to know what that world was up to: every day he asked his companions to bring him all the latest newspapers, which he devoured as if his life depended on a knowledge of their contents.

Reading these papers in the first days of the new year, Stavisky must have found ample justification for his flight and seclusion. His own name, first mentioned in connection with the Bayonne bond fraud on December 29, was now being bandied about by all the Paris dailies. They pointed out that Stavisky had worked closely in the fraud with the mayor and deputy of Bayonne, Joseph Garat, and that the man responsible for appraising the jewels used to back some of the bonds, Sam Cohen, was an old crony of Sasha's. Moreover, Stavisky's past was being dragged through the mud. On January 3 Sasha could read in *Le Petit Parisien* that the Bayonne fraud was simply "the end of a long chain of swindles" engineered by "Serge-Alexandre Staviski, alias Monsieur Alexandre." The paper discussed his arrest in 1926 at Marly-le-Roi, a previous bond scam at Orléans, his "weakness for jewels," and his flop-ridden theater. As for the latest swindle, the paper wanted to know "by what obscure connections" Stavisky had been able to set up the Bayonne scheme and get reputable insurance companies to purchase millions of francs' worth of bonds.

If Stavisky read this paper, as no doubt he did, he must have found reassurance only in the fact that its reporters seemed not to know where he had fled. The next day, *Le Petit Parisien* had him en route to Venezuela on board a luxury liner. How appropriate it seemed!

A NEW "AFFAIR"

On the same day that *Le Petit Parisien* asked how Stavisky could have sucked major insurance companies into his scheme, *L'Action française* provided the apparent answer. Maurice Pujo, one of the paper's most assiduous scandalmongers, published two letters written in 1932 by Albert Dalimier, currently minister of colonies in the center-left Chautemps government and formerly minister of labor under Premier Edouard Herriot in the mid-twenties. The first letter, addressed to the president of the General Insurance Company, recommended the purchase of municipal credit agency bonds as excellent investments. The second, addressed to Tissier, suggested that he approach major insurance companies in his campaign to market his bonds.

No additional commentary was necessary to provide what in more recent parlance is known as the smoking gun. Here was evidence not just of local wrongdoing, or merely of more skulduggery by that tireless swindler Stavisky, but of apparent involvement in criminal activities by a member of the national government. The Bayonne fraud was well on its way to becoming an affair.

No additional commentary may have been needed to smear the government of Camille Chautemps, but Pujo provided some anyway. It was Chautemps's brother-in-law (Pressard), Pujo pointed out, who as public prosecutor had protected Stavisky since 1927. Chautemps's brother, Pierre, served as a lawyer for one of Stavisky's companies. The least the premier could do now, insisted Pujo, was to cashier Dalimier and appoint an independent commission to investigate this murky business.

No government appoints an independent commission to investigate its own transgressions unless it is forced to do so; instead, leaders promise to conduct their own investigations, leaving no stone unturned, etc. etc. Questioned on the evening of January 3 about *L'Action française*'s damning revelations, Chautemps replied that "justice would run its course with inflexible rigor regardless of the people who might be adversely affected." To which, on the following morning, *L'Action française* responded that such phrases had been heard before: *Panama!* "On the day a republican government pursues justice without regard for personal consequences," it sneered, "chickens will grow teeth!"

Other papers took up the campaign against Stavisky, Dalimier, and the entire Chautemps regime. The cartoonist for the respectable *Echo de Paris* depicted Dalimier sitting at dinner and looking morosely at a huge sauceboat: "The Bayonnaise has turned," reads the caption. France's famous satirical weekly *Le Canard enchaîné* also had a field day with the blossoming affair. As one revelation succeeded another, the paper concluded that all these charges must be based on error or calumny. If this man was really such a mountebank, how could he have been on such good terms with deputies and even ministers? How could influential members of parliament have supped at his table and accepted his generous financial support? No, all this was an unfortunate misunderstanding; Stavisky would soon return to Paris, and cabinet ministers would again greet him as "Cher Ami."

In the first week of the new year, the international press also picked up the Stavisky story, which—especially in the Anglo Saxon countries—only confirmed certain established views regarding the nature of French political life. After reporting at length on the details of the Bayonne fraud and Stavisky's past swindles, the London *Times* noted laconically that "some of these circumstances required a great deal of explanation." The worry was that this latest scandal would add to the instability of French politics at a time of international insecurity. The *New York Times*'s man in Paris did not confine himself to the Tammany-like details of the Stavisky affair, but also retailed some of the legends already swirling around "this most sought-for swindler in the annals of the *Sûreté Générale.*" He reported that Stavisky had once escaped from the clutches of the police by doping his guards and "knocking them on the head." After his arrest at Marly-le-Roi, "where the police found their prey luxuriously dining with a Paris mannequin," Stavisky had again escaped "in the usual way." The *Times* man obviously picked up these fanciful morsels from the streets and cloakrooms of Paris, where it was also rumored that Stavisky held "a card as inspector in the French Secret Service." It would seem that in this latest triumph of fiction over fact, Stavisky was quickly emerging as a new Vautrin, Balzac's "Napoleon of Crime."

Not that the unfolding facts required much embellishment to put the government on the defensive. In an attempt to pacify the press and public, Chautemps ordered the arrest of Garat, the mayor of Bayonne. Yet Garat was too small a fish to satisfy the Parisian press's hunger for a large governmental catch. Dalimier, a more important target, defended himself in the time-honored fashion of political leaders: he insisted that he had acted in good faith, but if "mistakes were made," the responsibility lay with his subordinates. Premier Chautemps stood by his embattled minister, at least for a time. He also promised to launch an extensive (but not independent) investigation into the entire affair and to track down the culprit "wherever his flight may have taken him." To this end he ordered search messages sent to all French ships and consulates in North and South America.

None of these measures had its intended effect. Indeed, Dalimier's weak defense, and Chautemps's acceptance of it, inspired a new round of attacks. Again it was the antirepublican *L'Action française* that assumed the most militant posture, going so far as to call the people into the streets against their government. "At the beginning of this week parliament will reassemble," wrote Pujo on January 7, 1934, "and we urge the people of Paris to come in large numbers before the Chamber of Deputies, to cry 'Down with the Thieves,' and to clamor for honesty and justice."

In the face of such threats, Chautemps decided that his minister of colonies was expendable after all. In forcing Dalimier to resign on January 8, the premier hoped to save his government. But on the very day that Dalimier stepped down, events were under way in Chamonix that would dash any hopes for governmental continuity and domestic tranquillity.

"SUICIDE BY PERSUASION"

Reading the daily newspaper accounts of the mushrooming scandal, the man behind it all was giving way to despair. After a week or so in Chamonix there was little left of the elegant *homme du monde;* unshaven and sloppily dressed, Stavisky paced the floors of the Vieux Logis, cursing the cowardice and treachery of former friends and accomplices. In particular he condemned the politicians who had once "come begging" for handouts and now pretended not to have known him. "Ungrateful wretches," he fumed, "I could destroy them with a single word; that would be my right: I *made* the rotten bastards!"

On January 8 Lucette Almeras, who in the meantime had been let in on the true identity of "Monsieur Maurice," thought she saw two dark figures in the woods behind the Vieux Logis. Later she was sure she heard noises emanating from a neighboring villa, which was supposed to be uninhabited. Going into town for provisions and the daily papers, she and Henri Voix picked up a copy of *Le Petit Dauphinois,* which bore the headline "Stavisky is said to have passed the last few days in a villa at Servos." *"C'est la fin,"* Lucette gasped.

On the preceding day three policemen from Paris had indeed arrived in Servos. They had come on a tip from the woman who had rented the villa there to Pigalio. She had become suspicious because the latter, known in the region for his accumulation of bad debts, had paid in advance and in cash for the house, which he said he was renting for a "friend from Paris," whose name he listed on the registration as "M. Danger." The Paris police knew Pigalio as an accomplice of Stavisky. It looked as if their man was closer to hand than they had thought.

Once in Servos the Parisian policemen kept their presence secret from the local gendarmes. They traced their prey to Les Argentières, but only after Stavisky and company had decamped for the Vieux Logis. They then followed a number of false leads, gradually coming to fear that their quarry might no longer be in the area.

Meanwhile, Pigalio had again returned to Paris to scout out a new haven on the outskirts of the capital. In Paris, Pigalio contacted another Stavisky lawyer, the deputy Bonnaure, who apparently advised him to go to the police in order to strike a deal: information about the exact whereabouts of Stavisky in exchange for a mild judicial treatment for all concerned and an end to the official investigation. Bonnaure assured Pigalio that Chautemps would be only too glad to stifle the scandal, which was compromising too many important people.

It is unclear whether Pigalio then told the police precisely where they could find Stavisky, whether Bonnaure provided this information himself, or whether the Paris police inspectors in Chamonix obtained it—as they insisted they had—by comparing handwriting samples from all the recent lodging registrations in the region. In any event, Lucette Almeras had indeed seen figures lurking near the Vieux Logis, for on the morning of January 8 the police had traced Stavisky to his final hideaway.

They were not sure, however, that their man was in residence, for they saw no sign of him on the grounds or through any of the windows accessible to their inspection. Waiting until Voix and Lucette left for town, they persuaded the chalet's owner to let them in and have a look around. On the kitchen table they found a tally for a belote game with three columns headed "L," "H," and "S"—a sign they took to mean they were on the right track. A quick search revealed no further evidence of their prey, but one of the rooms on the second floor was locked. Trying to open it, they discovered it had been locked from the inside.

At this point the policeman in charge, a certain Charpentier, decided he had best ask the Sûreté headquarters for further instructions. After all, the man he had apparently run to ground had a history of judicial protection; this was not the time for independent initiative. Leaving a subordinate to guard the door, he went to a neighboring villa to make his call.

When he returned, he did something that later added to public suspicion that the police had not done all they could to take their man alive. He sent his assistants to other parts of the chalet and spent some time alone "guarding the door." Did he speak with Stavisky, try to get him to give himself up? Or, suspecting that Sasha was armed, did he suggest suicide as the only "honorable" alternative? Charpentier later insisted that he said nothing at all, just listened for sounds of activity inside.

After about a quarter of an hour, Charpentier called back his assistants and tried anew to gain entry with a passkey. This time they heard a faint "Who is there?" "Police!" they shouted. A bang resounded from inside the room, followed by the sound of a body hitting the floor. It was about four in the afternoon.

Unable to smash in the heavy wooden door, Charpentier gained access to the room through a window, which he reached with a ladder. There, according to his later testimony, he found Stavisky sprawled on the carpet near his bed, a gun clutched in his hand, a large hole in his head, blood dripping from his nose and mouth. Yet he was still alive.

The police procedure now became even stranger. Rather than immediately calling a doctor and ambulance (the local hospital was only a few kilometers away), Charpentier again telephoned Paris for instructions. Only after speaking at length with his superiors did he alert a physician, who concluded after a cursory examination that "nothing could be done" for the wounded man. Nevertheless, Stavisky *was* still alive, and one would have thought that the next step would have been to call an ambulance. Instead, Charpentier brought in a local photographer to take extensive pictures of the grisly scene, whose central figure lay softly panting in an expanding pool of blood. Here was an example either of exceptional care with evidence or of another case of calculated inertia: we do not know, after all, exactly what "instructions" Charpentier received from Paris.

Whatever the reasons for delay, by the time Stavisky was finally delivered to the hospital in Chamonix he had less than a liter of blood left in his body. There was certainly no hope of saving him now, and the doctors simply turned him over to a nun. Yet he lived for several more hours, finally expiring in the sister's arms at three-fifteen the following morning. While convinced that they could not have helped Stavisky after his arrival at the hospital, the doctors later told his wife that he might have lived had the police delivered him more swiftly into their care. In any event, the man who claimed he could bring down politicians by the utterance of a single word died without getting the opportunity to say what he knew.

But he did not have to. His death in such mysterious circumstances did for the Stavisky affair what Baron Reinach's had done for the Panama scandal: it gave it a whole new lease on life. Now leading politicians could be accused of murder along with financial corruption. For "police murder," of course, is just what most Parisian papers immediately assumed had transpired. Stavisky had been eliminated because he "knew too much."

Soon the suspicion of police murder hardened into conviction as all sorts of "facts" about the fatal events in Chamonix began making the rounds of the capital's cloakrooms and bars. It was said that Stavisky had been shot from a distance of three meters; that though left-handed he had been shot from the right side; that Voix had been in the room with him to act as executioner at the appointed time; or that the police had handed him one of their own revolvers and forced him to put it to his head. This last version was preferred by the *Canard enchaîné,* though the paper also allowed that the police might have done the shooting themselves to "expedite matters." Along with the public, most of Stavisky's former accomplices maintained that their boss had been brutally murdered by the authorities. The itinerant Russian journalist Ilya Ehrenburg, who knew Stavisky, insisted that "handsome Sasha" had been "shot by the police agent Voix" because the police feared Stavisky "would talk too freely, and men in high places were involved." Tissier's lawyer, originally convinced that Stavisky had been shot by the police, gradually accepted the official verdict of suicide after interviewing the doctors at Chamonix. But this desperate act had been, he insisted, "suicide by persuasion."

That Stavisky had left a suicide note for his wife and a farewell letter to his son, signed "Your Unhappy Daddy," hardly got the authorities off the hook. The letters were claimed to be fake; or it was said that they were "under lock and key" so that any important names they might contain could be erased. Finally, some Frenchmen had it on good authority that Stavisky was not dead at all—that he had been given vast sums by the government to make himself scarce. He was already on his way to some South Sea paradise where he would spend the rest of his life basking in luxury at the taxpayers' expense.

FEBRUARY 6, 1934

"Chautemps leader of a band of thieves and murderers . . . Down with the assassins!" shouted *L'Action française* on January 9. The cry was answered first by that royalist party's own paramilitary organization, the Camelot du Roi. That evening groups of Camelot demonstrators charged up and down the great Parisian boulevards, which had been laid out in the era of Napoleon III by Baron Haussmann in part to inhibit the construction of barricades and facilitate the dispersal of demonstrators by cannon fire. But the demonstrators this time frustrated police tactics by scattering into small side streets, then reconverging behind the police lines to build makeshift barricades from park benches, overturned cars, sidewalk urinals, and even uprooted trees. Their goal apparently was to storm that "bastion of corruption" the Chamber of Deputies in the Palais Bourbon. Although they did not achieve this end, they brought central Paris to a temporary standstill; the city had not seen such vicious rioting in years.

Nor did the demonstrations abate with a single, cathartic outburst. Over the course of the following two weeks the Camelots were joined by protesters from other right-wing paramilitary leagues, most of them bent on bringing down the Chautemps government, if not the entire parliamentary-democratic system. Watching these leagues in action, the American foreign correspondent William Shirer was reminded of the Italian Fascist Blackshirts and Nazi Brownshirts he had seen on previous assignments in the troubled postwar era. The French leagues did, in fact, have a certain derivative quality, with their various-colored shirts, jackboots, makeshift weapons, and would-be führers. Among the more prominent groups were the Jeunesses Patriotes, founded by a right-wing deputy named Pierre Taittinger and composed mostly of university students; the Solidarité Française, financed by the wealthy perfumer François Coty; Le Francisme, whose few thousand young toughs emulated most closely Hitler's SA, even eschewing wine for beer; and above all the Croix de Feu, a much larger association of decorated war veterans that claimed to be unpolitical but that tended strongly to the right.

In the 1930s the leagues had first shown their capacity to cause trouble by breaking up a meeting of the International Disarmament Congress in Paris's Trocadéro (1931). They would continue to raise havoc with the republic whenever they could, some of them eventually finding their true raison d'être in collaborating with France's German conquerors after 1940. Without for a moment underestimating their capacity for evil, we should however note that the French paramilitary leagues were not quite up to the standard set by their German and Italian prototypes. They were neither well armed nor very well organized. They lacked truly charismatic or resolute leaders. Some of them even had a slightly comic side. The Left mocked the Solidarité Française as "Silidarité Française" because many of its members were unemployed Algerian colonials ("Sidis"). The Francistes derived their name from a two-headed ax wielded by the ancient Franks; French politics might have been highly historical, but, as the historian D. W. Brogan observed, "they were not historical enough for a party of ancient Franks to get very far." Above all, the effectiveness of the militant French Right was undermined by rivalries among the various leagues, which often spent as much time attacking each other as they did the republic. Not all of them, however, wanted to eliminate the republic per se; some merely wanted to purge it of those liberal democratic features that they believed made it weak and flabby.

If not the republic itself, certainly Chautemps's government seemed threatened in the immediate aftermath of the Stavisky scandal. During the parliamentary debate that opened on January 11, Chautemps's response to the crisis further undermined his credibility with his many critics. Seeing both the escalating rioting and the press campaign against him as expressions of party politics—which in part they were—he not only refused to appoint an independent investigating committee but also tried to muzzle his opponents through stiffer libel laws. At the same time, he ordered a reorganization of the Paris police force, hinting that the powerful prefect of police, Jean Chiappe, might have to step down. These measures were widely interpreted as an effort by the government to cover up its own misdoings and to shift blame to the police, who were seen as mere pawns of corrupt politicians. Chautemps was able to avoid a full-scale investigation only by relying on votes from the Socialist party, a fact that undermined his position in France's conservative business community, which increasingly saw the premier as a captive of left-wing forces. Convinced that Chautemps could not be relied upon to keep the Communists down, some wealthy businessmen increased their financial contributions to the right-wing leagues that were fighting against the government.

The largest riots so far occurred on January 22, 23, and 27. On this last date Chautemps's position was further compromised by the disclosure that his minister of justice, Eugène Raynaldy, was implicated in yet another financial scandal. Raynaldy stepped down, as he said, "in order to have the freedom to respond to the attacks against [him]." But this did nothing to quiet the attacks against Chautemps. On January 27 the rightest leagues, joined by hundreds of indignant bourgeois, trashed the area around the Place de la Concorde in another effort to reach the parliament building across the Seine. Although they again failed to achieve this objective, they managed to injure some eighty policemen and terrify the deputies with their bloodthirsty little song:

> Les députés on les pendra
> Et si on ne pend pas
> On leur cassera la gueule
> La gueule on leur cassera!

> (Let's string up the deputies
> And if we can't string 'em up
> Let's beat in their faces
> Let's reduce 'em to a pulp!)

Chautemps himself apparently did not fear for his person, and his government, thanks to support from the Socialists, had received a narrow vote of confidence from the chamber on January 12. Nevertheless, he saw no way of ending the street violence and political chaos, which threatened to grow into full-scale civil war. Accepting the proposition that the country desperately needed calm, he and his cabinet resigned on the evening of January 27, 1934. The Right heralded this as a victory for political decency, while the Left saw it as a triumph of the street over the chamber. However Chautemps's fall was interpreted, Stavisky seemed already to be getting posthumous revenge.

The resignation of the Chautemps government left a political vacuum that was hard to fill, since most French politicians were understandably deciding that this was not the moment to assume governmental responsibility. President Lebrun finally managed to persuade one of the few Radical party politicians unbesmirched by the Stavisky scandal, Edouard Daladier, to form a new cabinet. Daladier was a former history professor who had previously served as defense minister and briefly as premier. Generally regarded as too unimaginative to be corrupt, this "bull from the Vaucluse" would, many believed, undertake a healthy charge through the dusty china shop of Third Republican politics. Others hoped that Daladier's good classical education might provide the intellectual vision that French politics sorely lacked. All were to be disappointed. In the end, gibed one journalist, Daladier's career could serve as proof that "culture does not suffice to create a great mind."

Daladier tried at first to form an "above party" government of leading personalities that would embrace both the Socialists and the parties of the Right. This proved impossible. The cabinet he eventually formed was dull and undistinguished even by the low standards of the Third Republic. Its most able member was the Socialist minister of the interior, Eugène Frot, but Frot would soon reveal himself as an ambitious schemer and something of a hothead.

The new premier also made some unfortunate personnel decisions affecting the Paris police and security administrations. He kicked Public Prosecutor Pressard upstairs to a cushier sinecure, thereby confirming the people's suspicion that corruption enhanced officials' careers as well as their bank accounts. Worse, he transferred the head of the Sûreté to the directorship of the Comédie-Française, whose previous director had irritated the government by mounting Shakespeare's *Coriolanus*, a play that could be seen as advocating the unseating of corrupt "bald tribunes" through popular revolution. Kicking a discredited official upstairs was poor public relations but hardly anything new; putting an errant policeman in charge of the "House of Molière" was an affront to the nation that only Molière himself might have found amusing. The people of Paris certainly did not.

As if these blunders were not enough, Daladier then went after one of the most popular officials in all Paris: Prefect of Police Chiappe. Although hated by the Socialists and the Communists, Chiappe had ingratiated himself with the middle classes by ordering prostitutes off the streets of Paris and into brothels, where the police could better supervise their activities. He had also instituted well-marked crosswalks to improve traffic control and cut down on the number of pedestrian fatalities. Most impressive, he had reformed the design of the notorious sidewalk urinals *(pissotières)*, in which many a gentleman had nearly succumbed from the suffocating stench. In addition to winning over the bourgeoisie through these innovations, he had also impressed the Fascist leagues by coming down much harder on rioters of the Left than on those of the Right. The leagues were apparently even prepared to forgive him his one major transgression: his known association with the arch-crook Stavisky.

Daladier did not want to tangle with Chiappe, but he was forced to because the Socialists, especially Frot, made their participation in his government contingent on his dismissing the popular police chief. The premier tried to placate Chiappe by making him resident general of Morocco. This move did not sit well with Chiappe, who perhaps recalled a former government's treatment of General Boulanger, whom he admired.* When Daladier proposed the Moroccan post to him, he refused it point-blank, adding that if the premier persisted in his intention he would find his former prefect of police "in the street." Although Chiappe later claimed he had meant to imply only that he would be unemployed and down and out, Daladier quite understandably interpreted this as a threat to join the antigovernment rioting. Now, goaded on by Frot and other Socialists, he had no recourse but to stick to his guns, even if this indeed meant that Chiappe would be "in the street" with the rightist leagues.

The tension inspired by Chiappe's dismissal was greatly increased by rumors that the government was preparing to contain future demonstrations with the help of security forces from the provinces and even black troops from Senegal. The rightist leagues, in particular the Action Française, worked themselves into a lather over the prospect of "French blood" being spilled by vicious rustics and

---

*When General Boulanger, a demagogic military officer with a wide popular following, challenged the republican system in the middle to late 1880s, the government sent him to a provincial command. Eventually he was tricked into fleeing to Belgium, where he committed suicide at the grave of his mistress.

licentious colonials acting at the behest of an "alien government" controlled by "leftists, Jews, Protestants, and Freemasons."

On February 4 and 5 several Paris papers urged their readers to demonstrate against the Daladier government on the sixth, when the premier was scheduled to deliver his ministerial declaration. The Action Française promised to be out in force in the Place de la Concorde despite, or because of, the prospect of a bloodbath. Foreign correspondents began to gather in the Hotel Crillon, on the north side of the Place de la Concorde, to witness what promised to be the best show in that historic square since the beheading of King Louis XVI and Queen Marie Antoinette. As it turned out, they were not to be disappointed.

The first demonstrators arrived at the square in the early evening. They were few in number, and their initial attempts to storm the bridge leading to the Palais Bourbon were easily repulsed by the security forces, which consisted exclusively of Paris police and republican guards. It appeared as if no blood would flow after all. But within an hour or so the early rioters were massively reinforced by contingents from some of the rightist leagues, as well as from the Communist party, which also despised the "bourgeois" government of Daladier. Now the fighting intensified, with rioters repeatedly rushing the Pont de la Concorde, the security guards responding with horse charges into the crowd. Dozens of police and demonstrators were severely injured in these charges and countercharges, but the real victims were the guards' horses, under whose hooves the demonstrators rolled marbles and tossed firecrackers, and whose haunches they slashed with razor blades attached to long canes.

As the attacks on the police lines intensified, the embattled security forces began to panic and fire their revolvers at their assailants. Some of the rioters were armed and fired back. Six demonstrators died in the first barrage. So did a woman standing among the foreign correspondents and American diplomats on the balcony of the Hotel Crillon. She was shot cleanly between the eyes.

By now the Place de la Concorde was bathed in darkness save for a small area near the obelisk where a bus had been set ablaze by the rioters. Another fire burned in the Naval Ministry, on the north side of the square. Firemen attempting to douse the conflagration were pelted with stones. Eventually, with the help of the naval troops on duty in the building, they put out the fire.

At about nine the demonstrators in the square were joined by several thousand ex-servicemen belonging to the Union Nationale des Combattants (UNC). They came marching into the square from the Champs-Elysées, mutilés in front to act as a shield for the middle-aged family men who made up the bulk of the column. Military decorations pinned to their breasts, they carried signs saying "WE WANT FRANCE TO LIVE IN ORDER AND HONESTY." (They did not know that the president of their organization was on the board of one of Stavisky's companies.) Seeing the bridge to the chamber well defended, they turned around and went up the Rue Royal on their way to the Elysée Palace, where they planned to present President Lebrun with a petition of veterans' grievances. They were prevented from doing so by a cordon of police, a development they interpreted as another sign of the republic's ingratitude for the sacrifices they had made in the Great War. Indignant and spoiling for a fight, they returned to the Place de la Concorde at about ten.

The next two hours saw the struggle for control of the Pont de la Concorde become more and more intense, as the demonstrators made over twenty charges against the exhausted and outmanned security forces. They accompanied these attacks with barrages of stones, pieces of asphalt, and iron railings torn from the fences around the flower beds in the Tuileries Gardens. Close to midnight, when it appeared that one more charge would carry the bridge, the police themselves rallied under a new leader, one Colonel Simon, and charged en masse through the mob, sweeping the square and sending rioters fleeing into the side streets. Lacking leadership or coordinated direction, the demonstrators gradually dispersed, relieving the chamber of the danger of invasion from at least this direction.

But there were other danger points as well. While rioters were storming the Pont de la Concorde, elements of the Croix de Feu had assembled on the other side of the river and tried to invade the Palais Bourbon from the opposite direction. They got as far as a police line in front of the neighboring Foreign Office, which they might have broken through had not their leader, Colonel de La Rocque, who had been directing operations over the telephone from the safety of a nearby house, called them back and ordered them to disperse. It seems that the colonel, like some of the other rightist leaders, was simply unprepared for the extent of the rioting or the actual prospect of victory.*

While the leagues were threatening the chamber, the deputies inside were attempting to hold a debate on the domestic and foreign policy the new government intended to adopt. In trying to deliver his ministerial declaration, Daladier was shouted down by the parties of the Right. "Assassin!" and "Long live Chiappe!" They screamed. Then the Communists began shouting *"Vivent les Soviets!"* and singing the "Internationale." Others countered with the "Marseillaise." A few deputies began pelting each other with ink bottles. Scrappy little Eugène Frot almost got into a fistfight. The scene inside the chamber was coming to resemble the scene outside.

During a recess necessitated by the pandemonium, the deputies streamed into the corridors and noted with horror that the crowd in the square was swelling and that the safety of the chamber itself was in question. Already the building's infirmary was filling with wounded police and guards. What if the mob broke in? What if it torched the place, as those crazed Germans had done to their Reichstag just the year before? Contemplation of these possibilities moved some of the deputies to call for early adjournment, but the debate dragged on into the night —a testament perhaps less to the deputies' courage than to their infatuation with their own rhetoric. Gradually, however, a number of deputies slipped out the back door and into the dark. Journalists covering the debate were duty bound to stay

---

*The leader of the Action Française, Charles Maurras, spent the evening of February 6 writing Provençal poetry for a colleague's wife.

to the bitter end, but as a precaution they put up a sign on the pressroom door: *"Avis à M.M. les Manifestants—Ici il n'y a pas de Députés!"* (Notice to demonstrators: there are no deputies in here!)

Finally, at about eight in the morning, the government was able to carry a motion that postponed all further parliamentary interpellations. The deputies still in the building ran for the back exit, the only one open. Most of them managed to elude the demonstrators and reach the safety of their homes or hotels. One who did not was the old Radical party war-horse Edouard Herriot. On his way home he was recognized by a group of rioters—including, as he huffed, "a young lady from good society"—who immediately began kicking and beating him. Then they packed him off in the direction of the Seine with every intention of drowning him. Incensed by the notion that a former mayor of Lyon should end his days "in any river but the Rhône," he managed to fight his way back to the police lines with the help of a passing Communist.

Can we take Herriot's narrow escape as symbolizing the fate of France on that bloody February night in 1934, when fourteen people died? Was the Third Republic in genuine danger of drowning in the swirling currents of political violence and popular indignation? We can only speculate about what might have happened had the rioters successfully invaded the chamber. It is conceivable (but by no means certain) that such a symbolic victory would have emboldened the republic's enemies to storm other bastions of governmental authority and perhaps even to declare a provisional government.

The success of such an adventure would ultimately have depended largely on two factors: the behavior of the army and the response of the rest of France. The French army in the 1930s, like the German Reichswehr in the preceding decade, felt alienated from the republic it was sworn to defend. Army leaders bristled at the revival of pre-1914 pacifism within the French Left and complained of a lack of respect for military virtues. They felt that France's security needs were being severely shortchanged in the national budgets. On a personal level, the commander in chief, General Maxime Weygand, despised Daladier and the new minister of war, Joseph Paul-Boncour, both of whom he saw as blind to the urgent need for a dramatic military buildup. On the evening of February 6, General Weygand acted just as General Hans von Seeckt had during the rightist Kapp Putsch of 1920 in Germany: he stayed away from the action, apparently waiting to see what would happen. But there is no clear evidence that Weygand or any other generals actively conspired with the leagues to bring down the Daladier government, let alone the republican system. What the army would have done if the leagues had tried to establish an alternative government cannot be known. It is possible that various generals and colonels would have gone in different directions, as they were to do after 1940.

As for the rest of France, its response to a full-fledged rightist coup would no doubt have been largely negative. Although Frenchmen outside the capital were not necessarily enthusiastic about the Daladier government, provincial France was not fundamentally antidemocratic or antirepublican. Much of the Midi (the south) was strongly republican or even Socialist, as was the "Red Belt" of working-class districts encircling Paris. The Fascist or royalist doctrines that so captivated many rightist intellectuals in Paris were not nearly so popular in the provinces. One should not forget, in other words, that in politics as in fashion and culture, "Paris" and "France" were by no means synonymous.

Another bar to the longer-term success of the militant Right was its chronic lack of internal unity and the absence of a single leader who might have played the role of führer or duce. The leagues generally failed to work together in coordinated fashion on February 6; cooperation after "victory" would have been equally difficult, particularly since conservative-nationalist groups like the Croix de Feu and UNC hardly saw eye to eye with the more strictly "Fascist" leagues or the royalists of the Action Française.

But to some extent these observations are the product of historical hindsight. On the night of February 6 the leaders of the Third Republic could credibly insist that the entire republican system was in danger of falling victim to a vast "Fascist plot." This perspective was shared by a great many Frenchmen at the time and has since passed into the mythology of the Third Republic. Daladier himself helped launch this interpretation through the communiqué he issued just before midnight on February 6: "There is evidence of an attempt by armed force against the security of the state. . . . The government is determined to maintain . . . the security of the population and the independence of the republican regime."

This sounded tough enough, but in fact Daladier was by no means sure how to proceed in the immediate aftermath of the rioting. Some of the younger members of his cabinet, especially Interior Minister Frot, advised him in the early morning hours of February 7 to put the rightist leaders under "preventative arrest" and to declare martial law. Though temporarily pulled in this direction, Daladier decided in the end against fighting fire with fire. In the first place, he was not sure that the army generals—especially his nemesis General Weygand—would protect the republic against a renewed rightist onslaught. And even if they would, the premier had no stomach for a full-scale civil war; as a veteran of World War I, he had seen enough bloodshed for one lifetime. He rejected his ministers' counsels on the grounds that these measures transcended his legal authority to act without prior parliamentary approval. This may have been technically correct, but it also reflected a broader tendency among Third Republic leaders, especially in the 1930s, to employ legalistic scruples to avoid decisive action.

Given what he perceived as weakness at the top, Interior Minister Frot decided to save the republic on his own. He ordered the new Paris prefect of police to begin rounding up a number of "subversives" who appeared on a list he had compiled for just such an occasion. Except for its rightist political hue, Frot's list recalled the notorious "Carnet-B" of 1914, which contained the names of Socialists to be arrested in the event of war. But even Frot, who apparently saw himself as a latter-day Robespierre, soon changed his mind about "saving the republic" through a preventative purge. Learning on February 7 that the opposition was arming itself for new battle and that the rightist leagues had put out a contract on his life, he now advised Daladier not to call in troops but to resign. In this counsel he was joined by several other "young Turks" in the cabinet who a few hours before had urged aggressive action. Only the Socialist leader, Léon Blum, who was later to head France's "Popular Front" coalition against fascism, advised the premier to remain in office. Blum feared, with good reason, that two victories of the "street" over the government in as many weeks could only further undermine the credibility of parliamentary democracy in France.

On February 8 the "bull from the Vaucluse" gave in to pressure from his cabinet, the press, and the streets, and laid down the reins of government. His announcement of resignation was reminiscent of King Louis-Philippe's abdication in 1848 in the face of popular insurrection:

> The government, which has the responsibility for maintaining order and security, refuses to assure it today by resort to exceptional means susceptible of causing a bloody repression and a new effusion of blood. It does not wish to employ soldiers against demonstrators. I have therefore handed to the President of the Republic the resignation of the cabinet.

In the end, Daladier's resignation may indeed have helped avert another major assault on the government, but it did not prevent additional bloodshed. On the night of February 8, sporadic rioting and looting claimed five more lives and caused hundreds of wounded. Those who were still ambulatory sauntered through the streets showing off their bandages and relating how they had come by them; one journalist suspected that some of the bandages might have been rather more elaborate than was necessary.

On the following evening the Communists tried to hold a mass demonstration against "fascism" in the Place de la République. Their purpose was to show that they would not stand idly by while the far Right—as in Rome and Berlin— took over the country. They were perhaps also motivated by a desire to clarify their own loyalties: groups of Communists, after all, had joined with the Fascist leagues in the rioting of February 6. Finding the square cordoned off by the police, the demonstrators retreated into the working-class districts stretching from the Gare du Nord and Gare de l'Est toward Belleville and Ménilmontant. There they erected barricades and fought pitched battles with the police, who did not hesitate to use live ammunition or bother to give any warning before opening fire. Four demonstrators were killed that night, and two died shortly thereafter of their wounds. An undetermined though large number of people were wounded. The police suffered no fatalities but claimed 141 injuries; most of these were bruises from kicks or missiles, but one policeman had been badly bitten. The significantly greater losses suffered by the rioters convinced the Communists that the police had been less hesitant to use their firearms than they had been on February 6. This only confirmed their belief that non-Communist Frenchmen cared not a sou for the lives of their Marxist countrymen. As the Communist wit

Charles Rappoport put it, *"Le sang communiste, ce n'est pas du sang français"* ("Communist blood is not French blood").

Alienated as they were from the republican system, including the rest of the French Left, the Communists nevertheless joined the Socialist-controlled trade union organization (CGT) in a twenty-four-hour general strike against the rightist leagues on February 12. This was the largest demonstration of its kind in French history, embracing all but two prefectures. It illustrated the depth of prorepublican sentiment throughout the country. It was also bloody, but less so than the February 6 riots. In Paris four persons died, all of them strikers.

The limited Communist-Socialist cooperation during this strike anticipated the Communist decision two years later to join France's Popular Front coalition government. The Communists took this step in response to the threat of fascism at home and abroad, a menace that Moscow, along with many rank-and-file French Communists, thought pressing enough to warrant their cooperation with the despised Socialists and bourgeois democrats. The Popular Front alliance was not long-lasting, but its very invocation greatly increased the far Right's hostility toward the republic. "Better Hitler than Blum" became the watchword of those on the right who let their hatred for the republic and its leftist Jewish premier outweigh fundamental considerations of self-preservation.

"A NEW LEASE OF DEATH"

Although the February riots had grown directly out of the Stavisky scandal, they quickly diverted public attention from that sordid business, since most Paris newspapers shifted their focus to the spectacular carnage in the streets. But though *l'affaire Stavisky* seemed safely buried along with the body of its central figure, it soon resurfaced to shake the republic once again.

After Daladier's resignation, President Lebrun turned for a new premier to Gaston Doumergue, a former president of the republic who was thought to be one of the only men in France with enough personal prestige to pull the divided nation together. In fact, Doumergue's prestige was based primarily on his intrepid affability—he had frowned once in public, but only, as he admitted, to give his face a rest—and on his advanced age. His appointment at seventy-one proved once again that, as the journalist Alexander Werth remarked, "in moments of great difficulty, France always plays for safety and falls back on old men." This is not necessarily a misguided policy—we have, after all, the examples of Clemenceau and Konrad Adenauer—but in Doumergue's case it was unfortunate because advancing years had not brought the added wisdom or political skill necessary to deal with the manifold ailments afflicting the nation. Although he tried to introduce constitutional reforms designed to enhance the power of the executive and reduce governmental instability, Doumergue lacked the decisiveness to see the changes through an obstreperous chamber.

Doumergue did, however, manage to appoint two committees to begin formal investigations into the Stavisky scandal and the riots of February 6. The first of these was known popularly as the "Thieves Committee" and the second as the "Murderers Committee." The goal of the Stavisky committee was to fix responsibility for the scandal as quickly as possible so that the ghost of the dead swindler would not haunt the republic for years to come. But just as the investigators were settling down to work, another grisly event occurred that, in the words of the historian Richard Cobb, gave the Stavisky affair yet another "lease of death."

On February 21 the engineer of a freight train noticed blood and bits of entrail on the front of his engine after completing a trip between Paris and Dijon. Having quickly established that this mess was human, the police began a search of the railway line. Not far from Dijon they found a man—or rather, several parts of a man—spread along the tracks. The body itself was cut into three sections, and the head, badly crushed, lay between the rails about twelve meters from the torso. Around the ankles of the corpse were pieces of rope, indicating that the man had been tied to the tracks. Nearby the police also found a large knife covered with blood, a briefcase, and, inexplicably, a blue powder puff. The briefcase was empty save for a summons from the "Thieves Committee." The document identified the dead man as one Conseiller Albert Prince, junior judge in the Paris Parquet (Public Prosecutor's Office).

The police had found Prince's body at a place called *la Combe aux Fées* (valley of the fairies), but no one assumed that fairies were responsible for what had happened there. The popular assumption was that yet another man who "knew too much" had been eliminated by highly placed people with much to hide. This assumption was strengthened when it became known that Prince was scheduled to testify about how his superior, the former prosecutor Pressard, had kept Stavisky out of jail for so long. His rendezvous with the freight train was explained by the fact that his wife had gotten a telephone call from a man who told her that Prince's mother in Dijon was about to be operated upon for a serious illness. Prince had left for work before the call came, but he returned home because he had forgotten his briefcase. Given the alarming telephone message by his wife, he took the first train to Dijon, where (according to witnesses at the station) he was met by two or three men who drove off with him in a car. At some point these men presumably killed him and then tied his body to the tracks, perhaps to cover their own. (A preliminary autopsy suggested that he had been dead before the train ran over him, but there were no wounds on the body indicating that he might have been knifed or shot.) Further investigation established that the phony alarm call had come from Paris, not Dijon, and suggested that Prince's briefcase might have contained papers relevant to his investigation of the Parquet's role in the Stavisky affair. Putting all this together, French and foreign newspapers alike concluded that Prince had been murdered both to prevent him from saying what he knew and to discourage others from coming forward. There was much talk in the rightist press about a "Sûreté-Masonic-Mafia" gang's having done the actual dirty work.

A new twist in the case developed when the authorities revealed that they were investigating the possibility that "Handsome Alex Stavisky had acted as an international spy, selling secret information to Germany and using women agents." To explain their suspicion, the police noted that Stavisky and two foreign actresses had been seen in a café frequented by Nazi sympathizers. Could it be that Inspector Prince was onto this foreign connection and therefore had to be silenced? (The presence of the actresses in the plot had the virtue of explaining the mysterious blue powder puff near Prince's body.) Or was it perhaps that French gangsters "inspired from abroad" had staged this latest piece of Grand Guignol not only to get rid of Prince but also to stir up more political unrest in France?

Speculation about Prince's grisly end prompted several French newspapers to launch their own "investigations" into the case. *Paris-Soir* hired three retired detectives from Scotland Yard and then brought in the Belgian detective-fiction writer Georges Simenon to assist them in their work. *Le Canard enchaîné* caught the proper spirit of the chase by claiming to have secured the services of two of the greatest detectives of China: Ki-san-fou, the *"homme de paille"* (man of straw), and Ki-mo-no, the *"homme de zinc du Bar de Shanghai"* (tin man of the Shanghai bar). Ki-san-fou's first report, which the *Canard* published in "the original Chinese," said (if read downward) "Getting on splendidly" or (if read upward) "Send more cash."

The Doumergue government could not afford to react so good-naturedly as the *Canard*. Although no ministers had been implicated in Prince's death, the entire republican leadership was again on trial for its apparent inability to prevent "gangsters" with possible police and chamber connections from behaving as if they lived in Chicago rather than in civilized France. And if espionage was involved in the affair, the security of the nation would be directly threatened. The Doumergue government therefore showed none of the hesitation that Chautemps had displayed when the Stavisky scandal broke: it offered a 100,000-franc reward for information leading to convictions in the crime, and it pulled in hundreds of uniformed police and detectives to work on the case.

But after an initial flurry of activity the investigations seemed to bog down and little more was heard about their progress. It has been suggested that the various inquiries may have come to the conclusion that—despite all the evidence pointing to murder—Prince could have killed himself, but done so in a way that looked conclusively like murder. Further investigation had poked many holes in the original suspicion of murder. A second postmortem examination showed that Prince was not dead after all when the train ran over him, but merely unconscious. He had apparently ingested a powerful anesthetic, and he could have tied himself to the tracks before losing consciousness. His briefcase might not have contained any documents incriminating higher officials; in any event, the information he was supposedly killed to suppress was well known to at least two other functionaries in the Parquet. His son promised to provide the "names" his father allegedly wanted to expose, but he never did. There were many other irregularities in the murder interpretation, but two questions above all others demand some response: If Prince indeed committed suicide, why did he do so? And if investigations privately reached a suicide verdict, why did not the investigators say so publicly?

Although the Paris newspapers, especially L'Action française, held Prince up as a model official and even a national hero, he had in fact been accused within the Parquet of negligence in his own conduct of the Stavisky investigation. Apparently he was anxious to exonerate his name by bringing forth startling new revelations in the case. He was also angry with Pressard, who had questioned his conduct. If he had found that he could not clear his name and tar Pressard by producing new evidence, perhaps he had decided that his "murdered" corpse would speak more eloquently on his behalf. Admittedly it seems farfetched that someone would use such elaborate, macabre, and (above all) permanent means to save face, but the Stavisky affair was bringing out the bizarre side of many a French official: at least three others connected with the case attempted suicide, one of them succeeding.

Why such a conclusion might have been hushed up is much easier to divine. The Doumergue government could hardly claim—*whatever* its investigation might have found—that another "suicide" had occurred. This would have brought the leagues back into the streets and perhaps ended the republic for good. In light of this threat, it was better to put up a reward for the guilty "gangsters" and round up all the usual suspects, which the police did with alacrity. If, as the journalist Alexander Werth has argued, the private newspaper investigations also found more persuasive evidence for suicide than for murder, they would have wanted to keep this quiet to protect circulation figures, which had soared in the wake of the Prince affair. As the publisher of *Paris-Soir* reportedly complained when his investigators told him that Prince had probably killed himself, "A suicide means the loss of two-hundred thousand readers. I have to have a *murder!*"

Among France's major political parties only the Socialists hazarded the view that Prince might have done himself in. The rightist parties and the Communists blamed different culprits—the Right said it was Chautemps, Pressard, and the Sûreté "Mafia"; the Communist newspaper L'Humanité fingered Chiappe, along with the rightist ministers Pierre Laval and André Tardieu—but all screamed bloody murder and held the republican leadership responsible. Just as they had in the February rioting, then, the far Left and the far Right could find common cause at least in their condemnation of the corrupt "system" that ruled France. The crisis of February 1934 showed once again that, as the French like to say, "the extremes touch."

IMPLICATIONS

It was not just Prince's gruesome death that kept the Stavisky affair alive; the parliamentary inquiry also had this effect, which was precisely why many leading politicians did not want it held. But the historian should be grateful for the inquiry's work, for the investigators not only clarified some of the hazier aspects of the case but also subjected the involved political and social institutions to penetrating scrutiny. In doing so, the inquiry pointed up what we can now see as some of the more far-reaching historical implications of the entire affair.

The widespread popular belief that Stavisky had been murdered by the police on higher orders was not confirmed by the inquiry, which came down solidly for a verdict of suicide. At the same time, however, the investigators concluded that the police had acted very negligently after they had tracked Stavisky to his final hiding place. One of the policemen on the scene proposed to the inquiry that Stavisky might have been saved had the detective in charge, Charpentier, acted more quickly to get the wounded man to the hospital. The inquiry accepted this proposition, adding that the policeman's own, hardly zealous efforts at first aid "could only render definitive the results of Stavisky's act." Taking all the police actions (or inactions) into account, one had to conclude that the authorities had done nothing "to conserve for justice a suspect of major importance." Whether this result was the product of low-level police negligence or orders from on high was not established, but the inquiry certainly implied that the Sûreté leadership had not wanted Stavisky taken alive.

The inquiry did not confine its investigation to police behavior in Chamonix. Delving into the entire history of Stavisky's activities, it found that his crooked schemes had at various times been abetted by high officials of both the Sûreté and the Parquet. Much of the investigation focused on the role of the rightist publisher Dubarry, who had often mediated between Stavisky and governmental officials. The investigators could not, however, precisely trace the flow of cash from Stavisky to his official protectors, because the evidence that might have allowed this—the famous bond counterfoils and check stubs—proved relatively unrevealing. But in the long run the inquiry's failure to connect each Stavisky check to a specific official was less significant than its broader finding that all of the relevant governmental agencies—the Sûreté, the Parquet, and the judiciary— had facilitated corruption and neglected to do their duty.

We might in turn attribute this failing to a historic deficiency in French administrative practice: the diffusion of responsibility to such an extent that no agency felt accountable for its actions or inactions. In this world, responsibility for any failing could either be shifted to another party (which would not accept it either) or be spread so widely that the fault would rest not with any individual or agency but with "evil fate." Alternatively, one could account for a crisis by invoking the "judgment of God." High French officials like Dalimier used these evasive tactics to defend themselves in 1934. As the historian Marc Bloch has shown in his classic account of France's "strange defeat" at the hands of the Germans, they would do so again in 1940. On that occasion French political figures blamed their nation's ignominious collapse variously on the system of parliamentary government, on the high command, on the "fifth column" of internal "subversives," or (better yet) on the British. Marshal Philippe Pétain, an aged rightist who headed the collaborationist Vichy regime, said France's defeat was God's punishment for the manifold sins of the Third Republic.

The parliamentary inquiry also looked into the behavior of nongovernmental institutions, particularly the press. It found that while venal publicists like Dubarry might have been guilty of oiling the wheels of Stavisky's machine, other journalists exploited the scandal for their own political or financial ends. In this respect *Paris-Soir*'s conduct came under special scrutiny. But again the problem was seen to be much broader than the exploitation of this or that scandal, something a free press was bound to do whenever it could. A number of French papers, many of which were owned by right-wing interests, not merely attacked corruption in high places but also did their best to undermine the public's faith in parliamentary democracy. This certainly was true of *L'Action française;* it held, too, for pro-Fascist weeklies like *Candide* and *Gringoire,* the latter owned by a brother-in-law of Chiappe, who was later made virtual chief of the Paris town council by the Germans.

The cynicism and despair fomented by the French press in 1934 did not simply vanish with the waning of the Stavisky scandal. Doubts about the legitimacy of the country's political institutions remained part of France's malaise through the late thirties to the moment of the German invasion. Added to this were the counsels of defeatism spread by the papers of the extreme Right and Left, which looked to the totalitarian states for their political inspiration.

Important as the inquiry was for a detailed understanding of the Stavisky affair, one need not read through its voluminous findings to see that this episode could only exacerbate France's most pressing problem: its persistent internal disunity and confusion over what the nation stood for, over what it meant to be French. In this respect the affair deserves comparison with a much more famous one: the Dreyfus case at the turn of the century.

Stavisky, of course, was no Alfred Dreyfus. Unlike the famous captain, Sasha was indeed guilty of most of the charges brought against him, though the accusation of espionage was never proven and was probably false. But more significant than the obvious differences in personal history and character are certain historical similarities in the treatment of the two cases. In both instances much was made of the "alien" background of the principal figures, though the Jew Dreyfus was a patriotic Alsatian and Stavisky a naturalized Frenchman and a convert to Catholicism. Both affairs, then, stimulated renewed outbursts of anti-Semitism and xenophobia. The insistence upon protecting the "true France" from alien influences also reignited the old battle over defining basic French values, reviving the chronic civil war of "France against Herself." In this struggle Frenchmen had traditionally battled each other with more passion (and perhaps more pleasure) than they had their various external enemies. During the Dreyfus era Frenchmen fought duels over the captain's guilt or innocence, and individual families split into rival camps. Rumors of a monarchist coup filled the air. No wonder Republicans of 1934 recalled that ominous time when they saw the rightist leagues massing in the Place de la Concorde! The republic had barely survived the Dreyfus affair, they said. Would it now survive Stavisky?

II

THE DEATH OF RED VIENNA

The Austrian Civil War of 1934

*"Dieser Dollfuss"—so sagte Chojnicki—"will das Proletar-
iat umbringen. Gott strafe mich nicht: ich kann ihn nicht
leiden. Es liegt in seiner Natur, sich selbst zu begraben."**

—Joseph Roth, *Die Kapuzinergruft* (1938)

On 12 February 1934 I was still limping from a skiing accident. It was a dark winter's morning. In the classroom at the
Landeserziehungsheim the electric lights were on. Suddenly, shortly after 11:00, the rooms went dark. We reacted
as schoolboys always do to any unexpected break in their
dreary routine—with cheers.

George Clare, *Last Waltz in Vienna* (1981)

The Austro-British writer George Clare (né Klaar), from whose family
memoir the above passage is taken, was naïvely cheering the beginning of
the Austrian civil war on that dark morning in February 1934. The sudden loss of electric power signaled a short-lived general strike and an armed
uprising of Austrian workers against the rightist dictatorship of Chancellor Engelbert Dollfuss. For the next four days Austria—especially its stately old capital,
Vienna—was to be the scene of some of the most vicious internecine fighting in
the 1930s. At its conclusion the workers' rebellion was thoroughly crushed and
the Austrian Socialist movement, headquartered in Vienna, forced into exile or
underground.

A witness to the action in Vienna who had just returned from Paris said he
was reminded of the recent carnage in the Place de la Concorde. In Vienna,
however, the fighting was concentrated not in a historic central square but in drab
proletarian suburbs ringing the city. In and around Vienna's huge municipal
housing projects, working-class armies squared off against police, military, and

---

*"This Dollfuss"—so said Chojnicki—"wants to kill off the proletariat. God have mercy on me; I
can't stand the man. It's in his nature to bury himself." The title of Roth's book may be translated as
"The Capucin Crypt."

rightist volunteer forces armed with howitzers, gas, and tanks. Once again, a great European city trembled in horror as citizens carried their impassioned political differences from parliament into the streets and made the gutters run with blood. And once again, the implications of the domestic turmoil were far more momentous than contemporary witnesses—by no means just naïve schoolboys—could have imagined.

RED VIENNA
AND BLACK AUSTRIA

"In no other European town," wrote the English poet Stephen Spender,

did the shabby contemporary life contrast so with the grandeur of the background of the past as in Vienna [of the interwar period]. The people in their suits and homburg hats or their leathery peasant costumes shifted like water at the very bottom of a tank against the exalted churches, palaces, monuments and galleries. To go to the Vienna Opera and see the weary audience like dwarfs against an ornate interior which demanded the parade of uniforms was to see the condition to which Vienna had fallen.

How could it have been otherwise? The Vienna of which Spender wrote had once been the center of a huge and cosmopolitan—if somewhat ramshackle and anachronistic—empire. When the Habsburg monarchy fell, in 1918, Vienna became the capital of a dwarf republic of some six million people, roughly a third of whom lived in the old imperial headquarters on the Danube. No wonder people called the city a "waterhead"! Vienna's grand architectural and cultural monuments had been extensively subsidized for generations by the city's wealthy aristocracy and upper bourgeoisie. Some of the aristocrats still maintained their palaces in the Inner City (the historic core of the town), although many had been reduced to genteel poverty because their agricultural estates in the eastern parts of the old monarchy had been confiscated by such postwar successor states as Hungary, Czechoslovakia, Poland, and Yugoslavia. Vienna's highly cultured upper-middle classes—traditional patrons of the city's famous opera and symphony orchestras—also suffered economic decline with the postwar shrinkage of Austria's marketplace for its manufactured goods. All Viennese, rich and poor alike, felt the terrible squeeze of inflation. In 1919 it took 6 Austrian crowns to buy a dollar; in January 1921 that figure had risen to 177; in August 1922, to 83,000. Although the crown's perilous skid was arrested by a League of Nations loan in late 1922, Austria was obliged to pay for this international largess by initiating austerity measures that cost thousands of civil servants their jobs.

Men who had exchanged substantive wealth and power for their shabby pretense understandably dreamt of recapturing the real article. G. E. R. Gedye, Vienna correspondent for the London *Daily Express*, observed,

In the decayed salons of inflation-battered Vienna, where one walked across precious oriental rugs to dine off costly plate on a little cold sausage and black bread beneath the eyes of the Old Masters, they [the aristocrats, high church officials, and business barons] whispered of the possibility of a . . . comeback of caste and privilege.

Whisper they might, but there seemed little likelihood that they would soon recover "their" Vienna: the Vienna of elaborate court ceremony, the Spanish Riding School, grand balls in the opera, banquets for two hundred guests in the Hotel Imperial on the Ringstrasse. This Vienna seemed to be lost forever not only because the empire had collapsed and the city's economy declined but also because real power in the Austrian capital had passed to a new social group, the working class.

Vienna's industrial workers had been on the political ascent since the waning days of the monarchy. In 1911 their party, the Social Democrats, had captured a majority of seats in the capital's city council. As long as the empire still survived, however, the Socialists' power was held in check by a constitutional system that gave the imperial government considerable control over Vienna's affairs. That changed in the early years of the republic. The new republican constitution apportioned extensive powers to the nation's individual *Länder* (states), of which Vienna became one in 1921. The stage was thus set for the appearance of "Red Vienna," one of postwar Europe's most ambitious sociopolitical experiments.

In the early 1920s, Vienna's Social Democratic mayor, Richard Seitz, and minister of finance, Hugo Breitner, launched a series of social reforms designed to improve the lot of the city's working classes, most of whom lived in crowded proletarian suburbs like Floridsdorf, Favoriten, and Ottakring. The municipal government built dozens of schools, kindergartens, and hospitals in the outer districts. It passed social-insurance legislation that protected the workers from cradle to grave. (Since burial fees were covered by the new insurance program, workers could now share in a hallowed Viennese tradition: that of going out in style as a *schöne Leich'*—a beautiful corpse.) Most important, the municipality constructed vast new housing projects that allowed working-class families to live in apartments of their own. Rents for these and other apartments in the city were kept within the workers' means through government-imposed rent controls.

The Viennese social-reform program soon became famous throughout Europe as a model of what progressive government could do. The left-leaning British intellectual John Lehmann summed up this sentiment when he wrote, "[Vienna's] experiment proved what had become so doubtful to us in London, that the working masses could find welfare and civilized conditions of life without a Communist revolution."

Although the Viennese reforms—unlike those in the Soviet Union—were not the fruit of violent and bloody revolution, they nevertheless exacted their price. To pay for all those free kindergartens, free hospitals, and free burials, to build housing projects and subsidize workers' lending libraries, the government introduced a "soak the rich" tax program. Since there were not that many rich left to soak, however, the heaviest tax burden fell on the middle classes. This did not endear Vienna's generous social-welfare system to members of the bourgeoisie. They especially cursed the municipal housing projects, which they claimed were so shabbily constructed that they would collapse in the first big storm, or, conversely, were built like military forts so that the workers could command the city like latter-day feudal lords.

There was, in fact, something fortresslike about the entire Social Democratic enterprise in postwar Vienna, but it was a beleaguered fortress. The Social Democrats may have dominated the capital, but they did not enjoy an equivalent influence in national politics, which increasingly was controlled by the conservative Christian Social party and its tough-minded leader, the prelate Ignaz Seipel. The Socialists' failure to play a significant role in the national political arena after 1920 led them to seal themselves off in Vienna and to carry on their reforms there in a kind of splendid isolation. The less power they enjoyed outside their "fortress," the more they insisted on maintaining strict control within. It looked, in other words, as if the anti-Socialist forces in Vienna would need help from outside if they were ever to regain mastery over their old preserve.

The Socialists' preoccupation with ruling Vienna did not prevent them from at least talking about extending their power to the country as a whole. Their chief theorist in that era was a Marxist dialectician of keen mental powers named Otto Bauer. With his high domed forehead, receding hairline, black soulful eyes, and sardonic smile, Bauer looked like an intellectual gypsy. When he climbed on his political soapbox, which he did often and with relish, he liked to talk as if free kindergartens in the capital were but a stepping-stone to the socialist millennium. The more his party settled down to a workaday existence of practical reformism in Vienna, the more Bauer insisted on retaining a commitment to Marxist theories of "inevitable" world revolution. This dualism between reformist reality and revolutionary rhetoric was evident even in the names the Socialists gave their municipal housing projects: one was called Goethe-Haus, after Germany's greatest poet, while another was named the Karl-Marx-Hof. It was bad enough that the Social Democratic leaders did not seem to know which of these names was closer to their heart; even worse, their enemies on the right decided that it was definitely Marx and that the Socialists meant what they said about revolutionary conquest.

In the mid-1920s Austrian politics settled into a sterile standoff between "Red" Vienna and the "Black" (or conservative) alpine provinces from which the national government of Chancellor Seipel derived most of its support. For their part the socialists announced a new party program in 1926, the Linz program, which bristled with Marxist phrases about the inability of the bourgeoisie to accept its "inevitable" loss of power without a fight, meaning that the workers must be prepared for "civil war." Socialist politicians like Bauer delighted in calling their conservative antagonists from the hinterlands *Dorftrottel* (village morons), an epithet recalling Marx's famous dictum regarding the idiocy of rural life.

The Socialists' chief opponent in the 1920s, however, was anything but a *Dorftrottel.* Ignaz Seipel, chancellor for most of the decade, was a shrewd and sophisticated political strategist, and one of his generation's most accomplished conservative thinkers. A Catholic priest, Seipel looked the part of a modern-day inquisitor. He had thin bloodless lips, a hawk nose, and piercing eyes. His black priestly gown hung over a frame emaciated by years of asceticism. To his many enemies he gave the appearance of a man whose sole goal in life was to crush all vestiges of free thought—not to mention free living—under the dark weight of Catholic orthodoxy.

Seipel actually had begun his political career as something of a progressive and after the revolution of 1918 had helped build the coalition between the Social Democratic and the Christian Social parties, which ruled Austria for the first two years of the republic's life. This coalition reflected the considerable continuity between empire and republic that marked the first years of the 1920s. It also pointed up the spirit of consensus that made the Austrian republic's early history much less violent than Weimar Germany's or, of course, Soviet Russia's. But Austria's "consensus" was born more of mutually perceived threats—particularly the threats of economic collapse and Communist revolution—than of genuine political agreement. As the pressing crises of the immediate postwar period abated somewhat, old polarities and antagonisms resurfaced. During the middle to late twenties Seipel countered ideological rigidity on the part of the Socialists—especially by his archrival Bauer—with ideological rigidity of his own. He came to see the Social Democrats essentially in religious terms, as enemies of the Christian order he hoped to impose on the chaos of Austrian politics. His own policy eventually amounted to a "mirror image" of the ingrown and one-dimensional vision of the Social Democrats.

Under Seipel's guidance, the Christian Social party countered the Social Democrats' Linz program with a countermanifesto that attacked Austrian socialism as a "revolutionary movement" bent on destroying all traditional Austrian institutions, including the church. Alluding to the fact that some of the Social Democratic leaders (like Bauer and Breitner) were Jews, it warned of "the decomposing Jewish influence" in Austrian politics.

Taken together, these two militant party programs revealed that the Socialists were more accurate than they realized in their rhetoric about civil war. Still, the ideological polarization in Austrian politics might have been less dangerous had the opposing parties contented themselves with heaping verbal abuse upon each other. As in France, though, in Austria politics became militarized in the 1920s through the creation of rival paramilitary organizations tied to the major parties. And in Austria, again as in France, this tendency to shift the chief arena of political confrontation from parliament to the streets undermined democratic institutions and weakened the country's ability to stand up to outside antagonists.

Austria's earliest paramilitary organizations had their origins in the immediate aftermath of the revolution of 1918, when peasants and villagers banded together to protect their crops, homes, and shops from marauding ex-soldiers, newly released prisoners of war, and hungry predators from the starving cities. Other groups were formed to defend the country's southern borders against attacks by the new Yugoslav army. Although initially lacking firm political definition, these so-called Heimwehren (Home Guards) soon assumed a pronounced anti-Socialist orientation in response to Red Vienna's attempts to commandeer food stores from the villages and extend its political control over the traditionally conservative and heavily Catholic countryside. The rural and small-town Heimwehren increasingly saw Vienna as a parasitic urban Babylon full of dangerous radicals, Jews, and foreigners. Large industrialists and bankers began funding the rightist paramilitary groups in the hope of turning them into an effective weapon for the reconquest of the Red citadel. With this support, the Heimwehren bought military weapons, including machine guns and howitzers, and even a couple of small aircraft. For "uniforms" they generally stuck with their traditional native costumes: green woolen coats, lederhosen, and alpine hats replete with jaunty cock feathers. (From these feathered hats derived their nickname *Hahnenschwänzler*, or "rooster tails.")

Opposing the rightist Heimwehren was the paramilitary organization of the Social Democratic party, the Republikanischer Schutzbund. This group was created in 1923 as a counterweight both to the Heimwehren and to the nation's regular army, the Bundesheer, which though at first heavily Socialist had increasingly fallen under the domination of the clerical-conservative Christian Social party. The Socialist party's army had its major strongholds in the country's industrialized regions: Upper Styria, Linz, and, above all, Vienna itself. Like the Heimwehren, the Schutzbund was well equipped with small arms, most of them gleaned from the huge stocks left behind after the dissolution of the old imperial army. Schutzbund members not content to wear their blue workers' overalls and leather caps put up a few schillings to outfit themselves in billed hats, gray windbreakers, and black or brown pants. They presented a less colorful picture than their rightist rivals, but they sang equally well as they marched through the streets of their urban strongholds.

Neither the Heimwehren nor the Schutzbund amounted to a truly formidable military force in the early 1920s, but each felt strong enough to risk periodic assaults on the other's territory. There were constant skirmishes between Right and Left, most of them provoked by attempts on the part of one group to steal or confiscate weapons belonging to its rival. The majority of these confrontations led to little serious bloodshed, though in 1923 three workers were killed in separate clashes with the rightist forces.

The small body count notwithstanding, this simmering civil war kept the little country in a state of nervous tension that belied Austria's proverbial reputation for tranquillity and gemütlichkeit (easygoing geniality). The *Neue freie Presse*, Vienna's leading liberal daily, complained in 1927 of a condition of "terror and counterterror." A popular cabaret artist of the period reaped loud cries of approval when he sang wistfully of a little town called Znaim, which "has no Schutzbund, no Heimwehr." Znaim, significantly, now belonged to neighboring Czech-oslovakia.

"BLOODY FRIDAY," JULY 15, 1927

One part of Austria, however, lacked a Schutzbund or Heimwehr, at least until 1926. In the Burgenland, Austria's easternmost province, the political parties had agreed in 1923 not to establish armies or distribute military arms. The political climate there seemed almost as placid as the surface of the Neusiedler See, the shallow lake across which the Austrian-Hungarian border now ran. But in 1926 the Frontkämpfer Vereinigung (Front Fighter's Association), a right-wing veterans' organization, extended its activities to the Burgenland. This provoked the Socialists, who loathed the Front Fighters as much as they did the Heim-wehren, to found branches of the Schutzbund in that province. By mid-1926 the Schutzbund and Front Fighters were busily breaking each other's heads in towns and villages across the region.

On January 30, 1927, the two groups decided to stage rival demonstrations in Schattendorf, a picturesque village hard on the Hungarian border. Since this was to be a test of strength, both groups brought in reinforcements from outside the province. The nervous authorities had pleaded with the leaders of the two organizations to stage their rallies at opposite ends of the village and to enter and leave town from different directions. But Schattendorf, like old Dodge City when rival gunslingers came to town, was not big enough for both these outfits, which in any event had no intention of keeping their distance from each other.

The Schutzbund was determined to prevent the Front Fighter leader, Colonel Max Hiltl, from addressing the veterans' rally. A group of *Schutzbündler* beat up some of Hiltl's followers as soon as they got off the train in Schattendorf. The Front Fighters, for their part, posted some of their men at an inn that lay beside the route that the Schutzbund would take in returning to the train station after their rally. The innkeeper and his two sons, all members of the veterans' group, stockpiled shotguns and ammunition in a house adjoining the inn.

As a Schutzbund column passed by in the late afternoon, Front Fighter men inside the tavern began yelling anti-Socialist slogans and making hand gestures of unmistakable significance. Enraged by this "provocation," a few *Schutzbündler* rushed into the inn, searching for their antagonists, while the rest of the column continued on its way. At this point the innkeeper's sons fled to the neighboring house, grabbed their weapons, and began blasting away from upstairs windows into the Schutzbund column below. One blast tore the head off a forty-year-old *Schutzbündler;* another ripped open the chest of an eight-year-old boy who happened to be watching the action from a nearby street corner. In addition to these two deaths, several men were wounded, five seriously.

When news of the Schattendorf events reached Vienna, the working-class suburbs ringing the city seethed in anger. Cries went up for a march on the wealthier districts in the center of town. The Social Democratic leadership, however, was able to prevent spontaneous disturbances by channeling the indignation into peaceful demonstrations. On February 2 it celebrated an impressive funeral for the Schattendorf victims, who were buried in places of honor in Vienna's Zentralfriedhof, the massive old cemetery that the natives liked to say was "half as large but twice as lively as Zurich." On the same day, the Socialist leadership called a brief general strike, during which the entire capital was immobilized. Tramcars halted in their tracks, telephone operators played deaf, shop girls deserted their counters, and waiters stopped serving coffee topped with *Schlag* (whipped cream). Such measures provided a momentary catharsis for the workers' rage, but tensions in the city remained extremely high as people awaited the results of the judicial proceedings set in motion by the Schattendorf tragedy.

In July 1927 three members of the Front Fighters Association went on trial in Vienna for the Burgenland killings. They were tried by jury, an innovation in Austrian judicial procedure introduced by the Socialists in 1920. On July 14, after a few days of heated legal argument and polemical editorials in the country's highly politicized press, the jury returned a verdict of not guilty. This may seem ironic given the provenance of the jury system, but Austrian courts—even those in Red Vienna—were dominated by a legal bureaucracy of prerevolutionary vintage that had little use for Socialism. Even the state prosecutor, while calling for a verdict of guilty, added that the moral responsibility for the Schattendorf events rested with the Schutzbund. No doubt this had its effect on a jury composed largely of middle-class citizens.

On July 15 the Socialist organ, the *Arbeiter Zeitung,* published an editorial bristling with indignation. "This verdict is a disgrace seldom, perhaps never, equaled in judicial history," declared the paper. "Apparently the jurymen thought it insignificant that some people shot point-blank at others—insignificant that is, as long as the killers were members of the Frontkämpfer, who must be allowed their hunting pleasure!" The jury members, concluded the editorial, were themselves "dishonorable criminals" whose verdict would bring down upon them, and upon the entire corrupt political system they defended, "hatred and contempt on the part of all justice-loving people."

These were provocative words, since many of Vienna's workers had already concluded that the Seipel government was intent upon strangling what was left of the Austrian revolution. The *Arbeiter Zeitung* editorial was probably not intended as a direct call to arms—the paper's editorial staff was firmly in the hands of the Social Democratic party's reformist leadership—but it had this fateful effect.

The night before, there was "much excitement" in the working-class districts, but no open manifestations of proletarian defiance. The following morning, however, commuters on the city's streetcar system waited in vain for the arrival of their trams. This was not simply another case of infamous Viennese *Schlamperei* (sloppiness): workers at the city's main power plant had cut off electricity to the entire transport system.

Having done this, the workers picked up their tools and headed for the Inner City. Workers in other plants did the same. By nine on that hot and sultry morning, columns of people dressed in dirty blue overalls and carrying heavy wrenches, hammers, and crowbars converged on the center of town. They showed no signs of coordinated leadership, having launched their march without consulting the Socialist party headquarters.

Reaching the Criminal Court Building, in the Alserstrasse, the first contingent of marchers shook their fists and shouted, "Down with the justice of shame!" They then marched along the Ringstrasse to the university, where Pan-German students had recently beaten up Social Democratic and Jewish students. "Down with the murderers of workers!" and "Down with the swastika bearers!" the marchers screamed. Prevented from entering the university building by police guards and hastily locked iron gates, the demonstrators rattled the bars and smashed windows. "A tough test for the poor students and professors inside," commented the Neue freie Presse. The timely arrival of police reinforcements induced the mob to move on once again, this time in the direction of the parliament building farther along the Ring.

Threatening as these actions were, the demonstration had not yet turned into a full-scale riot, largely because the mob was still small enough for the police to intimidate. But by late morning, as thousands more workers arrived on the scene, the demonstrators vastly outnumbered the police. The crowd that assembled in front of the parliament soon began to sense the power of its numbers. Indeed, some self-appointed ringleaders started yelling for an all-out assault on the templelike building, whose chief protection, aside from a vigilant statue of Pallas Athena,* consisted of a small group of mounted policemen.

Alarmed by the swelling mob arrayed against them, the police decided to rout the crowd before it could grow any larger. About twenty-five mounted police rode headlong into the demonstrators' ranks, slashing right and left with their sabers. Several people fell under the horses' feet, while others fled in panic to a park on the other side of the Ring. But their retreat was only temporary. The brutal police charge enraged the people, giving the mob a cohesiveness and unity of purpose it had hitherto lacked.

Having quickly regrouped, the mob stormed back across the Ring. On the way men dug up paving stones and pulled iron bars from the park fence. They hurled these, and any other heavy objects they could find, at the mounted police. "A hail of stones fell on [police] heads, knocking them defenseless to the ground," exulted one worker in a memoir of the battle. "The horses reared in terror and ran from the scene."

The mob could now have stormed the parliament; instead, it shifted its attention to a target more closely identified with the cause of its rage: the Palace of Justice, in the neighboring Schmerling Platz. Quickly surrounding the building,

---

*A contemporary joke ran, "Why does the Goddess of Wisdom stand outside the parliament?— Because there's no wisdom inside."

the huge crowd erected barricades out of park benches and overturned cars to keep police or military units from aiding the small contingent of bureaucrats and security guards locked inside. At first the rioters contented themselves with throwing rocks through the windows, but when the guards responded with pistol fire, they lost all restraint. With the help of a ten-foot-long tree trunk, they began to smash in the giant front doors of the palace. Meanwhile, other workers beat off potential police reinforcements. Wrote one witness later, "Pieces of uniform, police caps, pistols, broken sabers littered the ground—testaments to the impotence of the authorities. Riderless horses raced around the square."

The battering ram soon did its work, and enraged workers streamed into the building, searching for "officials." The few bureaucrats who had not managed to flee before the attack were barricaded in the upper floors with the police. For the time being the workers had to vent their rage on such symbolic items as desks and files. Gathering up armloads of documents, the workers made huge piles in the halls or simply tossed their booty out the windows. Suddenly the clear July sky was obscured by a rain of dusty court records. The rampaging rioters eventually found even more satisfying targets for their fury. Coming upon a room full of portraits of Habsburg emperors and empresses, they cut these into small pieces and pitched them out the window. A large oil painting of old Kaiser Franz Josef, who had loved nothing more than to pore over a good document, went the way of the emperor's beloved files.

The fate of the officials on the upper floors looked equally unpromising since the workers, unable to break into the police sanctuary, found another use for the piles of records, furniture, and paintings they had assembled in and around the palace: "Let's smoke them out!" someone shouted. It is unclear who set the first pile ablaze, but soon there were fires everywhere in and around the building.

While smoke curled from the windows of the Palace of Justice, another group of rioters attacked a small police station in the nearby Lichtenfelsgasse. This, too, they set ablaze, though not until they had cleared the building of its defenders. Yet another target was the editorial office of the *Reichspost*, primary mouthpiece for Austria's conservative-Catholic element. Demonstrators broke into the building, smashed furniture and files, and then started fires amid the rubble.

The Social Democratic leadership had certainly not intended its protest against the Schattendorf verdict to spark such a conflagration. Indeed, on the eve of July 14 it informed the federal police president, Johannes Schober, that no demonstrations were planned. The Socialist leaders' caution was motivated by fears—justifiable, as it turned out—that the party establishment would be held responsible by the government for any violence during a demonstration. The leaders also worried, with equal justification, that outbreaks of violence would enhance the influence of Communists and other extremist groups within the workers' movement. They therefore did all they could to contain the spread of violence and reassert their control once the spontaneous demonstration had begun. Mayor Karl Seitz personally accompanied a brigade of firemen who attempted to beat their way through the howling mob to the Palace of Justice. But the crowd booed Seitz's call for calm and forced him and the firemen to retreat. Julius Deutsch, chief of the Schutzbund, eventually managed to reach the palace with a fire brigade and a contingent of armed *Schutzbündler*. But Deutsch, too, was subjected to verbal abuse, and some of the *Schutzbündler* who tried to assist wounded policemen out of the building were themselves pummeled by the mob.

This turn of events came as a shock to the Social Democratic establishment, which had always taken pride in the "orderliness" and "discipline" shown by Viennese workers in their annual May Day marches and other ritual displays of Socialist power. Now, sitting helplessly in party headquarters, or watching from the windows of the besieged parliament, the Socialist leaders could only shake their heads in despair. Wilhelm Ellenbogen, a member of the party executive, captured this atmosphere perfectly when he recalled,

I was watching the crowd from the Social Democratic representatives' room in the parliament. I saw wild men with foam at their mouths and bloody-faced security guards writhing on the ground. Screaming women ran around like chickens with their heads cut off. The hysterical mob even attacked members of the Schutzbund and shouted down our popular mayor, Karl Seitz. Seeing all this, I had the impression I was witnessing an outbreak of mass psychosis.

Though as surprised by the July rioting as the Social Democratic leaders were, the government was quicker to regain its composure. Chancellor Seipel kept an icy calm throughout the turmoil. When, on the morning of the fifteenth, Otto Bauer and Mayor Seitz appealed to him to make concessions, including his own resignation, to appease the workers, he dismissed them with the cutting remark that he, a good democrat, could step down only after a vote of no confidence from the parliament. That afternoon he entrusted the security of the city to his president of police, Johannes Schober. The latter had already issued carbines to several hundred security guards and Police Academy students. Just at the moment when the Schutzbund men had begun to clear the Schmerling Platz and rescue the police from the Palace of Justice, Schober's police launched a full-scale attack.

For the remainder of the afternoon the Schmerling Platz resembled a scene from the First World War. Police advanced toward the Palace of Justice, "tree by tree, house by house," firing as they went. At first they fired over the heads of the mob, but they lowered their aim when the crowd failed to disperse. Some workers, armed with captured police pistols, fired back, but most began a disorderly retreat, leaving behind dozens of dead and wounded.

By late afternoon the Schmerling Platz had been cleared, and the fire department could free the remaining officials still barricaded on the top floor of the Palace of Justice. The men, most of them wounded or suffering from smoke inhalation, were freed none too soon, for the fire continued to burn out of control, and at six the entire roof caved in. The neighboring parliament building, meanwhile, had been transformed into an emergency hospital, as "one bloody body

Chancellor Engelbert Dollfuss *(second from left)* at a Heimwehr rally at Schönbrunn Palace (Vienna). He is accompanied by the Heimwehr leaders Emil Fey *(far left)* and Ernst Rüdiger von Starhemberg *(right).* *Austrian State Library*

Dollfuss and two military officers during the government's seizure of Floridsdorf in the February 1934 civil war. *Austrian State Archive*

Hitler crosses the city limits of Vienna following the *Anschluss* in March 1938. *AP/Wide World Photos*

Government artillery pounds the huge Karl-Marx-Hof apartment complex in Vienna during the civil war of February 1934. *UPI/Bettmann Newsphotos*

after another was carried up the graceful steps of this ordinarily so peaceful Greek temple."

A Viennese journalist touring the still-smoking battleground in the early evening encountered a group of Japanese and Chinese tourists gaping at the devastation. "They know this sort of thing happens frequently at home," opined the reporter, "but they must be amazed to see it in the heart of civilized Europe!" On his way across the Schmerling Platz the journalist stumbled over the corpse of a policeman, whose neatly slit throat was already crawling with flies, and whose glazed eyes seemed to ask, "Wozu?" ("Why?").

Senseless as the bloodshed may have seemed to many, it was by no means over. Workers streaming back to the suburbs late Friday night and early Saturday morning vented their bitterness on police stations in the outer districts. They descended upon a station in the Hernals district and tried to set it ablaze. The police inside fired "warning shots" out the windows, managing only to kill an old woman in a house across the street. When the workers shot an officer, the police began firing in earnest. Four more workers died.

The escalating violence and bloody police repression confronted the Socialist leadership with a new dilemma: should it, as many rank and file members were demanding, distribute arms to the workers? Late in the evening of July 15, the leadership debated this question and decided not to break out the munitions. Two days later Otto Bauer explained the party executive's decision to a group of workers: "Comrades, I have to justify our action in deciding not even to attempt a disorderly and irregular arming of the wildly excited proletarian masses. In this hour of extremely tense passions a wholesale distribution of arms would have meant to begin an open civil war. But it is our first duty, as long as we can, not to bring about civil war."

At the same time, however, the party leadership could not remain entirely passive, for this would have suggested utter impotence both to the workers and to the Seipel regime. Thus on the morning of July 16 a party information sheet appeared in the streets of Vienna announcing a twenty-four-hour general strike, as well as a transportation, postal, and telephone walkout of unlimited duration. "We do not want more blood to flow," said the proclamation. "The power of the workers consists in fighting with economic weapons."

The party leadership hoped by this action both to stop the flow of blood and to regain its own credibility. In the first aim it succeeded, but not in the second. The general strike went off as planned, and the workers resisted the temptation to combine this economic weapon with another march on the Inner City. The transportation walkout, which was designed to force the government to accept responsibility for the bloodshed of July 15 and to grant an amnesty to all workers arrested in connection with the rioting, did not succeed, because the Heimwehren intervened to keep the threatened services functioning. In Innsbruck the local rightists occupied the railway station and manned the trains; in Styria they mobilized twenty thousand men to run the transportation system and deliver mail. Reports that Italy and Hungary might intervene against the strike also had a sobering effect on the Socialists. Again the party leadership appealed to Seipel to negotiate a compromise solution, and again he refused. Unable to gain from Seipel more than a vague promise not to launch a wholesale attack on Vienna's social programs, the Social Democrats called off their action on July 18.

The end of the strike, which allowed the resumption of newspaper publication, inaugurated an orgy of mutual recrimination and finger pointing on the part of the Socialist and progovernment press. While admitting that the July 15 unheaval was not a product of a Socialist "conspiracy," the *Neue freie Presse* attributed the violence to the *Arbeiter Zeitung*'s "reckless" response to the "admittedly unfortunate" Schattendorf verdict. The Socialist party leadership, the paper insisted, had overestimated its ability to control the "rowdies and rabble" within the working-class movement. Once the rioting had begun, the party leadership should have immediately brought in the Schutzbund to disarm and isolate the mischief makers. Their failure to control the situation resulted in a "binge of violence" that cost lives and destroyed "valuable property," including the irreplaceable *Grundbücher* (central record books). The rioting had also terrified foreign visitors staying in the city's great hotels along the Ring. "What will our guests have to say about Viennese gemütlichkeit when they return home?" asked the paper.

The *Arbeiter Zeitung* understandably saw matters in a different light. It blamed the first incidences of violence on "Communist rowdies" who had "exploited the workers' justifiable rage." "Communists," said the paper, "are synonymous with undisciplined elements, who undermine working-class solidarity and at the first opportunity put the workers' hard-earned gains at jeopardy." But the paper also blamed the police for shooting into the crowd. It called Schober's forces "rabid" and insisted that they had been ordered by the government to fire on the workers.

In announcing the workers' return to their jobs on July 18, the *Arbeiter Zeitung* tried to depict this clear defeat for the Socialist movement as a victory of labor's vaunted "iron discipline." But nobody was fooled, least of all the workers. They saw the decision to return to work as an admission of failure and a confession of pusillanimity. A small but vocal contingent of radical workers denounced Bauer and company for their "conscious betrayal" of labor's cause. They concluded that in any future confrontations with the government, the workers would have to act entirely on their own.

But for now there were bodies to bury: fifty-seven Socialist workers, four policemen, and twenty-eight innocent bystanders. The city council organized a mass funeral for the dead Socialists. Municipal dignitaries, including Mayor Seitz, delivered eulogies. On the following day the Seipel government buried its four policemen in an elaborate ceremony attended by the entire cabinet and presided over by Federal President Wilhelm Miklas. The Socialists lost not only the battle of the streets and the transportation strike but the battle of the funerals as well.

Burial of the dead did not mean burial of the passions inflamed by the July rioting and police repression. On July 25 parliament met to hear government and

Socialist representatives blame each other for the tragedy. Most significant was the speech by Chancellor Seipel, who went out of his way to praise the police, thanking God that they had "done their duty." Then, by way of reply to Bauer's plea for amnesty for all those arrested, Seipel added, "Demand nothing from Parliament or the government which may seem merciful toward the victims and the guilty of the catastrophic days, but which would be cruel toward the wounded Republic." In taking this position, Seipel showed himself a churchman in the proud tradition of Cardinal Richelieu, acting by the hard rules of *raison d'état,* but he would have been better advised to expend on human suffering some of the sympathy he claimed to feel for the suffering of the state. By refusing any gesture of conciliation, he earned the epithet "Prelate without Mercy" and ensured that the wounds of Bloody Friday would remain unhealed.

MILLIMETTERNICH

"15 July 1927 was not a civil war. It was only a one-day revolt, but the events of that one desperate day made the civil war of 1934 inevitable." George Clare's assessment of the July events overstates the case. The interval of six and one-half years between the Palace of Justice rioting and the full-scale civil war of February 1934 offered several opportunities for political reconciliation. But these opportunities were not exploited, a failure attributable to flawed leadership on the parts of both the Socialists and the government authorities, and to pressures from outside the country, above all from Austria's aggressive neighbors to the north and south.

In May 1932 Austria elected a new federal chancellor, Engelbert Dollfuss. Dollfuss's most significant physical feature was his size, or rather, his lack of it: he stood five foot nothing on his tiptoes. This made him the butt of many jokes, including the one that insisted he mulled over his problems while pacing up and down under his bed. Dollfuss failed to see the humor in these jokes, and it is possible that John Lehmann was correct when he attributed Dollfuss's large ambitions to his tiny stature: "Does not example after example of conqueror and dictator in modern history—Napoleon, Dollfuss, Stalin among the foremost— demonstrate how unassuageable and remorseless is the lust for power when it wakes in a breast only four feet from the ground?" Putting Dollfuss in the same category with Napoleon and Stalin was no doubt stretching matters. The Austrians themselves preferred to call him Millimetternich, after their famous conservative statesman of the preceding century.

At the time Dollfuss assumed the chancellorship, he was thought to be capable of overcoming the dangerous rift dividing "Red" and "Black" Austria. As minister of agriculture in a previous cabinet, he had shown certain "democratic" leanings and earned a reputation for being realistic and flexible. He was, moreover, extremely personable and popular, a folksy son of the soil with a genuine love for his country. In his initial efforts to form a cabinet in 1932, he was tempted to invite the Social Democrats to join the government so that together they might address the tiny republic's severe economic and political problems.

The Social Democratic party also had its protagonists of coalition government, most notably Karl Renner, who had been postwar Austria's first chancellor, and would be chancellor and president after the Second World War. But the party executive, still under the intellectual domination of Otto Bauer, was disinclined to join forces with Dollfuss. Bauer was well aware that the tragic events of July 1927 had radicalized the party's rank and file, for whom memories of the bloody police repression remained a large obstacle in the path of reconciliation with the federal government. Bauer and many of his colleagues feared that any efforts at cooperation with Dollfuss would endanger party unity, which, in lieu of genuine political power at the federal level, had become the Socialists' overriding preoccupation. The Socialist leaders' hesitation to extend the olive branch was only heightened by the severe economic pressures that gripped Austria in the wake of the collapse of the country's leading bank, the Credit Anstalt, in 1931. The Left hoped to evade blame for the crippling effects of the ensuing Great Depression by avoiding governmental responsibility, a shortsighted strategy that animated the Social Democratic party in neighboring Weimar Germany as well. Personality conflicts also helped widen the rift between Left and Right. Otto Bauer, the urban intellectual par excellence, did not try to hide his disdain for Dollfuss, a farmer's son from Lower Austria who spoke with a provincial accent and who liked to wear rustic loden suits with bone buttons and feathered alpine hats. In parliamentary debates Bauer loved to bait his somewhat awkward rival by suggesting an equation of the latter's physical and mental dimensions. Then he would cackle derisively as the little chancellor went red in the face and sputtered in inarticulate rage. No doubt Bauer should have been more mindful of the danger of awakening large hatreds in a tiny breast.

Dollfuss, like Seipel before him, soon came to view the Socialists as implacable enemies with whom no compromise was possible. His initial flexibility gave way to an increasingly rigid posture defined by staunch Catholicism and an almost mystical conviction that he—and he alone—could save Austria from political and economic collapse. It was thoroughly appropriate that he took as his personal political symbol the crutched cross of the medieval Crusaders. Nor was it surprising that Otto Bauer, that latter-day infidel, stood high on a list of those to be purged from Dollfuss's Christian imperium.

Instead of a "grand coalition" of Christian Socials and Social Democrats, Dollfuss's first government was a shaky coalition composed of Christian Socials, the Agrarian League, and the Heimatbloc—the party of the Heimwehren. The last affiliation was especially significant, for the Heimwehren were determined to sabotage any reconciliation with the Socialists and to force an abandonment of parliamentary government.

Chief architect of the Heimwehr policy in the Dollfuss era was Prince Ernst Rüdiger von Starhemberg. Scion of one of Austria's most prominent families, the dashingly handsome Starhemberg had grown up in a military atmosphere. His first toys were tin soldiers, tiny swords, and miniature cannon. "Before I could even swim," he tells us in his memoirs, "I knew how to use my little sword and all the movements of cut, thrust and parry laid down in Austrian cavalry drill. When I was given a toy railway, I used it solely for the transport of my tin soldiers." This suggests a somewhat impoverished imagination, and young Starhemberg's political world was also one-dimensional. He confessed, "[I could] no more imagine Austria without the Emperor and his splendid army than I could believe in the existence of people who had not the same devotion to the Emperor, army and Habsburg Monarchy. If there were such people, they could only be wicked traitors."

After the revolution of 1918–19 Starhemberg quickly came to believe that such "wicked traitors" indeed existed and that they dominated the politics of the former imperial capital. An ancestor of Starhemberg's had helped save Vienna from the Turks in 1683; Ernst Rüdiger now dreamed of saving the city from the Socialists and Jews. In 1930 he delivered a speech at a Heimwehr rally in Vienna's Heldenplatz in which he attacked Hugo Breitner, the city's Social Democratic (and Jewish) director of finance. "Only when the head of this Asiatic rolls in the sand," he cried, "will the victory be ours."

Starhemberg believed that, in Dollfuss, Austria had finally found a leader capable of purging the country of its "Asiatics," along with the parliamentary system that the prince saw as an obstacle to genuine political progress. "Here at last," he wrote, "was a new man, one who had not been raised under the shadow of an antiquated party system." But Dollfuss was, as we recall, initially inclined to attempt a coalition with the Socialists. Starhemberg made his support of the new government dependent on the abandonment of such a policy. So Dollfuss was forced at the very outset of his government to choose between relying on the Heimwehren, whose leaders flattered his vanity and offered to provide the muscle for the achievement of his "Christian mission," and hazarding a reconciliation with the Socialists, who for their part did little to facilitate such an eventuality. The chancellor's choice of the former alternative has been called "the tragedy of Dollfuss," for the new leader might have used his great personal charm and popularity to strengthen Austria's fragile democracy rather than to dismantle it.

Dollfuss's policy was also influenced by Austria's international situation in the early 1930s. Less than a year after Millimetternich assumed the chancellorship in Austria, Adolf Hitler came to power in neighboring Germany. A native Austrian, the führer had never hidden his desire to see his erstwhile homeland united with the German Reich, an occurrence that presupposed the extinction of Austrian independence. In *Mein Kampf* (written in 1924), Hitler had declared, "In my earliest youth I came to the basic insight, which never left me, but only became more profound—that Germany could be safeguarded only by the destruction of Austria. . . . Even then I had drawn the consequences from this realization: ardent love for my German-Austrian homeland, deep hatred for the Austrian state."

Well before he came to power in 1933 Hitler had encouraged local Austrian

Nazis to agitate in favor of an *Anschluss* (connection or integration) between the two countries, a linkage explicitly prohibited by the Western powers in the postwar treaty system. In the 1920s the Austrian Nazi party was weakened by an internal power struggle between a faction that was completely subservient to Hitler and one that wanted to carve out a special Austrian "identity" within the Greater German Reich. After Hitler came to power, the group closest to the führer's views was able to gain ascendancy over its rival.

In 1933 and early 1934 the Austrian Nazis were doing all they could to destabilize the Dollfuss government, which openly proclaimed its intention to keep Austria independent. Their favorite tactic was to place bombs in places frequented by tourists, thereby undermining Austria's largest industry. When Dollfuss prohibited the Nazis from wearing their brown shirts, they paraded about bare chested and in tall silk hats. The exasperated chancellor banned the Nazi party entirely in June 1933, whereupon Hitler imposed a one-thousand-mark ($250) visa fee on all Germans traveling to Austria. This cost Austria 30 percent of its tourist income, a grave blow at a time when the Great Depression was devastating the fragile Austrian economy.

Where could Dollfuss turn for protection against the aggressive designs of his brutal northern neighbor and Hitler's equally brutal Austrian agents? The western European powers, having formally prohibited an *Anschluss,* seemed the likely choice, and Dollfuss indeed made appeals in their direction. The powers, through the League of Nations, eventually proved willing to assist Austria economically, but Dollfuss had reason to worry about the steadfastness of their political commitment in the early 1930s. Although France was genuinely concerned about Hitler's ambitions in Austria, it was too preoccupied with its internal political and economic turmoil in 1933–34 to pay close attention to the difficulties of the Dollfuss regime. England, France's chief partner in the postwar containment of Germany, was in the throes of the Great Depression and, in any case, reluctant to make major sacrifices to maintain the political status quo in Central Europe. The world's two emerging superpowers—the United States and the Soviet Union— were not partners at all in the treaty system designed to keep the Germans in their place.

One of the "Big Four" represented at the Paris peace conference was, however, more than anxious to keep Hitler's Germany and Dollfuss's Austria safely apart. This was Italy, which since October 1922 had been under the control of *Il Duce,* Benito Mussolini. It might seem odd that Mussolini would oppose the expansionist ambitions of Hitler, a fellow right-wing dictator who had often expressed his admiration for the duce. At first, in fact, Mussolini supported a union of Austria and Germany. But then it occurred to him that the absorption of Austria into Germany would constitute a threat to Italian security, for Italy would thereby exchange a weak northern neighbor for a strong and warlike one. This new neighbor might even demand the return of Italy's chief piece of territorial booty earned in the First World War, the ethnic-German South Tyrol. Hitler promised the duce that he had no interest in the South Tyrol, but Mussolini, quite rightly, did not trust him. Indeed, he believed that Italy could ultimately be secure on its northern frontier only if it extended its sphere of influence beyond the Brenner Pass into East Central Europe. His dream was the creation of a new South Central European Confederation consisting of Austria, Hungary, Yugoslavia, Albania, and Italy, with the last setting the political and cultural tone just as Austria had done in the preceding century.

Mussolini's strategic fears and dreams had implications for Austrian domestic politics, because the duce believed the Germans could be induced to keep their hands off Austria only if that country were to adopt the Fascist system of government and place itself firmly under the protection of Italy. If Austria were free of Marxist influence, he reasoned, Hitler could not claim the need to extend his influence there to "save" it from bolshevism. The key to Mussolini's policy in Austria, then, was the elimination of Socialist power—the smashing of Red Vienna.

In the late 1920s and early 1930s, the duce regarded the Austrian Heimwehren as the most promising tool for the execution of this policy. He heavily subsidized the Heimwehren and sent them arms from the supplies Italy had captured from Austria-Hungary in the First World War. His principal contact in these arrangements was Prince von Starhemberg, who claimed to share the duce's aversion for the "Prussians" and an Austro-German *Anschluss*. On the occasion of one of their early meetings, in 1930, Mussolini warned Starhemberg that Italy would not tolerate an expansion of German power in South Central Europe. Austria, he said, must retain its "independence." It had been, after all, "a bastion of Mediterranean civilization" when the Prussians were still baying at the moon. As for the Nazis, they managed to combine barbarism with effeminacy: "That bunch is full of homosexuals," confided the duce, rolling his eyes.

Mussolini clearly hoped that Starhemberg and the Heimwehren would stage a coup d'état and set up a dictatorship on the Fascist model. Indeed, one branch of the Heimwehr movement, the group headquartered in Styria, did attempt to overthrow the government in 1931. But this putsch was poorly organized and collapsed after a few hours. Even had it succeeded, it would not have served Mussolini's purposes, for the Styrian Heimwehr had close ties to the Nazis and strongly favored an *Anschluss*. Starhemberg opposed the Styrian putsch, whose leader, a hated rival, he likened to a "vulture who feeds on especially fly-blown carrion." The prince talked of launching his own coup but never quite managed to get around to it. Although a dashing and charismatic figure, Starhemberg proved an incompetent and easily distracted politician. His main interests, it turned out, were horses, houses, and women, though not necessarily in that order. He married the beautiful actress Nora Gregor, who made considerable demands on his time, money, and energy. The duce could sympathize with these passions, but he eventually realized that he would have to look elsewhere to ensure the triumph of Italian rather than German fascism north of the Brenner Pass.

When Engelbert Dollfuss became chancellor in 1932, Mussolini made urgent inquiries into his character and policies. "Who is Dollfuss?" he asked Starhemberg. "Is he a Jew?" Assured that Dollfuss was a good Catholic who shared his fears of the Nazis, Mussolini embraced Millimetternich as a fellow Latin and champion of Mediterranean civilization. He told Starhemberg to inform Dollfuss that the latter could count on his help. The new chancellor should come and see him, he said, adding, "I will let it be known in Berlin that Austria is to be left alone."

Dollfuss went to see the duce three times in 1933. On each occasion Mussolini personally assured Dollfuss of his support for Austrian independence, but he also made clear that Dollfuss must pay a price for this support. Austria would be expected to identify itself openly with Italy in its foreign policy; and at home it must establish an "authoritarian" regime capable of dealing more energetically with all those elements who might compromise its independence, directly or indirectly. Dollfuss claimed to have gotten the message: he would, he said, do all that was necessary to gain the support of Austria's "powerful and understanding friend."

Mussolini was not alone in urging draconian measures on the Austrian government. Pressure also came from the rightist Horthy regime in Hungary. Like Mussolini, Miklós Horthy saw the influence of the Socialists in Vienna as an obstacle to his own ambitions in Central Europe, which included pulling Austria into a Fascist federation dominated by Hungary and Italy. Horthy's minister of war, Gyula von Gömbös, had therefore assisted Italy in illegally transporting weapons to the Austrian Heimwehren. After Dollfuss's accession to power, Gömbös let it be known that he expected the Austrian chancellor to eliminate the "Bolshevist elements" in Vienna the way Hungary and Italy had done in their own countries during the preceding decade.

Yet another outside power urged a get-tough policy on the Austrian government. The Vatican's representative in Vienna took it upon himself to warn Austria's deeply religious federal president, Wilhelm Miklas (like Dollfuss a member of the Christian Social party, and the titular head of the government), that a continued Social Democratic domination of Vienna presented grave dangers to the moral and political health of the state. It was time, he suggested, to abandon a constitutional system that allowed "subversive elements" to undermine the nation's unity. When Miklas expressed reservations about violating his constitutional oath, the papal nuncio assured him that he need have no political or moral qualms regarding an action that would bring "an indisputable advantage for all."

The Dollfuss government quickly showed signs of having taken all this advice to heart. In October 1932, after a bloody confrontation between Nazis and Socialists in Vienna's working-class district of Simmering, Dollfuss appointed Major Emil Fey as state secretary in charge of public security affairs. Fey, bullet headed, hard eyed, and strongly built, was a holder of the coveted Maria Theresa Medal for Bravery in World War One. As head of the Vienna branch of the Heimwehr, he had become known for his hatred of the Socialists and his determination to run the Reds out of the capital. His first act after taking office was to ban all parades and demonstrations except those organized by the Heimwehr. Fey realized that this high-handed measure would enrage the Socialists. That, indeed, was its fundamental purpose, for Fey hoped thereby to goad the Reds to commit an act of self-destructive rebellion.

A few months later, Dollfuss enjoyed an unexpected opportunity to strike a more decisive blow at Austria's constitutional system. In early March 1933 the parliament maneuvered itself into a complicated dispute over a government bill to punish railway workers who had gone on strike. The government declared a negative vote on the bill as invalid because two ballots contained the name of the same parliamentarian. The delegate in question (a Social Democrat) had cast votes on behalf of himself and a colleague, whom nature had suddenly and irresistibly called to the bathroom. The voter had gotten confused and submitted two of his own ballot slips. This minor oversight could easily have been amicably resolved, but the Austrian parliament had a long history of turning procedural issues into matters of moment and impassioned confrontation. Visiting the old imperial parliament in 1897, Mark Twain had described a cacophonous "multitude of counsel" yielding nothing but "confusion and despair." So it was again. In the uproar that followed the government's invalidation of the disputed vote, Karl Renner, the Social Democratic president of the parliament, incautiously resigned his office. So did the two parliamentary vice-presidents, who belonged to the Christian Social and the Pan-German parties. This effectively put the parliament out of commission, and the body declared a suspension of its debates to sort things out.

Dollfuss had been searching for a way to close the parliament, and now he had it. He chose to regard the suspension of debates as permanent, announcing on March 8 that the country would henceforth be ruled by emergency decrees based on a wartime "Emergency Powers Act" that had never been revoked. When a few delegates tried to resume their meetings, Dollfuss sent in the police to clear the house.

The Social Democratic leadership protested against this governmental coup, but it chose not to call out the Schutzbund, as some leftist radicals advised it to do. In rejecting this measure, the Austrian Socialists resembled their German colleagues, who had allowed Hitler and his immediate predecessors to dismantle the Weimar parliamentary system without mobilizing their party's paramilitary organization, the Reichsbanner Schwarz-Rot-Gold. Otto Bauer later sorely regretted this decision. In his memoir on the Austrian civil war (written in exile in Prague shortly after the Socialists' defeat), he wrote, "We avoided confrontation [at that time] because we wanted to spare the country the catastrophe of a bloody civil war. Civil war came anyway eleven months later, a time much less favorable for us. We made a mistake—the most fateful of all our mistakes."

In abolishing parliamentary norms in favor of authoritarian government, Austria joined a host of European countries that had exchanged originally hopeful democratic experiments for repressive strongman regimes. The Europe of the interwar years was becoming the "Europe of the dictators." But there may have been something particularly "Austrian" about the ludicrous way that nation's democratic system assisted in its own destruction. As after the assassination at Sarajevo in the summer of 1914, the Austrians seemed to delight in pushing a minor crisis toward a major catastrophe. Arguing the importance of the absurd in history—especially Austrian history—G. E. R. Gedye wrote that "six million people eventually lost their freedom because of one man's weak bladder." This formulation, like that popular interpretation of Nazism that places so much stock in Hitler's allegedly defective genitals, puts too great a burden of guilt on the body's lower anatomy. The Austrian mind was the real culprit here, as Mark Twain had known it to be in 1897.

Dollfuss's Fascist advisers certainly approved of his dramatic action against parliament, but none of them was satisfied that he had gone far enough. The Italian ambassador to Vienna was not convinced that Dollfuss had the decisiveness to be a true Fascist. But he hoped that the momentum generated by his closing of parliament would force him, "if necessary against his will, to draw the consequences from this action . . . and establish a truly strong and courageous government." Gömbös sent Dollfuss a congratulatory telegram in early April urging him now to make a "tabula rasa" of the Social Democratic opposition. "Revolutions," he added, need to be made "with speed and vigor."

But few things in Austria, including revolutions and counterrevolutions, happen with speed and vigor. Despite continued pressure from his foreign "friends" and the Heimwehren (especially the impatient Major Fey), Dollfuss took a somewhat gradualist approach to the erection of "clerical fascism" in Austria. Much as he desired to curtail the Socialists' influence, he was not eager to provoke a full-scale civil war. At the end of March 1933 he outlawed the Schutzbund (thereby forcing it underground), a step that earned him more praise from Mussolini. But in general he inclined toward a governmental style of neobaroque posturing and grand gesture. His was, one might say, a fascism in keeping with Vienna's crumbling imperial architecture: monumental but not entirely convincing.

Highly representative of this style were several stagy demonstrations proclaiming the government's authoritarian resolve. At a celebration of the 250th anniversary of the salvation of Vienna from the Turks (in May 1933), Dollfuss declared that parliament had "died" and "would not return." Austrians, he said, wanted their government to be "based on new principles and ideals which in reality are very old ones for a Christian and German people." In September 1933 he staged a mass rally of his political supporters at Vienna's Trotting Horse Racecourse. There he announced the end of the "liberal capitalist order" and of "party rule." These would be replaced by a government "on the basis of estates and under a strong, authoritarian leadership." Competing political interests would disappear within a new "Fatherland Front"—a mass organization dedicated to maintaining Austria's independence as a Catholic corporative state. Dollfuss delivered this speech against a dramatic background of massed Heimwehr regiments dressed in loden green uniforms or traditional alpine regalia: a sea of lederhosen and cock-feathered hats. Wrote the British journalist G. E. R. Gedye, "Hundreds of thousands screamed 'Heil' as the diminutive Chancellor in his grey-green uniform of the *Kaiserjäger*, the Imperial Alpine regiment, a military cape over his shoulder and a white feather on his cap, traipsed up the speaker's dais."

One of those who screamed "Heil" that day was the young Viennese Jew George Clare. A Boy Scout at the time, Clare thought of Dollfuss as a kind of glorified scout leader, and he rejoiced at being part of what in retrospect he called "Millimetternich's mini-Nuremberg party rally."

It is hardly surprising that a young boy would get caught up in the panoply surrounding Dollfuss's patriotic crusade. Much of Austria at that time was engulfed in a wave of nostalgia for the good old days of imperial Austria. "Even real-life archdukes," recalled Clare, came back from exile: "Looking as if they had stepped straight off some operetta stage, they could be seen tottering from balls to bazaars, from memorial services to regimental reunions and patriotic rallies." Otto von Habsburg, the pretender to the vacated imperial throne, exiled in Belgium, returned too, but only in the form of picture postcards sold throughout the land. The monarchist faction in Austria hoped fervently that he might soon return in person to reclaim his ancient title and rehoist the black-yellow banners of the Habsburgs over the old Hofburg (imperial residence) in Red Vienna.

A politics of picturesque nostalgia was not what Mussolini, Gömbös, Fey, or even Starhemberg (despite his imperial upbringing) had in mind for Austria. At the end of January 1934, Starhemberg complained to Rome of the chancellor's "constant postponement of a final reckoning with the Social Democrats," who despite the ban on their party army still dominated Viennese politics and stood in the way of a true Fascist dictatorship. At the same time Mussolini dispatched his under secretary of state, Fulvio Suvich, to the Austrian capital. Suvich told Dollfuss that the hour was ripe for the destruction of Social Democracy and Red Vienna. A few days later, on February 11, the duce had his ambassador in Vienna instruct Dollfuss not to miss "the present propitious moment" to "clarify the situation" and make good on the promises he had given to Italy. The duce and his Austrian accomplices clearly wanted a drama in Vienna, and they did not envisage an operetta.

The Austrian Social Democratic leadership, aware of these pressures on Dollfuss, finally decided at this late hour that it had better attempt some kind of rapprochement with the chancellor. Otto Bauer let it be known that he would consider supporting a coalition government of Social Democrats and Christian Socials. Bauer's tentative overture found support in some quarters of the Christian Social party, particularly among those politicians, like the progressive Catholic Leopold Kunschak, who opposed Dollfuss's alliance with the Heimwehren and Mussolini. But when Kunschak and others urged Dollfuss to take up Bauer's offer, the chancellor replied, "If I were to do that, Mussolini [would] throw me right into Hitler's jaws."

CIVIL WAR

"Tomorrow we shall make a clean sweep of it." So bragged Major Emil Fey to the Vienna Heimwehr on the evening of February 11. Fey planned to launch a series of searches for Schutzbund weapons starting in Linz, capital of Upper Austria. He fully expected the Schutzbund there to try to prevent the search and, in so doing, provide the justification for his "clean sweep" of the Socialist organization throughout the country. Starhemberg, who had become jealous of Fey's influence on the chancellor, later claimed that the major's strike was an act of political grandstanding designed to "establish his popularity as the savior and liberator of Austria from Marxism." No doubt Fey did have such ambitions, but his strike was fully supported by Dollfuss and, for that matter, Starhemberg as well. All saw themselves as "saviors" of Austria. So would Adolf Hitler in 1938.

In the early morning hours of February 12, a Monday in the height of Austria's gay *Fasching* (carnival) season, about twenty policemen gathered in front of the Hotel Schiff, the Socialists' headquarters in Linz. At that moment the hotel was occupied by some fifty to sixty *Schutzbündler*. They played cards, threw darts at a Fatherland Front poster of Millimetternich, or slept. Clearly they were not planning any offensive action of their own, though their leader, a fiery and impatient war veteran named Richard Bernasek, had warned party headquarters in Vienna that his group would respond violently to any attempt by the police or Heimwehr to confiscate the Schutzbund's weapons. Bernasek also made it clear that if push came to shove in Linz, he fully expected help from Vienna. "If the Vienna workers leave us in the lurch, shame and disgrace to them," he declared. At two in the morning of February 12 the Vienna headquarters telephoned a coded message to the Hotel Schiff: "Ernst and Otto taken seriously ill; postpone the undertaking." Fey's police intercepted this message and had no trouble deciphering it. They knew that an attack on the Hotel Schiff was likely to provoke local resistance but that this resistance would not have the endorsement of the Socialist party leadership in Vienna.

At 7:00 A.M. the police burst into the hotel. Finding the first floor unoccupied, they rushed up to the second, where they heard cries: "To the weapons!" Richard Bernasek and one of his aides were immediately cornered in a small room, and they surrendered without firing a shot. So did Arthur Bonyhadi, chief of the Upper Austrian Schutzbund's intelligence service, and Otto Huschka, coordinator of mobilization. The latter was captured just as he was attempting to swallow a piece of paper containing plans for the Schutzbund mobilization. The rest of the *Schutzbündler*, now leaderless and without direction, retreated to a small theater in the center of the hotel and broke out their weapons, which included machine guns. Police attempting to root them out ran into a hail of fire, which they answered in kind. Men on both sides slumped to the floor, the first of dozens of casualties on that "Bloody Monday" in *Fasching* February.

Unable to dislodge the *Schutzbündler* from their stronghold in the Hotel

Schiff, the undermanned police called on assistance from the Austrian army, the Bundesheer. Within an hour a company of the Seventh Alpenjäger appeared on the scene. The company commander, a decorated war veteran, brought the hotel under systematic machine-gun fire. When the *Schutzbündler* continued to fire back, he brought up artillery and threatened to level the building. He did not have to do so, for the Socialist defenders soon decided that further resistance was futile. At about noon thirty-eight *Schutzbündler* walked out of the hotel, their hands in the air.

The battle of the Hotel Schiff, brief as it was, established a pattern for the rest of the fighting in the Austrian civil war. The Socialists lost their leaders in the early stages of the conflict and were obliged to fight without systematic direction or coordination. Bunkered down in their stronghold, they quickly found themselves cut off from the outside world and confronted with massively superior firepower. Lack of coordination meant lack of reinforcement for the isolated defenders; it also meant that only a small percentage of the *Schutzbündler* in Linz ever received their arms or actually joined in the fighting. But in one sense this first battle was untypical of what was to follow: the Socialists tended to surrender only after the government forces had made extensive use of their artillery.

When the men in the Hotel Schiff surrendered, they did not realize that fighting had broken out in other parts of the city. A battle raged at the Parkbad, a public bath complex occupied by about fifty *Schutzbündler*. Initially armed only with rifles, the Socialists had received a supply of machine guns hidden inside a manure cart that the police had been loath to search. Other battles took place at the docks along the Danube and at a school in whose strategically located tower the Schutzbund had mounted a machine gun. The army got rid of the machine gun (and much of the tower along with it) with a few rounds from a mountain howitzer. Throughout the fighting the police and army drew on assistance from Prince von Starhemberg's Upper Austrian Heimwehr, which had been concentrating men around Linz in preparation for Fey's showdown. These Heimwehr farm boys undoubtedly enjoyed their rampage through the streets of Linz, which for them was almost as alien an urban Babylon as Vienna.

Class hatred produced atrocities on both sides. There were also moments of tragicomedy inspired by Austrian *Schlamperei.* In one such instance, the military forces in Linz ordered reinforcements from nearby Wels. The requested troops were delayed in arriving because they had to travel in rented trucks that frequently broke down. Worried by the delay, the commander in Linz dispatched three men to find the relief column. The men hired a taxi and found the column outside town, but on their way back to the garrison they were stopped by a patrol of *Schutzbündler.* The Socialists pulled the men out of the taxi and dismembered them.

Sporadic fighting continued in Linz for two more days, but by Tuesday afternoon the government forces enjoyed the upper hand. The police and army had a somewhat tougher time of it in nearby Steyr, site of the huge Steyr-Werke, Austria's largest weapons factory. When news of the Linz fighting reached Steyr, the workers at the factory killed the plant director, and the Schutzbund launched an attack against the local army barracks. Eventually aided by an artillery company from Enns, as well as a company of Heimwehr, the army mounted a successful counterattack, gradually forcing the *Schutzbündler* from their positions throughout the town. At about 5:00 P.M. on February 12, howitzers and mortars were brought into action against the Socialists' last stronghold on a hill overlooking the town. Blasted into submission, some six hundred *Schutzbündler* capitulated, while hundreds more escaped into the surrounding woods.

News of the events in Upper Austria reached Vienna early in the morning of February 12. As in July 1927, the Social Democratic leaders suddenly found themselves confronted with a crisis that, despite their fiery rhetoric about the "inevitability" of civil war, they had tried desperately to avoid. This time, however, the Socialists were able at least to agree fairly quickly on a course of action. At about ten in the morning the party executive instructed Vienna's streetcar drivers to halt their trams. This was the recognized signal for a general strike, and within a couple of hours the city was without electric power and light. At the same time, the party called for mobilization of the Schutzbund, instructing its members to dig out their weapons and assemble at prearranged points around the city. But the orders also stressed that the men were not to use their weapons unless attacked. Bauer and Deutsch still hoped to avoid a bloody escalation of the conflict.

No doubt Chancellor Dollfuss also wanted to avoid a full-scale civil war, but he was equally determined to exploit this moment to destroy the Social Democratic party once and for all. He thus immediately proclaimed martial law and ordered a cordon of barbed wire thrown up around the entire Inner City. Citing the Socialists' "rebellion" in Linz, he declared the Socialist party illegal and ordered it dissolved. He froze its bank accounts and banned publication of the *Arbeiter Zeitung.* These were measures hardly designed to calm troubled waters.

Whatever Dollfuss or, indeed, his Socialist counterparts might have hoped to achieve by their various orders, events in the city quickly passed out of their control. On the government side, initiative went to Major Fey, the Heimwehren, and the military commanders in the field. Among the Socialists it fell to district Schutzbund leaders and militant trade unionists. None of these men was afraid to shed a little blood—to "turn the Blue Danube red," as a chilling contemporary phrase had it.

It seems clear, however, that it was the government forces that provoked the first bloody exchanges in the capital, just as they had in Linz. Whereas in July 1927 the workers had converged on the Inner City, this time the police, military, and Heimwehren marched out into the working-class suburbs. Their plan was to disarm the workers before the Socialists could coordinate their defenses in and around the huge municipal housing projects.

At about two in the afternoon on February 12 a contingent of police demanded entrance to the dance hall of the Reumann Hof, in the Margareten district, where some *Schutzbündler* had gathered to distribute weapons. When rifle fire through the building's windows drew counterfire from the workers inside, the police resorted to hand grenades. This tactic, which sent shattered legs flying around the Reumann Hof dance floor, forced the surrender of sixty-eight *Schutzbündler,* seven of whom were badly wounded. The government forces suffered casualties as well, but they had shown that a willingness to employ brutal measures could quickly effect the desired result.

Other Socialist strongholds, however, proved more resistant to government assault. The *Schutzbündler* ensconced in the Labor Temple in the Ottakring district kept up such a steady barrage of machine-gun fire on the streets around it that repeated police assaults, including one that employed a tank, were unable to drive the workers out. At 1:00 A.M. on February 13 Major Fey arrived at the scene and decided to call in the artillery. For an hour the army bombarded the building with field howitzers and heavy mortars. When the structure was thoroughly wrecked, Fey gave the order to storm it. The troops, however, took the final precaution of lobbing tear gas canisters into the rubble. By the time they finally attacked, most of the defenders had fled.

The toughest and most costly fighting in the Austrian civil war occurred in Floridsdorf, a southeastern suburb near the area where Napoleon had fought the battles of Aspern and Wagram 120 years before. The government troops could have used a Napoleon now, for the Schutzbund, occupying the huge municipal houses near the Floridsdorf bridge (spanning the Danube), had dug in with scores of heavy machine guns. For a time they were commanded by Julius Deutsch himself. The Socialists easily repulsed an initial government attack, then launched a counterattack that was halted only when the government troops brought up heavy artillery. Gradually, systematically, the big guns pounded the *Schutzbündler* out of their "forts" and forced them into disorderly retreat along the Danube. Journalists accompanying the advancing troops found scores of dead in the streets, and the small hospitals in the district crammed with wounded from both sides. There was neither time nor facilities, wrote one correspondent, to give medical attention to those wounded who still lay out in the streets. "Most of them," he reported, "are expected to die within twenty-four hours."

Toward the end of the four-day bloodletting in Floridsdorf, Dollfuss toured the battleground. According to some reports, the chancellor had initially opposed the use of artillery and gas, sanctioning their employment only after his military commanders convinced him that this would allow the quickest and most "humane" suppression of the uprising. Now, amid the rubble of Floridsdorf, he focused his concern on the government troops who were still encountering spirited resistance from isolated groups of *Schutzbündler.* He was reported by the *Reichspost* to have personally "closed the eyes" of one mortally wounded soldier. Emotionally caught up in the scene, he rushed back to his office and delivered the following message: "Full of reverence, we kneel before the heroes of these past few days, men who have sacrificed their lives and blood for their country. I will personally assume guardianship over all children who have lost their fathers [in this struggle]." To the Socialist rebels, with the exception of the "ringleaders,"

Dollfuss promised government pardon if the men would turn themselves in to the police before noon on Thursday, February 15. Few *Schutzbündler* took the government up on this offer, which it in fact never kept.

Floridsdorf saw the toughest fighting, but the most famous battle in the Austrian civil war occurred at the Karl-Marx-Hof in Heiligenstadt. This mammoth building, over a kilometer long and containing fourteen hundred apartments, was the pride of the Viennese workers. Foreigners admired it too. John Lehmann, who had friends who lived there, insisted that it was the only municipal housing project he had ever seen that did not remind him "in any sense of a barracks." Yet it had become a military compound for the Schutzbund, which stored weapons in the cellars and mounted machine guns atop the massive arches that gave the building the look of an impregnable castle. So formidable were the Karl-Marx-Hof's defenses that the *Schutzbündler* believed it could successfully ward off "any attacks of the fascists."

Like many Socialist convictions regarding the inviolability of Red Vienna, this turned out to be an illusion. In the opening phases of the battle, which began on the evening of February 12, the army posted mountain artillery on a hill overlooking the building and commenced blasting away at the so-called Blue Arch in the center of the complex. On the next day more artillery arrived, along with a machine-gun company and a battalion of infantry. Late that afternoon army troops successfully cleared part of the building but were pulled back for deployment across the Danube in Floridsdorf. Given this reprieve, *Schutzbündler* in the Karl-Marx-Hof held out until February 15, when the army returned with yet more heavy artillery pieces and infantry battalions. The white flag went up at about noon, and troops poured into the building to round up the remaining defenders. Of these they found very few, for most of the *Schutzbündler* had escaped into the city's sewer system—that vast labyrinth of echoing tunnels later immortalized by Graham Greene and Orson Welles in *The Third Man*.

Having thoroughly searched the Karl-Marx-Hof, Dollfuss's troops turned the complex over to the Vienna Heimwehr for occupation. When the regular occupants were allowed to return to their apartments several days later, they found their homes looted, and piles of human excrement on the floors and furniture. Parts of the building remained uninhabitable for many weeks because of the damage wrought by the artillery fire. Eventually the place was repaired, but it was not until after the Second World War that city officials afixed a plaque near the main entrance testifying to what had happened there in February 1934. It remains to this day the only such memorial in a city otherwise much given to commemorating its past.

A notable aspect of the battle for Vienna was the confinement of the fighting to the city's outer districts. Unlike the rioting in July 1927, the fighting in 1934 brought no Inner City bourgeois or Ringstrasse hotel guest face to face with Vienna's outraged proletariat. The writer Stefan Zweig, who was visiting Vienna during the February civil war, had to confess to his friends in Salzburg that he had seen none of the action, because he had stayed in the First (Inner City) District:

"Artillery fired away, houses were occupied, hundreds of dead bodies carried away—and I didn't see any of it." No doubt this was class war the way many Austrian middle- and upper-class citizens preferred to see it fought: that is, not actually to see it at all, but only to be aware that out there in the working-class wasteland "order" was being efficiently restored.

George Clare reports in his memoir that his parents, comfortable middle-class Jews, were horrified when they realized that the booming sound they heard in the distance was government artillery firing at working-class flats that surely contained women and children. Clare's family must have been the exception, for Vienna's bourgeois Jewish community was quick to rally around Dollfuss and assure him of its support. When the chancellor appealed to the Union of Jewish War Veterans to aid the government in its campaign against the Socialists, the group announced its readiness to "stand with the government." No doubt Vienna's middle-class Jews were eager to dissociate themselves from the likes of Bauer and Breitner, whose radical views they had never shared. Equally significant, they saw in Dollfuss (and behind him in Mussolini) their best protection against a Nazi triumph in Austria. Other Austrian patriots harbored this illusion as well, but none with such disastrous consequences.

While government forces were smashing the working-class strongholds in the suburbs of Vienna, other military and Heimwehr troops were routing the Schutzbund in the province of Styria, the third major battleground in the Austrian civil war. Among the roughly twenty Styrian communities that witnessed significant clashes, the most important was Bruck an der Mur, a mining town whose Social Democratic mayor, Koloman Wallisch, had previously incurred the Heimwehr's rancor by exposing its illegal weapons trade with Italy and Hungary. At Bruck the Schutzbund concentrated its forces on the Schlossberg, a hill overlooking the town. For two days the Socialists held off an assault force of regular army troops (including artillery batteries) and Heimwehren. But as their ammunition ran out, and the army's artillery fire began to take its toll, the Schutzbund abandoned the Schlossberg. Some surrendered, while others fled toward neighboring Yugoslavia over a high alpine pass. Poorly equipped for such a trek in the dead of winter, the men quickly returned to the lower valleys, splitting into small groups to evade police and pursuing Heimwehr. Koloman Wallisch himself hid for a time in the small village of Utsch but was soon recognized and denounced by a railway worker enticed by the 5,000-schilling bounty on the mayor's head. Hauled off to prison in Leoben, Wallisch joined a growing number of Socialist functionaries caught in the government's dragnet.

Some of the most prominent Socialist leaders, however, managed to evade capture by fleeing to Czechoslovakia, whose democratic leadership had openly (albeit not militarily, as many Socialists had hoped) sided with the rebels' cause. According to their own accounts, Bauer and Deutsch reached Czechoslovakia on February 15. They had gone into hiding as soon as it became apparent that the Schutzbund would be driven from its strongholds and the general strike fail to spread systematically across the land. Their flight contributed to the demoralization of the Austrian workers, many of whom were convinced that they had been left in the lurch once again by their leaders.

Karl Seitz, the Social Democratic mayor of Vienna, made no attempt to flee. In the early morning hours of February 13, policemen removed him from the town hall and packed him off to jail. Seitz's office, to which he had been legally elected, was summarily turned over to a federal commissar, who acted under the direct authority of the Dollfuss government. Richard Schmitz, the new commissar, promptly announced that he intended to run Vienna on principles quite different from those of his predecessors, who had "ruined the city." He gave some indication of what he meant when—not yet twenty-four hours in office—he reported that he had dismissed all Social Democratic officials in the municipal administration and replaced them with men he had "known for many years." The rightist *Reichspost* hailed Schmitz's appointment and opening moves as marking the "end of Red Vienna" and the beginning of the city's "reintegration" into the national body politic. This it certainly was, for Vienna was henceforth to share fully in all the central government's misguided policies—above all in its attempt to keep Austria "free" by emulating the repressive tactics of its Fascist neighbors.

The government's repression was by no means restricted to its military liquidation of the workers' uprising and its political destruction of Red Vienna. The Dollfuss government began a series of court-martial proceedings against captured *Schutzbündler* on February 14. At 10:00 A.M. the first group was tried, and at 4:41 P.M. the first execution took place. The victim was a minor Schutzbund figure who had been so seriously wounded in the fighting that he had to be held up by policemen during his trial and then carried to the gallows on a stretcher. Perhaps the government acted so quickly to execute him out of fear that he might soon die on his own and thus "cheat" the hangman.

The *Reichspost* acknowledged that this first execution was "fast work," and the work continued at a rapid pace. Over the next eight days, twenty-one men were tried and sentenced to death. Nine of the sentences were actually carried out; the rest were commuted to life prison terms.

Among those executed was Koloman Wallisch. He had been allowed to defend himself at his trial and had done so brilliantly but to little purpose: his gallows were being constructed outside during the proceedings. Once convicted, he appealed for clemency to President Miklas, but his petition never reached Miklas, because the minister of justice, Kurt von Schuschnigg, refused to send it. Only the condemned man's traditional "final wish" was granted. Wallisch was given a glass of wine, the first alcohol he had ever allowed himself. Showing a good sense of "gallows humor," he observed that there was now no danger of his becoming a drunkard. But the hangman got the last laugh: he tied the noose so badly that Wallisch took twelve minutes to die.

Although martial law was lifted on February 21, trials under regular judicial authority continued for months after the suppression of the upheaval. Well over a thousand Socialists were tried and sentenced to prison terms ranging from a few weeks to life. But trials and jail sentences were not the government's only means of ensuring the permanent emasculation of the Socialist movement. Social Democratic functionaries in the federal railway system were summarily fired, many without claim to pension benefits. Leftist trade unions were outlawed, their assets frozen. The law disbanding the Social Democratic party removed from office all those legislators, governors, and municipal authorities whose positions had been based on electoral victories of that party. Their places were filled by men proposed by the government parties, many of whom turned out to be Heimwehr members. The *Reichspost* celebrated this procedure as "the visible expression of the thanks that the patriotic population paid to the defenders of their homeland."

FOREIGN RESPONSE

Most Western foreign correspondents based in Vienna put the February events, from the outbreak of fighting to the executions, in a quite different light. Anglo-American journalists belonging to the "Louvre circle" (named after the now-extinct Café Louvre, where they liked to gather) made no secret of their pro-Socialist sentiments, and some even joined in the fighting. (Their "engagement" was a typical feature of 1930s journalism, filled with passionate commitment and open partisanship toward one side or the other, most often the Left. For many in the Louvre circle, the next stop would be Spain.)* In general the British and American papers carried stories from the Austrian "front" that reflected their authors' dismay over the bloody demise of Red Vienna. The two *New York Times* correspondents, Frederick T. Birchall and G. E. R. Gedye (who had joined the *Times* in 1929), reported at length on the government's assault against the municipal housing complexes, focusing on the indiscriminate use of artillery. They spoke of machine guns "blazing in the dark, rapping out the warning that the government intended to govern at all costs." Although the full costs in human life were not clear in the early reports, the journalists predicted massive losses. "Hourly," wrote Birchall on February 13, "[the civil war] costs a few more lives, and it is sowing seeds from which will come a harvest of bitter hatred and international strife."

Under the headline "Metternich Horrors Again Seen in Vienna," the *New York Times* suggested that the present atrocities in Vienna had a historical precedent in the "Vienna of Metternich, arch-enemy of freedom throughout Europe, with a horde of spies and informers, with his own police and his own executioners." Frank Knox, publisher of the *Chicago Daily News,* seemed to think that Millimetternich had outdone Metternich himself: "I saw the effects of the shell fire with which Dollfuss destroyed the Socialist government in Vienna, one of the most bloodthirsty, unwarranted, inexcusable employments of armed force against

*It is worth noting, however, that the Louvre circle's dominant figure, the American Robert Best, later served the Nazi cause in Austria.

helpless women and children in all history." Similar condemnations emanated from the British press, though the London *Times* insisted that the government's artillery bombardments had been "carefully controlled" to reduce property damage—apparently a significant virtue.

The entire Anglo-Saxon press, and the French press as well, strongly criticized the Dollfuss government's martial-law execution of the *Schutzbündler*. Typical was a *New York Times* story on the first two executions, which challenged the evidence upon which the men were convicted, as well as the dispatch with which they were killed. Dollfuss's recently appointed hangman would "soon be working overtime," the article predicted correctly.

Western press reports on the fighting also contained assessments of the possible political implications of Austria's civil war. In one of his first dispatches, Birchall suggested that after the defeat of Socialism the Austrian choice could "only be between two dictatorships—the home brand under the *Heimwehr* and the German variety bearing the Nazi stamp." The prospects, he said, were that the weaker domestic variety, now on top, would soon "be merged in the stronger, bringing Austria under German dominance to add to the power of Adolf Hitler." The French press was inclined to agree. *Le Temps,* a moderate-republican newspaper that often spoke for the government, warned that Dollfuss's actions would have a "profound repercussion on the international situation," since foreign powers sympathetic to the Austrian government's rejection of Nazism would be less inclined to back an administration that massacred its own people.

The Soviet press was predictably hostile to Dollfuss's actions, but it combined denunciation of the chancellor with fulminations against the Austrian Socialist leadership, which it accused of "betraying the workers to the bourgeois ruling class." The Russian propagandist Karl Radek (later to fall victim to Stalin's purges) equated the events of Vienna with those in Paris, insisting that Socialist behavior in both instances proved the hopelessness of expecting "Socialist leaders to defend the rights of democracy against the forces of reaction." That task, he implied, could be accomplished only by Communists and the Soviet Union.

In response to all this hostile comment, the Dollfuss administration orchestrated a countercampaign in the progovernment Austrian press. Reports from this quarter insisted that the government had acted as moderately as possible against a massive and well-coordinated assault. On February 17 Dollfuss himself broadcast a statement (also heard in the United States) in which he said that the government had used "utmost consideration in order to avoid unnecessary casualties" and that the responsibility for the deaths of women and children rested entirely with the Socialists, who had intentionally put them in the forefront of the fighting.

This interpretation made up the core of what might be called the "government myth" about the February civil war. In reality there had been no massive or coordinated assault; only about 10 percent of the Schutzbund members took up weapons, and their campaign lacked systematic planning and leadership from the outset. But the Left, too, generated myths about the tragic confrontation. Oft-repeated claims that the workers were "helpless," that they lacked arms or military training, were without foundation. Reports in the leftist or liberal press invariably cited Major Fey's provocative actions but rarely called attention to the Socialists' revolutionary rhetoric or rigidly sectarian policies. When the *Manchester Guardian* wrote that the Austrian Socialists had a "fine record," it conveniently overlooked a decade of militant posturing and self-isolating obstructionism. The tragic fact was that Austrian socialism, like the Austrian parliament, contributed significantly to its own destruction.

Like their respective presses, the French and the British governments took Dollfuss to task for the brutality with which he put down the Socialist uprising. According to the *New York Times,* one (unidentified) Western diplomat told Dollfuss "that any government that brought out artillery to deal with its Socialists ought not to need outside help to cope with a brown balloon filled with gas from Munich and Berlin." Alexis Léger, general secretary in the French Foreign Office, told the Austrian government that its repression of Social Democracy was a "bad mistake." Léger suggested that Dollfuss had launched his attack when he did because Europe's traditional protector of human rights, France, was itself in a state of debilitating turmoil.

One might argue that this chastisement came a little late: neither the French nor the British government had criticized Dollfuss for his high-handed elimination of parliamentary government and his proclamation of an authoritarian regime in 1933. They had undoubtedly hoped that these measures would make Austria more stable—better able to ward off the urgent embraces of its native son in Berlin. But it had become increasingly apparent to the French and the British governments that Dollfuss's policies were not only alienating large segments of his own population but also undercutting their efforts to "sell" him at home as Austria's best hope against Nazism. As soon as he learned how Dollfuss was dealing with the Socialist uprising, Sir John Simon, the British foreign secretary, warned that the bloodletting would lead, both in England and in France, to a "very marked cooling" of sympathy for the little chancellor, and that "any further attempts by His Majesty's Government to assist Dr. Dollfuss may be rendered increasingly difficult."

Britain and France therefore urged Dollfuss to retreat from his brutal tactics and extend the olive branch to the battered Socialists. On February 19, after two *Schutzbündler* had already been executed, Simon formally expressed his government's hope that "a policy of clemency and appeasement would follow the recent disturbances." The French ambassador to Austria pleaded with the Dollfuss government to employ "all possible mildness" in its treatment of the defeated opposition. France even tried to enlist the Vatican in support of this approach, but the papal nuncio in Vienna argued that any intervention on behalf of the Socialists would look like criticism of the Dollfuss government.

Dollfuss's blunt rejection of this advice—his hasty execution of another seven men and imprisonment of hundreds more—created a new outcry against him in

London and Paris. The little chancellor, once the subject of considerable affection as the "pluckish" defender of Austrian dignity, was now "the butcher of Vienna."

There was an outcry, too, in the United States, though it was largely confined to left-wing groups on the eastern seaboard. A joint Socialist-Communist demonstration on February 14 in front of the Austrian consulate in New York ended in a battle between police and demonstrators on the steps of the New York Public Library. On the following day several American labor unions organized a large protest meeting against the Dollfuss government in Madison Square Garden. The sponsors described the meeting as a demonstration against "the treachery and brutality of the attack of the Dollfuss government on the Austrian trade unions and Socialists."

Henry L. Stimson, America's once and future Secretary of War, expressed concern that Dollfuss's repression of the Socialists would "inevitably lead to a Nazi takeover in Vienna." By contrast, the American chargé d'affaires in Vienna (the American ambassador was back home in Pennsylvania during the civil war) remained unshaken in his admiration for Dollfuss. On February 13 he cabled Secretary of State Cordell Hull, "The Government's unusually vigorous and efficient suppression of the uprising has greatly restored confidence in the Chancellor, which he sorely needed." On February 22, after a private meeting with Dollfuss, the chargé wrote, "I am of the opinion that the Chancellor's feeling toward the Socialists is one of pity and charity, not bitterness or revenge. He impressed me with his sincere feeling for [the] interests of the workers and his simple peasant background still dominated his view." Chancellor Dollfuss, the chargé added, had told him, "I am charged with trying to imitate certain foreign dictators whereas my secret ambition is to help Austria like President Roosevelt is helping America."

Franklin Roosevelt, who might not have been entirely flattered by this comparison, was concerned primarily for the safety of the some seven hundred Americans residing in Vienna. He insisted that his ambassador to Austria, George H. Earle III, curtail his campaign for the governorship of Pennsylvania and return immediately to his post. After a quick *tour d'horizon* in Vienna, Earle echoed the American chargé's optimistic assessment of the situation. He reported that the government's military operations during the civil war "were conducted in a most humane manner." Since the conclusion of the fighting, Dollfuss had shown "amazing" clemency. "The relief and aid given to the insurgents' families by Dollfuss is almost unparalleled in Europe." Earle's prognostication ran as follows:

> Because of the demonstration of strength of the military forces of the Republic which brought fear of death to the Nazis and because of the efficiency and unswerving loyalty of the police and soldiers to the Government in this crisis, I believe Dollfuss' position is stronger than ever and that conditions are less threatening than at any time since my arrival last September.

Within less than five months Dollfuss would be dead, victim of an abortive Nazi putsch. Four years later Austria would be part of Germany.

The obtuse American diplomats notwithstanding, Dollfuss's loudest cheerleader remained Benito Mussolini. The duce told Dollfuss through Suvich that Italy considered his action "a very salutary movement that has brought to a head a situation which has been hanging over Austria for several years." Dollfuss's toughness would answer "the criticisms of the Nazis who have said that he was incapable of being ruthless and strong and unable to maintain order." On February 17 Mussolini encouraged Dollfuss not to be intimidated by criticism from abroad— "the usual twaddle of the European Left." Instead, he should move forward with the consolidation of fascism. This would, promised Mussolini, "be of fundamental importance for the independence of Austria."

So it would, but not in the way Mussolini had in mind. Hitler, the man whom Dollfuss's ruthlessness was supposed to impress, remained singularly unmoved. His central concern regarding Austria, after all, had never been that state's harboring of Marxists but its independent existence. And since the Socialists, not the rightist Austrian government, had been Nazism's most implacable opponent, Hitler and his colleagues could only welcome Dollfuss's crushing of Red Vienna. That the Nazis were not prepared to renounce their goals in Austria simply because Dollfuss had gotten tough with the local Reds was evident from the *Völkischer Beobachter*'s assessment of the February events. The Austrian government, it sneered, remained "democratic" despite its recent "illiberal" gestures. The Austrian Nazi party declared that it would continue to "fight the Dollfuss government tooth and nail so that a new Austria may arise after the Dollfuss system has met its deserved downfall." The implication was clear enough, though Dollfuss (and Mussolini) chose not to see it: Austria could never satisfy the Nazis by emulating their policies—it could do so only by "coming home to the Reich."

FINIS AUSTRIAE

According to official figures published by the government, the Austrian civil war claimed the lives of 115 members of the "executive" (military, police, and Heimwehren) and 196 *Schutzbündler* and other civilians. In addition, 486 government fighters were listed as wounded, 319 among the civilian population. Like much else relating to the February fighting, these numbers were hotly disputed. The Socialists claimed several hundred dead and thousands wounded. The best outside estimates suggested that the government had lost roughly what it claimed but that there were some 270 Schutzbund fatalities and almost 200 deaths among the unarmed civilian population, including 25 women and children. Whatever the quibbling about specific numbers, no one could deny that the Zentralfriedhof, already one of Europe's largest cemeteries, had experienced a sudden and substantial in-migration.

Austria's February *Fasching* season turned into a carnival of death. On February 21 the government staged an elaborate state funeral for the soldiers and policemen who had died in the fighting. Military trucks brought forty-one flag-draped coffins to the neo-Gothic town hall, where the archbishop of Vienna consecrated the bodies. Chancellor Dollfuss delivered a eulogy, declaring that the "fallen" had saved not just Austria and Vienna but "all Europe" from a terrible catastrophe. (His aim, presumably, was to draw a parallel between 1934 and 1683, when the successful defense of Vienna against the Turks allegedly saved Europe from the awful peril of Islam.) After the eulogy, the funeral cortege wound its way along the Ring, through the monumental Schwarzenberg Platz, past the Belvedere Palace (given to Prince Eugene in gratitude for his defense of Vienna in 1683), and on down to the Zentralfriedhof, where forty-one "graves of honor" had been freshly dug in the hard winter ground for these latest heroes of European Christendom.

At about the same time, Vienna's working-class population was also burying its dead, but with less fanfare, since the government forbade potentially disruptive "demonstrations." In Bruck an der Mur, Koloman Wallisch's unmarked grave was discovered by Socialist residents and bedecked with flowers. The Heimwehr promptly removed these, and people returned with more. No flowers covered the grave of the railway worker who had denounced Wallisch to the police. He had been found dead in a field ten days after the popular mayor's execution—presumably the victim of a Socialist vigilante squad.

If Austria's pageantry of death kept hatreds alive, so did the government's relief program for the families and dependents of men killed or incapacitated in the fighting. Most of the government aid went to the victims on the executive side, though far more working-class families had lost breadwinners or homes. On February 18 Cardinal Innitzer, Austria's leading prelate, announced that he and the wife of the chancellor had launched a fund for the benefit of widows and children of Social Democrats. According to the London *Daily Herald*, however, the relief parcels sent by Innitzer's fund contained—in addition to food and clothing—applications to join Dollfuss's Fatherland Front. Some families promptly returned the parcels.

In the end most of the aid reaching Vienna's working-class families came from abroad, from either the Quakers or the European Socialist parties, especially the British Labour party. But this help, too, sometimes had ulterior motives. Among the British Labour party emissaries sent to coordinate the relief effort was Kim Philby, the future Soviet spy. At that time he was already secretly working for Moscow, using the relief program as a cover for the establishment of a courier system between the underground Communist movement in Austria and exiled Communist leaders in Prague and the Soviet Union. Another source of aid was Nazi Germany. The Germans sent money and food to Socialist families as a way of convincing them that their (and Austria's) future lay with the Reich. Even the leftist relief workers admitted that this tactic registered some successes.

If the Nazis profited from Austria's civil war, this resulted less from their own efforts than from the legacy of hatred left by Dollfuss's actions. Determined to wreak revenge upon the diminutive chancellor and his followers, a number of former *Schutzbündler* joined the underground Nazi movement. Through them the Nazis acquired fresh arms and explosives for their continuing "tooth and nail" campaign against the Dollfuss regime. One of the *Schutzbündler* who cooperated with the Nazis, though only for a time, was Richard Bernasek, the man whose unauthorized resistance in Linz had sparked the Socialist uprising.*

Dollfuss himself was soon to discover that his crushing of the Socialists had done nothing to stabilize his regime. In the spring and summer of 1934 the Austrian Nazis increased their attacks, restless to exploit the government's weakness. On July 25 a small group of these Nazis—most of them members of the SS *(Schutz Staffel,* or security staff)—staged a putsch designed to overthrow the regime and effect an immediate *Anschluss.* The putsch was poorly organized and lacked the support of other local Nazi groups, particularly the SA (storm troopers), who were embittered over Hitler's recent purge of the German SA. The coup attempt quickly disintegrated, but not before a band of Nazis had managed to invade the Ballhausplatz and shoot the chancellor, who slowly bled to death in his office.

For a time it looked as if Dollfuss's death would bring his cause considerably more popular sympathy than he had been able to drum up for it in his life. According to George Clare, his funeral was "pompous," yet "somehow moving." There followed a kind of Dollfuss sanctification—a plethora of Dollfuss chapels, altar pictures, and eternal flames. Many villages got a Dollfuss street or square (just as Austrian towns were later to get streets and squares named after Adolf Hitler). But not all Austrians joined in this Dollfuss beautification: few Viennese workers wanted anything to do with the mythologizing of Millimetternich.†

The abortive Nazi putsch stunned Benito Mussolini, who was sure Hitler had ordered it as a prelude to marching on Austria. Denouncing the führer as a "horrible sexual degenerate," Mussolini rushed three Italian divisions to the Brenner Pass. The Germans must realize, he declared once again, that Italy would

---

*After his capture, Bernasek was imprisoned with 943 other *Schutzbündler* in the provincial courthouse in Linz. He soon escaped and made his way to neighboring Bavaria, where he worked for a time with refugee Austrian Nazis on plans for the overthrow of Dollfuss. He became alienated from the Nazi cause, however, after Hitler's purge of the radical SA on June 30, 1934, convinced him that National Socialism did not take its "socialism" seriously. From Bavaria he went to Czechoslovakia and then to Moscow, where he proclaimed his conversion to communism. After the *Anschluss* he returned secretly to Linz to work in the anti-Nazi resistance. Arrested in 1944, he was killed in the Mauthausen concentration camp in 1945, shortly before the end of the war.

†Exiled Austrian Socialists received the news of Dollfuss's assassination with vengeful delight. According to G. E. R. Gedye, they hailed his demise "as the death of a tyrant and murderer of liberty." "Austria is experiencing her June 30," they said, alluding to the Nazi Blood Purge of the SA; "as in the Reich, Fascists are murdering Fascists and we can look on in satisfaction at the process."

never tolerate an *Anschluss*. Hitler, anxious to avoid a confrontation with the duce at this point, hastily recalled his chief minister in Vienna and disclaimed all responsibility for the putsch attempt (which, indeed, he had not ordered or actively supported).

Mussolini, for a time, continued to assure Austria of his support, but his role as "defender of Mediterranean civilization" north of the Brenner Pass was rapidly coming to an end. He was soon to embark on a series of foreign-policy adventures that would isolate him from the West and lead him into an alliance with his erstwhile German rival, Adolf Hitler. As part of his blossoming friendship with Hitler he gradually abandoned Austria—just as he eventually abandoned Italy itself. When Germany annexed Austria in March 1938, Mussolini not only refused to intervene but even declared he had never been so "foolish" as to promise such a thing. The "totalitarian regimes," he added at that moment, must continue to "march in step together." Hitler, touchingly grateful for this demonstration of totalitarian solidarity, told the duce, "I shall never forget you for this, Mussolini. Never, never, never!"

Austria's Italian protector, we recall, had urged repressive internal policies on Chancellor Dollfuss as a way of strengthening Austria's ability to ward off German annexation. It was said in Italy, "The duce is always right," but rarely was the duce more wrong: the civil war he helped inspire in the Austrian republic had consequences precisely the opposite of those intended by Austria's "saviors."

The Austria that faced Hitler in 1938, like the France that faced him two years later, was a deeply divided and demoralized nation. Dollfuss's successor, Kurt von Schuschnigg, sought to continue the former's policy of maintaining an Austria at once "German" and independent. But Schuschnigg was even less adept at carrying off this intricate enterprise than Dollfuss. He was a cold, distant man, incapable of either giving or showing affection. More important, he was remembered in Vienna as the man who on the evening of February 12 had broadcast a speech denouncing the Social Democratic leaders as "hyenas" and urging that they be "chased to the devil." He was also remembered as the minister of justice who interpreted justice to mean sicking the hangman on the *Schutzbündler* with all possible speed. Schuschnigg's efforts to build up Dollfuss's patriotic Fatherland Front into a viable mass organzization faltered on these memories, which his government kept fresh by reminding Austrians how fortunate they were to have escaped the imposition of a "Bolshevist tyranny" in February 1934.

During the Schuschnigg era, the Social Democratic party remained proscribed, its leadership either in prison or in exile in Prague. Between 1936 and 1938 nearly two thousand Austrian leftists, mostly former *Schutzbündler*, went to Spain to fight on behalf of the republican government against the Franco rebellion. They founded their own unit, the *"Battalion 12. Februar,"* within the international brigades, and they liked to describe their engagement in Spain as their "revenge for February 1934." After the defeat of the Spanish republic most of the Austrians fled to France, where they were interned by the French government at a camp in Gurs. After the signing of the Nazi-Soviet nonaggression pact (1939) and the defeat of France, the Soviet government urged the Austrians to take the Germans' advice and repatriate to Austria. Most of those who accepted this advice were shipped straight to Dachau.

A number of Austrian radicals also fled to Moscow, where they divided their time between denouncing Schuschnigg and Otto Bauer, whom they (in keeping with the Soviet line) accused of having betrayed the workers' cause. They now put their stock in Stalin—an act of trust that the Russian dictator eventually repaid by including them in his brutal purge of foreign Communists in the late 1930s. In the meantime the Austrian Communists in Moscow maintained an active underground organization in Austria. Its function was to do what it could to destabilize Schuschnigg's hated regime. If Hitler profited from this, so be it: the Communist millennium, they were convinced, would only be hastened by the devastation Hitler was sure to wreak on the bourgeois world.

The Austrian Nazis also did what they could to keep Schuschnigg off balance. Distinctly unimpressed by his claims to have the nation solidly behind him, they belittled the staid Tyrolean with rude jokes focusing on the inadequacies of his brand of "fascism": "What good's the Hitler bra? (good for uplifting the masses); the Mussolini bra? (good for holding the masses together); the von Schuschnigg bra? (good only for covering false pretenses)." More ominous, after a brief rebuilding period following their abortive putsch, the local Nazis reverted to their terrorist campaign against the government. Once again Vienna's august boulevards resounded to the noise of bombs detonating, windows splintering, and rescue sirens howling.

The Austrian Nazis conducted their terror campaign over the protests of their German master, Adolf Hitler, who had decided that his annexation of Austria could best be effected by "peaceful" means: political intimidation and aggressive diplomacy. He focused his considerable talents in this domain on the hapless Schuschnigg, whom he invited to his mountain retreat near Berchtesgaden on February 12, 1938, exactly four years after the outbreak of the Austrian civil war. On this famous occasion the führer browbeat the Austrian chancellor into signing what Schuschnigg later admitted was Austria's death warrant. More specifically, Hitler threatened an invasion of Austria if the Vienna government did not remove its military defenses on the German border, lift its ban on the Austrian Nazi party, pardon the Nazi putschists of July 1934 (including the murderers of Dollfuss), and appoint Austrian Nazis to cabinet posts that controlled the police, the army, and the economy. During the course of the long meeting, Hitler often became hysterical, shouting that if Schuschnigg did not comply with his demands, he would "turn Austria into another Spain." He warned the Austrian chancellor that he could expect no support from Italy (the duce now being Germany's friend) or from England or France, which had shown their lack of backbone in 1936 when Germany remilitarized the Rhineland in open defiance of the Versailles treaty. As if this verbal assault had not been enough, Hitler refused to allow his guest to have a cigarette, further unnerving the chain-smoking Schuschnigg.

After the meeting, having acceded to all of Hitler's demands, the trembling Schuschnigg was told by Franz von Papen, Germany's ambassador to Vienna, to buck up: the "next time" Hitler would be more cordial and the Austrian would have an "easier time."

But there would be no "next time" for Schuschnigg: he was arrested by the Gestapo immediately after the *Anschluss,* imprisoned for a while in Vienna, then transported to the Sachsenhausen and Dachau concentration camps in Germany. There he had a chance to meet some of the Austrian Socialists against whom he had campaigned so bitterly in 1934.

As Hitler told Schuschnigg in February 1938, Germany had good reason to believe that the Western powers would "not lift a finger for Austria." But in addition to Western appeasement sentiment based on the fear of war, Hitler had another ally in his Austrian policy: the distinct international unpopularity of the Vienna regime. Like many working-class Austrians, large segments of the western European public were convinced that the Austria that appealed for help against German Nazism was all too close to Nazism in its own domestic policies. "Why support one Fascist against another?" was an oft-heard question. No doubt this question demonstrated political shortsightedness and a lack of strategic sophistication. It also obscured the genuine differences between Schuschnigg's "fascism" and that of his northern neighbor. Nevertheless, this kind of thinking made it much easier for appeasement-minded politicians in France and in Britain to stand on the sidelines when Hitler decided it was time to bring his native land "home to the Reich."

Might the Western powers have acted any differently had there been no Austrian civil war or Austrian fascism and had a democratic and westward-looking Austria stood more firmly united against an annexation? Of course, we cannot know the answer to this question, but such an Austria might have been willing to attempt some form of military resistance to Hitler's designs, and this would have put the Western powers in a very awkward position indeed. As it was, Austria was left to fend for itself, and for this it had few internal resources. At the last minute, as Hitler and his Nazi agents increased their pressure for an outright annexation, Schuschnigg turned for help to the Austrian workers, offering to restore their party and release their leaders from prison. But Austria's workers were not prepared to put their confidence in a man who had been very instrumental in their emasculation, and in any event it was too late.

Hitler used as his pretext for invasion Schuschnigg's call on March 9 for a plebiscite on Austrian independence. The Austrians would be asked if they supported a "free, independent, social, Christian and united Austria." They did not get the chance to answer, for two days later Hitler gave the order for "Operation

Otto," the military occupation of Austria. He claimed that he had done so because Schuschnigg's plebiscite would have delivered the nation to the forces of revolution.

Confronted by the prospect of imminent invasion, Schuschnigg went on the radio and in an emotional speech informed the Austrian people that he was giving in to "brute force," that he had ordered Austrian troops not to offer resistance if the Germans came over the border. "[We] refuse to shed German blood," he said, "even at this tragic hour."

Perhaps this "tragic hour" in March 1938 might have been averted had the Austrian government maintained the same disinclination to shed "German blood" in July 1927 and February 1934.

III

THE NIGHT OF
THE LONG KNIVES

Nazi Germany and
the Blood Purge, 1934

> Men may sleep, and they may have their throats about them
> at that time; and some say knives have edges.
>
> —Shakespeare, *Henry V*

> After the revolution, there is always the question of what to
> do with the revolutionaries.
>
> —Mussolini, letter to Oswald Mosley

June 30, 1934, dawned brightly for the SA *Obergruppenführer* (lieutenant general) Karl Ernst. He spent the morning in Bremerhaven, inspecting the *Europa,* the luxury liner on which he and his bride were about to embark on a honeymoon cruise to Madeira. That afternoon he attended a bon voyage party thrown by his comrades in the SA (*Sturm Abteilung,* or storm troopers), whose Berlin branch he commanded. During the celebrations the mayor of Bremen came by to wish Ernst and his bride "long life for the happiness of Germany." Among the guests was Prince August Wilhelm von Hohenzollern (Prince Auwi), fourth son of ex-Kaiser Wilhelm II and a deputy in the Nazi-controlled Reichstag (parliament). Consorting with Prince Auwi was quite a social coup for Ernst, a former hotel doorman and pimp who looked every inch the thug that he was. But the SA leader was beginning to take his prominence in Prussian society for granted; he ordered around titled landowners and was known to have seduced more than one heiress, despite a general preference for young boys. He liked to brag that he "owned" Berlin.

Upon returning to his hotel after the party, Ernst found an SS (*Schutz Staffel,* or security staff) officer waiting with a warrant for his arrest. Insisting that there must be some mistake, Ernst demanded a telephone to call his "good friend" Hermann Göring, head of the Prussian police and second man in the Reich behind Adolf Hitler. But the SS officer simply bundled him into a car, drove him to the Bremen airport, and put him on a plane for Berlin.

Arriving at Tempelhof airfield, Ernst jumped from the plane and into a wait-ing car, "smiling in every direction as if to show the world that he did not take his arrest seriously." Expecting to be taken to Göring, he was instead driven to the Lichterfelde Cadet School, in the southern part of the city. That evening, still demanding to see Göring, he was led into the school courtyard, stood against a wall, and shot. He fell to the ground shouting, "Heil Hitler!"

Karl Ernst was one of dozens of SA men to die in the so-called Blood Purge of June 30–July 2, 1934. The purge focused on the leadership of the plebeian, rabble-rousing SA, but it also swept up a number of conservative anti-Nazis who had nothing to do with the storm troopers. As a result of this copious bloodletting, which took place one and a half years after Hitler assumed the chancellorship, the führer was able to make his final breakthrough to total power in Germany.

ERNST RÖHM AND THE SA

When Adolf Hitler, then thirty, joined the fledgling German Workers party in 1919, he immediately set about the task of distinguishing this not very promis-ing band of radical rightists from the dozens of similar nationalist coteries in postwar Bavaria. To this end he established a personal guard within the party that he staffed with a few score "rough fellows"—tough young street-brawling types who shared his conviction that "the best defense [was] attack," that their "order troop must be known not as a debating society but as a dedicated fighting associa-tion." This was the true birth of the SA, though the group was not so christened until 1921 and did not begin wearing its characteristic brown shirts until a few years later.*

The men who joined the SA in the early years were not all war veterans, but the First World War, along with the revolution of 1918–19, which overthrew the German Empire and introduced the "Weimar Republic," made such a group possible. Postwar Germany was flooded with men who during the four long years of war had lived an existence at once revolting and strangely compelling. Along with rats, lice, mud, and boredom, they had experienced moments of extreme excitement and even joy—times when a man could "feel like a ferocious tiger of the trenches" and "employ the latest machines of mass destruction to quench his ancient thirst for blood." Then too, they had known the fierce comradeship born of living together through daylong barrages and sudden charges across "no-man's-land." During the war many of the soldiers had developed a pronounced con-tempt for the civilians at home—and even for the staff officers in the rear—who knew nothing of the "front experience" in the trenches. They had come to see

---

*Initially the SA wore windbreakers and ski hats designed by Hitler himself. They switched to khaki shirts because these could be cheaply purchased from the supplies of the former German colonial troops.

themselves as a breed apart, no longer entirely fit for anything but fighting and killing.

The soldiers' sense of apartness was heightened by what they found at home once the war had ended. Since the revolution, leadership over the country had passed from the kaiser and his generals to a coalition of Socialists, bourgeois democrats, and Catholics. To Hitler and the men attracted to his movement, the new leaders were "criminals" who had "stabbed the nation in the back" by staging a revolution during a time of war and who then added insult to injury by signing the humiliating Treaty of Versailles. Compounding these political grievances were severe economic dislocations engendered by remnants of the wartime Allied blockade and an inflation rate that by late 1923 had reduced the value of the German mark to roughly one-trillionth of a dollar. Work of any kind was difficult to find under these circumstances, and thousands of veterans, unable or unwilling to find a place in the 100,000-man army allowed Germany by the Treaty of Versailles, left the ranks of the military only to join the ranks of the unemployed.

For a brief time immediately after the war, some of these men found an outlet for their rapacious energies in the so-called *Freikorps* (free-corps) movement which comprised paramilitary forces recruited to defend German territories in the northeast under attack by the Poles. Later the free corps were active in the suppression of Communist-inspired revolts in Berlin, Munich, and central Germany. War veterans could find in these groups a welcome postponement of the dreaded return to civilian society, while younger men who had missed the wartime excitement could now become "veterans" too. The ethos of the free corps was perhaps best expressed by one of its leaders during a postbattle toast in Upper Silesia: "There's nothing better than a little war like this," he said as he raised his glass. "God preserve the theater of war. I'm threatening to become sober."

Like the free corps, Hitler's SA offered a haven to such men. To those who desired an extension or replacement of the war experience, it promised the chance to fight in the streets. To the unemployed and down-and-out, it provided a kind of "work" (albeit without pay), food, and a place to sleep. Above all, it gave this "lost generation" of young Germans a new direction and purpose in life, a cause for which to struggle with all the "heroic idealism" that Nazism claimed to demand of its stalwarts.

One of the most representative figures of this generation was the man who eventually came to head the SA—and to head the list of victims of the Blood Purge—Ernst Röhm. Though the scion of an old family of Bavarian civil servants, Röhm had never wanted to be a bureaucrat. From childhood on, his only dream was to become a soldier and to distinguish himself on the field of combat. The First World War allowed him to fulfill this dream. Wounded several times in battle, he advanced up the junior-officer ranks to become a captain on the general staff. Here he displayed great organizational ability and a keen grasp of logistics and military supply. Yet this was no stereotypical, bemonocled representative of the Prussian general staff. Battle-scarred, red-faced, and increasingly corpulent, Röhm preferred beer parties with his men to champagne evenings in the officers' casino. He prided himself on being a daredevil, a swashbuckler, a man who appreciated the thrill of a commando raid behind enemy lines. His experiences at the front left him contemptuous of the cautious calculation that he believed had enfeebled the general staff during the war and emasculated the civilian politicians at home. Throughout his life he retained an aversion for the civilian world of politics, yet he also believed that he and his comrades had an incontestable right, by virtue of their exalted experiences at the front, to play a commanding role in shaping Germany's political destiny. Röhm probably saw no inconsistency in this, yet his combination of "unpolitical" warrior bravado and far-reaching political ambition both fueled his rise to prominence and contributed to his downfall.

Another quality distinguished Röhm from most of his peers on the general staff: his open homosexuality. A sublimated homoeroticism, as the literary critic Paul Fussel suggests, may have played an important role in the front experience, especially in the relationship between gallant young officers and their men. But Röhm's homoeroticism was not sublimated, nor was his choice of partners limited to fellow officers who understood the importance of discretion. Particularly after the war, he was known to travel in a "dissolute" crowd, and there were rumors of "orgies" accompanied by prodigious bouts of gluttony and drunkenness. None of this would be terribly significant if Röhm had not eventually found in the Nazi SA an outlet for the full array of his passions: military, political, and sexual. According to one commentator, Röhm's influence stamped the SA as "a kind of wrestling club with a political bias."

Despite his reputation for dissoluteness, Röhm managed by virtue of his recognized organizational abilities to secure a place in Germany's much-constricted postwar army, the Reichswehr. His primary job was to help the army command circumvent the manpower limits imposed by the Versailles treaty, by building up a secret paramilitary reserve—the "black Reichswehr." Operating out of Munich, Röhm soon came into contact with Adolf Hitler, who was employed by the army to check up on radical rightist groups in Bavaria, including the one the future führer joined. Captivated instantly by Hitler's charismatic personality, fanatical patriotism, and revolutionary zeal, Röhm added the fledgling Nazi party to the list of organizations receiving financial and organizational assistance from the Reichswehr. Indeed, he soon made the Nazis, and particularly their SA, the focus of his largess. He saw Hitler's band of "rough fellows" as his kind of outfit. These were just the sorts of desperadoes one needed not only to build up Germany's shattered defenses but also to replace the country's government of bourgeois democrats and Socialists with a military dictatorship staffed by *Frontschweine* (front pigs) like himself and Hitler, who had won the Iron Cross (First Class) as a courier in the war.

Through Röhm's assistance the SA made rapid progress in expanding its numbers and improving its military training. In November 1921 it experienced its "baptism of fire" when (at least according to party legend) forty-six SA men beat up some seven or eight hundred Communists. Hitler valued Röhm as an important ally in this period and repaid the captain's admiration with genuine affection: Röhm became one of the few people he addressed in the familiar and intimate *du* form.

Nevertheless, Hitler and Röhm did not see eye to eye on all aspects of Nazi party strategy, especially with regard to the place of the SA in the National Socialist enterprise. Much as he wanted the SA to become a formidable "fighting association," Hitler did not see it primarily as a *military* unit and did not want the strictly military side of its activities to overwhelm what for him were its central functions: training young Germans in the values of National Socialism, protecting Nazi party meetings, and spreading the word through street marches, rallies, and demonstrations. For Hitler, in other words, the SA's focus should remain essentially political, a principle he sought to reinforce by ordering the organization's subordination to the party's political bureaucracy, the so-called Political Organization, or PO.

Röhm, on the other hand, dreamed from the outset of turning the SA and other rightist paramilitary forces into a massive popular militia that would, after the anticipated "revolution" against the current republican government, absorb the regular army into its ranks. In the meantime, the group must do all it could to develop its military potential through formal martial training, field maneuvers, and the like. In the first three years of the Nazi party's history, Röhm was in a better position than Hitler to further his vision of the SA because he controlled the largess from the Reichswehr and brought hundreds of his wartime cronies into the organization. By January 1923 the SA had emerged as a credible paramilitary force, with Hermann Göring, a highly decorated World War I pilot, as supreme commander. (Röhm himself, as an active army officer, remained somewhat in the background, though his connection to the Nazis and other radical rightist groups was well known.)

So mistrustful was Hitler of this development that he countered it with a characteristic move: in March 1923 he set up a new guard formation that assumed the SA's original task of protecting his person. Pledged to absolute loyalty, this so-called *Stosstrupp Hitler* (shock troop Hitler) was the ancestor of the infamous SS, which was not formally established until 1925. Significantly enough, it was this shock troop that stood guard next to Hitler when he launched his ill-fated "Beer Hall Putsch" from atop a table in Munich's Bürgerbräu Keller in November 1923.

This putsch, through which Hitler had hoped to gain control over Bavaria in anticipation of a march on Berlin, collapsed in its opening hours when Bavarian police broke up a Nazi column that was trying to reach the War Ministry, which Ernst Röhm had taken over with the help of another paramilitary group he controlled. Röhm and Hitler had counted on the Reichswehr to support their undertaking, but the army backed the Bavarian government and its police, ensuring the putsch's failure. The ignominious collapse of the revolt had a substantial impact on the future development of the Nazi party and its paramilitary formations. Hitler was convicted of treason and sentenced to five years in prison, thirteen months of which he actually served. When he emerged from Bavaria's Landsberg prison in 1925, he was determined to resist any further temptations to take power by armed force. He would assume control of the government "legally," securing the key office of chancellor by building his party into the largest and most powerful political organization in the state. He would be careful, too, to cultivate better relations with the army, whose solid backing he now deemed essential to his achievement of power and the fulfillment of his expansionist plans for Germany. Such strategy by no means ruled out the use of violence or terror tactics to intimidate enemies and win "respect" for his cause, but the violence would have to be carefully controlled and applied for best propagandistic effect. There was little room here for the indiscriminate brawling that Ernst Röhm and much of the SA held so dear.

As part of his reorganization of the Nazi movement in the mid-1920s, Hitler reestablished his authority over the SA and placed it firmly under the supervision of the party's Political Organization. He made it clear that the SA was to be no more than a "means to an end," a loyal "party tool" that would not shape policy or strategy. New guidelines published in 1925 prohibited the SA from carrying weapons (save for the odd rubber hose or pair of brass knuckles) and designated as its primary functions "hardening the bodies" of German youth and "training [young people] to accept the discipline and self-sacrifice demanded by our common great ideal." In short, the SA was to spend most of its time behaving like a kind of glorified Boy Scout troop, building "healthy bodies" rather than drinking beer and breaking heads.

This was too much for the old soldier Röhm. He would have liked to resist Hitler's new course, but having been released from the Reichswehr as a result of his support of the Beer Hall Putsch, he no longer had any political leverage. Rather than accept a leadership position in the SA under the conditions Hitler had set down, he withdrew from the political scene, then left Germany altogether to become a military adviser in Bolivia, which valued the services of skilled German officers in its endless wars with its neighbors.*

With Röhm in Bolivia and the SA trying—albeit with little success—to stay within its new guidelines, Hitler set about transforming his modest shock troop into a more elaborate praetorian guard: the SS. From the beginning this organization assumed a character quite different from that of the SA. The emphasis here was not on quantity but on quality, on the development of a truly elite force that would maintain strict standards in the admission and retention of members. Its elitism was evident in its smart black uniforms and in its motto "Our Honor Is Duty." In addition to providing personal protection for Hitler, the SS also moved

*In taking this step, Röhm contributed his small share to what was then, and would be again after 1945, one of Germany's more flourishing industries: the export of military talent. Bolivia itself became the postwar killing field for Klaus Barbie, the Nazi "Butcher of Lyon."

in on some of the SA's old turf, such as "hall security" during party meetings and distribution of the party newspaper, the *Völkischer Beobachter* (People's observer). Total membership remained small in the early years: at the time Heinrich Himmler assumed leadership of the SS, in 1929, the group had only two hundred men.

The SA, on the other hand, continued to grow during the second half of the 1920s. Profiting from the dissolution of most of the free-corps organizations, it had enrolled some seventy thousand members by 1930. The organization's new leader, Franz Pfeffer von Salomon, tried his best to keep the movement within the guidelines set down by Hitler in 1925, but he increasingly lost control over local and regional leaders who resented their subordination to the party's PO (which they derisively called P-Zero). The SA leaders also resented their financial dependence on the party, which doled out support payments that rarely covered the SA's needs. To achieve some financial independence and self-sufficiency, the SA established its own insurance program, housing complexes, clothing-supply company, and food distribution system. It also earned revenues by endorsing such mass-consumption products as Stürmer razor blades, Kampf margarine, and Sturm cigarettes, all of which store owners kept in plentiful stock if they knew what was good for them. Proceeds from such enterprises were kept within the SA, not turned over to the party. The storm trooper movement, in other words, was hardly revealing itself as a loyal "party tool." On the contrary, it was again asserting the essential restlessness and impatience with party supervision that had always made it so difficult to contain.

By the late 1920s it was also showing again its old proclivity for military forms and militarized street violence. This violence was rarely "surgical" in its precision, or even clearly ideological in its motivation: most often it was violence for the sake of violence, joyful bashing and brawling with groups like the Communist "Red Front," which seemed equally addicted to the carnage. Winston Churchill had a point when he observed that the SA "differed from the Bolsheviks whom they denounced no more than the North Pole does from the South." The mentality of the SA in this period was perhaps best captured by the group's most famous street brawler, Horst Wessel. He wrote with obvious enthusiasm of "one fight after another . . . high excitement . . . countless wounded and maimed, [and] even dead bodies piled in the public squares." Wessel himself would soon meet a violent death (though apparently at the hands of a pimp rather than a Communist) and as martyred hero would give his name to the Nazis' marching anthem, the "Horst Wessel Song."

Tensions between the rebellious SA and the Nazi party's political bureaucracy reached crisis proportions in 1930–31, when on two occasions the leader of the Berlin SA, Walter Stennes, actually revolted against the authority of the party's eastern German gauleiters (district leaders). Angry over inadequate subsidies from the party, and unwilling to take orders from the Berlin gauleiter, Joseph Goebbels, Stennes withdrew SA services from the party in August 1930. Goebbels turned to Hitler in Munich for help in quelling this upheaval, and Hitler duly gave it. The führer went to Berlin, called a meeting of the northeastern SA groups, and announced that henceforth he himself would take over supreme leadership of the storm troopers.* He was also careful to promise more generous financial allotments to the SA.

Hitler's personal intervention, as often in interparty battles, calmed the troubled waters—but only for a short while. In January 1931 Stennes revolted again, this time because Hitler had installed Ernst Röhm, recently returned from Bolivia, as his new chief of staff of the SA. Just as Stennes had no use for party tutelage, he resented being subordinate to Röhm in Munich. His resentment was partly a function of long-standing regional animosities, partly a matter of personal rivalry. To quell this second revolt Hitler expelled Stennes from the party and put Hermann Göring in charge of "purging" the northeastern SA of other rebellious spirits. (For this purpose Göring received the title "higher political commissar east.") Disruptive as these events were, they were just harbingers of harsher things to come.

A "SECOND REVOLUTION"?

Hitler's choice of Röhm to manage the Nazi party's troubled storm trooper organization seems hard to understand given the führer's earlier difficulties with the captain. It would seem, however, that Hitler believed his control over the SA was now firm enough that he could risk entrusting the group's day-to-day supervision to Röhm. Moreover, despite their falling-out in 1925, Hitler continued to trust his old friend. In justifying Röhm's appointment, Hitler recalled that the captain had stood loyally by him during the Beer Hall Putsch, even telling his military superiors that he would lay down his weapons only upon receiving a written order from Hitler or General Erich Ludendorff. "That's why I have unlimited trust in Röhm," said the führer. Such dedication on the part of his lieutenants would be necessary, Hitler believed, to help him win the chancellorship in the near future. Although the Nazi party had made great gains in the most recent elections (September 1930), Hitler was not yet in a commanding position. The Communists, moreover, had also made large gains, and the Nazis could expect to encounter stiffer resistance from the radical Left as they knocked on the doors of power. By dealing competently with this challenge and gaining absolute "control over the streets," they could show conservative Germans how indispensable they were in the common struggle against bolshevism. No one struck Hitler as being more competent in this domain than Ernst Röhm.

The captain, for his part, was more than ready to return to the SA. He wanted

---

*Hitler had neither the time nor the inclination to lead both the SA and the party. He therefore temporarily entrusted the day-to-day management of the SA to Otto Wagener, who kept the post of chief of staff that he had held under Pfeffer.

to be a part of the Nazis' final assault on the bastions of power. His designation as "chief of staff" rather than "supreme leader" of the SA did not bother him much, for he had confidence in his ability to run the organization as he saw fit.

When Hitler turned the SA over to Röhm, in January 1931, he was well aware that the captain had a reputation for "sexual irregularities." Claiming to despise homosexuality and pederasty as "entirely un-Germanic filth of the lowest order," he confronted Röhm in late 1930 "with the question of his tendencies." The captain swore that while he might once have had "such feelings," the "time of his aberrations [had] been overcome." Apparently Hitler believed him or, at least, trusted him to be discreet. This proved a vain hope, and in 1932 a French journalist published an embarrassing exposé on the subject of Röhm's retinue of handsome young aides-de-camp. Furious at his SA leader, Hitler called him in and (according to one witness) "yelled at him for hours." Yet he could not have believed this issue to be of crucial importance, for he left Röhm at his post, merely removing the Hitler Youth from his direct supervision. The journalist who wrote the embarrassing article, incidentally, was found murdered in the South Tyrol shortly after the Nazis came to power.

In the two-year period between Röhm's assignment as SA chief of staff and Hitler's appointment as German chancellor, the brown-shirted storm troopers rendered valuable services to the Nazi party. Vastly swollen in numbers by an influx of newly jobless young Germans, they helped the Nazi movement project an image of dynamic force. This was important at a time when the ravages of the world depression were also swelling the ranks of the far Left, raising fears among the German middle classes that their country might fall victim to a Bolshevik revolution.

While Hitler was prepared to unleash the SA against the Communists, provoking some spectacular street battles, he did not try to preempt a possible Red revolution by launching a Brown revolution of his own. On the contrary, he remained true to his post–Beer Hall Putsch vow to assume power legally—that is, to be appointed chancellor in the prescribed fashion by the president, old Field Marshal Paul von Hindenburg.

The intricate process by which Hitler achieved this goal on January 30, 1933, cannot detain us here. Suffice it to stress that his appointment required securing the support—or at least the toleration—of various conservative interests around the president who were concerned lest the Nazis' proclivities toward undisciplined radicalism exacerbate political and economic instability. Well aware of these concerns, Hitler relied for the most part on legal or pseudo-legal procedures to begin consolidating his power in the following months. Measures of outright physical terror were reserved primarily for the radical Left, whose brutal persecution many Germans found eminently justifiable, if not long overdue. For the time being, at least, Hitler seemed content to leave many of the traditional centers of conservative influence more or less intact. He did not order wholesale purges of the upper bureaucracy, judiciary, foreign service, officer corps, or churches. In short, the führer sought to quiet anxieties regarding his rule by acting more "sensibly" and "normally" than many of his conservative and liberal critics thought possible. These critics, understandably, were relieved.

Ernst Röhm, on the other hand, was disillusioned by what seemed to him a weak and overly cautious course on the führer's part. In May 1933 he instructed his storm troopers not to forget the unfulfilled goals of the Nazi revolution: "We have celebrated enough," he said. ". . . Your task is to complete the National Socialist Revolution and to bring about the National Socialist Reich." He could not imagine that this goal could be achieved without the salutary bloodletting that traditionally accompanied revolutions—without what he liked to call a "night of the long knives."

Röhm's men in the SA did not need to be reminded that the Nazi revolution was incomplete. They believed they had helped Hitler attain power so that he could liquidate the "reactionaries" and put *them* in positions of control. Like an army that had suffered privations while laying siege to a wealthy city, they expected their share of the spoils once the city had fallen. But instead of turning the long-sought prize over to plunder, Hitler was acting like a city father himself, wearing a frock coat and eschewing the company of his "old fighters" for that of fat industrialists and bemedaled generals. And he was saying that the ideas of National Socialist progress committed the party not to "behaving like fools and turning everything on its head but to proceeding carefully and intelligently with the realization of its program."

Some groups within the SA responded to this state of affairs by acting as if it did not exist. They began to make their own grass-roots "revolution," taking over small towns, replacing elected officials with their own people. They cashiered judges and prosecutors who dared call the SA men to account for brawling in the streets or looting Jewish-owned stores. True to the Nazi party's earlier campaign against large department stores (many of which were Jewish owned and all of which were said to hurt the small retailer), they organized boycotts against the big stores, terrorizing shoppers and employees alike. Another target was big finance: SA units blockaded the entrances to banks and stock-exchange buildings, while others occupied regional chambers of commerce.

Such activities did not go unopposed. Complaints about SA "outrages" poured into party headquarters. Industrial leaders warned that they could only deepen the depression, that they would produce yet more unemployment and endanger Germany's ability to raise credit abroad. Hjalmar Schacht, president of the Reichsbank and later Hitler's minister of economics, told the führer that the SA's "repeated interventions" in Germany's banking structure were producing chaos. He and others made clear that if Hitler was serious about dealing rationally with Germany's severe economic problems, he would have to take his SA in hand.

Hitler's response was not long in coming. On March 10, 1933, he issued a decree prohibiting the SA from taking "spontaneous" actions against economic enterprises. "Commerce must not be disturbed," he warned. On April 27 he gave the Reich Finance Ministry authority to use "all available means" to protect the banking system from interventions by party zealots and the SA. And, as if the implication of these measures were not clear enough, Hitler declared on July 6 that the Nazi "revolution" was not "a permanent condition." It was necessary, he insisted, "to direct the overflowing stream of revolutionary energy safely back into evolutionary channels."

Hitler's efforts to curb the SA angered and bewildered Röhm. At times he tried to make sense of the new orders by attributing them to the influence of those "reactionary philistines" who now surrounded the führer. He talked of "freeing" Hitler from the clutches of his "stupid and dangerous" entourage. Among these he included not just generals, businessmen, and bankers but also rival Nazi potentates like Goebbels, Himmler, and Hess. On other occasions, especially among his SA cronies, Röhm attacked Hitler himself. He complained that "Adolf [was] rotten," that he was making common cause with the reactionaries because as an inveterate civilian, artist, and dreamer, he did not want to be bothered with the rough and tumble of revolutionary renewal.

Harsh as this indictment was, Röhm hesitated to break openly or permanently with Hitler, and he combined continued acts of insubordination with efforts to impose *some* restraints on his storm troopers' activities. In June 1933 he promised to extend the Nazi revolution "with or without" the "gripers" around Hitler. But one month later, in response to reports about SA "excesses" in the streets, he ordered that rowdies who "disgraced the SA's honorable uniform" be subject to stiff penalties, including expulsion from the organization. He also tried to distract his men from their frustrations by organizing mass marches and rallies in which the SA legions could demonstrate their soldierly zeal without laying waste to villages or trashing department stores.

Röhm's irregular and somewhat halfhearted efforts to rein in his troops had little effect. One reason was that the organization had now grown so large it was almost impossible to manage. Shortly after Hitler came to power, in January 1933, the SA counted some seven hundred thousand members; within another year it had almost three million. Clearly standards of admission, never very high, had virtually ceased to exist. Röhm's purpose seemed to be to amass a horde so large that no one, not even Hitler, could contain it. He would swamp the entire state in a vast brown flood.

This intention also seemed inherent in Röhm's repeated cry in the spring of 1934 that a "second revolution" was urgently needed now that the original Nazi upheaval had apparently stagnated. As if to clear a path for this second revolution, Röhm ordered the SA's removal from the jurisdiction of the police and the courts. No SA man could be arrested or brought to trial without permission of the storm trooper leadership. Little did Röhm realize that this step, while apparently strengthening his position, actually helped seal his doom: now the police authorities could curb the SA only by eliminating its leaders.

Hitler was as reluctant to move decisively against his recalcitrant SA leader as Röhm was to cut himself adrift from the man he often cursed but still revered. The führer, however, realized that Röhm was now more a liability than an asset and that he posed a dangerous threat to his control over the Nazi movement. In January 1934 he ordered the Gestapo (secret state police) to begin assembling a dossier on "Röhm and his friendships" and on breaches of party discipline by the SA. "This is the most important assignment you have ever received," he told his Gestapo chief, Rudolf Diels.

The man who had created the Gestapo in 1933, Hermann Göring, needed no order from Hitler to collect incriminating evidence against Röhm. Though originally an admirer of the captain's, Göring had come to see him as an obstacle in the path of his own ambitions, which included being recognized as the Reich's number two man behind Hitler. He sought to achieve this aim by cultivating those traditional German elites—industrialists, large landowners, army generals—whom Röhm despised. He thus lent a sympathetic ear to his wealthy friends' complaints about the excesses of the SA and passed these eagerly on to Hitler. His zealousness in this regard was by no means inhibited by his own penchant for debauchery, which, though somewhat more conventional than Röhm's, greatly surpassed the captain's in scale. For example, if Röhm liked his sauerbraten and beer, the 280-pound Göring threw lavish banquets during the course of which he sometimes devoured an entire baby pig. If Röhm enjoyed hunting, bagging the occasional rabbit or deer, Göring built himself an enormous hunting lodge and organized shooting parties that decimated the wildlife for miles around. If Röhm sometimes exchanged his brown shirt for black leather, Göring decked himself out in bearskin robes or, during parties with a Roman motif, in toga and jeweled sandals. He had started taking morphine after the war; he then added cocaine and other drugs, which he liked to wash down with Dom Pérignon. It was almost as if Göring had originally taken the captain as an object lesson in libertinism, then shown him to be a piker.

Another man who saw Röhm as a rival was the SS leader Heinrich Himmler, also an old confidant of the captain's. During the Beer Hall Putsch the myopic, stoop-shouldered Himmler had joined Röhm in occupying the Bavarian War Ministry. At that time he said to Röhm, "It has been and always will be my greatest pride to be counted among your most faithful followers." Himmler's elite SS, though favored by Hitler since its founding in 1925, was technically an arm of the SA, and Himmler himself was in theory subordinate to Röhm. Whereas this relationship might have been acceptable in the early days, it had become increasingly intolerable to Himmler, who dreamed of creating a separate SS empire within the Nazi system. Since becoming SS chief, in 1929, Himmler had been expanding his organization's base of power, which lay primarily in its growing control over police and security operations. As the Third Reich's chief policeman, Himmler could not help clashing with Röhm, who had no use for policemen, even Nazi policemen. Himmler, moreover, shared with Göring certain military ambitions that were threatened by Röhm's dream of absorbing all armed forces in the state into an SA militia.

Like Göring, therefore, Himmler needed no encouragement from Hitler to discredit Röhm and his entourage. He focused his attack on the SA leader's sexual habits, which the prim and prissy SS chief found as repugnant as Hitler did. His agents circulated lurid reports about "fantastic orgies" at Röhm's headquarters. The captain's behavior, they noted, made a mockery of Nazi ideals regarding the purity of mind and body, the sanctity of the "healthy German family."

Here, as in the case of Göring, there was an element of hypocrisy, which did nothing to dampen the vendetta. Though Himmler did not share Röhm's sexual tastes, he was hardly without his own eccentricities, which included uninhibited passions for medieval mysticism, old Germanic cultic rites, Gothic castles, pseudo-scientific racism, King Henry the Fowler, and the Knights of the Round Table. While decrying Röhm's lamentable influence on the German family, Himmler eventually organized SS stud farms in which biologically acceptable couples could increase the "Aryan race" without benefit of matrimony. Röhm laughed and sneered at his rival's intellectual pretensions and cherished foibles. This was a mistake, for Himmler did not like to be laughed at.

Armed with an ever-growing dossier on the delinquency of the SA and its leader, Hitler was confronted with a dilemma. He could not simply disband the storm troopers, for that would throw hundreds of thousands of unemployed young men back on the resources of the state: the SA, after all, was among other things a giant welfare organization. The less drastic measure of dismissing Röhm was an alternative, and Hitler apparently considered doing just this on several occasions in the spring of 1934. But Röhm was a powerful figure in his own right, worshiped by his men and still possessed of influential contacts. Though at times he spoke of packing it in and returning to Bolivia, he might well refuse an order—even from Hitler—to give up the power he had come to cherish. Then the führer would be faced with open rebellion, a prospect he could hardly have welcomed. A solution to the "Röhm problem" had to be found—and soon.

One clear-eyed observer of Hitler's situation was certain that the führer would find a suitable way out of his dilemma. In February 1934 Benito Mussolini remarked, "Hitler's situation is not easy, but he is a good organizer; he'll find a way to deal with these people. . . . A state needs peace and discipline, and where there's a führer, there must be order."

THE CONSERVATIVE CAMP

Who among us would have imagined it possible that within four months the National Socialists would have taken over the entire German Reich, that all the middle-class political parties would have disappeared, that our democratic institutions would have been eliminated as with one stroke of the pen, that the new chancellor would have assumed a degree of power that no German emperor ever possessed.

So declared Vice-Chancellor Franz von Papen in a speech in Dresden in July 1933. Papen was a former page of Kaiser Wilhelm II and a doyen of Germany's

The SA leader Ernst Röhm and the SS chief Heinrich Himmler *(right)* lead a funeral of an SS *Gruppenführer* in February 1934. Four months later, Himmler and his SS were instrumental in the Blood Purge of the SA. *Bundesarchiv Koblenz*

Hitler and Röhm converse during an SS concert at Berlin's Sportpalast. Hitler ordered the execution of his SA chief in the Blood Purge. *Ullstein Bilderdienst*

Hitler greets President Paul von Hindenburg, who gave his blessing to the Blood Purge in the mistaken belief that it saved the nation from an SA insurrection. *The Warder Collection*

Röhm addressing members of the diplomatic corps in December 1933. Hitler accused Röhm of conspiring with foreign diplomats to subvert his regime. *AP/Wide World Photos*

aristocratic *Herrenklub* (Gentlemen's Club). His declaration showed that the traditional-conservative camp was in its own way as disillusioned by the National Socialist revolution as were Röhm and the SA. But while the latter complained that this revolution had not gone far enough, Papen and his friends fretted that Hitler was going much too far, that he was destroying valued German traditions and institutions in his efforts to create a National Socialist dictatorship.

There was a strong element of hypocrisy in this protest. The traditional Right had helped Hitler to power because it had no faith in the ability of democratic institutions to address Germany's pressing problems, in particular the threat posed by the radical Left. Conservative politicians, indeed, had begun to circumvent parliamentary institutions well before Hitler came to power. It was, after all, the Catholic conservative Chancellor Heinrich Brüning who in 1930 began ruling Germany on the basis of emergency decrees, a practice then followed by Papen himself when he became chancellor in 1932. To complain in the summer of 1933 that the man they had helped put in the chancellorship was abusing democratic norms was largely a cover for their real concern: the dawning realization that they had failed to "tame" Hitler so that they might use him to suit their own purposes.

Papen's complaint was not only hypocritical but also somewhat overstated. The Nazis had not yet assumed total control over the state; that would come later. Hitler had not hesitated to rule undemocratically, but he had resisted his SA's call for an immediate and wholesale assault on all bastions of traditional privilege and influence. Nevertheless, Papen was justified in his anxieties, for even the cautious and "sensible" Hitler had introduced certain policies that pointed toward the full-blown tyranny to come. He had facilitated the elimination not just of the leftist parties but of all parties except his own. The conservatives—never genuine believers in the party system—had willingly accepted the bourgeois parties' extinction in the expectation that they would find other vehicles (such as the regional governments, lobby organizations, and churches) through which they might exert influence over the regime. This was proving illusory, however, and Hitler was even taking the first steps that would lead to the "coordination" of these institutions within the power structure of the regime. He was also, according to Papen, not doing nearly enough to curb the revolutionary violence of his SA and other radical groups within the Nazi party. Indeed, Papen feared that the "growing revolution from below" would force Hitler to grant new concessions to his radical and undisciplined followers.

In the face of this threat, Papen turned his own office, the vice-chancellery, into what he called in his memoirs a "haven and assembly point for all those who feared for the future of their fatherland." His chief assistant in this enterprise was his press secretary, Herbert von Bose. Bose dreamed of replacing the plebeian Nazi regime with a restored monarchy and, to this end, sought to mobilize anti-Hitler elements across the Reich, particularly in the army. Among his most important contacts was Kurt von Schleicher, a retired Reichswehr general and political intriguer who had briefly held the chancellorship before Hitler's appointment and who still hoped to exert influence behind the scenes by playing off rival Nazi factions against each other.

Another possible, though less promising, focus of conservative resistance was President Paul von Hindenburg. Architect, along with Ludendorff, of Germany's successful campaign against the Russians in the First World War, Hindenburg had been elected president of the Weimar Republic in 1925. Lacking any real taste or gift for day-to-day political maneuvering, he had increasingly contented himself with a largely figurehead role in the administration of the state. This seemed to suit most of his countrymen ("Better a zero than a Nero," said some), and in 1932 the now eighty-four-year-old field marshal was elected for a second presidential term. One of his opponents in this election had been Adolf Hitler, a man the Prussian field marshal had once dismissed as "that Austrian corporal," and for whom he continued to have little use. To induce Hindenburg to appoint Hitler chancellor, the conservatives—in particular Papen himself—had had to use all their powers of persuasion, including promising to keep this vulgar ruffian in check.

Since assuming power Hitler had been very careful to flatter the old man and not to offend his prickly dignity. He had been largely successful in overcoming Hindenburg's distrust by promising to restore the monarchy "once Germany had recovered her full sovereignty." But there remained the danger that Hindenburg might, under the influence of his conservative friends, revert to his old hostility toward the führer. Papen claimed in his memoirs that when he last saw Hindenburg, in May 1934, the president took his hand and said, "Things are going badly, Papen; try to restore some order." Hitler thus needed to be sure that the president had no cause to turn against him and use his immense prestige to thwart the consolidation of his power.

Hitler had another reason to curry the president's favor. The old man's health was failing, and he would soon be passing from the scene. Hitler was determined to succeed him as president and to combine the presidential powers, which included supreme command over the army, with those he already possessed as chancellor. Hitler wanted Hindenburg to bestow his blessing on this plan before he died; this would ensure that such a "revolutionary" step found acceptance in conservative military circles and in the nation as a whole.

The key to Hindenburg's heart, and thus to Hitler's immediate political ambitions, was the army. The military was also the key to Hitler's broader goal of turning Germany into an expansionist world power. The führer had therefore cultivated the military leadership just as he had the president. He had zealously attended field maneuvers and flattered the generals' vanity. Shortly after taking power, he had promised top army and navy officers that he would not interfere in their affairs, though he would do all he could to further rearmament. On March 21, 1933, Hitler attended a religious ceremony in the tradition-laden church of the Potsdam garrison. There, in the presence of Germany's aged field marshals, he addressed President von Hindenburg, "Sir, the union between our new strength and the symbols of ancient grandeur has now been celebrated."

Many of the Reichswehr's generals were soon won over by Hitler's flattery and promises of restoration of national grandeur. At the end of one of Hitler's speeches, Admiral Erich Raeder, later to be tried at Nuremberg for his role in Hitler's war of aggression, remarked, "No Chancellor has ever spoken so firmly on behalf of the defense of the Reich."

But here, too, the ambitions of the SA threatened to come between Hitler and a key conservative partner. The military leadership was well aware of Röhm's desire to establish a revolutionary "people's militia" to replace the traditional army. They knew he talked boldly of "engulfing the gray rock [the Reichswehr] in the brown flood." They were aware that Röhm was fond of pointing out that the Reichswehr had not been a part of the "National Socialist revolution" and that he claimed for his SA control over Germany's mobilization planning and border defenses. To such claims the Reichswehr generals reacted with horror and disgust. When Röhm dared compare his SA to the volunteer forces that helped defeat Napoleon at the Battle of Nations in 1813, General Walther von Reichenau, the pro-Nazi head of the Reichswehr's "Office of Troops," exploded, "Napoleon was beaten by regular Prussian soldiers!" The implication, of course, was that Germany's future enemies would also be defeated by regular troops—not by a bunch of pot-bellied brawlers.

Hostility between the Reichswehr and the SA manifested itself also in frequent clashes between regular army soldiers and storm troopers in the streets of garrison towns. In the East Prussian village of Ratzebuhr, for example, a column of SA men attacked two soldiers who seemed to be jeering at their military pretentions. One of the soldiers defended himself with his bayonet, while the other yielded passively to his assailants. Significantly, the soldier who fought back was rewarded by his superiors, while the one who did not was punished. Members of the army must realize, the Reichswehr leadership seemed to be saying, that the "honor" of the military was at stake in its confrontation with Röhm's civilian street fighters tricked out as soldiers.

Like their conservative counterparts in the civilian sector, Germany's military leaders swamped Hitler's office with complaints about the SA and demanded that the führer take action against his brown-shirted legions. In January 1934 the minister of war, General Werner von Blomberg, threatened to resign if Röhm was allowed to continue interfering in the army's affairs and insulting the dignity of the officer corps. His resignation would have meant for Hitler the loss of vital Reichswehr support in his campaign to succeed Hindenburg as president. Indeed, the enmity of the Reichswehr might have forced him out of the chancellorship before he had time to consolidate his power, let alone launch the Third Reich on its mission of military conquest. It was high time for the führer to bring peace between the SA and the army.

On February 28, 1934, Hitler called a meeting in the Reichswehr's headquarters between the army leadership and various SA potentates. Göring was also present, resplendent in the uniform of an infantry general (one of the dozens of military uniforms he now affected). The führer delivered a long speech in which he pleaded with his SA leaders not to "cause him difficulties" during this critical period. Then he announced that Germany's military requirements could not be met through the creation of a people's militia; the nation needed a regular army, which must be recognized as the "sole bearer of military arms" in the state. He reaffirmed earlier promises to expand the army's numbers dramatically, to reintroduce conscription, and to supply the Reichswehr with the latest weaponry. The SA, for its part, also had "valuable services" to perform. In addition to its various political and propagandistic duties, it would provide millions of Germans with "premilitary training"—this, however, under the supervision of the army.

Needless to say, the SA was not pleased with this arrangement. Although Röhm extended his hand to General von Blomberg after the meeting, he let it be known among his SA intimates that he had no intention of bowing to Hitler's will. Indeed, he once again vented some highly intemperate comments about Hitler, calling the führer an "idiot corporal" and suggesting darkly that he (Hitler) needed "a long vacation."

One of Röhm's "intimates" present on this occasion turned out to be a spy for Hitler. He immediately went to the führer with this latest evidence of Röhm's insubordination, if not downright treachery. Surprisingly enough, Hitler did not explode into rage and demand Röhm's head. Rather, he said suggestively, "We must let this matter ripen." Perhaps he still hoped his SA leader might come to his senses. More likely, he believed that the preparations necessary to bring the "SA problem" to an acceptable resolution were not yet complete. But it is also quite likely that he was still not exactly sure how this resolution should proceed.

The following three months witnessed a significant escalation in the tensions between the SA and the army. Showing that he indeed had no intention of honoring the February 28 agreement, Röhm began to amass new armaments for his storm troopers. More and more SA units came into possession of military carbines and even heavy machine guns, which Röhm purchased on the international black market and smuggled into Germany. These weapons procurements did not go unnoticed by the Reichswehr leadership, which protested to Hitler. Attempts by the army to confiscate some of the SA's weapons induced the storm troopers to hide their arms, but not their hostility toward the generals. SA leaders openly cursed the entire military establishment. "The army," said one SA group leader at a giant storm trooper rally in May, is "nothing but a pile of shit." Röhm, in a drunken state, called General von Reichenau a *Sauhund* (literally, "pigdog").

Against this background of increasing tensions between SA and army, Germany's generals sought allies against the storm troopers wherever they could find them, including in the Nazi party leadership and in the SS. Hitler's deputy, Rudolf Hess, became a key supporter of the Reichswehr's cause, as did Heinrich Himmler and the SS security service (SD) chief, Reinhard Heydrich. These were strange bedfellows indeed. Hess and Himmler had never served in the postwar military, and the sinister Heydrich had been drummed out of the navy in 1931 for violating its code of honor. (He had compromised, then refused to marry, the daughter of a wealthy shipbuilder.) Germany's conservative generals would come to learn just how self-destructive their partnership with the SS really was, but in the spring of 1934 they saw only advantages in their cooperation with the zealous Himmler and Heydrich.

The SS leaders, for their part, were pleased to have military backing as they maneuvered to free themselves from formal SA tutelage and to promote their own organization as a separate power in the state. With Himmler's encouragement, Heydrich took charge of the SS campaign to break the influence of the SA. It is probable that from the outset Heydrich saw this operation as culminating in the physical liquidation of the storm trooper leadership. But to justify such a draconian solution to Hitler he would have to show that SA insubordination was ripening into an actual conspiracy against the regime. From May 1934 onward, Heydrich's SD kept the SA leadership under constant surveillance, looking for signs of imminent rebellion. When it failed to find more than the usual open bluster and tough talk, it became creative, assembling a dossier rich with secret plans for putsch and assassination.

The führer, meanwhile, seemed to be searching for ways to postpone a final reckoning with his old friend Röhm. In early June he called Röhm to the chancellery and in the course of a five-hour meeting ordered him to place the SA on an extended furlough. Röhm meekly acquiesced, announcing shortly after the meeting that the SA would suspend all public activities during the month of July. He also declared that because of ill health he would take an extended "cure" at Bad Wiessee, a spa on the shores of the Tegernsee, in southern Bavaria. But he appended to this announcement a statement that could easily be interpreted as a sign of continued intransigence, indeed as a warning: "Once my health is restored," he said, "I will resume the full scope of my activities." As for the SA, it would find the "proper answer" to give to those who thought its days were numbered. "The SA is and remains the destiny of Germany," he proclaimed.

Whatever Röhm's intentions after the completion of his cure, Hitler could not have allowed the SA problem to hang in limbo for too much longer, since something had to be done to gain the army leadership's complete confidence before Hindenburg took his appointed place in Valhalla. As it turned out, however, Hitler's hand was forced less by Hindenburg's declining health than by new signs of life from the conservative opposition around Franz von Papen.

By early June 1934 Papen had concluded that since Hitler was apparently unwilling or unable to control his SA, he, the vice-chancellor, would have to move the government into action by calling public attention to the regime's misdeeds. As a forum for this challenge, he chose the auditorium of Marburg University, one of the few German universities that had shown any reluctance to give the new Nazi regime an intellectual stamp of approval. On June 17, before what he called "the intellectual aristocracy of Germany," Papen delivered a speech written for him by the Christian conservative intellectual Edgar Jung. Papen began by defending the conservatives' role in helping Hitler to power, explaining that they had hoped to "reform" the discredited Weimar democracy by "unifying" the divisive party system under the banner of National Socialism. They had meant this only to be a "temporary" measure designed to clear the way for the creation of a "new spiritual and political elite." They had certainly not intended to introduce an "unbridled dictatorship" and a "revolution against order, law, and church." After cataloging more precisely the ways in which the Nazis had violated fundamental values and institutions of "European civilization," Papen appealed to Hitler to distance himself from those of his followers who were "falsifying" his ideas. "No people," he warned, "can live in a condition of permanent upheaval; perpetual dynamism can create nothing. Germany must not climb aboard a train traveling into the void, no one knowing where it might finally stop."

From our vantage point well beyond the place where Germany's train finally came to a halt, we can see that Papen's speech was both prophetic and myopic: it showed a clear apprehension of growing danger but also betrayed continued blindness regarding Hitler's true character and intentions. In an important sense the Marburg speech must stand as a monument to the intellectual and spiritual bankruptcy of German conservatism. Yet Papen's audience was impressed. Students and professors, after recovering from their initial shock at witnessing an anti-Nazi proclamation, warmly applauded the vice-chancellor. So did selected guests from the diplomatic community. William Dodd, the American ambassador, judged the speech a "moderate and entirely reasonable criticism of the Hitler autocracy."

The Nazis, in their own way, were also impressed. Joseph Goebbels, Hitler's minister of propaganda, immediately prohibited the speech's distribution and ordered German newspapers to make no mention of the oration. He confiscated copies of the one paper that had managed to publish excerpts of the speech before this order was issued. On June 21 the propaganda minister heaped vituperation on Papen and his conservative allies. "Thank God that the gentlemen in the club armchairs do not possess all the brains," he jeered. These men had failed the country in the past, he noted, and there was no reason to think they were "strong enough" to run it now.

Papen was shocked by Goebbels's actions because the regime had apparently promised not to prevent the vice-chancellor from getting his point of view across to the German people. He still failed to understand completely what National Socialism was all about. Full of righteous indignation, he threatened to resign and to complain personally to President von Hindenburg about Goebbels's "breach of trust."

Hitler, for his part, was also shocked—shocked by the audacity of Papen's gesture. Although he had known that the vice-chancellor's office constituted a nest of doubters when it came to the Nazi mission, he had not expected these fastidious and fainthearted "reactionaries" to throw down the gauntlet quite so blatantly. He could surmise only that Papen had acted with the blessing of Hindenburg (which was true) and the connivance of the Reichswehr leadership (which was not true). To him it seemed that a dangerous alliance was in the making between Papen's people, Hindenburg, and the military—an alliance he could not allow to mature if he expected the Third Reich to last another month, let alone "one thousand years."

Two days before Papen's speech Hitler had conferred in Venice with Mussolini, a man he greatly admired. The duce had advised him to reestablish order in his party and to solidify his position with the army. Hitler agreed that the army must be placated and that this would involve dealing decisively with Röhm. But the conservatives' impertinence had to be checked just as decisively. Papen's speech, it seems, had rekindled all of Hitler's old contempt for the traditional Right, for those "dwarfs" and "little worms" who were trying to "sabotage" the new Germany. In short, the führer could no longer let matters slowly "ripen." He would have to act as quickly as he could to put this entire business behind him.

PURGE

On June 21 Hitler paid a call on President von Hindenburg at the latter's East Prussian estate, Neudeck, a gift to the hero of Tannenberg from a "grateful nation" (more precisely, from a circle of wealthy industrialists and landowners). The führer went to Neudeck in order to reingratiate himself with the president in the wake of Papen's speech and to check on the old man's health. He was pleased to discover that Hindenburg was too feeble mentally to grasp the implications of Papen's challenge, which Hitler's lieutenants had hastened to describe to him as a "severe breach of discipline." But though Hindenburg was now more or less out of commission—spending most of his waking hours reminiscing about the wars of 1866 and 1870—General von Blomberg, who was also present at Neudeck, took this occasion to remind the führer of his commitment to deal with the SA. A month's vacation for the storm troopers would clearly not suffice to put this organization in its proper place.

This reminder was undoubtedly superfluous, for Hitler had already decided to act. But he had probably not yet decided exactly how he would proceed, or what the full scope of his operation would be. In this regard his lieutenants Himmler, Heydrich, and Göring were more precise in their calculations. They were busy drawing up lists of "undesirable persons," which they circulated among their friends for additional suggestions. These were invariably forthcoming, for everyone seemed to know a few "subversives," or at least someone who was thinking of becoming one. Soon the "Reich list" took on the dimensions of a letter to Santa written by an especially greedy child. A witness to this process recalled that the entire party leadership seemed to be intoxicated with "the smell of blood."

To push Hitler to quick action, Himmler and Göring took their "evidence" of SA putsch plans to Generals von Blomberg and von Reichenau, who in turn called an emergency meeting with the führer on June 27. At this meeting Hitler took an important step closer to his solution of the SA problem. He told the generals that he would soon order all the SA leaders together for a showdown in Bad Wiessee. If he was not satisfied with their behavior, he would arrest the lot, including Röhm. But he did not talk of physical liquidation, and it is unclear whether he now believed this would be necessary.

Anxious to expedite Hitler's reckoning with the SA, SS leaders put together a plan of attack that would enable them to cripple their rivals with a few well-aimed blows. For weapons and transportation they turned to the Reichswehr, which was only too happy to provide assistance. Blomberg and Reichenau promised logistical support and also put regular army troops in Bavaria on alarm status. The generals seemed to smell blood themselves.

During these last days of June the conservative camp, too, was restless. Papen's aide Bose was determined to persuade President von Hindenburg to take drastic action against Hitler. Through the president's son, Oskar, he tried to arrange a meeting between Hindenburg and Papen, who would urge the president to declare a state of emergency, depose Hitler, and proclaim a new government dominated by conservatives. Unfortunately for Bose, however, Oskar von Hindenburg told General von Blomberg about this plan. Blomberg alerted the SS, which now knew it had to act by June 30, the day Papen had proposed to meet with the president.

Himmler and Heydrich immediately put SS units throughout the Reich on alert. At the same time they sent the Gestapo to arrest Edgar Jung, the man who had written Papen's Marburg speech. In Jung's apartment the Gestapo found more details regarding the conservatives' "plot," including the names of men they hoped to rely on in bringing down Hitler's regime.

When Hitler, who was at that moment attending a wedding in Essen, heard about Papen's plan to see Hindenburg, he flew into a rage. "I've had enough," he screamed. He instructed Göring to return to Berlin and await further orders. Then he telephoned Bad Wiessee and ordered Röhm to call together all his top aides for a conference with their führer. The meeting would take place on June 30.

On the same day (June 28) units of the Reichswehr in Munich received orders to stay in their barracks on full alert. The SA, it was said, was about to attack the army. Röhm and his men had allegedly already decided which officers they would execute. In the army's headquarters in Berlin's Bendlerstrasse, General von Blomberg gave his approval to the text of a statement to appear in the *Völkischer Beobachter* the following day:

The Reichswehr considers itself in close harmony with the Reich of Adolf Hitler. The time has passed when people from various camps could pose as spokesmen of the Reichswehr. The role of the Army is clearly determined: it must serve the National Socialist State, which it recognizes. The hearts of the Reich and the Army beat in unison. . . . The Reichswehr wears with pride the symbols of Germany. It stands, disciplined and faithful, behind the leaders of the state, behind the Marshal of the Great War, President von Hindenburg, its supreme leader, and behind the Führer of the Reich, Adolf Hitler, who, coming from the ranks of the Army, is and always will be one of us.

What was the SA up to on the eve of the Blood Purge? Many storm trooper leaders were aware that they were under close scrutiny by the Gestapo and that the army was arrayed against them. To this state of affairs they responded by placing their own units on alert and by ordering demonstrations of SA strength in the streets of many German cities. In Munich, for example, thousands of SA men went on the march, shouting their revolutionary slogans and giving themselves over to isolated acts of violence. But by the night of June 29 they had returned to their homes. There was no sign that they planned an imminent putsch.

Hitler, meanwhile, had repaired to the Hotel Dreesen on the Rhine River near Bonn to plan his confrontation with Röhm. He looked awful, his face gray and pouchy, his eyes red from lack of sleep. After hours of consultation with Goebbels, who kept reminding him of the need to strike quickly, he called in the SS *Obergruppenführer* Sepp Dietrich and ordered him to proceed to Bad Wiessee with Hitler's personal guard, the SS *Leibstandarte Adolf Hitler.* He left the Hotel Dreesen late that evening for a nearby airfield, where an airplane stood ready to fly him to Munich.

The führer arrived at the Munich airport at 3:30 A.M. on June 30 and was told that the Munich SA had already attempted a putsch. This, fortunately, had been put down, but the situation was "still critical." Hitler did not question the veracity of these reports. "This is the darkest day of my life," he muttered. He then drove off to the "Brown House," Nazi headquarters in the "capital of the movement".

Assembled in the Brown House at this early-morning hour were dozens of local SA leaders; they had been told that their führer wanted personally to speak with them regarding their grievances. In fact, Hitler had very little to say: as soon as they were brought before him, he began tearing off their insignia and calling them traitors. Without further ado, he ordered two of the men to be shot. *Now* there was no question about how he would solve his SA problem! As the dawn broke over Munich, he set off for Bad Wiessee and his final reckoning with Röhm. Later he explained this action by saying, "Only one decision was open to me. Only I, no one else, could deal with this treachery."

Hitler was so eager to settle accounts that he left for Bad Wiessee even before his personal SS guard had reached the spa. He drove down to the Tegernsee in a column of three cars; he, Goebbels, and Viktor Lutze (the man Hitler had designated to replace Röhm) sat in the first; the second and third cars were filled with police and SS men. They arrived at Bad Wiessee around 6:30 A.M. Tradesmen were making early deliveries to the spa hotels, but otherwise the streets were deserted.

Tranquillity reigned as well in the Pension Hanselbauer, the chalet-style hotel where Röhm was taking his "cure." The SA leader and his entourage were still sleeping soundly after their usual heavy consumption of beer and sausages. Röhm slept alone in a large room on the second floor; down the hall reposed the *Obergruppenführer* Edmund Heines, leader of the Silesian SA, his arms around a young boy recently recruited into the SA ranks. Neither of these men, nor any of the other SA leaders who had arrived early for their conference with the führer, slept with a gun under his pillow; they expected a verbal duel with Hitler, nothing more.

Suddenly the Hanselbauer's corridors echoed to the sounds of police and SS men kicking in doors and shouting commands. Heines was one of the first to be pulled from his bed, naked and cursing. "A disgusting scene, which made me feel like vomiting," said Goebbels later. As Heines tried to defend himself, he was beaten to the floor, a bloody lump.

Hitler himself led the assault on Röhm's room. The next day, still in a state of high emotion, Hitler would talk of how he and his men entered Röhm's lair "unarmed, not knowing whether those swine might have armed guards to use against us." In fact, Hitler had a revolver, as did the policemen accompanying him. They pounded on Röhm's door and, as soon as the befuddled and half-naked man released the lock, stormed inside, Hitler waving his pistol in the air. "You are a traitor!" he yelled. "You are under arrest!" Allowing Röhm no time to protest, he stormed out of the room and ran down the hall, peering into other rooms. Like Goebbels, he claimed to be disgusted by what he saw. "In one room," he gasped, "we found two naked boys." Later he and Goebbels would spread the rumor that Röhm himself had been found in bed with a male lover.

In a matter of minutes Röhm and his men, now dressed, were herded into the hotel's cellar and placed under guard. At this moment a truck filled with SA men, part of Röhm's personal guard, arrived on the scene. They outnumbered Hitler's people and were heavily armed. This was clearly a precarious moment for Hitler, but the führer rose to the occasion by personally confronting the storm troopers and ordering them to leave. Though torn in their loyalties and bewildered by Hitler's claim to have foiled a putsch attempt by Röhm, the SA men withdrew as ordered. Had they not done so, deciding instead to liberate their leader, world history in the twentieth century might have been quite different.

With the departure of the SA guard, Hitler's men bundled the SA leaders into cars and dispatched them in the direction of Munich's Stadelheim prison. The arrival of Sepp Dietrich and the *Leibstandarte Adolf Hitler* provided the führer with enough men to establish checkpoints on the roads to the Tegernsee, so that other SA leaders, arriving for their "conference" with Hitler, could be intercepted and packed off to Stadelheim. Hitler himself left Bad Wiessee by a circuitous route in case members of Röhm's guard should change their minds and try to intervene against the roundup of their leaders.

Upon arrival at Stadelheim, Röhm and his colleagues were assembled in a central courtyard to await assignment to individual cells. Though some of the men spoke bitterly of their treatment, even cursing the führer, most held their tongues. Old killers themselves, the majority of them must have suspected that they would not leave this prison alive. But they seemed reconciled to their fate, offering little or no resistance to their SS guards. Their passive behavior should be noted in light of later charges that Hitler's most prominent victims, the Jews, showed special cowardice in allowing themselves to be "led like lambs to the slaughter." In fact, many Jews, particularly those who revolted at Treblinka or in the Warsaw ghetto, displayed much more willingness to resist their fate than did Hitler's brown-shirted retainers.

By ten on the morning of June 30, Hitler was back in the Brown House, its entrances and hallways still heavily guarded by SS men. There he spoke briefly with Goebbels, who in turn put through a call to Göring's headquarters in Berlin. "Colibri," he shouted. This was the signal that the purge could commence in the Reich capital.

Unlike Munich, where the atmosphere had been tranquil in the last days of June, Berlin seemed to be tense and edgy. Ambassador Dodd, by profession a historian, observed on June 28 that the mood in Berlin resembled that of Paris on the eve of the Great Terror, when the Jacobins were about to strike. Albert Speer recalled that there were soldiers in battle dress encamped in the Tiergarten, while others cruised the streets in trucks. There was an air of "something cooking," he remembered having concluded.

Something was indeed cooking. Early in the morning Franz von Papen was called to Göring's Berlin residence, which lay behind the Air Ministry complex. As he approached, he noted that the entire complex was sealed off by SS guards armed with machine guns. Göring received him in the company of Heinrich Himmler, who kept getting whispered messages from SS aides. A witness to the scene described the corpulent Göring, his white blouse bulging and his jackboots reaching up his bloated legs, as looking like a "Puss-in-Boots, or some character in a fairy tale." But this was no fairy tale. Göring informed Papen that Hitler had just flown to Munich to put down a putsch by the SA. The führer had entrusted him, Göring, with "full powers" to deal with the rebels in the capital. Papen protested against this arrangement, claiming that he, as vice-chancellor, had the duty to take whatever measures were necessary, including asking President von Hindenburg to proclaim a state of emergency. Göring replied that this would not be necessary: he and Himmler had things well in hand. Papen should simply repair to his villa and stay there until he was told he could venture out. With uncharacteristic insight, Papen now realized that he was being placed under house arrest and that he had undoubtedly been called away from the vice-chancellery so that the SS could search his offices and occupy the building without having to put up with his tiresome protests.

Papen left Göring's headquarters but did not go immediately to his home. Instead, he hurried back to the vice-chancellery in order to secure his private papers. He was too late. The building was already occupied by the SS, and he learned that his press secretary, Bose, had been shot while "offering resistance" to his arrest. At this point some of Göring's men arrived and took Papen to his villa, which in the meantime had been occupied by Prussian police. Here he was locked away, his telephone cut, his mail intercepted. He did not realize at the time that this was Göring's way of protecting him from the zealous SS. Although he had no use for Papen, Göring recognized that the vice-chancellor had too many important contacts, especially in the diplomatic community, for Göring to allow his simple liquidation.

In the Gestapo building in the Prinz-Heinrich-Strasse, Reinhard Heydrich received Goebbels's order as relayed by Himmler from Göring's headquarters. He now sent word to his agents in Berlin and eastern Germany to break the seals on their special-orders packets, which contained the names of people to be liquidated. Of course, the killer squads were not instructed to hold trials, even mock trials. Their orders were simply to round up the designated "subversives," drive them to designated sites (prisons, SS barracks, forest retreats), and shoot them. It was to be expected, however, that some of the targets would never make it to their assigned execution sites; they would be shot "while trying to escape."

One of the first to hear the fatal knock on the door was Erich Klausener, head of the Catholic Action and friend of Jung and Bose. Apparently he offered no resistance to the Gestapo men who came to his office to arrest him, but when he turned to get his coat they shot him in the back. Perhaps they feared they would fall behind schedule if they did not dispatch a few of their victims on the spot.

Another early victim was Gregor Strasser, an old companion of Hitler's and codeveloper of the Nazi party. His offense had been to resist Hitler's efforts to make the party more acceptable to conservatives and to be identified with Hitler's immediate predecessor as chancellor, the arch-intriguer General Kurt von Schleicher, who had hoped to play off Strasser against Hitler. Picked up by the Gestapo on the afternoon of June 30, he thought he was being taken to Hitler for a reconciliation. Instead, he was driven to the main Gestapo prison and shot through a hole in his cell door. The official explanation for his death was suicide.

Kurt von Schleicher was spending the morning of June 30 at home in the company of his young wife, with whom he had just returned from a holiday excursion. He had been warned by friends to stay out of politics since his fall from power, but he could not resist the occasional meeting with anti-Nazi contacts and imagined that he might soon be recalled to high office to save the nation. He should have extended his holiday. At about eleven-thirty, five men dressed in long black raincoats (despite the eighty-six-degree temperature) walked calmly into his study and shot him to death. As his wife ran screaming into the room, they shot her too. The report they submitted to Himmler said Schleicher had been killed while trying to resist arrest; his wife had unfortunately fallen in the cross fire. A maid who had witnessed the bloody scene was found dead a few months later, allegedly the victim of suicide.

Another Schleicher associate and the second Reichswehr general to die in the purge was Kurt von Bredow. Although he had heard rumors of Schleicher's murder, and must have guessed that the Nazis planned a similar fate for him, he refused to leave Berlin. In fact, he openly showed himself in a popular Nazi haunt, the Hotel Adlon, and refused a foreign diplomat's offer of sanctuary. The Gestapo arrived at his door at five in the afternoon; as he answered their summons, they shot him in the head.

Neither Bredow's death nor Schleicher's provoked any opposition from the Reichswehr; indeed, the army leadership was quick to endorse the killings as necessary countermeasures by the regime. It accused Schleicher and Bredow of complicity in Röhm's "plot" and supported the regime's claim that the men had been killed resisting arrest.

Elsewhere in the Reich the SS and Gestapo killers were also hard at work, going down their lists supplied by Himmler, Heydrich, and Göring, knocking on doors, dragging men off to prison, often shooting their victims "while trying to escape." In Munich they descended upon the villa of Gustav von Kahr, a former Bavarian official who had been instrumental in foiling Hitler's Beer Hall Putsch in 1923. Three men pulled the frail old man out of his house, bundled him into a car, and sped off in the hot June morning in the direction of the Munich suburb of Dachau. Kahr's body was found in a swamp near the concentration camp (opened by Himmler in March 1933) a few days later; he had apparently been hacked to death with an ax.

Kahr owed his fate to having eleven years earlier thwarted the Nazis' will. Another victim of the purge in Munich owed his fate to having a name similar to that of an SA leader on Himmler's list. The prominent music critic Dr. Willi Schmid, mistaken for an SA leader named Willi Schmidt, was taken from his home by four SS men, who gave no explanation for his arrest. A few days later his wife received his coffin, along with an apology and an offer of a pension. In the meantime the SS had found the right man and killed him.

As the SS killers were making their rounds in the Bavarian capital, Hitler remained sequestered in the Brown House, haranguing his entourage about the evils he had seen at Bad Wiessee and the treacherous conspiracy he had managed to root out in the nick of time. His need to justify the actions he had so far taken was eagerly served by minions like Hess and the party secretary Martin Bormann, who talked of extravagant SA expenditures and habitual visits to bordellos. Bormann told Hitler that the SA potentates were in the habit of slipping out of performances of Wagner operas to go whoring. Another member of the führer's entourage, Wilhelm Brückner, showed him menus from SA banquets featuring frog legs, bird tongues, and vintage French wines. This was just the thing to send the vegetarian, teetotaling, and ascetic Hitler into a paroxysm of rage. "So here we have those revolutionaries!" he shrieked.

In his fury he demanded the list of SA prisoners assembled in Stadelheim and proceeded to place an x next to five names. These men, he announced, were to be shot immediately. Röhm's name was not among them. "I have spared Röhm for past services rendered," he explained.

At seven in the evening Hitler left the Brown House to return to Berlin. As he was flying back to the capital, a radio announcer gave the people of Munich their first official account of what had happened in Bad Wiessee that morning. Elements in the SA, they were told, had tried to foment conflict between the Brownshirts and the state. Röhm had done nothing to halt this dangerous development; indeed, he had abetted it. The führer had therefore gone to Bad Wiessee and arrested the most compromised SA leaders. In the process he had encountered scenes of moral dissoluteness that aggravated these men's political crimes. In order to restore decency to the Reich, he had ordered this "diseased abscess lanced and drained."

Such were the metaphors of totalitarian butchery. At once euphemistic and sinister, they anticipated the language of later, yet more comprehensive purges: Stalin's offhand comment that one could not chop wood without making chips fly; Mao's observation that to rid a pond of "bad fish" one needed to drain the water.

The draining operations inaugurated by Hitler on the morning of June 30 were not confined to Munich and Berlin. Another major focus of the purge was eastern Germany, where local SA units had been especially vocal in calling for a "second revolution." The SS in eastern Germany had been on alert since June 24, its leaders told to prepare for action against the SA in cooperation with the Reichswehr. Here, too, lists of "politically unreliable people" had been drawn up and circulated among Himmler's and Göring's minions. On the morning of June 30 Heydrich gave the code word for the operation in eastern Germany: "Hummingbird." On that command, SS patrols occupied various regional SA headquarters and orders went out to all SA leaders from the rank of *Standartenführer* (colonel) upward to make their way to their command posts. By late afternoon, police offices in towns like Breslau were filled with SA men who had obediently answered this summons. Those who were to be executed were stripped of their SA insignia, bundled into vans or trucks, and driven to nearby forests. There, again without significant resistance on their part, they were lined up and shot, usually in the back of the head. The men who had not been forced to make this fatal excursion were quick to declare their "absolute obedience" to Hitler and to distance themselves from the "unheard-of state of affairs" that had prevailed before this moment of necessary cleansing.

In eastern Germany, as in Berlin and Munich, innocent bystanders died along with the "guilty." In Lower Silesia local SS leaders used the occasion to kill three Jews. In one small town a butcher and local SS leader decided this was the moment to get revenge on a business rival who had prevented him from controlling the village slaughterhouse; he killed the man and dumped his body by the side of a country road.

By the evening of June 30 Hitler was back in Berlin, where throughout the day SS firing squads had been dispatching their SA comrades at places like the Lichterfelde Cadet School. Now, as he toted up scores with Himmler and Göring in the Reich chancellery, Hitler finally seemed to have quenched his lust for blood. The man in whose name most of the blood had been spilled, Ernst Röhm, was still alive in Stadelheim, and Hitler seemed disinclined to alter this situation.

Could it be that Röhm, despite his "crimes," still meant too much to the führer for him to share the fate of his murdered colleagues? Himmler and Göring feared that this might be so. Again they cataloged Röhm's offenses, harping on his dissoluteness. Perhaps more important, the army leadership also restated its case againt Röhm, whom Blomberg now struck from the list of retired military officers, as if to wash the army's hands of the ex-captain's fate. Indeed, having acquiesced in the murder of two of their own generals, Schleicher and Bredow, the military leaders could hardly allow Röhm to survive.

Under this combined pressure, Hitler finally relented. No doubt he had also become convinced that Röhm was too dangerous to be left alive: he still had thousands of devoted followers, and he knew a great deal about Hitler's and the party's weaknesses. In the early afternoon of the next day, July 1, Hitler telephoned to Munich, where Theodor Eicke, commandant of the Dachau concentration camp, was standing by for orders from Berlin. The order Eicke now received said that Röhm was to die, though as a final gesture of the führer's friendship he would be invited to die by his own hand.

Three hours later Eicke and two other SS men appeared at the door of Röhm's cell in Stadelheim. They gave the SA leader a copy of the *Völkischer Beobachter,* which reported his own dismissal and the executions of the five SA men approved by Hitler in the Brown House. They also placed on his table a revolver loaded with a single bullet. The führer, they explained, wanted his old friend to make "honorable" use of it.

Ten minutes later, having heard no sound from Röhm's cell, they returned to find him sitting quietly, the gun untouched. According to one account, Röhm said that if "Adolf" wanted him dead, Adolf ought to do the shooting himself. The SS men told him to stand up and strip to the waist. He did so, exposing his bare chest to three bullets fired in quick succession. *"Mein Führer, mein Führer,"* he managed to gasp as he fell to the floor.

AFTERMATH

On July 2, the day after Röhm's execution, Joseph Goebbels ordered the cities of the Reich to hang out flags in celebration of the führer's "victory over a criminal revolt." State-controlled German newpapers obediently praised the regime's "preventative strike" without intimating the extent of the butchery, which ultimately claimed some eighty-five victims. In the absence of reliable sources of news, people turned to the rumor mill, an engine of information that even Goebbels could not shut down. But the wildest rumors did not do full justice to the grisliness that had occurred during the preceding two days. Had people known more clearly what had happened, there might have been a few protests, although this is not very likely. The majority of the victims were SA members, and the undisciplined and dissolute storm troopers inspired no affection among the order-loving German population. Even the outlawed Social Democratic party, which conducted clandestine surveys of German public opinion during the Third Reich, admitted that people were generally pleased by the results of the Blood Purge. One of their surveys reported,

> The immediate result of the murders was great confusion, both as regards the way they were viewed and as regards their future political consequences. On the whole, Hitler's courage in taking decisive action was stressed the most. He was regarded practically as a hero. Hitler's slandering of the victims, their homosexuality and their 30,000 Mark meals, was at first also adjudged heroic. As to what the repercussions of the events of 30th June and their aftermath will be, an agreed and definitive answer cannot yet be given. Our comrades report that Hitler has won strong approval and sympathy from that part of the population which still places its hopes in him. To these people his action is proof that he wants order and decency. Other sections of the population have been given cause for thought.

The victims' immediate families, of course, were less inclined to see matters this way, and wives of men who had disappeared haunted the ministries asking for news of their husbands, or at least for a body to bury. Many of them were turned away because the regime refused to acknowledge the full extent of the purge, records of which were immediately burned. Not a few Blood Purge victims thus vanished without a trace—their fate anticipating the lot of millions of men, women, and children who would over the course of the next eleven years disappear into *"Nacht und Nebel"* ("night and fog"), as the ominous Nazi phrase had it.

Representatives of the foreign diplomatic corps in Berlin were not much better informed than the Germans about what had transpired during the Blood Purge. On July 2 William Dodd reported to Secretary of State Cordell Hull that "energetic intervention" on the part of Hitler had liquidated a "conspiracy" masterminded by Röhm. Dodd then had this to say of Röhm's murder:

> Röhm was considered as a man of the left wing of the party and one of those who believed that a second more radical revolution was necessary. His elimination therefore, while primarily a stern lesson in party discipline, would seem to indicate the temporary dissolution of a call for strength of the radicals, and to that extent increased strength to the conservative elements which desire a more liberal domestic and foreign policy with eventual monarchist leanings.

A few days later, after learning of the killings of prominent conservatives, Dodd amended his original assessment, suggesting now, "The results of the abortive revolt do not seem to have favored either side." The more he learned about the killings, the more appalled he became. "[The American] people," he noted in his diary, "cannot imagine such things happening in their country as have happened here." Eventually the historian and Baptist Dodd could put these horrors into perspective only by comparing them to the abuses of the Catholic tyrants of old. The world had seen nothing so evil, he suggested, since the Stuart kings were expelled from England in 1688. He wondered if he should not resign in order to show his contempt for the Nazi regime.

Dodd's French counterpart, Ambassador André François-Poncet, was not in Germany when the purge occurred and was only gradually able to piece together what had happened. Like Dodd, he became increasingly alarmed the more he learned, especially because German newspapers began claiming that *he* had been engaged in traitorous dealings with Schleicher and Röhm. Indignant that the German Foreign Office would not formally distance itself from these charges, he too contemplated resignation. Indeed, he confided to Dodd at this point that he would "not be surprised to be shot on the streets of Berlin." "The Germans hate us so," he added, "and their leadership is so crazy." François-Poncet would have loved to see this regime fall, but he knew that his own government, still shaken by the Stavisky scandal and the February riots, would do nothing to encourage such a result.

The British ambassador, Sir Eric Phipps, was equally appalled by the killings, but he confined his protests to acid remarks about a regime he was coming to detest. Shortly after the purge he had a dinner date with Göring, who showed up late, saying that he had just gotten back from shooting. "Animals, I hope," grunted Sir Eric.

The Western ambassadors were not the only foreigners shocked by the Nazis' bloodletting. The London *Times,* later a bastion of appeasement sentiment, ran a violently anti-German editorial on July 3 that prompted an official protest from the German government. Ten days later General Hugh Johnson, head of President Roosevelt's National Recovery Administration, delivered a speech in which he said,

> A few days ago, in Germany, events occurred which shocked the world. I don't know how they affected you, but they made me sick—not figuratively, but physically and very actively sick. The idea that adult, responsible men can be taken from their homes, stood up against a wall, backs to the rifles and shot to death is beyond expression. I have seen something of that sort in Mexico during the Villa ravages and among semi-civilized people or savages half drunk on sotol and marijuana—but that such a thing should happen in a country of some supposed culture passes comprehension.

Johnson's outrage over "responsible adults" being shot in the back might strike us—with our knowledge of much greater barbarities to come—as almost quaintly innocent. But the Germans of 1934 did not relish being compared to Mexican bandits and drug-crazed savages. They protested sharply to Cordell Hull, who was quick to express his regret that Johnson's governmental position "made it possible for remarks uttered by him as an individual to be misconstrued as official."

Officially, indeed, none of the Western governments did anything to protest Hitler's action. On the contrary, they made it clear that this was not their affair, that it was an "internal matter" involving only the Germans themselves. Moreover, like many Germans, the Western powers hoped that Hitler's elimination of some of the more unsavory elements in his regime would make the Third Reich a more "responsible" state. The route to the Munich conference of 1938, in other words, began with the Western powers' response to the Nazi bloodletting of 1934.

If Western statesmen tried to put the best light on the Blood Purge, so did the German conservatives—at least those who survived. For some of them the fact of survival itself seemed all that mattered. Hitler's Harvard-educated press secretary, Ernst ("Putzi") Hanfstaengl, returned to Germany in early July from a society wedding in Newport to find his conservative friends "in a trance," just thankful they were still alive. "You can thank God you weren't here," they told him. Despite his shock over the murders, Putzi stayed on to serve the führer. Another conservative servant of Hitler, Foreign Minister Konstantin von Neurath, justified the purge by insisting that Schleicher and Röhm had intended to take over the armed forces; by killing them, Hitler had avoided "civil war." The hapless Franz von Papen, after being released from house arrest, again threatened to resign but then allowed Hitler to persuade him to stay in office for the time being in order to demonstrate the "unity of the government." Three weeks later, in the wake of the abortive Nazi putsch in Vienna, Papen consented to become Hitler's ambassador to Vienna; his task was to smooth things over with the Austrian conservatives until Hitler was ready to absorb his old homeland into the Reich.

Hitler's primary concern in the immediate aftermath of the purge was to secure a retroactive "legalization" of the killings. On July 3 he brought a bill before the cabinet that contained just one line: "The measures taken to put down the treasonous attacks of June 30 and July 1–2, 1934, shall be classified as legal acts of state security." Hitler explained that the purpose of this initiative was "not to cover a violation of law, but to legalize an action that saved the nation and prevented untold disasters." Hitler's ministers promptly accepted his bill, which the parliament then made law of the land. In so doing, commented one historian, Germany's legislators "officially sanctioned crimes of the government and made murder a legal recourse of the state."

Another concern of the führer's was how old President von Hindenburg would respond to the purge, whose victims, after all, included two Reichswehr generals. Hindenburg received early reports of the bloodletting with relative calm. He remarked that he had long ago urged Hitler to "get rid of this immoral and dangerous Röhm and lock him up." The führer's failure to do this had now "cost much blood." But he added, "He who wants to make history like Hitler

must be prepared to let guilty blood flow and not be soft." When he learned that
Schleicher's blood had flowed as well, he temporarily lost his calm and demanded
an investigation. But after checking with General von Blomberg on the accuracy
of Hitler's claim to have crushed a vast conspiracy against the state, he allowed his
name to be signed to a telegram to Hitler (probably written by Goebbels's office)
that said, "According to reports sent to me, it appears that, thanks to the firmness
of decision and courage which you showed, exposing your own person [to danger],
the attempted high treason was crushed. You have saved the German people
from grave danger. I am obliged to express to you my profound thanks and
recognition."

Hindenburg's blessing on the Blood Purge meant a great deal because the old
man seemed to personify rectitude and decency amid all the uncertainties and
moral chaos of those days. "That Hitler's action was approved by this supreme
judge was highly reassuring," recalled Hitler's architect, Albert Speer, who
counted himself among those "unpolitical" Germans who "snatched avidly at
excuses" to justify the Nazis' brutalities.

The key to Hindenburg's approval was the position taken by the Reichswehr
leadership, particularly by Generals von Blomberg and von Reichenau. Putzi
Hanfstaengl had expected Reichenau to be indignant at the murders of
Schleicher and Bredow, but Reichenau eagerly accepted Hitler's promise (never
kept) to look into "those activities of the purge that were illegal." Blomberg
showed no hesitation whatsoever in endorsing everything the Nazis had done in
connection with the purge. At the cabinet meeting on July 3 he thanked the
"statesman and soldier" Hitler for his "courageous intervention," which had
"saved the German people" and reassured them in their expectation of "great
future exploits." Among senior officers only old Field Marshal August von Mack-
ensen and General Kurt von Hammerstein protested against the cold-blooded
murder of their colleagues. In response to their protest, Hitler privately admitted
that the generals' murders had been an "error" and promised their posthumous
"rehabilitation." Like Hitler's other promises to rectify "mistakes" in connection
with the purge, this one was never kept.

Endorsement of Hitler's actions by the military, combined with the cowed
complicity of conservative politicians connected to the government, could not
help reassuring the führer, who according to contemporary accounts was "inwardly convinced" that he had come through a "great danger" in the past few
days. Hitler nevertheless felt the need repeatedly to justify the killings, both to his
own people and to the rest of the world. On July 13 he delivered a major radio
address before the Reichstag and foreign diplomatic community in the Kroll
Opera House (the old Reichstag building had burned down in February 1933). In
this speech Hitler took "full responsibility" for what his regime had done but
placed all blame for the bloodletting on Röhm, whom he accused of fomenting a
"mutiny" within the SA and of "conspiring" with a foreign government (clearly
France). He also spoke luridly of Röhm's homosexuality, the excesses of his entourage, the threat posed by men who favored revolution for its own sake and as a

permanent condition. Finally, he raised the issue of Röhm's impossible demand for a militia to replace the Reichswehr, which he again insisted must be the sole bearer of arms in the state. He said nothing directly about the murders of conservatives like Bose, Jung, and Klausener, let alone the victims of private grudges. But toward the end of his speech he made clear that he and he alone had the right to identify the "enemies of the state" and to take whatever action was necessary to deal with them. "Let it be known for all time to come," the führer concluded, "that if anyone raises his hand to strike the state, then certain death is his lot."

Roughly two weeks after the delivery of this aggressive apologia, Hitler went to visit President von Hindenburg, who lay on his deathbed, a simple army cot. The old man was barely conscious and addressed Hitler as "Your Majesty." This form of address was not entirely inappropriate, for Hitler had already presented to the cabinet a law that would combine the offices of chancellor and president as soon as Hindenburg passed from the scene, which he obligingly did on August 2, 1934. In its official commentary on Hindenburg's death, the Nazi government acknowledged his "almost incalculable services" to Germany, which included opening "the gates of the Reich to the young National Socialist Movement."

Hindenburg had certainly performed this service, and now his death opened the gates to Hitler's assumption of absolute power in the state. The departed field marshal's presidential powers devolved on Hitler, though in deference to the "greatness of the departed," the ex-corporal modestly announced that he would be content to be addressed simply as "Führer and Chancellor."

Among the first to congratulate Hitler on his new powers were the Reichswehr generals who had stood by him during the purge. Having already acquiesced in his killing not just of their rival Röhm but of their comrades Schleicher and Bredow, they now hastened to offer him the army's unconditional loyalty. A new military oath instituted by Blomberg replaced traditional fealty to "nation and fatherland" with a personal oath of obedience to Hitler himself. Under the power of this oath the German Wehrmacht (successor to the Reichswehr) would collaborate with Hitler in a war of aggression that featured the slaughter of millions of innocent civilians and the calculated starvation of prisoners of war.

In attempting a long-term assessment of the Blood Purge, one might ask whether it represented a turning point in the history of National Socialism. In one sense it seemed that it had. The perpetually dynamic and undisciplined SA was so cowed by the killing of its leaders that it never again held a position of importance or threatened the "order" of the state. Röhm's replacement by Viktor Lutze brought with it a new discipline, even prudery, to the storm trooper ranks. Henceforth SA men who publicly conducted themselves "in an unworthy manner" or who "offended against paragraph 175" (the state's ban on homosexuality) were to be expelled immediately from the organization.

But though this transformation of the SA was important to the internal development of that organization, it hardly meant that the Nazi Reich had decided to become law-abiding or to reject terror as a means of achieving political ends. Perhaps no one made this clearer than Hermann Göring, who in a speech on July 12 described the "legal" implications of the purge as follows: "We don't recognize the oft-repeated proposition that everything in the state can break apart, just as long as law is respected. We don't see law as something primary; rather, the *Volk* is our primary concern. . . . Laws, after all, were created by people, and where a people finds laws that no longer reflect its worldview, it can get rid of these laws."

With this bold pronouncement Göring made clear that if the Third Reich had negotiated a turn in June 1934, it was only a turn toward a more open revelation of its true character. The road that led to the Second World War and the Holocaust had been laid out when Hitler assumed power, but now it was much more plainly marked. Now it was evident that this regime would recognize no traditional laws or limits in the pursuit of its ideological ends. Thus the historian Joachim Fest is surely correct when he writes, "It is by no means a fabrication of hindsight to see a direct connection between the killings of June 30 and the subsequent practice of mass murder in the camps of the East."

Another link between the Blood Purge and the war and Holocaust involved the organization that profited most directly from the emasculation of the SA: the SS. Shortly after the purge, Hitler officially freed the SS from its subordination to the SA; he did so "in view of its great services . . . especially in connection with the events of June 30." At the same time he promised the SS that it could develop its own military divisions armed with the latest weaponry. This was the birth of the so-called *Waffen-SS* (Weapons SS), which went on to play an important role in Hitler's ideological crusade in the East, as well as in the administration of the concentration camps.

If the true loser in the rise of the SS was European Jewry, another loser, at least in terms of rivalries within the Third Reich, was the army. In supporting the SS's purge of the SA, the army leadership had expected to eliminate the sole threat to its monopoly over armed force in the state. Instead, the generals promoted the rise of a new monster rival whose powers and influence would vastly transcend those of the storm troopers and, indeed, of the Wehrmacht itself.

In 1934 the SS's development as a state within the state was still several years off. Important for the immediate future was Hitler's success in consolidating his personal dictatorship through a comprehensive and bloody purge. Although many Western politicians failed at first to understand the full implications of these events, one observer from the East did not: Joseph Stalin. The Russian dictator understood immediately why Hitler had acted as he did, and he would soon emulate him by staging an even more comprehensive internecine bloodletting.

Another fascinated onlooker was Benito Mussolini. He was aghast at the way Hitler had applied his advice to discipline his followers and create "order." The Blood Purge, and even more the Nazi putsch attempt in Austria, convinced him that Hitler was a madman and "a horrible sexual degenerate." Yet on another level Mussolini also understood what Hitler had done, and he would soon embark on a bloody imperial crusade that had as one of its purposes the consolidation of his personal control over the Italian Fascist state. Thus, if the Blood Purge provided any historical lesson to Hitler's fellow tyrants in the 1930s, it might have been that the führer was right when he argued that a political movement willing to use "heroic" terror was more likely to succeed than a meek one, just as a "courageous man could more readily win the heart of a woman than a coward."

IV

"REVENGE FOR ADOWA"

Italy and the Opening of the Ethiopian Conflict

> The conquest of the earth, which mostly means the taking it away from those who have a different complexion or slightly flatter noses than ourselves, is not a pretty thing when you look at it too much.
>
> —Joseph Conrad, *The Heart of Darkness*

Twenty years after General George Custer and his Seventh Cavalry were annihilated by Sioux and Cheyenne Indians at the Battle of the Little Big Horn, a large army of Italians met crushing defeat at the hands of another "primitive" people: Ethiopian warriors under Emperor Menelik II. Italy, united some twenty-five years earlier with critical assistance from France and Prussia, had launched an invasion of Ethiopia* in hopes of expanding its colonial empire and demonstrating to the world that it should be taken seriously as a great power. Like Custer, the Italian generals had expected an easy victory, for the Ethiopians were an "inferior race," while the Italians, heirs of Caesar and Columbus, had the most powerful colonial army in Africa—sixteen thousand men and fifty-two heavy guns. They were also supported by thousands of native troops recruited from their colony of Eritrea.

On March 1, 1896, this proud force threw its full weight against one hundred thousand Ethiopians encamped around the town of Adowa, which lay in mountainous country not far from the Eritrean border. When the daylong battle was over, nearly four thousand Italian soldiers were dead and nineteen hundred had been taken prisoner. The remnants of the Italian force managed to limp back into Eritrea only because the Ethiopians elected not to pursue them and wipe them out. But there was no disguising the fact that Italy had suffered a humiliating defeat, indeed the "greatest single disaster in European colonial history." The

---

Ethiopia is the modern name for the ancient empire of Abyssinia. I will use the modern term in this chapter except when quoting sources that employ the earlier name.

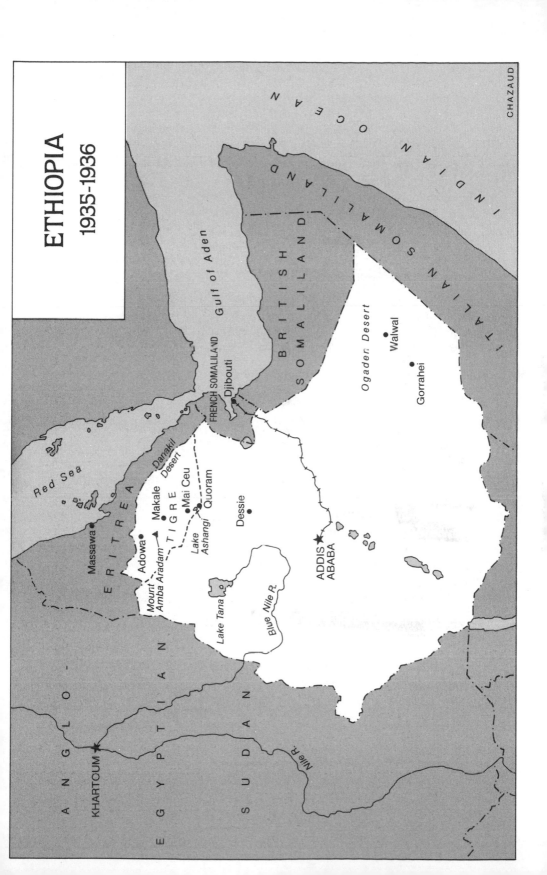

ETHIOPIA
1935-1936

INDIAN OCEAN

CHAZAUD

Gulf of Aden

ITALIAN SOMALILAND

BRITISH SOMALILAND

FRENCH SOMALILAND

Djibouti

Ogaden Desert

Walwal

Gorrahei

Red Sea

Massawa

ERITREA

Adowa

Makale

Danakil Desert

TIGRE

Mount Amba Aradam

Mai Ceu

Quoram

Lake Ashangi

Dessie

Lake Tana

Blue Nile R.

ADDIS ABABA

ANGLO-EGYPTIAN SUDAN

KHARTOUM

Nile R.

ignominy was such that the commanding general, Oreste Baratieri, a vain and pompous man, might have wished that he had personally suffered the same fate as General Custer on the blood-soaked hills of the Little Big Horn.

"Revenge for Adowa" became a central preoccupation for Italian nationalists in the early twentieth century. Italy's most prominent patriot, the poet-warrior Gabriele D'Annunzio, spoke of "the scar, yes, the shameful scar of Adowa." Only by returning to Ethiopia and reversing the outcome of that horrible encounter could Italy prove that the 1896 battle had been a fluke, that poorly armed "black folk with woolly hair" were in fact no match for a modern European army.

In the year after Adowa, Italy participated with France and Great Britain in a partition of Somaliland that gave Italy a stretch of territory along the Indian Ocean. A few years later, in 1911, Italy managed to enlarge its African empire in the north by seizing Tripolitania and Cyrenaica (Libya). But Ethiopia, protected by its rugged terrain and its fierce native armies, remained outside the Italian orbit. In any event, Italy had all it could do to "pacify" the colonies it already possessed. Revenge for Adowa seemed an unrealizable dream.

IL DUCE

No Italian of the postwar era desired revenge for Adowa more fervently than *Il Duce*, Benito Mussolini. Though in his youth he had been a socialist, pacifist, and vocal anti-imperialist, dismissing talk of a return to Adowa as a "jingoist dream," Mussolini had changed his political spots during the First World War. He insisted Italy must enter the war (on the Entente side) to reap "immense booty" and to show the world that Italians were capable of fighting a "really great war," one that would obliterate the tenacious image of Italy as a nation of sybarites. No doubt this volte-face was also a function of Mussolini's mercurial and volcanic nature, his predilection for violence and aggressive posturing that had always belied his theoretical commitment to pacifist internationalism.

The Fascist state that Mussolini built up in the wake of his "March on Rome" in October 1922 was designed, among other things, to display a "tougher," more "streamlined" Italy—one worthy of its Roman imperial heritage. The duce wanted nothing less than to transform the Italian people into lean, mean characters who did not dance, shake hands, or drink tea. He ordered the Italian national tennis team to wear black shirts and the Italian army to introduce the goose step, suitably rechristened the *passo romano* (Roman step). Italian men were to go around saying, *"Me ne frego"* ("I don't give a damn"); Italian women were to give up "negro dances" and devote themselves solely to producing and raising young soldiers for the nation; Italian children, dressed in miniature black shirts, were to learn to adopt a "fierce gladiatorial pose."

Perhaps it need not be said that this campaign to transform the Italian people was not entirely successful—indeed, not much more successful than another Mussolini project: to make Rome the "most moral city in the world." At times the duce recognized that the task was probably hopeless because of unsuitable material. "Even Michelangelo needed good marble," he sighed.

But if his people often fell short of the mark, he, at least, would not. He turned his life as duce into a kind of permanent exhibition of model Fascist behavior. He wore military uniforms of dashing design; he strutted; he thrust out his prominent lower jaw and scowled ferociously; he did calisthenics, rode horses, drove fast cars, and fenced. He kept the light in his study burning long after he had retired to bed with his wife, Rachele, or his mistress, Clara Petacci.

Mussolini was without question a consummate showman, an arch-poseur. Most of the time he was aware of this, and relished his role-playing. Perhaps he liked playing tough because in reality he was rather soft. In times of stress he sought "refuge" in playing the violin, which he confessed brought "tears to [his] eyes" (and no doubt to others'). He had an ulcer, a weak stomach, and poor eyesight. For his bad stomach he drank liters of milk daily, and to assist his faltering eyes he had his speeches typed in extra-large print.

Not all contemporary observers were as impressed by Mussolini's poses as they were meant to be. The noted Italian journalist Luigi Barzini met him in 1932, and his impression was not favorable:

He wore a white yachting cap, a wing collar, the double-breasted jacket of a businessman, grey green army breeches, and black boots. He looked like a circus-performer in off-hours. Perhaps his clothes were meant to symbolize the multifarious variety of his interests: horses, business, the sea, the economic life of the nation, and the army. He looked small, thick, rude, and stubborn. I remember the large ivory-colored bald head, the bulging black eyes in the pale face, the protruding jaw, the yellow teeth set wide apart (a sign of good luck, according to popular belief), a little potato-like excrescence on his cranium, and the large black mole under his chin. He moved his arms and legs as a wrestler does to make his clothes fit better.

Roughly ten years earlier Ernest Hemingway had come away from a first encounter with Mussolini equally unimpressed. He had noticed that the duce, trying to appear the voracious reader to a group of visiting journalists, was ostentatiously absorbed in a French-English dictionary that he held upside down. Hemingway spent the next twenty years belittling the duce.

Although some other journalists and contemporary opinion makers also saw through the duce,* Mussolini was on the whole revered at home and respected abroad. Barzini was obliged to admit that (at least until the Second World War) Mussolini was "more popular in Italy than anybody had ever been and probably

---

*The most vitriolic Mussolini debunker in the twenties was the American journalist George Seldes. After being expelled from Italy for his hostile reporting, he wrote a biting attack on the duce called *Sawdust Caesar.* Significantly enough, no American or British publisher would publish the book until after the Italian invasion of Ethiopia had undermined Mussolini's foreign reputation.

ever will be." When he went out in public, mothers lifted babies up for him to touch, men flocked behind him, and girls swooned. This was a man the Italians desperately wanted to believe in. Mussolini made this easy for them because he rarely let sober reality spoil the show. To govern Italians, he once remarked, "you need only two things: policemen, and bands playing in the streets."

Outside Italy, Mussolini inspired widespread admiration, though perhaps not love. Adolf Hitler was by no means the only influential foreigner to praise him effusively. After a visit to Rome in 1927, Winston Churchill confessed to being "charmed . . . by Signor Mussolini's gentle and simple bearing and by his calm and detached pose in spite of so many burdens and dangers." Lord Rothermere, the conservative publisher of the *Daily Mail,* declared Mussolini to be "the greatest figure of our age." And George Bernard Shaw, though hardly a man of the Right, thought he saw something of his revered Nietzsche in Mussolini's tough-guy stance.

Mussolini thus had influential admirers in Europe, but he was more consistently revered in America. No doubt this stemmed largely from his image as Europe's most dedicated anti-Communist. Americans also perceived him as a skillful pragmatist and man of action—a kind of Latin version of the Yankee go-getter. In general the U.S. press treated him almost as favorably as his own did. He appeared on eight *Time* magazine covers between 1923 and 1943 (though, much to his disgust, he was never named "Man of the Year"). The *New York Times* might have been run by his own office of propaganda. In the mid-twenties Mayor Jimmy Walker of New York confessed to admiring Mussolini "without reserve." The duce "stands high above the political men of the whole world," he said, adding, "I long to shake his hand." During the next decade many influential Americans did get to shake his hand, since the duce, a former journalist, understood the public-relations value of personal interviews. After meeting him, the corn pone sage Will Rogers declared, "Dictator form of government is the greatest form of government; that is, if you have the right Dictator." Mussolini was the right dictator for the American ambassador to Italy, Richard Washburn Child. An indefatigable duce booster, Child went so far as to ghost-write (along with Mussolini's brother, Arnaldo) the dictator's self-promoting memoir, *My Autobiography.* In the preface to that work Child wrote, "He [Mussolini] has built a new state upon a new concept of a state. He has not only been able to change the lives of human beings, but he has changed their minds, their hearts, their spirits."

FASCIST COLONIAL POLICY

Despite his popularity at home and acclaim abroad, Mussolini had managed to solve few of the severe political and economic problems that had afflicted Italy for generations. Behind a dazzling facade of public works projects and forced industrial growth, Italy remained a poor nation, with millions of its inhabitants living in medieval squalor. This was especially true in the south, where the regime built new factories but could do little to raise living standards, improve literacy, or stem political corruption. Banditry and the Mafia were still facts of life in Sicily, though fascism's elimination of elections undercut at least one source of the crime families' power: their manipulation of the electoral system. In Sardinia, malaria epidemics (described by the government as "intermittent fevers") continued to rage unchecked. In fact, malaria was the regime's best weapon against the spread of illiteracy.

On the international level Italy had come to be recognized as an important power, but not a "great power." Its economic weaknesses, questionable military prowess (Italian claims notwithstanding), and lack of a large or significant empire put it in the second rank behind the United States, Great Britain, Japan, and France. Most troublesome of all, Mussolini's Italy faced a major Continental rival with the rise of Nazi Germany, and Mussolini himself had to wonder whether Hitler's accession to power in 1933 did not severely compromise his claim to be "Europe's most dangerous man."

The duce faced difficulties even within the Fascist movement he appeared to control so decisively. Like Hitler, he had come to power by winning the acquiescence of conservatives who hoped to use him for their own purposes. And again like Hitler, this self-proclaimed "revolutionary" found that his courting of the establishment—the king, army, church, and senate—alienated his more radical Fascist followers, especially since Mussolini could not "coordinate" Italy's traditionalist powers the way Hitler managed to do in Germany. Frustration with Mussolini's lack of revolutionary zeal ran high among his paramilitary retainers, the Blackshirts, who took seriously fascism's original commitment to nationalizing big businesses, confiscating church property, and abolishing the stock exchange. Like the German SA, the Blackshirts also had a strong predilection for street brawling, and they deeply resented Mussolini's efforts to curb this in favor of less violent propagandistic functions.

The restless Blackshirts sometimes received encouragement from regional Fascist leaders—the *ras**—who since the March on Rome had built up semi-independent fiefdoms and resented Mussolini's efforts to bring them under centralized control from the capital. The duce had expelled some of the most rebellious elements from the party in the late 1920s, but in the early 1930s he still commanded anything but a tight ship. His immediate subordinates in the Fascist government realized this; they noticed that despite all his strongman posturing he was often obliged to change policy suddenly to accommodate this or that special interest. They said derisively that his was a "dictatorship of soft cheese."

Mussolini's adventurous colonial policy can best be understood against this backdrop of grand pretensions and genuine weaknesses. Although the duce never admitted it, he came to see imperialist expansion much the way many nineteenth-century imperialists had seen it: as a panacea for national failings and insecurities.

---

*The term *ras*, interestingly enough, was derived from the Ethiopians' name for their tribal chiefs.

Colonies would solve the nation's domestic problems and assure it great-power status.

In the late 1920s and early 1930s, Mussolini began to combine generalized claims for Italian greatness with specific demands for a larger and more prominent place in the imperial sun. He insisted that colonies were a necessity for Italy because the country needed more space for its growing population. (He then promptly undercut this argument by insisting that Italy could afford to increase its birthrate because there was room for at least twenty million more people in the country.) He spoke also of the economic rewards of colonialism, and perhaps he really believed that imperialism paid. Even if it did not, colonial expansion would help curtail unemployment by giving the nation's jobless something to do. It would also, of course, give those rebellious Blackshirts something to do—something more "constructive" than shaking down shopkeepers and clamoring for the nationalization of banks. Perhaps the patriotic enthusiasm engendered by a new colonial crusade might even rub off on the obstreperous *ras*—get them thinking about the needs of the nation rather than about feathering their nests in Ravenna or Bologna. And with the duce orchestrating this great enterprise, all that snickering about his being a dairy product dictatorship might cease.

Imperial conquest, Mussolini also believed, would transform Italy into an uncontested great power. He let it be known that Italy could not breathe easy until it controlled a vast colonial empire in northern and central Africa. Then Britain and France, which also had colonies in northern Africa, would have to recognize that the Mediterranean was once again a "Roman lake." And Germany, which had been stripped of its colonies after World War One, would have to content itself with second-class status behind the New Rome.

If achieving this exalted status required war, so much the better. War, Mussolini now liked to say, was an ennobling experience and imperialistic war the supreme test of a nation's vitality. He told army conscripts that it was better to live "one day as a lion than a hundred as a sheep"; to the party he said, "The more enemies, the more the honor."

In Mussolini's expansionist plans Ethiopia figured prominently; indeed it was the key to his imperial mission. A successful conquest of Ethiopia would enable Mussolini to step forward as avenger of the Adowa defeat, that blot of shame on Italy's martial record. Moreover, Ethiopia lay between Italy's existing colonies of Eritrea and Italian Somalia, obstructing communication between them. "If the Mother Country was to derive the desired advantage from her two colonies," wrote General Emilio De Bono, who was later to lead the Italian invasion, "it would be necessary to abolish the inconvenience [of Ethiopian independence]." Abolishing Ethiopian independence would allow Italy to create a huge colony stretching across the Horn of Africa from the Red Sea to the Indian Ocean. To add to the attractiveness of this enterprise, Ethiopia was thought to be a gold mine of mineral riches, easily exploitable by an industrious conqueror.

But what of its present inhabitants? In Italian eyes they were a benighted race of savages living under a ruler of unequaled corruption and brutality. Their land was ripe for a "civilizing mission" on the part of a European nation eager to take up the White Man's Burden. The duce believed that none of the other European powers could object too much to such a useful undertaking. Had they not all conducted similar missions themselves?

But time was of the essence. Mussolini wanted his conquest of Ethiopia to be concluded rapidly so that Italy could grab its colonial booty and return its armies to the Continent before Germany had rearmed and reasserted itself in European affairs. Hitler's accession to the chancellorship made haste all the more necessary, because the führer was apparently bent on a rapid reestablishment of German power and influence. The Austrian Nazis' July 1934 putsch attempt in Vienna (which, as we have seen, Mussolini blamed on Hitler) seemed to show that the Germans were anxious to move their southern border to the Brenner Pass. The duce did not want to be tied down in Africa if Hitler moved on Austria.

Mussolini started planning an Ethiopian invasion as early as 1925. Three years later Italy signed a "treaty of friendship" with Ethiopia designed to mask its true intentions and to facilitate economic and political penetration in anticipation of military conquest. By the early 1930s the duce was declaring to his generals that he wanted to gain full control over Ethiopia no later than 1935. And he made clear that he preferred an invasion to winning the colony through negotiation. He wanted "war for war's sake, since fascism needs the glory of a victory." "My objective," he said at the time, "is simple: I want to make Italy great, respected, and feared."

ETHIOPIA AND
EMPEROR HAILE SELASSIE

The African country upon which Mussolini focused his imperial ambitions was itself one of the oldest empires in the world. The Ethiopian rulers traced their ancestry to Menelik I, said to be the son of the queen of Sheba and King Solomon of Jerusalem. During the fourth century A.D. the people of Ethiopia were converted to Christianity by their ruler, who declared fealty to the Coptic church of Egypt. In the twelfth century the Amhara people, who thought of themselves as Caucasians, became the dominant political group and established control over the northern part of what is now Ethiopia. During the next few centuries the "Solomonic" dynasty expanded its influence to the southern and southeastern regions of the Ethiopian plateau. In the nineteenth century Ethiopian emperors doubled the size of their territory by incorporating vast stretches of the Ogaden Desert, in Somaliland. As one historian of Ethiopia has observed, this African power was "the only state south of the Sahara that utilized classic techniques of imperialism and expansion through military conquest to determine its geographical boundaries."

Like that in many empires elsewhere in the world, rule in Ethiopia did not remain uncontested by the various peoples forced to subordinate themselves to it.

Non-Amharic ethnic groups like the Galla, the largest Ethiopian tribe, deeply resented their inferior status and felt little or no loyalty to the central government. They represented a strong centripetal force that the government was always at pains to contain.

In the spring of 1924 Ras Tafari Makonnen, regent and future emperor of Ethiopia, made a tour of Europe. The man who was to become known to the world as Haile Selassie ("Power of the Trinity") was thirty-two years old at the time of his tour. Though very small, he radiated strength. Wilfrid Thesiger, the renowned British traveler whose father was British minister in Ethiopia, spoke of Haile Selassie's "physical distinction," his "sensitive and finely molded face," and above all his "dignity, a dignity entirely unassumed." Compared with the balding, bug-eyed, thick-lipped duce, Ras Tafari was a study in refinement and poise.

On his tour of Europe, Ras Tafari was accompanied by a retinue of lesser Ethiopian nobles and six lions, which he presented as tokens of his esteem to various European potentates. His itinerary included Berlin, Brussels, Amsterdam, Stockholm, London, Geneva, and (significantly enough) Rome. He arrived in the Italian capital just after the mysterious disappearance of one of Mussolini's sharpest critics, the Socialist Giacomo Matteotti, about whose whereabouts the Italian press was feverishly speculating.* One newspaper ran a cartoon showing Ras Tafari whispering to the Italian chief of police, "Tell me, in all confidence, did you eat him?" This was highly emblematic of the Italian attitude toward Tafari and Ethiopia.

Elsewhere in Europe, however, the Ethiopians were well received and aroused favorable comment. The tour was significant in that it introduced Ethiopia's future emperor to Europeans and taught Ras Tafari the value of publicity abroad, which he sorely needed over the course of his long career. Twelve years later he returned to Europe under much less happy circumstances.

At the time of his first European tour, Ras Tafari had been regent of Ethiopia for eight years. He ruled in the name of Empress Zauditu, daughter of Menelik II, the victor at Adowa. His regency had begun with a bloody civil war when a rival for the throne, Menelik's grandson, Lij Yasu, tried with the backing of another powerful *ras* to seize power. Tafari managed to win the war by enlisting the support of his tribe, the Shoa, which had become the strongest of the Amharic peoples. But fierce ethnic rivalries, regional particularism, and feudal opposition to centralized control were to remain prominent features of his reign.

Once he had put down Lij Yasu's rebellion, Ras Tafari began to devote himself to what he regarded as his life's calling: the modernization of Ethiopia. Like an African Peter the Great, he sought to pull a vast land from the depths of primitive backwardness into a new and alien world of technical progress, eco-

---

*Matteotti, it turned out, had been murdered by Fascist thugs and buried in a shallow grave near Rome. Though this crime temporarily shook the Fascist regime, Mussolini eventually took "personal responsibility" for it, just as Hitler later took responsibility for the Blood Purge.

nomic efficiency, and cultural modernity. Yet his efforts to introduce such startling novelties as paved roads, plumbing, and hospitals—not to mention central political control—aroused grave misgivings among more traditional-minded Ethiopians. The arch-conservative Coptic clergy supported Tafari's appointment as regent but did what it could to sabotage his reforms. A number of *ras* opposed his centralization of authority, particularly after he had himself crowned negus (king) in 1928.

Despite the best efforts of his reactionary opponents, though, Tafari managed during the 1920s to make improvements in such fields as transportation and medical care. He also undertook to curtail slavery, the aspect of Ethiopian life that most scandalized foreigners. In 1923 he issued a decree making the buying and selling of slaves a crime punishable by beheading. However, slavery was so bound up with the social and economic life of Ethiopia that little actual progress was made in eliminating this evil. The Italian government harped on this failing, for it seemed to underscore the urgency of Italy's civilizing mission.

Ras Tafari achieved more genuine and noticeable success in the realm of diplomacy. In 1923 Ethiopia became a member of the League of Nations. Significantly, it did so through the support of Italy, which hoped to curry favor with the young regent and turn his nation into an Italian protectorate. Tafari, for his part, welcomed Italian economic and political assistance but also sought to keep Italy from exerting more than a friendly influence in Ethiopian affairs. In case Italy had other ideas, he could call on the League for protection. Nobody had ever believed in the League more fervently than Ras Tafari—unless it was Woodrow Wilson, the man who had originally sponsored its creation, only to see his own country refuse to join it.

In 1930 Empress Zauditu died and Negus Tafari ascended the imperial throne as His Imperial Majesty Haile Selassie I, Negus Negusti, King of Kings. His coronation ceremony, a high point in the modern history of Ethiopia, was a spectacular testament to his skills as a self-promoter. The British writer Evelyn Waugh, who had gone to Ethiopia in search of the exotic, witnessed the event and wrote a vivid account of it in one of his travel books. He noted that the response of the world powers to the coronation invitation was surprisingly gratifying—perhaps a result of Ras Tafari's earlier European tour. Delegations arrived from all the major European capitals and from Washington, which sent "a gentleman of experience in the electric installation trade." The delegations presented their gifts: the Germans a signed photograph of Hindenburg and eight hundred bottles of hock; the British a pair of elegant scepters with an inscription composed, almost correctly, in Amharic; the Italians, prophetically enough, an airplane. The reception for the visiting dignitaries featured a slightly soiled red carpet and a body of troops turned out in "well-cut khaki uniforms," the Lion of Judah (Haile Selassie's symbol) shining in polished brass on cap badges and buttons. "But for the bare feet below their puttees," wrote Waugh, "they might have been the prize platoon of some public school O.T.C. [officers' training corps]." Equally impressive was the fact that the city's twenty thousand prostitutes had hired language teachers to learn a few necessary phrases in English, French, and Italian.

The coronation took place in Ethiopia's new capital of Addis Ababa. Located on a high plateau in the center of the country, Addis Ababa in 1930 was essentially a shantytown consisting largely of mud huts, some of them covered in the garish strips of corrugated iron that had recently become fashionable in Africa. Few buildings had more than one story, and the only ornate structures were St. George's Cathedral and Menelik II's tomb. The town's shops were all in the hands of foreigners, mainly Armenians and Levantines. Its one nightclub, the Robinson, was run by a Greek and staffed by Hungarian, Czech, Romanian, and White Russian cabaret girls. There was also a hotel called the Imperial, which "fell short of its name except in the lavishness of its fleas and lizards." The air was pungent from open drains, rancid butter, red peppers, and burning cow dung. Every third hut was a mead salon, which sold "fermented honey in front, dusky girls with pomegranate-sized breasts in back."

The coronation ceremony, conducted according to the ancient and (for foreigners) utterly baffling rites of the Coptic church, was immensely long and complicated. "Psalms, canticles, and prayers succeeded each other, long passages of Scripture were read, all in the extinct ecclesiastical tongue, Ghiz." The visiting diplomats shifted uncomfortably from ham to ham in the immense heat of the coronation tent. Finally the bishops fumbled among some cardboard boxes and withdrew from one a crown. The emperor was presented with this, along with lion robe, orb, spurs, and spear. As the ceremony dragged to a close, Waugh examined the diplomats once again: "Their faces were set and strained, their attitudes inelegant. . . . Their clothes made them funnier still. Marshal d'Esperez [France] alone preserved his dignity, his chest thrown out, his baton poised on his knee, rigid as a war memorial, and, as far as one could judge, wide awake."

Also present at the coronation ceremony were some of the new emperor's foreign advisers, the white men he had brought from Europe and America to help him transform his ancient and unruly kingdom into a modern state. His economic adviser was an American, his military experts came from Sweden and Belgium, and his bandmaster was a Swiss. It is significant that he chose his advisers not from France, Great Britain, or Italy but from smaller or more remote nations that had no colonies bordering on Ethiopia. He did not want foreign help to turn into foreign control. And if Italy tried to weaken his regime by stirring up discontent among Ethiopia's lesser nobles, Haile Selassie would try to keep afloat by playing off one European power against another.

Less than a year after he was crowned emperor, Haile Selassie inaugurated his most celebrated reform: the promulgation of a constitution, Ethiopia's first. As a model for this innovation he chose the Japanese imperial constitution of 1889. He looked in this direction because Japan's modernization under the Meiji emperor (1867–1912) impressed him as an experience that Ethiopia might emulate. There was considerable irony in this aspiration, for Japan's invasion of Manchuria in the same year (1931) delivered the first major blow to the League of Nations, the body in whose protective powers Haile Selassie placed such faith. If, moreover, the Ethiopian leader wanted to enhance his image abroad, setting himself up as an African Hirohito was not a good idea.

With the promulgation of a constitution, Haile Selassie redoubled his efforts to bring his nation into the modern world. He drew up a new penal code that defined more precisely (and somewhat more leniently) which limbs might be lopped off for which offenses. His Belgian military advisers struggled to create a reasonably competent army, but apparently only the small imperial guard looked impressive to European observers. The army as a whole, opined the Italian military command in East Africa, could be discounted as an effective force, though its soldiers were fanatical and "oblivious of death."

Europe—not just Italy—remained to be convinced that Haile Selassie was making significant strides in the direction of the twentieth century. The London *Times* wrote that Ethiopia was still "backward in culture and progress," that its communications were "hopelessly bad," its bureaucracy shockingly corrupt. "Ethiopian officials," it noted with high-minded disdain, "have yet to discover anything derogatory to their dignity in taking presents of money from perfect strangers." Lord Mottistone, former British secretary of war and now a prominent voice on the extreme right, depicted Ethiopians as "committing the most frightful atrocities," among them "a peculiar form of torture constantly practiced on women who are suspected of untruthfulness. . . . The women die by slow degrees. Their shrieks are literally heard for miles." G. B. Shaw weighed in with the observation that Ethiopia was "not a nation," that its emperor was incapable of controlling warlike tribes who "shot travellers on sight" and whose warriors were not allowed to marry until they had produced "phallic evidence [of having slain] four fullgrown men." The French press, too, was filled with sneering comments about Ethiopia's "barbarism," its "feudal" political structure, and its continued toleration of slavery.

Most of these accusations were true enough, yet unjust. Haile Selassie had hardly been in power long enough to transform his impoverished, divided, and reluctant nation into a place acceptable to high-minded Europeans. If he were to make substantial and lasting changes, he would need both more Western support and more time. Europe, especially Italy, was not prepared to give him either.

DIPLOMATIC PRELUDE

In late November 1934 a British-Ethiopian commission visited a well complex called Walwal, in the Ogaden Desert. The wells, vital desert properties, lay at a point where the territories of Ethiopia, British Somaliland, and Italian Somaliland converged. The British-Ethiopian commission's intention was to establish the exact boundaries separating the three entities. When the commission arrived at Walwal, it found the region partly occupied by native Somali troops under Italian command. The Italians, it seemed, regarded the wells as theirs. As the

Mussolini leads a procession of his Blackshirt followers. *The Warder Collection*

Emperor Haile Selassie addresses the League of Nations, urging it to intervene on Ethiopia's behalf against Italy. *UPI/Bettmann Newsphotos*

Ethiopian dead amid the ruins of Addis Ababa, following the city's capture by the Italians in May 1936. *UPI/Bettmann Newsphotos*

Mussolini and Hitler. The "brutal friendship" between the two dictators began during Italy's invasion of Ethiopia, which Hitler publicly supported. *The Warder Collection*

commission's Ethiopian guards set up camp across from Italy's Somali troops, tensions began to mount, for Ethiopians and Somalis could not abide each other. On December 5 an Ethiopian threw a bone at a Somali. This was enough to provoke a general melee—in which the weapons were guns, not bones. Ten minutes later three Italian planes and two light tanks appeared on the scene. When the shooting finally stopped, both sides had suffered heavy losses. (The Ethiopians registered 107 dead and 45 wounded; the Somalis, 30 dead and 100 wounded. No Italians were killed or injured.) This became known as the incident at Walwal.

No doubt it was a relatively minor incident, but then so was the murder of Archduke Francis Ferdinand at Sarajevo in 1914. Like the Austrians on that occasion, Mussolini was looking for an excuse to bully a minor power that stood athwart his imperial ambitions. Ethiopia, noted General De Bono, had been causing Italy no end of grief. It was giving important building contracts to foreign powers other than Italy. Italy had not "experienced any beneficial results" from the "treaty of friendship" it had signed in 1928. It was time to remind those black men with woolly hair just who was the "superior race" in the Horn of Africa.

Immediately following the Walwal incident, Ethiopia "insulted" Italy once again by requesting that the dispute be submitted to the League of Nations for arbitration. Mussolini was in no mood for arbitration. Two days later (December 11) he handed Ethiopia a draconian ultimatum demanding that the Ethiopian detachment at Walwal apologize and salute the Italian flag. He also insisted that the Ethiopians pay a large indemnity and punish the guilty parties. Without waiting for a reply, he drafted the "Directive and Plan of Action for the Resolution of the Italo-Ethiopian Conflict," which called for "the destruction of the Ethiopian armed forces and the total conquest of Ethiopia." At the same time Mussolini ordered General De Bono to sail for Africa. He told him to go "with the olive branch" in his pocket, but also to make preparations "for an adverse outcome of the affair." If Ethiopia does not offer a satisfactory solution, said the duce, "we shall follow subsequent events exclusively in accordance with our own standpoint."

Mussolini had no reason to think that his colonialist "partners" in Africa, France and Great Britain, would object too strenuously to his solving the Ethiopian problem as he saw fit. Since the early twentieth century those two powers had made clear that they regarded Ethiopia, the one African state not yet under European domination, as belonging to Italy's sphere of interest. As recently as 1925 Britain had let Italy know that it did not object to Italian economic penetration of Ethiopia as long as this did not adversely affect the British Sudan's right to draw water from the Blue Nile, whose headwaters were in Ethiopia.

There was another reason why Mussolini thought he had a free hand in Africa. He knew that the Western powers considered him an invaluable ally in their effort to keep Adolf Hitler in line. He had shown just how useful he could be in this regard by sending troops to the Brenner Pass following the Nazi putsch attempt in Vienna. Surely the Western powers would not let a minor dispute in black Africa jeopardize their close association with the man whom Hitler (according to Mussolini) "feared most."

There were, however, other factors in the diplomatic calculation concerning the Ethiopian crisis to which the duce did not pay sufficient attention. One was the sanctity of the League of Nations, to which Haile Selassie had submitted the Walwal dispute, and whose covenant would be grossly violated by an Italian invasion of a member state. The duce had not the slightest respect for the League, but other European powers saw it as a useful mechanism for keeping the peace. They did not want to see it severely tested, let alone humiliated. A related factor was public opinion. The duce controlled public opinion in his own country, but he could not control it abroad (though he did his best to influence it by favoring friendly foreign correspondents and expelling critics). Much as many western Europeans and Americans admired Mussolini's achievements in Italy, they tended to be less impressed by his bluster in Africa. Certainly there would be a public outcry if he put his hands on Haile Selassie, the dignified little man with the many lions.

At first, however, Mussolini's optimistic expectations regarding Europe's response to his Ethiopian challenge were solidly confirmed. On January 7, 1935, the day General De Bono sailed for Africa, Foreign Minister Pierre Laval of France signed an accord in Rome with Mussolini. According to this agreement France would support Italy's endeavors to keep Austria independent of Germany. In exchange, Italy would have a free economic hand in Ethiopia as long as it allowed that state a facade of independence. Laval's other condition was the continuation of France's control of the railway running from Addis Ababa to Djibouti, in French Somaliland. Laval clearly hoped that this piece of diplomatic horse-trading would help secure the "Latin alliance" of France and Italy against that Teutonic upstart both countries had reason to fear. "What I sought to do," he explained later, "was to preserve a working agreement with Italy which would keep her on France's side in the event of a grave crisis in Europe." The French press hailed the agreement as "the cornerstone in the structure of Franco-Italian amity." Moreover, Italy's military cooperation meant that France could transfer some seventeen divisions from the Alps to the north and to the Maginot Line— that great system of bunkers it was building along its border with Germany.

Next it was Great Britain's turn to court Italy at the expense of Ethiopia. While many Britons admired Haile Selassie, the British government was not inclined to make any sacrifices on his behalf. As Samuel Hoare (foreign secretary from June to December 1935) noted in his memoirs, British colonial governments in Africa found the Ethiopians to be "bad neighbors." Haile Selassie could not control the various tribes in the south and west or the "wandering gangs, disloyal Rases, anti-Christian Moslems, Arab slave traders and intriguing adventurers, who one and all did much as they liked in this remnant of medieval Africa." Sir Robert Vansittart, permanent under secretary in the Foreign Office, insisted that London should placate Mussolini in Ethiopia because Britain could no more be serious about defending black men in 1935 than it had been about defending yellow men in Manchuria in 1931. Moreover, Vansittart feared that if Britain did not allow Mussolini to take Ethiopia, Mussolini would allow Hitler to take Austria—a much more serious blow to European security. "My real trouble," he wrote, "was that we should all have to choose between Austria and Abyssinia, if Mussolini stuck to his mania for fame and sand."

In late January 1935 Mussolini put out feelers in London to ascertain the British government's position on Ethiopia. He got no response, which led him to believe Britain did not care about that country. He was not far from wrong. In that very month Sir John Simon, then foreign secretary, cabled Britain's minister in Addis Ababa, "It is becoming increasingly important that the Emperor should appreciate the necessity in his own interest of doing everything to conclude an agreement with Italy at the earliest possible date. . . . His Majesty should face facts in a spirit of realism."

Roughly three months later, April 11–14, the prime ministers of Italy, Britain, and France gathered in Stresa to discuss forming a common front against Germany. The immediate stimulus was Hitler's recent announcement that Germany would no longer be bound by the Versailles treaty's limitations on its armaments. The conferees issued a strong protest against Germany's action. The British and French might also have taken this opportunity to warn Mussolini about proceeding too rashly in Ethiopia, but they did not. Vansittart insisted in his memoirs that this decision made sense because no pressures at this point "would have deterred [Mussolini] from making of himself the fool he was becoming. He had decided to attack Abyssinia long—perhaps eighteen months—before Stresa."

No doubt he had, but the duce was not the sort to attack unless he thought he faced easy odds. The suggestion, at this crucial moment, that he might face British and French military sanctions would certainly have given him pause. However, the powers had no intention of making such threats, even as a bluff. France remained firmly opposed to any initiative that might alienate the duce. As for Britain, two months after the Stresa conference a committee chaired by Sir John Maffey, former governor general of the Sudan, issued a report stating, "No vital [British] interests in or around Ethiopia . . . would make it essential for His Majesty's Government to resist an Italian conquest."

Such unflinching acceptance of Mussolini's ambitions, however, did not accord with a growing sense in some sections of western European opinion that Italy's African policy threatened the League of Nations and, therefore, the entire system of collective security. The leftist press in France was "uniformly hostile to the idea of an Italian conquest of Ethiopia." *Le Populaire* called for the League to "come out of its torpor." In June 1935 the British League of Nations Union announced the results of a "peace ballot," which showed that ten million people favored economic sanctions against a member state that violated the League covenant; another six million were ready to apply military sanctions. Rightist papers like the *Daily Mail* and the *Morning Post* attacked the peace ballot as a "ballot of blood" and conducted polls of their own that registered strong opposition to the League. Yet these attracted much less attention than the peace ballot. As one historian has noted, this moment represented a high point in British enthusiasm for an activist League—for Woodrow Wilson's vision of a militant defense of "the Rule of Law in the international community."

In the same month the British cabinet went through a shuffle. Stanley Baldwin returned as prime minister, Hoare replaced Simon as foreign secretary, and Anthony Eden became minister for League of Nations affairs. Neither Hoare nor Eden was a consistent supporter of an activist League, but both were at least somewhat receptive to public demands for a show of principle, particularly since a general election was in the offing. The two politicians seem to have believed that they could pacify both the duce and domestic public opinion through a compromise arrangement that allowed Italian penetration of Ethiopia, but not its outright annexation. To explore this possibility Eden was dispatched to Rome in July with an offer to the duce. Britain would cede Ethiopia "a narrow tract of territory in British Somaliland as an outlet to the sea in compensation for substantial Abyssinian concessions to the Italian demands." More precisely, Ethiopia would be asked to cede large tracts of its Ogaden territory to Italy. At the same time, Eden warned the duce that he must not flagrantly challenge the League by openly invading Ethiopia.

Mussolini was impressed by neither the offer nor the warning. He told Eden that Laval had promised him a free hand in Ethiopia, and not just in the economic realm. Nor did he want a few more acres of sand and palm trees in the Ogaden. He dismissed Eden's warning about the League as bluff, for he knew that the British cabinet, along with the French, opposed mobilizing the League in matters not vital to the great powers' security. His mission a failure, Eden left Rome full of contempt for the vulgar duce, while Mussolini began referring to Eden as "Lord Eyelashes." (As for Eden's countrymen, Mussolini dismissed them as a "degenerate race" with more women than men and a high percentage of people over fifty—the "age limit for bellicosity.")

As Eden was coming up empty in Rome, Hoare was facing difficulties at home, for the British press had gotten wind of the government's plan and published an outline of it. The House of Commons was up in arms, some members opposing any cession of British territory to Ethiopia, others railing against the accommodation of a bully at the expense of a weak African state.

Chastened by this response, Hoare went to Geneva on September 12 and delivered what one historian has called "the most ringing assertion of collective security ever made by a British statesman." He said that the League, like his country, stood "for steady and collective resistance to all acts of unprovoked aggression." But he also said something that was universally ignored by the pro-League journalists who celebrated his tough sanctionist line: "If risks for peace are to be run, they must be run by all." This was an important qualification, for Hoare knew that the French were unprepared to take the risk of war to keep Italy out of Ethiopia.

And what of the United States, a power that was not a member of the League, that maintained few commercial interests in Ethiopia, but that had strong ethnic ties to Italy? The primary concern of the American State Department was to prevent U.S. involvement in the Italo-Ethiopian dispute, which it saw as a traditional colonial conflict. The U.S. government was also well aware that Great Britain and France seemed willing to sanction Italian penetration of Ethiopia. The State Department's chief of the Division of Near Eastern Affairs wrote on December 17, 1934, "There seems little reason to doubt that Italy has been given a free hand in Ethiopia, at least by France and possibly by Great Britain, and in any case there would appear to be little likelihood that either Great Britain or France would take very effective measures to prevent Italian aggression in Ethiopia." If Ethiopia invokes the Kellogg Pact* in this dispute, he went on to argue, "we ought to leave such invocation to the League of Nations and make every effort to avoid having the matter dumped in our lap on the score that we were the original initiators of the Pact." Secretary of State Hull concurred: after the incident at Walwal he instructed the U.S. chargé d'affaires in Ethiopia to "scrupulously refrain from taking any action which would encourage the Ethiopian Government to request the mediation of the United States."

Italy clearly hoped that American racism would place the United States on its side in this conflict. The New York correspondent for the *Corriere della sera* (Milan) argued that America, because of its extensive experience with "the primitive psychology of the colored races," would appreciate Italy's policies in Ethiopia more than the western European countries did. But just in case Americans should fail to grasp the necessity and nobility of Italy's mission in Ethiopia, the Italian government hired a New York advertising agency to enlighten them. Its campaign stressed the great "cultural and humanitarian benefits" that Italy had brought to its other African colonies and now proposed to extend to Ethiopia. The Italian coordinator of the campaign was confident of its success, for—as everyone knew—Americans "were more susceptible to advertising than any other people."

Plausible as this Barnumesque observation might have been, not all Americans were swept off their feet by the Italian propaganda. While the right-wing press, led by the *Chicago Tribune*, applauded Italy's African imperialism on the grounds of "commercial, evangelical, scientific, and humanitarian purposes," many other influential papers condemned Mussolini's aggressive intentions. American blacks were especially incensed by Italy's bullying, which many of them found familiar. In some American communities blacks vented their hatred of Mussolini's Italy by attacking Italian shopkeepers and peddlers. Blacks taunted Italo-Americans when Joe Louis easily knocked out Primo Carnera in the summer

*The Kellogg-Briand Pact (1928), jointly sponsored by Secretary of State Frank Kellogg and Foreign Minister Austride Briand, of France, formally renounced war as an instrument of national policy and provided for the peaceful resolution of disputes.

of 1935. Italo-Americans responded by claiming that Mussolini would kayo Haile Selassie in one round.

The Roosevelt administration, while holding firm to a policy of no direct U.S. engagement, became increasingly concerned that war in Ethiopia might spread to Europe and undermine the world's collective security system. Secretary of State Hull accordingly appealed for a peaceful resolution of the dispute, as did FDR himself. These appeals prompted Mussolini to observe that his "worst opponents [came] not from the Harlem Negroes . . . but from many genuine white men in Europe and America."

But Mussolini needed have no fear that the white men in Washington would go beyond pious appeals for peace and understanding. FDR wanted to embargo U.S. arms supplies to Italy and not to Ethiopia, but Congress, still strongly isolationist, insisted on a nondiscriminatory embargo. Thus the United States forbade shipments of arms to *both* parties. It was like denying David his rock as he went off to face Goliath.

The one important power that encouraged Mussolini's violent conquest of Ethiopia was Nazi Germany. Hitler realized that Mussolini's dream of military glory in Africa was likely to alienate the Western powers and send the duce scurrying for new partners. He expected, too, that Italy's aggression would distract world attention from his own military buildup. Finally, he hoped that an act of brutality by Italy would help end the moral isolation in which Germany had found itself since the Röhm purge. Hitler thus ordered the German press to cease all attacks on Italy, particularly on its Ethiopian ambitions. (Some German papers, it seems, had been making fun of Mussolini's imperial pretensions, which one publication called Italy's "sickly striving to pass for a nation that is great and important.") Hitler instructed his ambassador in Rome, Ulrich von Hassell, to tell Mussolini that an Italian invasion of Ethiopia would meet with Germany's "benevolent neutrality." Under no conditions would Germany do anything to aid the negus.

Mussolini responded positively to these overtures, particularly as the Western powers began to make quibbling objections to his African plans. He ordered, for his part, a cessation of Italian press attacks on Germany. No longer should the Germans be reminded that they had still been baying at the moon when Italy was civilizing the world. As a personal concession, the duce grudgingly acknowledged Hitler's political abilities and stopped referring to him as a sexual deviate. He even lifted the ban on Italian distribution of the *Völkischer Beobachter,* long a thorn in Italy's side.

With these encouraging developments, the German government's most pressing fear was that Italy and Ethiopia might reach a negotiated settlement, thereby curtailing Italy's deepening isolation from the West. For this reason Hitler decided on a policy of utmost duplicity: while subtly encouraging Italian aggression, he at the same time strengthened the negus's willingness to fight by secretly giving him military hardware that could be used against an Italian invasion. In the summer of 1935 he sent the Ethiopians some 350 million reichsmarks worth of Mauser rifles, ammunition, pistols, and hand grenades. The arms were paid for through a secret Foreign Office fund and shipped clandestinely to Ethiopia.

Haile Selassie was appropriately appreciative, and did not fail to delight in Hitler's betrayal of the duce. Later he noted that Germany was the only country to give Ethiopia "concrete support" in the form of arms and ammunition. "All the while endorsing Mussolini's enterprise," he wrote, "Hitler was secretly doing his utmost to sabotage it." Such was the opening of the "brutal friendship" between Hitler and Mussolini: it could hardly have been more indicative of things to come.

GIRDING FOR WAR

Mussolini did not order an attack on Ethiopia immediately following the Walwal incident, because Italy's preparations for an invasion were yet to be completed. The duce wanted to be sure that when he did move, he would have the weight of numbers, firepower, supplies, and careful preparation on his side. "For the lack of a few thousand men, we lost the day at Adowa," he claimed. "We will never make that mistake [again]. I am willing to commit a sin of excess but never a sin of deficiency."

Accordingly, Italy spent the period between the Walwal incident and the invasion moving thousands of men and mountains of supplies into place in Eritrea and Italian Somaliland. The harbor at Massawa (Eritrea) was rebuilt to accommodate the flood of men and material. Airplanes were shipped to Massawa piece by piece in crates, then reassembled by Italian mechanics. Fiat supplied hundreds of "mules"—all-terrain vehicles designed to operate on the rough paths and dry creek beds that passed for roads in Ethiopia. Mules of the more traditional variety were procured as well, along with Muslims to drive them, for Christians would not do such "degrading work."

An important part of Italy's war preparation involved the recruiting and training of native Eritrean troops. But Mussolini did not plan to rely primarily on black soldiers commanded by white officers; he would send two Italians for every native, thereby guaranteeing "racial superiority" over the predominantly black Ethiopian forces. Together with 100,000 natives, 200,000 Italians would fight a "war of mass formations," deploying well-armed infantry closely supported by tanks and aircraft. Mussolini did not use the term *blitzkrieg*, but this was clearly what he had in mind.

To ensure that their enemy was internally divided, the Italians spent a great deal of time and money fostering "ambitions and dissensions" among the feudal *ras* of Haile Selassie's empire. They sought to turn local lords' heads with bribes and promises of spoils after the emperor's defeat. According to General De Bono,

their task was easy, for "venality [was] a natural characteristic of inferior peoples."
In fact, they succeeded in winning over only one major Ethiopian lord: Ras Haile
Selassie Gugsa, a debauched twenty seven-year-old who had fallen out with the
emperor because the latter had taken away some of his lands. As compensation
the emperor had given Gugsa his thirteen-year-old daughter in marriage, but
Gugsa beat her so severely that she died two years later. Angry at having been
forced to exchange large tracts of land for a frail woman, he vowed to get even
with the emperor. For one million lire he promised to turn his province in Tigre
(bordering on Eritrea) over to the Italians once the invasion began. Haile Selassie
learned of this treachery but refused to see it as such. "Most of my chiefs," he
said, "take money from the Italians. They pocket Italian money and remain
steadfast to Ethiopia." In the case of Gugsa, this was a misjudgment.

Ethiopia also prepared for war, though Haile Selassie continued to press for a
diplomatic solution through the League. Ethiopia's attempt to amass a creditable
arsenal was impeded by the western European powers' decision to emulate the
Americans in embargoing arms to both prospective belligerents. This measure,
undertaken to force the disputants to the bargaining table, succeeded only in
ensuring that Ethiopia would be woefully undersupplied and ill equipped at the
time of the Italian invasion. In the crucial area of air power, for example, Ethiopia
went to war with twelve planes, only eight of which were operational, and none of
which was effectively armed. As for his enthusiastic but undisciplined army, Haile
Selassie did his best to beat it into shape. He hired more military experts from
Europe, including Germany, which pending Hitler's great rearmament surge still
had surplus military talent for export. The emperor's German and Swedish advisers established an officer cadet school near Addis Ababa in January 1935, but the
young students were not terribly promising. Their chief instructor, a Swede,
found them "more intelligent than Swedish boys of the same age" but physically
weak (as a result of no school sport and too much syphilis), mechanically inept,
unable to take criticism, and hopelessly untidy. In any event, the first class could
not be graduated for over a year, and the Italian invasion came in nine months.

Despite these inadequacies, Haile Selassie's warriors were recklessly confident
of victory. They had been nurtured on tales of Adowa, when the spears of their
ancestors had triumphed over the rifles of the invaders. Some of them, no doubt,
owned one of the dried Italian ears, noses, fingers, or penises that were still being
hawked in the bazaars of Addis Ababa forty years after that momentous battle. So
contemptuous were they of the Italian fighting spirit that their battle artists
always painted the Italians in profile, "because they are looking with the other eye
where to run away." Should the Italians be so foolhardy as to attempt invasion
again, the Ethiopians thought, "they only had to swoop down like a troop of lions
and the macaroni melted." Although they had not kept up with the latest military
technology—with tanks, planes, and poison gas—this did not seem to worry
them: at Walwal they had tried to saber an Italian armored car; and whenever an
Italian reconnaissance plane landed off in the distance, many believed that they
had forced it to crash with a shot or a curse.

There was much warlike enthusiasm in the general populace as well. The Ethiopian Boy Scouts sent a letter to their leader, the eleven-year-old *ras* of Harar, lamenting that their training was not sufficiently martial and asking for rifles. A noble lady organized a "Battalion of Death," while another claimed to have recruited a "Legion of Amazons." All Ethiopia seemed hungry for macaroni.

Haile Selassie himself was much less confident of victory than his people; he never believed that Ethiopia could defeat Italy without substantial help from abroad. But the Lion of Judah could not say this at the moment he was calling his armies together for the confrontation Italy would not let him avoid. So he combined his League appeals with bellicose speeches designed to show that he would make no dishonorable accommodation with the enemy. He was also concerned that initial Italian military successes might quickly demoralize his armies, for he knew that these tribal warriors' bravado was likely to evaporate as soon as they lost their chiefs. Thus he warned, "Soldiers, when you have heard that in the battle-fire a loved chieftain has fallen, do not weep or despair. The man who dies for his country is happy. . . . Rather die free than live as slaves."

As the Ethiopians and Italians feverishly girded themselves for battle in the spring and summer of 1935, Haile Selassie's exotic African empire caught the attention not just of the Western world's diplomats and would-be peacemakers but also of its newspaper publishers. Ethiopia, hardly known to most Europeans and Americans, was now news, and editors were desperately trying to satisfy the sudden curiosity. As Evelyn Waugh recalled, "Files were being searched for photographs of any inhospitable looking people—Patagonian Indians, Borneo head-hunters, Australian aborigines—which could be reproduced to illustrate Abyssinian culture." Anyone who had any experience of Africa (not necessarily of Ethiopia) might be hired as a "special correspondent" and sent off to Addis Ababa to put together some local-color pieces in anticipation of the more vivid color sure to come. Addis Ababa's two or three seedy hotels were suddenly crawling with a new and particularly twentieth-century infestation: war correspondents. They came, as Waugh reported, "with their rifles and telescopes and ant-proof trunks, medicine chests, gas-masks, pack saddles, and vast wardrobes of costume suitable for every conceivable social or climatic emergency." They were nevertheless unprepared for what Ethiopia had in store for them: most of the correspondents, it seems, wrote their stories without leaving the uncertain safety of the Imperial Hotel bar.

Along with those who hoped to report the news came others who hoped to make it: military volunteers. It is common knowledge that the Spanish civil war attracted international volunteers but not that Ethiopia did so as well. They came from all over the world, but primarily from Europe and America. In England three thousand men volunteered to fight for Ethiopia, though few actually went. In New York's Madison Square Garden, nine thousand whites and blacks held a recruitment rally featuring the dismemberment of a Mussolini effigy. A few dozen blacks actually went to Addis Ababa, no doubt without realizing that the Amharic chieftains considered themselves Caucasians and had until very recently kept black slaves.

Perhaps the most important of the military volunteers was one Theodore Konovaloff, a Russian officer who served as chief adviser to Haile Selassie's forces in Tigre Province. Unlike most volunteers, Konovaloff was to stay with the emperor until the fall of Addis Ababa, not only providing intelligent (though rarely followed) technical advice but also, on one occasion, spying behind enemy lines disguised as a Coptic deacon.

Among the American volunteers was a group of black pilots under the command of Colonel Hubert Julian. Known as the Black Eagle of Harlem, Julian managed to persuade Haile Selassie to allow him and his group to join the Ethiopian army in the summer of 1935. Soon, however, Julian had a falling-out with a rival American black aviator, John C. Robinson, who called himself the Brown Condor of Ethiopia. After a public fight with Robinson, Julian left Ethiopia and was replaced by his rival as head of the "American-Ethiopian Air Force." This enthusiastic organization, however, did little to affect the outcome of the war: it seems that Hubert Julian crashed the outfit's one plane before he left.

On the eve of the war, Italy had two divisions on the southern front in Italian Somaliland under the command of Marshal Rodolfo Graziani, Italy's best-known (and perhaps most brutal) colonial general. His was supposed to be a purely "defensive" front, but Graziani knew that the Italian public would never forgive him if he did not advance. Since his public reputation mattered more to him than the duce's orders, he secretly prepared an offensive campaign, ordering trucks and Caterpillar bulldozers from the United States.

In the north, along the Ethiopian-Eritrean frontier, the Italians amassed "the largest expeditionary force ever brought together for a colonial campaign." Joining two fully equipped Eritrean divisions and a battalion of Libyans were tens of thousands of freshly arrived Italians. The latter were organized into five regular army divisions and five Blackshirt divisions. Along with the troops came Fascist leaders and Fascist celebrities, most of whom tried to get into the air corps, by far the most glamorous branch. Mussolini's two sons graced this service, as did the Futurist poet Filippo Marinetti. These men rightly considered the 150-machine Italian force vastly superior to its tiny African counterpart—"even when," as General De Bono noted contemptuously, "various black, white and yellow amateurs consented to enrol themselves" in it.

Reviewing his assembled forces shortly before the invasion, General De Bono could not help crowing with pride. Here were thousands of men and machines, all ready to be thrown into battle for the sake of Italian greatness. "The miracle of today is explained by the change that has come over the spirit of the Nation, which knows it can look with confidence to the glittering future toward which the Duce is leading it," he declared.

REVENGE FOR ADOWA

The Italian command expected that the Ethiopians, despite Haile Selassie's appeals to the League for mediation, would be unable to resist committing some "stupid act of aggression" that would justify an invasion. Although there were several minor border incidents in the months following the Walwal clash, the Ethiopians held themselves back. Their unexpected patience forced Mussolini, who feared that time was on the side of the Ethiopians, to make the first move. In September 1935 he ordered De Bono to mobilize his troops for invasion. De Bono asked if he should withhold his attack pending an Italian declaration of war. "No," replied the duce, "no more hesitations; I order you to begin your advance early on [October] 3."

Mussolini did not, as he had once promised to do, go to Africa and lead the Italian invasion himself. But he was no less bellicose for being safely out of danger. On the afternoon of October 3 he appeared on the balcony of the Palazzo Venezia in Rome and told an excited crowd, "We have been patient for forty years. Now we too want our place in the sun."

Some of the Italian troops who crossed the Mareb River into Ethiopia in the gray dawn of October 3 also had trouble containing their enthusiasm. "At this historic hour," gushed one soldier, "all Italy is with us, the dead of Adowa call us. . . . A new cycle is beginning for our country, the Roman legionnaires are again on the march. This narrow dusty track shut in by thorny hedges is the road to empire." A few of the troops picked up pieces of Ethiopian soil and ran it through their fingers; it would, they concluded, be suitable for the cultivation of good Italian crops.

As Italian and Eritrean troops streamed across the Ethiopian border, General De Bono sent up two airplanes to drop copies of a proclamation over enemy territory. The proclamation, signed by the general, blamed the opening of hostilities on Ethiopia, which had "treacherously attacked" Italian posts. It insisted that the soldiers of Italy were entering Ethiopia to defend its people "against molestation" and to "punish those guilty of provocation." Pleading for cooperation with the Italian "liberators," it urged the people not to listen to "false rumors" and to pray for a quick Italian victory. But it ended with a warning: "Woe to him who disturbs public order. I shall be pitiless."

Even as some Italian planes were dropping proclamations, others were dropping bombs. De Bono insisted that the targets were exclusively military ones, sites "where groups of warriors had been observed." Yet one of the first targets was the town of Adowa, which was filled with women and children. Mussolini's eldest son, Vittorio, participated in the opening raid, which he saw as "revenge . . . for the heroic death of our soldiers, who forty years ago fell victim to overwhelming odds." But young Mussolini was disappointed by the results of his raid: "I noticed with regret," he reported, "that [my bombs] did not create any sensational effects. Perhaps I was so disappointed because I had expected the huge explosions and flames I had seen in American war movies. Unfortunately, the mud-and-grass Ethiopian houses were just not designed to provide a satisfactory target to a bomber."

Unspectacular though these raids might have been to the bombers, they were impressive enough to the people on the ground. Even Ras Seyum, one of Haile Selassie's most valiant chiefs, was shaken as Italian planes bombed his position in northern Tigre: "Dear God of Ethiopia," he cried, lifting his eyes to the sky, "what will happen next?" In Addis Ababa the diplomatic community sent an urgent appeal to the duce to desist from bombing the capital. Greek and Levantine shopkeepers painted red crosses on the roofs of their shops, and even on their strawhats, in hopes of securing immunity from Italian bombs.

Buildings marked with red crosses, however, seemed to attract rather than deter Italian pilots, and they were one of the few targets the bombers managed to hit with any consistency. The British minister in Ethiopia telegraphed London that the first Italian bombs had fallen precisely on a house containing hospital stores and flying the red cross. European and American newspapers sent up cries of indignation over this "barbarous" behavior and over Italian air attacks that claimed the lives of defenseless women and children. General De Bono dismissed these complaints with equal indignation. In reality, he insisted, the only victims of the first raids "were one woman, one child, and several cattle." He said nothing about warriors.

Unlike the brash bomber pilots, Italy's infantry soldiers were for the most part relieved that their opening foray into enemy territory produced few spectacular effects. Indeed, there was very little serious fighting at all, because Haile Selassie had ordered his commanders to withdraw their troops as the Italians advanced. He did this in order to respect a thirty-mile "zone of neutrality" proposed by the League. But withdrawal was also part of his military strategy. He planned to draw the enemy away from their sources of supply, ever deeper into a country whose rugged landscape and inhospitable climate would take a high toll on the invaders. "We will fight like the Russians against Napoleon in 1812," said one of the emperor's aides. The problem with this strategy was that most Ethiopian commanders found it dishonorable. One of them, Ras Seyum, disobeyed the emperor and sent a few hundred men into the "neutral zone," where they fought minor skirmishes with the Italians. During the course of these, they managed to kill an Italian lieutenant. According to the Ethiopian warrior who proudly displayed the dead Italian's uniform, this man had been a true *gobos* (someone very brave). "He stared out from atop his mule as if nothing could intimidate him." Unfortunately for the Ethiopians, this *gobos* was the only Italian officer to die in the opening phases of the invasion.

The first days of the campaign also witnessed the treachery of Ras Haile Selassie Gugsa, though his betrayal of the emperor did not amount to the spectacular coup he had promised. He was supposed to have opened the road to Makale, the capital of eastern Tigre, and to have delivered to the Italians thousands of warriors. Instead, he fled immediately to the Italian lines with only twelve hundred men. The Italian press made the best of this by multiplying the number of defectors by a factor of ten. De Bono, however, was not even sure that the few troops Gugsa brought him were of any value. "Have you complete trust in your men?" he asked the *ras*. Gugsa said yes, but De Bono remained doubtful: "It is difficult to read a black man's face," he admitted. He appointed Gugsa governor of Tigre but kept him under close supervision.

Italy's first major goal in the Ethiopian invasion was the conquest of Adowa. De Bono was prepared to use native troops for the taking of other towns, but not this one: "Adowa must be captured by Italian troops," he declared, "so that the unfortunate events of 1896 [can] be redressed." Haile Selassie's strategy of withdrawal meant that the town was hardly defended, and it fell on October 6. The Italian flag was rehoisted over the city by a general (Ruggero Santini) who had seen it taken down forty years earlier when he was a lieutenant. Then followed what one pro-Italian English war correspondent called a "touching little ceremony." A few native Eritrean troops who had fought with the Italians at Adowa, and been held prisoner ever since by the Ethiopians, were taken from their cages and lined up before the general. Each one of them was missing one hand and one foot, amputated by the Ethiopians as punishment for their service with the Italians. Santini gave the men one hundred lire apiece. "Their faces beamed with pride and happiness," gushed the journalist, "as the General said a few words to each." Meanwhile, back in Rome, Mussolini exultantly cabled Gabriele D'Annunzio, "Fascist Italy has freed itself of its sackcloth."

Shortly after taking Adowa, General De Bono issued a proclamation freeing the slaves in northern Tigre Province. "You know that where the flag of Italy flies, there is liberty," he announced. Technically this proclamation freed some fifteen thousand slaves. But De Bono quickly discovered that his writ in this regard was no more powerful than Haile Selassie's. "I am obliged to admit," he wrote later, "that the proclamation did not have much effect on the owners of the slaves, and still less, perhaps, on the liberated slaves themselves." As soon as they were set free, the slaves appeared before the Italian authorities asking, "Who feeds [us] now?"

In the opening phase of the campaign in the north, the Italians encountered serious resistance only once. A column commanded by General Oreste Marriotti was given the assignment of advancing on Makale through the Danakil Desert. The American war correspondent Herbert Matthews, traveling with Marriotti's column, described the route as a "Val d'Inferno"—a "prehistoric landscape" of deep gorges and fantastic hills, "scattered as if sown by some gigantic hand." The heat was so fierce that the wine the soldiers drank "might have been heated on the stove." On the morning of November 12 the column, exhausted and bedraggled, entered a small gorge created by the Ebna River. As the main body of the column was about halfway through the gorge, it began hearing birdcalls of two notes, insistently repeated. Suddenly the dry air was filled with rifle and machine-gun bullets. The Italians scurried for cover behind rocks and thorn bushes, but not before some of them dropped in their tracks. The column remained pinned down in the gorge all day, occasionally fighting fierce hand-to-hand battles with Ethiopian warriors who dropped down on them from the cliffs that flanked the gorge.

By nightfall the situation seemed hopeless; the Italians expected to be wiped out one by one during the night, or to face certain annihilation the following day. But there was no more fighting during the night, and at dawn a scouting party sent out to explore the heights discovered that the enemy had simply disappeared. The soldiers could not believe their luck. Reviewing their losses, they were also relieved to find that they had suffered relatively few fatalities. Matthews attributed this to poor marksmanship on the part of the Ethiopian troops—"emotional savages in a frenzy of excitement." Whatever the cause of the Italian deliverance, Matthews claimed to have found the experience the "thrill of a lifetime." Chances are that most of the Italian troops did not.

On the southern front the Italians did not advance so rapidly. Their one significant success was the capture of a stone fort at Gorrahei, which was commanded by Afework, a legendary chieftain of great bravery. Before their advance against this fort, the Italians bombed it, in the process mortally wounding Afework. With his death the Ethiopians lost their resolve and abandoned the fort. It seemed that Haile Selassie's fears regarding the disastrous results of a chieftain's death had not been misplaced. The emperor himself was obliged to make an appearance in the Ogaden to restore morale. In mid-November he flew down from Addis Ababa and distributed awards to those soldiers who had distinguished themselves by capturing Italian tanks. Those who had fled were flogged, and one of the chief officers was executed by bayonet. The southern front firmed up, at least for the moment.

Although there had been relatively little serious fighting in the opening phase of the war, a number of Ethiopian military deficiencies were already manifest. Matthews was right about the poor marksmanship. Ethiopian warriors tended to fire quickly without taking aim. Perhaps it would not have helped much if they had done so, for their weapons were in very poor shape, owing to their owners' habit of using gunsights for can openers and pushing the rifle muzzles into the mud. They wasted what little ammunition they had by firing copiously into the air before and after battles and when drunk. Although the Ethiopian soldiers often displayed insane élan, hurling themselves into assaults against murderous cannon and machine-gun fire, their tactics were sloppy and poorly coordinated. The commanders tended to stay well to the rear and were generally out of touch with battlefield events because of bad telephone connections and a lack of signaling equipment. Perhaps most grievous of all, the Ethiopian commanders did not follow up initial victories. As at Adowa in 1896, and more recently in the Ebna gorge, they were so gratified by their opening successes that they went off to celebrate and allowed their battered enemy to slip away.

All was not entirely well with the Italian army either. Their little Fiat tanks turned into mobile ovens, slowly cooking their occupants at a steady 120 degrees. The mechanical "mules" often broke down, and the live ones sometimes refused to budge despite Islamic curses and many *"Figli di puttane!"* imprecations from the Italians. Morale was generally high, but there were severe strains between the regular army conscripts and the Blackshirt "volunteers," who received better food and pay. (These tensions anticipated the hostility between Blackshirts and conscripts during the Second World War.)

Although General De Bono made substantial advances during October and early November, taking Makale on November 8, the duce was not satisfied with his progress. He wanted the conquest of all Tigre to be accomplished without further delay. De Bono, on the other hand, knew that his troops needed rest and hesitated to overextend his supply lines. On November 9 he refused an order from Mussolini to advance immediately on Amba Alagi (a town the Italians had lost in the Adowa disaster), because the place had "no strategical importance." This was De Bono's last decision as commander of expeditionary forces. A week later Mussolini informed him that his mission was completed and that he would be replaced by Marshal Pietro Badoglio.

SANCTIONS

On October 7, 1935, the League of Nations council declared Italy in violation of Article 12 of the covenant, which required that member states submit disputes to arbitration. Two days later the League's general assembly confirmed the council's finding by a vote of fifty to one, with two states, Hungary and Austria,* abstaining. The assembly also voted to establish a coordination committee to work out the exact nature and timing of economic sanctions to be imposed on Italy if it did not desist from its aggression in Ethiopia. This was a momentous occasion in the history of the League—the first time it had voted to apply Article 16, the covenant's provision for sanctions against a member state. It was also to be the last.

The purpose of the economic sanctions was not, strictly speaking, to "punish" Italy, much less to destabilize its regime. The point was to convince that state to seek arbitration in the Ethiopian dispute by making it too costly for Italy to continue the war. Therefore, no attempt was made to expel Italy from the League, and no state broke diplomatic relations, let alone advocated a declaration of war. It was thought that the sanctions would have plenty of time to make an impact because Italy could not possibly win the war in less than two years. Some European leaders, particularly Laval, hoped the sanctions would never actually come into effect, because Mussolini would be content with a few face-saving victories and end the war early of his own accord.

---

*Austria abstained in the vain hope of retaining Italian support for its independence against Germany. In refusing to condemn Mussolini's invasion of Ethiopia, it further undermined its own moral stature, making it easier for the Western powers to abandon it in 1938. Germany did not vote on the sanctions question, because it had already left the League.

By mid-October the coordinating committee was able to agree on a set of proposals that included an embargo on the sale of arms to Italy, the repeal of the embargo on arms to Ethiopia, prohibition of loans to Italy, the exclusion of Italian imports, and an embargo on exports critical to Italy's war effort. The precise nature or scope of the export embargo—by far the most controversial and far-reaching proposal—was to be determined by yet another committee.

Although the League's assembly voted to accept these proposals, not all member states applied them. Switzerland refused to prohibit Italian imports, on the grounds that this would cost some ten thousand Swiss their jobs and alienate the populace in the Italian-speaking cantons. More significantly, Britain elected to continue, for all practical purposes, its embargo against arms sales to Ethiopia. By the end of November 1935 His Majesty's government had granted only three export licences for arms shipments to Haile Selassie's regime: these were for ceremonial swords and two million rounds of ammunition. The emperor's request to buy war surplus rifles and airplanes was rejected. Anthony Eden objected to this policy, noting that the Ethiopians were getting "a consistently raw deal from us in the matter of arms." The Ethiopians agreed. One of their officers fumed to the British war correspondent George Steer, "You have let us down like savages in the matter of arms. When you give up your pious embargo it will be too late." Indeed it would.

If the purpose of the sanctions resolution was to chasten Mussolini without thoroughly alienating him, the opposite effect was achieved. Insisting that the Western powers were punishing Italy for doing precisely what they had always done, he ordered an "austerity campaign" to counteract the sanctions' effects. Italians were exhorted to eat less meat, to use less electricity, and to "buy Italian." Anticipating shortages of certain imported raw materials, the government launched a drive to make synthetic fibers and collect scrap metal. To build up its gold reserves, it asked Italian women to turn in their wedding rings in exchange for steel ones stamped with the duce's initials and blessed by the pope.

These campaigns were not uniformly successful, but in general the Italian people rallied around the regime in this moment of self-generated "crisis." As the historian Denis Mack Smith has observed, "The sanctions seemed to show that Italy was encircled and persecuted, that the nation itself, not only the regime, was in danger, and the campaign of austerity envisaged by the autarchy was not pure caprice, but a vital national interest." The duce had never been more popular.

At the same time Italian diplomats around the world bitterly attacked the League's intervention. They were particularly active in Britain, which they regarded as the most hypocritical and anti-Italian of all the European powers, and yet susceptible to influence because of its strongly conservative foreign-policy establishment. In mid-November a member of the Italian embassy in London thus gave a speech to the Royal Institute of Foreign Affairs entitled "British Foreign Policy through Italian Eyes." A compendium of Italian grievances, the speech lamented Britain's alleged preference for the "nordic" over the "Latin" races, no doubt a result of a "falling off in classical education." Britain, said the speaker, was "apt to be more just toward [its] late enemies in the Great War" than it was toward Italy. Now it was assuming a "high moral attitude" regarding Italy's invasion of Ethiopia, but this was an act of sheer hypocrisy. "While you stick to the loot that you acquired even so recently as in 1919," the Italian went on, "you hold up your hands in horror, if anyone tries to follow, not your new principles, but your old example." Britain's opposition to Italy's "justifiable penetration" of Ethiopia was also highly baffling because Britain had opposed that "barbarous state's" admission to the League (on Italian sponsorship) in 1923. "We Italians think . . . that England should have been consistent with her former attitude. Her superiority-complex should have been satisfied by saying: 'I told you so.' "

Italy's campaign of self-justification also involved the recruitment of foreign "experts" to speak out in favor of its mission in Africa. One of these experts, a retired British officer named Major E. Polson Newman, returned from an Italian-subsidized trip to Ethiopia with the following comments on Italy's invasion:

> Everybody knows that if Italy had appealed or were to appeal now to the League of Nations to secure the territories which are necessary to her she would have had no chance of obtaining satisfaction. Yet, knowing this, Italy is blamed for trying to acquire those territories in the only way which is possible for her. It is the League of Nations which should be blamed and not Italy. . . . Considering the supreme efforts and the enormous sacrifices made by Italy during the [Great War], considering the fantastic and unprecedented progress achieved in every field since the advent of Fascism, and considering the fact that Italy has been a powerful bulwark against the spread of Bolshevism at the most critical moment, it is a very poor reward to tell her that she may not enjoy the colonial privileges enjoyed by all other nations.

Italy's truculent and defiant response to the League's initial sanctions proposals forced the Western powers to consider tightening the screws by applying more far-reaching export restrictions. The French government, however, was strongly opposed to any extension of the sanctions measures beyond those already proposed. Public opinion in that country was severely polarized by the crisis. Bourgeois and upper-class audiences in Paris movie theaters shouted "Vive l'Italie" at newsreel scenes showing Italian victories in Ethiopia. Groups on the Left demonstrated in the streets of Paris against Italy and for sanctions, though some leftist deputies feared that tough sanctions would drive Mussolini into the arms of Hitler and thus weaken French security. As one of them told a meeting of the Independent Radical Federation, "We must look out for our own security. It is not right that we should become more isolated because of an African quarrel in which we are not directly interested." The far Right was unequivocally pro-Italy and anti-League. On October 4, representatives of the rightist veterans' organizations and Fascist leagues told President Albert Lebrun that "sanctions meant war." *L'Action française* asked why France should support "a bunch of cannibals" against Fascist Italy, which along with France represented the "best of Latin civilization." A "Manifesto of French Intellectuals for the Defense of the West and Peace in Europe" attacked a "false judicial universalism" in Geneva that had placed "superior and inferior, civilized and barbarian, on the same footing." Pierre Laval, while admitting that these views did not perhaps show France in the best light, agreed that sanctions must not go too far. Indeed, he continued to search for ways to placate Mussolini even after Italy's invasion. He proposed to Anthony Eden that the League give Italy a mandate for those parts of Ethiopia not inhabited by the dominant Amharic peoples; the rest of the country should be "administered" by the League, but with "Italian participation."

In his memoirs Eden claimed to have been scandalized by Laval's proclivity "to reward the aggressor." "It did not appear to occur to him," he wrote, ". . . that anyone other than Mussolini had to be content." But the British government was divided on the question of pursuing more extensive sanctions. Eden championed a widening of sanctions to include nonmilitary items and the lifting of Britain's embargo on arms to Ethiopia, but he was still a junior minister without a great deal of clout. Foreign Secretary Hoare continued to believe that Britain must not be more aggressive than France in attempting to curb Mussolini. The British chiefs of staff advised the government that it would be folly to provoke Italy in the Mediterranean when Japan was becoming more aggressive in the Far East. A warning by Laval that the French navy might not support Britain if Italy attacked Royal Navy ships compounded British fears of "going it alone." Vansittart supported Hoare in all his reservations. Though he despised the French government, especially Laval, he agreed that Britain could not afford to isolate itself in a quixotic pursuit of international justice. In this he and Hoare had the widespread backing of the rightist press, parts of which, as in France, were subsidized by Italy.

Despite these trepidations by its two most powerful members, the League of Nations could not allow Mussolini to pursue his aggression in Ethiopia without at least *considering* further measures to stop him. Most members realized that the most effective measure—short of closing the Suez Canal, which neither France nor Britain would accept—would be an embargo on oil. Italy was wholly dependent on oil imports and possessed only a two-month surplus for its campaign in Africa. Oil exporting powers in the League like Britain, France, Holland, Romania, and the Soviet Union (which had joined the League in September 1934) supplied Italy with most of its petroleum. Why not simply cut it off?

In debating this question, the League powers kept returning to an unpleasant fact: oil-exporting nations outside the League could elect to step in and supply Italy with the oil that the League states refused to sell it. This would both undermine the oil sanctions' effectiveness and transfer the Italian petroleum market to non-League competitors. The nation most likely to profit from this transfer was the United States.

How did the United States stand on sanctions, particularly the possibility of oil sanctions, against Italy? It must be said that Italy's invasion of Ethiopia was for the most part ill received in the United States. Even many of those Americans who had applauded the duce's domestic policies now turned against him. American businessmen were no longer so eager to lend him money, nor the American Catholic press so eager to defend him. Ernest Hemingway summed up American disgust with the duce's civilizing mission when he dismissed it as an attempt to make Ethiopia "a land fit for Fiats." But condemning his aggression and taking hard-nosed economic measures to stop it were two quite different propositions. Realizing that it lacked authority from Congress to extend the existing military embargo to nonmilitary items like oil, the Roosevelt administration called for "voluntary" cutbacks in U.S. trade with Italy. But this appeal had little effect on New York importers and exporters. In the fall of 1935 U.S. trade with Italy increased sharply, with the largest increase, significantly enough, coming in oil shipments. When Roosevelt, frustrated by the collapse of his "moral embargo," tried again to get authority for an oil embargo, isolationists in Congress beat down his initiative. Their efforts were supported by thousands of Italo-Americans who bombarded their congressmen with letters opposing revision of the American Neutrality Act. The duce himself thanked the Italians of America for standing with their "mother country" during its time of trial.

European politicians like Hoare and Laval used America's sanctions policy as justification for not pursuing an oil embargo through the League, but in fact they would not have taken this step even had America been willing to go along with it. Their goal, after all, was to find a way to bring Mussolini back into the fold, not to force him farther into the wilderness. And apparently they took seriously a warning from the duce that he would consider an oil embargo "an act of war."

In the end the Western powers did not succeed in placating Mussolini, but they did succeed in rendering the entire sanctions policy ineffective by excluding oil. Italy's operations in the African war were hardly affected by the League's various financial and economic measures. But an oil sanction would have been a different matter. Three years later, on the eve of the Munich conference, Mussolini admitted to Hitler, "If the League of Nations had . . . extended economic sanctions to oil, I would have had to withdraw from Abyssinia in a week." The duce's earlier threats to go to war over an oil embargo were probably just bluster. His navy was a fourth the size of the Royal Navy, and his army was preoccupied with Ethiopia. Churchill was undoubtedly correct when he observed that if there was ever an opportunity for "striking a decisive blow in a generous cause with the minimum of risk," this was it. Churchill, however, made this observation after World War II. In 1935–36 most Western politicians, including Churchill, regarded the permanent alienation of Italy as a serious risk indeed.

The West's almost desperate effort to prevent Italy's loss to the Stresa Front reached its apex (or nadir) in December 1935 with the so-called Hoare-Laval pact, one of modern European diplomacy's most disreputable agreements. During the preceding month the British Foreign Office had instructed its chief Ethiopian expert, Maurice Peterson, to work out possible compromise solutions to the Italian-Ethiopian dispute with his counterpart in the Quai d'Orsay. By early December the diplomats had come up with another plan to buy off the duce with non-Amharic Ethiopian territories and to compensate the emperor with a port in British or Italian Somaliland. Vansittart, who followed these negotiations, justified the sacrifice of the non-Amharic lands on the grounds that they had never been under effective Ethiopian control. "Their negro tribes were desolated by every form of disease and brutality, including phallus-hunting," he added, no doubt to suggest that inheriting disease-ridden phallus hunters was just what Italy deserved. Hoare, still clinging to his "double policy" of negotiation with Italy and "loyalty to the League," believed this latest plan might work. So did Laval, but he was prepared to give the duce even more territory.

In early December, Laval asked Hoare if he could visit London to finalize the compromise plan before presenting it to the duce, the emperor, and the League. Hoare, at that moment facing a physical and mental breakdown, suggested instead that he (Hoare) stop in Paris on his way to a much-needed vacation in Switzerland. Unfortunately for Hoare, Laval agreed.

On December 7–8 Hoare and Vansittart met with Laval and several diplomats from the Quai d'Orsay. Laval sat with a telephone within reach and on several occasions called Mussolini to keep him abreast of the negotiations. On the basis of what he heard from the duce, Laval insisted that the Peterson plan would have to be modified. Italy should be allowed to keep all the territories it had already overrun in Tigre Province. Hoare agreed to this since these territories, especially Adowa, "were dear to the Italian heart." They also agreed that Italy should have economic control over all the non-Amharic regions, though in this capacity it would be "acting under the League." Ethiopia, in compensation, would get a port, though it was unclear exactly where.

It was also unclear whether Mussolini would accept this package despite its generosity toward Italy. He had let it be known that he wanted the outright annexation of all the non-Amharic lands and a mandate over the rest. Should these demands not be accepted, he would "wipe Abyssinia off the map." How Haile Selassie would respond to this proposal was unclear as well, but it did not seem to matter so much.

In the end it mattered little how either of the contending parties felt about the Hoare-Laval plan because its details were leaked to the French press by anti-Laval elements in the Quai d'Orsay before it could be secretly discussed in Rome or Addis Ababa. The British press picked up the story and raised a storm of protest over this new, and to date most far-reaching, effort to pacify an aggressor nation at the expense of its victim. Letters to the editors of major British papers reflected widespread popular indignation. Typical was a missive from a provincial schoolmaster asking how he could ever again speak to his boys of "an Englishman's honor." Politicians of all political shades professed their disbelief that Britain and the League could have been so badly served. "It is really disgraceful," wrote the National-Labour MP Harold Nicolson in his diary. "Sam Hoare was certified by his doctors as unfit for public business, and on his way to the sanitorium he stops off in Paris and allows Laval to do him down. My God!" A cruel joke quickly made the rounds: "No more coals to Newcastle, no more Hoares to Paris!"

In response to this outcry the Baldwin government decided to back away from the Hoare-Laval plan and even to cashier poor Hoare, who, to add injury to insult, had broken his nose while skating in Switzerland. As Anthony Eden stepped in to replace Hoare, Europe's attention turned once again to the battlefields of Ethiopia, where the real carnage was taking place.

THE FALL OF ADDIS ABABA

With De Bono's replacement by Marshal Badoglio* in late November 1935, the character of the Italian campaign in Ethiopia changed. De Bono was not entirely the humanitarian he claimed to be in his memoirs, but he generally tried to avoid atrocities and truly believed Italy had come to Ethiopia to "civilize" it rather than simply to subjugate it. Badoglio, though not a member of the Fascist party, was a political general par excellence; he knew that the duce wanted quick successes and was prepared to countenance any means to achieve them. Badoglio, and Graziani in the south, thus turned increasingly to terror tactics: bombing raids on undefended villages and the widespread use of poison gas.

Yet Badoglio was also cautious. Concluding that De Bono's "rapid, bloodless advance" had dangerously exposed Italy's forces to Ethiopian counterattack, he ordered their shift into a defensive posture until more "preparations" could be made on the transport and supply system. At the same time he sent Italian planes to bomb the town of Dessie, where Haile Selassie was coordinating his country's chaotic mobilization. The emperor was photographed personally firing a machine gun at Italian planes circling over his headquarters. These photographs, along with reports that Italian bombs had fallen on Dessie's American Red Cross hospital, helped rally Western opinion against Italy just at the moment the Hoare-Laval proposals were leaked.

Badoglio's concern about an Ethiopian counteroffensive was warranted. In early December, Haile Selassie decided he could withdraw no farther, that it was

---

*Marshal Pietro Badoglio had an odd career. Though generally held responsible for Italy's disastrous defeat at Caporetto in World War One, he managed to become chief of staff of the army after the war. Despite his lack of Fascist credentials, Mussolini made him governor general of Libya, where he earned a reputation for brutality. During the Second World War he lost his job as chief of the general staff for criticizing Mussolini's amateurish handling of the Italian campaign in the Balkans. In July 1943 he took over the Italian government when the Fascist grand council overthrew the duce. Various postwar attempts to celebrate him as Italy's savior should not obscure that he was always a calculating opportunist with no fixed political or moral principles.

necessary to strike a crushing blow before Italy could amass any more men and material in Tigre Province. Hoping somehow for another Adowa, he ordered three armies under three of his most trusted chieftains to cut off the Italian advance south of Makale.

An initial skirmish between Ethiopian troops and an Italian armored column seemed to suggest that another Italian debacle might indeed be in the offing. The Ethiopians caught the Italians in a mountain pass and managed to disable some of their tanks by tearing off the treads. "The tanks might have been animals," wrote the emperor later. "It was an incredible spectacle: men in flimsy cotton shammas attacking these steel monsters with their bare hands." One Ethiopian warrior jumped on top of a tank and pounded on the turret. When the driver unwisely popped his head out, the Ethiopian lopped it off with his long sword. Other Italians were killed in the act of surrendering, their hands-in-the-air gesture being understood as an invitation to disemboweling.

Badoglio insisted in his memoir of the war that this encounter was of "little importance to the general situation," but in fact he was worried that the intiative might pass to the Ethiopians. What would the duce do if he learned that the Italian advance was threatened? To forestall such an eventuality Badoglio ordered new bombings, but this time the bombs contained dichlorodiethyl sulfide— popularly known as mustard gas. One of the Ethiopian chiefs later described his troops' reaction to this aspect of Italy's civilizing mission:

> On the morning of December 23 . . . we saw several planes appear. We were not unduly alarmed as by this time we were used to being bombed. On this particular morning, however, the enemy dropped strange containers that burst open almost as soon as they hit the ground or water, releasing pools of colorless liquid. I hardly had time to ask myself what could be happening before a hundred or so of my men who had been splashed by the mysterious fluid began to scream in agony as blisters broke out on their bare feet, their hands, their faces. Some who rushed to the river and took great gulps of water to cool their fevered lips, fell contorted on the banks and writhed in agonies that lasted for hours before they died. . . . My chiefs surrounded me, asking wildly what they should do, but I was completely stunned. I didn't know what to tell them. I didn't know how to fight this terrible rain that burned and killed.

As reports of the first gas attack percolated out of Ethiopia, the Italian command quickly denied their veracity. Later it admitted to using some forms of gas, but only of a type that caused no lasting damage. In fact, the Italians continued to drop mustard gas until the fall of Addis Ababa—and to drop it not only on troop concentrations but also on densely populated villages. The effects of these attacks on Ethiopia's civilian population were described by J. W. S. Macfie, a doctor with the British Ambulance Service:

The first [gassing patient] I examined, an old man, sat moaning on the ground, rocking himself to and fro, completely wrapped in a cloth. When I approached he slowly rose and drew aside his cloak. He looked as if someone had tried to skin him, clumsily; he had been horribly burned by "mustard gas" all over the face, the back, and the arms. There were many others like him; some more, some less severely affected; some newly burned, others older, their sores already caked with thick brown scabs. Men and women alike, all horribly disfigured, and little children, too. And many blinded by the stuff, with blurred crimson apologies for eyes.

The Ethiopian population had no effective protection against the gas attacks. The few available gas masks were defective. In the capital the wife of the British minister assembled volunteers to make gauze bandages impregnated with soda, which could be held over exposed areas during an attack. Soldiers in the field were told to urinate on their shammas and hold them over their faces. Ethiopia appealed to the International Red Cross committee for gas masks, but the committee, chaired by a pro-Fascist Swiss, turned down the request on the grounds that Ethiopia had not specified "for what purposes the masks were to be used."

Foreign correspondents accredited to the Italian campaign did their best to play down the horrors of the gas attacks. Herbert Matthews insisted that they had played a minor role in the war, burning only "several thousand peasants, more or less badly." They did not, he declared, prevent the native population from "welcoming [the Italian invasion] with satisfaction."

The Ethiopians attempted two major offensives in December and January, but they were stalled by skilled Italian defensive tactics and massive air attacks. These were great days for the young Italian air force. Vittorio Mussolini was overjoyed when he and his comrades began using incendiary bombs: "I was always satisfied with the effects created by incendiary bombs," he wrote. "At least with them one saw fire and smoke." One also saw "wild flights of men and animals" and groups of natives "opening up like petals of a flower" when bombs landed in their midst. Understandably the Ethiopians came to hate these "sky devils" who rained fire and poison down on their heads. They captured an Italian pilot in December and promptly beheaded him in a village square. This act of primitive vengeance was exploited by the Italian press as renewed evidence of the urgency of Italy's civilizing mission.

By the end of January 1936, General Badoglio was ready to resume his advance southward. He chose as his immediate objective the mountain of Amba Aradam, on whose rugged summit Haile Selassie's minister of war, Ras Mulugueta, had dug in with an army of some eighty thousand men. Badoglio decided to force Mulugueta either to fight or to abandon his strong position. "I hope he will fight," Badoglio cabled Mussolini on January 31, "in which case there will be an important battle, upon which I shall enter with the greatest determination, with absolute confidence in the valour of our soldiers."

But Badoglio did not trust simply in the valor of his soldiers. Before attacking, he subjected Mulugueta's position to weeks of heavy air and artillery bombardment. When his 280 guns and 170 airplanes had "softened up" the enemy's lines, he sent four regular army and two Blackshirt divisions up the mountain. Elite *alpini* (alpine troops) scaled a sheer rock face that the Ethiopians had not bothered to defend. There were pockets of fierce Ethiopian resistance, but the weeks of bombardment had demoralized Mulugueta's troops and caused many to slip away before the Italian attack. Enough remained, however, to provide the victors with a gratifying body count: when they reached the summit, they found over eight thousand corpses. Italian planes then went to work on the retreating Ethiopians, strafing them as they fled down the mountain. Among the victims was Ras Mulugueta himself.

Successful as this assault was for the Italians, it was not the "battle of annihilation" that Badoglio wanted to mount. That came in late March at a place called Mai Ceu, a few miles north of the emperor's new headquarters at Quoram. Though by no means a skilled military commander, Haile Selassie had decided to lead his troops personally into battle; he hoped his presence would inspire his men to heroic feats of valor and compensate for Ethiopia's technical deficiencies. Badoglio, for his part, again put his trust in careful preparation and superior firepower. Having intercepted communications from the enemy camp, he knew that Haile Selassie planned a massive attack. He therefore surrounded his positions at Mai Ceu with artillery and machine-gun installations. These he placed behind rows of sturdy thorn hedges, Ethiopia's answer to barbed wire.

The Ethiopians attacked on Saint George's Day (March 31), in the hope that Saint George, patron saint of Ethiopia, would bring them victory, as many believed he had done at Adowa. Wave upon wave of brilliantly clad tribesmen advanced across rolling, slightly wooded hills in the direction of the Italian lines. They came on, wrote Herbert Matthews, "in grim fury"; and they kept coming on as the Italian machine guns cut through them like scythes through dry grass. Soon the dead were piled so high in front of the Italian lines that the machine gunners "had to raise the muzzles of their weapons on the shoulders of their comrades to fire over and into the new waves sweeping inexorably up the hill." A few Ethiopians broke through the first Italian lines, but then "bayonets and hand-grenades did their deadly work." This was not reminiscent of Adowa; it was more like the Battle of the Somme, with the Ethiopians in the role of the British.

Haile Selassie wanted to press on with his attack despite the disastrous losses incurred in the opening assault, but his feudal generals had had enough. The emperor was obliged to order a retreat from Mai Ceu across the plain of Lake Ashangi to the south. This retreat turned out to be even more harrowing for the Ethiopians than their assault. As they fled across the plain, the Italian air force pursued them with machine-gun fire, bombs, and more mustard gas. Stragglers were attacked by Galla tribesmen—vicious human hyenas who habitually swept down on anyone weakened by wounds or exhaustion. Often the Galla preferred to mutilate rather than kill, chopping off testicles for their brides, leaving their living but helpless victims to be picked apart by the flocks of vultures that followed them on their grisly rounds. Mutilated men left lying on their backs always tried to roll over, for they knew that the vultures tended to go first for the eyes.

After the battle of Mai Ceu, Haile Selassie's armies began to melt away, the men simply drifting back to their villages. The Swedish officer who commanded the emperor's cadet school hoped with his fifteen-year-old charges to stage a Thermopylae on a high mountain pass north of Addis Ababa, but the cadets retreated in trucks when the Italians appeared. Now there was nothing but another stretch of nasty country between the invaders and the capital. Badoglio reported to Mussolini on April 11, "The battle upon which the Empire depends is over."

Badoglio meant by this the "Italian Empire," but it applied to the Ethiopian as well. Stunned by his defeat at Mai Ceu, Haile Selassie retreated to a mountain sanctuary to pray. He emerged two days later prepared to continue fighting a guerrilla campaign in the rugged mountains of the southwest, but his wife and most of his advisers persuaded him instead to make a personal appeal to the League for support against the invader. On May 2 he and a large entourage boarded a special train for Djibouti, in French Somaliland. From there they would sail via Palestine to Europe. His decision to leave made political sense, since any hope of regaining his empire lay in Europe and not in the mountains of Ethiopia. But this step was a humiliating one, for it violated the Ethiopian tradition that an emperor must seek death in battle rather than flee. Haile Selassie was to be haunted by charges of cowardice for the rest of his life.

The emperor's departure was the signal for an orgy of rioting, looting, and killing in the capital. Drunken soldiers roamed the streets looking for white faces, because whites were held responsible for Ethiopia's humiliation. Most of the emperor's white advisers had left even before he did, but other European and American officials, along with their families and dozens of Greek and Levantine shopkeepers, barricaded themselves in the various foreign legations. There they stood off haphazard attacks by small bands of soldiers and sent out desperate appeals to the Italians to hurry their advance on the city.

Badoglio's forces finally arrived in Addis Ababa on May 5. They could have gotten there sooner, but the marshal wanted to give the rioters and looters more time to work their havoc: this would enhance his role as "liberator."

Most of the Europeans in Addis certainly saw the Italians as their saviors. The French legation gave Badoglio a hero's welcome, the minister greeting him in full dress uniform. Badoglio was pleased that the devastation of the capital seemed to confirm the validity of Italy's civilizing mission. "If any doubts had still remained as to the state of barbarism of these people," he wrote later, "the condition in which we found Addis, destroyed and sacked by the express order of the Negus before he left, was quite enough to dispel them."

With the fall of Addis Ababa, Italy had avenged Adowa and found its place in the sun. On May 9, 1936, the duce told a delirious crowd massed before the

Palazzo Venezia that King Victor Emmanuel III was now emperor of Ethiopia. *"Imperatore! Imperatore!"* screamed the crowd.

THE WORST OF ALL WORLDS

A month after his capital fell, Haile Selassie arrived in Europe. His first stop was England, the country he regarded as most sympathetic to his cause. In London, however, he was snubbed by a conservative political establishment that feared that any official courtesies extended toward the emperor would offend Italian sensibilities. Prime Minister Baldwin fled a tea party in order to avoid greeting him, and the new king, Edward VIII, refused to invite him to Buckingham Palace.

Europe's leaders, in fact, had more or less decided to abandon Haile Selassie's cause even before the emperor arrived in London. Italy's dramatic military advances in the early spring had made it clear that the war would not last as long as had originally been thought. If existing sanctions were having no effect on Italy's behavior or on the progress of the war, why continue them? France was now pressing Britain to drop sanctions altogether. Eden was disgusted with the French foreign minister Pierre Flandin's eagerness to defend Italy at the expense of Ethiopia; the Frenchman, he huffed, presented "the Italian case with confident cynicism." But there were leading British politicians who were equally prepared to do whatever was necessary to "save Italy for Europe." One of these was Neville Chamberlain, then chancellor of the Exchequer. At a cabinet meeting on May 27 he argued that Mussolini "would probably respond if we offered to raise sanctions and come to terms, and that he might be very ready to cooperate again with France and ourselves in Europe."

Instead of being "cooperative," Mussolini showed what he thought of the League and its sanctions by declaring the outright annexation of Ethiopia and then, since Ethiopia "no longer existed," demanding its immediate expulsion from Geneva. The League council passively accepted Italy's annexation of a member state but refused for the moment to bless this act of rapine by expelling Ethiopia. As one council member put it, "The Italians want us to eat shit. So be it. We will eat it. But they want us also to declare that it smells like roses. That is too much."

Thus Ethiopia, in the person of Haile Selassie, was allowed to put its case before the League assembly. When the emperor rose to give his speech on June 30, Italian journalists, who referred to him as Signor Tafari, tried to shout him down. But he managed nonetheless to tell the assembled delegates what they undoubtedly did not want to hear:

It is not merely a question of a settlement in the matter of Italian aggression. It is a question of collective security; of the very existence of the League; of the trust placed by States in international treaties; of the value of promises made to small states that their integrity and their independence shall be respected and assured. It is a choice between the principle of equality of States and the imposition upon small Powers of the bonds of vassalage.

Two weeks later the League made its choice. As of July 15, all sanctions against Italy were formally lifted.

Haile Selassie's speech can be seen in retrospect as a fitting though tragic epitaph for the League of Nations. That institution had now failed twice (the first instance being Japan's invasion of Manchuria) to act decisively against violations of its covenant, because key member states thought it was not in their vital interests to do so. In future international crises the major powers would simply ignore the League and resort to ad hoc conferences to try to resolve their differences. The fateful Munich conference of 1938 would be the last of these before the onset of World War II.

The purpose of abandoning Ethiopia was to keep Mussolini from straying from the Stresa Front. Instead, the Western powers got the "worst of all worlds," as Robert Vansittart put it. They undermined the League's credibility by refusing to impose effective sanctions but alienated the duce by slapping his wrist. He came away from the sanctions fiasco more than ever convinced of the West's anti-Italian bias and hopeless degeneracy. England had shown itself to be "perfidious Albion." France, despite its "Latin" blood, was no more virile or trustworthy than England. The United States was a "country of niggers and Jews, the forces which disintegrate civilization." As for the League, it was such a farce that one need not even pay lip service to its flabby principles of peace and international cooperation: Italy left the League in 1937, becoming (after Japan and Germany) the third major power to do so.

Mussolini's growing contempt for the Western democracies was accompanied by a growing admiration for his former nemesis: Hitler's Germany. In March 1936 Hitler had remilitarized the Rhineland in direct violation of the Treaty of Versailles. This bold step, which the Western powers meekly tolerated, greatly impressed the duce. Germany, he began to believe, was more suited as a partner for Fascist Italy than the effeminate Western democracies. Both Fascist powers, after all, were "have not" nations struggling for their fair share of power and influence in the world. Both were virile young nations to which the future legitimately belonged. By the end of the century, Mussolini confidently predicted, there would be only four "great powers": Italy, Germany, Japan, and the Soviet Union.

The führer did his best to encourage the duce's budding infatuation with Germany. In early April he sent an aide to Rome to explore the development of an "anti-Bolshevist front" between the two Fascist powers. During the course of this meeting, Hitler's emissary assured Mussolini that the führer wanted to see Italy become stronger and that he fully sympathized with Italy's "legitimate campaign" in Africa. How different from the Western powers' schoolmarmish finger wagging! Mussolini responded to Germany's overture the way Hitler later received the duce's blessing upon the *Anschluss:* "Tell the führer that I thank him from the heart for his support in this trying hour," he gushed. "I will never, never forget it."

V

"RED ELLEN" WILKINSON AND THE JARROW CRUSADE

Great Britain in the Great Slump

> England is a very good country
> when you are not poor.
>
> —George Orwell,
> *Down and Out in Paris and London*

O n Halloween day 1936, 197 men arrived in London after having walked for twenty-five days over three hundred miles from their homes in Jarrow, in the northeastern corner of England. The Jarrow men were truly ghosts of a departed era, for their town, once a major shipbuilding center, had lost its industrial livelihood in the depression and become one of the poorest towns in the country. The marchers—or crusaders, as they liked to call themselves—carried with them a petition asking the government to resuscitate industry in their town. They wanted work, they insisted, not charity.

People all along the crusade route were impressed by the marchers' determined spirit, courage, and orderliness. Upon their arrival in London one journalist was moved to comment, "No one can see these men—clean, decent, orderly, self-disciplined, with their poor but well-darned and carefully patched clothes—without being profoundly moved." He declared that no government could "lay aside the ghost" of Jarrow while there were "two-hundred marchers to resurrect it as they have done in every village and town which they passed."

The "Jarrow crusade" was by no means the only such perambulatory protest against unemployment in Britain. Since the early twenties, and increasingly during the Great Slump of the thirties, Britain had witnessed dozens of "hunger marches" on the capital. The Jarrow march was one of the last such demonstrations, and it was also one of the smallest. Nevertheless, it became far and away the most famous—indeed, the only one that generated much publicity at all.

The main reason for this was that it was led by one of the most extraordinary figures in twentieth-century British politics: Ellen Wilkinson. Red Ellen, as she

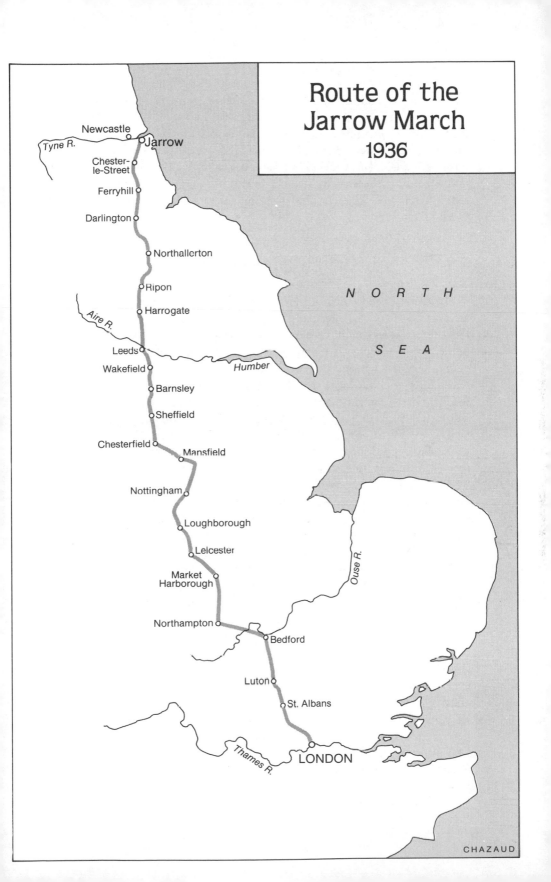

Route of the
Jarrow March
1936

Tyne R.
Newcastle
Jarrow
Chester-le-Street
Ferryhill
Darlington
Northallerton
Ripon
Harrogate
Aire R.
Leeds
Wakefield
Barnsley
Sheffield
Chesterfield
Mansfield
Nottingham
Loughborough
Leicester
Market Harborough
Northampton
Bedford
Luton
St. Albans
Thames R.
LONDON

N O R T H

S E A

Humber

Ouse R.

CHAZAUD

was called, was a diminutive, fiery, redheaded woman who knew how to attract people's attention to whatever cause she happened to champion. In the mid-thirties she was championing Jarrow in her capacity as the town's newly elected member of Parliament. She walked almost the entire three hundred miles of the Jarrow crusade, giving impassioned speeches at stops along the way. No wonder *Jarrow* became a byword for depression-era suffering, and the Jarrow crusade a lasting symbol of protest against mass unemployment and poverty during the Great Slump.

TWO BRITAINS

In the fall of 1933 the British writer J. B. Priestley traveled around England to assess at first hand the effects of the Great Slump on his native land. He found that in some areas conditions did not seem to have deteriorated significantly. The port city of Southampton, for example, was "a town that had not let the universal depression master it and that was contriving to enjoy its unique situation, between forest and heath and deep blue water, a lovely bay window upon the wide world." Of the bucolic Cotswolds he reported, "There is not, I imagine, much distress anywhere in this region. The men on the land are not well paid, but they can live on their wages. People looked comfortable there. The children were noticeably in good shape." Industrial Coventry had plenty of unemployed, but it seemed to have passed its worst period of depression. Factories that had been working on short time a year earlier were now back on double shifts. "I saw their lights and heard the deep roar of their machinery, late [in the] night." Coventry made Daimler automobiles, and Priestley saw many of them on the roads, along with processions of other fancy cars and comfortable new buses.

But as Priestley headed north into England's old coal-mining, iron-making, and shipbuilding regions he saw little evidence of comfort or prosperity. County Durham, which offered to the bus traveler nothing but "distant glimpses of coal-pits and mining villages," was a "nightmare place that seemed to have been constructed out of small army huts and unwanted dog kennels, all sprawling in the muck outside some gigantic works." He was not sure what was made in the huge works, "but even a Kafir would not have envied the employees if it was they who lived in these forlorn shanties." Gateshead, near Newcastle in the far northeast, was "nothing better than a huge dingy dormitory—a dormitory for the working-class." Central Newcastle itself had a certain "ebony dignity," but its outskirts were all mean streets where "slatternly women stood gossiping at the doors of their wretched little houses or screeching for their children playing among the filth of the roadside." "If T. S. Eliot ever wants to write a poem about a real wasteland instead of a metaphysical one," observed Priestley, "he should come here."

At the center of this urban wasteland were the giant steel mills and shipbuilding yards that had once made the region prosperous, though at the expense of its natural beauties. Now many of the mills and yards were shut, and their former workers, if not on the "dole," were trying to eke out a living by engaging in such preindustrial trades as fishing. This means, noted Priestley, "that these men, who were once part of our elaborate industrial machinery but have been cast out by it, are starting all over again, far away from the great machine, at the very beginning, out at sea with a line and a hook." But these sons of industry were not Robinson Crusoes, and England was not a South Sea island. These men had "trade in their fingers," and every time they went out with their primitive hooks and lines they declared "once again the miserable bankruptcy" of England's industrial system.

In essence, what Priestley had encountered on his journey was not one England but two: on the one hand, primarily in the Midlands and the north, a bleak nineteenth-century manufacturing England with many of its "satanic mills" now closed, their former workmen on the dole or in fishing boats; on the other, mainly in the south, a surprising "new England" of filling stations, bungalows with tiny garages, cocktail bars, Woolworths, modern motor coaches, wireless sets, greyhound racing, swimming pools, and "everything given away for cigarette coupons."

Impressed as we are with history's most prominent images of the "Hungry Thirties" in Britain—images of long bread lines and men standing about shiftlessly on street corners—we may be inclined to overlook the fact that the British economy registered substantial growth over the decade as a whole. Although the period 1930–34 was one of severe economic dislocation, the mid-thirties witnessed what one study of depression-era Britain has called "the largest and most sustained period of growth in the whole inter-war period." This resulted essentially from the rapid development of new industries like motor vehicles, aircraft, electricity, and chemicals. There was also a "retailing revolution," which inundated Britain with American-style chain stores and department stores. A general decline in the prices of consumer goods enabled the British to buy mass-produced items, from radios to automobiles, in record abundance. They bought houses, too. After a bad slump in home construction during the twenties, some three million new homes were built and sold in the next decade. The housing boom transformed the urban landscape, ringing cities with suburban "estates" where Englishmen could have their semidetached castles and their precious gardens as well. The families that lived in these houses were generally smaller than before, since the middle classes were having fewer children in order to increase their disposable incomes and enjoy higher standards of living. (A baby Austin rather than a baby human," as one historian put it.)

The thirties also witnessed the appearance of fads or crazes that bespoke greater prosperity. While thousands of Britons took to the roads to protest unemployment, many thousands more took to the roads (and trails) to keep fit. In 1930 Britain established the Youth Hostel Association, along with the Ramblers' Club, which sponsored all sorts of hikes—mass hikes, competition hikes, birdwatching hikes, and patriotic hikes to Portsmouth during navy week. The Great Western

Railway organized a "Hikers' Mystery Express" from London that dropped off hikers at some unspecified place in the country for a ramble and then, if all went as planned, returned to pick them up in the evening. Fearing a fitness gap, a team of British observers went to Nazi Germany in 1935 to study that country's ambitious fitness program. Though critical of the maniacal discipline with which the Germans pursued sport and fitness, the British team urged that Britain do its best to keep up, and Parliament accordingly passed a national physical-fitness bill.

Another craze of the thirties was nudism. This fad, like walking for exercise rather than for work, was practiced largely by the relatively affluent, for only people who could afford to buy plenty of clothes found much pleasure in taking them off. That the British took up this craze in spite of their climate was a testament to the virulence of the affliction and the intrepidity of its practitioners. The nudists assembled at first in muddy, insect-ridden woods and later in nature camps; in winter they held indoor meetings under sunlamps. During these gatherings they engaged in earnest conversations about health and ate lettuce and tinned-salmon teas. "At the superior nudist camps," reported two chroniclers of the interwar period, "a nice class distinction was made: the butlers and maids who brought along the refreshments were forced to admit their lower social standing by wearing loin-cloths and aprons respectively."

For many Britons the depression era was also a great party era. In this respect the thirties simply carried over a tradition of the twenties, when England's postwar generation of "bright young people" seemed to have embarked on a permanent binge fueled by the fashionable new "cocktail." "Oh Nina, what a lot of parties," gasps a character in Evelyn Waugh's *Vile Bodies,* a roman à clef of the Roaring Twenties: "Masked parties, savage parties, Victorian parties, Greek parties, Circus parties, parties where one had to dress up as somebody else, almost-naked parties in St. John's Wood, parties in flats and studios and houses and ships and hotels and night clubs, in windmills and swimming baths. . . ." By the thirties the bright young people had gotten older but—if Waugh's *Diaries* of the period are to be trusted—no wiser. Waugh and his rich friends like Diana Guinness, Eddie Marsh, Harold Acton, Cecil Beaton, and Nancy Cunard partied furiously and no less exotically than in the twenties. Occasionally they enjoyed, reported Waugh, parties with "masses of little lesbian tarts and joyboys."

It is safe to say that there was little nudism in Newcastle, few joy boys in Jarrow. While Waugh's Britain—essentially the Britain of the "new" industrial south—was enjoying a substantial recovery by the mid-thirties, most of the north, parts of the Midlands, and much of Scotland and Wales remained locked in grim depression. One of the reasons for this disparity is that the economic problems in the depressed areas stemmed not from the Great Slump alone but also from long-term weaknesses and structural inadequacies that predated the crash of 1929. Staple British industries like coal mining, metal manufacturing, textile production, and shipbuilding—most of which were concentrated in the English Midlands and northeast and in Lowland Scotland and southern Wales—had been suffering at least since the early twenties and, in some cases, since well before that. Over the course of the late nineteenth century, Britain had seen its supremacy in heavy manufacturing gradually undermined by the rise of competitors—most notably Germany and the United States—which made better use of more modern and sophisticated techniques. The industrial world's gradual conversion from coal to petroleum-based sources of energy undercut one of Britain's primary export branches and rendered its newer oil-fired industries dependent on costly imports. In any case, the newer oil- or electricity-fired plants tended not to locate in the old industrial regions, because they no longer had to be near the coalfields; instead, they went south to the markets.

The First World War hurt Britain's economy in general and its old industrial economy in particular. Traditionally lucrative markets for manufactured goods slipped away as trade was disrupted and other countries moved toward industrial self-sufficiency. Factories and machine tools were worn down by wartime production demands. These might have been replaced or modernized after the war, but victory itself militated against this: what was "good enough to win the war" was thought to be good enough to keep Britain on top. In any event, a substantial upgrading in industry would have been expensive, and a general decline in trade after 1921 forced companies to reduce infrastructure investments. Nor was the government in a position to help with generous subsidies. It had borrowed so extensively to fund the war (there was an elevenfold increase in the national debt between 1914 and 1918) that it felt obliged to cut spending back dramatically in the early years of the peace.

This meant that the Roaring Twenties did not roar economically for Britain, and particularly not for the industries that had made Britain great. In the heavy industrial regions unemployment sometimes ran as high as 40 or 50 percent. Government retrenchment and individual companies' attempts to cut costs by lowering wages fueled a host of labor disputes. The most notorious of these—the general strike of 1926—had its origins in a confrontation between coal miners and mine owners over wages, work hours, and reorganization of the mines. The general strike not only exacerbated class tensions but further weakened the British economy.

The prospects for taking the steps necessary to renew Britain's ailing older industries were not enhanced by many Britons' refusal to look their problems in the eye. Rather than concentrating on the real causes of their country's industrial decline, they tended to blame their ills on Britain's wartime loss of its best and brightest young men. An entire generation of "golden youth" was said to have vanished in the war. The absence of this "lost generation," it was further said, meant that power in Britain had remained in the hands of those "tired old men" who had brought on the disastrous war in the first place. The American historian Robert Wohl has pointed out that this explanation lacked much basis in fact: England's losses had been proportionately smaller than Germany's or France's; and plenty of younger men survived the trenches to assume leading roles in postwar politics, business, and the arts. (One of them was Mussolini's nemesis

Anthony Eden.) What *had* occurred, Wohl notes, is that a disproportionately large number of public school and Oxbridge men died at the front because as junior officers they had the fatal duty of leading their men "over the top." The country's increasing fixation upon these departed elites reflected a widespread nostalgia for the Edwardian past and provided a "means of accounting for the disappointments of the present." Accounting for them, one might add, without doing anything about them.

The worldwide Great Depression, brought on by the American stock market crash of October 1929, compounded Britain's commercial and industrial weaknesses by drying up yet more markets and further reducing investment resources. As trade and production plunged, bankruptcies mounted. Financial panic opened a monetary hemorrhage in the city of London: by the summer of 1931 the Bank of England was losing gold at the rate of two and a half million pounds a day. The government was obliged to abandon the gold standard in an effort to save the pound.

In the wake of these developments, unemployment, high enough since 1921, assumed catastrophic proportions. In the winter of 1932–33 Britain had about three million out of work (almost 25 percent), and the figure did not fall below two million until after 1935. In the ailing heavy-industrial fields the unemployment percentage varied considerably but was consistently well above the national average. Among coal miners it reached 42.4 percent in 1932 and remained at 34.4 percent in 1935. The two Britains drew further apart as high unemployment or underemployment impoverished parts of the work force and made the country's traditionally uneven distribution of wealth more uneven still. In the mid-thirties eight million of the twelve million families in Great Britain possessed among them less than one-twentieth of the personally owned wealth.

Startling as these statistics are, they do not tell us anything about the conditions of life for the poor and unemployed during the Great Depression. The first consequence of joblessness was generally a drop in income, for the level of government unemployment relief was lower than that of wages except in some of the least-skilled trades. Decline in income required "economies" in what were often already tight domestic budgets, and it was not always "frills" that got cut out: dietary standards plunged in most of the high unemployment areas. "So far as the evidence goes," wrote one contemporary student of the problem, "it suggests that people living at the economic level of the dole are living near or below the threshold of adequate nutrition." A Newcastle study found that unemployed families were "living on a diet below the standard considered necessary to maintain health and working capacity." The depressed areas suffered higher rates of serious diseases like tuberculosis, though it is not clear that this was directly related to unemployment, for in some of these areas TB rates were high even under full employment.

For the former family breadwinners, the most debilitating and lasting effects of unemployment were often psychological. Contemporary observers reported high rates of depression and anxiety. Men complained of feeling useless, bored, isolated, and directionless. A young American sociologist who studied the effects of unemployment on the daily lives of British workers recorded the following comments from the afflicted:

"Us men that's learned to work are lost without it." "It ain't the money any more than it is the fact that you don't have nothin' to do." "You've heard tell that the worker today don't get no satisfaction out of his work. Well, let me tell you something. He gets a lot more satisfaction out of it than he does living without it on unemployment benefit."

The psychological situation tended to be different for those younger men who had rarely worked in their lives and for whom, therefore, work did not have the same meaning. Priestley was told by older workers that the young unemployed "were undisciplined and carefree, the dingy butterflies of the backstreets." These men had "no sense whatever of waste and tragedy in themselves. . . . They cadged cheerfully from relatives, and so managed to find a few coppers for cigarettes and pictures and a bit of betting. . . . They knew nothing about responsibility. They [were] the new playboys of the western world."

The distractions touched upon by Priestley—gambling, the cinema—were indeed extremely popular among the unemployed. Moving-picture houses did as lively a business in the depressed areas as pawnshops. Betting on football matches and greyhound races consumed all too many dole checks. Then, of course, there was the pub, though consumption of spirits and beer actually declined in the thirties because alcohol was one of the few consumer items that did not go down in price. Engaging in these activities brought the unemployed much high-minded censure from the tax-paying classes, who complained of "extravagant and profligate" ways among those on the dole.

Less problematical, perhaps, was a source of amusement the unemployed shared with all other Britons: following the latest murder trial in the popular press. The most sensational of these in the thirties was the Rattenbury case, which involved the stabbing of a country squire by a young groundsman who had been sleeping with the squire's wife. What made the case so piquant was not the stabbing itself but the theme of a young man's corruption by a lust-crazed older woman. There were other juicy cases as well: "Mahon the Mumbles villa murderer, . . . Armstrong the poisoner who put arsenic on tea-time sandwiches, Maltby the tailer who failed to keep a suicide pact with his mistress and lived in a barricaded house for six months with her decomposing body in the bathroom, where he took his meals. . . ." There were also many "trunk murders": killings in which the victims were cut into small pieces and packed away in footlockers. The unemployed followed these stories with particular relish because they had plenty of time to read the newspapers and entangle themselves vicariously in the sordid dramas of the day. In his classic report on poverty and unemployment in the coal-mining districts, *The Road to Wigan Pier*, George Orwell observed, "The

Scotch miner was a bore when you got to know him. Like so many unemployed men he spent too much time reading newspapers, and if you did not head him off he would discourse for hours about such things as the Yellow Peril, trunk murders, astrology, and the conflict between religion and science."

The British government was hard-pressed to cope with the problem of mass unemployment. In 1920 the government had extended Britain's existing Unemployment Insurance Law to cover virtually the entire work force. Financed by contributions from employers and employees, this program was designed to cover short-term unemployment and assumed a jobless rate of about 4 percent. When over the course of the twenties and early thirites unemployment rates reached several times this figure, and men found themselves without work for years on end, the government began covering the inevitable shortfalls in the original program with subsidies from the Exchequer. This practice contributed significantly to the government's escalating budget deficit in this period. In 1931 a Labour government fell when the cabinet proved unable to agree on retrenchment measures, including cuts in unemployment benefits. The succeeding "National Government," which drew together representatives from all three major parties (Labour, Conservative, and Liberal), introduced new regulations that raised employee contributions and reduced benefits by about 10 percent. It also imposed a new screening procedure for benefit recipients known as the means test.

This means test was by far the most controversial of the new cost-cutting measures. As its name implied, it was designed to structure benefit payments according to the financial "means" of potential recipients. In calculating the amount of relief, the local public-assistance committees that administered the means test took into account all sources of family income, including pensions and earnings from wives and children. They also assessed the value of household goods and personal property.

Many of the committees seem to have pursued their task with a diligence worthy of the heartless Mr. Scrooge. But what particularly infuriated the unemployed was that the system penalized thrift and rewarded improvidence. Those who had laboriously accumulated some personal assets received lower benefits than those who had squandered everything. Perhaps even worse was the system's implicit assumption that the unemployed were personally responsible for their loss of work. As one commentator wrote, "Behind this system is still the notion that unemployment is somehow the fault of the unemployed, from which they are to be deterred if possible; and an attempt is made to persuade their relations to help in deterring them, because they will be made to contribute to their support."

In fact, the means test was not applied with equal severity across the land. Since administration of the procedure was left to local committees, practices varied from district to district. Some Labour-controlled committees were quite lenient in imposing the test; others hardly imposed it at all. These anomalies led to changes in the system in 1934. Neville Chamberlain, then chancellor of the Exchequer, took unemployment relief "out of politics" by transferring responsibility for its administration from local public-assistance committees to the National Unemployment Assistance Board. Unfortunately for the recipients, relief scales were often lower under the new system.

The government saved money through the cost-cutting measures inaugurated in 1931. The means test reduced payments for half a million recipients, took another quarter million off the rolls entirely, and deterred an untold number from applying for benefits. In the first year of operation twenty-four million pounds was saved, an achievement the government hailed as a major success. But the new regulations generated a great deal of ill will toward the government. Ramsay MacDonald, a veteran Labour party politician who assumed the prime ministership in the National Government, earned the enduring enmity of most workers: he was seen as a "traitor" to Labour's cause, the very personification of governmental insensitivity to the plight of those who suffered most in the "bankruptcy of the system."

The one policy inaugurated by the National Government to cut unemployment was the Special Areas Act of 1934. Under this act two new special-areas commissions were set up to explore ways to bring new jobs to the depressed areas. But both their resources and their powers were severely limited. Operating with a grant of only two million pounds, they were not allowed to supplement state relief programs or subsidize firms working for profit. The Labour party politician Aneurin Bevan dismissed the initiative as "an idle and empty farce," and the lord mayor of Newcastle declared it "a mere flea-bite and a sop."

JARROW AND
THE PALMER'S SHIPBUILDING COMPANY

Although conditions were depressed in most of Britain's heavy-manufacturing districts, they were particularly bad along the Tyne River, in the northeast. And within the Tyneside the town of Jarrow was undoubtedly the grimmest of the grim: a black shrine of poverty and decay. Visiting there in 1933, Priestley commented that the very air was "thick [and] heavy with enforced idleness, poverty and misery." One of its black streets might have been "a little more wretched than another," but to the outsider "they all looked alike." Every other shop appeared to be permanently closed. "Wherever [I] went," wrote Priestley, "there were men hanging about, not scores of them but hundreds and thousands of them. The whole town looked as if it had entered a perpetual penniless Black Sabbath."

Jarrow had originally gained recognition not as a center of industry, idle or otherwise, but as the home of the Venerable Bede (d. 735), father of English education and scholarship. The town did not take on any industrial importance until the eighteenth century, when it began to build ships for the salt and coal trade, and for Britain's "wooden navy." It became a shipbuilding center because of its favorable position on the Tyne, close to the northeast coast, but in fact, it was coal mining, rather than shipbuilding, that fueled the town's first major expansion in the early nineteenth century. Jarrow's population doubled between 1801 and 1811 and reached 3,350 by 1821, holding roughly at this figure until the mid-nineteenth century.

In the early nineteenth century Jarrow emerged as a classic English coal town, the sort of place that Dickens was later to denounce in his novel *Hard Times.* In exchange for a backbreaking and lung-destroying job, the miners "bound" themselves to a colliery on an annual basis. Under the terms of their bondage, they were paid for each basket ("corf") of coal they brought to the surface. But the corfs all had to meet a specified weight; subweight baskets were forfeited to the mine owner without payment to the miner. The owners hired overseers ("keekers") to check the corfs; and since they paid them according to the number of subweight baskets they detected, the miners invariably worked part of the time for nothing.

Labor disputes were frequent and sometimes violent in the Jarrow coal pits. "Binding strikes" occurred when the miners discovered that the owners had not kept to the terms laid down when the men were hired. A binding strike in 1810 resulted in so many arrests that the bishop of Durham lent the Jarrow authorities his stables as a pen for the strikers. Hunger generally drove the strikers back to the mines on the same terms on which they had left them. They worked in the pits until physically unable to wield a pick or haul a corf. Of course, their servitude might be cut short by mine accidents, of which Jarrow had its frequent and bloody share. In 1826 a large explosion killed thirty-four of the forty-nine men and boys working in one pit; an explosion in 1830 killed forty-two. Sudden cave-ins and floods also claimed numerous lives.

Poor safety conditions in the Jarrow pits, in fact, was one of the reasons for their decline in the late nineteenth century. Another was rising water in the ever-deeper shafts, which were built close to the seacoast. Competition from newer and more efficient mines in the Midlands, whose products could be sent to London via the expanding rail network, also helped doom coal mining in Jarrow. By the early twentieth century Jarrow was on its way out as an important mining center.

Well before then, however, Jarrow's shipbuilding industry had "taken off" and thus guaranteed the town a second industrial life. In 1851 Charles Mark Palmer, son of a prosperous shipowner and merchant, established a new shipbuilding company in Jarrow called (modestly enough) Palmer's. The Palmer's shipyard specialized in the construction of a new, screw-driven iron steamship designed by Palmer himself. Palmer's ships revolutionized the coastal coal-shipping trade because they were much faster and more reliable than the traditional sailing vessels; they could get coal from Newcastle to London in five days, whereas the sailing ships generally needed a month. Soon Palmer's was building steam colliers in such quantities that it was said they "built them by the mile and cut them off in required lengths."

A second factor in the rise of Palmer's was the construction of fighting vessels for the British Admiralty. During the Crimean War (1854–56), Palmer's received an Admiralty contract to build an ironclad floating battery for use in the siege of Kronstadt. Though the war was over before this vessel, the HMS *Terror,* could see action in the Crimea, the navy was pleased with its new *Terror,* and would order many more ships from the Palmer's yard in the future.

As the Palmer's Jarrow yards expanded, C. M. Palmer vertically integrated his enterprise by installing rolling mills and blast furnaces and by setting up his own shipping firm. In its heyday the Palmer's yard was one of Britain's most self-sufficient, maintaining in-house control over the production process from iron manufacture to carpentry and rigging. As the overseer of this entire operation, Charles Palmer earned a deserved reputation for dynamic entrepreneurship. He was clearly one of those "men of enterprise" beloved by nineteenth-century political economists.

Jarrow, the town C. M. Palmer put on England's heavy-industrial map, now became a typical "company town." It was one of those small places where everything—local trade, social life, housing, cultural amenities, politics—revolved around the Great Firm. One admirer of C. M. Palmer wrote in 1904, "So completely is the town identified with the works, that it might more appropriately be called 'Palmer's Town.' " Not surprisingly, the company controlled the town council, and Palmer himself became Jarrow's first mayor after incorporation, in 1875.

But if Palmer "made" Jarrow as the support community for his sprawling works, what kind of town did he make? A reporter from neighboring Newcastle had this to say of "Palmer's Town" in 1858:

> There is a prevailing blackness about the neighborhood. The houses are black, the ships are black, the sky is black, and if you go there for an hour or two, reader, you too will be black. The architecture of the place has a strong tendency to extreme simplicity—the straight up-and-down brickism common to manufacturing districts—and the atmosphere is of smoke—smoky.

Jarrow's proletarian streets were not just black but also cramped and disease ridden. As the town's population expanded along with the shipbuilding yards,* the incoming workers, most of them Irish, crowded into rows of "pit cottages" built in the early nineteenth century. These dwellings had one room and a ceiling not more than six feet from the floor. Since there were no toilets, sewage was dumped on the ground in back. Occupancy varied greatly according to activity at the yard, but it was not uncommon for fourteen people to live in these hovels, all sleeping together regardless of age or sex. Medical officers sent by the government

---

*Jarrow had a population of 3,834 in 1851. By 1891 it had risen to 33,675, an increase of almost 1,000 percent.

The Jarrow crusaders set off on their 300-mile walk to London. *Inset:* Ellen Wilkinson and Mayor Thompson. *South Tyneside Libraries*

Ellen Wilkinson regales the Jarrow marchers during a lunch break en route. *South Tyneside Libraries*

As they arrive in London, the crusaders are described as "looking like a walking Depressed Area." *South Tyneside Libraries*

The Jarrow crusade's mongrel dog mascot. He wears a tag saying "Jarrow Protest March to London." *South Tyneside Libraries*

to inspect conditions there were appalled by the crowding and, even more, by the unsanitary conditions the workers lived in. One of the doctors wrote of a "most foul liquid . . . oozing through the walls and running according to the level of the ground either into the yards and beneath the houses, or into the back streets." Even when sanitary conditions improved somewhat in the late nineteenth century, the incidence of deaths in Jarrow due to contagious diseases (smallpox, scarlet fever, typhoid, and so on) was much higher than in other British towns of comparable size. In 1883 it stood at 51 per 10,000, as opposed to 24.6 per 10,000 nationwide. Annual plagues of diarrhea swept away many children. The town council, controlled by Palmer's, refused to tax property owners for a modern sewage system until the early twentieth century.

When he visited Jarrow in 1933, Priestley guessed that this town, moribund in the Great Slump, could "never have been alive" as "a real town, a piece of urban civilization." For the most part, he was right. Busy and productive though Jarrow was in its heyday, it lacked community vigor and even the most rudimentary urban amenities. For most of the nineteenth century, it had no hospital, and it had no municipal library until 1937. There were no public parks. What nineteenth-century Jarrow *did* have in abundance was pubs—thirty-one in 1865. Drunkenness on the streets and on the job became such a problem that in 1904 Palmer's finally opened a company coffee room to compete with the pubs and gin houses.

Jarrow's Dickensian grimness was making the town's name a byword for industrial squalor by the late nineteenth century. Yet there was another side to this place that was much less publicized. For its foremen and highly skilled workers, the Palmer's yard built some two hundred detached houses, which the occupants bought rather than rented. In the late 1850s Jarrow actually had more property owners than any other town of its size in England. Palmer's also sponsored a local mechanics' institute (a self-help educational center) and financed an imposing new town hall. There was a great deal of local pride in these institutions, and much resentment that outsiders seemed unaware of them when they made Jarrow synonymous with black blight and squalor. However, this pride reflected a certain narrowness of vision, a class-based myopia that focused on Jarrow's few amenities for the better-off rather than on the horrifying conditions under which most of the town's inhabitants lived.

Palmer's paternalistic innovations did not prevent the local shipyard from suffering a number of labor disputes in the middle to late nineteenth century. In 1865 Palmer's "locked out" its employees in order to discourage union organization. But workers were in short supply at that time, and Palmer's was forced to permit formation of the Amalgamated Society of Engineers. The organization grew so rapidly that by the 1870s Palmer's had become a "union shop." In that same decade the union waged a major strike for the nine-hour day. It won this struggle partly because Palmer's was going through one of its periodic slumps and had to cut back production.

These labor disputes, significant though they were, by no means turned Jarrow into a hotbed of political radicalism in the late nineteenth and early twentieth centuries. Not only was C. M. Palmer, a member of the Liberal party, elected mayor in 1875; he also served as the town's MP from 1876 until his death, in 1907. In 1892 he easily won reelection to his parliamentary seat against an opponent sent up from London. His supporters included not just the town's relatively small middle-class population but also hundreds of skilled laborors from the Palmer's yard. These men supported Palmer for a number of reasons: he was genuinely charismatic and much respected in the region; he was, for better or worse, the town's central "provider"; and, most of all, he belonged to Jarrow and the Tyneside—not to distant London or the alien south. C. M. Palmer's successes also stemmed from the political impotence of the unskilled Irish workers, who did not become a significant voting force in Jarrow until after the First World War, when most of them voted Labour.

During the first forty years of its existence, the Palmer's yard grew along with the booming British shipbuilding industry, though both suffered occasional minor slumps. A more serious slump hit the industry in the 1890s. At this point C. M. Palmer, who had sold his firm to a limited partnership in 1865 but stayed on as managing director, retired. Chairmanship of the company passed in 1897 to a London lawyer who, according to one authority, "treated the firm merely as a field of investment and hired specialist aides." There was nothing unusual in this—it was part of becoming bigger—but it meant that Palmer's sailed into the rougher waters of turn-of-the-century shipbuilding without a dynamic and experienced captain at the helm.

Soon it hit real trouble. Another big slump in the early twentieth century brought the company to the verge of bankruptcy. Afflicted with a deficit of £128,413 in 1912, Palmer's was saved only by mortgaging its assets and taking out short-term loans at high interest.

These measures kept the company afloat until the First World War spurred a wealth of orders from merchant shippers and the Admiralty. By 1915 Palmer's had turned its prewar deficit into a credit of £42,772. Throughout the war, it continued to make handsome profits, and in 1918 it was riding high, increasing its mortgage stock by one million. The following year it paid a 12 percent dividend to its shareholders. A "spirit of euphoria and limitless expansion" reigned.

The euphoria was premature, to say the least. It soon turned out that the war boom was itself a hidden curse. To meet surging demand Palmer's, along with other British yards, dramatically expanded production capacity. But shipbuilders in other countries did the same. The United States, in particular, emerged as a major competitor, responsible between 1914 and 1918 for some 86 percent of the net increase in world tonnage. Once the war was over, the world's shipbuilding industry had much more productive capacity than was necessary. Demand in Britain was particularly low because that country had confiscated a good part of the German merchant fleet in war reparations. A further dramatic decline in demand for new shipbuilding was one result of the Washington naval agreement of 1922, according to which the nine major industrial nations consented not to build capital naval ships for ten years.

By the mid-twenties, therefore, British shipbuilding was in serious trouble. A report issued in July 1925 described the situation in the northeast as "extremely depressing." Nine of the fifteen firms on the river Wear were without work of any kind. In October of that year there were no new vessels in any of the berths. It was also in that year that a British shipping company placed an order for five ships with a German yard that could deliver the ships at three-fourths of the cost projected by the lowest British bidder. Britain was rapidly pricing itself out of the world shipbuilding market.

Palmer's suffered along with the other British yards. In 1925, a "black year for Jarrow," it built only three small ships and lost a total of £206,946. Much of the trouble Palmer's encountered stemmed from the general malaise afflicting the British shipbuilding industry but was compounded by its poor management decisions. In the expansionist euphoria at the end of the war, Palmer's had begun buying up subsidiaries. It bought a shipyard at Amble, a colliery in Durham, an iron-ore mine in Spain. Wrote one commentator, "To buy so often and so recklessly when the market was in boom conditions was hardly the mark of wise management. . . . And these profligate decisions made the company even more vulnerable to the cruel blows that were about to fall. In 1920–21 profits fell to £85,000 and in the next two years there was an aggregate deficit of £109,000." By 1925 the company's debt had risen to £462,000, and it rose another £211,000 in the following year. Facing bankruptcy again, the company reduced the value of its shares from one pound to five shillings and suspended some of its interest payments.

Perhaps these measures would have enabled Palmer's to recover and rebuild its fortunes had there been nothing ahead except smooth economic sailing. But 1929, a good year for many industries, was so bad for Palmer's that it extended its moratorium on debt payments. All that the managers at Palmer's could do now was hope that the worst was over. In fact, it had barely begun.

The world depression of the early thirties hit shipbuilding even harder than most industries. Dependent as they were on the health of the export trade, shipbuilders were among the first heavy manufacturers to lose business in the Great Slump. In 1930 northeastern shipbuilders launched just over 600,000 gross tons, but in 1931 that figure was only 68,000. Unemployment in British shipbuilding as a whole was almost 50 percent in 1931; in the Tyneside it was 60 percent. Weeds were already starting to grow in the berths.

With the onset of the depression, leaders of the British shipbuilding industry recognized that their branch had a production capacity far in excess of market demand. Dozens of firms were competing for orders that a handful could easily fill. In light of this situation, they collectively decided to cut back production capacity by phasing out some of the weaker yards. The agency that presided over this process was the National Shipbuilders' Security Limited (NSS), and the guiding spirit behind NSS was Sir James Lithgow, owner of Lithgow's of Port Glasgow, one of Britain's largest shipbuilding yards.

Sir James, called by his biographer "the last of the tycoons," may have come of age in the anxiety-ridden twentieth century, but he really belonged to the more confident world of the Victorians. He ran his business the way he organized the shooting parties on his estate in Scotland: with military precision and little margin for slackers. *He*, at least, had no trouble identifying the reasons for Britain's economic troubles in the modern era; they included rampant profligacy among the lower orders and a tendency on the part of weak-willed politicians to give in to the workers' every demand. In a statement entitled "Our Present Economic Condition" (1925), which Sir James inserted into the cornerstone of his new country house, he argued that postwar improvements in workers' wages and working conditions had given "rise to the belief, not only amongst the wage earners themselves, but also amongst large sections of politicians, that the standards of earlier days had been unduly depressed, and could be permanently improved upon without detriment to the industrial activity of the country." The inevitable consequence of this development was that those British industries (like shipbuilding) which had to compete with foreign producers were "severely handicapped," while government was "too fearful of popularity to call boldly for an all-around reduction of costs."

When Lithgow's colleagues first raised the possibility of "rationalization" in adjusting to the severely depressed conditions in the shipbuilding industry, Lithgow was hesitant to go along: he claimed to dislike "combinations" of all sorts, even those among industrialists. What changed his mind was his growing conviction that if the owners did not take drastic action to cut surplus production capacity, the entire industry would continue to lose profits and—equally frightening—the government might intervene. "If the owners could [rationalize]," he now argued, "they could keep their industrial independence and avoid damaging bankruptcies." But he warned that the actions of the NSS would not bring quick riches. Employing a characteristic military analogy, he told his colleagues that he saw the production cuts "as reserve trenches upon which troops fall back when unable to hold the advanced, more extended, lines. In the process the feeble at least have to be sacrificed, and perhaps many more. Once we are all in the reserve trenches, we ought to be perfectly safe and comfortable, ready to advance as our strength increases to occupy our former position."

With Lithgow as its presiding officer, the NSS began operations in late 1930. According to its charter, it would purchase obsolete or redundant yards, scrap their equipment, and close them to further shipbuilding activity for a minimum of forty years. The corporation started with £1,000,000 in debenture stock, which was augmented by a levy of 1 percent on the price of all British ships laid down after November 1, 1930. Eventually NSS raised enough money through the levy to avoid having to issue more stock.

In its first year of operation NSS bought up and closed down three yards, all of them in Scotland. Lithgow had promised that NSS "would not put a man out of work," that concentration "would actually improve chances of employment." In fact, unemployment in the industry continued to rise. At the end of 1930 some 92,000 British shipbuilding workers were out of work; by 1931 the number had increased to 117,000. Some of this was the result of NSS closings, for not all the men put out of work by them could or would migrate to other yards, and in any case the remaining "healthy" firms were in no position to employ them.

Soon NSS turned its attention to the Tyneside, where conditions continued to deteriorate. Palmer's led the pack of weak firms there. In 1931 it built only one ship and in 1932 only two, both for the Admiralty. On July 19, 1932, Palmer's launched the HMS *Duchess*, its last. Another six-month moratorium on its debt payments kept the company alive until mid-1933, but when no more orders materialized the company's directors had no choice but to declare bankruptcy. NSS became the "receiver" of the bankrupt firm in a London courtroom on the last day of July 1933. Palmer's immediately closed its doors and began liquidating its assets. It never produced ships again.

A great cry of protest arose in the black streets of Jarrow. The townspeople accused NSS generally, and Lithgow personally, of killing off the shipyard in order to enhance profits elsewhere. A delegation from Jarrow made this charge in the House of Commons shortly after the closing of Palmer's, and Ellen Wilkinson repeated it in her book on Jarrow, *The Town That Was Murdered* (1939). Here she also argued that Palmer's was technically a good company, its workers "in the front rank of their craft." Palmer's, she claimed, was "killed because it was a powerful competitor . . . rooted out, not because it was inefficient, but because it stood in the way of a group of big financial interests, who wished to consolidate their grip on the shipping industry and get control of shipping prices."

One can understand and sympathize with this charge. NSS seems to have been a ruthless operation and Lithgow himself almost a caricature of the capitalist ogre. On a more objective level, though, the accusation makes little sense. The workers at Palmer's may indeed have been capable, but their company was not. It had been mismanaged since the war and was no longer technologically advanced, even by British standards.* Moreover, the yard was corrupt. When he visited Jarrow shortly after Palmer's closed, Priestley heard stories about lorry loads of valuable material having been driven in one gate at Palmer's, signed for, and then quietly driven out another. He heard about jobs so blatantly rushed that the builders had used wooden pegs in place of steel rivets. And of course the company had been financially on the skids, indeed bankrupt. Even the ruthless Lithgow could not kill a corpse.

Palmer's might have been saved by government subsidies, but it made more sense, if the government was going to subsidize shipbuilding, to help the yards

---

*In the thirties British-built ships no longer ruled the waves. France had the fastest service on the South Atlantic run, and Germany, with the *Europa* and the *Bremen*, had the two fastest and most sophisticated North Atlantic liners.

that had the best chances of survival. In fact, the government did introduce a modest loan program in 1935, but firms that received loans had to promise to scrap two tons for every ton they built. Although this helped some yards get by, Britain's share of world production continued to decline. The northeast, which before the war had built a third of the world's shipping, built about 12 percent in 1936. In that year only twenty-two berths out of fifty-six on the Tyne were occupied.

Meanwhile Jarrow was in dire straits. Almost 70 percent of its work force was now unemployed. One of the jobless later recalled that there was nothing to do in Jarrow but "stand at the top of Ormonde Street . . . talk about our woes and troubles . . . then go back [home] and get fed." What few amenities the town had were closing down. The musical society was disbanded and the debating club suspended. Jarrow's one claim to cultural fame in this period seems almost pathetic. In 1936 it celebrated the centennial of the publication of Dickens's *Pickwick Papers* by inviting Mr. Barnaby Williams to impersonate Dickens's comic characters. In this same month the local paper reported a rash of teenage crime and wife beatings. Clearly the town needed what comic relief it could find.

Against this grim background the Jarrow town council launched a desperate appeal in London for the reopening of the Palmer's shipyard. Walter Runciman, the head of the Board of Trade, answered this appeal as follows: "Nothing is to be gained by giving Jarrow the impression that its shipyard can be revived. The best thing is to make a clean sweep of the premises, and throw open to purchase one of the best sites in the world for the establishment of prosperous new industries."

For a moment it seemed that a new enterprise might be built on the site of the Palmer's yard. Late in 1934 a syndicate proposed to build a new Thomas steelworks on the Palmer's site. The syndicate hoped to be able to offer lower-than-standard prices for its products because of more efficient production techniques. This may have been its undoing, for the Iron and Steel Federation, which had a near-monopoly on steel production in Britain, did not want another modern steel plant opened. While negotiations were under way between the Jarrow syndicate and the federation, two firms already in the cartel began rolling the kinds of products contemplated at Jarrow. Undoubtedly this increased the cartel's unwillingness to see another plant started in Britain. Yet membership in the federation was crucial for the prospective Jarrow operation, for without it the new plant would lack access to markets and raw materials controlled by the cartel.

When it became aware of the federation's resistance, the Jarrow town council appealed to the government to force the cartel to open its doors. It sent a resolution to the prime minister urging him to use his powers "to call upon the Steel Federation to cease blocking the plans for a Jarrow steel works." The upshot of this appeal was another statement by Runciman: "Jarrow must look elsewhere than at iron and steel for her new industries." The government, added an aide to the prime minister, "was not prepared to force iron and steel into Jarrow against technical industrial opinion."

To this the mayor of Jarrow responded, "I hope the people of Jarrow will not accept the decision of the Government as they did when the shipyards were closed. We as a town are going to see that notice is taken of us. That is what we elect a parliament for." Members of the council seconded this view. Several spoke of "walking to London" to give the government Jarrow's reply to this latest cruel rebuff. One of them, however, suggested that more than an "ordinary walk" might be needed. "I am willing enough to march," he said, ". . . but now I think we should try to get down to London with a couple of bombs in our pockets. Yes, I am perfectly serious. We should go down there with bombs in our pockets. These people at Westminster have no use for us anyway. These people do not realize that there are people living in Jarrow today under conditions that a respectable farmer would not keep swine." Yet another council member noted bitterly that sanctions against Italy for her invasion of Ethiopia had been lifted, "but sanctions against Jarrow are not withdrawn."

The proposal that Jarrow men go down to London with bombs in their pockets may have been seriously made, but it was also made in the heat of the moment. The man who proposed this new edition of the Gunpowder Plot (Councillor David Riley) turned out later to be an advocate of moderation. Indeed, what is notable about Jarrow's response to its setbacks was its final determination to stick to *parliamentary* measures as a way of expressing its outrage.

This decision reflected a broader and equally intriguing aspect of the Jarrow scene: the town's disinclination in the midst of grim depression to support extremist political parties, of either the Left or the Right. A Communist party candidate polled well in Jarrow's North Ward, its poorest, in the 1933 municipal elections; but there was never any prospect that the town as a whole would go Red. In fact, the CP despaired of making a serious impact in the Tyneside, which it declared "the weakest and least satisfactory of all Party Districts." In Jarrow the Communist party had only seven members in 1940. The British Union of Fascists, which also made a concerted effort to capitalize on unemployment in the northeast, fared even worse than the Communists. It had no members in Jarrow at all.

Instead of moving to the extreme left or right, Jarrow sent a moderate Labour party man to the House in the 1920s, and in 1931, at the beginning of the depression, elected a Tory to represent them. In subsequent general elections (beginning with 1935), Jarrow drifted back into the Labour camp, where it has remained ever since.

Perhaps the main explanation for Jarrow's rejection of radical solutions, especially of the Communist variety, lay in the strong anti-Communist influence of the Catholic church among the poorer Irish laborers. Jarrow's craft unions, particularly the boilermakers, were also militantly anti-Communist. It was significant, too, that the town's Conservative party was not cut off from the local work force, and identified with its frustrations. Thus, though Jarrow was an angry town in the mid-thirties, it was not a revolutionary one.

"RED ELLEN"

Just as Jarrow's sad history encapsulated the rise and decline of Britain's traditional heavy industries, so the career of Jarrow's most famous member of Parliament, Ellen Wilkinson, embodied key developments in the history of the British Left in the twentieth century. Over the course of her thirty-year career she was associated with a variety of leftist institutions and causes, including the Independent Labour party, the trade union movement, women's emancipation, the British Communist party, Fabianism, Guild Socialism, the general strike of 1926, antifascism, and, above all, the crusade against mass unemployment. She became one of Britain's first female members of Parliament, a pioneer in the women's trade union movement, and, in 1945, Britain's second woman cabinet minister. Summing up her career, one authority on modern British politics suggested that she was arguably twentieth-century England's "most important woman politician." Though she never attained Margaret Thatcher's supreme political office, in a sense she paved the way for Thatcher (not, of course, for Thatcher's politics) because she "made the role of women in high politics credible and effective." She did this through a combination of unrelenting hard work, finely honed political instincts, great oratorical ability, and tremendous personal charisma. She needed all these assets to make her mark, for the British Left was every bit as male dominated and unreceptive to woman politicians as the Tory Right.

Contemporaries described Ellen Wilkinson as a tiny but powerful human dynamo. Even shorter than Engelbert Dollfuss, she had a slight but well-proportioned body and a head of brilliant red hair. Her physical features and her hard-driving, impetuous nature earned her epithets like "Elfin Fury," "Fiery Particle," and "Little Miss Perky." Tough as she was, she also had a softer side. Her secretary claimed that she could "charm the birds off trees." Apparently she could also charm the pants off men, for she had affairs with several of her political colleagues. Nevertheless, politics, rather than politicians, remained her consuming passion, and she never married.

Ellen Wilkinson often boasted that she was "born into proletarian purple"; it would be more accurate to say that she was born into the poor but respectable lower middle class. Her father was an insurance salesman who voted Tory and her mother a housewife with "a passion for cleanliness of house and person." Hers was a home that kept the aspidistra—George Orwell's symbol for obsessive petit bourgeois propriety—flying prominently in the window box.

Wilkinson was brought up a strict Methodist, and she maintained her faith even after she discovered agnostic or atheistic writers like Darwin and T. H. Huxley in her teens. "This [discovery]," she later confessed, "never upset my cheerful faith in my friend God. . . . I didn't get this fuzzy mess sorted out until I discovered Karl Marx in my early twenties." Precisely how Marx managed to reconcile Darwinism, materialism, and Methodism she does not tell us, but the answer might lie in her biographer's admission that Miss Wilkinson was "no intellectual." Whatever the explanation, Wilkinson remained in the church all her life. "I am still a Methodist," she told the Left Book Club in 1939; "you can never get its special glow out of your head."

As a child, Ellen rebelled against authority and tended to identify with the downtrodden. But she did not rebel against her family's belief in the value of education. Through a great deal of hard work, she managed to gain admission to the University of Manchester in 1910—an unusual accomplishment for a woman of her social background. At university she became active in the Independent Labour party, finding in socialism "the answer to the chaotic rebellion of [her] school years." She also plunged into the campaign for the enfranchisement of women, thereby launching a lifelong commitment to feminist causes. Surprisingly enough, the fiery Wilkinson did not condone the use of violence to achieve the vote for women. She preferred parliamentary agitation to the smashing of windows, the burning of letter boxes, or the slashing of paintings in the National Gallery. Thus she spent no time in prison under the "cat and mouse law," never went on a hunger strike or suffered the indignity of forced feeding.*

At this time Wilkinson took up another lasting commitment—Fabianism. As a member of the university's Fabian Society, she met George Bernard Shaw, who later recalled her somewhat dismissively as "an amusing and interesting little red-haired spitfire." She continued to work on behalf of the Fabian Society even after she became committed to a more radical brand of socialism in the twenties. Here again we find evidence of an intellectual eclecticism that might have lacked doctrinal rigor but that had the advantage of keeping her from becoming a narrow sectarian.

During the First World War, Wilkinson threw herself passionately into the cause of antimilitarism. While many other women were presenting white feathers—symbols of cowardice—to conscientious objectors, Ellen was doing her best to get the men out of the trenches as quickly as possible. She joined the Women's International League for Peace and Freedom (WIL), which campaigned for an immediate truce without annexations or indemnities. The WIL later developed close ties to the League of Nations, an institution that Wilkinson, like Haile Selassie, came to regard as the world's greatest hope for lasting peace. During the war Wilkinson also took up the cause of female workers on the home front. As a functionary of the Amalgamated Union of Co-operative Employees, she campaigned for equal pay for women shop assistants and better working conditions for munitions workers, the majority of whom were women. She saw these campaigns as "breaching the wall of prejudice that ordains a woman must be paid less, irrespective of work done . . . simply because she is a woman." In her union

---

*The "cat and mouse act" was a measure introduced in 1913 to provide for the release on license of "suffragettes" who refused to take food while in prison for violent offenses. The license would be revoked if the released prisoner committed a further offense.

activities her sex was certainly a handicap, for the male labor union bosses tended to regard her as an intruder. At the same time, however, they learned to respect her courage, drive, and organizational talents. Gradually she was able to overcome the prejudices.

In the early twenties the British Left became increasingly radicalized, as workers and demobilized soldiers found that their country was far from "the land fit for heroes to live in" that Prime Minister David Lloyd George had promised it would be. Some left-wing intellectuals, moreover, found *their* promise in revolutionary Russia, which they believed offered a model for the rest of the industrial world. As one of them put it, "There might be something good coming out of the war after all; for if the Russian people could overthrow their government, could not the Germans, the French, or the British?" Wilkinson shared this enthusiasm, at least for a time. Impatient with the Labour party's slow pace toward the socialist millennium, she became a founding member of the British Communist party. She then went to Moscow in 1921 to attend the founding of the Red International of Labour Unions, which was organized to "win unions from the policy of class collaboration to class struggle." Wilkinson fully accepted this principle. She condemned the moderate Labour leaders' calls for compromise between workers and employers as "working with the enemy" and "whoring with capitalist forces."

Wilkinson's Communist affiliation also brought her into contact with the National Union of Working Men (NUWM), a Communist-backed protest group led by Walter Hannington. Under Hannington's direction the NUWM took to the streets in the twenties and early thirties to force the government to provide more public-service jobs and higher unemployment benefits for those who remained without work. It also staged "commando raids" on factories where workers were putting in overtime. Its sometimes violent tactics brought it into conflict not only with the police but also with the Labour party and trade union leadership. The group seemed not to know whether its chief goal was improving the lot of the unemployed through piecemeal reforms or smashing the entire capitalist system. Wilkinson shared in this ambivalence: she urged the unemployed to agitate in favor of reforms but also insisted that the system could not be changed without a revolution.

Committed as she apparently was to the Moscow line, Wilkinson did not remain a Communist for long. Like many British leftists, she soon came to resent Moscow's orders to "bolshevize" the European Communist movement by purging national parties of all but the most militant and faithful followers. By 1924 she had dropped out of the party and distanced herself somewhat from the NUWM. Nevertheless, she continued to believe that the more moderate Labour party executive and Trades Union Council (TUC) were not doing enough to help the unemployed, that they could learn something from Hannington's militant confrontationism. When it came time to organize the Jarrow crusade in the mid-thirties, she would remember Hannington and consult him.

Wilkinson broke into mainstream electoral politics in the mid-twenties. After serving briefly as a city councillor in her native Manchester, she stood as Labour party candidate in 1924 for the constituency of Middlesbrough East, a depressed steel-making region in the northeast. She was then thirty-three, but looked so young that one of her opponents dismissed her as a "school girl." Her campaign focused on Middlesbrough's high unemployment and its higher-than-average rates of tuberculosis and infant mortality. "What a town to have the privilege of fighting," she said. "Here capitalism reveals all its hard ugliness and the struggle for bread is bitter. Middlesbrough is a book of illustrations to Karl Marx."

Although Middlesbrough might also have provided the illustrations for a Victorian primer on the "proper" place of women in society, Wilkinson managed to win the election by going door-to-door, speaking to the voters in a language they understood, breaking down prejudices with wit, tough talk, and sheer determination. Her victory was all the more remarkable because it cut against the grain of a national Tory landslide sparked by the Zinoviev letter* and a new Red scare. When she joined the three other female MPs in the House of Commons, the august *Times* was moved to comment, "The advent seems almost worthy of a commemorative mural painting in the lobby [of the House] by Sir William Orphen, alongside that of Queen Elizabeth, as both have the same attractive shade of bright red hair." Reading this, Wilkinson must have known that she had her work cut out for her if she was to be taken seriously by the establishment she meant to turn upside down.

Her agenda in the House committed her not only to a fight against the ruling Tory establishment but also to struggles against the leadership of her own Labour party. In opposition to the Labour party executive, which was dominated by the right-wing Labourite Ramsay MacDonald, she campaigned for an extension of the franchise to women under thirty, "because women with no vote are so neglected." Her feminist stance also led her into a battle to open the House of Commons' Strangers' Dining Room to female guests and to improve working conditions for the women members, who were forced to share an office. But her major preoccupation remained unemployment. She spent much of her time trying to persuade her own party to concern itself less with attaining political respectability than with finding employment for the nation's jobless workers. To this end she favored massive public works programs and the nationalization of major industries.

If Wilkinson's militant posture on unemployment and women's rights put her at odds with the moderate Labour party leadership, her role in the general strike of 1926, which climaxed several years of labor unrest centered in the coal-mining industry, confirmed her reputation as Red Ellen. The Labour party executive

---

*On October 25, 1924, extracts of a letter allegedly written by the Comintern's chief, Grigori Zinoviev, appeared in the British press. The letter urged local Communists to promote revolution through acts of sedition. Appearing right before the general election, it undoubtedly contributed to the massive Tory victory. Labour politicians charged that the letter was forged, and indeed it was probably written by anti-Soviet émigrés. Zinoviev himself later became one of the first victims of Stalin's purges.

council, like its counterpart in Vienna a year later, was reluctant to endorse confrontationist measures, such as a general strike, over which it might well lose control. But Wilkinson and her colleagues in the left wing of the Labour party believed that the general-strike weapon offered Labour an opportunity to lead the working classes toward a radical restructuring of the economy. Accordingly, she rushed around the country speaking before local strike committees and encouraging the workers to stay away from their jobs.

One can get a vivid sense of her activities—and her own perception of them—from an autobiographical novel she wrote about the strike, called *Clash*. On the eve of the strike "Joan," the heroine, is somewhat jaded by all her experiences as a labor organizer. "At the age of twenty-six she had begun to think of her fellows simply as pink faces before a platform, or as lines of dark figures into whose hands she thrust meeting bills." But the self-sacrificing spirit of the strikers renews her radical commitment, turning her into "a living red flag, the spirit of revolution." Joan is terribly embittered by the TUC's decision to call off the general strike after only nine days. Wilkinson vented this bitterness more systematically in *A Workers' History of the Great Strike*, which she wrote with two of her radical colleagues. "No attempt was made by Mr. Citrine [head of the TUC] or any other speaker [at a poststrike inquest] to explain or justify why the strike was called off," the authors complained. The Labour party leadership refused

> to realize that the whole working class is engaged in a bitter struggle for its standards of life in which no quarter will be given by either side. . . . Our leaders must frankly prepare for struggle on a class basis. The corpse at the "Inquest" was not the Theory of the General Strike, but the nineteenth century trade union leadership, which refused to face up to the class issues involved in the . . . struggle.

Since the coal strike, which had kicked off the general strike, continued well after the broader walkout ended, Wilkinson now turned her attention to relief operations for the miners' families. With a group of militant Labour party politicians and trade unionists, she visited labor groups in America in search of financial support for the British miners. Wilkinson and her colleagues proved effective fund-raisers, and the American Federation of Labor made a substantial contribution to their cause. This did not prevent the miners' strike from collapsing a few months later, but it helped confirm America's reputation as a soft touch for needy old-world politicians, from Winston Churchill to Bernadette Devlin.

In the late twenties Wilkinson focused much of her considerable energy on feminist issues. She tried to get more women appointed as police constables, but with little success: British police apparently were not called Bobbies for nothing. Wilkinson fought as well to get women admitted to the diplomatic corps, from which they had been excluded on the grounds that they could not keep a secret. She worked—with more success—to eliminate the inequity by which British women who married aliens traditionally lost their citizenship, while men did not. Her special concern for working-class women was evident in her attack on Winston Churchill, then chancellor of the Exchequer, for his decision to tax the cheap artificial silk on which poorer women tended to rely for their underclothing. On the domestic front, Wilkinson provoked a major uproar by suggesting that under existing conditions the married state for women was tantamount to slavery. One women's issue that Ellen did not pursue was the question of contraception and state-sponsored advice on birth control. The Labour party executive council elected not to take a stand on this hotly debated question, for fear of splitting labor ranks. For once, Ellen agreed with the council and ducked the issue every time it came up. No doubt she did so because her constituency included a high percentage of Roman Catholics, although she must have understood the correlation between oppressed conditions and large families among the poor.

Wilkinson's preoccupation with women's issues did not prevent her from carrying on her fight to reduce unemployment and to better the lot of those who remained without work. She was indignant over the new National Government's Unemployment Insurance Bill (1931), which not only reduced benefits but deprived married women who had lost jobs of any relief at all. She also opposed the government's retrenchment program, which she rightly feared would result in yet higher rates of unemployment.

These were stirring times for Wilkinson: the "Hungry Thirties" were her "golden age." For most of the first half of the decade, however, she was in the political wilderness because she lost her parliamentary seat in the Labour debacle of October 1931. Like many of her colleagues, she blamed MacDonald for Labour's defeat, arguing that his efforts "to put patches on the social fabric" were "treacherously wrong." It is no use, she declared, "building Jerusalem in perorations; the average voter wants to see the blueprint of the city."

In fact, Labour's loss in 1931 was the result not of a wholesale desertion from the Labour ranks on the part of working-class voters but of a massive middle-class vote for the National Government. The middle-class flight to the National Government was propelled partly by fears that Labour might reverse its financial orthodoxy and inaugurate dramatically higher unemployment benefits. Walter Runciman played on this fear when he claimed that depositors in the Post Office Savings Bank would lose their savings by Labour withdrawals to finance the dole. Significantly enough, a high percentage of those voters who did desert the Labour party were women. Ellen Wilkinson had helped secure the vote for women under thirty (and over twenty-one) through the Equal Franchise Act of 1928. Now these women helped turn her and her party out of power.

Wilkinson's defeat in 1931 by no means suspended her political career, for she remained active in Labour party and trade union politics. But it did give her a little more time to pursue a social life that was as eclectic as her intellectual makeup. She went to parties at H. G. Wells's house and visited her friend Nancy Astor at her country mansion, Cliveden, a name soon to become synonymous with upper-class appeasement of Nazi Germany. She went to tea parties with

Bertrand Russell in Bloomsbury, played golf, and mingled socially with Winston Churchill and Lord Beaverbrook, the conservative newspaper publisher. She drove an Austin Seven between a furnished flat in Bloomsbury and a small country house in Buckinghamshire. But even in this social whirl, politics was never far from her mind. She sometimes crashed her car because she was concentrating on her next political move when she should have been concentrating on the road.

Wilkinson's visits to Cliveden notwithstanding, one of the issues that preoccupied her most in the thirties was the menace of fascism. She was one of England's most vocal opponents of Mussolini, whose invasion of Ethiopia she denounced in the strongest terms. Hitler's rise to power frightened her even more, and she was appalled that her countrymen seemed unconcerned by what was happening in Germany. In 1934, a year after Hitler's assumption of power, she wrote (with Edward Conze, a fellow socialist) a call to arms called *Why Fascism?* This turgid little book offered a traditional Marxist interpretation of fascism as "one response to the breakdown of liberal laissez-faire capitalism in the war and postwar era." Fascism, the authors argued, developed most successfully "in those countries where imperialism has either lost its colonial basis, as in Germany, or is struggling to obtain a sufficient one, as in Italy." The question, then, was how fascism might fare in capitalist countries that maintained significant but crumbling empires. In other words, how would it fare in England?

Wilkinson and Conze devoted the last part of their book to an analysis of British fascism. Their fundamental concern was less with the leader of the British Union of Fascists, Oswald Mosley,* than with "well-marked tendencies in Britain which may lead to a different type of fascism from Mosley's." She and Conze went on to argue that the National Government itself might emerge as that "different type of fascism." "The conditions of [the National Government's] birth and the size of its majority are reminiscent of the elections which swept Hitler into power," they argued. "Stripped of all the theatricality which surrounds fascism, the National Government may develop into a distinctly British form of fascism. It has all the features which distinguish fascism from pure and simple reaction." The chances that the National Government would move in this direction, they believed, depended largely on the extent to which the British economic system managed to hold its own. Should capitalism continue to founder on its internal "contradictions," and the unemployed become more rebellious, then Britain's middle and upper classes would undoubtedly demand a "strong hand," just as they had in Italy and in Germany. The Labour movement, having made a "fetish of democracy," might be unable to resist this trend. The danger, then, was great: "It is simply absurd to rest on the cushion of English national character—the boarding house comfort that 'Englishmen don't do such things.'"

---

*Oswald Mosley founded the British Union of Fascists in 1932 after the political failure of his progressive New Party. Impressed first by Mussolini, then by Hitler, he moved the BUF in an increasingly anti-Semitic and militarist direction. In 1936 the BUF provoked violent riots in London's East End. Mosley's following declined after the Public Order Act of 1936 banned private armies.

It may indeed be a mythical piety that the British are more civil than other people, but Wilkinson's analysis of Fascist prospects in Britain suggests that she greatly exaggerated her countrymen's vulnerability to this movement, just as she misrepresented the essential nature of the National Government. The real danger in the mid-thirties was not that MacDonald or his Conservative successor, Stanley Baldwin, would become dictators and overturn traditional British liberties but that returning prosperity in much of Britain would allow the government to continue to neglect those areas that were not recovering. At the Conservative party conference of 1936, Baldwin's parliamentary secretary insisted that people should stop harping on unemployment and start taking note of "the important thing, and that is the positive achievement [of the government] in increased employment." Even if such neglect did not produce a serious revolutionary challenge to the existing order, it demanded to be redressed.

Ellen Wilkinson may have misunderstood the final political implications of Britain's Great Slump, but she instinctively appreciated the human cost of mass unemployment. This appreciation brought her back into parliamentary politics in the mid-thirties, now in the constituency that had become synonymous with depression-era suffering: Jarrow.

Although it is understandable why Wilkinson should have turned to Jarrow, it is perhaps less obvious why Jarrow might have turned to her. Albeit no longer affiliated with the Communist party, Red Ellen still stood well to the left of any of the politicians who had represented Jarrow in the past. Of course, she was also an "outsider" and, most damaging of all, a woman. In fact, her nomination to stand as the Labour party candidate for Jarrow in the 1935 general election created a great deal of dissension in the town's Labour ranks. Some worried about her Communist past; others expressed doubts that a woman could understand the financial and economic issues affecting Jarrow's future.

Just as in Middlesbrough East, however, Wilkinson quickly overcame doubts and prejudices in Jarrow by plunging headlong into the local political scene, addressing countless meetings, banging on doors, striding the black streets of her adopted town in an old, threadbare coat that "she kept for Jarrow to make her equal to the Jarrow folk and they to her. . . ." Apparently she had the good sense to leave her car and golf clubs in Bloomsbury.

Wilkinson not only won over her party but won her constituency by a healthy margin. Her victory was in part a measure of Jarrow's radicalization since the preceding general election, in 1931; in part it also reflected Wilkinson's skill as a politician. In essence she won by focusing on Jarrow's sense of having been passed by in the nation's economic recovery. Her central campaign promise was to make sure that the leaders in Westminster did not continue to forget the people of Jarrow. Jarrow's population immediately understood that Wilkinson was a fighter and that she would fight hard on their behalf. Red Ellen quickly became "Our Ellen."

Immediately after her election Wilkinson led a small delegation of Jarrow officials to Westminster to plead for government assistance in revitalizing Tyneside industry. The government, she insisted, should regard the entire region, with its coal, steel, chemicals, and shipbuilding, "as one big experimental area . . . dovetailing the various industrial interests." If private industry could not be induced to reclaim the region's economy, then the government should do so by nationalizing the relevant industries and pumping in new resources. "I am sick of hearing about the sacred rights of private property," she declared. "I want to hear about the sacred rights of human life."

This statement, which could have served as Ellen Wilkinson's epitaph, would have been fitting, too, as her personal slogan in the Jarrow crusade, the most dramatic and best-remembered event in her political career.

ORGANIZING THE MARCH

Although Ellen Wilkinson may be remembered most of all for her participation in the Jarrow crusade, one should not assume that she was primarily responsible for either its initial organization or the shape it eventually took. Inspiration came from the Jarrow city council, which was considering ways to call the nation's attention to the town's difficulties. The city magistrates might refuse to sit in judgment of their fellow citizens; town officials could boycott a planned visit by the duke of Gloucester; or former shipyard workers might go down to the derelict Palmer's yard and "build a ship of some description, just to show they could still do it." Finally, in a meeting of July 20, 1936, the council voted to mount a march to London as a means of gaining "maximum publicity" for Jarrow's plight.

It was proposed that the march should last a month and reach London just as the new parliamentary session was opening. Money for the enterprise would be raised through donations from institutions and individuals in the region. Jarrow's mayor, J. W. Thompson, a devout Anglican, initially opposed the plan but swung firmly behind it when he was assured that the march would be "nonpolitical" and that it enjoyed the support of the town's entire political and religious establishment. Ellen Wilkinson, having consulted with Wal Hannington, considered an "expert on Hunger Marches," recommended that the Jarrow crusade join up with a march that Hannington's NUWM was planning for the same period. The council flatly rejected this advice. It wanted nothing to do with the Communist-backed NUWM; nor did it like to think of the Jarrow crusade as a hunger march, which conjured up images of emaciated people begging for handouts. The "right to work," not charity or handouts, was to be the theme of the demonstration.

On September 3, six days before the march was set to begin, a little over 200 men took medical examinations to assess their fitness for the rigors of a 300-mile walk in cool and no doubt rainy weather. Only 180 passed the first medical screening, and those who were rejected protested vigorously, but to no avail. The council wanted only "good stout fellows" who would not break down on the journey and discredit the town. The restriction to "fellows" dismayed Ellen Wilkinson, the committed feminist, who argued that women should march, too, since they had suffered in the slump as much as, if not more than, the men. But the council said no: the women should stay home and support their men with encouraging letters and packets of freshly darned socks.

In the first days of October, complaints began to surface in the local press that planning for the march was still incomplete even though the departure date was imminent. An editorial in the *Shields Gazette* attacked the march organizers for not having announced the exact route or the amount of money raised to date. It was also unclear whether the marchers would continue to receive their unemployment benefits when they were on the road. Resolution of this question was crucial, for few men would join the march if it meant sacrificing a month's worth of relief payments. The march organizing committee, led by Councillor David Riley, a big, good-natured Irishman rarely seen without his bowler hat, did his best to reassure the prospective marchers and their families that all these matters would be resolved as quickly as possible. One thing was certain, said Riley: the men would walk to London but return home by bus or train.

There were also complaints from the march organizers. Alderman J. Symons launched a bitter attack on the young men of Jarrow for not volunteering en masse for the march. "I notice," he fumed, "that most of our marchers are middle aged. The young men do not seem to be bothered, and I must say we are very disappointed. They have let us down badly." The young men's inadequate response expressed the irresponsibility that came from having never held a job and supported a family. The mayor touched on this problem when he warned of an "attitude of apathetic resignation adopted by so many." The organizers were also discouraged with the results of their fund-raising campaign. One thousand pounds was needed, but by late September only £757 had been raised. Though the Jarrow march was meant to dramatize the plight of the entire Tyneside, neighboring Newcastle's city council had refused to give the enterprise a grant.

Despite these difficulties and disappointments, the organizers pressed on with their preparations. Reports issued to the local press made it clear that the march was to differ significantly from previous NUWM-sponsored demonstrations against unemployment. These had resembled old-fashioned military campaigns in that the marchers essentially lived off the land, scavenging for food, drink, and women, as they went. The Jarrow crusade, by contrast, would be "respectable." The men would be given pocket money so that they would not have to beg along the route. At their nightly rest stops they would be guests of town officials. If they had to sleep at casual wards, they would not be treated like vagrants and made to do menial tasks for their upkeep. Each marcher would carry towels, brushes, and shaving gear in order to keep up a good appearance. "Appearance is going to have a most amazing effect on people as we go down," said Riley. Since good appearance also required sobriety, the men would carry no alcohol. Finally, to ensure that the march remained "unpolitical," Jarrow's men would avoid all contact with other marchers or local political demonstrations along their route. Declared Riley, "We are going to mind our own business very strictly."

Two days before the departure date, Riley announced the exact route, stop-off points, and other final details. The men would walk a total of 297 miles from the town hall of Jarrow to Hyde Park in London. Their route would take them through large cities like Darlington, Sheffield, and Leeds and through cathedral towns like Durham and Ripon. Their arrival in these places would be prepared by an advance team including both Labour and Conservative party representatives. A secondhand bus filled with equipment, food, camp stoves donated by the Boy Scouts, and medical supplies would accompany the march. So would two medical student volunteers from the Inter-Hospital Socialist Society. Councillor Riley and Alderman Symons would lead the march the entire way. Ellen Wilkinson, who originally thought she would be able to join the march only on "odd days," announced that she could make the entire journey, except for two or three days when she would have to attend the Labour party conference in Edinburgh. Riley was also able to quiet the men's fears regarding payment of their unemployment benefits: their wives or other dependents could claim their checks while the men were away.

Preparations for the march were supported by Jarrow's Conservative party almost as wholeheartedly as by the local Labour movement. Conservatives in Jarrow had been hurt by the depression along with the Labourites, and they absorbed a political blow with the failure of the steelworks initiative, which local people blamed on Tory politicians in the Board of Trade and Ministry of Labour. At the Conservative party conference in Margate in early October, Jarrow's Conservative agent declared, "It was difficult to be a Conservative in Jarrow when [the steelworks plan] failed." He moved a resolution calling for the government to "reestablish the steel or other industries in Jarrow." Instead, the conference passed a general resolution calling blandly for the government "to intensify its efforts to establish industries in the Special Areas."

Frustrated by this rebuff from the central Conservative leadership, the Jarrow Conservatives joined the local Labour party in pushing for a march on London. At the Jarrow Conservative Club's annual leek and vegetable show, the Conservative agent insisted that "all political differences were being sunk in an effort to assist Jarrow industrially." The Labour party "could rest assured that so long as political propaganda was kept out of things, the Conservative Party would loyally collaborate with them in the object that they were all hoping to achieve."

Nothing the Labour party's representatives on the march organizing committee had said could have alarmed the Conservatives. Even Ellen Wilkinson had reluctantly accepted the idea of a nonpolitical march. As a final demonstration of this principle, the march organizers elected to employ "neutral colors" in their banners and insignia. The men would carry large white banners with "Jarrow Crusade" emblazoned in blue letters across them. Blue and white, it seemed, were the colors of the Jarrow Football Club.

WALKING TO WESTMINSTER

On October 5, 1936, a headline in the *Shields Gazette* proclaimed, "Hopes, Fears, Leave-Taking, Last-Minute Jokes—Jarrow said good-bye today to the 200 men who started out gravely on their 300 mile trek to London." Shortly before the departure there was a special religious service in Christ Church. The rector of Jarrow blessed the endeavor, and the congregation sang "O God, Our Help in Ages Past." Mayor Thompson gave the men a last-minute inspection, no doubt looking for any outward signs of inner failings. He told them to remember that "they were going on behalf of Jarrow, and they were being relied upon to maintain Jarrow's good name."

As the column, led by Ellen Wilkinson in a bright green dress and Mayor Thompson in his ceremonial robes, headed for the outskirts of town, the Palmer's band played march music, and children from Ellison Elementary School cheered wildly. An old woman pressed a small silver coin into the march marshal Riley's hand for good luck. It looked as if they might need it: the secondhand equipment bus was so heavily loaded that it could not get up a hill near the edge of town, and the marchers had to push it.

In addition to their blue-and-white banners proclaiming "Jarrow Crusade," the marchers carried an oak box with gold lettering saying "Jarrow Petition." Signed by 11,572 townsfolk, the petition noted that Jarrow had for the last fifteen years "passed through a period of industrial depression without parallel in the town's history." The persistence of unemployment had reduced the people to "a deplorable condition." It had not only "placed a severe mental strain on the strongest of men" but had also taken a terrible toll on the youth, who, "owing to the restriction of facilities for their being apprenticed," were "tending to grow up with no trade to their calling." The petition concluded,

> Wherefore it is with the deepest concern not only in their own plight, but for the nation, that a town should be for so long a period stricken with unemployment and a valuable opportunity for industry left unavailing, that your petitioners humbly and anxiously pray that His Majesty's Government realise the urgent need that work be provided for the town without further devastating delay, actively assist resuscitation of industry and render such other actions as may be met.

The first morning after departure found the men on their way to Ferryhill, having spent the preceding night at Chester-le-Street. A *Shields Gazette* reporter who accompanied the marchers waxed enthusiastic: "The tramp, tramp of Jarrow men, going forwards today to Ferryhill, marching half the length of England, carrying the woes and troubles of not only their own town but of all the distressed areas . . . is beating out history as it awakens the echoes of the villages and towns on its route." The men's spirits, said the reporter, were at "concert pitch." They had marched steadily on the first day, joined en route by a mongrel dog whose presence they took to be a sign of good luck. The hound trotted beside the lead marchers "with a carefree air as if it knew its paws were treading the road to adventure like those of Dick Whittington's cat." The men marched to tunes played by the marchers' own mouth organ band. Ellen Wilkinson, leading the procession, struck up lively songs. At their first stop, in Chester-le-Street, the arrangements had been "the last word in efficiency." The men's only complaint was that they had eaten tinned beef for every meal. Their cook, it turned out, was a retired Spam slinger who had served twenty-five years with the Fifth Royal Northumberland Fusiliers. Though the *Shields Gazette* reporter claimed the cook's "hand had not lost its cunning," apparently this meant only that he could still open a can.

More penetrating comments on the spirit and meaning of the march came from a reporter for the *Newcastle Chronicle*. As to the motivation of the men, he noted, "One cannot help feeling that many of them—especially the younger men—had seized the opportunity to escape from their drab surroundings and risk hardship in action, in new surroundings, and even, if possible, adventure." It was surprising, he added, how small a proportion of the men had been south before. Two young men saw Durham Cathedral (thirty-five miles from Jarrow) for the first time, and almost none had ever been to London. If it did nothing else, the Jarrow crusade would show a few men from the north of England what the southern part of their country looked like.

A few days into the march, another side benefit materialized. Though most of the men suffered from blisters, their overall health was actually improving. At their nightly stops they were fed wholesome meals by their hosts, and they had persuaded their own cook to expand his repertoire. Their steady exercise in the fresh air also helped improve their constitutions. "Our men are getting sturdier every day. The next few days will see them fit as fiddlers," said the Shields reporter. Only the dog seemed to be in any serious trouble; it had developed bad blisters on its paws but kept going.

On October 8 the men's spirits were dampened somewhat by rainstorms, the first (oddly enough) they had encountered. To protect themselves against the elements, they carried mackintoshes and ground cloths. Considerably more depressing and less easy to cope with was the news that they received from Edinburgh, where Ellen Wilkinson had gone to attend the annual Labour party conference. At the conference the party's national executive council addressed the issue of unemployment but offered no coherent solutions; rather, it proposed another "inquiry"—Labour's traditional answer to difficult problems. Wilkinson was furious. "This is not the moment for more resolutions, more reports, a new kind of inquiry," she shouted in her speech. "What we want is something that would fling a challenge to the National Government and say 'Our people shall not be starved.' . . . If we can't do this, what use are we?" She appealed to the executive council to place its full authority behind the crusade. "If you do this," she said, "you can have a revival instead of what this conference has been up to now."

Wilkinson's speech irritated the party bosses, one of whom retorted that it was folly to send "hungry and ill-clad men on a march to London." A more useful measure would be "to muster religious bodies and the teaching profession in support of new initiatives against unemployment." This was too much for Wilkinson. "Liars!" she screamed, and fled the hall with tears streaming down her face.

When they learned of these events, the marchers were indignant. "These people have let us down," Riley cried. "They are attempting to pauperize us and the attack has come from a quarter from which it was least expected. But never mind. We have to keep our chins up and our dignity." The men decided to send a telegram to the Labour party headquarters in London declaring, "We sons of England's most famous town resent the attack [at Edinburgh] on our Member, and the attempts to pauperize our marchers."

The national Labour party's refusal to endorse the Jarrow crusade contrasted sharply with the words of praise for their endeavor that the men heard at most of their nightly stops. Town and village politicians were full of compliments on the men's spirit and discipline. Most interesting, perhaps, was the blessing given the march by local Conservatives. The chairman of the Leeds Conservative Association said, "The wisdom of placing the strain of so long a march upon untrained men is not for us to judge, but it would be a poor thing for this country if a time should arrive when a constitutional and orderly appeal to the Government . . . should fail to impress those at the head of our land." Noting that the Jarrow appeal was likely to have just this effect on Conservative leaders in London, the Tory agent in Sheffield declared, "I say this march is a good thing whether my head office or other people like it or not." What *he* liked about the crusade was that politics did not enter into it. "There can be no politics," he said, "when people are fighting for their bread and butter."

This was nonsense, for the unemployment issue had always been political. At its heart lay the most fundamental of all political questions: Lenin's famous distinction between "who and whom"—between the wielders of power and those on whom it is imposed. The Jarrow crusade was "unpolitical" only in the narrow sense that it eschewed Communist connections and was not the exclusive province of the Labour party. It is understandable, however, that this reassured many Conservative politicians, for they liked to think that their nation was not divided by any fundamental class differences. They were also very grateful for the marchers' "discipline," because they had genuinely feared that this small army of unemployed men might tear up their towns—might loot and pillage as their ancient ancestors, the Vikings, had done when they came south.

Local police officials had reason to be pleased by the men's discipline as well, and they heaped praise on the Jarrow men. The chief of the Ripon police wished the marchers "every success in their effort to get work." And the Special Branch of Scotland Yard, which kept the march under observation, reported with relief that "the demonstrators were warmly welcomed by the inhabitants of the places through which they passed, and no untoward incident calling for police action occurred. . . ."

Local clergymen were, for the most part, hardly less congratulatory than the politicians and police. No doubt they were pleased to see that though these men were jobless, they were not godless. It seems that in addition to their mongrel dog the marchers had picked up an itinerant Methodist preacher named Tom Sykes who "constituted himself unofficial padre for the men." At the Methodist Hall in Northallerton, Preacher Sykes blessed some sixty of the men and led an inspiring hymn. (What the other 140 men were doing at this moment one can only guess; there were reports that some of the Jarrow men were taking advantage of their celebrity status to make inroads with the local girls.) In the cathedral town of Ripon the archdeacon conducted a private service for the marchers, and the local bishop wished them Godspeed. Other local clergy did the same. A significant exception, however, was the bishop of Durham, who wrote a nasty letter to the *Times* in which he offered, "The policy of the marches is, in my view, a revolutionary policy. It involves substituting for the provisions of the Constitution the method of organized mob pressure. If generally adopted . . . it may bring us before the winter is out into grave public confusion and danger."

The bishop of Durham's suspicions were contradicted not just by the men's upright discipline and proper Christianity but also by their determination to keep their distance from Communist groups and from participants in an NUWM-sponsored national protest march that coincided with the Jarrow crusade. In Chesterfield local Communists held a meeting to mark the arrival of the Jarrow marchers, who they claimed sympathized with their cause. There was little basis for this claim. One of the march organizers, Paddy Scullion, had once been close to the NUWM and had chaired meetings for Walter Hannington. Riley, the march marshal, had been active in the general strike of 1926. But when the Chesterfield Communists tried to claim common cause with Jarrow, Riley was indignant. He announced that if necessary he would get the police to prevent such "attempts to make political capital out of the Jarrow March." When Communists in Harrogate placed their red banner next to Jarrow's blue-and-white standards, Riley made them take it down. "I would have done the same thing had it been a Conservative or Labour banner," he insisted. Special Branch reported that Riley had expelled one Communist from the Jarrow march. And when some haggard NUWM men who had marched all the way from Scotland crossed paths with the Jarrow crusade, the Jarrow men gave them a wide berth.

"Nothing is too good for marchers!" headlined the *Shields Gazette* on October 21. The paper was hardly exaggerating. In Leeds the marchers had been given a large financial donation that would fully cover their train fare for the return trip to Jarrow. The Leeds town council had also laid on a five-course dinner served on tables decked with "snowy linen" by "neat waiters in evening dress." After the meal the men were given cigarettes, cigars, and pipe tobacco. "It was reminiscent of a huge Christmas party," said the Shields reporter, but it was probably unlike any Christmas party these men had ever witnessed. The manufacturers of Nottingham showered the Jarrow men with new clothes, underwear, cigarettes, and sweets. Not surprisingly, a headline the next day (October 22) announced that the marchers were "Suffering from Good Food." The medical students' major task now was ministering to stomach troubles caused by overeating. For those still having foot trouble, the shoemakers of Leicester stayed up all night repairing boots. The town council gave the men new trousers. As the crusade made its way through the traditional hunting preserves of the English aristocracy, wealthy residents threw money at the men. One local baron pulled up in his Bentley and handed over a large contribution he had raised among his fox-hunting friends. "We shall be the smartest body of men that ever marched into London," said Riley proudly.

So popular did the Jarrow crusaders become that attempts were made to exploit them commercially as well as politically. Several agents for firms making proprietary medicines approached the marchers' medical students and offered presents of ointments if they would sign a statement saying "Used in the Jarrow Crusade." The marchers felt that their welcome in Luton (north of London) was "tinged with a calculating business-like air."

This last observation pointed up an interesting shift in the spiritual positions of northern and southern England on the nation's mental compass. In her mid-nineteenth-century novel *North and South*, Elizabeth Gaskell had depicted the booming north as commercially grasping and the aristocratic south as lazy and self-indulgent. In some ways the images had now been reversed, but one should not exaggerate this shift. The northern crusaders were not above a little business-like exploitation themselves: they signed a contract with a recording company for rights to the stirring marches played by their mouth organ band. A reporter accompanying the march later recalled, "As we got nearer London, the men were more determined than ever to take part in the prosperity which was apparent on every side."

The only marcher now having difficulty was Ellen Wilkinson. She had, as promised, walked almost the entire distance. She had been very chipper most of the time, leading the singing in her arching soprano voice. But by the twentieth day she was so fatigued that she limped noticeably. The men tried to persuade her to ride in a car the rest of the way, but she refused. She continued to limp along in front, sometimes leading the mongrel dog on a leash.

One other problem troubled the marchers as they approached the capital. Virtually all the men had been offered work by industrialists or merchants along the way. The work, however, was in such fields as baking or bricklaying. By law, unemployed men would lose further benefits if they refused to accept work that was related to the jobs they had been trained to do. None of the Jarrow men wanted to retrain to become bakers or bricklayers, nor did they want to move to the south, its relative prosperity notwithstanding. Hence they refused these offers, continued their march, and eventually returned to unemployment in Jarrow.

Their decision to do this is perhaps understandable, but it also helps explain why England's recovery was so uneven and unemployment in the depressed areas so tenacious.

DISAPPOINTMENT

Reports vary as to how the Jarrow marchers looked when they reached London. It had been raining steadily during the last day (October 31) of their march, and Ellen Wilkinson joked that the men—exhausted, soaked, and shivering—looked like "a walking depressed area." The *Times,* however, declared that the men arrived in the capital "still stepping out briskly and cheerfully," and the *Daily Herald* gushed, "With a song on their lips and courage in their hearts . . . two hundred men [walked] through the streets of London." All commentators agreed that London gave the crusaders a warm welcome. As they strode along Edgeware Road, said the *Times,* hundreds of people cheered them—"Good old Tyneside." "People of all parties, of all creeds," declared the *Daily Herald,* "welcomed [the marchers], took them into their hearts." The *Shields Gazette* reporter enthused, "Our march over the boundary of the capital was like a triumphant procession. People acclaimed the men of Jarrow as heroes. We were received with no less enthusiasm than the Crusaders of the Middle Ages. Women wiped their eyes and men on the pavements waved a salute as the column swung trimly along the busy streets."

London, like the smaller cities the marchers had visited, went out of its way to make the men comfortable during their stay. They were put up in pleasant lodgings in Mile End Road. A tailor came to measure them for new suits, which they paid for with some of the money they had collected en route. A West End cinema owner gave them tickets to see *The Call of the Flesh* and *Bed and Sofa.* Commented Riley, "I never thought there was so much generosity and good nature in the world."

On November 1 the marchers held a demonstration near Hyde Park's Speakers' Corner, a famous meeting ground for political protesters, Bible thumpers, and various hawkers of utopia. Riley described the rally as "unpolitical"; it would give the Jarrow men an opportunity to "tell a London audience the facts about a town which had suffered severely from industrial depression." Nearby another rally was in progress, this one organized by the Communist party to protest Britain's embargo on arms to the beleaguered Spanish republic. The Communists invited the Jarrow men to join the rally, but they declined. So the Communists suspended their meeting and joined the Jarrow rally. Riley could not prevent this, for Hyde Park was free and open territory.

Two days later the Jarrow men found themselves standing on Pall Mall to watch King Edward VIII drive by on his way to open Parliament. Edward, soon to abdicate his throne in order to marry the American divorcée Wallis Simpson, was popular with the British unemployed because he had urged the Baldwin government to create more jobs. As Edward drove by, the Jarrow men "cheered lustily," according to a police report.

That evening the men attended a public meeting in Farringdon Street. On this occasion Canon R. H. L. ("Dick") Sheppard, one of Britain's more left-leaning clerics, assured the crusaders that "the heart and mind of every thinking person in England" was with them. "I only wish to God we could march the people of London down to Jarrow to see the conditions there," he added. Jarrow's councillors also spoke, reiterating that they were "not here for charity" but for "the right to work."

Another speaker that evening was Sir John Jarvis, lord lieutenant of Surrey. Sir John was well known to the people of Jarrow. He belonged to the syndicate that had proposed the ill-fated steelworks scheme. He had also persuaded his rich county of Surrey (south of London) to "adopt" Jarrow and subsidize a beautification of the place. Surrey money had been used to put in a park and a cricket arena and to renovate some of the more deteriorated Jarrow houses. Ellen Wilkinson, perhaps sensing in Sir John a competitor for Jarrow's favor, had dismissed these projects as window dressing. To this charge Sir John's secretary had angrily responded that Jarvis's good works had "brought brightness and hope into many Jarrow homes," that Jarvis had "always sought to get more permanent employment for Jarrow," and that his efforts might have had more success "had Miss Wilkinson and her political friends cooperated with Sir John." Now Jarvis suddenly announced yet another scheme to save the town. He said that he had purchased part of the old Palmer's shipyard and planned to build there a new steel-tube plant. At first it would employ "hundreds but it might lead to thousands" of new jobs. And he would, he added, accept no profits on his investment. The *Times* promptly declared him to be Jarrow's "fairy godfather."

Generous and promising as Jarvis's announcement sounded, Jarrow's representatives greeted it with skepticism. "I have been called a doubting Thomas but I say now, as I said when the steel works were mooted, I shall believe it when I see the chimney smoking," said Mayor Thompson. Jarrow's representatives were suspicious as well as skeptical. Was it not possible that Sir John, a Conservative, was trying to undercut the Jarrow crusade's raison d'être by leaping in with glamorous promises that he might or might not be able to keep? Would not his intervention let Parliament off the hook? Certainly Ellen Wilkinson felt this way. Why, she asked, had not Sir John consulted her, Mayor Thompson, or the town clerk before making his announcement? Mayor Thompson was also bitter over Jarvis's intervention: "Why did he not act first and speak afterwards?" he complained.

In any event, Mayor Thompson and the men of Jarrow had come to London not to listen to John Jarvis but to present their petition to the House of Commons. Before leaving Jarrow, Ellen Wilkinson had worked out with the Metropolitan Police the logistics of this operation. The men could enter the House only in small groups to meet with specific MPs named in advance. There would be no assault en masse. Nor would the men be received by any cabinet ministers, let alone the prime minister. While the march was in progress, Prime Minister

Stanley Baldwin had made clear his view of this and similar demonstrations in a ponderous statement printed in the *Times:*

> Ministers have had under consideration the fact that a number of marches on London are in progress or in contemplation. In the opinion of His Majesty's Government such marches can do no good to the causes for which they are represented to be undertaken, are liable to cause unnecessary hardship to those taking part in them, and are altogether undesirable in this country, governed by a Parliamentary system, where every adult has a vote and every area has its representative in the House of Commons to put forward grievances and suggest remedies, processions to London cannot claim to have any constitutional influence on policy. Ministers have, therefore, decided that encouragement cannot be given to such marches whatever their particular purpose, and Ministers cannot consent to receive any deputation of Marchers, although of course, they are always prepared to meet any members of Parliament.

On the afternoon of November 4, Ellen Wilkinson formally presented the Jarrow petition to the House of Commons. In an emotional speech, she reminded her colleagues of the blows that had fallen on Jarrow. She noted that its shipyard was closed and its application for a new steelworks rejected. Where formerly eight thousand men had been employed, one hundred now worked on temporary schemes. She concluded, "The town cannot be left derelict, and therefore your petitioners humbly pray that His Majesty's Government and this honourable House, should realise the urgent need that work should be provided for the town without further delay."

Wilkinson claimed that her speech was witnessed by "as many marchers as could be packed in to the galleries," but in fact very few Jarrow men were present for this culmination of their long journey. Most of them were on a sight-seeing excursion down the Thames, courtesy of Sir John Jarvis. They did not even know that they were missing their great moment.

In reality, however, they had not missed much. The House politely accepted Jarrow's petition. But Walter Runciman, speaking for the government, dismissed the entire crusade as unnecessary: "The unemployment problem has been solved," he declared.

When the men returned from their excursion, they were told of the government's response. "It means you have drawn a blank," Riley told the men, "but they are not going to do this with Jarrow. It does not matter what the consequences are, we are determined. We are not going to suffer this kind of thing." It seemed that Riley had suddenly remembered his days in the general strike. Other Jarrow men were equally rebellious. One of them called out, "Let's stage a stay-in strike." Another shouted, "Don't move boys, we want to see the Prime Minister." But in the end the men were, as a police report put it, "prevailed upon not to create a scene." They quietly returned to their billets.

That evening a deputation led by Mayor Thompson and the town clerk met with selected MPs in the House of Commons. The town clerk retailed Jarrow's grievances yet again. Then the mayor held up his ceremonial chain of office and said, "Its links form a cable, its badge is an anchor . . . symbols in gold of the cables and anchors of the thousands of ships we built at Jarrow. Now owing to NSS the Jarrow shipyard is closed." Thompson dropped his heavy chain with a crash. "If you are not going to help us," he cried, "this means nothing."

The next morning Jarrow's crusaders boarded a train to return home. Sir Malcolm Stewart, commissioner for special areas, saw them off. "Your march will remind the country of the courage and the patience with which you have endured unemployment," he declared. The Metropolitan Police were especially pleased with the Jarrow men's "patience." Their report on the march concluded, "During the marchers' stay in London their conduct was exemplary and no incident occurred necessitating police action."

SYMBOLISM

A few days after the Jarrow marchers left London, fifteen hundred men and women affiliated with the NUWM's national protest march arrived in the capital. Unlike the Jarrow crusaders, they had not been lionized en route. Few people had given them money, and no one had offered them a recording contract for their Red marching songs. The police had kept them under close surveillance and did not wish them well.

They had been, however, treated rather better than previous NUWM marchers. This was, after all, 1936—the year when Ethiopia fell to Mussolini, Franco's Fascists attacked the Spanish republic, Hitler remilitarized the Rhineland, and Mosley's BUF marched in East London. Fear of fascism produced an upsurge of vigilant activity on the left. Across western Europe "Popular Front" alliances of socialists, Communists, and bourgeois democrats committed themselves to the containment of fascism. In Britain anti-Fascist politics easily blended in with a new cultural aesthetic dedicated to radical change. Victor Gollancz founded the Left Book Club, John Lehmann started *New Writing,* and modernist London artists mounted the Surrealist Exhibition. For radical intellectuals like Julian Symons, 1936 was "not only the middle of a decade, but also the heart of the Thirties Dream"—a dream in which fascism would be checked "by a great concerted movement for democratic action supported by all men and women of good will." The NUWM marchers, who claimed to be protesting fascism along with the depression, profited from this spirit, particularly in bastions of the young leftist intelligentsia like Oxford and Cambridge. Women students at Oxford's Lady Margaret Hall peeled the marchers' potatoes; in Cambridge male undergraduates marched a couple of miles in the NUWM ranks—the first steps, one might say, that were to carry some of them off to fight and die in the Spanish civil war.

During their stay in London a delegation of NUWM marchers demanded—

and received—a meeting with the minister of labor. This was ironic, for the much less militant Jarrow men had been denied that privilege. This anomaly prompted one commentator to suggest that the Jarrow men had not made enough of a nuisance of themselves: had they paraded up and down Whitehall like the NUWM marchers, they might have gotten a ministerial hearing as well.

Perhaps they might have, but this would not have made much difference in the larger scheme of things. None of the "hunger marches" in the 1930s had a significant effect on government policy. Minor adjustments in the relief scales and a more lenient application of the means test at the end of 1936 helped some unemployed families improve their standard of living. In 1937 a new special-areas act sought to encourage industrial relocation in the depressed regions through government rent subsidies and tax concessions. But these measures were mere palliatives and did not substantially reduce the misery in the high-unemployment. areas. Significant recovery was achieved only at the end of the decade as Britain began rearming in earnest for a possible war with Germany. There was considerable irony in this, too, for the protest marchers had identified arms races and militarism as scourges of the capitalist system.

In Jarrow itself the crusade did little to change the bleak economic situation. John Jarvis actually delivered on his promise to build a steel-tube plant, but this was not directly connected to the march. Moreover, this innovation was no panacea for Jarrow's problems, for it employed only about eight hundred people, not the thousands Sir John had projected. For Jarrow, too, genuine delivery came only through rearmament and war, which filled the Tyneside yards with the gray hulls of new naval vessels. Thousands of Jarrow men now found work in the immediate vicinity, though not in Jarrow itself, for the Palmer's yard stayed closed.

Can we conclude from Jarrow's unhappy fate that the crusade had no significance at all? One of the participants argued that even if the march did not do much to relieve the depression in Jarrow, it relieved the marchers' own sense of uselessness, giving them a new sense of purpose and dignity. "It enabled us to keep our self-respect," he said. The men were also proud that through their march Jarrow had become the "symbol" of people's unwillingness to accept their lot without protest.

The Jarrow crusade was symbolic in another way. It was emblematic of the British workers' willingness to seek solutions to their difficulties within their country's constitutional framework. This approach had a long history in Britain, dating back to the "Chartists" of the mid-nineteenth century.* Events like the Jarrow march help us understand why in the twentieth century Britain did not produce a strong or widespread revolutionary movement even at its moment of greatest

---

*The Chartists demanded, among other reforms, the enfranchisement of all adult males. Though they had a radical wing that engaged in violent riots, the Chartists devoted most of their energy to circulating massive petitions that were repeatedly submitted to Parliament between 1839 and 1848. These "charters," with millions of signatures, might be seen as the ancestors of the Jarrow petition.

economic malaise. It was not so much—as one commentator later charged—that these unemployed men let themselves be fobbed off with crumbs from rich men's tables but that they genuinely believed that their nonviolent and "unpolitical" protest could have a positive effect. As long as they maintained this belief, it was unlikely that they would try to dismantle the system from the ground up.

The Jarrow crusade also showed a willingness by Conservative and Labour politicians to work together, at least at the grass-roots level. In this respect England differed dramatically from the various Continental dictatorships, as well as from France. A viable political middle also helps explain why Britain did not fall victim to "revolution" from left or right, or even to that chronic political instability that weakened France in the interwar era.

As if to dramatize Britain's essentially constitutionalist and anti-extremist bent, the Jarrow crusade's most famous participant, Ellen Wilkinson, moved closer to the center of the Labour party in the late thirties and forties. She was not, noted the historian Kenneth Morgan, "swayed sentimentally towards Russia by the wartime achievements of the Red Army." Instead, she showed a "growing repugnance to Communism." During the war she directed Britain's civil defense program, and in 1945 she joined Clement Attlee's Labour cabinet as minister of education. Her importance for the Labour party, suggested Morgan, lay "in the way she helped translate the passions of the thirties into the experience of power from 1940 onwards." He saw a direct line from Ellen Wilkinson, who died in 1947, to Michael Foot and his successor Neil Kinnock. "Through them and their successors," Morgan concluded, "Ellen Wilkinson may yet win a posthumous victory."

VI

DEATH IN THE AFTERNOON

The Spanish Civil War and the Destruction of Guernica

> The tragedy of Spain remains to haunt the conscience of mankind.
>
> —Albert Camus

At about four-forty in the afternoon of April 26, 1937, two nuns on the roof of La Merced Convent in Guernica rang a bell and shouted *"Avión! Avión!"* For the next three hours Guernica, a small town in the Basque region of northern Spain, was attacked by planes belonging to Germany's "Condor Legion." Bombers dropped tons of high-explosive and incendiary bombs, while fighters swooped in low to strafe people running from their burning houses. When the raid was over, roughly two-thirds of Guernica's buildings were leveled or in flames. The attackers had failed to hit a strategic bridge, arms factory, or barracks on the outskirts of town, but they *had* managed to knock out an orphanage, a candy factory, a pelota fronton, and La Merced Convent.

The name *Guernica* could now be added to the growing list of atrocities produced by that spectacularly brutal war between the wars, the *guerra civil* in Spain. Yet there was nothing about this tragedy—not the military importance of the target, the motives of the raiders, the number of people killed, or even the final responsibility for the town's destruction—that was not subject to wildly conflicting interpretations. Indeed, the war of words over Guernica, which lasted long after the war of bullets and bombs had ended, is as much a part of this story as the bombardment itself.

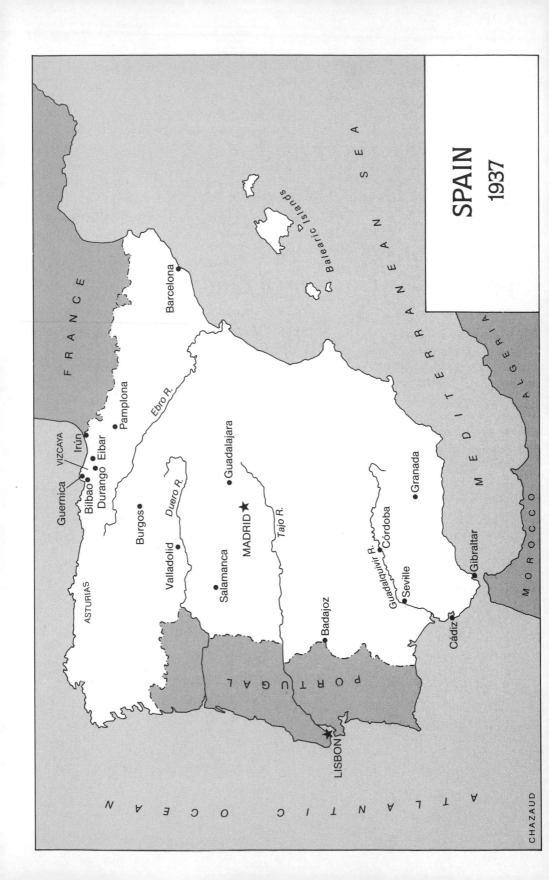

SPAIN
1937

FRANCE

ATLANTIC OCEAN

MEDITERRANEAN SEA

Balearic Islands

ALGERIA

MOROCCO

PORTUGAL

ASTURIAS

VIZCAYA

Guernica
Bilbao
Durango
Irún
Pamplona
Eibar

Barcelona

Ebro R.

Burgos

Duero R.

Valladolid

Salamanca

Guadalajara

MADRID

Tajo R.

Badajoz

LISBON

Granada

Córdoba

Guadalquivir R.

Seville

Gibraltar

Cádiz

CHAZAUD

SOL Y SOMBRA

The Condor Legion planes that destroyed Guernica had been sent by Adolf Hitler to help General Francisco Franco and his Spanish Nationalist forces conquer Republican Spain and install a pro-Fascist regime in Madrid. In this effort Franco also received help from Mussolini, who sent him Italian aircraft and ground troops. The Republican government, for its part, was supported by the Soviet Union, as well as by thousands of volunteers from Europe and America. The conflict was thus very much an international one, a kind of dress rehearsal for the command performance that began only five months after the Spanish war ended with Franco's victory.

The Spanish civil war had its origins, however, not in international rivalries but in Spain's own, tormented history. It was the bloody culmination of long-standing antagonisms between Spaniards of starkly contrasting political, religious, and social outlooks. It was also the product of regional animosities between the central government and separatist enclaves like Catalonia and the Basque country. The vicious civil war unleashed by these ancient rivalries and hatreds shocked many outsiders, but not the Spanish. They attributed their prolonged orgy of bloodletting to *casticismo*—that peculiar "purity" in the Spanish character that made all social and political differences seem as sharply divided, and as mutually antagonistic, as the *sol* (sunny and cheap) and *sombra* (shady and expensive) seating sections in a Spanish bullring.

During the half decade immediately preceding the outbreak of the civil war, Spanish politics had become even more overheated than usual. In April 1931 King Alfonso XIII abandoned his throne, in the wake of municipal elections that revealed widespread dissatisfaction with his ineffectual rule. The king's precipitous departure opened the way for the establishment of a democratic republic dominated in its early years by liberal and leftist parties in the Cortes, the Spanish parliament.

The new republic lived a precarious existence from the outset. Its early attempt to separate church and state earned it the unbending hatred of the Spanish Catholic hierarchy, whose bishops, like Cervantes's Don Quixote, saw themselves as the defenders of an ancient Catholic culture against modernist innovations like civil marriage, divorce, and the enfranchisement of women. Spain's clerical establishment spoke openly of the need for a latter-day *reconquista*—a new crusade against those twentieth-century liberal and radical infidels who were corrupting the Spanish soul with their blasphemies and perversions.

Equally embittered by the politics of the new republic were the officers of Spain's once-glorious, but now sadly diminished, army. The monarchy collapsed in 1931 partly because members of the military establishment held the king responsible for the army's gradual loss of prestige and influence in the state. But the republic soon proved even less supportive of military ambitions than the monarchy. The new minister of war (and later president and prime minister), Manuel Azaña, attacked the army's power by abolishing the Supreme Military Council and reducing the number of officers. These measures understandably alienated the military leaders, who, like the bishops, identified their own privileges with a "true" and timeless Spain.

Another source of anti-Republican agitation lay in the countryside, where the owners of agricultural estates saw their vast latifundia and semifeudal privileges threatened by land-reform programs and agrarian strikes. Not surprisingly, the estate owners joined the generals and bishops in evoking that most potent of all Spanish myths—the myth of a "true Spain."

The Spanish republic had the misfortune to be despised by the radical Left almost as fervently as by the Right. A large percentage of the Spanish working classes were anarchists who had little use for the liberal parliamentary order established in 1931. Like their enemies on the right, the anarchists pined for a simpler, preindustrial Spain, but their ideal was not absolutist Old Castile but the decentralized village society that had flourished before the rise of the central monarchy. They attacked all modern political institutions as intolerable impositions on the freedom of the self-governing pueblo. Their repeated strikes, plant occupations, and church burnings terrified and enraged the upper and middle classes.

The anarchists were particularly strong in the agricultural regions of Andalusia, in Barcelona ("the city of bombs"), and in the mining center of Asturias. Their ranks increased dramatically in the 1930s because the Great Depression, though less severe in Spain than in most of western Europe, exacerbated unemployment in a society that had virtually no unemployment relief. Against a backdrop of increasing impoverishment, anarchist groups proclaimed general strikes in Madrid and Barcelona in 1934. In October of that same year leftist forces in Asturias staged a full-scale revolution under the rallying cry "UHP" ("¡Uníos, Hermanos Proletarios!"). Armed with rifles and sticks of dynamite, Asturian miners attacked civil-guard posts, town halls, convents, churches, and even the university. In the process they killed a few businessmen, scores of policemen, and a dozen priests.

Faced with this challenge to its authority, the central government called in a young general named Francisco Franco Bahamonde to deal with the rebels. Physically, Franco was a Sancho Panza type—short and pot-bellied, with dewlaps under his chin and a prominent bald spot on his oversized head. He spoke in a high-pitched voice and walked like a man suffering from prostate trouble. But Franco was anything but a softy. He was a tough, dedicated soldier who did not chase women or drink. Like many ascetics, he was also brutal, ruthless, and ambitious. He had proven himself in Spain's bloody colonial campaigns in Spanish Morocco, where he was known to have praised one of his men for hacking off a prisoner's ears. When called to Asturias in 1934, he ordered his trusted Moroccan and foreign-legion troops to show no mercy in bringing the miners to terms.

In about fifteen days the Franco forces smashed the rising, then indulged in an orgy of killing and rapine that dwarfed the atrocities committed by the rebels. Franco's troops shot between fifteen hundred and two thousand people, many of them after the actual fighting had ended.

The Asturian anarchists were joined in their rebellion by local Socialists and Communists, but for the most part these three leftist factions were deeply suspicious of each other and went their separate ways in pursuit of the revolutionary millennium.

The Spanish Socialist movement was itself divided between a faction that supported the parliamentary republic and one that sought to overthrow it in favor of a leftist dictatorship. Unfortunately for the republic, the second group attained dominance in the mid-1930s as Spain's most influential Socialist, Largo Caballero, abandoned a posture of moderate reformism for a confrontationist pose designed to curry favor with hotheaded young extremists. Caballero was also motivated by events outside Spain. For him the lesson to be learned from Hitler's and Dollfuss's destruction of Social Democracy was the need to preempt violence from the right through "direct action" from the left. Accordingly, he threw his considerable influence behind the strikes in 1934. "If legality is no use to us," he said at the time, "if it hinders our advance, then we shall by-pass bourgeois democracy and proceed to the revolutionary conquest of power." Caballero allowed his followers to flatter him as the "Spanish Lenin." In fact, however, he had none of Lenin's incisiveness, and his radical posturings only undermined Spain's fragile democracy by continually testing the government's ability to maintain order.

Caballero's move to the left did not take him far enough to suit the Spanish Communist party, which, like the other European Communist parties, had little use for any leftist organizations not directly tied to Moscow. Thus the Communists derided the Socialists as "Social Fascists" and the anarchists as "sterile dreamers." Spanish communism's militant intransigence also reflected the influence of its most famous leader, Dolores Ibarruri, popularly known as La Pasionaria. Formerly a devout Catholic, La Pasionaria had married an Asturian miner, abandoned Mary for Marx, and become an advocate of violent and total revolution. The Right spread rumors that she had cut a priest's throat with her teeth, which was probably untrue, although La Pasionaria made no effort to deny it.

Confronted by destabilizing challenges from the left and the right, Spain's Republican government sought friends wherever it could, including among the champions of regional autonomy in Catalonia and the Basque country. Catalonian nationalists, proud of their region's relative economic prosperity and rich cultural tradition, had long been campaigning for regional control of the school system and recognition of Catalan as an "official" language within Catalonia. In 1932 the Cortes, prodded by the Azaña government, passed a Catalan statute that contained these and other concessions. But this innovation alienated conservative centralists and Castilian intellectuals, who saw it as a blow to the integrity of old Spain. Moreover, while the statute pleased Catalonian federalists, it did not go far enough to satisfy the local separatists, who continued to agitate for a completely independent Catalonian state.

In the Basque country the republic encountered and tried to accommodate another campaign for home rule. This campaign was especially significant in connection with the Guernica story, for the Basques claimed that their efforts to restore "ancient Basque liberties" had a great deal to do with the destruction of their most sacred town in 1937.

The Basques are an ancient race whose language has nothing in common with Spanish—or, for that matter, with any other Indo-European tongue. Their mountainous provinces, on the Bay of Biscay and the border with France, were among the most industrialized in Spain in the 1930s. Like Jarrow, the Basques had a great shipbuilding tradition, constructing some 45 percent of Spain's merchant fleet by the early twentieth century. But the Basques' greatest source of pride was their long tradition of democratic liberty, chief symbol of which was "El Arbol," an ancient oak tree standing next to the parliament house in Guernica. José Antonio de Aguirre, president of the Basque Confederation in the 1930s, wrote, "Long before France and Spain existed as states, centuries before Christopher Columbus discovered America, the Basques, beneath the Tree of Gernika, were recording for posterity those laws of equality and justice which they had heretofore known only among themselves." Until the middle to late nineteenth century the Basques had managed to protect their special liberties against encroachments from the Spanish crown, but they lost the last of their autonomous privileges in 1876. Nevertheless, as Aguirre pointed out, the Basques "never accepted [this] de facto situation imposed by superior forces." For them "the fact remained that the traditional pact between the Crown and the [Basque] country was broken."

When the monarchy fell, in 1931, the Basques saw a new opportunity to claim some of their ancient rights. Though the Basque lands were solidly Catholic and socially conservative, the republic was prepared to court them by offering concessions similar to those given the Catalonians. In 1932 three of the four Basque provinces (Navarre was the exception) approved a Basque statute that restored most of their ancient liberties. Yet here, too, federalist concessions enraged conservatives in the rest of Spain, igniting a countercampaign to restore central control.

In the parliamentary elections of 1933 the Cortes fell under the domination of center-right politicians belonging to the CEDA (Confederation of Autonomous Right Parties). The CEDA's leader, Gil Robles, was no Republican; for him the republic had legitimacy only so long as it was controlled by the Right. He and his associates in the CEDA proceeded to annul many of the reforms instituted by earlier leftist governments: they suspended land reform, restored the death penalty, revived clerical education, and abolished Catalonian autonomy.

Two years later, in February 1936, Spanish voters went to the polls again. The elections were necessary because members of the ruling center-right government of Alejandro Lerroux had been caught accepting bribes to grant permits for the operation of electric gambling wheels called *straperlo*. The *straperlo* scandal was Spain's answer to France's Stavisky affair; it seemed to point up the rottenness of elective, parliamentary government.

In the period immediately preceding the election, the Spanish Communist party had abandoned its isolationist stance on orders from Moscow, which now believed that the threat of fascism throughout Europe demanded hasty marriages of convenience between Communists, Socialists, and bourgeois democrats. The Comintern leader, Georgi Dimitrov, justified this "Popular Front" strategy by likening it to the capture of ancient Troy. "The attacking army was unable to achieve victory until, with the aid of the Trojan Horse, it penetrated to the very heart of the enemy camp. We, revolutionary workers, should not be shy of using the same tactics." Ominous as this metaphor sounded, however, the Comintern was not anxious to foment a Communist revolution in Spain, at least not for the time being. This would only frighten the Western democracies, with which Moscow now hoped to cooperate in the containment of fascism. As for the Spanish Communists, they retained a commitment to the "inevitable" revolution, but for the moment they toned down their revolutionary plans in order to find common ground with the Socialists and bourgeois democrats.

Had Spain's Communists wanted to take power in 1936—as the Right claimed they did—they would have been hard pressed to do so. Though the party had added significantly to the roughly one thousand members it had in 1931, it remained very small (perhaps one hundred thousand members in 1936) compared with the Socialists and anarchists. The Socialists and radical Republicans, moreover, were reluctant to join forces with the CP, which had recently denounced them as "Social Fascists." In the end they agreed only to a limited electoral alliance, since this seemed the most likely way to recapture control of the republic. Together the Popular Front parties waged a vitriolic campaign full of warnings about "Vatican fascism" and threats that if the Right won the Left would "proceed to civil war."

The Right responded to the Popular Front challenge with some tough talk of its own. Bishops fulminated ex cathedra against the leftist coalition, advising Catholics that a vote for the Popular Front would ensure their eternal damnation. José Antonio Primo de Rivera, leader of the far-right Falange party, declared that his group would consider a Popular Front victory "dangerously contrary to the eternal destinies of Spain."

The Right's warnings and fulminations notwithstanding, the Popular Front coalition won a narrow victory over the rightist parties arrayed in a "National Front." The biggest losers, as so often in the thirties, were the moderate parties in the center. Indeed, the February 1936 election results documented that process of polarization that had been gaining momentum in Spain since the republic was founded.

The victory of the Popular Front led to the establishment of a new government under Manuel Azaña, the Right's old nemesis. Azaña's cabinet contained no Communists (the Communist party had only fourteen deputies in the parliament), but the narrowness of the victory made the government dependent on Communist "toleration" of its policies. To keep the support of the radical Left, Azaña ordered the release of prisoners jailed in connection with the 1934 strikes and Asturian rebellion. His government also revived the land-reform program abandoned when the rightist parties took over in late 1933.

The unintended effect of these measures was to generate a popular upheaval that the government was unable to control. Anarchists staged peasant expropriations of rural properties and worker occupations of factories. They also resumed their torching of churches and convents, which they justified by reviving old horror stories like the ones about nuns poisoning chocolates meant for workers' children. A new wave of strikes engulfed the land, threatening the fragile economy. Surveying the chaos, Azaña adopted a characteristically fatalistic mood: "Always I had been afraid that we would come back to power in bad conditions. They could not be worse. Once more we must harvest the wheat when it is still green."

The Right ensured that Azaña's problems derived not only from popular insurrection and leftist militancy. Spain's wealthy financiers began pulling their money out of the country. The youth group of Gil Robles's CEDA declared the Popular Front to be "anti-Spain" and vowed to bring it down. "Either [we] smash Marxism or Marxism will destroy Spain. . . . Let us annihilate Marxism, Freemasonry, and separatism so that Spain may continue her immortal road!" Like the early *squadristi* in Italy and the Heimwehren in Austria, young Spanish rightists now drove into working-class barrios and fought pitched battles with their enemies. So eager were the young Falangists to smash the republic that some of them joined forces with anarchist militants to gun down Socialist politicians. Here was a Spanish confirmation of the French wisdom regarding the proximity of extremes.

Spain's top army officers, meanwhile, began reviving old plans to replace the republic with a military junta. Their chief conspirator was not yet Franco, whom the Republican government had sent to the Canary Islands to keep him from making trouble, but General Emilio Mola, another veteran of the colonial wars in Morocco. Mola, every bit as ambitious as but considerably less patient than Franco, began circulating plans for a "rising" in which all "good Spaniards" were invited to participate. According to this plan, Mola would be *el director* in a new junta. Franco was not included, because he was characteristically still testing the winds before deciding how to trim his sails. "With Franquito or without Franquito," declared one of the conspirators, "we will save Spain."

THE RISING

While walking to work on the evening of July 12, 1936, Lieutenant José Castillo of the Republican assault guards was shot dead by four Falangists. Castillo, who had recently helped quell a rightist riot, had been marked for assassination for some time. At the time of his marriage a month earlier, his bride had received an anonymous letter asking why she was marrying a man "soon to be a corpse." In revenge for Castillo's murder, some of his colleagues in the assault guards waylaid a prominent rightist politician named Calvo Sotelo, shot him in the back of the neck and dumped his body in Madrid's East Cemetery. The following day Spain's capital witnessed two funerals: one featuring a crowd of Socialists raising clenched fists and red flags, the other boasting equally vast crowds saluting with arms outstretched in the now-familiar Fascist style. As in Vienna two years before, the destruction of a tenuous young democracy was symbolized by rival burials.

Sotelo's murder was not just a symbolic event: it gave Spain's rightist generals the dramatic incident they needed to justify their long-planned rising against the republic. On the night of July 18, Franco, having finally decided to join the rebels, left Las Palmas for Spanish Morocco in an English airplane chartered by the rightist industrialist Juan March. There he took control over native and foreign-legion troops with whom he planned to invade the Spanish mainland. On the same day, rebel army units on the mainland began seizing control of key buildings in selected cities.

As the rebellion spread, the government dithered. Prime Minister Santiago Casares Quiroga, who had said when first informed of a generals' plot, "So there is to be a rising? Very well, I, for my part, shall take a lie-down," declined to order emergency measures. When pressed by left-wing unions to issue arms to young Socialists and Communists, he refused. This policy earned him the hatred of the Left, who called him Civilón (Civilian), after an infamous bull who refused to fight. Casares clearly held back arms from the militants because he feared they would use them to take over the republic. This was an understandable fear, but since significant components of the regular military had gone over to the rebels, arming the leftist militants constituted the government's best hope of quelling the rebellion before it had a chance to gain important footholds.

By the time Casares could be induced to resign, the rebels were already taking over conservative bastions like Burgos, capital of Old Castile, Seville, Valladolid, and Pamplona, the old monarchist center in Navarre where Mola had his headquarters. This was also the town where young bucks allowed bulls to chase them through the streets during the annual festival; now young rightists played bull to the town's leftists.

Barcelona and Madrid, Spain's largest cities, witnessed some of the more vicious fighting in the first days of the civil war. In the Catalonian capital anarchist groups, which loathed the rightist military even more than they did the Madrid government, seized several arms depots and went out to confront rebel battalions that had been ordered by their officers to converge on the Plaza de Cataluña, in the center of town. The anarchists were joined by some athletes who had come to Barcelona to compete in the "People's Olympics," organized by labor unions to protest the upcoming Nazi Olympics in Berlin. By nightfall on July 20 the Plaza was littered with dead, and in the broad, leafy Ramblas, one of

Europe's most handsome avenues, bodies were piled in front of the numerous flower kiosks. The rebellion had been swiftly crushed—a testament perhaps to what might have happened across Spain had the government acted with similar dispatch.

In Madrid, where the rising was poorly coordinated among the anti-Republican generals, rebel forces assembled on July 19 in the massive Montana barracks west of the capital. Their plan was to march into the city and quickly take it over, but they had not counted on the resourcefulness of the leftist labor unions, which stole some 65,000 rifles from the ministry of war. Alerted to the presence of the well-armed workers, the rebels elected to delay their attack.

That night La Pasionaria delivered a speech calling on "workers, peasants, anti-fascists, and patriotic Spaniards" to put down the rising of the "hangmen of Asturias." "¡No pasarán!" ("They shall not pass") she cried, echoing the French garrison's watchword at Verdun in World War I.

Whipped to violent enthusiasm by La Pasionaria's rhetoric, crowds in Madrid's Plaza de España decided that the lance of Don Quixote, whose statue stood in the square, was pointing provocatively in the direction of the Montana barracks. Soon Republican forces had the barracks under artillery bombardment and cut off from smaller rebel garrisons elsewhere in the city. When a white flag finally appeared on the fortress, a huge mob swelled forward, only to be met by machine-gun fire. Incensed, the attackers now broke down the fort's heavy doors, stormed inside, and began killing soldiers by the scores. One huge worker carried rebel officers to the very top of the high stone fortress and threw them down. As in Barcelona, fury like this quickly ended the local rising, a devastating blow to the rebels' hopes for a rapid conquest of the country.

Another blow to the rebel forces was their failure to win the Spanish navy over to their cause. Rebel officers of the Mediterranean fleet tried to turn their ships over to Franco, who had since decided to join the rising, but the men, ordered by Madrid not to obey their officers, rose up and took control of the vessels. Now run by their crews, several ships stationed themselves in Gibraltarian waters to prevent Franco's troops from making a crossing to the mainland.

Thus, after the first few days of fighting, the rising had reached an impasse. The rebels under Mola controlled only about one-third of Spain—a wide band in the north (excluding Asturias and the Basque country), and enclaves in the south such as Cádiz, Seville, Córdoba, and Grenada. About 23,000 troops had gone over to the rebellion, but some 33,000 stayed loyal to the republic. Further progress for the rebels clearly depended on getting Franco's colonial forces—the best in the Spanish army—from northern Africa to the mainland, where they could join Mola. Yet Franco lacked the ships to do this, because of the naval mutiny, and the "air force" at his disposal consisted of three old Breguets, a Dornier flying boat, and the English Dragon Rapide in which he had flown to Morocco. Franco lacked a vivid imagination, but it was clear to him that he needed help from outside Spain if he was to "save" the nation from "foreign influences." When asked what he proposed to do, he replied, "Everything that might be feasible and necessary. Everything, except surrender."

INTERVENTION
AND NONINTERVENTION

In their search for foreign assistance, the Spanish rebels turned to the only powers that might be willing to provide it: Italy and Germany. Their hope was that these two Fascist states would see in the rebel movement a kindred spirit and in the republic an enemy worth helping the rebels to overthrow.

On July 19, 1936, Franco sent Luis Bolín—London correspondent for Madrid's monarchist paper *ABC,* and his chief press spokesman—to Rome with a request for transport planes, bombers, fighters, and munitions. Mussolini had earlier sent money and arms to Spanish rightists to encourage a rebellion, but this time the duce was reluctant to help. His earlier assistance had provoked no uprising; moreover, he had come to see the Spanish as an "inferior race" with "Arab blood" in their veins. On July 20 Mussolini replied to Franco's request with one word: "NO."

In desperation Bolín turned to Count Ciano, Mussolini's son-in-law and recently appointed foreign minister. Citing the urgency of Franco's need, Bolín promised to pay full price for whatever Italy might send. Ciano, for his part, saw the blossoming Spanish conflict as giving him an opportunity to show off his organizational talents. He promised to intervene on Franco's behalf with his father-in-law. After a number of meetings with Ciano, and following a new appeal from General Mola, the duce reversed his position and decided to send Franco the equipment he had requested.

Mussolini's volte-face was very likely motivated by traditional strategic and political interests, buttressed by ideological considerations. The duce believed that an alliance with Spain would bolster his crusade to turn the Mediterranean into an Italian lake. His conquest of Ethiopia made a Spanish alliance all the more important, for Italy's new colony could be best supplied through southern Mediterranean ports. He may also have seen intervention in Spain as a way of gaining control over the Balearic Islands (Majorca, Ibiza), near Gibraltar, thus decisively countering British influence in this strategic region. Even if this did not happen, intervention in Spain would give Mussolini a new arena in which to strut and bully, and remind the world that he was still "Europe's most dangerous man." A refusal to help Franco, on the other hand, might spell the rebels' defeat and the consolidation of the Popular Front government, which Mussolini saw as little more than a front for Bolshevik interests. Apparently he believed that Republican Spain was in the process of "going Communist" and that a Communist victory in Spain would encourage Communist ambitions throughout western Europe, including Italy. He said at the time that he decided to help Franco because "Bolshevism in Spain would mean Bolshevism in France, Bolshevism at Italy's back, and the danger of Bolshevization of Europe."

Three days after sending Bolín to Rome, Franco made his first contact with the German government. Unlike Italy, Germany had never assisted Spanish rightists in their crusade against the republic. Nor, contrary to oft-repeated accusations, had Hitler's regime encouraged the rising. Germany's Foreign Office and military leadership, indeed, were strongly opposed to helping the rebel forces. The diplomats feared that intervention, however limited or veiled, would endanger German relations with the Spanish republic, while the generals believed that Germany's own rearmament drive had not progressed far enough to warrant its sending any arms to foreign states. Nor did either of these groups have much confidence in the success of Franco's rising. Thus the Foreign Office flatly rejected Franco's initial request for transport aircraft.

Even before receiving this unwelcome answer, Franco had dispatched a second aid request to Germany through less orthodox channels. In the hope of bypassing the German Foreign Office, Franco enlisted the help of two members of the Nazi party "Foreign Organization" living in Spanish Morocco. The first of these men, Johannes Bernhardt, was a failed kitchen-stove salesman and unpaid member of the SS; the second, Adolf Langenheim, was a mining engineer and local chief of the Nazi Foreign Organization. Franco persuaded these two Germans to fly to Germany in a requisitioned Lufthansa airliner with a personal appeal to the führer for ten transport planes. The men also carried a hand-drawn map outlining (more optimistically than conditions warranted) the rebels' military situation.

When the German Foreign Office and War Ministry learned of this mission, they urged that the emissaries be denied access to any top party leaders. But Franco's messengers managed to get in touch with Hitler's deputy, Rudolf Hess, who had a weakness for quixotic enterprises. Hess immediately arranged for Bernhardt and Langenheim to deliver Franco's request to Hitler, who was then in Bayreuth attending the annual Wagner festival.

The meeting with the führer took place on the night of July 25 in the Wagner home Villa Wahnfried. Hitler, having just returned from a performance of *Siegfried*, listened patiently while Bernhardt nervously translated Franco's letter, which stressed his and the führer's common cause against bolshevism. After studying Franco's map, Hitler asked some questions about the rebels' situation and about Franco personally, of whom he knew little. The German emissaries did their best to instill confidence in the rebels' cause without undercutting the urgency of Franco's appeal. In the process they mentioned that Franco was also appealing to the duce.

At first Hitler, like Mussolini, seemed reluctant to come to Franco's aid. Then suddenly, without consulting anyone, he announced that he would accommodate Franco's request—that he would indeed send *twenty* transport aircraft, along with pilots and technical personnel. Only after announcing this decision did he ask whether Franco could pay for the German aid. When informed that Franco had a war chest of only twelve million pesetas (about four million reichsmarks, or one million dollars), Hitler was aghast. "You can't start a war with so little money!" he cried. But he did not rescind his offer.

Hitler's decision to help Franco, like Mussolini's, was partly based on the belief that the Spanish republic was in danger of becoming a western outpost of pro-Soviet bolshevism. Should that happen, Germany would be "encircled" by Communist adversaries. "The Straits of Gibraltar can't turn Red," he is said to have told Bernhardt and Langenheim. "An Iberian Peninsula dominated by the Soviets would pull along France and would lead to a Communist bloc in western Europe that would endanger Germany." This reasoning sounded defensive in spirit, but Hitler was undoubtedly also thinking offensively: his ultimate goal was to attack the Soviet Union and secure lebensraum (living space) in the east for the German people; while attempting this, he could not afford to have a strong anti-German Franco-Spanish bloc on his western flank. Very likely the news that Franco had appealed to the duce influenced Hitler as well. He did not want to be upstaged by Mussolini, nor did he want to leave the Mediterranean arena entirely to the Italians. Moreover, joint intervention with Italy would strengthen the bonds between the two Fascist states that had been forged during the Ethiopian conflict. Of course, there were risks in fulfilling Franco's request—the Western democracies would undoubtedly object—but Hitler apparently believed that France and England were too caught up in their domestic difficulties to do more than protest. Had they not meekly acquiesced to his remilitarization of the Rhineland and allowed the duce to grab Ethiopia?

Hitler was nevertheless careful to accompany his aid offer with very specific conditions on how it was to be used. The German assistance was to go to Franco alone, not to the other rebel generals. Moreover, it was to be defensive only: German personnel were not to play an active combat role. Finally, the entire effort must be kept secret; Bernhardt was made to swear that he would tell no one that he had even seen the führer.

Before their meeting ended, Hitler called in Air Marshal Göring and War Minister von Blomberg. He curtly informed them of his decision, then asked for comments. Though he shared his military colleagues' reservations, Blomberg said nothing. Göring, however, objected that Germany lacked military equipment to spare and that any assistance to Spain would cause "international complications." But when Hitler made it clear that his mind was made up, Göring suddenly developed enthusiasm for the idea. Much later, at his postwar Nuremberg trial, he claimed that he had supported the plan from the outset because it would enable him to "test [his] young Luftwaffe." In fact, Göring came to this conclusion only well after Germany's initial intervention had dramatically escalated. Only then, too, did he and Hitler begin to appreciate the economic gains—such as access to Spanish iron ore—that Germany might achieve by helping the rebels overthrow the republic. In the meantime, Spain's troubles might so galvanize the world's attention that little notice would be paid to Germany's own, ongoing rearmament.

Nationalist troops walk through the ruins of Guernica following the city's fall to Franco's forces. *UPI/Bettmann Newsphotos*

A poster advertising the Communist Thaelmann Brigade, which fought against Franco's rebel forces in the Spanish civil war. *The Warder Collection.*

Franco bids farewell to members of the German Condor Legion, who originally entered Spain as "tourists." *UPI/Bettmann Newsphotos*

Hitler and Franco meet at Hendaye in October 1940. Although Hitler gave Franco crucial support in the Spanish civil war, Franco kept Spain neutral in World War II. *The Warder Collection*

Göring's flip-flop on the Spanish aid issue should not disguise the fact that this was Hitler's decision and that it was made in the face of clear opposition from his Foreign Office and top military advisers. That the military should have been overruled was particularly revealing: it showed once again just how shallow the army's "victory" over the SA had been two years before.

If the Spanish rebels could call upon Italy and Germany for help in attacking the republic, the Republican government believed it could rely on France to help it survive the rebellion. France, after all, also had a Popular Front government dedicated to containing the Fascist challenge in Europe. Its leaders could hardly favor the creation of a right-wing state on its southern border. Thus on the same day that Franco appealed to Italy (July 19), José Giral, the republic's new prime minister, sent a telegram to Prime Minister Léon Blum of France: "Surprised by dangerous military *coup*. Beg of you to help us immediately with arms and airplanes. Fraternally yours Giral." Spain's ambassador to France then delivered a shopping list to the French government that included Potez bombers, Hotchkiss machine guns, howitzers, rifles, and bombs.

Blum was sympathetic to the Spanish Republican cause and agreed almost immediately to Giral's request. Shortly after doing so, however, he received a call from his ambassador in London, who informed him that the British government was alarmed by the prospect of French arms shipments to the Spanish republic. Pro-Franco elements at the Quai d'Orsay had set off warning bells in Britain in the hope that London would persuade Blum to change his mind. Now Prime Minister Stanley Baldwin urged Blum to come to London to discuss Spain. Blum did so and was duly counseled by Foreign Minister Anthony Eden to be "prudent" in any help he might give Madrid.

The British government's response to Blum's initiative reflected long-standing suspicions of the Spanish republic. Since the fall of the monarchy, in 1931, London had kept a watchful eye on events south of the Pyrenees, fearful that Madrid's new rulers would undermine Britain's extensive economic interests in Spain. Repeated threats to nationalize British companies—in particular its vast Rio Tinto copper mines—left conservative politicians in London hoping for a return to the monarchy or for the creation of an "orderly" military regime. When Spain instead elected a Popular Front government, Britain's ambassador to Madrid, the arch-conservative Sir Henry Chilton, likened conditions there to those in "Russia prior to the Bolshevist Revolution." There would be "hell to pay," he warned, if the Left was not checked.

While Eden counseled Blum to be "prudent," most of his colleagues in the cabinet were hoping Paris would send no aid to Spain at all. Samuel Hoare, now reinstalled in the cabinet as first lord of the Admiralty, agreed with Chilton that the Madrid government was a "Communist regime" that neither France nor Britain should assist. Conservatives outside the cabinet shared this view. Winston Churchill later recalled that he was "not in favor of the Communists" in 1936.

"How could I be," he asked, "when if I had been a Spaniard, they would have murdered me and my family and friends?" On the other hand, Churchill and Conservative members of the Baldwin cabinet realized that the Labour party and the majority of the British public favored the republic, if not direct British intervention to save it. In the end, therefore, the British government decided to ban arms shipments to both sides in the Spanish conflict and to adopt a policy of "strict neutrality." Its justification for this was the need "to prevent an uncontrollable internationalization of the war." This stance, amounting to a refusal to help a legitimately elected government stave off an aggressive right-wing predator, echoed London's position on the Ethiopian conflict.

Despite British warnings, Léon Blum went ahead with his preparations to send planes, and even French pilots, to Spain. But when news of this leaked out in Paris, the right-wing press, which had hailed the generals' uprising as an inspiring development, sent up a loud cry against lending any support to "Bolshevists and anarchists." More significantly, the French senate, dominated by conservatives who had no use for the Spanish Popular Front (or, for that matter, its French equivalent), came out strongly against aid. So did influential Radical party (that is, non-Socialist) ministers in Blum's cabinet. Now Blum was torn between his instinct to help a fellow Popular Front regime and a growing concern that such aid might endanger his own government and its good relations with Britain. In the end he struck a weak compromise: the French government would not officially send planes to Spain, but it would not prevent private sales of aircraft, so long as the planes were unarmed.

In fact, these restrictions were not observed. Over the course of the next two weeks, the French air minister, Pierre Cot, secretly sent a number of military planes to the republic in exchange for Spanish gold. Chief intermediary in this transaction was the novelist André Malraux, the "Byron of the Age," who applied his writer's inventiveness to the business of gunrunning. In addition to Potez and Dassault bombers, and Dewoitine fighters, Malraux and Cot sent along the one-time private aircraft of Haile Selassie, who hardly needed it in his exile in Bath. The French planes were flown by a motley collection of international volunteers and mercenaries organized by Malraux into the Escuadrilla España.

Among the reasons French and British conservatives opposed sending aid to the Spanish republic was the assumption that the Soviet Union would become an active partner in the Republican cause. Baldwin, for example, told Eden that he must not "bring [Britain] in to fight on the side of the Russians." As it turned out, there were good grounds for the belief that Russia would help Madrid, though that aid was always qualified and in the end a mixed blessing for the republic.

The Soviet government analyzed the Spanish generals' rising in terms of its effect on Russian national interests. Though we have no firsthand account of Soviet decision making in this matter, we can safely assume that Stalin and his colleagues viewed the rising as a potential danger to Russia. A Nationalist victory, after all, would mean that Russia's chief ally, France, was surrounded by three hostile nations. This in turn would make it difficult for France to move against Germany should that power embark on its threatened *Drang nach Osten* (drive to the east). If aid to the republic could prevent this from happening, it was certainly in Russia's interest to provide it.

On the other hand, Stalin undoubtedly realized that helping the republic also had its disadvantages. Too much Soviet aid would alarm Britain and France, Russia's potential partners in the containment of Germany. The Soviet dictator, moreover, had pressing domestic priorities on his agenda: he was about to embark on his Great Purge of the Old Bolsheviks.

These considerations probably explain why Stalin decided to help Spain, but to do so cautiously. He would send enough aid to prevent the republic from losing, but not enough to gain it a quick victory. Unlike Germany and Italy, which ultimately sent large units of military regulars, Russia dispatched primarily equipment and supplies, along with a limited number of military experts, pilots, tank crews, and technicians. As he was preparing to dispatch this aid, Stalin warned the new Spanish prime minister, Francisco Largo Caballero (who had just replaced Giral), to avoid any radical policies that would allow Madrid's enemies to portray Spain as a "Communist Republic."

As the Spanish republic's potential allies were taking their first, cautious steps toward intervention, Franco's allies were hastily completing their plans to transport the rebel general and his troops from Africa to Spain. Under the code name Feuerzauber* (Magic Fire), Germany established a number of ad hoc agencies to facilitate the world's first large-scale military airlift. The Luftwaffe general Helmuth Wilberg's Sonderstab W (Special Staff W) gathered the men and machines (twenty Junkers 52 transport aircraft and six Heinkel 51 fighters) that Germany would contribute to the operation. A German-Spanish holding company innocuously called Compañia Hispano-Marroquí de Transportes was created to handle the transport of equipment, which was conducted in the tightest secrecy. A total of ninety-one German pilots, ground personnel, and technicians—all classified as "businessmen and photographers"—embarked for Spanish Morocco under the auspices of the Reisegesellschaft Union (Union Travel Agency). Historians have tended to call these men "volunteers," but in fact most of them were "volunteered" for this duty by their superiors, who gave them twenty-four hours to pack their bags.

The Italians, meanwhile, were also pushing ahead with their contribution to the Franco airlift, but this operation proceeded less efficiently than its German equivalent. Only nine of the twelve Italian Savoia bombers dispatched to Mo-

---

*In Wagner's *Die Walküre*, Brünnhilde sleeps on a rock surrounded by a "magic fire" that only the hero, Siegfried, can penetrate. Hitler undoubtedly identified with Siegfried, but it is hard to see Franco as Brünnhilde.

rocco made it. Two crashed with the loss of all hands, and one made an emergency landing in French Algeria. It seems that the Italian technicians had loaded the planes with too many bombs and too little gas. This was not the last of the Italian miscalculations in the Spanish civil war.

The airlift itself was anything but smooth. Troops were crammed into planes from which everything dispensable, including seats, had been removed. Some of the men became sick as soon as the planes left the ground, and their example caused most of the others to follow suit—a messy business since they were all sitting on the floor. On several occasions the planes encountered antiaircraft fire from Spanish-Republican warships. At one point two of the German pilots loaded bombs into their planes and attacked a Spanish vessel, thereby violating the führer's order against direct combat involvement. Moreover, the German fighter pilots, who were supposed to instruct Spanish pilots in the operation of the Heinkels, took over the aircraft themselves when the Spaniards began crashing them one after another into the sea.

Despite all the difficulties, this pioneering military airlift proved a great technical success. When it was completed in early October 1936, roughly twelve thousand tough, experienced soldiers had been ferried to Nationalist bases in mainland Spain. The rebels were now in a position to pursue the war in a much more aggressive fashion.

This Nationalist success notwithstanding, Franco's airlift was riddled with ironies. Not only were the Nationalist xenophobes using foreigners to help them recover a "pure" Spain; they also were effecting their new *reconquista* with the aid of the Moors, whom the Spaniards had driven from the country (along with the Jews) in the original *reconquista*. One of Hitler's airmen insisted that his Moorish passengers "could not hear enough about Adolf Hitler and the new Germany." Perhaps so; but had these dark-skinned men lived in Hitler's new Germany, they would certainly have been persecuted as "racial inferiors."

On the day that Hitler launched his Operation Magic Fire, leaders of the Profintern (the Moscow-sponsored international trade union organization) decided to raise money for the Spanish republic. Entrusted with the propagandistic side of the fund-raising drive was one Willi Münzenberg, a German-born Communist and public-relations expert. Münzenberg immediately established an array of "front" organizations in western Europe and America, the most significant of which was "International Red Help." Wherever possible, Münzenberg drew on the services of literary and artistic celebrities to give his campaign added glamour and cultural panache.

The majority of pro-Republican intellectuals who aided the Republican cause, however, needed no coaxing from Münzenberg. They saw the Nationalist rising as a new stage in fascism's crusade to crush democratic liberties throughout Europe. To the French writer André Chamson, the Franco rebellion was a "shock still more profound than that of February 6 [1934]. We saw the symbol of liberty in peril and the prefiguration of our future." C. Day Lewis in England declared the Spanish struggle a "conflict of light and darkness," while Stephen Spender said it "offered the twentieth century an 1848."

Some of the writers and artists who aided the republic did so with more than their money, pens, and brushes; they joined the "international brigades" that were being formed across Europe and America to provide the republic with additional (albeit often poorly trained) manpower. Others fought directly with Spanish-Republican units. George Orwell, for example, packed a rifle for the POUM (Partido Obrero de Unificación Marxista) and was wounded in the neck. The British poet W. H. Auden went to Spain to drive an ambulance but was so shocked by the atrocities on both sides that he soon became disillusioned and returned to England. Two young Cambridge intellectuals, John Cornford and Julian Bell, stayed long enough to be killed. (The first English volunteer to die, however, was a woman: the painter Felicia Browne.)

The bulk of the international brigades consisted not of poets or painters but of working-class men recruited under the aegis of the Profintern and Comintern. Some joined simply because, in the persisting depression, they had nothing else to do; others wanted to put themselves through a "test" similar to that experienced by the previous generation in World War I. "We had a greater need of going to Spain than the Spanish republic had of us," said one of them. Many of the volunteers were exiles from European Fascist or authoritarian regimes who saw the Spanish war as an opportunity to strike a blow at fascism and thereby begin a crusade that might lead to the liberation of their own countries. Italian anti-Fascists in the "Garibaldi Brigade" shouted, *"Oggi in Spagna, domani in Italia"* ("Today in Spain, tomorrow in Italy"). Former Austrian *Schutzbündler* called their unit the Bataillon 12. Februar and hoped to find in a Franco defeat revenge for their own defeat in 1934. Julius Deutsch himself headed the Austrian contingent, of whom a very high percentage died. (Indeed, more Austrians were killed in the Spanish civil war than in their own civil war.)

America's left-wing community, though having no similar domestic defeats to avenge, also sent volunteers to Spain in the form of the "Abraham Lincoln Brigade." Carrying passports stamped "Not Valid for Travel in Spain," some three thousand Americans found their way to the Spanish front. One of their leaders was a young westerner named Robert Merriman, who had become a convert to the leftist cause while studying economics in Moscow. Merriman was to become the model for Robert Jordan, the protagonist in Ernest Hemingway's classic Spanish war novel, *For Whom the Bell Tolls.*

Mention of Hemingway reminds us that the Spanish civil war—even more than the Ethiopian conflict—was a foreign correspondents' war, one in which most correspondents displayed unabashed partisanship for one side or the other (most often for the republic). Hemingway himself, representing the North American Newspaper Alliance, divided his time between writing pro-Republican dispatches, making a propaganda film called *The Spanish Earth,* and instructing international-brigade volunteers in weapons drill. He also found time to court a journalistic colleague, Martha Gellhorn (later to become his third wife), who lobbied extensively for the *causa* among American liberals, including the Roosevelts. Like many of her European colleagues, Gellhorn saw the conflict in apocalyptic terms: "We knew, we just *knew*, that Spain was the place to stop Fascism. This was it. It was one of those moments in history when there was no doubt."

Conviction like this bred lofty contempt for that credo of journalistic "objectivity" that the historian and journalist Phillip Knightley has lamented as "the first casualty" in war correspondence in the modern era. The *New York Times* reporter Herbert Matthews, whom we last encountered glorifying Mussolini's rape of Ethiopia, took a 180-degree turn in Spain and became a passionate advocate not only of the Republican cause but also of the "engaged" journalist's duty to fly his colors openly:

> All of us who lived the Spanish Civil War felt deeply emotional about it.
> . . . I always felt the falseness and hypocrisy of those who claimed to be
> unbiased and the foolish, if not rank stupidity of editors and readers who
> demand objectivity or impartiality of correspondents writing about the
> war. . . .

Matthews ran into trouble with his editors at the *Times* not because he was biased but because he was biased in the wrong way. In those days the *Times*'s editorial "bullpen" was dominated by right-wing Catholics who wanted a Franco victory. They sent another reporter to Spain, the Catholic William Carney, to "balance" Matthews's dispatches with stories about Republican atrocities against the clergy, of which there were many. The result was a polarization of the *Times* readership that mirrored a broader polarization over Spain in American society as a whole.

Before the international brigades began pouring into Spain, Franco's forces were able to make substantial advances in the southern part of the country. In town after town they defeated the Republican army and militia units, butchered their prisoners, and even massacred civilians. In the fortress town of Badajoz, Franco's Moors were given free rein following their victory. They roamed through the streets, pulling off men's shirts to look for rifle bruises on the shoulder; those with any marks were shot on the spot. Others were herded into the town's bullring and systematically executed by machine gun. Some twelve hundred were killed on the first night alone.

The Nationalists' most prominent victim was the Grenadan poet Federico García Lorca. Though not a member of a political party, he was identified with the literary Left and therefore hated by Franco's self-appointed guardians of a "true" Spain. He was shot by the Falangist militia and thrown into an unmarked grave in a remote part of Grenada. (The exact whereabouts of the grave remains unknown even today.)

As Nationalist troops were completing their grim "cleansing" of the towns they had "liberated," Francoist officials embarked on a cultural *limpieza* (purge) designed to rid Spanish life of foreign influences. Ragout and *tortilla à la francesca* were banished along with décolleté dresses and short skirts. Priests made glorious bonfires of books written by foreign atheists and Protestants. In all, the National-ist cultural purge was much more convincing than Mussolini's equivalent efforts to replace handshakes with the Fascist salute and the goose step with the *passo romano.*

The Nationalists' military progress was aided by the first appearance of Italian Fiat fighters, which were more effective than any planes the republic then pos-sessed. In the north the rebels made effective use of their Junkers 52s (now converted to bombers) and German tanks to take the town of Irún, hard on the French border. Before abandoning Irún to the Nationalists, Asturian anarchists set parts of it ablaze—a tactic the Nationalists would later recall when interpret-ing the destruction of Guernica.

Significant as these military developments were, they had less impact on the course of the war than did a series of diplomatic maneuvers that accompanied them. In early August the French government, pressured ever harder by the British, announced that it would push for a "nonintervention pact" to contain the ominous escalation of the war. Paris presented drafts of its plan to the govern-ments of Britain, Italy, Germany, and the Soviet Union. At the same time France declared that it would suspend all deliveries of war materials to Spain.

After some delay for consultation (and to allow more men and arms to pour into Spain), Italy and Germany agreed to join the pact. They never, however, had any intention of abiding by it; indeed, they accompanied their diplomatic gesture with secret orders to escalate their commitment to Franco's cause. Russia joined the pact, too, and with equal cynicism. As he signed the agreement, Stalin sent military advisers to Spain to prepare the groundwork for Russia's intervention on the side of the republic.

At this point the United States was forced to take a formal position on the Spanish conflict. Like the British, the U.S. government had been suspicious of the republic from the outset. America's ambassador to Madrid in the early thir-ties, Irwin Laughlin, feared that the republic would be captured by "Bolshevistic influences," since "Communistic falsities" had captivated the "seventeenth-cen-tury-minded Spanish people." The Roosevelt administration thought its worst fears were confirmed when the Azaña government threatened to nationalize a Spanish subsidiary of ITT, which ran Spain's telephone system. Only Washing-ton's threat to break diplomatic relations caused the Spaniards to relent.

At the time of the Popular Front electoral victory in 1936, the United States had a new and rather pro-Republican ambassador in Madrid—Claude Bowers, a journalist and popular historian of the Jeffersonian era. Yet even Bowers, who fled to Biarritz during the civil war, became alarmed at what he took to be "Commu-nistic elements in Spain . . . working toward another French Revolution with its terror." American suspicions of the new government deepened when armed workers commandeered ITT's facilities following Franco's rebellion. Though Bowers himself remained pro-Republican, many other American diplomats in Spain cabled warnings of growing anarchy and Communist influence.

It was against this ominous background that the Giral government attempted to buy arms from the United States. There should have been no difficulty with this, since the neutrality legislation the Congress passed in connection with the Ethiopian conflict did not apply to civil wars. But the State Department had already decided that a Republican victory would be counter to American interests. As Under Secretary of State William Phillips noted, "The critical part of the situation is that if the [Spanish] Government wins, as now seems likely, communism throughout Europe will be immensely stimulated." Hence Phillips told the Spanish ambassador that neither side in the war would be allowed to buy American weapons; America would maintain an attitude of "strict neutrality." FDR, who knew little about Spain, later confirmed this posture even though he had personal sympathies for the republic. But despite FDR's talk of a "moral embargo" against the sale of any materials that might benefit either side, ITT helped Franco run his communications system, and Texaco sent him his gas and oil—all on credit.

In early September the European powers formally established the "Nonintervention Committee" and charged it with preventing arms shipments to either side in the Spanish war. But this committee was a charade from the beginning. First Germany and Italy, then Russia, used it as a smoke screen to cover their continuing intervention. Britain and France were aware of the violations but let them proceed because they were more concerned with the appearance of nonintervention than with actually stopping the arms flow. Hitler's representative on the committee, Joachim von Ribbentrop, joked with considerable justification that this agency should have been called "The Intervention Committee."

THE CONDOR LEGION

While the Nationalist airlift was still in progress, Germany increased its commitment to Spain by sending more planes and pilots. By late August 1936 Germany had sent so many men and machines to Spain that War Minister von Blomberg ordered one of his top aides, Colonel Walter Warlimont, to oversee the German commitment in person. Warlimont was also to function as Germany's chief liaison with Franco.

On the eve of Warlimont's departure, Hitler lifted his ban on direct German participation in the fighting. (Officially, however, Germany continued to deny any involvement in Spain.) Hitler was prepared to take off the gloves, he told intimates, because the French were sending aircraft and advisers to the republic. His own military advisers, however, believed that he might have been motivated more by Italy's decision to allow its pilots an active combatant role: the führer did not want to play second fiddle to the duce.

With this change in their mission, the Germans created a bomber squadron called the Flight Pablo. The Pablos' commander was Captain Rudolf von Moreau, a fragile little Bavarian who was known in Germany for his record-breaking flights from Berlin to Tokyo and New York. Soon he was to gain fame among his fellow pilots in Spain for dropping emergency supplies to Nationalist troops under siege in Toledo's Alcázar fortress. His colleagues likened this feat to hitting a postage stamp with a pebble during a one-hundred-meter sprint. In September the Germans added a fighter squadron called the Pedros.

Competent as the Pedros and the Pablos were, they soon met their match in the men and planes sent to Spain by the Soviet Union. The German Heinkels in particular were outclassed by the faster Soviet Chato fighters. Also formidable were the Russian Katiuska SB-2 bombers, which could carry larger loads than the converted German Junkers 52s.*

Extensive Russian involvement prompted Hitler to raise the German commitment another notch. On October 24 he told Count Ciano that he was "prepared for any effort that barred the door for Moscow." He and his advisers feared that without more help Franco would be unable to capture Madrid in the fall, as planned. Berlin therefore created a new military force for deployment in Spain. It was primarily an air unit, but attached to it were antiaircraft, ground-support, and tank groups. Like Germany's initial commitment, this one came with certain conditions: the German forces would operate under a single German commander responsible only to Franco, their bases would be protected by Nationalist troops, and the Spaniards must pursue the war in a more systematic and aggressive fashion. Franco, who had not been asked if he even wanted such a force, agreed to these terms.

Germany's new force was called the Legion Condor, apparently because Air Marshal Göring, who oversaw its creation, liked bird names and could readily identify with the world's largest vulture. The Condor Legion's personnel were the crème de la crème of the Luftwaffe. Most of them were young (average age, twenty-two), and many came from an aristocratic background. Though idealistically committed to their mission, few were volunteers in the strict sense; like their predecessors, they were assigned this duty and not told its specific nature until they shipped out. One of their number insisted that they kept their mission secret—even from their families—out of that "sense of duty" that was "the pride of Adolf Hitler's entire Wehrmacht." At its height the Condor Legion comprised a little more than five thousand men. Personnel were rotated out and replaced after nine months in order to give fighting experience to as many men as possible.

---

*Stalin, incidentally, did not send this fine equipment out of the goodness of his heart. The Spanish were obliged to pay for it with a portion of their enormous gold reserves, the rest of which Stalin kindly consented to "store" for them in Moscow for the duration of the war. "The Spaniards," he confided to his colleagues, "will never see their gold again, just as one cannot see one's own ears." Of course, he was right: Moscow no more returned this gold to Spain than Spain returned it to the New World Indians from whom they had originally plundered it.

The commander of the Condor Legion was General Hugo Sperrle (code name Sanders), a huge, shaven-headed, monocled man who, Hitler bragged, was Germany's "most brutal-looking general." Like Ernst Röhm, whom he admired, Sperrle had fought with the Freikorps after World War I, then joined the Reichswehr and worked his way up through the ranks. Sperrle's chief of staff was Colonel Wolfram von Richthofen, cousin of the legendary World War I air ace Manfred von Richthofen. Physically, Richthofen could hardly have been more different from Sperrle. He was slim, handsome, always elegantly turned out in hand-tailored flying suits. One of his admirers insisted that he would have "made a good figure at a diplomatic function." Such outward polish notwithstanding, Richthofen was both a hardened soldier and a devoted National Socialist. For him there was "no higher calling than that of a warrior," and "no freedom beyond the opportunity to serve the führer and the volk."

The Condor Legion personnel did not wear field-gray German uniforms. Rather, they wore the olive-brown outfits of the Spanish army, replete with insignia in the Nationalist colors of red and gold. Their ceremonial flags, however, betrayed the legion's country of origin: they bore in the center a large Iron Cross, trimmed with a Luftwaffe eagle holding a swastika in its talons. In one lower corner was the Falangist Yoke and Arrows, in the other the initials *LC*.

After helping Franco's forces gain control of southern Spain, the German pilots threw themselves into the battle for Madrid, which was heavily defended by Republican ground troops, international brigades, Soviet tanks, and an air force consisting largely of Russian and French planes. The Germans flew sortie after sortie over Madrid, anxious to see how civilians would react to almost daily bombardments. Like their Italian equivalents in the Ethiopian war, they loved the colorful effects their "eggs" made when properly laid on targets below. But the air assault on Madrid proved to be less of a lark than the Germans had expected. Very quickly they found themselves outclassed—if not in skill, at least in equipment—by their Republican adversaries. Count Max von Hoyos, one of the Pablos, claimed that his squadron of six Dornier 17s regularly encountered sixty to seventy enemy planes over Madrid. Hoyos's own plane was shot up and the count put temporarily out of commission with a bullet in his leg. Hoyos was lucky, for several of his colleagues were killed. In an effort to avoid more losses, the Germans switched to night raids, but this limited their effectiveness. They hit few of their military targets—though they managed to kill over two hundred people and wound some eight hundred more.

On the ground the Nationalist attack stalled in the outskirts of the capital. Some of the most ferocious fighting took place in Madrid's University City, where battalions of the international brigades fought hand-to-hand battles with Franco's Moors and legionnaires. In the Clinical Hospital, members of the German Thälmann international brigade put bombs in elevators and sent them up to the Moors on the higher floors. Many other Moors died from eating laboratory animals inoculated for experimental purposes.

The Nationalists' failure to take Madrid in late 1936 and early 1937 prompted Franco's Italian and German allies to expand their commitment in Spain once again. Mussolini decided that he could win the war quickly by sending Italian ground troops to the Iberian peninsula. At first he sought to rely primarily on the Blackshirts, as he had tried to do in Ethiopia. He ordered his regional leaders to select especially tall men so the Italians would look impressive when standing next to the squat Spaniards. But Mussolini's Blackshirt "volunteers," many of whom were sent to Spain against their will, proved to be such reluctant and inefficient fighters that regular troops had to be sent out to support them. In the end the Spanish were not impressed by their strapping Latin allies. "The Germans behave with dignity and avoid showing off. The Italians are quarrelsome and despotic bullies," declared a Nationalist officer.

Germany elected to rely on more and better aircraft rather than on ground troops. In early 1937 the Condor Legion received a few brand-new and still experimental Bf-109s, made by Messerschmitt and later to become famous as Me-109s. With the delivery of these planes Germany indeed began using the Spanish war as a "European Aldershot" (the main British proving ground). In the earliest stages of their Spanish deployment, however, the new planes suffered too many mechanical breakdowns to be of much use.

The increasing internationalization of the Spanish civil war in late 1936 and early 1937 made a "dishonest farce," as Ambassador Bowers put it, of the Nonintervention Committee, whose Fascist and Communist members repeatedly charged each other with violations, while openly committing violations themselves. The British and the French continued to issue pious platitudes about the importance of containing the conflict. Equally sterile was the contribution of the hopelessly discredited League of Nations, which urged its members to "secure genuine non-intervention" and recommended arbitration.

Recognizing that nonintervention was meaningless as long as Spanish ports remained open to shipments of men and material, Anthony Eden proposed in a cabinet session that the British navy "supervise" the harbors around the Spanish coast. This plan was immediately scuttled by his Tory colleagues, who quite rightly feared that it would hurt Franco more than the republic. Nothing should be done, said Samuel Hoare, "to stop Franco from winning."

Failing to secure support for unilateral action, Eden advanced a new proposal for international supervision of the Spanish ports. This plan was eventually accepted by all members of the Nonintervention Committee, but only after thousands more "volunteers" poured into Spain. And since the supervising navies included the German and the Italian fleets, the project amounted to little more than putting foxes in charge of the henhouse. As Bowers noted, "The patrol system was a farce from the beginning, and Italian and German ships continued to pour men, arms, and ammunition into Spain."

At the time he made his abortive proposal for British supervision of Spanish ports, Eden advanced what turned out to be a very prescient analysis. Noting that the Condor Legion's activities in Spain showed that the "cautious" influences in the German army and foreign office were being overruled by Hitler, he concluded,

If on this occasion no attempt is made to check this further German adventure, then we may be certain that when on subsequent occasions the Nazi Party urges extreme courses the more cautious influences will have no opportunity to make themselves felt. The Spanish conflict apart, Memel, Danzig, and Czechoslovakia are Europe's present danger points. If German interference is not checked in Spain, there will be no chance of moderating in that country any similar aggressive tendencies in respect of any of these three danger points.

THE WAR IN THE NORTH

In early 1937 the Nationalists and their allies mounted three campaigns designed to facilitate the capture of Madrid. The most important of these took place near Guadalajara, where in mid-March a combined Spanish and Italian army attempted to encircle the capital. Mussolini had pressed for this offensive in hopes of showing off Italian military superiority and bringing the war to a rapid close. Though the Italian forces were well armed, their tanks lacked sufficient fuel and their commanders refused to work closely with the Spaniards. The result was a humiliating defeat for Italy. Hemingway, newly arrived in Spain, promptly declared it the "biggest Italian defeat since Caporetto." The jubilant Republicans renamed the Italian CTV (Corps of Voluntary Troops) "¿Cuándo Te Vas?" ("When are you leaving?"). There were jokes about the Italians in the tanks needing rearview mirrors in order to see the battle. Even the Nationalists, who had long been smarting under Italian arrogance, quietly welcomed their ally's humiliation. Members of Franco's staff toasted the success of the Republicans, who "had demonstrated that Spaniards, even Red Spaniards, could always get the better of Italians." (In fact the Italians of the Garibaldi division in the international brigades played a key role in the defeat of their Fascist countrymen.) For Mussolini, Guadalajara was like Adowa: a defeat to be avenged with all possible speed and at all costs. He vowed that no Italian commander would return home alive if Italy did not win a major victory in the immediate future. In early April he sent another seventy-two fighter planes to Spain in order to make such a victory more likely.

The failure of the Guadalajara offensive convinced Franco that further assaults on Madrid would be fruitless for the time being. Instead, he turned his attention to the northern front, which had been relatively quiet since the early days of the war. Victory in the north would give the Nationalists control over Spain's largest coal and iron-ore reserves, its most productive steelmills, and key port facilities still in the hands of the republic. Bilbao, in the center of a highly fortified area called the Iron Ring, was the primary goal of the campaign, but to get within striking distance of Bilbao the Nationalists had to establish footholds in the rugged mountains of Vizcaya. On March 22 Franco ordered General Mola to prepare a devastating attack on the Basque country that would make use of every airplane and artillery piece the Nationalists could spare. "The entire Northern Front," said Franco, "had to be obliterated before the autumn."

Franco's German allies strongly supported this decision. Sperrle and Richthofen knew that Berlin wanted to secure Nationalist control over the Basque ore fields, whose products would then be exportable to Germany. Sperrle promised to commit the Condor Legion's entire resources to the campaign.

As Mola prepared his battle plan, he had good reason to be optimistic. Though the ground forces of the two sides were about equal, the Nationalists had clear air superiority—some 150 aircraft to the Republicans' 25. The Republican forces would have difficulty getting fresh supplies, for the Nationalist navy had blockaded the Basque ports. The British Admiralty chose to honor this cordon even though Britain had not accorded the Nationalists "belligerent status." Here was another example of how "nonintervention" worked to the advantage of the rebels.

On March 31, General Mola, whom Bolín described as a man of exceptional "charm and kindness," issued the following statement: "I have decided to terminate rapidly the war in the north: those not guilty of assassinations and who surrender their arms will have their lives and property spared. But, if submission is not immediate, I will raze all Vizcaya to the ground, beginning with the industries of war."

On this same day the Condor Legion bombers put Mola's threat into practice. Against the town of Durango, a rail and road junction southeast of Bilbao, they launched what Claude Bowers called "the most terrible bombardment of a white civil population in the history of the world up to March 31, 1937." German bombs killed a total of 127 civilians, including 14 nuns in the Chapel of Santa Susana and two priests, one of whom was blown apart while he was elevating the Host in the Church of Santa María.

The Nationalist ground troops, however, had difficulty following up the successes achieved by the Condor Legion pilots. The terrain in Vizcaya was treacherous and coordination between air and ground forces poor. The Germans, for their part, became convinced that the Spanish were being too cautious. Richthofen went to see Mola and (according to his diary) "demanded stronger action and accused him of want of energy." Eventually Richthofen was able to work out an agreement with Mola's chief of staff, Colonel Juan Vigón, that placed control of all air forces in German hands and guaranteed better coordination between air, artillery, and ground forces. The agreement also stated that German and Italian bombers would attack enemy troop concentrations "without concern for the civilian population."

As the Nationalists resumed their offensive, Mola demanded that the Condor Legion bombers combine ground-support operations with massive assaults on the industries of Bilbao. He wanted half the city's factories destroyed. Richthofen thought this made no sense, for the Nationalists hoped to capture and make use of these factories in the near future. Franco, too, opposed the wholesale destruction of Spanish industry. But Mola was adamant; he said that Spain had been dominated for too long by the industrial centers of Bilbao and Barcelona, that the country already had "too much industry, which brought only social discontent." Here was the authentic voice of old Spain.

Through the first three weeks of April, German and Italian planes divided their time between support operations and assaults on Bilbao. The bombing of Bilbao was hampered by cloud cover, however, and the ground offensive continued to proceed more slowly than the Germans had hoped. Frustrated, Sperrle proposed that the Nationalists break off the offensive and return to the Madrid front. But Franco insisted on a continuation of the Bilbao offensive. Richthofen now concluded that if the Spanish command was serious about taking the Basque country, it might indeed be necessary "to reduce Bilbao to soot and ashes."

By late April, however, it became clear that the Basques were in trouble. The Nationalist command noted extensive retreat movements in the direction of Bilbao. On April 25 Richthofen, studying his battle map, thought he saw an opportunity to prevent the retreating Basque units from reaching the heavily defended area immediately around Bilbao. The map showed that the three main roads leading toward Bilbao from eastern Vizcaya converged at one point: the Rentería bridge near the town of Guernica. Richthofen marked this site as a "possible target." On that same evening, Nationalist troops stood fifteen kilometers from Guernica. "Our hopes have risen a great deal," wrote Richthofen in his diary.

THE BOMBARDMENT

On the evening of April 26, 1937, the British foreign correspondent George Steer, who like many of his colleagues had followed the stink of war from Ethiopia to Spain, was having dinner with a few friends in Bilbao's stately Torrontequi restaurant. The room, he wrote, was "peopled by the near-ghosts of women and old men of the Right, who talked in a whisper and glided rather than walked." Suddenly a government official ran into the restaurant shouting, "Gernika is in flames!"

Steer and three other journalists—Noel Monks of the *Daily Express,* Christopher Holme of Reuters, and Mathieu Corman of *Ce Soir* (Paris)—jumped into a car and raced toward Guernica, thirty miles to the northeast. Fifteen miles from their destination they noticed that the night sky was beginning to glow a fleshy pink—"the sort of pink that Parisians have dreamed of for centuries."

Soon they could see Guernica itself. The town was "a trembling, wild red disorder," windows and roofs "trailing locks of fire." Driving down the road leading into town, they saw "black or burning beams and tattered telephone wires rolled drunkenly, merrily across it." Four dead sheep lay in a trickle of blood. As they crossed over bomb craters and "volcanoed fresh earth" to reach the Casa de Juntas (the Basque parliament building), they saw "a dazed score of militiamen . . . standing by the roadside, half waiting for, half incapable of understanding, their orders. The fire of the houses lit up their spent, open faces." Other militia-men were laying out bodies riddled with bullet holes; one victim was a "lovely girl," and the men cried as they covered her with a sheet.

Steer went into the garden behind the Casa to check on the fate of El Arbol, the petrified oak trunk symbolizing Basque liberties that had been partly burned in Napoleon's peninsular war. "Untouched. The black old trunk, under which, when it flowered, the Catholic kings promised to respect Basque democracy, stood there in its mummified death, untouched between thick white pillars. . . . A few rose petals lay on the stones around—pink confetti blown there in the twi-light by the bombardment of Gernika."

Steer and his colleagues immediately began interviewing townspeople who were not too dumbstruck or feeble to talk. The people made "the funny noises of bombers poising, fighters machine-gunning, bombs bursting, houses falling, the tubes of fire spurting and spilling over the town." Between interviews, Steer played with some silver tubes he had found on the ground. Thermite, an incendi-ary agent, leaked from their bases. Their stamps said they had been made in the German RhS factory in 1936. "And over the legend stood a symbol in miniature, the Imperial eagle with wings spread."

On April 28 the London *Times* and the *New York Times* carried a long story by Steer about what he had seen and learned in Guernica. The London paper had been reluctant to publish the story because its editor, Geoffrey Dawson, was an arch-appeaser who, by his own admission, did his "best, night after night, to keep out of the paper anything that might hurt [the Germans'] susceptibilities." But this story was too important to "spike," whatever the effect it might have on German susceptibilities. It stated, in part,

> Guernica, the most ancient town of the Basques and the center of their cultural tradition, was completely destroyed yesterday afternoon by insur-gent air raiders. The bombardment of this open town far behind the lines occupied precisely three hours and a quarter, during which a powerful fleet of airplanes consisting of three German types, Junkers and Heinkel bombers and Heinkel fighters, did not cease unloading on the town bombs weighing from 1,000 lbs. downwards and, it is calculated, more than 3,000 two-pounder aluminum incendiary projectiles. The fighters, meanwhile, plunged low from above the center of the town to machine-gun those of the civilian population who had taken refuge in the fields. . . .
>
> In the form of its execution and the scale of the destruction it wrought, no less than in the selection of its objective, the raid on Guernica is unparal-leled in military history. Guernica was not a military objective. A factory producing war material lay outside the town and was untouched. So were two barracks some distance from the town. The town lay far behind the lines. The object of the bombardment was seemingly the demoralization of the civil population and the destruction of the cradle of the Basque race. Every fact bears out this appreciation, beginning with the day when the deed was done.

Monday was the customary market day in Guernica for the country round. At 4:30 P.M., when the market was full and peasants were still coming in, the church bell rang the alarm for approaching airplanes, and the population sought refuge in cellars and in the dugouts prepared following the bombing of the civilian population of Durango on March 31st, which opened General Mola's offensive in the north. . . .

Five minutes later a single German bomber appeared, circled over the town at a low altitude, and then dropped six heavy bombs, apparently aiming for the [railroad] station. The bombs with a shower of grenades fell on a former institute and on houses and streets surrounding it. The airplane then went away. In another five minutes came a second bomber, which threw the same number of bombs in the middle of the town. About a quarter of an hour later three Junkers arrived to continue the work of demolition, and thenceforward the bombing grew in intensity and was continuous, ceasing only with the approach of dusk at 7:45. The whole town of 7,000 inhabitants, plus 3,000 refugees, was slowly and systematically pounded to pieces. . . .

The tactics of the bombers, which may be of interest to students of the new military science, were as follows: First, small parties of airplanes threw heavy bombs and hand grenades all over the town, choosing area after area in orderly fashion. Next came fighting machines which swooped low to machine-gun those who ran in panic from dugouts, some of which had already been penetrated by 1000 lb. bombs, which make a hole 25 ft. deep. Many of these people were killed as they ran. A large herd of sheep being brought in to the market was also wiped out. The object of this move was apparently to drive the population underground again, for next as many as 12 bombers appeared at a time dropping heavy and incendiary bombs upon the ruins. The rhythm of this bombing of an open town was, therefore, a logical one: first, hand grenades and heavy bombs to stampede the population, then machine-gunning to drive them below, next heavy and incendiary bombs to wreck the houses and burn them on top of their victims.

Steer's colleagues on the scene in Guernica sent out similar reports, though not as thorough or graphic. The Basque president, José Antonio Aguirre, immediately issued a widely reproduced declaration condemning the bombing as an "attempt to wound us in the most sensitive of our patriotic sentiments, once more making it entirely clear what Euzkadi [Basques] may expect of those who do not hesitate to destroy us down to the very sanctuary which records the centuries of our liberty and our democracy." A few days later the canon of the cathedral of Valladolid, Father Alberto de Onaindia, who happened to have been in Guernica on April 26, came forth with a detailed account of the bombing that closely resembled Steer's description. His report said in part,

The airplanes came low, flying at two hundred meters. As soon as we could leave our shelter [Onaindia and some militiamen had hid in a sewer], we ran into the woods, hoping to put a safe distance between us and the enemy. But the airmen saw us and went after us. The leaves hid us. As they did not know exactly where we were, they aimed their machine-guns in the direction they thought we were traveling. We heard the bullets ripping through the branches, and the sinister sound of splintering wood. The milicianos and I followed the flight patterns of the airplanes; and we made a crazy journey through the trees, trying to avoid them. Meanwhile women, children and old men were falling in heaps, like flies, and everywhere we saw lakes of blood.

I saw an old peasant standing alone in a field; a machine-gun bullet killed him. For more than an hour these eighteen planes, never more than a few hundred meters in altitude, dropped bomb after bomb on Guernica. The sound of the explosions and of the crumbling houses cannot be imagined. Always they traced on the air the same tragic flight pattern, as they flew over all the streets of Guernika. Bombs fell by the thousands. Later we saw the bomb craters. Some were sixteen meters in diameter and eight meters deep.

On April 27, even before the first news stories from Guernica had begun to circulate in America and western Europe, the Spanish Nationalist command in Salamanca issued a declaration flatly denying that Guernica had been bombed at all. Franco's chief press spokesman, Luis Bolín, insisted, "Our planes, because of the bad weather, have not been able to fly today [sic] and consequently could hardly have bombed Guernica." Bolín also tried to clear the Germans, by claiming, "There is no German or foreign air force in National Spain. There is a Spanish air force, a noble, heroic Spanish air force, which constantly fights against Red planes, Russian and French, piloted by foreigners." How then did Bolín explain the fires that destroyed Guernica? "The incendiarists are those who, last summer, burned Irún, and yesterday, Eibar. Unable to hold back our troops, the Reds have destroyed everything. They accuse the Nationals of deeds which are but the realization of their own criminal intentions."

During the next two days the Nationalist command repeated these charges, insisting that "data" they possessed showed that the fires in Guernica originated from below and spread upward and that there were no holes in roofs or craters in the streets that might have pointed to a bombing attack. Embellishing its original theme of Red culpability, the rebel press office insisted that the destruction "was carried out by Asturian dynamiters, employed by the Marxists, in order afterward to attribute the crime to us." Another Nationalist statement added that the Franco forces had no reason to bomb Guernica because the town was far from their lines and not a military target—the one point on which their story agreed with Steer's and Aguirre's.

On April 29 Franco's forces entered Guernica and incorporated it into the Nationalist zone. Now they let correspondents attached to their forces view the ruins and conduct interviews with the inhabitants. Pembroke Stephens of the *Daily Telegraph* wrote a vague dispatch quoting some "excited and distracted women" who told him that their homes had been "destroyed at night by fire"—testimony that could have supported either side's version. A story by William Carney of the *New York Times* tended toward the Nationalist line, though not emphatically: "This writer found that most of the destruction could have been the result of fires and dynamiting," he concluded. In a dispatch dated May 4, James Holburn of the London *Times* wrote that though the fires in Guernica had destroyed much of the evidence of their origins, it seemed that the town *had* been bombed intermittently. On the other hand, since he could not find many craters or bomb fragments, Holburn opined that it was "difficult to believe that Guernica was a target for a bombardment of exceptional severity and was selected by the Nationalists for an experiment with incendiary bombs."

Holburn's last reservation notwithstanding, what was significant about this report was its suggestion that some bombing had probably taken place. Since the Nationalist command exercised very strict censorship on all correspondents accredited to it, one can only assume it was now prepared to admit that Guernica might have been bombed. Indeed, the official version out of Salamanca had begun to change even before Holburn filed his dispatch. A Nationalist communiqué dated May 2 said, "It is possible that a few bombs fell upon Guernica during days when our airplanes were operating against objectives of military importance." Now Guernica was reported to have been an important military target after all. Allegedly only six kilometers "from the first line of combat," it was described as "an important crossroads filled with troops retiring towards other defenses." The town's munitions factory and barracks were also mentioned. The communiqué therefore insisted, "It would not have been surprising if the National airplanes had marked Guernica as an objective. The laws of war allowed it, the rights of the people notwithstanding. It was a classical military objective with an importance that thoroughly justified a bombing." The Nationalist statement failed to note, however, that none of these "military objectives" had been destroyed, only houses and public buildings.

The Nationalist line was changing because Bolín's original position had simply been untenable; even pro-Nationalist correspondents had filed reports on April 26 about rebel air activity and bombing missions. It must have seemed more credible to admit that some bombs might have fallen on Guernica in the course of a mission to hit legitimate military targets near the town. Nevertheless, the Nationalists stuck to their insistence that the bulk of the destruction had been carried out by the Reds themselves. Their May 2 communiqué concluded, "The destruction of Guernica was the work of . . . incendiary dynamiters."

Accounts by participants in the raid belie these denials. Wolfram von Richthofen's diary contains the following entry for April 26, 1937:

Deploy immediately: A/88 [reconnaissance squadron] and J/88 [fighter squadron] over roads in the area of Marquina-Guernica-Guericaiz. Deploy K/88 [attack-bomber squadron] (after return from Guericaiz), VB/88 [experimental bomber squadron] and Italians against roads and bridges (including suburb) hard eastwards of Guernica. That [area] *must* be closed off if we are finally to achieve success. . . . Vigón agrees to advance his troops in such a way that all roads south of Guernica are closed. If that works, we'll have bottled up the enemy around Marquina.

Richthofen's diary contains another entry relating to Guernica, dated April 30:

Guernica, city of 5,000 inhabitants, literally leveled [*buchstäblich dem Erd-boden gleichgemacht*]. Attack was launched with 250-kg [high-explosive] bombs and firebombs, these about ⅓ of the total. When the first Jus [Junkers 52s] arrived, there was already smoke everywhere (from the experimental bomber squadron, which attacked first with three planes). Nobody could see roads, bridges, or suburban targets anymore, so they just dumped their bombs in the midst of it all [*warf nun mitten hinein*]. The 250s knocked down a number of houses and destroyed the municipal water system. The firebombs now had time to do their work. The type of construction of the houses—tile roofs, wooden decks, and half-timbered walls—facilitated their total destruction.—Inhabitants were generally out of town because of a festival [*sic*]; most of those [in the town itself] fled at the outset of the attack. A small number died in wrecked shelters.—Bomb craters in the streets are still to be seen—absolutely fabulous [*toll*]! City was completely closed off for at least 24 hours; that would have guaranteed immediate [conquest] if troops had attacked right away. But at least [we had] a complete technical success with our 250s and EC.B1s [firebombs].

Colonel Hans Henning von Beust, leader of Bomber Squadron Number 1, stated in 1955 that he and his colleagues had dropped bombs on Guernica from a height of thirty-five hundred meters. The pilots could, he said, only "estimate" where the bombs would fall because there was so much smoke and dust. He added that a strong easterly wind blew the bombs from the primary target area over the city center. Lieutenant Colonel Karl von Knauer, leader of Fighter Squadron Number 1, wrote in his diary for April 26, 1937, that a sortie carried out against the "bridge at Guernica" had had a "good effect." After visiting the site on May 1 and seeing the massive devastation, he opined that some of the bombs might have set off ammunition dumps in the town.

This evidence alone should be enough to prove that the Condor Legion bombed Guernica. It also shows that the Germans were quite proud of what they had achieved. Since it turned out that neither the bridge near Rentería, nor the arms factory, nor the barracks had been hit at all, the "success" and "good effect" noted in the German sources can only refer to the destruction of the town itself.

These sources tell us yet more. The bomb mixture Richthofen describes—two-thirds high explosives and one-third incendiaries—suggests that the Condor

Legion wanted to knock out more than a bridge (which was made of stone and steel) and road crossings: buildings were to be smashed and burned. The stated goal of the attack—"closing off" Guernica to retreating troops—could have been achieved only through large-scale devastation; a few craters in the roads would not have been adequate. The Condor Legion pilots knew, in any event, that their bombers lacked bombsights sophisticated enough for pinpoint bombing; Beust said it was a "wonder [they] ever hit anything at all."

Having had the chance to view the Guernica ruins on April 30, Richthofen said nothing in his diary to suggest that any (not to mention most) of the destruction had been caused by Republican troops on the ground. Both Beust and Knauer stated explicitly that in their opinion the Reds had not burned the town. Could the Germans simply have missed the "data" cited by the Nationalist command? It is impossible to state categorically that no fires were set by people on the ground, but it is highly improbable that any were. Why would the Red soldiers want to destroy the haven in which some of their army had found refuge, and toward which other Republican forces were retreating? And if the Republicans wanted to impede the Nationalist advance by burning Guernica, why not destroy the bridge at the same time? And if they were aiming at a propaganda coup, why not torch El Arbol?

It is significant that none of the Condor Legion personnel availed themselves of the "Red arson" argument even though it would have limited their responsibility for this atrocity. As for their technical ability to do what they claimed to have done, ex post facto analyses of the legion's destructive power that were carried out by a German researcher suggest that the bombers' load on April 26 was indeed powerful enough to level the town without the "help" of Asturian dynamiters and arsonists.

While evidence from the German side makes it clear that the Condor Legion destroyed Guernica, it does not suggest—as Steer, Aguirre, and other pro-Republican commentators claimed—that an annhilation of the entire town was the goal from the outset. On the contrary, it suggests that the Condor Legion wanted to close off the town by knocking out the Rentería bridge, the incoming roads, and the eastern suburbs.

The German sources also reveal that the Condor Legion command saw Guernica as a legitimate military target, not as a candidate for an experiment in the terror bombing of helpless civilians. They attacked on April 26 not because it was a market day but because it was the first day they could organize sorties designed to cut off the Republican retreat in that area. Hermann Göring is said to have admitted at his Nuremberg trial in 1946 that Germany regarded Guernica as a "testing ground," but in fact he said only that he regarded the Spanish civil war in general as an opportunity to try out new machines and techniques.

There is even less evidence that the Condor Legion wished to bomb Guernica in order to "wound" the Basques in "the most sensitive of [their] patriotic sentiments." None of the pilots seems to have known what this town meant to the

Basques. They were imported military technicians, not students of Spanish history.

On the other hand, "terror" and psychological warfare cannot have been entirely absent from the pilots' minds as they approached their target. They had bombed and strafed defenseless civilians often enough in the past: Durango was a grim case in point. In fact, they had orders to wreak terror wherever they could, for their commanders believed that this might break the enemy's morale and expedite final victory. The Germans, we know, were frustrated with the Nationalists' slow progress in the north; they were looking for a quick breakthrough. As for the Italians, they had a recent humiliation to avenge and a warning from the duce that they had better do so quickly. It seems reasonable to assume that once the main strike force arrived over Guernica and found the primary targets obscured by smoke and dust, the bombadiers had no compunction about dumping their "eggs" in "the middle." Nor, apparently, did the fighter pilots hesitate to machine-gun people—and even sheep—running helplessly on the ground.

Although it is clear that Condor Legion planes carried out a massive attack against Guernica, the question remains whether the Germans (and, to a lesser degree, the Italians) bear sole responsibility for what happened. Undoubtedly they bear a large share of it, for the Condor Legion command had demanded and received a "significant influence" over Nationalist tactical operations in the north. But all Condor Legion sorties were cleared through the Nationalist command in Salamanca. The Guernica attack was no exception: Vigón, Mola's chief of staff, ordered the attack, and he and Richthofen worked out its details. Mola himself apparently did not participate in this planning session, but he must have known that Guernica (or its environs) was on the list of targets. This town stood between his forces and Bilbao, the great prize, and he had signed leaflets dropped on Basque towns warning that he would "raze all Vizcaya to the ground" unless submission was immediate. Moreover, he and Vigón must have known something of Guernica's historical significance. Although there is no evidence that their primary motivation was the destruction of the Basques' most sacred symbol, as Nationalist centralists they surely welcomed the opportunity to strike a blow at Basque autonomy.

A related question concerns General Franco's role in this entire affair. Two historians of the raid have insisted that Richthofen and Vigón made their decision "without reference to higher authority." Franco's English biographer George Hills claims that the Germans attacked Guernica without consulting any Spaniard at all. He claims Franco first learned about the bombing from foreign news reports and initially dismissed these as "Red propaganda." When informed by his own command that the Condor Legion had in fact carried out the attack, he allegedly called in Colonel Funk of the legion and gave him a dressing down. Reportedly "pale with anger," Franco told the German that he would "not have war made on [his] own people." (An odd comment, if true: what did he think he had been doing since July 1936?) Franco insisted that Sperrle, whom he held responsible for the raid, be recalled to Germany.

While it may be that Franco did not personally order the attack on Guernica, or even know of it in advance, one cannot reasonably insist, as many of Franco's defenders have done, that he bears no responsibility for the atrocity. He had authority over the Nationalist campaign in general and the war in the north in particular. He was the only Spanish general to whom the Condor Legion was responsible. He had made the decision to conquer the Basque country, and he held to this goal even when the Germans wanted to break off the offensive. Although he apparently hoped to spare the war industries for use after their capture, he was not opposed to the massive destruction of human life, Spanish or foreign. If he indeed was "pale with anger" over the bombing, his anger undoubtedly stemmed less from sympathy for the victims than from a perception that this was a public-relations fiasco of the first order. That he would want to deny any responsibility for it is quite understandable.

Although parceling out responsibility for the tragedy of Guernica seemed important to Franco—as it has seemed to commentators and historians ever since—this issue was not uppermost in the minds of the raid's victims. Richthofen's assertion notwithstanding, there were roughly two thousand more people than usual in Guernica on that April afternoon. In addition to market-day visitors, hundreds of soldiers and refugees from the war zone filled the town. The refugees brought tales of how Franco's Moors looted, raped, and disemboweled and of how in one town they had "nailed the tongues of some women to a table." When those two nuns on the roof of La Merced Convent shouted their warning, some of the people in town must have feared that a similar fate might soon be in store for them.

According to witnesses of the attack, within a few moments of the warning a single Heinkel 111 appeared over the eastern end of town. Guernicans could not have known that it was piloted by Moreau, the Condor Legion's ace. The plane passed once over the city, then returned and dove in the direction of the Rentería bridge. Though there was no flak—Guernica had no antiaircraft guns whatsoever—Moreau's bombs landed not on the bridge but about three hundred yards to the west, in a plaza fronting the railroad station. One bomb tore up the Julian Hotel across the plaza. A volunteer fireman reported seeing women and children blown high in the air, come apart, and then rain down in "legs, arms, heads, and bits and pieces everywhere."

About twenty-five minutes later three more Heinkel 111s appeared low in the sky. Releasing their bombs at about two thousand feet, they hit a candy factory near the Rentería bridge. Incendiary bombs ignited caldrons of sugar solution, turning the factory into an inferno. Young female workers began stampeding from the building; one of them, her hair and overalls ablaze, collapsed in a fiery heap. The central marketplace, not far away, was also hit. Two bulls, sprayed with burning thermite, charged through the canvas-walled stalls. Soon the entire market was on fire.

Next, five pairs of Heinkel 51 fighters zoomed in very low over parts of the town not yet obscured by smoke. As one witness reported, two of the planes "just flew back and forth at about one hundred feet, like flying sheep dogs rounding up people for the slaughter." One Heinkel zeroed in on a woman and her three small children, killing them all in a single burst. Another plane wiped out the town band.

At about six the first bombers—Junkers 52s and Italian Savoias from the Soria Squadron—neared their target. They came in groups of three, wave after wave, carrying among them almost 100,000 pounds of explosives. These they dropped helter-skelter through the smoke and dust hanging above the town. One group of bombs hit a pelota fronton; another blew up the Bank of Vizcaya; and still another demolished the Residencia Calzada, killing forty-five orphans and elderly citizens. Bombs dropped by Beust's Squadron Number 2 hit La Merced Convent, which fortunately had just been evacuated. A 550-pounder demolished the town hall. By the time the last of the bombers had headed home to their base in Burgos, seven out of every ten buildings in Guernica had been destroyed or set on fire.

People were now streaming from the town into the nearby fields and hills. Running along, they presented irresistible targets to a squadron of six Messerschmitts, which swooped down almost to ground level to spray them with machine-gun fire. Soon the Messerschmitts were joined by another squadron of Heinkel 51s. Sometimes the planes flew singly, sometimes in pairs. They executed daring maneuvers as they pursued their quarry up rocky hillsides and along twisting roads.

The fighters finished their sport at about seven-thirty. The raid on Guernica was now over. It had lasted about three hours, with intervals of a few minutes between each wave of fighters and bombers. The forty-three planes that took part in the raid may have failed to hit their primary target, but they managed to obliterate a small town and in the process kill over a hundred people. The exact number of dead, like much else about this atrocity, is still disputed.*

RESPONSES

The bombing of Guernica provoked widespread outrage in the Western democracies, though the Nationalist apologia also quickly found its defenders in these countries. Indeed, sharply contrasting interpretations of the Guernica tragedy divided public opinion throughout the West, just as the Spanish war in general had done.

During the first week in May 1937, many American newspapers published indignant commentaries on the Guernica bombing. Typical was an editorial in

*Estimates of the death toll range from under 100 to 1,600 (undoubtedly far too high). Vincente Talon, in his *Arde Guernica* (Madrid, 1970), claimed that 200 died, while Hugh Thomas suggests about 1,000. The most recent and authoritative account, Jesús M. Salas Larrazabal, *Guernica* (Madrid, 1987), insists that no more than 120 people died in the raid.

the *Wheeling Intelligencer,* which said that though there had been "terror on both sides . . . nowhere . . . has one read of such fiendish ferocity as that exhibited at Guernica and Durango. . . . All other issues in Spain have been sloughed away by this Nazi-Moor-Fascist attack on the Basques." *Time, Life,* and *Newsweek,* which heretofore had straddled the fence on the Spanish war, now declared their support for the republic.

Some American diplomats and politicians were also quick to condemn the raid, along with the Nationalist claim that the Reds had destroyed the town. On April 30 Ambassador Bowers cabled Secretary of State Hull, "Guernica 'holy city of the Basques' totally destroyed though an open country town with unarmed population by huge bombs dropped from insurgent planes of German origin and pilotage. . . . Denials by insurgents and Germany following world reaction incredible. The extermination in line with Mola's threat to exterminate every town in province unless Bilbao surrenders."

A few days later (May 6), Senator William E. Borah, of Idaho, brought the matter before the Senate. Idaho had America's largest Basque population, and Borah had come to regard the Nationalist campaign against this people as typical of Fascist bestiality. "No language," he said, "can describe the scene at Guernica, and Guernica was not a single instance; it was simply a culmination of a long line of unspeakable atrocities. It was not a military maneuver. . . . An unarmed, non-combatant city was singled out for the most revolting instance of mass murder in modern times. It was Fascist strategy." Senator Gerald P. Nye, of North Dakota, inserted into the *Congressional Record* a letter signed by seventy-six prominent Protestant politicians, educators, and clergymen, condemning the raid as an atrocity "outside the pale of morality and civilization." In the House of Representatives, Jerry J. O'Connell, of Montana, another state with a large Basque population, told his colleagues that he and three other congressmen had written Secretary of State Hull alerting him "to the massacre of Guernica, reported by all the foreign correspondents of accredited newspapers to be the work of German planes, German bombs, and German pilots." Unfortunately, added O'Connell, the secretary had replied that there was "no evidence" that Germany and Italy were "participating in the Spanish invasion."

Hull answered in this fashion for diplomatic and political reasons. Although he knew full well that Germans and Italians were fighting on behalf of Franco, and had bombed Guernica,* he could not publicly admit this without undercutting the justification for America's "strict neutrality" and its "moral embargo" on weapons to the republic. Hull also realized that any official condemnation of the attack would arouse the ire of Franco's many defenders in the United States, some of whom were beginning to echo the Nationalist line on this event.

For example, H. Edward Knoblaugh, an AP reporter in Madrid, admitted

---

*Hull had extensive reports from his own State Department attesting to the bombing, not to mention the presence of German and Italian personnel in Spain. In his memoirs he wrote of "the savage bombing of the Basque city of Guernica by the Franco forces employing German and Italian planes."

that an attack had taken place but insisted that most of the destruction had been done by the Reds. This view eventually became gospel among conservative American Catholics. Shortly after the bombing, Father Wilfrid Parsons, editor of the Catholic magazine *America,* wrote that the charges of a Fascist bombing amounted to "the greatest propaganda hoax (after Badajoz) in the whole merry game of misleading the public." The "facts," he said, were that "dynamiting Anarchists" planted mines in the houses and streets, soaked the buildings in gasoline, then set the whole business off "and departed." Another Catholic spokesman, Father Joseph F. Thorning, a professor at Mount St. Mary's College, in Maryland, told the American Catholic Historical Association that though Franco's planes might have dropped some bombs on Guernica, the damage they did "was insignificant in comparison with the havoc perpetrated by gasoline flames kindled by Spanish anarchists in their retreat."

America's response to Guernica—whichever direction it took—was less important than France's and Britain's, for America was not a member of the Nonintervention Committee. France and Britain were now confronted with an atrocity that seemed to signal more boldly than ever the bankruptcy of their "nonintervention" policy. The question was what they would do about it.

In France, where pro-Republican circles had long been fuming over Paris's abandonment of Madrid, leftist and liberal newspapers saw Guernica's destruction as a confirmation of their direst warnings regarding Fascist bestiality. With this atrocity, declared *L'Humanité,* fascism had "beaten all its records." This reaction was predictable enough; more interesting and significant was the response of the moderate press, especially the moderate Catholic press. Following a series of interviews in Paris by Father Onaindia, the Basque priest who had been in Guernica on April 26, several moderate Catholic papers came out strongly against the bombing. In *L'Aube,* Georges Bidault, the future Resistance leader, declared, "For three hours, the German air fleet bombed the defenseless town. For three hours, the German airplanes fired their machine-guns on the women and children in the streets and in the fields. All of this in the name of civilization. And even, for the Crusade, as they say." *L'Oeuvre* regarded the bombing as an example of "total war"—the new military doctrine that advocated terror attacks on civilian populations as a means of expediting victory.

Prominent Catholic intellectuals like Jacques Maritain and François Mauriac joined in the condemnation. Mauriac's admonition "One does not exterminate an old Christian people such as the Basques simply because they believed they were not duty-bound to revolt" struck a receptive chord among many French Catholics, but it also introduced an agony of the soul, for the Vatican continued to side with Franco's "crusade" regardless of its tactics. Indeed, Pope Pius XI refused to receive two Basque priests who had brought a letter about Guernica, and Cardinal Pacelli (soon to become Pope Pius XII), dismissed the Basques' protest with the remark "The Church is persecuted in Barcelona." Sympathy for the republic, therefore, amounted to a rebellion against church leadership, especially when, in August 1937, the Vatican extended de facto recognition to Franco's Nationalist government.

The French right-wing press experienced no agonies of conscience over Guernica. After initially saying nothing at all about this issue, the rightist papers soon fell into line behind the Nationalist claims of Red arson. "It was the Reds who burned Guernica just as they burned Irún," declared the *Journal de Toulouse*. On May 6 *L'Action française* told how "honest French reporters" had exposed "Red lies" about Guernica. *Je suis partout,* edited by the future collaborator Robert Brasillach, expressed astonishment that any good Frenchmen could believe the "legend" about Guernica's bombing spread by "Masonic agencies" rather than "all the rectifications of our invincible *caudillo* and fervent Catholic, General Franco."

France's pro-Franco forces could count on their government to take no significant action over Guernica. Blum, under pressure from Britain and anti-interventionist elements in his cabinet, remained deaf to calls from fellow Socialists in and outside France for a vigorous response to the atrocity. Though Foreign Minister Delbos had solid information from his consul in Bilbao regarding the bombing, he brushed off appeals for a formal protest with vague suggestions that an "inquiry" into the affair ought to be conducted. He did nothing, however, to ensure that such an inquiry took place.

France's chief ally, Great Britain, witnessed a dramatic public upheaval over Guernica, just as it had over Ethiopia. Steer's *Times* dispatches brought a barrage of indignant letters to the editor, many from clergymen. One of them wrote presciently, "If a European war comes, as seems all too likely, the scenes in Guernica will be repeated in every big town in Europe." Leftist intellectuals and Labour party politicians excoriated the Franco forces and demanded that the British government do so as well.

British right-wing opinion, on the other hand, rallied around a pro-Franco Catholic publisher named Douglas Jerrold, who claimed on the basis of information supplied by a Nationalist spokesman that Guernica had been shelled and bombed "in the proper course of the operations against Bilbao" before April 26, but that the actual destruction was the work of retreating Basque and Asturian troops. Jerrold's claim showed another interesting shift in the evolving Nationalist interpretation, but such slight changes did not undermine Nationalist credibility in the eyes of the British Right. Pro-Franco forces in the press and in Parliament—including a number of retired military men—continued to insist that Guernica could have been destroyed only by Red arsonists and dynamiters.

Britain's division of opinion on Guernica put Foreign Secretary Eden in a difficult position. In his memoirs he calls Guernica "the first blitz of the Second World War" and notes that Foreign Office reports at the time placed the blame on "German aircraft." On May 3 a Labour party politician asked him in Parliament whether he would "initiate immediately proposals for an international commission to investigate the circumstances of the recent air attack on Guernica and, in particular, the charges made by the Basque government." Eden replied evasively that his information was not yet complete but that the government was "considering what steps [could] be taken in co-operation with other Powers to prevent re-currence of such happenings."

On the following day Britain brought the matter before the Nonintervention Committee. There was some talk of an international investigation into the Basque charges, but the German and the Italian delegations would have none of this. The most the Fascist powers would agree to was a general appeal to both sides in the Spanish war to forgo bombings of "open cities." Guernica was not to be referred to as a justification for the appeal. Berlin eventually approved this gesture because, as a German War Ministry cable put it, "a completely intransigent position would make [Germany] responsible in world opinion for the failure of a humane action. In any case [this action] has no practical relevance, since neither side will be able to agree on the definition of an 'open city.' "

Britain lamely accepted this "solution" and did not push for an investigation into the Guernica affair. Neither Stanley Baldwin nor Neville Chamberlain, who became prime minister on May 28, 1937, wanted to ruffle German sensibilities in this delicate matter. Even Eden, who remained foreign secretary until February 20, 1938, was prepared to turn a blind eye to the grossest German violations of "nonintervention." On June 1, in response to a colleague's question whether "Germany and Italy were genuinely in favor of maintaining non-intervention arrangements in Spain," Eden replied that one must distinguish between Italy and Germany: while the former was clearly a violator, "Germany throughout had cooperated loyally, efficiently and zealously in all the arrangements adopted in the Non-Intervention Committee." With positions like this, it is astonishing that Eden later managed to convince most of the world that he had been Europe's greatest "anti-appeaser" of the thirties.

Aside from promoting the Nonintervention Committee's innocuous humanitarian declaration, the British government, under pressure from Ellen Wilkinson and other Labour leaders, launched an evacuation of Basque women and children from the war zone. British ships brought thousands of evacuees to Southampton under protection of the Royal Navy. Franco objected strongly to this operation, as did the pro-Franco British ambassador to Spain, Sir Henry Chilton. He argued that by removing useless mouths from Bilbao, Britain would prolong that city's ability to withstand the Nationalist siege. As for the evacuees, they became celebrated in England as "the children of Guernica." They were among the first of millions of war refugees who would be displaced from their homes over the course of the next decade.

The Spanish Nationalist command, for its part, continued to maintain both that Guernica was a military target worthy of bombing and that it had not been destroyed by bombs. A "commission" established by the Nationalists issued an "official report" a year later that did not admit to any Nationalist bombing. It concluded only that one or several "unidentified" planes "appeared" over the town and caused the inhabitants to flee into shelters. Then the Republican soldiers, it alleged, went to work and burned the town.

Nationalist officers in the field, however, sometimes spoke with an embarrassing candor about what had happened to Guernica. In August 1937 a Franco staff officer told the American correspondent Virginia Cowles, "Of course [Guernica] was bombed. We bombed it and bombed it and bombed it, and *bueno,* why not?" A Nationalist press officer traveling with Cowles said to her later, "I don't think I would write about that if I were you."

PICASSO'S *GUERNICA*

Pablo Picasso had never been to Guernica, but when he read of the town's bombardment he decided at once to use this event as the subject for a mural he had been commissioned to produce for the Spanish pavilion at the 1937 Paris World International Exposition. The project would, as he put it, allow him to express his "abhorrence of the military caste which has sunk Spain in an ocean of pain and death." He began making preparatory sketches on May 1 and finished his great work roughly one month later.*

The result of Picasso's sustained burst of creative activity was a huge (eleven by twenty-five feet) canvas in black, gray, and white, featuring a woman hurtling from a burning house with flames licking at her hair, a disemboweled horse, a stoic bull, and a mother clutching her dead child. This was no traditional "battle scene" but a vivid rendition of modern warfare as seen through the terrified eyes of the victims, both human and animal. Historically it bears comparison with great antiwar paintings like Rubens's *Horrors of War,* Goya's *The Third of May, 1808,* and, more recently, Max Ernst's *The Angel of Hearth and Home,* which was also inspired by the Spanish civil war.†

After it was put on display at the Paris Exposition, *Guernica* was exhibited in London in 1938, moved to New York's Museum of Modern Art in 1939, and finally sent to post-Franco Spain in 1981. (Upon its transfer to Madrid's Casón del Buen Retiro, Spanish newspapers spoke of a "liberated *Guernica,*" but the painting is now encased in a bulletproof glass box and guarded by policemen with machine guns.)

---

*During his labors, incidentally, Picasso's two mistresses showed up in his Paris studio and began quarreling over right of place. Picasso refused to say which he preferred, telling them to fight it out for themselves. This they quite literally proceeded to do, while Picasso kept on painting. The art historian James Lord noted the irony in this scene: Picasso's two lady friends engaged "in a fistfight in his studio, while he peacefully continued to work on the enormous canvas conceived to decry the horrors of human conflict."

†In 1967, thirty years after painting this work, Ernst wrote, "One picture that I painted after [sic] the defeat of the Republicans in Spain, is *The Angel of Hearth and Home.* This is of course an ironic title for a kind of juggernaut which crushes and destroys all that comes in its path. That was my impression at the time of what would probably happen in the world, and I was right."

After the end of World War II, and perhaps with Picasso's painting in mind, people began to view Guernica's destruction not just as another atrocity but as a prelude to the greater horrors to come. "Guernica" is often cited both as a precedent-setting example of "terror bombing" and as a precursor of the raids on Coventry, Rotterdam, Hamburg, and Dresden.

Yet momentous and tragic as the Guernica bombing was, in some ways it is surprising that it should have taken on such vast symbolic weight. Despite claims to the contrary, it was by no means the first large-scale bombing of a civilian population. In the Ethiopian war the Italians made a regular practice of bombing undefended towns and even Red Cross centers. The earlier bombing of Durango in the Spanish war probably killed about as many civilians as the Guernica attack. Though the Guernica raid certainly took on terrorist dimensions, "demoralization of the civil population" was not its initial or primary purpose, as it was in many World War II attacks.

What makes the Guernica case special is primarily the historical and political significance of the target. But the foreign airmen who laid waste to the city had little or no notion of this significance. Nor, obviously, could they have known that their act would shock world opinion and become the subject of the twentieth century's most celebrated painting. Picasso's *Guernica* helped make this moment emblematic of the horrors of modern warfare, but perhaps it ought also stand for war's bitter ironies.

VII ～━～

"THE REVOLUTION EATS ITS CHILDREN"

Stalin's Great Purge

> THE WHITE QUEEN: He's in prison now being punished; and the trial doesn't even begin til next Wednesday; and of course, the crime comes last of all.
>
> ALICE: But suppose he never commits the crime?
>
> THE WHITE QUEEN: That would be all the better, wouldn't it?
>
> —Lewis Carroll, *Through the Looking Glass*

In 1936 Mme Marcelle Vinal, astrologer for the French newspaper *L'Intransigeant,* predicted that the following year would be a bad one for Europe's dictators. "Their power will be weakened," she announced, "because Saturn is no longer in the sign of the fishes and opposed to Neptune."

One of Europe's most brutal dictators, Joseph Stalin, was apparently unaware that the stars had turned against him. In 1937 his "Great Purge" of alleged political "oppositionists" reached its peak with the second of three spectacular show trials. These trials, in which prominent Communist party figures confessed to crimes they could not have committed, have been called "the most ambitious and concentrated attempt to destroy and distort the historical truth that history has known." But the infamous trials constituted only one dimension of Stalin's Great Purge. The cream of the Red Army was liquidated without public trial, and tens of thousands of minor party officials, state bureaucrats, economic experts, and ordinary citizens disappeared into forced-labor camps.

Certain aspects of Stalin's Great Purge suggest similarities to Hitler's Night of the Long Knives, but in the modern era the massive scope of Stalin's internecine bloodletting can be compared only to that of Mao's "Cultural Revolution" of the 1960s and perhaps that of Pol Pot's "killing fields" in Cambodia in the 1970s. Although the Great Purge did rid Stalin of various opponents or critics, it followed earlier repressions that had already eliminated most resistance to the dictator's policies. The crusade's focus on "Old Bolsheviks," moreover, made the terror seem cannibalistic—a reenactment of that grisly period in the French

Revolution when the revolutionaries turned against themselves and "ate their children."

THE KIROV ASSASSINATION

In the late afternoon of December 1, 1934, a young Communist named Leonid Nikolayev appeared at the entrance to the Smolny Institute, a former school for daughters of the aristocracy that now served as the headquarters of the Communist party in Leningrad. Nikolayev, emaciated and trembling, showed his pass to a guard and entered the building, whose windows shone brightly in the early December darkness. The young man walked down strangely empty corridors until he found the office of the Leningrad party boss, Sergei Kirov. Nikolayev hid in a corner near Kirov's door and pulled a Nagan revolver from his briefcase. When Kirov came out of his office and turned down the hall, Nikolayev shot him cleanly through the back. He then collapsed in a faint a few yards from his victim.

News of Kirov's murder was immediately relayed to Joseph Stalin in the Kremlin. Stalin ("Man of Steel"), who had been ruling Russia with an iron hand for the past half dozen years, was now fifty-five. He had a pockmarked face, uneven teeth, and a stiff left arm. Like many other dictators, he was quite short, and wore thick-soled shoes to give him an extra inch. One of his rivals (and later victims), Nikolai Bukharin, suggested that Stalin was made miserable and mean-spirited by his short stature, by his inability to "convince everyone, including himself, that he [was] a taller man than anybody else." Stalin's personality was also shaped by his harsh upbringing as the son of a drunken cobbler in wild Georgia, a mountainous region that had been controlled by the Mongols and Turks before becoming a part of the expanding Russian Empire in the early nineteenth century. As a young boy, the future dictator identified with the Georgian rebels who had resisted their land's "Russification." Later he became a zealous Russifier in his own right, but he always spoke with a Georgian accent and retained something of the provincial rebel in his character. His personality was further molded by his education at a repressive theological seminary famous for its production of rebels and by his long years in czarist prisons and Siberian exile. Well before he embarked on his Great Purge, he had established a reputation for cruelty and vengefulness: his enemies compared him to Tamerlane and Genghis Khan.

Immediately upon receiving word of the Kirov assassination, a shocked and angry Stalin rushed by train to Leningrad. At the station he was met by Philip Medved, head of the Leningrad NKVD (secret police). As Medved opened his arms in greeting, Stalin punched him in the face. From the station he went directly to the NKVD headquarters and began questioning Nikolayev. "Why did you kill such a nice man?" he is said to have asked Nikolayev. According to one account the young man fell on his knees and pointed at a group of NKVD men standing behind Stalin and shouted, "They forced me to do it." Another account has Nikolayev insisting that he had "fired at the Party" when he shot Kirov. To Stalin's query about where he got his revolver, he replied, "Why do you ask me? Ask Zaporozhets [second in command of the Leningrad NKVD] that!" To which Stalin, reportedly "green with anger," cried, "Take him away!"

All existing accounts of this scene in the Leningrad NKVD building are secondhand. No one present at the meeting left a reliable memoir. We do know, however, that Kirov's assassination led to a wave of arrests and executions. At first the government blamed the deed on Russian "White Guard terrorists" who had allegedly sneaked into the Soviet Union from Finland and the Baltic States. In early December, Soviet newspapers announced that 104 White Guardists had been executed for their role in this counterrevolutionary plot. Then the investigation shifted to the Ukraine, where twenty-eight men were charged with "organizing acts of terror against officials of the Soviet government." They too were immediately executed.

Two weeks later, however, the Soviet press offered an entirely different explanation for Kirov's murder. Two prominent Old Bolsheviks, Grigori Zinoviev and Lev Kamenev, were said to have "encouraged" Nikolayev's act by fomenting dissension within the party.

Why this sudden attack on two former luminaries of the Bolshevik party? The explanation must be sought as much in earlier party history as in more recent developments. Zinoviev and Kamenev had been Lenin's closest associates during his years in exile before the Bolshevik Revolution. Although they had angered Lenin by opposing his insurrection in October 1917, after the revolution they returned to favor and assumed key positions in the new Soviet regime. Zinoviev, indeed, had fancied himself Lenin's successor. Stalin, who had similar ambitions, could not help resenting Zinoviev's and Kamenev's influence with Lenin, especially since he knew that Lenin saw *him*, the raw provincial from Georgia, as too uncouth and heavy-handed to inherit his mantle of leadership.

In the years immediately following Lenin's death, Stalin had to share power with Zinoviev and Kamenev, but he quickly sought to undermine their influence by maligning them as coffee-house revolutionaries who had spent most of their careers talking about revolution in Western cafés. He also made derogatory reference to their Jewish origins, tapping a vein of anti-Semitism that was almost as rich among Russia's revolutionaries as among the old defenders of czarist autocracy. In matters of policy Zinoviev and Kamenev had incurred Stalin's hatred by opposing his position of "Socialism in One Country," which held that the Soviet Union could and must become an advanced industrial country before Communist revolutions had triumphed abroad. By careful backstairs maneuvering, Stalin managed slowly to isolate his opponents and set them up for their political fall, which came at the Fifteenth Party Congress, in 1927. After this moment they never again exercised genuine influence, but Stalin, in his paranoid insecurity, saw them as potential troublemakers. It seemed that he had long been waiting for an opportunity to ensure that these former oppositionists never became oppositionists again.

The Kirov assassination offered this opportunity, and Stalin seized it. Exposure of the Zinoviev-Kamenev "plot" led to a new wave of arrests and executions, though initially the focus was on lesser "allies" of the two discredited leaders. In Leningrad, corpses began to pile up in the NKVD cellars. The press launched a campaign for increased vigilance toward the "hidden enemy." A Central Committee directive entitled "Lessons of the Events Connected with the Evil Murder of Comrade Kirov" called on party members to hunt down all former oppositionists who remained in the party. Within the next month thousands of party members and ordinary citizens were arrested and deported to Siberia. Since Leningrad was said to be the main site of the oppositionist plot, the purge focused on that city. A Soviet journalist told the American Communist Louis Fischer that right after the Kirov assassination, well-to-do Muscovites traveled to Leningrad to buy up the furniture, carpets, and paintings of the people sent into exile. "The purge almost solved that city's housing problem," he added.

On December 28 and 29 Nikolayev and thirteen other men accused of being directly involved in the Kirov assassination were tried in a secret military court. The published account of their trial said that they had "confessed" to plotting against Kirov in order to open the way for Zinoviev's and Kamenev's return to power. Oddly enough, however, the press also mentioned a diary carried by Nikolayev that suggested he had acted alone. Immediately following the trial, Nikolayev and the others were shot.

Zinoviev and Kamenev, on the other hand, were not tried for the murder until mid-January 1935. Before their trial they were ordered by the NKVD publicly to assume full responsibility for the Kirov murder, but they agreed to accept only "moral responsibility." In the trial Zinoviev reportedly admitted, "The former activity of the former opposition could not, by the force of objective circumstances, but stimulate the degeneration of those criminals." As punishment for their subversive behavior, Zinoviev was sentenced to ten years' imprisonment and Kamenev to five. A week later Medved and Zaporozhets, the Leningrad NKVD men, were charged with dereliction of duty for their failure to protect Kirov. Their sentences were three and two years' Siberian exile, respectively.

Most Russians apparently accepted the various official explanations for the Kirov murder. One NKVD official who later defected to the West, however, claimed to have smelled a rat from the outset. Alexander Orlov, an operative in the NKVD's Foreign Department, had been out of the Soviet Union at the time of the murder. Upon his return to Moscow in the fall of 1935, he began asking friends in the secret police about the assassination. Though told it was "healthier not to know too much," he pressed on with his investigation. He learned, he said, that Kirov had alienated Stalin in the summer of 1934 by challenging his authority. Without Moscow's permission, he had apparently requisitioned scarce food supplies for the workers of Leningrad. A gifted orator, he had become extremely popular in Leningrad, which he had turned into his personal fiefdom. As a party "moderate" he had opposed internal purges and the introduction of the death penalty for oppositionists.

As for the assassin, Orlov learned that Nikolayev had been apprehended by the NKVD in an earlier attempt to kill Kirov. Rather than detain him, the police had returned his revolver and allowed him to go free. A few days later he was found by Kirov's guards snooping around the Smolny. Turned over to the secret police, he was advised by an undercover agent posing as his friend to try yet again. This time the police were careful to clear away most of the Smolny guards. Even Kirov's personal bodyguard was removed from the scene. This explained the ease with which Nikolayev could enter the Smolny and gun down his target.

On the basis of this information, Orlov surmised that the Leningrad NKVD had "allowed" Kirov to be murdered on orders from Stalin himself. The dictator had gotten rid of a bothersome rival, then used the murder as a pretext to launch a campaign against Zinoviev and Kamenev. The entire operation was a giant "frame-up."

Another NKVD agent turned defector, Walter Krivitsky, advanced a similar theory in 1939. Noting that Zinoviev and Kamenev had remained figureheads of an inchoate "opposition" to Stalin's one-man rule, Krivitsky opined that the dictator was searching for a way to destroy the Bolshevik Old Guard once and for all. Hitler's Blood Purge of June 30, 1934, suggested a solution: "Stalin was profoundly impressed by the manner in which Hitler exterminated his opposition, and studied minutely every secret report from our agents in Germany relating to the events of that night." Hitler therefore "showed the way," and Stalin proved an adept pupil.

Orlov's and Krivitksy's revelations smacked of insider information, and they convinced many students of Stalinism that the dictator had orchestrated the Kirov assassination. Nevertheless, there are reasons to doubt that this was so. Kirov was not, it turns out, the "moderate" anti-Stalinist that Orlov made him out to be. He had supported the dictator in his consolidation of power, which he never really challenged. Of course, Stalin may have still wanted him out of the way, but assassination was a dangerous and clumsy way to achieve this: it might encourage the murder of other high officials. Had he nevertheless chosen this method, Stalin would probably have been more efficient in its execution and would not have let loose ends, like Nikolayev's dead-end diary, confuse the issue. His initial response to the murder—an immediate trip to Leningrad and a wild striking out at all sorts of alleged culprits—suggests confusion, panic, and un-focused retaliation. Only gradually did more coherent and focused uses for this event become clear to him.

In the end, at any rate, Stalin's possible complicity in the Kirov assassination is less important than his exploitation of the affair. Krivitsky was certainly correct when he noted that "the murder of Kirov was a turning point in Stalin's career. It ushered in the era of public and secret trials of the Bolshevist Old Guard, the era of the confessions."

THE TRIAL OF THE
TROTSKYITE-ZINOVIEVITE
UNITED CENTER

Not long after the Kirov assassination, orders went out from Moscow to every party organization to step up efforts at exposing "deviations" from the party line. In her memoirs of the purge period, Eugenia Ginzburg, one of its victims, speaks of an "orgy of breast-beating and self-criticism." Lecture halls were turned into "public confessionals" where people "repented" for misunderstanding the theory of permanent revolution, or for underrating the importance of the Second Five-Year Plan, or for showing signs of "rotten liberalism." A new "verification of party documents" led to the exclusion of thousands of people accused of poor discipline, lack of revolutionary zeal, association with counterrevolutionary elements, or drunkenness and hooliganism.

The worst offense, however, was maintaining contact with what was now called the Trotskyite-Zinovievite United Center. The addition of the discredited and exiled Lev Trotsky to the anti-Soviet conspiracy was a significant development. Much more than Zinoviev or Kamenev, Trotsky had played a key role in the Bolshevik Revolution and in the subsequent civil war. As commissar for war, he had created the Red Army, which ultimately defeated the White forces and saved the revolution. In Stalin's eyes this was Trotsky's first sin, for Stalin had not been one of the central figures in the October Revolution, and in the civil war he had displayed more brutality than military ability. Trotsky compounded this sin by openly accusing Stalin both of "calculated caution" in the revolution and of reckless insubordination in the civil war. He also harped on Stalin's lack of sophistication in socialist theory, dismissing one of his essays as "a hopelessly provincial analysis." Trotsky found it hard to imagine that Stalin, a "third-rate provincial mind," an uncouth rustic who did not even know German, might try to lead the party of Marx and Engels once the great Lenin had passed from the scene.

When it became evident that Stalin would try to do just this, Trotsky did his best to stop him. He conspired, intrigued, and let it be known far and wide that Lenin had thought Stalin an impossible brute. He heaped ridicule on Stalin's theory of "Socialism in One Country": Did this not signal an abandonment of that worldwide socialist upheaval without which Soviet communism could not long survive? Was not Stalin the "gravedigger of the revolution"? But whatever the force of his arguments, Trotsky lacked Stalin's talent for political infighting and organization; instead of isolating Stalin, he increasingly isolated himself. In the decisive showdown at the Fifteenth Party Congress, in 1927, Trotsky tried to gun down Stalin with his famous oratory but found that his salvos all missed the mark. Now he was "the Prophet Unarmed," and soon he would be driven from the party and then (in 1929) from the country. Yet even in exile in Turkey, Norway, France, and Mexico, he seemed to Stalin a dangerous adversary whose nefarious influence had to be countered with all possible means.

Though initially somewhat inchoate, Stalin's campaign against deviations from the party line soon focused firmly on Trotsky and his alleged coconspirators, Zinoviev and Kamenev. A decree of March 7, 1935, ordered the removal of all works by these men from Soviet libraries. Other decrees gave the regime new legal tools to deal with suspected deviationists and plotters. A revision of the criminal code declared the death penalty for attempts by Soviet citizens to flee abroad. If the flight involved a military man, members of the man's family would be subject to arrest whether or not they knew of the impending flight. Another revision extended the death penalty to children over twelve—an ominous sign of Stalin's intentions.

Accompanying these legal measures was a sharp intensification in the official veneration of Stalin—that "cult of personality" that Khrushchev was later to identify as the starting point for Stalin's crimes. He was heralded by the Soviet press as the "wisest of leaders," "beloved father," "great helmsman," "reformer of the world," and "forger of peace." Soviet newspapers and magazines invariably carried Stalin's picture, along with gushing letters, speeches, and greetings from "ordinary citizens." His oversized portrait stared down from innumerable billboards and building facades. Like the ubiquitous television screens in George Orwell's *1984*, these portraits also reminded the people that their chief was always watching.

The chief's vigilance was responsible for the exposure early in 1935 of an apparent "conspiracy" against the regime within the very walls of the Kremlin. A number of the Kremlin guards, it seems, were discovered to have been former White Guardists and Trotskyites. The official in charge of Kremlin personnel, Abel Yenukidze, was an old friend of Stalin's who sometimes protected dissidents from the full force of "Soviet justice." Exposure of the "Kremlin plot" led to Yenukidze's arrest and expulsion from the party. With this rough treatment of Yenukidze, Stalin established an important precedent: he showed that he was ready to sacrifice personal friends who had in some way become obnoxious.

Yenukidze's fall and the repressive legal measures that preceded it might have seemed alarming to some Soviet citizens, but most Russians, especially those outside the party, had reason to regard the year and a half or so following Kirov's murder as an "idyllic interlude." The economic situation improved considerably after the disruptive initial phases of forced industrialization and agricultural collectivization in the late twenties and early thirties. The 1935 harvest was relatively bountiful. Food rationing ended, and the collective farms were permitted to sell grain on the open market. On the political front a new "Stalin constitution," which the Soviet press hailed as "the most democratic in the world," promised free, equal, and secret elections, as well as the protection of individual rights and the guarantee of employment for all citizens. "Life has become better, Comrades, life has become gayer," said the chief; and apparently many Russians agreed.

Events were brewing on the international horizon, however, that helped bring this "idyll" to an end. Hitler's Germany was now emerging as a genuine threat. Stalin had been inclined initially to discount Hitler's importance, but the führer's

Blood Purge suggested that he was not a man to be trifled with. Hitler's remilitarization of the Rhineland in 1936, which by fortifying Germany's western border opened the possibility of a push to the east, suggested that Russia might once again have to reckon with aggression from its old enemy. As if this were not frightening enough, the Japanese were threatening Russian interests and territory in the Pacific. The Western democracies seemed unable or unwilling to counter the designs of the Fascist powers. They had not stopped Hitler from remilitarizing the Rhineland, Mussolini from raping Ethiopia, or Japan from moving into Manchuria.

For Stalin these developments had significant diplomatic as well as domestic implications. In foreign policy they led him to adopt the Popular Front strategy and to intervene in Spain. At home they kindled his fears of a "fifth column" that might cripple Soviet defenses at the moment of foreign attack. He believed he would have to liquidate in advance any individuals who might turn against him in time of war. In this respect he was prepared to be even more brazen than Hitler. So far the führer had liquidated only a few dozen troublemakers within the Nazi movement; Stalin knew that he would have to be more thorough.

In the spring of 1936 G. A. Molchanov, chief of the NKVD's Secret Political Department, called together about forty of his colleagues and informed them that a vast plot against the Kremlin leadership had been uncovered. At the center of it stood Trotsky, Zinoviev, and Kamenev, along with a few lesser accomplices. Full details of the conspiracy, however, were as yet unclear. The NKVD's job was to flesh out the bare bones of this plot and, more important, to secure the "confessions" of the ringleaders. Molchanov told his men that Stalin himself would supervise the investigation, though direct control would be in the hands of Genrikh Yagoda, chief of the NKVD. Yagoda's assistant would be one L. M. Zakovsky, who had once bragged that if he had Karl Marx to interrogate, he could make him admit to being an agent of Bismarck.

Such claims notwithstanding, it seemed that Stalin did not fully trust his policemen, for he instructed Nikolai Yezhov, secretary of the party Central Committee, to keep an eye on the investigation. A tiny man with a cruel streak that rivaled Stalin's own, Yezhov was called "the bloodthirsty dwarf." Stalin said that his prominence showed that "out of filth you can make a prince."

On Stalin's orders, Molchanov, Yagoda, and company began their investigation by bringing some three hundred former oppositionists to Moscow and subjecting them to inquisitorial grilling. According to Orlov, who had contacts among the interrogators, Stalin's plan was to identify by these methods roughly fifty or sixty oppositionists who would testify that they had engaged in conspiratorial activities under the direct control of Trotsky, Zinoviev, and Kamenev. Armed with these "confessions," the NKVD would then try to force Zinoviev and Kamenev themselves to admit their guilt. If they resisted, which was only to be expected, they and their families would be threatened with execution. If, on the other hand, they agreed to accept the charges against them at a public trial, they would be allowed to live. Stalin was not an aficionado of American gangster films, but he knew how to make an offer one could not refuse.

In the event, only sixteen men (including Zinoviev and Kamenev, who had been in prison since January 1935) actually appeared in court at the first Moscow show trial, in August 1936. Among these sixteen, five were "fictitious defendants"—that is, NKVD plants whose assigned duty was to pressure the real defendants to confess, then to confirm and embellish those confessions at the public trial.

The first of these five stooges was one Valentin Olberg, a former agent of the Foreign Department of the NKVD who had previously worked in Berlin as a secret informer against exiled Trotskyites. When told in 1936 that his services were again needed to unmask Trotsky's evil designs, he readily agreed to cooperate. In preparation for his upcoming "trial," he signed a deposition that he had recently received an order from Trotsky's son to recruit an anti-Stalinist hit squad among the students of the Gorky Polytechnic Institute. He also confessed to being a secret agent of the Gestapo, adding that this German connection "followed the [Trotskyite] line of organizing terrorism in the USSR against the leaders of the Communist Party of the Soviet Union." As a reward for his testimony, the NKVD promised Olberg a new posting in the Far East—not, one would think, a terribly attractive proposition. But he was also undoubtedly given to understand that if he resisted or bungled his assignment, he would quickly be transformed from a "fictitious" defendant into a real one.

The NKVD's next pigeon initially proved much less willing to coo for his keepers. Isak Reingold, a trade official and personal friend of Kamenev's, resisted police efforts to get him to admit that his once-powerful friend had drawn him into a terror organization that planned to kill Stalin. In frustration Molchanov turned Reingold over to an especially brutal interrogator, who grilled him for long periods without allowing him food, water, or rest. Still he resisted, saying he would sign a confession only if ordered to do so by the party leadership. He remained uncooperative even when confronted with a signed order for the arrest of his family and his own execution. Finally Yezhov intervened, informing Reingold in the name of the Central Committee that he could prove his loyalty to the party only by signing the deposition required of him. Suddenly he dropped all resistance and confessed that Kamenev and Zinoviev had ordered the murder of Kirov and planned to kill other party leaders, including Stalin, Molotov, Voroshilov, and Kaganovich.*

As their third tool the NKVD chose one Richard Pickel, a writer and theater

---

*Reingold's deposition was forwarded to Stalin, who promptly struck Molotov's name from the list of assassination targets. Everyone who learned of this assumed it meant the worst for Molotov—that Stalin's next move would be to add him to the list of conspirators. Instead, Stalin allowed Molotov to twist in the wind for a while, then restored him to grace. Molotov continued to act as Stalin's right-hand man, signing the death warrants for thousands of "enemies of the people," negotiating the infamous nonaggression pact with the Nazi foreign minister, Joachim von Ribbentrop, in August 1939, and outliving his master by some thirty-three years (he died in 1986).

manager who had once been chief of Zinoviev's secretariat. The police asked
Pickel to confess that he, along with Reingold and another accomplice, had
received written instructions from Zinoviev to kill Stalin. Pickel was not eager to
denounce his former boss, but eventually agreed to do so on the promise that *he*,
at least, would not suffer as a result of his testimony. He signed a statement that
the "Trotskyite-Zinovievite bloc" had planned in 1934 to "strike a crushing blow
at the CPSU by committing a number of terroristic acts with the aim of beheading the leadership and seizing power."

With the signed depositions of Olberg, Reingold, and Pickel, the NKVD was
ready to force the ringleaders of the "Trotskyite-Zinovievite Center" to admit
their guilt. Before doing so, however, they were told by Stalin to firm up their case
against the absent Trotsky, whom the chief wished to depict as the mastermind of
the entire conspiracy. In reviewing Olberg's testimony, Stalin noted that he had
confessed to receiving assassination orders from Trotsky's son, not from Trotsky
himself. Yagoda offered to rewrite Olberg's deposition to implicate Trotsky directly, but Stalin was oddly fastidious about these documents: there should be no
tampering with the "evidence." Instead, he agreed to an NKVD proposal to
recruit two additional fictitious defendants—the former NKVD agents Fritz
David and K. B. Berman-Yurin, who swore to have separately visited Trotsky in
Copenhagen in 1932 and received from him orders to kill Stalin.

Having gotten all their decoys in a row, the NKVD now set out to do the same
with their real targets. They started with the Trotskyite side, which because of
Trotsky's absence had to be represented by his former associates within the grasp
of the police. One of these was Ivan Smirnov, a distinguished Old Bolshevik and
revolutionary hero who had fought in the revolution of 1905, suffered for years in
czarist prisons, and led a Red Army unit to victory in the civil war. After Lenin's
death Smirnov had joined with Trotsky's followers in demanding that Lenin's
Testament, which urged the removal of Stalin from his post as general secretary,
be fulfilled. Exiled with Trotsky in the late twenties, he had recanted and returned to Moscow, only to be arrested and imprisoned in January 1933. Since that
date he had never been out of prison, which caused some police officials to
question his suitability as a defendant in the upcoming trial. "I am afraid," said
one NKVD man to Stalin, "that we won't have a strong case concerning Smirnov; he's been in prison for several years." But Stalin was impatient with such
niceties: "Don't be afraid," he reportedly said, and ordered the police to extract a
confession from Smirnov in whatever manner they could. If this required
"mounting"—that is, torture—so be it.

In the event, Smirnov's interrogators resorted chiefly to psychological torture.
They confronted him with the testimony of his former wife, Safonova, who in the
hope of saving both herself and Smirnov swore that the latter had received terrorist orders from Trotsky. Then the police brought Smirnov and his wife face to
face so that Safonova could reinforce a promise from Stalin to spare them both if
Smirnov confessed. The Old Bolshevik finally relented but agreed only to confirm
part of the charges against him.

Distinguished and prominent as Smirnov was, he was a small fish compared with those former chief lieutenants of the great Lenin—Zinoviev and Kamenev—who languished in prison for the Kirov murder. Much of the previous "investigation" had been designed to set the scene for the interrogation of these two men. Now it was their turn fully to learn how much the Red Dictator had assimilated the wisdom of the White Queen.

The NKVD agent in charge of interrogating Kamenev confronted him with the depositions of Olberg and company attesting to his and Zinoviev's murder of Kirov and attempts to murder Stalin. "That is a lie, and you know it is a lie!" exclaimed Kamenev. He pointed out that since he and Zinoviev had been imprisoned or constantly shadowed by the police for the past five years, they could hardly have been preparing terrorist acts. He added that he would never again take part in a "judicial farce" or enter into any "deals" with Stalin. When the NKVD reported this to Stalin, the chief replied that no prisoner could withstand the "astronomical pressure of the state." But it was not with the weight of the state that Stalin proposed to squeeze cooperation out of Kamenev. "Tell him," Stalin said to Kamenev's interrogator, "that if he refuses to go to trial, we'll find a suitable substitute for him—his own son, who will testify at the trial that on instructions from his dad he was preparing terrorist acts against the leaders of the Party. . . . This will bring him to his senses at once. . . ."

Stalin was right: Kamenev quickly relented. His deposition stated that he and his fellow conspirators had come to hate Stalin because of his great successes in leading the Soviet Union out of its "difficulties" in the mid-twenties. They knew that the only way they could come to power "was to organize terroristic acts against the leaders of the CPSU, and primarily against *Stalin.*"

Zinoviev's interrogation was handled personally by Yezhov. Claiming that the Soviet Union was in danger of being attacked by Germany and Japan, and that all internal subversion must cease immediately, Yezhov demanded in the name of the Politburo that Zinoviev confirm at a public trial that he had been planning to kill Stalin in collusion with Trotsky. Yezhov added that if Zinoviev agreed to do this, Stalin would spare his life; if not, he would be tried by a secret military court and "annihilated." Zinoviev refused.

Now the NKVD literally turned up the heat. Although it was very hot that July, Zinoviev's jailers turned on the radiators in his cell. Suffering acutely from asthma and liver disease, Zinoviev began tossing about on the floor of his cell. Prison doctors gave him injections that increased his pain. Finally Zinoviev had had enough: he joined Kamenev in agreeing to make confessions and go to public trial if—and only if—Stalin personally confirmed the Politburo's promise to spare their lives.

A meeting was accordingly arranged between the prisoners and the chief. An NKVD man who witnessed the meeting reported that Zinoviev and Kamenev tearfully recalled their services to the party and pointed out the brazen implausibility of the charges. "Just think of it," cried Zinoviev, "you want to portray members of Lenin's Politburo and his personal friends as unscrupulous bandits

Stalin and members of the Politburo on the occasion of Stalin's fiftieth birthday (December 1929). *Left to right:* Sergo Ordzhonikidze, Klementi Voroshilov, Valerian Kuibyshev, Stalin, Mikhail Kalinin, Lazar Kaganovich, Sergei Kirov. *Bildarchiv Preussischer Kulturbesitz*

Grigori Zinoviev, Karl Radek, and Béla Kun at a meeting of the Comintern in 1924. All were to fall victim to Stalin's Great Purge. *Bildarchiv Preussischer Kulturbesitz*

Nikolai Bukharin, Russian communism's greatest theorist and one of Stalin's most prominent victims. *UPI/Bettmann Newsphotos*

Russian victims of the 1941 German invasion, whose initial success was partly a result of Stalin's purge of the Red Army leadership. *Society for Cultural Relations with the USSR*

and our Bolshevik Party, the party of the proletarian revolution, as a snake pit of intrigue, treachery, and murder. If [Lenin] were alive, if he saw all this!" Unimpressed, Stalin reminded them of their factional struggles against the Central Committee and informed them curtly that only full cooperation could spare them "and the lives of those [they] led into the swamp." When Zinoviev and Kamenev asked for guarantees that they would not be shot, Stalin exploded, "A guarantee? Maybe you want an official treaty, certified by the League of Nations?" But he ended the meeting by declaring, "We Bolsheviks, disciples and followers of Lenin, do not want to shed the blood of old Bolsheviks, no matter how grave their past sins against the Party."

The trial of the Trotskyite-Zinovievite United Center opened on August 19, 1936, and ran until August 24. It took place in the October Hall of the Trade Union House in Moscow, formerly a club for the nobility. The courtroom, replete with baby blue walls, white columns, dancing-girl frieze, and crystal chandeliers, had previously been the club's ballroom. Now it was fitted with rough wooden benches on which sat about 150 Soviet citizens and some 30 foreign journalists, handpicked for their pro-Stalinist views. The Soviet spectators were mostly minor NKVD officials and clerks. Some of them were apparently assigned the duty of raising a commotion in case any of the defendants unexpectedly began saying things that might embarrass the trial's organizers.

Presiding over the court was V. V. Ulrikh, whom one foreign witness described as follows: "His shaven head rose to a point; his neck bulged out over the collar of his tunic in rolls of fat; his little pig's eyes darted here and there, from the prisoners to the crowd and back again." To the right of Ulrikh and two lesser judges* stood Andrei Vyshinsky, the public prosecutor. Vyshinsky cut a dapper figure, dressed in a well-tailored suit, his trim gray mustache and hair setting off a rubicund complexion. If Ulrikh looked like a pit bull, Vyshinksy resembled a "prosperous stockbroker accustomed to lunch at Simpson's and golf at Sunningdale." Across the room from Vyshinsky sat the prisoners, guarded by NKVD soldiers with rifles and fixed bayonets. The defendants looked pale and worn, although they had been allowed to catch up on their sleep and eat hearty meals in the period immediately preceding the trial.

Ulrikh opened the proceedings by asking the accused if they wanted to be defended by lawyers. In fact, the defendants had already been privately told that they could not have lawyers, and the court had rejected requests by several noted foreign jurists to defend the men. Thus they were obliged to "defend" themselves and to do so in a way that fully confirmed their guilt. Just before the trial opened, Yezhov had warned them that any act of "treachery" would result in certain execution for the entire group.

The secretary of the court then read the indictment. It stated that "newly

*One of these judges, I. I. Nikitchenko, was later to appear on the bench of the Supreme Allied Tribunal at Nuremberg. His presence there lent some credence to the German charge that in these trials the kettle was calling the pot black.

revealed circumstances" had established that these members of the so-called Moscow Center had not simply known "that their adherents in Leningrad were inclined towards terrorism, but were the direct organizers of the assassination of Comrade S. M. Kirov." Recent investigation had also shown that the accused "were the initiators and organizers of attempts which were being prepared on the lives of other leaders of the Communist Party of the Soviet Union and of the Soviet Government as well." Throughout their conspiracy they had "been acting on direct orders from L. Trotsky." Their motives were rooted in their hatred for "the Socialist victories of our country," their eagerness to wallow in the "swamp of white-guardism," and their identification with the "last remnants of the exploiting classes." Soviet vigilance had fortunately uncovered this conspiracy before it could run its course. Confronted with conclusive evidence of their criminal deeds and intentions, the defendants had "freely confessed" to all charges.

In light of the regime's elaborate preparations for this trial, it is not surprising that the actual proceedings yielded little in the way of "courtroom drama." For the most part the defendants did what they had agreed to do: they confirmed their confessions and elaborated on details of their nefarious plots when asked to do so by the public prosecutor.

Comrade Reingold proved especially zealous in incriminating himself and his colleagues. He said that the Moscow Center, of which he, Zinoviev, and Kamenev were members, planned to arrange Stalin's murder, place Kamenev at the head of the state, make Zinoviev chief of the Russian Communist party and the Communist International, and put T. Bakaiev (another defendant) in charge of the secret police. Then Bakaiev would put to death all the actual assassins and any secret police functionaries having "dangerous knowledge" of the plot. It sounded, noted one journalist, like something from the era of Ivan the Terrible.

Reingold also took pains to add some new "accomplices"—Alexei Rykov, Nikolai Bukharin, and Mikhail Tomsky, all prominent party figures and members of the so-called Right deviation. This was an important (and no doubt rehearsed) addition, for two of these men were to become the central defendants in the third show trial, in 1938.

Asked by Vyshinksy how he and his fellow plotters "reconciled terroristic activities with Marxism," Reingold answered that they knew terror was "incompatible with Marxism," but had to resort to it because Stalin's immense popularity precluded his being removed from power by legal means. "There are no other methods available of fighting the leaders of the Party and the Government at the present time," declared Reingold. "Stalin combines in himself all the strengths and firmness of the present Party leadership." Reingold added that Zinoviev and Kamenev had hoped to conceal their continuing conspiratorial activities after their initial exposure by "crawling on their belly to the Party" and securing Stalin's forgiveness.

Following Reingold to the dock, Zinoviev and Kamenev were asked if they admitted the "grave crimes" in which their colleague's testimony had implicated them. Zinoviev, his face puffy and sickly gray, quietly said yes. He later added, "My defective Bolshevism became transformed into anti-Bolshevism and through Trotsky arrived at fascism. . . . We filled the place of the Mensheviks, Socialist Revolutionaries, and White Guards who could not come out openly in our country."

Kamenev also confirmed Reingold's testimony. Ponderously, "like a professor lecturing his class," he told the court how his group had decided on assassination to win power because the Soviet Union's economic prosperity and Stalin's popularity with the masses "made an [open] opposition movement impossible." Later, during his special examination, Kamenev elaborated on his "monstrous crime," careful to stress his connections with Trotsky. Asked if his claims to be a party loyalist were not "deception," he replied, "No, worse than deception." "Perfidy?" prodded Vyshinsky. "Worse," said Kamenev. Vyshinsky: "Worse than deception, worse than perfidy—find the word: Treason?" Kamenev: "You have found it."

For its part, the prosecution offered no evidence for the guilt of the accused beyond the various depositions the defendants were required to confirm. Vyshinsky did not produce letters from Trotsky or copies of written plans for the assassination of party leaders. This seems odd, for incriminating documents would have been easy to fabricate, as indeed they had been fabricated in famous political trials of the past, including the Dreyfus trial. This strange fastidiousness, already noted in connection with the pretrial investigation, may have reflected, as one scholar suggests, a Marxist desire to "keep control over the facts, to be able to distinguish what might be called real reality from the 'objective' [that is, politically necessary] one." More likely, the authorities simply did not think they needed more "evidence" than they already had.

Their confidence was by no means misplaced, but there were minor hitches in the proceedings. Smirnov initially denied another defendant's testimony that he, Smirnov, had conveyed Trotsky's instructions about terrorism to the Moscow Center. Indignant, Vyshinsky called Smirnov's attention to his sworn deposition, in which he had confessed to just this offense. Confronted with this discrepancy, Smirnov at first remained silent, then recanted his recantation. Yet he apparently did so in a "sarcastic" manner that revealed his contempt for the charges against him.

Another complication arose when one of the secondary defendants, a certain S. Holtzman, testified that he had met Trotsky at the Hotel Bristol in Copenhagen in 1932 to arrange terrorist attacks in the Soviet Union. Soviet and foreign newspapers duly reported Holtzman's testimony, which allowed Trotsky (then in Norway) to claim that he had not been in Copenhagen in 1932, and the Danish government to point out that Copenhagen's Hotel Bristol had been demolished in 1917! Apparently the hapless Holtzman had been given the name "Hotel Bristol" by the NKVD, which in turn had gotten it from a hotel list supplied by the Soviet Foreign Office. The list covered hotels in Oslo, Norway, not Copenhagen. Stalin was not amused. "What the devil did you need a hotel for?" he is said to have asked Yagoda. "You ought to have said that they met at the railway station. The railway station is always there!"

Minor setbacks such as this hardly disrupted the progress of Soviet justice. Following Vyshinsky's examinations the defendants were allowed to make "last pleas." Here they engaged in new orgies of self-abasement, prostrating themselves before the party and its all-powerful chief. "We didn't listen to *him* at the proper time—and he taught us a lesson!" cried one defendant. Kamenev said nothing in his defense; instead, he addressed his children, instructing them not to "look back" but to "go forward with the Soviet people [and] follow Stalin!" Zinoviev took pains to explain how a famous Old Bolshevik like himself could have become a "traitor." The answer was that his good Bolshevik record was a "myth"—he had always valued personal power over the success of socialism, and he had started "fighting against the Party" as soon as he saw that it was succeeding under Stalin. In the process he had begun "telling untruths," but at least now, in reciting his errors, he was telling "the whole truth." That was more than he could say for his accomplice Smirnov, who seemed to have "adopted a different decision." So in the end Zinoviev combined self-abasement with denunciation of a colleague—a tour de force of toadyism in the name of self-preservation.

But though self-preservation lay at the core of this unseemly display, such a simple and understandable instinct was probably not the whole story behind these extraordinary confessions, or those that followed. As Robert Conquest has pointed out, "surrender and self-abasement" were integral aspects of the "Party mind" in Stalin's Russia. These show trial confessions were not exceptional acts "but rather the culmination of a whole series of submissions to the Party made in terms [these men] knew to be 'objectively' false." Having already submitted to the party's rigorous discipline, they could see "no political possibilities outside the Party," and their willingness to "crawl in the dust" sprang from a desire not just to go on living but also to remain in or return to the Communist fold.

In this vein Eugenia Ginzburg, a loyal Communist, recalled her unwillingness to take flight after having been "exposed" for neglecting to denounce an unreliable colleague. "But I must prove my innocence to the Party," she said. "How can I, a Communist, hide from the Party?"

A determination to provide a final service to the party, then, may have helped pave the way to the Stalinist Canossa for some of these men. But even if the errant Communist did not see false confession as a service, he was disinclined to protest his innocence for he knew that he was guilty of many offenses, if not to Stalin then to old friends and colleagues whom he had betrayed in his time. Perhaps he had denounced a confederate to the secret police, or helped Stalin purge the kulaks (rich peasants), or sent some cement plant manager to the Gulag for failing to reach his production quota under a five-year plan.

This deeper guilt is a central theme in Arthur Koestler's *Darkness at Noon,* that haunting fictional account of Stalin's Great Purge. Koestler's condemned Communists parrot the accusations of their judges, for they see in them a kind of righteousness that has little to do with literal truth. "They were too deeply entangled in their own past, caught in a web they had spun themselves, according to the laws of their own twisted logic; they were all guilty, although not of those deeds of which they accused themselves." What Koestler describes here, and what at least some of the show trial defendants seem actually to have felt, is a sense of sin—sin in a secularized, post-Christian form.

Like Koestler's Comrade Rubashov, Zinoviev, Kamenev, and their "accomplices" did not save themselves by their prodigious feats of self-abasement. Nor did the five fictitious defendants receive medals or sinecures for helping to incriminate the real targets. Vyshinsky demanded that all the accused be convicted and shot like "mad dogs," and the court duly sentenced all sixteen to death. According to Soviet law, persons sentenced to death were to be allowed seventy-two hours in which to file a plea for a pardon or a stay of execution. But on August 25, twenty-four hours after the verdict had been pronounced, the Moscow papers carried an official announcement that all sixteen had been executed. According to NKVD gossip, Kamenev was "stunned" when taken from his cell to be shot. He cried and made a scene. Smirnov, on the other hand, was calm and composed. "We deserve this for our unworthy attitude at the trial," he reportedly said.

The reaction to the trial and executions in the Soviet Union was predictable enough. Before the trial had even ended, letters to the editor in *Pravda* were urging the death penalty for these "rotten agents of the *Gestapo.*" After the executions more letters applauded this quick reckoning with treason. Most of these letters were no doubt planted by the authorities, but this does not mean that they did not reflect genuine popular sentiments. After all, most people everywhere are fascinated with crimes in high places and often believe their top politicians capable of the nastiest skulduggery. In the totalitarian systems, moreover, there was a strong popular tendency to trust in the leader, but not necessarily in his henchmen. "If he only knew . . ." was a commonly heard phrase, both in Germany and Russia. Many Russians were relieved that their chief, at least, seemed to know.

While the Zinoviev trial was still in progress, Leon Trotsky, alleged mastermind of the entire conspiracy, derided the proceedings as "humbug." "For political vengeance," the exiled Bolshevik added, "the trial puts the Dreyfus scandal and the Reichstag Fire in the shadow." He noted that he had copies of every letter he had sent in the past seven years, and would soon prove the fraudulence of the charges against him. "I will make the accusers the accused," he warned.

Trotsky's fulminations notwithstanding, Moscow's first show trial found acceptance among many foreign observers. *Pravda* recorded with much fanfare a statement by "the English jurist Pritt" to the effect that the trial and sentences were perfectly in order. The Moscow correspondent for the London *Observer* agreed that the government's case against the Zinovievites was genuine. Sir Bernard Pares, a British expert on Russia hardly known for his pro-Bolshevik views, reported after visiting Moscow that Zinoviev and the others were undoubtedly guilty as charged. "Zinoviev was now finally brought to book and died, still fawning, like the coward he had always been. . . ." Harold Denny, a correspondent for the *New York Times,* entertained and then quickly dismissed the notion that the confessions might have been bogus. "These defendants do not testify like men coerced and the stories they tell extemporaneously on their feet dovetail as fabricated stories hardly could. If there is more here than meets the eye, not even the most skeptical observer can guess what it is." As for the defendants' willingness to confess even though it probably meant their "doom," Denny could only point to the "traditional Slavic-Oriental indifference to death."

Foreign Communists and fellow travelers who had come to believe in the legitimacy and necessity of Stalin's system tended to applaud the Zinoviev trial. The French intellectual Left spoke with almost one voice (André Gide was a notable dissenter) in favor of Stalin's action. In England, Sidney and Beatrice Webb reaffirmed their oft-stated admiration for Soviet justice: "the Soviets must be right, Beatrice Webb said; they must know . . ." Reaction among pro-Stalinists in America was typified by the views of a friend of Alfred Kazin (called Francis in the author's memoir of the thirties). Reading about the trial in the *New York Times,* Francis could "not doubt the reiterative, hallucinatory charges that such people were outside, mad dogs, criminal oppositionists, heretics, unbelievers, seditionists, driven to conspiracy against the State and murder of the leaders because they had gone against the Party." In Norway the local Communists joined the Nazis in demanding Trotsky's expulsion from the country. The Norwegian Communist party newspaper said, "Trotsky ought to share the dock with Zinoviev and Kamenev. Even death and annihilation are too good for him."

But a great many foreign observers, including some on the left, were shocked and dumbfounded by the Zinoviev trial. The *Manchester Guardian* and the British Labour press refused to be taken in; so did George Orwell, Ellen Wilkinson, and Edmund Wilson. The American philosopher John Dewey established a committee of inquiry to look into the Moscow Center case after the Danish government reported the nonexistence of the Hotel Bristol. Dewey's committee determined that Holtzman could not have met Trotsky in Copenhagen; from this, in good philosophical fashion, Dewey concluded that there was something fishy about the entire proceeding.

But if Dewey thought that his exposure of this "hole" in the government's case would have any effect on the progress of Soviet justice, he was sadly mistaken. It only made Stalin wonder whether Yagoda was the right man after all to run his Great Purge.

THE CASE OF THE ANTI-SOVIET TROTSKYITE CENTER

Stalin played such a key role in planning and orchestrating the Zinoviev-Kamenev trial that he must have known that the central charges against the defendants were false. Yet on a deeper level he undoubtedly believed in these men's guilt. Had they not once resisted his policies? Did they not remain potential rivals for power? And since Stalin identified his own policies and power with the progress of the Soviet state—indeed, with the progress of history—he regarded all personal opponents, even those who claimed to have seen the error of their ways, as enemies unto death.

But the trial and execution of the members of the Zinovievite-Trotskyite United Center did not relieve Stalin of his anxieties concerning subversion within the party. In hopes of saving themselves, Zinoviev and company had denounced other former oppositionists, some of whom remained in positions of influence. Kamenev had insisted that Rykov and Bukharin (still editor of *Izvestia*) thought "just as [he] did." To Stalin this could mean only that the fifth-column danger remained potent and menacing.

In the late summer and fall of 1936, Stalin was therefore prepared to extend his purge to the former Right deviationists mentioned in the Zinoviev-Kamenev trial. To this end he sought once again to unsheath his "sword of the revolution"—the NKVD. At the end of August, Molchanov summoned his inquisitors and stunned them with the announcement "This year you will have to forget about vacations. The investigation has not yet ended; it has just begun."

But Stalin, already suspicious regarding the requisite sharpness of his revolutionary sword, soon learned that it was even duller than he had feared. One of the Right deviationists, Tomsky, was allowed to kill himself, thereby evading interrogation. Yagoda, backed by some members of the Politburo and the Central Committee, was dragging his feet in the new investigation. It seemed that he had friends in the Rykov-Bukharin camp. Was he trying to put off their trial, hoping that Stalin would change his mind? Or was he trying to save his own skin? After all, he was an Old Bolshevik himself and could not have welcomed an open season on the species. Moreover, he had apparently believed Stalin's promises that Zinoviev and Kamenev would be spared if they cooperated with the chief. Now he knew what such promises meant.

On September 10, while Stalin was away from Moscow on vacation, *Pravda* suddenly announced that the investigation into the charges against Rykov and Bukharin was being suspended for lack of evidence. Reference was made to "pressure from some members of the Politburo."

Confronted with an apparent palace rebellion, Stalin seemed to give in. He acquiesced in the suspension of the "Right opposition" investigation. But he was determined that his purge should not lose momentum. On September 25 he sent the following telegram to the Politburo:

> We deem it absolutely necessary and urgent that Comrade Yezhov be nominated to the post of People's Commissar for Internal Affairs. Yagoda has definitely proved himself to be incapable of unmasking the Trotskyite-Zinovievite bloc. The [police] is four years behind in this matter. This is

noted by all Party workers and by the majority of the representatives of the NKVD

Yagoda was named minister of post and telegraphs, an ominous transfer since this was the position from which Rykov had just been removed. More ominous for all Old Bolsheviks was the appointment of Yezhov to replace Yagoda as head of the secret police. Unlike Yagoda, Yezhov was a "new man" with no ties to the group who had made the October Revolution. As Stalin's creation, he would do the chief's bidding without question. Thus his appointment signaled the beginning of the so-called Yezhovshchina ("cleanup" regime of Yezhov, 1937–39). In its thoroughgoing brutality, this period might be seen as a twentieth-century reincarnation of Ivan the Terrible's Oprichnina (ca. 1564–72), when Ivan's personal henchmen, dressed in black tunics adorned with dog-and-broom insignia, "sniffed out treason" and "swept it away" in a massacre of the czar's enemies, real and imaginary.*

The Yezhovshchina commenced with preparations for a second public trial not, as Stalin had originally planned, involving the Right opposition—but focusing on a new group of former Left oppositionists said to be tied to the Zinovievite-Trotskyite camp. This group was described as the Reserve Center—a collection of second-string subversives who were to take over leadership of the anti-Stalinist conspiracy in the event that the first team was exposed and taken out of the game. Though they held positions of influence in the party, they were less august than Zinoviev or Kamenev. But two of the accused, Karl Radek and Grigori Pyatakov, had figured rather prominently in party history.

Karl Radek, born Karl Sobelsohn in 1885 in Galicia (Austrian Poland), was one of international communism's best-known journalists. He began his career in 1908, editing two German Social Democratic papers. During World War I he fell in with Lenin in Switzerland, and after the October Revolution he began writing for *Izvestia*. He quickly gained a reputation for wit and brilliant invective but was so given to clownishness and self-parody that most of his colleagues found it hard to take him seriously. Physical characteristics added to his buffoon image. According to one colleague, Radek was instantly recognizable as "the little man with the huge head, his beard encircling his clean-shaven face like a monkey's, his protruding ears, his spectacles, his pipe held between tobacco-stained teeth."

In 1918 Radek went back to Germany, where he helped organize the new German Communist party. Arrested by the republican authorities, he turned his jail cell into a contact point for Germans who wanted to do business with the new

*Stalin admired Ivan the Terrible and identified in many ways with his brutal regime. In a conversation with the actor who played Ivan in Sergei Eisenstein's film about the czar, Stalin noted that Ivan "was a great and wise ruler, who guarded the country from the penetration of foreign influence and strove to unify Russia." But Ivan had shown weakness in failing to liquidate all the feudal families who stood in the way of Russia's progress. Religion, Stalin opined, had made Ivan less "terrible" than he ought to have been. "God got in his way."

Soviet state. Soon he was helping the Reichswehr (new German army) establish ties to the Bolsheviks, a service that facilitated his quick release and return to the Soviet Union. Following Lenin's death Radek allied himself to Trotsky and championed the latter's vision of "permanent revolution." With Trotsky's fall Radek was exiled to Siberia, from which he initially wrote caustic letters denouncing Stalin's policies. But Siberia did not suit the cosmopolitan Radek, and he was soon condemning Trotsky and praising Stalin with all the rhetorical brilliance at his command. For good measure he also exposed a middle-level secret-police officer as an anti-Stalinist subversive. By the early thirties he had burned all his bridges to the opposition and was back writing for *Izvestia*.

Radek could not have seemed a serious threat to Stalin, and it is hard to understand why the chief ordered his arrest. Perhaps Stalin was short on prominent names for the second trial and needed a well-known figure. Perhaps, too, Stalin despised Radek precisely because he seemed so spineless: the Russian dictator both demanded and distrusted sycophancy. Radek's cosmopolitan background and Jewish origins were no doubt also held against him. Stalin resented showy men of the world who were always dropping references to restaurants in Berlin, London, and Paris. And though he was not yet the dyed-in-the-wool anti-Semite he later became, Stalin harbored an instinctive distrust of Jews.

Grigori Pyatakov, the second show trial's other star attraction, was as serious and disciplined as Radek was clownish. An outstanding leader of the Red Army during the civil war, he had been president of the Soviet government in the Ukraine, then head of the coal industry in the Don basin. In his Testament, Lenin characterized him, along with Bukharin, as one of "the most able forces (among the youngest) [in the party]." In the twenties Pyatakov helped set up the first two five-year plans for the industrialization of the country, and in 1931 Stalin appointed him deputy commissar for heavy industry. Pyatakov did not head this agency, because he had once sided with the Trotskyites against Stalin. But he had abandoned all opposition by 1928 and worked efficiently for the regime ever since.

Why, then, did Stalin include him in the circle of conspirators? The answer undoubtedly lies in Pyatakov's prominent role in Russia's industrial development. He could be made a scapegoat for all the disasters, privations, and failures that attended Stalin's campaign to make the Soviet Union into a first-rate industrial power. He could also be portrayed as a holdover from those scientific and industrial "specialists" whom Stalin had been attacking ever since the revolution and who had been the objects of an earlier show trial—the so-called Shakhty trial of 1928.* Though he understood the need for industrial expertise, Stalin was deter-

---

*In the Shakhty trial fifty Soviet engineers, as well as five German nationals working for German firms in the Soviet Union, were charged with sabotaging the economy at the instigation of foreign interests. They were also accused of perpetuating "bourgeois" attitudes and values. On the eve of the trial Stalin said, "We have internal enemies. We have external enemies. We cannot forget this for one moment." All but four of the defendants were convicted. Sentences, however, were more mild than in the later trials: five were executed and the rest imprisoned for terms varying from one year to life.

mined to keep his technical specialists in their place, determined that they should not develop "technocratic" notions about running the state themselves. "The engineer, the organizer of production, does not work as he would like to but as he is ordered, in such a way as to serve the interests of his employers," wrote the chief. Since Stalin's rivals Rykov and Bukharin had opposed his purge of the industrial specialists, a new trial involving a prominent manager like Pyatakov would refocus attention on the treachery of the two and lay the groundwork for a more concerted action against them later on.

As in the Zinoviev-Kamenev trial, prospective defendants in the Trotskyite Center case were made to confess their guilt before the trial opened. Pyatakov refused to do this for several weeks. Eventually the police brought in Pyatakov's former boss, the people's commissar for heavy industry, Sergo Ordzhonikidze. Ordzhonikidze was a close friend of Stalin's, and he apparently promised Pyatakov in the name of the chief that his life would be spared if he confessed. Whether Pyatakov believed this is impossible to say; knowing the fate of Zinoviev and company, he could not have been optimistic. In any event, the police also turned his wife against him by threatening to kill their son if she did not incriminate her husband. Faced with these pressures, Pyatakov finally signed a deposition saying that he had met Trotsky in Oslo in 1935 and received from him instructions to sabotage Soviet industry. According to the deposition, Trotsky told Pyatakov that he was working in concert with the Germans, who had promised to go to war against a weakened Soviet Union and to put the Trotskyites in power.

Karl Radek, though hardly known for his inner fortitude, also resisted police pressures to make him sign the deposition they had prepared for him. In their effort to break him, they brought him together with another prospective defendant, Grigori Sokolnikov, former Soviet ambassador to Great Britain, who had already "confessed." Though Sokolnikov did his best to bring Radek around, the latter insisted that he would not yield until he had had a personal interview with Stalin, in whose benevolence he continued to believe. A meeting was accordingly arranged. Radek emerged from it ready not only to sign a deposition but also to rewrite his confession in a way that heightened his guilt.

The Trotskyite Center trial, which opened on January 23, 1937, looked in some ways to be a reenactment of the Zinoviev-Kamenev affair. It, too, was held in the ornate October Hall, and presiding again was the uncouth Ulrikh, with the dapper but equally ferocious Vyshinsky as chief prosecutor. This time, however, the audience was considerably larger, and it included more foreign journalists and diplomats (among them the new American ambassador, Joseph Davies). Three of the seventeen defendants had lawyers; the rest had "waived" this right. Instead of publishing a mere summary of the proceedings, as it had in the Zinoviev trial, the Stalin government now produced a lengthy "verbatim report." These changes undoubtedly reflected Stalin's growing confidence in the trials' credibility in the eyes of the world.

The formal indictment charged the seventeen defendants with "treason against the country, espionage, committing acts of diversion, wrecking activities and the preparation of terrorist acts." This conspiratorial "parallel center," acting "under the direct instructions of L. D. Trotsky," and with the collusion of "foreign states," had as its main goal "the forcible overthrow of the Soviet Government with the object of changing the social and state system existing in the USSR." The indictment contained long excerpts from the written confessions of the defendants, all of whom pleaded guilty.

First to testify was Pyatakov. One of the foreign correspondents covering the trial described him as looking "like a professor, with his scholar's stoop, high forehead, black-rimmed glasses and short reddish beard and waved-back hair, both flecked with gray." In a "clear, colorless voice," Pyatakov gave a "detailed recital of conspirative action, little less terrible and more convincing than the indictment." The high point in his testimony came when he described a secret visit he made to Trotsky in Oslo in December 1935. Pyatakov said that he flew to Oslo from Berlin on instructions from a "Trotsky agent" named Heinrich or Gustav. During his two-hour meeting with Trotsky, the Old Bolshevik complained of the dilatory fashion in which the conspirators in Russia had thus far proceeded. "When we came to the subject of wrecking activity," said Pyatakov, "[Trotsky] delivered himself of a veritable philippic, made cutting remarks such as: 'You can't break away from Stalin's navel cord; you take Stalin's construction for socialist construction.'" Trotsky went on to urge more concerted subversion in preparation for a "fascist attack" scheduled for 1937. He said he had worked out all the details with Hitler's deputy, Rudolf Hess. In exchange for "wrecking" the Soviet economy and "diverting" Stalin's attention from the attack, the Germans would install Trotsky and his friends in power. They in turn would compensate Germany with territory in the Ukraine and rights to "exploit in the Soviet Union the raw material resources it needs." Near the end of Pyatakov's testimony, Vyshinsky asked him how he would categorize his activities: were they "crimes against the state?" Pyatakov said they were. "Was [Pyatakov] helping the aggressor, helping fascism?" asked Vyshinsky. "Undoubtedly," answered the defendant. Vyshinsky had no further questions.

While Pyatakov's testimony focused on collusion with the Germans, Radek brought in the Japanese. Pyatakov had already mentioned letters Radek had allegedly received from Trotsky spelling out concessions to Germany and Japan that the conspirators would make to secure those states' support in bringing them to power. Radek now testified that the new Trotskyite regime would revive "private capital" concentrated around "German and Japanese concessionaires." As he talked, Radek warmed to his role, which after all he had written himself. He admitted to conspiring with the other defendants in the wrecking of trains, mines, and chemical plants. He and his confederates had discussed with Japanese and German agents the "wartime use of bacteriological means for the purpose of infecting troop trains, food supply depots and sanitary stations with bacilli to cause highly contagious diseases." The Germans were to gain control over the

Ukraine, and the Japanese would get Russia's maritime provinces, Sakhalin oil, access to Siberian goldfields, and carte blanche in China.

Radek also confessed to having helped assassinate Kirov, adding that he had realized at the time that this act could be only a first step, that the entire Soviet leadership would have to be liquidated. He understood, too, that the Kirov killing would commit the conspirators to a full-scale "guerrilla war" against the NKVD, since the police would realize that "such things as the assassination of Kirov are not like pimples which burst out for a short time and then disappear." In another colorful metaphor, he professed belated indignation over his willingness to overthrow Stalin and thrust Russia into the clutches of capitalist and foreign exploiters "for nothing at all, just for the sake of Trotsky's beautiful eyes."

Perhaps because Radek's flamboyant mea culpa had upstaged his inquisitors, Vyshinsky took it upon himself to needle the defendant. Noting that Radek had failed to confess for three months after his arrest, he wondered if this did not make him an unreliable witness. To this Radek pointed out that the court had learned of Trotsky's instructions only from him, Radek. Here he obliquely exposed the central weakness of the entire trial: the charges were all based exclusively on personal testimony of the defendants (no written evidence was produced), and if the testifiers were unreliable, the government's case was worthless.

Radek's testimony sometimes amused the audience, for he could not, even in these grim circumstances, resist occasional flashes of his old wit. But more systematic comic relief was provided by another defendant, one Valentin Arnold, a self-professed Russian army deserter, sometime South American sailor, veteran of Verdun, Hollywood stuntman, Los Angeles Mason, and (most recently) Trotskyite agent serving as chauffeur for party leaders. Arnold testified that he had been ordered by the Trotskyite Center to kill both Molotov and Ordzhonikidze by involving them in auto accidents. In both cases, however, he had lost his nerve and "muffed" his assignment. For Molotov, Arnold's testimony must have been especially welcome, for it seemed to reestablish his credentials as a worthy enemy of Trotsky and thus a friend of Stalin.

Three other defendants, all former railway officials, testified that they had supplied secret information concerning the Russian railway system to Japanese agents. I. A. Kniazeff, former chief of the southern railways, told of causing the deaths of sixty-three persons in a widespread train-wrecking program involving some thirty-five hundred accidents between 1935 and 1936. Another wrecking plot, this one in the coal mines, was divulged by one A. A. Shestov, a member of the board of the Eastern and Siberian Coal Trust. Shestov spoke of sabotage operations in the Kuzbas coal district sponsored by Pyatakov, Trotsky, and various German mining engineers. The conspirators had, he said, set fires and caused explosions in the coal pits that claimed many lives and significantly retarded coal production.

After five days of testimony, Vyshinsky put the trial in perspective. The proceedings, he declared, illuminated "like a searchlight" the "most remote re-

cesses, the secret by-ways, the disgusting hidden corners of the Trotskyite underground." They "revealed and proved the stupid obstinacy, the reptile cold-blood-
edness, the cool calculation of professional criminals with which the Trotskyite
bandits [had] been waging their struggle against the USSR." This was the "abyss
of degradation," the "last boundary of moral and political decay," the "diabolical
infinitude of crime!" Comrade Stalin had fortunately seen through the Trotskyite-Zinovievite Counterrevolutionary Center as early as 1931 and had kept his
vigilant eye on these traitors ever since. Now their nefarious plans and deeds were
exposed for all to see. The young workers and peasants, the toilers of all countries,
would realize with whom they were "really dealing."

After four hours of such fustian, Vyshinsky lodged a passionate appeal for
"death by shooting" for all the defendants. "I am not alone in this demand," he
cried.

> I feel that by my side here stand the victims of the crimes and of these
> criminals: on crutches, maimed, half-alive, and perhaps legless, like Comrade
> Nagovitsina, the switch-girl at Chusovskaya Station, who appealed to me,
> through *Pravda*, today, and who, at twenty years of age, lost both her legs in
> averting a train disaster organized by these people! . . . The victims may be in
> their graves, but I feel they are standing here beside me, pointing at the
> dock, at you, accused, with their mutilated arms, which have mouldered in
> the graves to which you sent them!

In their "last pleas" the defendants made no serious effort to defend themselves. On the contrary, they competed with one another in self-laceration and
praised the court, police, and Stalin for exposing their conspiracy before it could
do yet more damage. Typical was Pyatakov's final statement: "In a few hours you
will pass your sentence. And here I stand before you in filth, crushed by my own
crimes, bereft of everything through my own fault, a man who has lost his family,
who has lost his very self."

Vyshinsky was correct in his claim not to be alone in demanding the death
penalty for the accused. As after the Zinoviev trial, mass meetings around the
country called for the defendants' blood. Some of the meetings were led by young
Nikita Khrushchev, then a Stalin protégé. "We will uncover and annihilate [the
oppositionists] and reduce to dust every one of them and scatter them to the far
winds," declared Khrushchev.

On January 30 the court announced that it found all the defendants guilty. All
but four—Radek, Sokolnikov, Arnold, and Stroilov—were given the death sentence. These four received prison terms varying from eight to ten years. Stalin
undoubtedly dictated the penalties, and one must wonder why he showed "le-
niency" toward some of the accused. NKVD rumor had it that he spared Radek's
life on a special appeal from the prominent German writer Leon Feuchtwanger,
who made this his price for agreeing to write a book justifying the trials. As for
Arnold, he may have been spared just because Stalin was entertained by his

fanciful testimony. In any event, clemency of this sort was not worth much. Radek died in an Arctic labor camp in 1939, as did Sokolnikov. Arnold simply disappeared—presumably not back to Los Angeles.

During the proceedings, Leon Trotsky, now in Mexico, publicly attacked the trial as a "cruel fiasco" and a "gigantic frame-up being carried out in the same manner as a chess puzzle." Stalin, in struggling to maintain his personal dictatorship, had "taken recourse to the methods of Cesare Borgia." Trotsky denied ever having written to Radek, with whom he said he had broken off all relations in 1928. "No one among the leaders of the Communist Party ever took Radek seriously," he added. "Why should I have considered Radek as a person worthy of my special confidence?" He dared the Soviet court to produce the Radek letters it claimed to have found, and he demanded "in the name of elementary political hygiene" the formation of an international body of investigation to look into the charges against him. He promised to demonstrate before such a commission that Stalin was "the organizer of the greatest political crimes in world history."

The Soviet regime could write off Trotsky's attack as the defensive posturing of an obvious traitor. Less easily dismissed was the revelation produced by a Norwegian newspaper that Pyatakov could not have flown to Oslo to meet Trotsky in December 1933, because no civil aircraft had landed at Oslo's airport in that month. Again it seemed that Stalin and his henchmen had unnecessarily discredited their case by insisting upon too much detail. In an important psychological sense, though, they were right to have done so. As Adam Ulam has pointed out, "People are often willing to believe the most thinly established slander when it comes to human motivations, but when it comes to actual plots, credulity and interest grow in proportion to the richness of detail."

Whether it was the satisfying complexity of the alleged plots or a willingness to see Stalin more as an embattled statesman than as a Borgian schemer, this second Moscow show trial found its influential supporters around the world, just as the first one had. The *New York Times* correspondent in Moscow, Walter Duranty, offers a case in point. He noted that some people abroad had said that the Zinoviev-Kamenev trial seemed somehow phony. "But this trial," he declared, "does stand up and the evidence rings true." He described Vyshinsky as "serious-minded and an earnest seeker after truth." When one of the defendants insisted that he had not been "treated roughly" by the police, and had confessed only because he realized he "had been wrong and Stalin right," Duranty editorialized, "His words rang true as gold." It bothered him, however, that the defendants made little effort to defend themselves as Americans supposedly would have done. "Why do they act like that, these Russians? Why don't they fight back and defend themselves as we should in a similar case? The only answer I have is that they are Russians, who are a different breed from us. Or have you not read Dostoevsky?"

Duranty was not the only Western correspondent to accept this trial as juridically correct. The Moscow correspondent for the left-leaning London *Daily Herald* argued that the defendants confessed because the state's collection of evidence "forced them to do so. No other explanation fits the facts." A British Labour party MP insisted that all foreign correspondents, with the exception of the Germans and the Japanese, "expressed themselves as very much impressed by the weight of evidence presented by the prosecution and the sincerity of the confessions of the accused." This was an exaggeration, for the London *Times* and the *Manchester Guardian* correspondents had their doubts. Yet it is safe to say that the Western press did little to subject this trial—or, for that matter, any of the Moscow show trials—to the critical scrutiny that the audacious charges and bizarre confessions might legitimately have called forth.

Duranty claimed that the foreign diplomats attending the trial—the Germans and the Japanese again excepted—unanimously agreed that Vyshinsky had "put it over." The new American ambassador, Joseph Davies, certainly thought so. In a long report to the secretary of state, Davies insisted that the prosecutor "conducted the case calmly and generally with admirable moderation." The accused, Davies further reported, "all appeared well nourished and normal physically." In his general assessment of the trial, Davies admitted that he had been "predisposed against the credibility of the testimony of these defendants." But his experience of previous trials (as a jurist in the United States) and the application of "tests of credibility" led him to the conclusion "that the state had established its case, at least to the extent of proving the existence of a widespread conspiracy and plot among the political leaders against the Soviet government, and which under their statutes established the crimes set forth in the indictment." Despite his lingering "reservations" based on the possibility that the Russian "psychology" might be different from the American, he stated, "To have assumed that this proceeding was invented and staged as a project of dramatic political fiction would be to presuppose the creative genius of a Shakespeare and the genius of Belasco in stage production."

Like the Zinoviev trial, this one also found its defenders among the fellow-traveling intelligentsia in the West. Upton Sinclair was certain that good Bolsheviks would not confess to crimes they had not committed. Theodore Dreiser declared that Trotsky was guilty of all charges brought against him. After the Dewey commission found the second Moscow show trial—like the first—to have been a "frame-up," thirty-eight American intellectuals published a letter in *Soviet Russia Today* denouncing the commission and urging Americans not to cooperate with it. The letter asked, "Should not a country recognized as engaged in improving conditions for all its people, whether or not one agrees with all the means whereby this is brought about, be permitted to decide for itself what measures of protection are necessary against treasonable plots to assassinate and overthrow its leadership and involve it in war with foreign powers?"

The brilliant German novelist Heinrich Mann defended Vyshinsky's tactics and the confessions as a mutual "Dostoevskian" struggle "for the possession of the subterranean truth." His countryman and fellow novelist Leon Feuchtwanger, who as we noted may have interceded with Stalin on behalf of Radek, was nonetheless convinced of Radek's guilt. He said that his initial doubts about this "melted away as naturally as salt dissolves in water" once he heard Radek's testimony. "If that was lying or prearranged, then I don't know what truth is." In his book *Moscow 1937* he declared, "There was no justification of any sort for imagining that there was anything manufactured or artificial about the trial proceedings."

Left-leaning intellectuals who dared cast doubt upon the trials—most notably, Orwell, Stephen Spender, and Kingsley Martin—tended to be hounded by their colleagues as traitors or dupes of the Gestapo. It seemed that the Fascist challenge, particularly the war in Spain, ruled out for the majority of leftist intellectuals any criticism of the Soviet Union. As Louis Aragon wrote, with much passion but little logic, "To claim innocence for these men [in the Pyatakov-Radek trial] is to adopt the Hitlerian thesis on all points. . . . [Those who do this] reprieve Hitler and the Gestapo of the Spanish rebellion, they deny fascist intervention in Spain."

THE MILITARY PURGE

Six months before the Pyatakov-Radek trial, the NKVD arrested a Red Army divisional commander in Kiev named Dmitri Shmidt. Son of a Jewish shoemaker and swashbuckling veteran of the civil war, Shmidt had associated briefly with the Trotskyite opposition in the mid-twenties. In 1927, following the expulsion of the Trotskyites from the party, Shmidt had personally insulted Stalin, telling the chief that one day he would lop his ears off. His arrest in 1936 could therefore be understood as another example of Stalin's vengefulness and, more precisely, of his adherence to that old Sicilian maxim "Revenge tastes best when it is eaten cold." Little did anyone suspect that Shmidt's arrest was the first step in a Stalinist purge of the Red Army that would decimate its leadership, leaving it ill prepared to meet the German onslaught in 1941.

On June 11, 1937, Soviet newspapers published a short communiqué announcing that Russia's most esteemed military figure, Deputy War Commissar Marshal Mikhail Tukhachevsky, had been arrested along with seven other prominent generals. All would be brought before a military tribunal on charges of spying for a "foreign state" and preparing the defeat of the Soviet Union. The next morning another communiqué announced that the trial had already taken place and that all the accused had been convicted and executed.

These announcements came as a great shock to the Soviet people. Unlike the politicians belonging to the Trotskyite Center, the generals had not been subjected to an extended vilification campaign prior to their execution. They were military "heroes" one day, "traitors" the next. One top officer recalled asking himself how it could be that men who had "done so much to improve our army" could suddenly become "enemies of the people." No wonder some diplomats began to speak (sotto voce) of Stalin as "the sick man of the Kremlin."

But Stalin was neither mad nor quite so precipitate in his military purge as it may have seemed. In retrospect it can be seen that the NKVD had gradually and carefully undermined the military leadership before Stalin made his move against Tukhachevsky and his colleagues in June 1937.

After his arrest, Commander Shmidt was grilled for information concerning an alleged army plot to kill War Commissar Klementi Voroshilov, a close Stalin associate. Eventually Shmidt made the confession demanded of him and, in the process, implicated other military leaders. He was shot in May 1937.

In the course of the Zinoviev trial a more senior military leader, E. A. Dreitzer, implicated Corps Commander Vitovt Putna in the Trotskyite conspiracy. Since both Dreitzer and Putna were close to Tukhachevsky, it is not surprising that the marshal's name came up during Radek's testimony. Radek testified that Tukhachevsky had no relations with the Trotskyites, but, as one veteran intelligence officer noted at the time, having a positive character reference from Radek was a mixed blessing.

In a party plenum meeting in March 1937, some military men, including Yona Yakir, commander of the Kiev Military District, apparently spoke out against Stalin's purge of the Old Bolsheviks. The chief, for his part, grumbled ominously about what harm "a few spies in the Red Army could do." The next month Corps Commander Gekker, head of the Red Army foreign liaison and a close Yakir associate, was arrested. On April 28 *Pravda* urged the Red Army to become more ideologically vigilant and to fight the "internal" as well as the external foe.

An astute observer of Stalin's tactics might have seen in these moves the proverbial "handwriting on the wall" for the Red Army leadership. No one outside the NKVD, however, could have known of a yet more insidious maneuver against the military establishment: the compiling of a dossier "proving" pro-Nazi subversion in the army.

This story reads like bad spy fiction. As best as it can be reconstructed, the tale began in late 1936 when a Soviet triple agent (he worked for the NKVD, the Gestapo, and a czarist émigré group) planted hints with Reinhard Heydrich's SD (the SS security service) suggesting a conspiracy between the Soviet high command and the German general staff to undermine both the Hitler and the Stalin regimes. Heydrich, whose SS was already competing with the German army, was only too eager to use this information to discredit the Wehrmacht leadership. But he also saw that it could be used against Tukhachevsky and his colleagues in the Soviet Union, with the probable result that Russia's military defenses would be weakened. Accordingly, Heydrich and Himmler forwarded the file to Hitler, after "improving" it with a few more compromising details. The führer in turn decided to send the material on to Stalin, whom he trusted to make good use of it. He did this through Eduard Beneš, president of Czechoslovakia. Upon receiving the material, Stalin apparently asked how much he had to pay for it. To "preserve appearances" the Germans asked for three million gold rubles, which Stalin promptly paid.

It seems unlikely, however, that Stalin accepted the German dossier as entirely legitimate. When it came time to "expose" the "counterrevolutionary Fascist organization" in the military, he made no direct use of the Nazi material. At a meeting of the Military Revolutionary Council (June 1–4), where he called for the generals' arrest and execution, he based his charges exclusively on confessions supplied by military men like Shmidt and Putna. He may, however, have used the dossier to persuade other Soviet generals to act as judges against their colleagues and to sentence them to death. It is not certain whether the military Revolutionary Council held a trial to pronounce the sentences or simply rubber-stamped them after the men were already executed. It is certain only that eight high officers collaborated with Stalin in this unseemly business and that six of them were later liquidated themselves.

If the details of the Tukhachevsky "trial" are somewhat murky, harder to fathom still are the motives that might have led Stalin to liquidate his best generals, the very men who had been helping him to build up the power and effectiveness of the Red Army. One must speculate here, as with most of Stalin's motives, for unlike Hitler he produced no *Mein Kampf* or *Table Talks* spelling out his designs and inner thoughts.

Even if Stalin did not accept at face value all the innuendo contained in Heydrich's voluminous dossier, he (like Adolf Hitler) harbored a long-standing distrust of military men and was always prepared to believe the worst of them. This distrust had several sources. Military men, like engineers and technical specialists, had a way of becoming so proud of their expertise that they often saw themselves as more important to the health of the state than the leading politicians. They held themselves "above politics," developed self-perpetuating cliques, and created their own agendas based on their specialized view of the world. In the Russian case, Stalin's regime had actually encouraged these tendencies by abolishing the Leninist system of political commissars in the army and allowing commanders full control of their units. Stalin also made senior officers exempt from arrest by civilian authorities without special authorization from the people's commissar of defense. Having allowed his generals to become somewhat independent, and to forget the demands of political vigilance, Stalin seems suddenly to have realized that the Red Army might become a "state within the state" rather than a pliable political tool. Just as he had to remind his industrial specialists that politics always came before economics or technology, so he had to remind his generals of their subordinate status.

But it seems that Stalin feared more than his generals' potential independence. He knew that Tukhachevsky and his colleagues had spent a great deal of time in Germany during the twenties, attending German military schools and socializing with German officers and diplomats. This close German-Soviet military relationship had more or less ended after Hitler came to power, though Tukhachevsky had paid a brief visit to some of his old Reichswehr friends as recently as January 1936. On that occasion he had gone out of his way to praise the accomplishments and effectiveness of Hitler's new Wehrmacht. *"Ils sont déjà invincibles!"* he told a French journalist. Stalin must have wondered, upon learning of such effusions, how Tukhachevsky and his colleagues would behave if Hitler made good on his threat to secure lebensraum in the east.

Paradoxically, Stalin seems to have worried both that his army might not effectively stand up to the Germans and that it might not allow him to evade such a confrontation. Despite deteriorating relations with Nazi Germany, Stalin hoped to keep his options open for an eventual rapprochement with the Reich. Russia carried on extensive trade with Germany in the early thirties, and Stalin secretly sent emissaries to Hitler to negotiate a resumption of military and technical cooperation. In December 1936 an NKVD agent told his colleague Walter Krivitsky in Paris, "We have set our course toward an early understanding with Hitler. It will only be a matter of three or four months. There's nothing for us in this rotting corpse of France, with her Front Populaire." Stalin's top generals, on the other hand, had gradually adjusted to the notion that war with Germany was inevitable. Despite his German contacts, Tukhachevsky in particular opposed any opening to the Reich; instead, he favored firming up Russia's alliance with France. He and his colleagues therefore threatened to tie Stalin's hands when it came to dealing with Hitler. Stalin's decision to eliminate this obstacle to his freedom of action can thus be seen as an important step toward the Nazi-Soviet pact of August 1939.

In addition to these strategic considerations, Stalin may also have been motivated by personal animosities toward the Tukhachevsky circle. Though Stalin often praised Tukhachevsky and allowed him to become a marshal, he certainly remembered that in the civil war Tukhachevsky had performed much more brilliantly than he had. Indeed, Stalin believed that Tukhachevsky had spread the word in the Red Army officer corps that he, Stalin, was responsible for the Reds' failure to conquer Poland in 1920. The more megalomaniacal Stalin became, the more determined he was to erase any memories of his less-than-glorious martial and revolutionary past.

Finally, it is worth noting that three of the nine officers executed in August 1937 were Jewish. On the one hand this made the charges against them seem all the more preposterous: why would Jews want to collaborate with the Nazis? But to Stalin, whose growing anti-Semitism was already evident in his campaigns against Trotsky, Zinoviev, Kamenev, and Radek, the Jewish generals' ethnic origins would have helped confirm their guilt.

The behavior of the victims in this case seems as baffling and troublesome as that of the purge's chief architect. Tukhachevsky and his colleagues, all tough veterans of bloody military campaigns, submitted passively to arrest even though they must have known what was in store for them. When their fears were confirmed, they made no effort to escape their fate. It is reported that Yakir exclaimed before the firing squad, "Long live the Party! Long live Stalin!" As we noted above, several of the condemned officers' colleagues gave the purge a measure of legitimacy by serving on the military court that formally passed the death sentences (though the accused may already have been dead). Why did the army, the one agency that might have effectively resisted Stalin, fail to do so at the very moment when its integrity was being liquidated along with its leadership?

Perhaps the best answer is that—like the party leaders who meekly acquiesced in their own destruction—the military hierarchy had already sacrificed its integrity on the altar of Stalinist loyalty. The Soviet officer corps had zealously followed orders to shoot unarmed peasants during the collectivization of agriculture; they had helped massacre the kulaks; they had followed the zigzags of Soviet foreign policy without a murmur of dissent. Moreover, during the years when they were helping Stalin consolidate his dictatorship, they were given special privileges—servants, dachas, cars, access to the Bolshoi corps de ballet—that they must have seen as rewards for their complicity in these brutal policies. Another reward, interestingly enough, was a lack of party interference in military business, a development that may have lulled the generals into a false sense of security. In any event, Soviet Russia's military leadership proved even less prepared to defend itself against political terror than was Germany's. A number of Wehrmacht officers, after all, did plot against Hitler, and some of them eventually tried to kill him. The Red Army, alas, produced no Becks or Stauffenbergs, no legacy of military resistance to totalitarian terror.

When Hitler crushed the military conspiracy that culminated in the assassination attempt of July 20, 1944, he extended his fury to the conspirators' families. Stalin anticipated this brutal policy in 1937 by arresting, imprisoning, and (in some cases) liquidating relatives of the purged officers. Yakir's wife was murdered, along with a brother, the wife of another brother, and her son. Two of Tukhachevsky's brothers perished, while his aged mother, teenage daughter, and three sisters were sent to labor camps.

Stalin's military purge by no means ended with the liquidation of the Tukhachevsky circle. Indeed, the campaign immediately extended to all senior and junior officers who had once served with the executed generals—a huge number, given these men's extensive experience. Among the first victims were Old Bolshevik soldiers who had fought with distinction in the civil war. These men were replaced by officers slightly their juniors, but soon they, too, started to disappear. By 1939 many Soviet regiments were under the command of lieutenants.

Another target was the military education system, particularly the top military academies. A student at the Frunze Military Academy recalled how in 1936 instructors began to disappear. One day the class commissar announced that Lecturer Vatsetis had been arrested as an "enemy of the people." The students found this incredible, for Vatsetis had "fought all through the Civil War for Soviet power." Then the wave of arrests engulfed the student body. A young man who had fought with the international brigades in the Spanish civil war and received the decoration "Hero of the Soviet Union" suddenly vanished.

This Spanish veteran was not alone: Soviet soldiers who had fought in Spain were particularly vulnerable to the purge because Stalin distrusted their contacts with foreigners, especially with Spanish Trotskyites. He sent the NKVD to Spain to keep close watch on the Red military contingent, an assignment the police seem to have taken up with relish. General J. K. Berzin, commander of the Red Army force in Spain, ran afoul of the vigilant police and was sent home to be shot. A Soviet officer named Stern, who under the nom de guerre Kleber took charge of the international bridages, was executed in Spain itself. Brigade Commander Vladimir Goriev, who had commanded the successful Republican defense of Madrid, was called home, awarded the Order of Lenin, and promptly shot.

Soviet officers who had helped train "partisans" for possible deployment after an invasion also began to disappear. Stalin had concluded that the training of partisans showed a "lack of faith in the Soviet state," for it acknowledged the possibility that an enemy might successfully penetrate Russian territory. When one officer nevertheless asked his superior how these loyal men could suddenly be condemned as "enemies of the people," he was told to keep his mouth shut: "Comrade Stalin has taken charge of this operation himself, and he will not let innocent people be wronged."

But Comrade Stalin was hardly inclined to allow a few men's possible "innocence" stand in the way of a thorough military housecleaning. Particularly thorough was his "cleansing" of the Kiev Military District, Yakir's old command, where some six to seven hundred officers were arrested on charges of treachery, sabotage, and treason. Here the purge even swept up long-retired veterans, most notably General Bougetsky, a civil war hero who had lost an arm fighting the Whites. Accusing him of plotting with the Nazis to kill Defense Commissar Voroshilov, the NKVD pinned a swastika on Bougetsky's chest and emptied a spittoon over his head.

While officers stationed in western Russia were accused of conspiring with the Germans, those in the Far Eastern Command were charged with treasonous dealings with the Japanese. In June 1937 the NKVD began arresting members of Marshal Vassily Blyukher's Far Eastern Red Banner Front. An interested observer of this process was the Japanese Command in Manchuria. Sensing that the purge was significantly weakening the Red Army, the Japanese Command began to "test" the Russians with several probing attacks along the Amur River. This prompted Stalin to relax his Far Eastern purge for the time being, though he resumed it with redoubled vengeance in 1938.

Stalin's purge not only embraced all regions of the country but also decimated all branches of the military. The Soviet navy had committed the grave error of adjusting its strategy to the limits of Russia's technical and industrial capacity. The naval command had developed a relatively small force, based primarily on submarines, committed essentially to a coastal defense. For Stalin this doctrine amounted to a refutation of his own achievement as Great Builder and to sabotage of his ambitious plan to launch a powerful oceangoing fleet. Clearly he could not become a latter-day Peter the Great with a naval strategy based on short-range submarines. He also distrusted his naval leaders for their "cosmopolitan" connections, though it was hard to see how a navy, especially one instructed to extend its international range, could avoid contacts with foreigners. In any event,

Admiral R. A. Muklevich, a leader of the drive to modernize the Soviet navy, and V. M. Orlov, naval commander in chief, were accused of conspiring with the Tukhachevsky circle to prevent the creation of a large surface fleet. Their arrest (and eventual execution) opened the way for a purge of all their staffs and of all naval installations and educational institutions. Compared with a holocaust like this, the Battle of Tsushima in the Russo-Japanese War had been a minor setback.

While attacking the naval leadership for its defensive timidity, Stalin faulted the Soviet air force for the opposite failing: for overreliance on the strategic bomber and insufficient emphasis on the defensive fighter. The two officers who had developed Russia's respected strategic bomber capacity, Generals Alksnis and Khripin, were removed from command and probably executed. The country's most accomplished aviation designer, A. N. Tupolev, was imprisoned on trumped-up charges of having sold Soviet aviation secrets abroad. Even the heads of the Moscow Aeroclub, which tested new models of light and sport aircraft, were charged with sabotage when the club lost some planes in a competition and two female parachutists died in a jumping exhibition. The fact of the matter, protested a club member, was that the planes simply went astray and the women jumpers, "trying to outdo one another, opened their parachutes too late."

If many officers were killed because they held the wrong views, or knew people who held the wrong views, others died because they stood in the way of an ambitious colleague's advancement or simply stumbled into the cross fire of denunciation and personal vendetta. Marshal Blyukher, proletarian general, lord of the Far East, and brilliant strategist, apparently fell victim to an intrigue launched by Voroshilov and the army commissar L. Z. Mekhlis. When he was shot in late 1938, there was no talk of treason or sabotage—no talk at all. Twenty years later Khrushchev "rehabilitated" him, without, however, mentioning that Blyukher had been one of the "judges" who condemned Tukhachevsky.

While Stalin closely supervised the Red Army purge, he received much zealous assistance from the NKVD, which—like its German counterparts, the SD and the Gestapo—relished every opportunity to undermine the military. The NKVD was particularly anxious to damage the rival military-intelligence agency of the Red Army, many of whose foreign agents it accused of spying for the countries where they were stationed. Most of these men were called home and shot. The NKVD also attacked the political commissars, who had been reintroduced in the military system in 1937. Charged with being too "independent-minded," all twenty-eight army political commissars were liquidated.

As the military leadership reeled under these attacks, the NKVD added to its already considerable powers. Like the German SS, it developed its own military units, managed vast forced-labor camps and factories, and maintained "scientific institutes" in prisons like the one described in Alexander Solzhenitsyn's *The First Circle*. After 1937 the NKVD supplanted even the party as the dominant institution in the Soviet state.

Yet even the powerful NKVD was not immune to the Great Purge. When he succeeded Yagoda, Yezhov immediately began culling the police leadership of Yagoda loyalists. Some three thousand NKVD officers were executed in 1937–38. Yagoda and Molchanov were thrown into prison. Meanwhile Yezhov, aware that he had made some enemies, instituted new security measures at the NKVD headquarters in the Lubyanka. To reach his office on the third floor, one had to take an elevator to the fifth floor, ride back down to the first floor, then finally proceed to the third. This circuitous passage was rendered all the more difficult because the elevator often broke down.

Before the military purge had run its course—the last officer was executed two weeks before the German invasion in 1941—roughly one-third of the Red Army officer corps had been executed, imprisoned, or dismissed from service. Among those liquidated were three of the five Soviet marshals, all eleven deputy people's commissars of defense, and thirteen of fifteen generals of the army. All commanders of military districts, all corps commanders, most brigade and division commanders, half the regimental commanders, and all but one fleet commander were purged or shot. A Soviet historian later observed that no army officer corps in wartime ever suffered the devastation that the Soviet military experienced in peacetime. Indeed, the Red Army lost many more senior officers in the Great Purge than in the Great Patriotic War against Germany.

Stalin was apparently aware that the scope of his military purge would undermine martial efficiency, but he believed this problem could soon be solved through the appointment of new men—"simple" men he could trust. Even if rebuilding took some time, the internal security of his regime, which he seemed genuinely to believe threatened, claimed his primary attention. The chief was also aware that some innocents were being purged along with the "guilty." But for this, as for many other of his barbarities, he had a ready proverb: "If you cut off the head, you do not worry about the hair."

WHIRLWIND

Many Russians no doubt believed that the storm of Stalin's purges would subside now that it had carried away the military "traitors," along with their oppositionist accomplices. Who was left to purge? "Stalin cannot shoot everybody," it was said. As it turned out, however, Stalin was just reaching his stride. In the spring and summer of 1937, the "whirlwind"—as one victim called the Great Purge—began sweeping over the reigning Communist party leadership, the trade union organization, the Comintern apparatus, the "national minorities," the managerial, intellectual, and scientific elite, and the community of foreign Communists who had sought refuge from fascism in the Soviet Union.

But it did not stop with party apparatchiks or social-intellectual elites. Tens of thousands of ordinary people—peasants, factory workers, schoolteachers, petty bureaucrats—also languished in prisons and camps or, like Boris Pasternak's Lara in *Doctor Zhivago*, "vanished without a trace and probably died somewhere, forgotten as a nameless number on a list that afterwards got mislaid." In some areas the police simply rounded up a certain percentage of the entire population. "Day and night," recalled one victim, "GPU [secret police] vans raced through the streets of town and village, taking their victims from their homes, factories, universities, laboratories, workshops, barracks and government offices." In distant Azerbaijan a British diplomat saw "striking proof of the long arm of the Kremlin"—a succession of trucks deporting Turko-Tartar peasants to camps in Central Asia. No part of the Soviet Union, it seemed, was safe from this foul wind.

Leningrad, that "window on the West" built by Peter the Great, was certainly not safe. Russia's second city was now under the control of the local party boss Andrei Zhdanov, an especially brutal thug whom Stalin had brought in to replace Kirov. Zhdanov proceeded to gut the entire Leningrad party apparatus, from minor functionaries up through all seven municipal members of the Central Committee. They were either liquidated or sent to Siberia, where they joined the hundreds of Leningraders deported in the wake of the Kirov assassination. The thorough Leningrad operation was particularly unnerving, since the subarctic nights provided no shadowy cover for those small-hour knocks on the door. Light at midnight, it seemed, was even worse than darkness at noon.

Zhdanov's purge was then emulated by Stalinist henchmen in other Russian provincial party committees and in all the Soviet republics. Lazar Kaganovich (the "Black Tornado") descended on Ivanovo, Smolensk, and the Kuban; Georgi Malenkov, one of Stalin's successors, took care of Belorussia, Armenia, and Azerbaijan; Lavrenti Beria, later head of the secret police, swept through Georgia. Like Ivan the Terrible's *oprichniki*, they "sniffed out treason" and "swept it away." According to one Soviet historian, they liquidated 90 percent of the provincial and republican Central Committee memberships in 1937–38. Eugenia Ginzburg met the entire former government of the Tartar Republic in prison.

The Ukraine, whose leaders were especially vocal in opposing the purges, and where Stalin (rightly) suspected considerable anti-Soviet sentiment, was subjected to an even greater fury. The purge there was conducted by the unholy trinity of Molotov, Khrushchev, and Yezhov, who arrived in Kiev in August 1937 with a large band of NKVD troops. They quickly cashiered the local Politburo and installed Khrushchev as first secretary. Over the course of the following year, Khrushchev saw to the arrest of all seventeen members of the Ukrainian government and most members of the Central Committee. Of the 102 members and candidate members of this latter group, only 2 were to survive the purge. They were replaced by young ideologues who could be trusted to enforce Stalinist and Great Russian authority. Among them was Leonid Brezhnev, who, as the saying goes, never looked back.

Watching Stalin and the rest of the Politburo review troops on May Day, 1937, the British diplomat Fitzroy Maclean, was struck by how anxious Stalin's colleagues looked. They "grinned nervously and moved uneasily from one foot to the other, forgetting the parade and the high office they held and everything else in their mingled joy and terror at being spoken to by him." Their nervousness was understandable. One of their number was already missing and his dacha reassigned. Their subordinates were being arrested in droves. Commissars and vice-commissars of trade, industry, education, justice, and transport were experiencing the same fate. Soon more members of their own, select company would cease appearing at public functions, indeed would simply vanish from sight. It would be like "Ten Little Indians" in the Kremlin, though the strange disappearances in this case eventually stopped with five.

If this harsh culling of the top party ranks could perhaps be explained in terms of the victims' past transgressions, the extension of the purge to low-level party members and nonparty citizens seemed bereft of all rhyme or reason. It has been estimated that for every party member who was purged, eight or ten ordinary citizens went to prison. This was because in one sense the Great Purge was more like a snowball than a whirlwind: as soon as a person was arrested, all his acquaintances immediately became suspect. Those who were denounced to the police promptly denounced others in an effort to save themselves. "Accuse one another, denounce one another, if you wish to remain among the living," was the word of the day.

Indeed, virtually anyone in the Soviet Union in 1937 was vulnerable to the purges. Nevertheless, just as some Soviet citizens were (in Orwell's phrase) "more equal than others," some were also more likely to be purged than others. Suspect categories included former members of non-Communist parties, active Orthodox church members, Theosophists, Tolstoyans, Jehovah's Witnesses, artists or intellectuals belonging to an ethnic minority, Jews, and, above all, anyone with foreign contacts, past or present. These categories were admittedly somewhat arbitrary. Eugenia Ginzburg thought that a fellow prisoner had been arrested because she knew Ginzburg. But no, the woman said, "I'm a Tartar, so it was simpler to put me down as a bourgeois nationalist. Actually, they did classify me as a Trotskyist at first, but Rud [a policeman] sent the file back, saying they'd exceeded the quota for Trotskyists but were behind on nationalists, even though they'd pulled in all the Tartar writers they could think of." People in the prisons and camps vied with one another in thinking up ingenious reasons to justify their arrests: they apparently believed that if they could identify the reason for their predicament, they could perhaps reclaim some control over their fate. But Nadezhda Mandelstam, wife of the purged poet Osip Mandelstam, recalled one victim who understood the futility of this exercise: "What do you mean, *what for?*" this woman asked a cellmate puzzling over her arrest. "It's time you understood that people are arrested *for nothing!*" As the NKVD liked to boast, "Give us a man, and we'll make a case," or, more colorfully, "So long as you have the neck, the rope will be found somewhere."

It was relatively easy for the police to make cases against intellectuals, scientists, and writers, because they were suspect in general as thinking people, and they were apt to cross over the aesthetic-methodological lines that the regime had established in all scientific and artistic fields. Among the academic intelligentsia, historians were especially vulnerable, for the past had become an ideological minefield in which the mines' locations were always subtly shifting. An eminent professor of ancient history wandered onto dangerous terrain when he described Joan of Arc as mentally unstable. This would have been acceptable enough before the Popular Front, but when Russia was trying to cultivate good relations with France it seemed dangerously provocative. The police also noted that this same professor had lectured on Alexander the Great and Hannibal to Red Army officers and had met foreigners at academic conferences. He was locked away as a spy and a terrorist, along with dozens of similarly incautious colleagues.

Historians were no doubt expendable enough, but the regime also sacrificed hundreds of natural scientists in the interest of "security" or ideological purity. Leading physicists whose skills were vital to the nation's technological development were arrested as "German spies" or as "intellectual deviationists." Critical fields like atomic physics and radio technology suffered enormous setbacks as their best Soviet practitioners ended up breaking rocks in the Gulag. In biology the ideological battle was particularly vicious, since Trofim Lysenko, a fanatical quack, campaigned with Stalin's blessing against those of his colleagues who doubted his claim to have disproved the basic laws of heredity. The most prominent victim of this mania was V. I. Vavilov, Russia's greatest geneticist. He was first expelled from his research institute and the Academy of Sciences, then repeatedly interrogated, and, in 1940, imprisoned. He introduced himself to his cellmates as follows: "You see before you, talking of the past, Academician Vavilov, but now, according to the opinion of the investigators, nothing but dung."

Reduced to dung, too, were many of Russia's most brilliant writers and poets. Among the seven hundred authors who attended the First Writers' Congress, in 1934, only fifty survived to attend the second, in 1954. Isaac Babel, Russia's finest short-story writer since Chekhov, made the mistake of writing truthfully about the revolution and civil war. He was arrested in 1938 and died in a camp in 1941. The country's most gifted poet, Osip Mandelstam, wrote a poem about Stalin that ended with the lines "And every killing is a treat/For the broad-chested Ossete."* The police found this poem in a search of Mandelstam's apartment in 1934. After his arrest his wife appealed to Bukharin for his release. "He hasn't written anything rash, has he?" asked Bukharin. Of course, Mandelstam had written his death warrant, though his demise was agonizingly protracted. After a second arrest, in 1938, he was sent to a labor camp in the Far East, the kind of place described horrifyingly by Solzhenitsyn in *One Day in the Life of Ivan Denisovich* and *The Gulag Archipelago.* On his way to the camp he was beaten and robbed by a gang of criminals, then driven to near-madness by starvation, and finally allowed to die in a psychiatric hospital. In an artistic sense he had died earlier, since after his arrest he was not allowed to publish any work, and his name was no longer mentionable in public.

---

*The Ossetes lived in the Caucasus, north of Georgia, and were thought to be particularly barbarous. There were persistent rumors that Stalin had Ossetian blood.

Many of the purged intellectuals were guilty of "cosmopolitan leanings," a heinous offense in the eyes of Stalin's xenophobic regime. Xenophobia was also strongly evident in Stalin's decimation of the Comintern, the Moscow-based umbrella organization to which most foreign Communist parties belonged. Stalin never had much use for this institution. Its inherent cosmopolitanism and its former control by Zinoviev and Bukharin made it doubly suspect. In 1927 some members of the Comintern executive committee had refused to denounce Trotsky without seeing the charges against him. Although after this mildly defiant gesture the Comintern leadership raised no more objections to Stalin's policies and, indeed, helped him discipline potential troublemakers in the various constituent parties, Stalin continued to see the Comintern—like the army—as a source of potential danger.

Among the ironic perversities of Stalin's purge of the Comintern was its focus on those foreign Communists who had suffered most from the rise of fascism in Europe. Soviet Russia was filled with leftist exiles from Mussolini's Italy, Hitler's Germany, Dollfuss's and Schuschnigg's Austria, Franco's Spain, and Horthy's Hungary. Numerous, too, were refugees from authoritarian Poland and Yugoslavia. Stalin could easily attack these people because their governments would not lift a finger to protect them.

Among the first to go in the purge of foreign Communists in the Soviet Union were the Germans—important KPD (German Communist party) politicians and obscure refugees alike. In 1937 Heinz Neumann, a former member of the KPD's Politburo, was arrested at the Hotel Lux, the dingy headquarters of Moscow's foreign Communist community. Three other former German Politburo members disappeared at about the same time, as did the editors of *Die Rote Fahne* (The red flag), Heinrich Susskind and Werner Hirsch. All were executed. After questioning Neumann, Susskind, and Hirsch, who were all Jewish, one of their interrogators reportedly concluded, "The Jewish refugees are Hitler's agents abroad." Equally grotesque was the NKVD's persecution of powerless German refugees whose only notability lay in their previous persecution by the Gestapo. Eugenia Ginzburg met one of these poor wretches in prison. Her calves and buttocks were covered with deep scars left by Gestapo torture, and her fingernails had been torn out by the NKVD. Most of the German Communists in Russia who survived the purge period were turned over by the NKVD to the Gestapo after the Nazi-Soviet pact in 1939. (The Nazis returned the favor by giving the Soviet government some of the anti-Stalinist Russians they held.) Among the few German Communists in Moscow to escape this fate was Wilhelm Pieck: he helped the Russians purge his countrymen and, as a reward, was installed as head of the Communist party in East Germany after the war.

One German Communist who almost got away was the propaganda genius Willi Münzenberg, who as we recall orchestrated the Comintern's public-relations campaign for the Spanish republic during the civil war. He had enough sense not to return to Moscow when summoned there in 1937. Expelled from the party, he was interned in France as an enemy alien after the outbreak of war in

1939. Released in 1940, he tried to flee to Switzerland but was murdered, probably by NKVD agents, on the way.

Austrian leftists, particularly former *Schutzbündler,* fared no better than their German colleagues. They had fled to the Soviet Union after vainly fighting against the Right in Austria and Spain. They expected to lick their wounds in Moscow and prepare for an eventual triumphant return to their homeland. One of them noted at the time, "We were knocked down, but we are not beaten, because out of defeat we will learn how the proletariat fights and wins." Instead, they learned that their host regarded them as a nuisance. It seemed that despite their protestations of Stalinist loyalty, they might still harbor their old Social Democratic ideals. Moreover, they might raise inconvenient objections were Stalin to attempt a rapprochement with the hated Hitler. They could not understand Stalin's subtleties and must have been shocked when the NKVD started rounding them up in late 1937.

Among the first to be arrested was Gustav Deutsch, son of Julius Deutsch, the former Schutzbund leader. Young Deutsch was an enthusiastic apostle of Soviet policies, including Soviet criticism of his father's "betrayal" of the February 1934 uprising. Nonetheless, Gustav Deutsch was forced to admit to being a spy and Trotskyite agent. He was executed in 1939. Another prominent victim was Heinz Roscher, former deputy leader of the Schutzbund in Floridsdorf. Having led the first Schutzbund contingent to Moscow, he insisted that he and his comrades felt "right at home in the fatherland of the world proletariat." Like Deutsch junior, he had done his part to denounce the Austrian Social Democratic leaders as "Social Fascists." He declared that his experience in the Soviet Union had taught him that "reformism [was] the false path to socialism," which could "march to victory only under the leadership of the Communist party." Little good it did him: one week before the fourth anniversary of the February 12 uprising, three men arrived at his apartment in the middle of the night and took him away. His wife and son never saw him again.

Italian Communists in Moscow, whose countrymen back in Italy were in the process of linking their destiny to Nazi Germany, shared the fate of the exiled German and Austrian Communists in the Soviet Union. Almost two hundred Italian Communists perished in the Great Purge. Their destruction was abetted by Palmiro Togliatti, who, like Wilhelm Pieck, kept himself alive by denouncing his people to the NKVD. Among those arrested was Togliatti's brother-in-law. The police smashed his teeth and permanently injured his spine, but he survived and returned to Italy after the war. Incredibly, he refused even then to speak out about his suffering, insisting that it was not for an Italian, but only for a Russian, to complain about Soviet actions.

Among all the groups in the Comintern, the Polish Communist party suffered the heaviest casualties. Poles had played an important role in the history of Russian communism, and they constituted by far the largest foreign contingent in Moscow. Between 1937 and 1939 about fifty thousand of them were shot; among them were all the Polish Politburo members resident in the Soviet Union. Behind this extraordinary brutality lay not only ancient national hatreds but also Stalin's understanding that most Polish Communists would oppose a new partition of their country between Russia and Germany.

Stalin did not limit his purge of foreign Communists to men and women living within easy grasp of the NKVD in the Soviet Union. His secret police established "mobile groups" charged with the hunting down of oppositionist (or potentially oppositionist) Communists in foreign countries. One of their first victims was an NKVD resident agent in Switzerland named Ignace Reiss, who had broken with Stalin and denounced the dictator as a "traitor to the cause of the working class and of Socialism." Reiss's body was found riddled with machine-gun bullets on a road near Lausanne. Another NKVD foreign agent, Walter Krivitsky, who had warned Reiss to flee and who defected from Soviet service after the Reiss murder, was found shot in a Washington, D.C., hotel room in 1941. His death was ruled a suicide, but according to the erstwhile American radical Sidney Hook, Krivitsky had told his American friends, "If I am ever found apparently a suicide, you will know that the NKVD has caught up with me." Four years before Krivitsky's death, Soviet agents murdered a former czarist officer named General Eugene Miller in Paris. Miller led a White Russian émigré group called the Russian United Military Union, which had connections to the Nazis. He may have been killed because, as Krivitsky asserted, he "knew too much" about NKVD collaboration with Heydrich; or the NKVD may have wanted him out of the way so that it could put one of its own double agents at the helm of the United Military Union.

Members of the Spanish POUM, the dissident Marxist unit fighting in Barcelona during the Spanish civil war, also stood high on Stalin's hit list. The NKVD sent agents to Barcelona to smash this group and secure the preeminence of pro-Stalinist Communist forces in the Catalan capital. They began by murdering the POUM's main leader, the prominent Catalan writer Andrés Nin. Orlov, the NKVD's chief agent in Spain, then orchestrated the interrogation and torture of other POUM leaders in the convent of Saint Ursula in Barcelona, "the Dachau of republican Spain."

Dissident Spaniards and apostate NKVD agents were small game compared with the man whom Stalin still regarded as his most dangerous rival: Leon Trotsky. In exile in Mexico since 1937, Trotsky had surrounded himself with security guards in a bunkerlike compound outside Mexico City. An NKVD agent named Leonid Eitingon was given virtually unlimited funds to crack Trotsky's defenses and liquidate him. After one abortive attempt involving a full-scale assault on Trotsky's villa, Eitingon managed to infiltrate a subordinate into Trotsky's household. On August 20, 1940, this young man struck Trotsky in the back of the head with an ice ax as the latter was reading a paper his assailant had brought him to critique.

FINAL ACT: TRIAL OF
THE ANTI-SOVIET BLOC OF
RIGHTS AND TROTSKYITES

Trotsky may have been Stalin's most prominent victim, but two years before his murder Stalin had staged a third and final show trial that featured defendants only slightly less august than Trotsky. This trial's central figures—Nikolai Bukharin, Alexei Rykov, and Nikolai Krestinsky—had all been members of Lenin's Politburo. Bukharin was arguably Bolshevism's greatest theorist. Another prominent defendant was Genrikh Yagoda, the former NKVD head who Stalin believed had been insufficiently zealous in persecuting his fellow Old Bolsheviks. Less well known, but still politically important, were five people's commissars and high economic administrators, none of whom had a record of opposition to Stalin. Rounding out the list of accused were a leading agronomist, a trade union official formerly posted in Berlin, Yagoda's private secretary, and three elderly Kremlin doctors charged with the "medical murders" of the famous writer Maxim Gorky and three other Communist luminaries. The charges against these men were so extensive, their alleged conspiratorial connections so labyrinthine, that Stalin needed a special diagram with colored lines and arrows to keep it all straight.

The central themes of the "Right oppositionist" trial were familiar enough, but the prosecution allowed itself some intriguing embellishments and innovations for this final performance. In addition to spying and wrecking for Germany and Japan, the principal defendants were accused also of working for the Poles and the British. Bukharin was charged with having tried to kill Lenin as well as Stalin. (This, no doubt, to put Stalin on an equal footing with Lenin.) Two Asian Communist leaders from Uzbekistan were added to the list of European-Russian "bourgeois nationalists" who supposedly plotted to turn Soviet border regions over to foreign powers. The accusations of medical murder added a bizarre twist that apparently diverted some observers' attention from the more serious aspects of the trial. The central purpose of this extravaganza, after all, was to identify the primary defendants with all opposition to Stalin—past, present, and potential. The entire Old Bolshevik leadership except Stalin was to be condemned forever as a "foul-smelling heap of human garbage."

The trial opened on March 2, 1938, in the October Hall with Vyshinsky again in the role of prosecutor. As usual, confessions had been secured in advance through a combination of "conveyor" interrogations (nonstop grillings conducted by teams of inquisitors), appeals to patriotism and party loyalty, and threats against family members. The "evidence" against the accused was voluminous: it filled fifty thick volumes stacked impressively on the judges' table. If the judges nevertheless needed additional motivation to convict the defendants, they had only to glance at a small curtained window in the back of the courtroom. Behind it sat Joseph Stalin.

The judges and prosecutor were prepared to do their duty, and so, apparently, were the defendants. And yet the trial had hardly gotten under way before one of the accused, the former vice-commissar of foreign affairs Nikolai Krestinsky, shocked everyone by retracting a confession he had made during his pretrial interrogation. Asked if he pleaded guilty to the charges against him, Krestinsky, a "pale, seedy, dim little figure, his steel-rimmed glasses perched on a beaky nose," said spiritedly, "I plead not guilty. I am not a Trotskyite. I was never a member of the bloc of Rights and Trotskyites, of whose existence I was not aware. Nor have I committed any of the crimes with which I personally am charged, in particular I plead not guilty to the charge of having had connections with the German intelligence service." Krestinsky's codefendants gasped in amazement. A shocked Vyshinsky asked him about his pretrial confession. Krestinsky admitted that he had confessed to Trotskyite transgressions during his interrogation, but now he wanted it clearly understood that he had not committed "a single crime."

Vyshinsky quickly moved on to other defendants, and after two of them bent over backward to implicate Krestinsky, he was recalled to the stand. Now he addressed the discrepancy between his confession and his present plea of not guilty. In his pretrial interrogation, he said, he had given "false testimony several times." His explanation was even more shocking: "I simply considered that if I were to say what I am saying today, my declaration would not reach the leaders of the Party and the Government." A hush spread over the court. Never, noted one foreign observer, had such a thing been said in public before.

Krestinsky's testimony was suspended until the following evening. When he returned to the stand, Vyshinsky asked him if he persisted in his refusal to confirm his pretrial testimony, as well as the incriminating statements made by other defendants. "I fully confirm the testimony I gave in the preliminary investigation," answered Krestinsky. What then, pressed Vyshinsky, was the meaning of the "piece of Trotskyite provocation" he had delivered on the preceding day? Krestinsky replied,

Yesterday, under the influence of a momentary keen feeling of false shame, evoked by the atmosphere of the dock and the painful impression created by the public reading of the indictment, which was aggravated by my poor health, I could not bring myself to tell the truth, I could not bring myself to say that I was guilty. And instead of saying, "Yes, I am guilty," I almost mechanically answered, "No, I am not guilty." . . . I request the Court to register my statement that I fully and completely admit that I am guilty of all the gravest charges brought against me personally, and that I admit my complete responsibility for the treason and treachery I have committed.

If any statement was "mechanical," it was this one and not Krestinsky's original not-guilty plea. His words, noted one witness, "were reeled off like a well-learned lesson." Apparently the NKVD had not wasted the intervening evening.

No refresher lessons were required to make Mikhail Chernov, former people's commissar of agriculture, admit to the most far-reaching economic "wrecking" campaign yet chronicled in the Moscow trials. He declared that Rykov and other Rights had instructed him to stir up the middle peasants against the government by treating them in the same, harsh fashion in which Moscow had treated the kulaks. "I was to accentuate the distortions of policy, to incense the middle peasants, to take special account of the national feelings of the Ukrainian population and to explain everywhere that these distortions were a result of the policy of Moscow. . . ." Chernov said that he had also embarked on a program—"drawn up in accordance with the demands of the German intelligence service"—to "wreck" operations in livestock breeding, seed and crop rotation, and tractor stations. Chernov and his coconspirators had sabotaged horse breeding "in order . . . not to provide horses for the Red Army." They had infected cattle and pigs with bacteria. To reduce crop yields the plotters had "muddled up seed affairs" and ordered incorrect crop rotation. At tractor stations they had sabotaged agricultural implements and brought in supervisors who were "members of our Right organization."

Isaac Zelensky, ex-chairman of the state planning board and self-confessed former agent of the czarist Okhrana (secret police), was not to be outdone as a wrecker by Chernov. He admitted that his agency had ensured shortages of sugar and sabotaged butter distribution by mislabeling grades and lacing thousands of cases of the most expensive grade with glass and nails. "And what about eggs?" prodded Vyshinsky. Had not Zelensky and his band of Rights "taken measures to ensure that Moscow would be without eggs?" Yes, admitted Zelensky, in 1936 they had allowed "fifty carloads of eggs" to spoil before shipment to the capital. The purpose of all this, added Zelensky, was to foment an uprising against the Soviet government and to bring the Rights to power. Zelensky claimed to have secured promises of support for the rightist coup from a representative of the British Labour party.

Whatever the Russian people might have thought about the machinations of the British Labour party, at least it now had an explanation for all those shortages, poor or rotten products, and high prices they had endured over the last few years. Vile "wreckers," not the inadequacies of Comrade Stalin's five-year plans, were to blame.

Through most of the Moscow trials, the Germans and Japanese had been presented as Russia's most dangerous enemies: voracious Fascist-imperialist pigs eager to poke their snouts into Stalin's "socialist garden." But now, as Zelensky's testimony indicated, another foreign danger had emerged: Great Britain. Britain's suspect status was confirmed when an Uzbek Communist leader confessed that he and a colleague had been instructed by the bloc of Rights to conspire with the British for the secession of Uzbekistan from the Soviet Union and its incorporation into the British Empire. This charge may have seemed a little far-fetched—Britain, after all, was having enough trouble holding together what remained of its far-flung empire—but the British lion had served nineteenth-century Russian leaders as a convenient bogey often enough: why not let it roar again? This would have the added advantage of explaining why Russia's Asian republics seemed somewhat restless under Great Russian rule.

The third show trial was well under way before Nikolai Bukharin, its central figure, was examined. Bukharin's testimony was deferred so that a number of defendants could thoroughly blacken his name before he appeared. He was depicted by his colleagues as an "archfiend" who "had his hand in every plot." When Bukharin finally stood before him, Vyshinsky picked up this theme with a vengeance. Bukharin's career, said the prosecutor, represented "the acme of monstrous hypocrisy, perfidy, jesuitry and inhuman villainy." This man, who had the temerity to invoke the great Lenin's name (and who, with his bald head and red beard, looked somewhat like Lenin), had actually plotted to kill Lenin in 1918. He had also taken part in the assassination of Kirov and planned to kill Stalin.

Preposterous as these charges were, Stalin had every reason to hate and distrust Bukharin. The Old Bolshevik had been closer to Lenin than Stalin had ever been. Moreover, when Stalin launched his brutal policy of collectivization and forced industrialization in the late twenties, Bukharin began espousing a "socialist humanism" that put people's needs before production goals and state power. And while Stalin tried secretly to maintain cordial relations with Nazi Germany, Bukharin publicly opposed any rapprochement with Hitler, who he insisted had "cast a dark and bloody shadow over the world."

Stalin had begun laying the groundwork for Bukharin's elimination at a Central Committee meeting in February 1937. Here the chief and his supporters demanded Bukharin's and Rykov's arrest as "hired murderers, saboteurs, and wreckers in the service of fascism." Bukharin responded by charging Stalin and Yezhov with establishing a brutal police state and with engaging in "acts of torture on a scale hitherto unheard of." A Central Committee commission appointed by Stalin quickly decided the men's fate: "arrest, try, and shoot." They were immediately thrown into the dreaded Lubyanka prison. Bukharin was apparently not tortured beyond the usual rounds of endless interrogation. But Yezhov (on Stalin's orders) threatened to kill his wife and newborn son if he did not confess and stand trial.

As soon as Bukharin began testifying on March 5, 1938, it was apparent that he would not follow his script. On the one hand, he declared, "I plead guilty to . . . the sum total of crimes committed by this counter-revolutionary organization, irrespective of whether or not I knew of, whether or not I took a direct part, in any particular act." This was a rather more fulsome confession than Vyshinsky could have wanted. On the other hand, Bukharin flatly denied some of the particular charges against him. He insisted that he had not planned to kill Lenin or Stalin, had no complicity in the assassination of Kirov or other Soviet leaders, did not work for any foreign intelligence service, and did not commit wrecking activities to promote fascism. He also implied that confessions from some of the other defendants had been extracted through torture. On several occasions he frustrated the prosecution by launching into learned dissertations on Marxist theory. At other times he brazenly insulted his interrogators, observing, for example, that what Vyshinsky called "logic" was mere "tautology." Most important, in his "last plea" Bukharin managed to inject into his statement a challenge to the regime's central myth: the proposition that Stalin and Stalinism were the legitimate heirs to the Bolshevik Revolution. He did this by insisting that the prosecution's accusatory terminology—"anti-Soviet bloc," "counter-revolutionary organization," and so forth—referred to the true carriers of the Bolshevik heritage. No wonder one foreign correspondent could describe Bukharin as "proud and defiant," as "the first of the fifty-four men who have faced the court in the last three public treason trials who has not abased himself in the last hours of the trial."

Still to testify among the major defendants was Genrikh Yagoda. An American correspondent noted that Yagoda had sat through the previous testimony "as if in a daze." Having spent the last ten months in prison, sharing cells with men he himself had imprisoned, he now looked much older than his forty-seven years. His hair was white and his face "lined with despair." Since he had made the preliminary arrangements for this trial, he now resembled "a playwright who suddenly finds himself mixed up in the plot of his own play." But the plot had taken an adventurous turn that was not of his making. Yagoda stood accused of plotting to seize the Kremlin in collaboration with the Tukhachevsky group, and of arranging through three Kremlin doctors the "medical murders" of Maxim Gorky, Valerian Kuibyshev (an aide to Molotov), and two other Soviet leaders who had recently died. Moreover, he had allegedly tried to murder Yezhov by spraying his rival's office with mercury. No doubt Yezhov wrote this part of the trial script himself: being a murder target would enhance his prestige and give him something in common with the chief. Yet the story was somewhat baroque even by the standards of the Moscow trials. Vyshinsky must have realized this, for he reminded the court of other bizarre murders, such as that of Pope Clement II, who died by inhaling the fumes of a poisoned candle.

When called upon to corroborate the charges raised against him, Yagoda confirmed most of them but insisted for some odd reason that he bore responsibility for only two of the "medical murders." Reminded by Vyshinsky that he had confessed to all the charges in his pretrial interrogation, Yagoda announced that he had been lying on that occasion. Asked why he had lied, he said, "Permit me not to answer that question." The audience gasped at this answer, for they knew well what Yagoda, an old torturer himself, was alluding to. The court quickly adjourned; when it reassembled, Yagoda was called back to the stand. If before he had looked cowed, now he seemed crushed. In a voice that was "utterly weary and so faint that it could scarcely be heard in the hushed court," he read a statement confirming all the charges. Again Yagoda's former pupils "had done their work well."

In his concluding speech Vyshinsky—undoubtedly still indignant over the impertinent comments made by some of the defendants—demanded that all but two of the accused be shot like dirty dogs! Our people are demanding one thing: crush the accursed reptile! Time will pass. The graves of the hateful traitors will grow over with weeds and thistles. . . . Over the road cleared of the last scum and filth of the past, we, our people, with our beloved leader and teacher, the great Stalin, at our head will march as before onwards and onwards, towards Communism!

The court found all the defendants guilty after one day's deliberation. Three lesser figures were given prison sentences of fifteen, twenty, and twenty-five years. The rest were condemned to death and promptly shot.

Despite the predictable outcome of the "bloc of Rights" trial, Stalin had reason to regret some of its aspects. Bukharin had managed to use the trial to deliver his own political message. The inclusion of Britain among Russia's foreign predators must have seemed foolhardy in light of Hitler's annexation of Austria on March 11, 1938. Stalin, after all, might need British support against Germany if he failed to find an accommodation with the Reich. The introduction of the medical-murder motif proved misconceived because it highlighted victims other than Stalin and was so grippingly bizarre as to distract people's attention from the more important charges.

Stalin blamed Yezhov for the Bukharin trial's shortcomings. In December 1938 he removed Yezhov from his post as chief of the NKVD. A few weeks later the former policeman simply disappeared. Stalin later told a protégé, "Yezhov was a scoundrel. He killed our best people. . . . For that we had him shot." The real reason for his liquidation was his emergence as a rival to Stalin. Evidently he saw himself as a possible successor to the chief; unfortunately for him, so did the chief.

Despite the outrageousness of the charges and the prominence of the principal defendants in the "bloc of Rights" trial, some foreign witnesses were as convinced by this performance as by the others. Ambassador Davies, who attended all the sessions, wrote his daughter on March 8,

It [the trial] is terrific. I have found it of much intellectual interest, because it brings back into play all the old critical faculties involved in assessing the credibility of witnesses and sifting the wheat from the chaff—the truth from the false—which I was called upon to use for so many years in the trial of cases, myself. . . .

The extraordinary testimony of Krestinsky, Bukharin, and the rest would appear to indicate that the Kremlin's fears were well justified. For it now seems that a plot existed in the beginning of November, 1936, to project a *coup d'état*, with Tukhatchevsky at its head, for May of the following year. Apparently it was touch and go at that time whether it actually would be staged.

Two other foreign witnesses, the British diplomat Fitzroy Maclean and the American embassy official Charles E. ("Chip") Bohlen, were not so easily taken in, but even they found it hard to assess the trial's credibility. If the charges were true and the whole regime was riddled with treachery, why had the conspirators achieved so little success? And if they were innocent, why did they confess? Even extensive experience in the Soviet Union did not make it easy for these Western observers to penetrate the Alice in Wonderland world of Stalinist Russia. (Bohlen, however, was not so nonplussed by the purge trials as to miss exploiting the unusual opportunity they afforded the American diplomatic community in Moscow: as soon as Russians with choice apartments were arrested, Bohlen applied to take over their quarters. "I felt like a vulture," he confessed, "but we needed the space.")

Ambassador Davies's approval notwithstanding, the response from abroad to the last of the show trials must have given Stalin some cause for concern. The Anglo-American press gave prime coverage to attacks on the trial by Trotsky and Alexander Kerensky.* John Dewey published depositions contradicting the charges against Krestinsky and declared this latest trial to be a "frame-up" similar to that of the Zinoviev-Kamenev affair. Eighty members of the (Trotskyite) Socialist Workers party picketed the Soviet consulate in New York. Great Britain officially protested against the charge that it had fomented secessionist activities in the Soviet Union. France's chief Socialist newspaper vehemently attacked the "whole of the accusations and confessions as untrue," thereby endangering the Socialist party's Popular Front alliance with the Communists, who loyally defended all the trials. Trotsky's and Kerensky's attacks may not have meant much to Stalin, but hostile reactions from the Western democracies could not have been welcome when his efforts to mend fences with Germany seemed not to be bearing fruit.

But perhaps they were bearing fruit. Germany ridiculed the Bukharin trial and showed its displeasure with Moscow by closing its last two consulates in the Soviet Union. Yet Germany must have noted that while various Soviet officials were being condemned for conspiring with the Reich, one of the defendants, a former counselor in the Soviet embassy in Berlin, pleaded guilty to obstructing a "normalization of relations between the Soviet Union and Germany." The implication was that Stalin was eager to do business with Hitler. Germany could also hardly fail to notice that the show trials were wiping out those Russians who were most strongly anti-Fascist. Anti-Nazi diplomats in Berlin's Moscow embassy were indeed appalled that the Soviet officials they trusted most were being eliminated. And for all their anti-Fascist rhetoric, the trials did not bring an end to secret negotiations between German and Soviet officials. Hitler made no public men-

*Kerensky, who had led the provisional government overthrown by the Bolsheviks in October 1917, told a New York audience that the purges attested to "the continuous struggle between the people and the dictatorship" and represented "the last stage of the evolution of the Bolshevik regime." Kerensky died in 1970 in the United States, still waiting for the Communist regime in his homeland to fall.

tion of any possible "positive" effect the purges might have on Russia's relations with the Fascist powers, but his partner Mussolini was less circumspect. Writing in the *Popolo d'Italia* on the Bukharin trial, he observed, "Stalin is doing a notable service to fascism by mowing down in large armfuls his enemies who have been reduced to impotence."

Russians have long shown a fascination with the cleansing power of flames. The anarchist Mikhail Bakunin prophesied in 1848 that "tongues of flame" would burn down the citadels of power across Europe. Fire was central to the artistic visions of Scriabin and Stravinsky. Lenin's prerevolutionary magazine was called *Spark*. Stalin, too, was fascinated with fire, and he liked to compare his purges to the conflagrations that had periodically swept through Moscow, forcing its reconstruction with new timbers. But by 1939 Stalin's "cleansing fire" had begun to burn itself out. Combustible materials in the form of Old Bolshevik stalwarts, hostile party bureaucrats, veteran Red Army leaders, "bourgeois nationalists" in the provinces, and technocratic "specialists" were now so meager that only localized hot spots continued to smolder. There was already fresh growth in the burned-over places: new men in the party and military bureaucracies whose prime qualification for office was an unquestioning loyalty to Stalin.

This wholesale restructuring of civilian and military leadership undoubtedly consolidated Stalin's position, leaving him the sole arbiter of his nation's fate. His new associates, however, were inexperienced and often incompetent. They were also determined to do nothing to provoke their chief's distrust. Below the leadership level, ordinary citizens were so utterly terrified of somehow running afoul of the omnipresent police that they guarded every word and gesture, frantically seeking safety in isolation and conformity. Stalin's consolidation of power, in other words, was purchased at a terribly high price: the emasculation of an entire nation.

VIII

"PEACE FOR OUR TIME"

Appeasement and the Munich Conference

> And here we are—safe in our skins;
>   Glory to God for Munich.
> And stocks go up and wrecks
>   Are salved and politicians' reputations
> Go up like Jack-on-the-Beanstock; only the Czechs
>   Go down and without fighting.
>
> —Louis MacNeice, "Autumn Journal: 1938"

Early in the morning of September 29, 1938, several members of the British cabinet gathered at Heston airport outside London to wish Godspeed to their prime minister, Neville Chamberlain, who was off to meet Adolf Hitler and Benito Mussolini in Munich. The sixty-nine-year-old Chamberlain, his tall frame stooped and his hands red and gnarled with rheumatism, delivered a brief speech to his colleagues. "When I was a boy," he said platitudinously, "I used to repeat 'if at first you don't succeed, try, try, try again.' That's what I'm doing." Then he reached for a nobler tone, one more commensurate with the loftiness of his mission: "When I come back, I hope I may be able to say, as Hotspur says in *Henry IV*, 'Out of this nettle, danger, we pluck this flower, safety.'"

With his "try, try, try again," Chamberlain was referring to two flights he had recently made to Germany in pursuit of a peaceful solution to the so-called Sudeten crisis. The Sudetenland was an ethnic-German part of Czechoslovakia that the führer claimed belonged "home in the Reich" but that the Prague government insisted remain in Czechoslovakia. The Munich conference itself proved to be something of an anticlimax, for Chamberlain had already conceded most of Hitler's demands at the earlier meetings. The result of these efforts was not "Peace for Our Time," as Chamberlain promised upon his return from Munich, but war in eleven months. The nettle, it seemed, was much more tenacious than the flower.

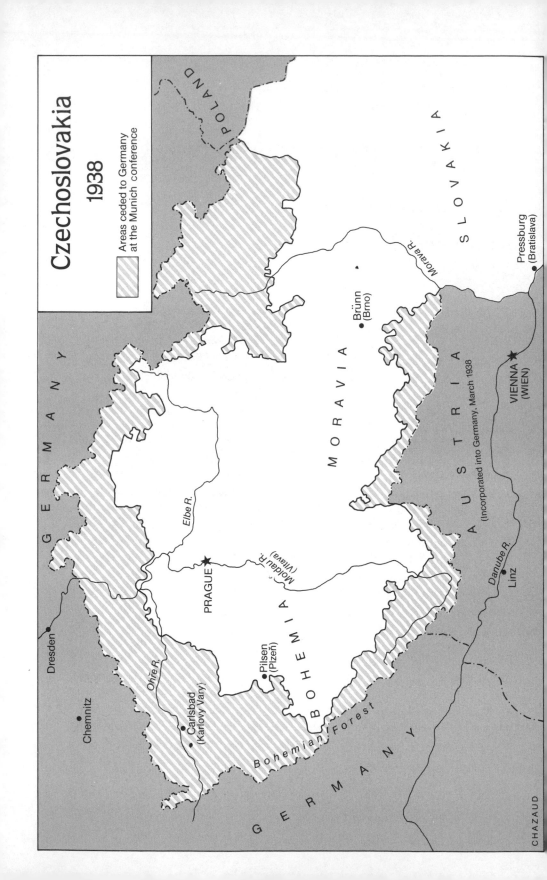

Czechoslovakia
1938

Areas ceded to Germany at the Munich conference

POLAND

GERMANY

Dresden

Chemnitz

Carlsbad (Karlovy Vary)

Ohře R.

Pilsen (Plzeň)

Bohemian Forest

B O H E M I A

PRAGUE

Elbe R.

Moldau R. (Vltava)

M O R A V I A

Brünn (Brno)

Morava R.

S L O V A K I A

Pressburg (Bratislava)

VIENNA (WIEN)

A U S T R I A

(Incorporated into Germany, March 1938)

Danube R.

Linz

G E R M A N Y

CHAZAUD

AN "AFFAIR OF THE HEART"

In contemporary parlance the word *appeasement* has distinctly negative con-
notations: it suggests a craven submissiveness in the face of political bullying. But
for much of the period between the two world wars appeasement struck many
western Europeans as an eminently reasonable policy. Did it not, after all, seek to
solve problems through negotiation and compromise rather than through armed
confrontation? For some this policy was more than just reasonable: it was a moral
and emotional commitment—an "affair of the heart." Pascal observed that the
"heart knows reasons that reason knows not." But in this case the heart and the
mind erred together.

The diplomatic strategy that culminated in the Munich conference of 1938
had its origins in the Western democracies' response to the terrible carnage of
World War I. The Great War was said to be the "war to end war," a cataclysm so
devastating that the industrial nations could never again contemplate using warfare as an instrument of policy. The apparent "lessons" to be derived from the
war included a new appreciation of the evils of arms races and rigid entangling
alliances, as well as a determination not to let another minor disagreement in an
out-of-the-way country mushroom into a casus belli among the great powers.
This imperative was strengthened by the conviction that wars were no longer
containable in scope or intensity and that a new war might destroy Western
civilization altogether. As Winston Churchill wrote shortly after World War I,

[The war had] established that henceforward whole populations will take
part in war, all doing their utmost, all subjected to the fury of the enemy. It is
established that nations who believe their life is at stake will not be re-
strained from using any means to secure their existence. It is probable—nay,
certain—that among the means which will next time be at their disposal will
be agencies and processes of destruction wholesale, unlimited and perhaps,
once launched, uncontrollable.

Air power was the most frightening innovation in warfare, for new terror-
bombing techniques made civilians in their cities as vulnerable to the horrors of
war as soldiers at the front. Prime Minister Stanley Baldwin of Britain summed
up this anxiety when he insisted in 1932 that Europe's civilians would be virtually
defenseless in a future war: "I think it is well also for the man in the street to
realize that there is no power on earth that can protect him from being bombed.
Whatever people may tell him, the bomber will always get through. . . ." Accounts of terror bombing in the Spanish civil war, particularly the destruction of
Guernica, confirmed people's worst fears. It was significant that the *Germans*
bombed Guernica, for no new monster of war seemed so terrifying as Hitler's air
force. When in the mid-thirties Charles Lindbergh warned the West of Ger-

many's "overwhelming strength . . . in the air," he touched a nerve. So did a 1936 film based on H. G. Wells's book *Things to Come*, which showed a European "Everytown" leveled like Guernica by waves of bombers. Three years later, on the eve of the war, George Orwell's protagonist in *Coming Up for Air* spoke for his generation when he predicted massive bombing raids, squalid air-raid shelters, and food queues. "It's all going to happen," he sighs. "I know it."

Western European policymakers realized that modern war entailed not only vast physical destruction but economic devastation as well. Painfully aware that World War I had left their countries saddled with huge debts, they convinced themselves that even preparations for renewed military conflict could threaten domestic socioeconomic stability.

This conviction was especially strong in Great Britain, whose "Ten Year Rule" of 1919, which instructed Britain's military planners to draw up their estimates "on the assumption that the British Empire would not be engaged in any great war during the next ten years," reflected the treasury's determination to hold down military spending. Britain's defense budgets fell from £766 million in 1919–20, to £189 million in 1921–22, and to £102 million in 1932. The proportion of defense spending in the total budget dropped from 29.9 percent in 1913 to 10.5 percent in 1933. The Great Slump of the early thirties made military economies seem all the more necessary. Even when the Manchurian crisis prompted an abandonment of the Ten Year Rule in 1932, the treasury warned, "Today's financial and economic risks are the most serious and urgent that the country has to face."

France, which had lost a million and a half men and suffered the destruction of its northern provinces in World War I, was in considerably worse shape than Great Britain. In the mid-thirties, when France began to rearm in earnest, debt charges left over from the war still consumed half the national budget. This forced the Popular Front government to hold down new military expenditures. The new commitments that Paris did make were primarily defensive—bunker systems like the Maginot Line designed to prevent the Boche from wrecking the country once again.

Another by-product of World War I, the rise of Bolshevik Russia, also crucially affected Anglo-French attitudes toward war and peace. Many western Europeans believed that the only nation that would profit from a new war was the Soviet Union. After the next war, it was said, "the Cossacks will rule Europe." For some this even produced a willingness to revive Germany as a bulwark against possible Soviet expansionism. Not a few British conservatives agreed with ex-Kaiser Wilhelm II that the "Teutonic nations" of England and Germany had the duty to protect Europe from the "barbaric Slavs." When France signed an anti-German defense treaty with the Soviet Union in 1935, some Frenchmen, particularly on the right, complained that the government was simply choosing the Devil over Beelzebub.

A resolute and united determination to hold down the Germans, indeed, was an early casualty of postwar reassessments of political and economic realities. Though the majority of Britons were no doubt happy enough to "squeeze the German lemon until the pip squeaked" in the immediate aftermath of the war, many soon developed qualms about imposing a "Carthaginian peace." Germany, it was argued, had not been exclusively responsible for the war, as the "war guilt clause" in the Versailles treaty had charged. Moreover, the victorious Allies had acted unwisely and shortsightedly in depriving the Weimar Republic of all but a token army, saddling it with a huge reparations bill, and denying ethnic Germans in Austria and Czechoslovakia the "right" to join Germany if they so wished. The bible of the revisionist school was John Maynard Keynes's *Economic Consequences of the Peace*, which argued that a strong Germany was vital to the strength of the rest of Europe, including Britain. As for the collective security imperatives that the treaty system was supposed to protect, these might better be guaranteed by the League of Nations than by the unilateral enfeeblement of Germany.

Those Englishmen who believed that Germany had been wronged at Versailles tended to blame this injustice on France, which, they alleged, insisted on keeping Germany down so it could dominate the Continent itself. Germany had to be revived, they argued, to counterbalance French, as well as Soviet, power.

France, indeed, was initially determined to keep Germany as weak as possible through a rigorous enforcement of the Versailles terms. In 1923 it sent troops into the Ruhr industrial district when Germany defaulted on its reparations payments. But the Ruhr occupation, which France pursued over the objections of Britain, cost the French treasury heavily and provoked almost as much discontent in France as in Germany. Why, many Frenchmen asked, should they be saddled with the main responsibility for keeping the Germans in their place? Had not France suffered more grievously in the last war than Britain, not to mention isolationist America? France might have been a victor in the First World War, but, as one historian put it, "she had in many respects the psychology of a defeated power."

Failing to achieve a strict enforcement of the Versailles treaty, France sought to hem in Germany by forging military alliances with the smaller "successor states" of eastern Europe: Poland, Czechoslovakia, Yugoslavia, and Romania. This so-called Little Entente had genuine strategic value only so long as France was prepared to back up her Eastern allies should they be threatened by Germany. France's participation in the Locarno treaty of 1925, which guaranteed Germany's western borders but not its eastern frontier, already signaled danger for the Little Entente. Germany's remilitarization of the Rhineland in 1936 undercut this system much more dramatically, since Germany could be much bolder in the east if it was fortified in the west. By the middle to late thirties many Frenchmen were indeed suggesting that it would be better to reappraise the nation's foreign policy than to embrace security commitments in eastern and central Europe that exceeded France's actual capacities.

Even had France been committed to a rigorous containment of Germany, its domestic political situation made a strong or consistent foreign policy difficult if not impossible to maintain. The Stavisky affair was one episode in a kind of low-grade civil war that beset France throughout much of the thirties. Ideological polarities and widespread contempt for the "system" meant that any strong policy was likely to bring rioting to the streets. Moreover, the French premier's need to base his cabinets on ever-shifting coalitions of several parties guaranteed chaos at the top: Paris saw twenty-four changes of ministry between 1930 and 1940. None of these governments, including the Daladier ministry that faced Hitler at Munich, believed it had a solid mandate for decisive action.

France's internal weaknesses made it strongly dependent on its main European partner: Great Britain. Increasingly Paris found itself deferring to London in matters of foreign policy. Since Britain was generally less committed to containing Germany than was France, this dependence contributed to the growth of appeasement sentiment in France. For some French leaders this was a source of frustration and shame; for others it was a convenient excuse to avoid doing what in any case they had no stomach to do.

"THOSE BLASTED CZECHS"

If there was any aspect of the postwar treaty system that seemed calculated to arouse feelings of guilt among western Europeans, it was the Allied decision to prohibit rump Austria and the ethnic-German regions of Czechoslovakia from becoming part of Germany. This seemed a blatant transgression of the principle of "self-determination of peoples," one of the new pieties of Wilsonian politics. The victorious powers had nonetheless imposed these restrictions to prevent Germany's expansion and to contain its power. Moreover, the Allies wanted to ensure Czechoslovakia's economic viability by incorporating within that new state the heavily industrialized western areas that were populated largely by Germans. They also hoped to enhance Czechoslovakia's security by placing its border with Germany outside the mountain chain that surrounds historical Bohemia.

The Western powers had good reason to be concerned about the viability of Czechoslovakia. In addition to its three and one-half million Germans, the state also harbored substantial Ruthenian and Hungarian minorities. The seven million Czechs lived on uneasy terms with the country's two million Slovaks. Czechoslovakia was, observed the historian A. J. P. Taylor, "a state of nationalities, not a national state." In that sense it was a microcosm of the Habsburg monarchy, of which it had been a part until 1918.

The German minority posed the largest problem. After the collapse of the Habsburg monarchy, many, perhaps the majority, of the Sudeten Germans wanted to join the Austrian republic, which in turn hoped to become incorporated into Germany. In late October 1918 their representatives declared the creation of two independent provinces, German Bohemia and the Sudetenland, whose leaders boycotted the Czech provinical assembly in Prague.

A significant minority of Sudeten Germans, however, was prepared to remain in Czechoslovakia virtually from the outset. Industrialists and exporters whose raw materials and markets were in historical Bohemia chose to cast their lot with the new Czech state. The imperial German ambassador to Vienna noted in October 1918, "[The Bohemian Germans] are not irredentists. . . . [They] fear competition from the superior German industry" and are disinclined to "abandon all [their] important interests in Bohemia." They would, he concluded, simply "have to make the best of things, get on with the Czechs and learn Czech."

This would not be easy. The Germans considered themselves superior in every way to their Slavic neighbors, whom they had economically dominated during the centuries of Habsburg rule in Bohemia. The Czechs, for their part, would undoubtedly want to turn the tables on the German minority now that they were in control. One could only hope that both groups, recognizing the practical necessity of cooperation, would do their best to turn this state of nationalities into a national state.

During the Paris peace conference of 1919, the Czech representatives promised to adopt a liberal policy toward Czechoslovakia's minority groups, including the Germans. In an aide-mémoire, the Czech delegation, led by Foreign Minister (later, President) Eduard Beneš, even suggested that Czechoslovakia would emulate Switzerland in setting up cantonlike, semiautonomous regions for its ethnic minorities. The Czechs' employment of the Swiss example was unfortunate, for the German minority dwelled upon this promise when it became evident that Prague would not grant such far-reaching autonomy. Where was the Czech "Switzerland," asked the Germans, when Prague closed German schools in the Sudeten region, sent in Czech officials, and awarded government contracts disproportionately to Czech firms?

Despite such complaints, most Sudeten Germans increasingly combined demands for greater autonomy with expressions of guarded loyalty to the Czech state. In local and national elections held during the twenties, the so-called activists, who espoused participation in the Czech government, consistently defeated the intransigent irredentists, who held out for incorporation into Germany. The two main activist parties—the Agrarians and the Social Democrats—entered the national government in the mid-twenties and remained in it through the early thirties. One of the activist leaders, the Agrarian Franz Spina, justified political cooperation as follows:

We have lived with the Czechs for a thousand years, and through economic, social, cultural, and even racial ties, we are so closely connected with them that we really form one people. To use a homely metaphor: we form different strands in the same carpet. Of course it is possible to cut the carpet into pieces, but one cannot remove the flowers woven into the pattern. We lived with the Czechs in a form of symbiosis: we have entered into a marriage of convenience and nothing can separate us.

The Czech-German "marriage of convenience" survived also because the German governments of the twenties were not inclined to disturb it. Foreign Minister Gustav Stresemann, the dominant figure in Weimar German foreign policy in the twenties, would not even receive a delegation of Sudeten German nationalists who wanted his support in 1926. "I have always made it clear," he wrote at the time, "that I would welcome an attempt to bring about the collaboration of the Germans in Czechoslovakia." The Prague government responded to this German support by working for the inclusion of Weimar Germany in the League of Nations. In 1928 President Beneš visited Berlin and reaffirmed the friendship between the two democratic republics.

Hitler's seizure of power five years later did not immediately change this relationship, for the führer wanted to consolidate his domestic position before embarking on an adventuresome foreign policy. The Czech government tried its best to get along with the new regime in Berlin. Beneš declared in 1933, "We have not had a single grave conflict with Germany in fourteen years, we have no frontier dispute with her and we wish to be on the same terms of friendship with the Germany of today as with that of Stresemann."

In the long run, however, Beneš and the Czechs found it impossible to live on harmonious terms with Hitler's Germany. The führer, who had first encountered Czechs during his youthful vagabond days in cosmopolitan Vienna, despised this people along with Habsburg loyalists, papists, Social Democrats, and Jews. After he came to power he developed new grievances against Czechoslovakia, for the Prague government was giving shelter to hundreds of German anti-Nazis who had fled the Third Reich. Czechoslovakia's alliances with France and the Soviet Union were clearly oriented against Germany. Most important, Czechoslovakia stood geographically athwart Hitler's plan to gain German "living space" in the east. Shortly before he assumed power Hitler had told a supporter that he intended to resettle the Czechs in Siberia.

A little less than five years later Hitler made his intentions regarding Czechoslovakia clearer in a secret military-political *tour d'horizon* with his top officers at the so-called Hossbach conference, held on November 5, 1937. Germany's need for living space, he said, could be solved only by force, and the military campaign to achieve this goal must start no later than 1943–45 but might begin as early as 1938. Expansion would commence in Austria and Czechoslovakia, historical German areas where racial "sterility" was already setting in. Although Czechoslovakia was allied with France, the führer believed that both France and Britain had "tacitly written off the Czechs and were reconciled to the fact that this question would be cleared up in due course by Germany." The incorporation of Czechoslovakia and Austria into the Reich "would mean an acquisition of foodstuffs for 5 to 6 million people, on the assumption that the compulsory emigration of 2 million people from Czechoslovakia and 1 million people from Austria was practicable." Militarily the annexation of these areas would mean "shorter and better frontiers, the freeing of forces for other purposes, and the possibility of creating new units up to a level of about 12 divisions." Though two of Hitler's top generals, War Minister Werner von Blomberg and Army Chief Werner von Fritsch, questioned the führer's plans, the Wehrmacht leadership obediently drew up a war scenario that called for an invasion of Czechoslovakia through "surprise attack" as soon as political conditions allowed.

Before attacking Czechoslovakia, however, Hitler hoped to weaken it by aggravating tensions between the Sudeten German minority and the Prague government. In reality, he cared little for the Sudeten Germans' plight, but he realized that he could exploit their grievances as a pretext for interference in Czech affairs. Just as with the pro-German Austrians, in other words, he would claim that "intolerable conditions" in Czechoslovakia "forced" him to bring the Sudetens "home to the Reich." (In fact, the Sudetenland had never been part of the German Reich.)

Hitler's campaign to destabilize Czechoslovakia by courting the Sudeten irredentists was significantly bolstered by the world economic crash, which fell with particular force on industrialized Bohemia. As unemployment levels among the German factory workers soared, Sudeten politicians lambasted the Prague government for failing to effect adequate relief measures. Czechoslovakia's economic difficulties made Nazi Germany, with its ambitious public works programs, look all the more attractive. Not surprisingly the parties that demanded the Sudetenland's integration into Germany—the Nationalist party and the local branch of the Nazis—made rapid headway at the expense of the parties willing to work within the Czech framework. At the same time, however, Hitler's accession to power hardened the Sudeten Social Democrats' determination to resist a "German solution," which they knew would destroy democratic socialism in Czechoslovakia, just as it had in Germany. One of the Social Democrats' parliamentary representatives declared in April 1933, "Our policy of reconciliation [with Prague] . . . is the only one which the German population can follow if it understands its interests correctly. Our policy of the closest possible association with the Czech proletariat is therefore the only road for us."

As the influence of the Social Democrats waned and that of the radical irredentists grew, the Prague government banned the Nazi party, which (as in Austria) had been engaging in terrorist tactics against the central government. But this proved a futile gesture, since another group immediately appeared that incorporated many of the Nazi party's goals, as well as most of its membership. This was the Sudetendeutsche Heimatfront (Sudeten German Home Front).

The SDH was led by Konrad Henlein, a former gymnastics teacher who firmly believed in the racial and cultural superiority of Germans over Czechs. (Ironically enough, Henlein's mother was Czech, an inconvenient fact he was careful to conceal.) Henlein saw in Hitler a kindred spirit. Shortly after the führer came to power in Germany, Henlein's *Turnzeitung* (Gymnastic newspaper) enthused, "Beyond these frontier posts the bells are now joyfully heralding in a new era full of hope for the future. . . . Germany has today entered upon the path to freedom."

Profiting from the same economic and political dislocations that had favored the Nazis, Henlein's Home Front, which changed its name to the Sudetendeutsche Partei (Sudeten German party) in early 1935, rapidly gained ground. In the 1935 elections the SDP won 65 percent of the votes cast in the German parts of Czechoslovakia. With this triumph it emerged as the single largest party in the state.

The SDP also changed direction as it grew. Though always radically pro-German, the party had initially maintained some independence from Berlin, no doubt because Henlein feared Hitler might try to place the movement under the control of local Nazis. By late 1935, however, the Nazi element in the SDP had become so strong that Henlein found it prudent to angle for Hitler's favor. In that year the German Foreign Office began subsidizing the SDP on a monthly basis, and in the following summer, at the Berlin Olympic Games, Hitler personally awarded Henlein an honorary Olympic medal (for his "services to German sport"). In late 1937, at the same time that the Wehrmacht was refining its plans for the invasion of Czechoslovakia, Henlein prepared a secret report for the führer on "current questions affecting German policy in the Czech republic." Here he declared that an understanding between Germans and Czechs was "practically impossible" and that a solution to the Sudeten problem was achievable "only through the Reich." The Sudetenland, he added, was now "oriented toward Nazism and dominated by a unified National Socialist party built upon the leader principle."

It seems clear, then, that by 1936–37 Henlein's goal was nothing less than the incorporation of the Sudetenland into Nazi Germany. But Henlein was no fool; he understood that an open proclamation of this policy could lead to the banning of his party. He also realized that a more limited goal—political autonomy for the Sudetenland within Czechoslovakia—could serve as a giant step toward eventual incorporation into the Reich. Hence in his public proclamations Henlein was careful to combine his demands for "Sudeten self-determination" with declarations of loyalty to the Czech state. In an interview in 1934 with a Czech newspaper, Henlein insisted that he had "nothing in common with Hitlerism" and that he had no interest in "any revision of [Czechoslovakia's] borders." As late as 1937 he was still assuring the Prague government of his loyalty and claiming that his party was not an "appendage of either National Socialism or fascism, but wholly a national movement of long standing."

Henlein sounded this "moderate" note abroad as well as at home. Realizing that the Prague government was unlikely to yield autonomy to the German-dominated territories without external pressure, he turned for support not only to Germany but also to the Western powers, especially Great Britain. Here he hoped to trade on British doubts about the Versailles treaty and on local sympathies for the "persecuted minorities" in central Europe. In a speech before the Royal Institute for International Affairs in December 1935, Henlein accused Prague of running roughshod over minority rights. But he also claimed to oppose Pan-Germanism as much as Pan-Slavism and categorically denied rumors that he was a "local representative of Hitler." In discussions with a British expert on Central Europe, R. W. Seton-Watson, Henlein ruled out any unification with Germany and declared "the Nazi program as unsuited for exportation beyond the frontiers of the Reich." In three further visits to London in July 1936, October 1937, and May 1938, Henlein met with various British politicians, always giving his "word of honor" that he took no directions from Berlin and desired no Sudeten separation from the Czech state.

Henlein made a very favorable impression upon the British politicians with whom he spoke. Robert Vansittart, permanent under secretary in the Foreign Office, came away convinced that Henlein was a "reasonable man." Lord Halifax, foreign secretary at the time of the Munich conference, said Henlein "gave the impression of being genuinely anxious for a speedy settlement." More important, Henlein induced the British government to take an openly pro-German position on the Sudeten question. In March 1937 Foreign Secretary Anthony Eden urged Prague to accept the necessity of a "far-reaching settlement" with the Sudeten Germans.

Henlein returned to the Sudetenland and told his followers that the coast was clear for further pressure on the Prague government. "No serious intervention in favour of the Czechs was to be feared from England or probably from France," he announced, and he was right. Foreign Minister Yvon Delbos of France said in October 1937 that France would fulfill her treaty obligations to Czechoslovakia if Germany committed "unprovoked aggression" against it. Short of that, however, Paris would not intervene. Britain was even less likely to make trouble. On November 26, 1937, Sir Neville Chamberlain, who had become prime minister in May of that year, wrote that he was inclined to tell the Germans, "Give us satisfactory assurance that you won't use force to deal with the Austrians and Czechoslovakians and we will give you similar assurance that we won't use force to prevent the changes you want, if you can get them by peaceful means."

The British ambassador to Berlin, Sir Nevile Henderson, who liked to refer to "those blasted Czechs," claimed that he had spoken to people in England who thought Czechoslovakia was a "variety of exotic flower." One of his diplomatic colleagues, insisted Henderson, had begun a dispatch in 1937 by saying, "There is no such thing as Czechoslovakia." Within two years he would be right.

IN THE WAKE OF THE *ANSCHLUSS*

By invading Austria on March 12, 1938, Hitler showed how he intended to deal with questions of ethnic-German "self-determination" in Central Europe. Many Europeans assumed that he would simply continue his march into the Sudeten regions of Czechoslovakia. Certainly the Czechs feared he would, and they braced for war.

For the moment, however, Hitler was content to swallow Austria and to digest it without complications. Göring called in the Czech ambassador and gave him his "word of honor" that Prague had "not the slightest reason for concern." The business with Austria, said Göring, was purely a "family matter," and Germany continued to harbor nothing but "friendly intentions" toward Czechoslovakia. Göring also called on the British ambassador, Henderson, and conveyed to him Hitler's "earnest desire . . . to improve Czech-German relations." But Berlin coupled these benign reassurances with renewed demands for better treatment of the German minority. The implication was that improved relations between Germany and Czechoslovakia depended on a satisfactory resolution of the Sudeten question.

In fact, Hitler had no interest in bettering the lot of the Germans in Czechoslovakia; he was simply playing for time until he could absorb the Sudetenland, which in turn would put him in a position to destroy Czechoslovakia. On March 28 he held a secret meeting with Henlein, informing the SDP leader that he intended "to settle the Sudeten problem in the not-too-distant future." Henlein, who henceforth would be Hitler's *Statthalter* (viceroy), was instructed to make demands on Prague that were "unacceptable to the Czech Government." These would include an insistence upon separate German regiments commanded by German officers. Noting Henlein's successes in England, Hitler also suggested that he return to London "to use his influence with a view to ensuring nonintervention by Britain."

In accordance with Hitler's instructions, Henlein launched a series of negotiations with Prague that were designed to fail. Every time the Czechs made concessions, Henlein upped the ante. On April 23, at an SDP congress in Karlsbad, Henlein put forth eight demands as a basis for further negotiation. They embraced not only "full autonomy" for the Sudetenland but also "compensation for the injustices committed against the Sudeten Germans since 1918." Henlein concluded his speech by declaring his allegiance to "the National Socialist principles of life, which govern our thoughts and feelings and according to which our people will shape its laws."

The Prague government rejected most of Henlein's demands, which it knew had been framed in Berlin. But the Czechs had no choice but to continue negotiating with Henlein, since his SDP had now absorbed all the Sudeten parties except for the Social Democrats. Czechoslovakia, moreover, was now surrounded on three sides by the Greater German Reich, and its elaborate, French-built fortification system was outflanked by German military installations. To make matters worse, Prague was under increasing pressure from the Poles, who wanted to absorb the coal-rich Teschen district, and from the Hungarians, who had territorial ambitions along Czechoslovakia's southeastern border.

Czechoslovakia's position was also rendered precarious by the apparent inability or unwillingness of the European powers to protect it against German intimidation. Prime Minister Léon Blum of France, who returned to the premiership briefly between mid-March and mid-April 1938, gave some thought to supporting the Czechs, but he was undercut by the French military leadership, which informed him that direct military aid to Prague would be "impossible" given

France's lack of a common border with Czechoslovakia. The most the French army could do, said General Maurice Gamelin, would be to hold down parts of the Wehrmacht in the west. But Gamelin and his colleagues were convinced that Germany could not be dissuaded from pursuing its ambitions in southeastern Europe by a French holding action, and they were dead set against any genuine offensive campaign against the Reich.

In any event, Blum's second government was too short-lived to be of any use to the Czechs. It fell victim to the deep class and ideological antagonisms that beset France throughout the thirties. Blum, a Jew, also found himself the target of vicious anti-Semitic attacks. Xavier Vallat, a rightist parliamentarian who had launched his political career during the Stavisky scandal and would end it as Vichy's commissioner general for Jewish affairs, announced that it was tragic for France that it should be led by a man whose "race was condemned by divine malediction never to have a motherland." Fearing Blum might lead France into a war with Germany over Czechoslovakia, Léon Daudet of the Action Française lamented that "Jack Clod, the guinea pig of bloody democracy," might have to go to his slaughter "at the nod of a Jew he hates in some obscene, faraway dump about which he hasn't the least notion."

Shortly before Blum's government gave way to Daladier's, the Soviet foreign minister, Maxim Litvinov, announced at a news conference that the Soviet Union was prepared to take part in a collective action—inside or outside the League—aimed at keeping the peace. In the wake of the *Anschluss,* he said, the main threat to peace came from Germany's designs on the Sudetenland. In these circumstances, added Litvinov, Soviet Russia favored the creation of a grand alliance designed to keep Hitler in his place. This alliance would complement the Russian-Czech pact of 1935, which obligated Russia to come to Prague's defense if it was attacked by Germany, but only if France did so first. Journalists at the conference asked how Russia could aid Czechoslovakia when it, like France, lacked a common border with that state. Would Russia seek permission to send its troops through Poland or Romania? Litvinov was vague on this point, as indeed he had to be: he knew that neither Poland nor Romania would allow passage of Russian troops through its territory.

The Western powers knew this as well, which led them to suspect that the Soviet Union wanted to involve them in a war from which it would keep its comfortable distance—waiting to pick up the pieces. Even if the Soviet Union could get troops to the front, would they fight effectively considering the chaos and demoralization in the Red Army engendered by Stalin's purges? Few Western military analysts had much faith in the fighting capacity of the Red Army. Litvinov's intervention, in other words, did nothing to rally the Western powers behind beleaguered Czechoslovakia; it only strengthened their objections to confronting Germany in alliance with the Soviet Union.

The key to countering Hitler's ambitions in Czechoslovakia remained Great Britain, since France would not act without British support, and Russia, if it acted

The Führerbau, where the Munich conference took place in September 1938.
Bundesarchiv Koblenz

Top right: Chamberlain and Germany's foreign minister, Joachim von Ribbentrop; map of Czechoslovakia, showing regions ceded following the Munich agreement; *bottom:* Chamberlain announcing that he has brought "peace with honor."
Deutsche-Presse-Agentur

Participants in the
Munich conference.
Left to right: Neville
Chamberlain, Edouard
Daladier, Adolf Hitler,
Benito Mussolini,
Galeazzo Ciano (Italian
foreign minister).
Deutsche-Presse-Agentur

Konrad Henlein, pro-Nazi
leader of the Sudeten
German party. *The
Warder Collection*

at all, would not do so unless France did. The man chiefly responsible for shaping British policy in this period was Neville Chamberlain, prime minister from May 1937 to May 1940. Tall, thin, and always elegantly turned out, Chamberlain had the sort of disciplined, priggish character that sometimes inspires admiration but rarely affection. Lloyd George, who hated him, called him a "pinhead." Even his defenders admitted that he had been "weaned on a pickle." His upbringing was indeed sour and bracing. He was the son of Joseph Chamberlain, a self-made manufacturing millionaire from Birmingham who built a political career as an imperial expansionist and advocate of Anglo-German cooperation. Young Neville became a successful brass dealer in Birmingham, which like his father he represented in Parliament. From 1931 to 1937 he served as chancellor of the Exchequer, following in general a policy of financial retrenchment and sanctioning increased arms expenditures only after 1936. Upon becoming prime minister he devoted himself above all to securing better relations with Germany, which he, like many Englishmen, believed had been treated unfairly in the peace settlement.

As for his intellectual style, Chamberlain was an exceedingly high-minded man who believed that his policies were guided and sanctioned by divine Providence. This conviction tended to inure him to the criticism—and often to the advice—of his colleagues. According to one recent biographer, he also embodied the Victorian belief in the power of reason over passion, which in reality meant that he did not acknowledge the role of passions in his policy. Yet he did have one strong passion: a loathing for war that sprang from his memories of the Great War. At a National Government rally in May 1938 he said,

> When I think of those four terrible years and I think of the 7,000,000 of young men who were cut off in their prime, the 13,000,000 who were maimed and mutilated, the misery and suffering of the mothers and the fathers, the sons and the daughters, and the relatives and the friends of those who were killed and wounded, then I am bound to say again what I have said before, and what I say now, not only to you, but to all the world—in war, whichever side may call itself the victor, there are no winners, but all are losers.
>
> It is those thoughts which have made me feel that it was my prime duty to strain every nerve to avoid a repetition of the Great War in Europe. And I cannot believe that anyone who thinks what another war would mean, can fail to agree with me and to desire that I should continue my efforts.

The *Anschluss* came as a shock to Chamberlain, though he was convinced that Britain could have done nothing to stop it. At any rate, it was not the annexation itself but the aggressive way in which it was brought about that concerned him. Such tactics, he said, "made international appeasement much more difficult." He was determined that the Czechoslovakian situation should not be handled in the same manner.

In this Chamberlain was firmly supported by his new foreign secretary, Lord Halifax, who had taken office in February 1938 upon the resignation of Anthony Eden. Halifax had long been convinced that the Germans had legitimate complaints regarding the Versailles settlement and that once these had been resolved the Germans would be easier to live with, indeed would become an invaluable bastion against the spread of bolshevism in Europe. At one point he expressed the wish "to see, as the culmination of his work, the Führer entering London, at the side of the English King, amid the acclamation of the English people." In November 1937 he had visited Hitler in Berchtesgaden and intimated that Britain would allow Germany a laissez-passer in Austria. Hitler's rude manner in effecting the *Anschluss* did not dispose Halifax to take a tougher stance regarding the Sudetenland. On the contrary, at a British foreign-policy committee meeting on March 18 he urged his colleagues not to offer any guarantees to Czechoslovakia or to encourage the French to move toward a hard line. Rather, Prague should be told to meet the German demands as expeditiously as possible.

If Halifax was prepared to sacrifice the Sudetenland, Britain's minister in Prague, Sir Basil Newton, seemed prepared to write off Czechoslovakia entirely. "If I am right in thinking," reported Newton directly after the *Anschluss*, "that Czechoslovakia's present political position is not permanently tenable, it will be no kindness in the long run to try to maintain her in it." If France believed it "worthwhile to try to perpetuate the *status quo* in her own interests," he added, she should do so unaided.

Chamberlain was not prepared to dismiss Czechoslovakia *tout court*, but he agreed that Britain should offer it no guarantees. On March 20 he wrote, "I have abandoned any idea of giving guarantees to Czechoslovakia, or the French in connection with [their] obligations to that country." Chamberlain favored not only forcing the Czechs to negotiate with their German minority but also pulling the Reich government into the settlement. Once the Sudeten problem was disposed of, he suggested, Czechoslovakia's new borders might be secured by an Anglo-German guarantee. This proposal stemmed from the prime minister's conviction that Hitler cared only about integrating ethnic-German areas into the Reich; it illustrated his complete misunderstanding of the führer's true motives.

Chamberlain's determination to include Germany in the Czech-Sudeten discussions was enthusiastically endorsed by Ambassador Nevile Henderson in Berlin. Henderson was perhaps the most single-minded of all the British appeasers. When he received notice of his appointment to Berlin, he decided this "could only mean that [he] had been specially selected by Providence [to] . . . preserve the peace of the world." On his way from Buenos Aires (his previous posting) to Berlin, he read *Mein Kampf*, but this did not prevent him from urging his fellow countrymen to see National Socialism as "a great social experiment" rather than as a brutal dictatorship. "Guarantee us peace and peaceful evolution in Europe," he said, "and Germany will find that she has a no more sincere, and I believe, more useful friend in the world than Great Britain." When Henderson learned that his counterpart in Prague had urged London to press the Czechs to "readjust their relations with Germany," he had no hesitation in telegraphing that he "concurred wholeheartedly and unreservedly in the sage counsel given by Mr. Newton."

Since Chamberlain, like Henderson, was convinced that he was acting on behalf of Providence, such sage advice was not entirely necessary. His mind was made up, and it remained only to convince the rest of the cabinet, the nation, the French, and (last of all) the Czechs that his course was the only reasonable one.

Less than a week after the *Anschluss*, Chamberlain told the foreign-policy committee that a glance at the map of Europe revealed how impossible it would be to send military aid to Czechoslovakia in an emergency. All Britain could do would be "to make war on Germany," but it was "in no position from the armament point of view to enter such a war." But why even talk of war? "If Germany could obtain her desiderata by peaceful methods," said Chamberlain, "there was no reason to suppose she would reject such a procedure in favour of one based on violence."

Chamberlain set forth his arguments without having formally consulted with Britain's chiefs of staff, but he knew they would agree with him. After all, they had long been insisting that Britain's shortage of arms necessitated a cautious policy, especially since a confrontation with Germany might pull in Italy and Japan as well. When, the day following his analysis to the foreign-policy committee, he did call in the military chiefs, they fulfilled his expectations. The chiefs presented a document (Halifax called it "an extremely melancholy document") arguing that the *Anschluss* had rendered Czechoslovakia's military position hopeless. Nothing the Western powers can do, it said,

> can prevent Germany either from invading and overrunning Bohemia or inflicting a decisive defeat on the Czech army. If politically it is deemed necessary to restore Czechoslovakia's lost territory, this aim will entail war with Germany, and her defeat may mean a prolonged struggle . . . by a slow process of attrition and starvation.

In addition to Britain's military weaknesses, Chamberlain could also cite official U.S. policy on appeasement as a reason for coming to terms with Hitler. President Roosevelt privately disapproved of the "city man" Chamberlain's eagerness to make a "business deal" with Hitler, but he put forth no alternatives to this policy, nor did he give any indication that a harder line would find official U.S. support. The fact was, whatever FDR may personally have wanted, Congress did not want America to become entangled in sordid European quarrels. FDR's ambassador to the Court of Saint James's, Joseph P. Kennedy, was unabashedly pro-German, even offering to go to Germany to speak with Hitler about the "prospects of a European settlement." Kennedy told his German counterpart in London that FDR sympathized with "German demands for justice."

The same position was being taken by William Bullitt, Washington's ambassador to France. Obsessed with the Soviet danger (he had previously been ambassador to Moscow), Bullitt said the United States should help France find a way to evade its responsibilities to Russia's ally Czechoslovakia. In the event of a German invasion of Czechoslovakia, FDR should summon a great-power conference in The Hague, which would arbitrate the dispute. If Prague refused to accept the conference's decision, France would be justified in refusing to come to her aid. America, as the honest broker in these arrangements, might be accused of "selling out a small nation . . . to produce another Hitler triumph," but this was preferable to seeing "an Asiatic despotism established on fields of dead."

Bullitt's proposal for a great-power conference—presumably minus Czechoslovakia—anticipated the "solution" that was eventually to materialize at Munich. Chamberlain's argument that Britain must be cautious because it could expect no support for a tougher line from the United States recalled British claims during the Ethiopian crisis that the League should not impose oil sanctions on Italy, because America would undercut them. In the end America's apparent unwillingness to take on Hitler proved as compelling an argument for British (and French) appeasers as Russia's apparent eagerness to do so.

Reassured by all these arguments, Chamberlain had little difficulty convincing his cabinet that Hitler should be accommodated in the Sudetenland. The strongest opposition came from Duff Cooper, his first lord of the Admiralty. Cooper urged the government to make "a more friendly gesture to France," which might encourage Paris to live up to its obligations toward Prague. "I insisted that when France fought Germany [as Cooper thought inevitable] we should have to fight too, whether we liked it or not, so that we might as well say so. . . ." But Cooper, isolated and often ill, was in no position to put some backbone into British policy. He was eventually to resign from the government over the Munich settlement, the only minister to do so.

Having lined up his cabinet, Chamberlain turned his attention to Parliament and the public. He delivered a major address on the Sudeten question to the House of Commons on March 24. In it he firmly opposed Britain's undertaking any "new and specific commitments" to Czechoslovakia. Quoting Anthony Eden, he noted that "nations cannot be expected to incur automatic military obligations save for areas where their vital interests are concerned." Czechoslovakia—unlike France, Belgium, Portugal, Iraq, or Egypt—was not such a place. On the other hand Chamberlain admitted that war in Czechoslovakia could very well pull in countries that did not have direct obligations to that state. Hence it was imperative that war be avoided. The British government was "ready to render any help in their power, by whatever means might seem most appropriate, towards the solution of questions likely to cause difficulty between the German and Czechoslovak Governments." In the meantime there was "no need to assume the use of force, or, indeed, to talk about it." Such talk could "only do harm."

The British press did not unanimously applaud Chamberlain's speech. The *Manchester Guardian* and the *Economist* were sharply critical. The strongly pro-appeasement London *Times,* however, weighed in with a glowing commentary, as did John Maynard Keynes in the *New Statesman.* Chamberlain had an ear only for the yeas; he claimed that no British statesman "had ever made a crucial policy statement as widely acclaimed" as his own. While clearly exaggerating his public-relations success, Chamberlain was correct in assuming that the majority of Englishmen stood behind him at this time.

If Chamberlain had little difficulty convincing his cabinet and public that appeasement was the correct policy, he also had no real trouble in winning over the French. France's new premier, Edouard Daladier (who had held this office before, in the wake of the Stavisky affair), might have been called the Bull of the Vaucluse, but at this point in his career he was a neutered bull. So afraid was he of German power that he longed for a Franco-German rapprochement. Anticommunism also led him in this direction. Even if Germany were to be defeated in war, he argued, "the only gainers would be the Bolshevists." Daladier's foreign minister, Georges Bonnet, was a former finance minister who (like the premier) had gotten ensnared in the Stavisky affair. This experience was said to have made him "hard-boiled and cynical," determined to please the Right, which had once attacked him. Now he sided with the Right's opposition to foreign commitments that might involve France in war with Germany. Such a conflict could only lead to "social revolution," he warned, to "the disappearance of the privileged class." In any event he was certainly not prepared to confront the Germans without solid British backing.

Chamberlain effectively played on French fears and hopes when he met with Daladier and Bonnet in London on April 28–29. His grim message was that France could not expect significant British support if it allowed its difficulties with Germany to result in war. He reminded the Frenchmen that Britain's rearmament had focused on defensive air power rather than on a land army capable of taking the offensive. France could not expect Britain to send an expeditionary force to the Continent "on the same scale as in the Great War." Britain was in no position to prevent a German conquest of Czechoslovakia if Hitler chose to invade there. Though admitting that a tough, united stance on the part of Britain, France, and Czechoslovakia might induce Hitler to back down, Chamberlain concluded that as long as there was one chance in a hundred that he would not, provocations must be avoided. On the more optimistic side, Chamberlain added that if the Western powers could ascertain what the Germans wanted, he was "not without hope that we may go through without a fresh demonstration of force."

Daladier did assert that France was willing to fight if necessary, and he argued against underestimating Czechoslovakia's ability to resist a German invasion. He also pointed out that if Germany absorbed Czechoslovakia it would be greatly strengthened. Nevertheless, he soon accepted the British line. Bonnet did not need to be convinced at all. Long an advocate of a four-power pact embracing France, Britain, Germany, and Italy, he saw the Czech imbroglio as a chance to realize this goal. Making his own view that of the vox populi, he said, "People in France and Great Britain saw in this very crisis an opportunity of reaching an understanding with Germany which would finally assure the peace of Europe."

While it may be true, therefore, that Britain took the lead in pursuing appeasement, France was a rather more eager follower than many commentators—especially French commentators—have been willing to admit.

United now in their resolve to reach a negotiated solution to the Sudeten question, Britain and France increased their pressure on Czechoslovakia to treat generously with Henlein and his backers. Their ministers in Prague made clear that Czechoslovakia would find no support in the West for intransigence.

In response Prague continued to make one concession after another, but with little hope of finally satisfying the German minority—or, more important, the German government. As tensions continued to mount, Czechoslovakia's pessimism turned to intransigence. When, in mid-May, Prague thought it detected menacing German troop movements on the Czech-Bavarian border, it mobilized the army. All Europe went on alert, fearing war. A message was hastily sent from London to Berlin warning that if war broke out and France went to the defense of Czechoslovakia, the British government "could not guarantee that [it] would not be forced by circumstances to become involved also."

But there was no German invasion; indeed, the German troop movements had not been designed to facilitate one. Berlin immediately and indignantly denied that Germany had provoked Prague in any way; it was Czechoslovakia that was being "provocative."

On reviewing the situation, London and Paris were inclined to agree. By the end of the month they were blaming the Czechs for the so-called May crisis. Henderson denounced the Czechs as a "pigheaded race" and Beneš as the "most pigheaded of the lot." Now the Western powers sought to smooth Hitler's ruffled feathers and resumed pressure on Prague to negotiate a settlement. Henderson assured Berlin that the Sudeten Germans were "a matter of indifference" to London.

Hitler, however, was not easily placated. Furious over Czechoslovakia's act of defiance, he called his generals together and reminded them of his decision "to smash Czechoslovakia by military force in the near future." But now he identified Czechoslovakia as an impediment to Germany's designs in the west, rather than in the east. "In the event of war between Germany and the Western Powers, the aim of which is the extension of our coastline (Belgium and Holland), Czechoslovakia, as an enemy in the rear, stands in the way of a certain German victory. She must be removed."

Among the generals who listened to Hitler's ravings was one who was shocked: Ludwig Beck, chief of the general staff. Beck believed that a war against Czechoslovakia could not be limited and that a general war pitting Germany against the Western democracies would lead to the Reich's annihilation. He saw Hitler's Czech policy as the triumph of irresponsible radicalism and adventurism over sound military strategy. Convinced that the moment had finally come both to thwart Hitler's war plans and to assert the officer corps's supremacy over Nazi radicals like Himmler and Heydrich, who had been in the ascendancy since the Röhm affair of 1934, Beck pleaded with his colleagues to threaten resignation en masse unless Hitler changed his course. But his efforts were in vain. Beck failed primarily because his colleagues were receiving reports from London and Paris contradicting the chief of staff's contention that those powers would inevitably intervene if Germany moved against Czechoslovakia. It should also be noted that the officer corps had shown—most recently in the Blomberg and Fritsch affairs* —that it was unlikely to assert its collective authority against Hitler and his henchmen. Thus only Beck resigned over the Czech crisis; and his departure was a symbol more of impotence than of effective defiance.

While Hitler was secretly planning the military conquest of Czechoslovakia, his Western counterparts were despairing over their apparent inability to ensure a peaceful and permanent resolution of the Sudeten dispute. Convinced that time was running out, Chamberlain and Halifax decided to send an investigator-mediator to Czechoslovakia to expedite the peace process. Their choice fell on Lord Runciman, the ex-president of the Board of Trade, who (we will recall) had earned a reputation for toughness in his dealings with Britain's unemployed. Runciman turned out to be rather more generous with the Sudeten Germans than with the men of Jarrow. So biased in their favor was he that Sudeten children sang a song about him: *"Was brauchen wir 'nen Weihnachtsmann,/Wir haben unser'n Runciman"* ("We don't need a Santa-man; we've got our Runciman"). Runciman's entourage was equally pro-German. His secretary declared his sympathy for the Sudeten Germans' dislike of Czech Jews, while Lady Runciman displayed (according to a local report) "remarkable understanding for the Sudeten Germans and spoke of Bolshevik influence in Czechoslovakia."

Over the course of their visit, which lasted from August 3 to September 16, Runciman and his colleagues heard the Czech government insist that it was doing all it could to placate the Sudeten Germans, and the SDP representatives claim that Prague was clearly "not prepared to make concessions of a kind that would lead to a real pacification of the state." Prodded by Runciman, President Beneš agreed to appoint more Germans as officials in the Sudetenland and to raise a loan to pay the German minority compensation for economic "damage" inflicted upon them since 1918. The Sudeten negotiators, faced with such far-reaching concessions, asked for advice from Berlin on how to answer. Foreign Minister Joachim von Ribbentrop reminded them of Berlin's general instructions to Henlein, "namely, always to . . . demand more than could be granted by the other side."

This the Henleinists did, but Beneš then came back with his "fourth plan,"

---

*War Minister von Blomberg and Army Chief von Fritsch had, as we noted above, questioned Hitler's plans at the Hossbach conference in 1937. In January 1938 Blomberg was suddenly dismissed—allegedly for having married a woman who had posed for pornographic photographs. Shortly thereafter Fritsch was unjustly accused of homosexuality and dismissed as well. Hitler now became commander in chief of the armed forces, and the officer corps grew ever more subservient to the führer.

which fully accommodated the Karlsbad demands of April 1938 (outlined above), along with more recent Sudeten claims. Realizing that they could not turn this down without exposing their determination to avoid any settlement short of separation, the Henleinists fomented anti-Czech riots in the Sudetenland, then used Prague's declaration of martial law as a pretext for breaking off negotiations.

At the same moment, Hitler delivered a speech at the annual Nuremberg party rally in which he demanded "self-determination" for the Sudetenland and branded Czechoslovakia an "irreconcilable enemy." "I am in no way willing that here in the heart of Germany a second Palestine should be permitted to arise," shouted Hitler. "The poor Arabs are defenseless and deserted. The Germans in Czechoslovakia are neither defenseless nor deserted, and people should take note of that fact."

During the rally the British Foreign Office decided to warn Hitler again that if his actions in Czechoslovakia pulled France into a war, Britain might not be able to "stand aside." But Ambassador Henderson, attending the rally, voiced strong objection to giving Hitler this message: it might "provoke" him. The Foreign Office accepted Henderson's advice and left the message unsent. "We refrained from a possible irritant effect," explained the new permanent under secretary, Alexander Cadogan.

Four days later the Runciman mission returned empty-handed to London. Of course, Runciman was unaware that his efforts had never had the slightest chance of success.

FROM BERCHTESGADEN
TO GODESBERG

Even before Hitler delivered his truculent Nuremberg speech, Chamberlain was mulling over a new plan to save the peace: a personal meeting with Hitler in Germany. It was not that Chamberlain looked forward to sharing the führer's company; he now considered Hitler "half-mad," and he agonized over the thought that "the fate of hundreds of millions" depended on him. Rather inconsistently, however, he also believed that Hitler was open to reason and that he was "a man who could be relied on when he had given his word." Moreover, Chamberlain was excited by the prospect of an "unconventional and daring" stroke that might enable him to reclaim the diplomatic initiative. At one point he even considered departing for Germany without telling the führer he was coming.

In one sense Chamberlain's plan was not so unconventional or daring as he claimed. Many influential Englishmen had visited Hitler and lived to tell the tale. Indeed, most of them had returned singing his praises. Lloyd George had called him "the greatest living German." The historian Arnold Toynbee had found Hitler to be a "man of peace." Lord Lothian, an imperial administrator and one of Britain's more prominent appeasers, agreed that Hitler "did not want war."

Vernon Bartlett, a popular journalist close to the "Cliveden set,"* reported that
Hitler was concerned only about German "security." (What was more, added
Bartlett, Hitler had eyes "so large and so brown [actually blue] one might grow
lyrical about them if one were a woman.") Still Chamberlain was right to think
his idea bold. No sitting prime minister since Disraeli had visited Germany, and
Disraeli had not embarked on a personal "summit" with his German counterpart
(Bismarck) at a time of great tension between the two nations.

By mid-September, Chamberlain had decided that the moment had come for
him to implement his daring plan. Fighting in the Sudetenland between Czechs
and ethnic Germans threatened to produce the "justification" Hitler seemed to
want in order to send in the Wehrmacht. On September 13 the prime minister
dispatched a personal note to Hitler, in which he said, "I propose to come over at
once to see you with a view to trying to find a peaceful solution." He added that
he would come by air and could depart the very next day. Two days earlier he had
presciently confided to his diary:

> I fully realise that, if eventually things go wrong and the aggression takes
> place, there will be many, including Winston [Churchill], who will say that
> the British government must bear the responsibility, and that if only they
> had had the courage to tell Hitler now that, if he used force, we should at
> once declare war, that would have stopped him. By that time it will be
> impossible to prove the contrary, but I am satisfied that we should be wrong
> to allow the most vital decision that any country could take, the decision as
> to peace or war, to pass out of our hands into those of the ruler of another
> country, and a lunatic at that. . . .

Hitler, for his part, immediately put himself at Chamberlain's disposal, speci-
fying that the meeting take place at his mountain retreat near Berchtesgaden,
hard on the border of the Austrian state he had just annexed. Later Hitler confessed to having been "thunderstruck" by Chamberlain's gesture, which threatened to complicate his plan for the rapid destruction of Czechoslovakia. On the
other hand he no doubt believed he could bully Chamberlain the way he had
bullied poor Schuschnigg, the Austrian chancellor who had come to Berchtesgaden to bargain for his country's independence, only to be sent back down the
mountain like a beaten dog. At the same time, Hitler was apparently flattered that
a British prime minister would drop everything and come running to treat with
him. Britain, after all, was not Austria.

The day before his departure, Chamberlain met briefly with his cabinet and
informed them of "Plan Z," his proposed journey to Berchtesgaden. He told his
colleagues that he hoped his gesture would "appeal to the Hitlerian mentality,"

*The "Cliveden set" was an informal group of pro-appeasement politicians, publicists, and high-
society figures who gathered periodically at Lord and Lady Astor's country house, Cliveden. A contemporary cartoon depicted some of them dancing to a foreign-policy tune conducted by Joseph
Goebbels.

that it might be "agreeable to [Hitler's] vanity that the British Prime Minister should take so unprecedented a step." Lest his colleagues worry that the British prime minister was more likely to be bowled over than Hitler, Chamberlain promised to make no specific commitments and certainly to make "no agreement on the direct transfer of Czech territory."

Although some British politicians doubted the wisdom of Chamberlain's plan—Robert Vansittart called it a "new Canossa"—the nation as a whole was instantly captivated by the sheer drama of this enterprise. At the age of sixty-nine, Chamberlain was making his first flight—and this to Hitler's "eagle's eyrie" in distant Bavaria! The British press cheered him on as if he were a new Lindbergh, but a Lindbergh with the fate of the world riding on his shoulders. France was equally worshipful. Parisian newspapers thanked him on behalf of France's mothers and children. M. Frossard in the *L'Homme libre* wrote, "This move, unprecedented in the history of the world, points to the tragic gravity of the situation and earns for the grand old man the respectful admiration of the civilized world. I am now convinced that war has been rendered impossible."

After a seven-hour flight Chamberlain and his party arrived in Munich and transferred to a special train for the remainder of their trip to Berchtesgaden. When they finally reached the Berghof, they had to ascend a long staircase before being greeted by Hitler, who ominously stood next to General Keitel, his new chief of the Wehrmacht. Then began what one of the British party, Lord Strang (head of the Central European Department of the Foreign Office), called a "somewhat macabre tea-party at a round table in the room with the great window looking out towards Austria." Soon Hitler and Chamberlain, accompanied only by Hitler's interpreter, retired for their tête-à-tête.

According to Chamberlain's personal record, Hitler opened the meeting by asserting his faith in the "racial affinity" between the English and the Germans, though of late that affinity had suffered some "very severe blows." Chamberlain countered with the assurance that whatever some Englishmen might think, he "looked on the Führer as a man who, from a strong feeling for the sufferings of his people, had carried through the rebirth of the German nation with extraordinary success."

These hypocritical pleasantries taken care of, the two men got down to business. Hitler stated bluntly that he would integrate Czechoslovakia's three and a half million Germans into the Reich "at all costs." He would "face any war, and even the risk of world war, for this." Chamberlain asked whether, this goal having been achieved, "the differences with Czechoslovakia would be at an end." People were asking in Britain, he added, "whether [Germany] was not aiming over and above this at the dismemberment of the Czechoslovak State." Hitler replied that the Polish, Hungarian, and Ukrainian minorities in Czechoslovakia would undoubtedly make their own demands, but he "was not their spokesman." The question of the hour was "whether Britain would agree to the secession of [the German] areas."

Chamberlain expressed his satisfaction that they "had now got down to the crux of the matter at last." Though he could not make categorical statements for the entire British government, or for the French, he "could give it as his own personal view that, now that he had heard the Führer's motives and now that he saw the whole situation in a clearer light, he was prepared to ascertain whether his [favorable] personal opinion was also shared by his colleagues in the Cabinet." He could state personally that he "recognized the principle of the detachment of the Sudeten areas." As for the practical details of effecting their transfer, these could be worked out at a second meeting after Chamberlain had consulted with his government and the French (he said nothing about the Czechs). The prime minister had clearly gone much beyond his mandate, forgetting his promise not to make any overtures regarding the cession of Czech territory. Hitler, perhaps gratified by Chamberlain's generosity with another country's territory, proposed that their next meeting take place in Cologne or Bad Godesberg; that way the prime minister would not have so far to travel.

Upon his return to London, Chamberlain was hailed as a hero. Bouquets of flowers and letters of encouragement descended on 10 Downing Street. Chamberlain was not above patting himself on the back. "I have no doubt whatever," he told his sister, ". . . that my visit alone prevented an invasion."

But he still had to convince the rest of his government that he had done the right thing. At a cabinet meeting on September 17 he reviewed his meeting with Hitler, whom he variously described as "the commonest little dog" and as an excitable but rational man who "meant what he said." Chamberlain insisted that Hitler had left Britain with only two options: accept self-determination for the Sudetenland or go to war. The prime minister did not admit that he had agreed in principle to the cession of the Sudetenland—a calculated deception.

Not all the ministers immediately accepted Chamberlain's contention that Britain had no real choice but to accept Hitler's terms. Duff Cooper noted that it had always been Britain's concern to "prevent any one Power from obtaining undue predominance in Europe," a principle that Chamberlain seemed ready to discard with respect to Germany. Cooper repeated his earlier contention that since Britain would undoubtedly have to fight Nazi Germany at some point, it was better to make the stand now, because Germany's superiority in arms would only grow. Other ministers worried about Britain's honor. In the end, however, all elected to back the prime minister.

One of the reasons they did so was a new report, dated September 14, from Britain's military strategists, who again argued that the empire's resources would be overstrained in a confrontation with the Axis powers. Especially alarming was the growth of German air power. The strategists calculated that the Luftwaffe could rain down five hundred to six hundred tons of bombs per day on Britain. The military put little stock in the usefulness of Britain's potential allies. (Nor, for that matter, did some members of the government: "Pray God," wrote Alexander Cadogan, "we shall never have to depend on the Soviet, or Poland, or—the U.S.")

Britain's chief ally, France, now had to be briefed on the Berchtesgaden meeting and convinced of the rightness of Chamberlain's course. On September

18 Daladier and Bonnet were summoned to Downing Street. Chamberlain gave them the same options he had given his own government. Daladier expressed the fear that "self-determination" through plebiscites would be demanded by all the minorities in Czechoslovakia and lead to the dismemberment of that state. At this point Chamberlain finally admitted that he had already agreed to the cession of the Sudetenland to Germany but not to plebiscites across the land. He also proposed that Britain and France guarantee the integrity of what remained of the Czech state, if Germany would do so as well. Daladier seized upon these last points to legitimize his acceptance of the British position. Now it might appear that France had not abandoned its Czech ally after all.

In fact, this "guarantee" idea was largely a sham, involving as it did German cooperation. Moreover, if Britain and France would not risk protecting a heavily fortified Czechoslovakia, they would hardly protect the much more vulnerable rump. Chamberlain certainly had no intention of doing so. As for the probable Czech response, it seemed hardly to concern the British and French leaders that Czechoslovakia might not find the proposed "solution" attractive. Like Ethiopia, Czechoslovakia was a "minor" state that could not be allowed to disrupt the workings of great-power diplomacy.

On September 19 Britain and France sent a joint note to Prague insisting that the Czechs accept without amendment the cession to Germany of all Czech territories where Germans constituted a majority. When Prague refused this demand, the British and French ambassadors informed the Czech government that if it continued to resist, it would be "left to its own fate," which it had "brought on itself." The West, Prague was told, would certainly not go to war "just to keep the Germans in Czechoslovakia."

Prague had no choice but to capitulate, but it did so with great bitterness. The Czech ambassador to France said upon learning of the ultimatum, "Here you see the condemned man. He has been sentenced without even being heard." Violent anti-French demonstrations broke out in Prague. President Beneš grasped the broader implications of what was happening, even if London and Paris did not: "I felt very keenly the fact that there were at that time so few in France and Great Britain who understood that something much more serious was at stake for Europe than the retention of the so-called Sudeten Germans in Czechoslovakia."

Having managed in an amazingly short time to secure acceptance of all Hitler's demands, Chamberlain was eager personally to deliver the good news to the führer. On September 22 he flew back to Germany to meet Hitler at Bad Godesberg, a small spa town on the Rhine just south of Bonn. He and his party stayed across the river at the Hotel Petersberg,* an opulent pile of masonry then owned

*Eleven years after housing Chamberlain and his party, the Petersberg again assumed a historic role: as headquarters of the Allied High Commission in West Germany. Ivone Kirkpatrick, who had been seconded from Henderson's staff to translate for Chamberlain, returned to the Petersberg in 1950 as British high commissioner. After the high commission was disbanded in 1955, the Petersberg gradually fell into ruin. In the late 1980s, however, it was restored to serve as a government guest house for official visitors to Bonn—all in all, an intriguing symbolic progression.

by the proprietor of 4711, the famous eau de cologne. The visitors' spacious rooms overlooking the Rhine were stocked with fruit, cigars, cigarettes, and fifteen samples of 4711 products. This would be the only generosity the Englishmen encountered during their visit.

The Godesberg meetings took place in the Hotel Dreesen, where Hitler had plotted his Blood Purge with Goebbels. As Ivone Kirkpatrick, Chamberlain's translator for the talks, related, the hotel hall was filled with "Third Reich nabobs in variegated uniforms." To Kirkpatrick this scene suggested something out of decadent Rome, while for Lord Strang it brought to mind "the domestic establishment of some great barbaric chieftain of Germanic heroic legend." When Hitler entered, the retainers suddenly fell silent and shrank toward the walls. Ignoring his resplendent satraps, the führer immediately led Chamberlain upstairs to a room with a long table, sat down at one end, and looked at the prime minister as if to say, "Your move."

Chamberlain happily reported that he had secured agreement from his own government, the French, and even the Czechs to Hitler's Berchtesgaden terms. Now all that remained was to work out ways to transfer the relevant territories in an orderly manner. The prime minister sat back in his chair and beamed expectantly at Hitler.

The führer looked perplexed as his interpreter translated Chamberlain's message. He had always believed that the West was flabby and timid, but he had not expected such total submission. Nor had he wanted it; he was spoiling for an excuse to show the world what his vaunted Wehrmacht could do to the Czechs. Stalling for time to consider his response, he asked whether Prague had really agreed to all this. Yes, said Chamberlain, it had. There was an embarrassed silence. Finally the führer said in a rasping voice, *"Es tut mir leid, aber das geht nicht mehr"* ("I'm sorry, but this will no longer suffice").

Now it was Chamberlain's turn to be perplexed. He inquired why an arrangement that Germany had just accepted had suddenly become unsatisfactory. Hitler, after another pause, replied that in the meantime Hungary and Poland had raised new claims against Czechoslovakia. These states, he added, "were good friends and Germany would insist that their claims be met." This was nonsense: there were no new Polish or Hungarian claims, and Hitler had in any case said at Berchtesgaden that he was not their spokesman. The führer was clearly fumbling for an adequate monkey wrench to toss into the gears of Chamberlain's well-greased diplomacy. Soon he found it: the previous arrangements for territory transfer, he said, involved an "intolerable delay." Sudeten Germans were being killed every day by the Czechs, he claimed. No, the Sudeten "territory must be ceded at once, without any delay, and occupied by German troops!"

Aghast, Chamberlain replied that he could not accept an immediate military occupation. Hitler might send in his police, but the British public would be outraged if he sent in the army. Kirkpatrick admitted to himself that this stance did not make a great deal of sense. "If we were prepared to agree to the cession of the territory, it seemed illogical to object to its military occupation and to insist on inflicting the Gestapo rather than the Army on its inhabitants." But illogical as this position was, Chamberlain stuck doggedly to it, with the result that the first session broke up in a stalemate.

That evening the cabinet cabled Chamberlain with word that public opinion in England seemed to be "hardening" in the sense that people felt the government had "gone to the limit of concession," and that it was time for Hitler to give something in return. Moreover, though Chamberlain did not know it, at that moment a group of anti-appeasement politicians led by Churchill was vowing to urge a declaration of war against Germany if Chamberlain did not secure a *gradual* transfer of the Sudetenland and no military occupation. When one of the group suggested that it might be inconvenient to start a war when the prime minister was still on German territory, Churchill, waving a whisky and soda, grumbled, "Even the Germans would not be so stupid as to deprive us of our beloved Prime Minister."

Thus Chamberlain had been right to worry about his country's reaction to an immediate military occupation. Aware of the need for a German quid pro quo, he pressed Hitler for concessions on the timing and the nature of occupation; he asked the führer for a written statement of his demands, pleading that they be modified.

Later that evening Hitler produced a memorandum, but it made no significant concessions. It called for, inter alia, the withdrawal of all Czech forces from an area designated by an accompanying map. This area was to be turned over to Germany by October 1 and in "present condition"—that is, without the removal or destruction of any military or economic facilities. The departing Czechs were not even to take away foodstuffs, farm equipment, or cattle. No later than November 25, plebiscites would be held in those areas where ethnic domination and national allegiance were disputed; these plebiscites could be conducted by an international commission. Nothing was said about the nature of the occupation, leaving the Germans free to send in the army.

Chamberlain called this statement a "Diktat" in the tradition of the Versailles settlement. His indignation may have reflected a need to recover some measure of self-esteem, but his punctiliousness was both quixotic and a bit belated—rather like an effort to restore virginity after pregnancy. In any case, the prime minister quickly returned to his old self. As he left Godesberg, he promised to submit Hitler's new demands to his government and to the French.

This time Chamberlain returned not to cheers and flowers but to grim preparations for a war that many Britons now feared was imminent. In London civil defense crews were handing out gas masks and digging trenches in Green Park. Antiaircraft guns lined the Victoria Embankment, hospitals were readied for massive casualties, and Parliament considered a plan to move to Stratford-on-Avon. At the same time, however, Britain's chiefs of staff finally threw off their strategic gloom and submitted a new report that was much more optimistic about the West's ability to prevail over Germany. The Reich was weak on the western front, said the report, and the German general staff could probably not correct this deficiency quickly. In short, the chiefs had "confidence as to the ultimate outcome" of a war. As if to document this new determination to stand firm, the government (in Chamberlain's absence) mobilized the fleet.

This toughness frightened rather than encouraged Chamberlain. Meeting with the full cabinet on September 24, he argued for acceptance of Hitler's terms. Astoundingly, he tried to convince his colleagues that Hitler, who had obviously led him down the primrose path, "would not deliberately deceive a man with whom he had been in negotiations." Since Hitler meant business when he threatened war, only an immediate Anglo-German understanding could prevent a catastrophe. To capture the conscience of his colleagues, Chamberlain evoked vivid images of German bombers laying waste to London. He wondered aloud what degree of protection the government could provide for its citizens. He concluded that "we were in no position to justify waging a war today, in order to prevent a war thereafter."

Eloquent as Chamberlain was, the cabinet began to balk. Cooper and some of the other younger ministers threatened resignation. During two days of meetings Chamberlain could not win his government's endorsement of his proposal to ask the Czechs to accept Hitler's terms. Nor could he persuade the usually quite persuadable French. Daladier and Bonnet told the British cabinet that if Germany attacked Czechoslovakia, France would "fulfill its obligations." Unable to sway the French and threatened with a rebellion in his own government, Chamberlain acquiesced: his government would announce that if France went to war, Britain would support it.

As this announcement was being made, Paris was emulating London in preparing for war. Municipal authorities distributed sand to be spread around buildings to counter the effectiveness of incendiary bombs. Queues formed outside banks as depositors withdrew their gold; readers in the Bibliothèque Nationale dove under tables at the sound of every passing plane. The far Right, which had found the Godesberg demands perfectly acceptable, howled in rage: "Must Frenchmen really die for f—— Beneš?" asked an Action Française zealot, who like many of his ilk would soon also prove unwilling to die for Poland and, later, even for France. Undeterred, the government declared partial mobilization and sent troops to the Maginot Line. Just as in August 1914, the streets of Paris were clogged with young men carrying military kits, trudging off to the train stations. But 1938 was not 1914: "Nobody shouted à Berlin this time," noted one observer. "It was all rather sad and solemn, and nobody had any illusions about the romance of modern warfare."

Nor were there any illusions in Czechoslovakia, but the Prague government, buoyed up by this very belated show of support from the West, announced its own rejection of the Godesberg demands. Czechoslovakia ordered general mobilization and began manning its extensive fortifications. It looked as if Hitler might have his war after all, albeit a larger one than he had bargained for.

"A HUGGER-MUGGER AFFAIR"

Preparations for war notwithstanding, Chamberlain was still determined to find a peaceful way out. On September 26 he sent his éminence grise, Sir Horace Wilson,* to Berlin with a personal letter to Hitler. The letter reiterated Chamberlain's willingness to do business on the basis of the Berchtesgaden proposals, while insisting that the Godesberg memorandum was unacceptable to Western public opinion and to Czechoslovakia. Convinced, however, that Hitler wanted to "avoid the human misery and suffering that would inevitably follow on a conflict," he urged the führer to agree to a conference with the Czechs designed to define acceptable ways for the Sudeten "territory to be handed over." Wilson delivered the letter to Hitler that afternoon.

Hitler's immediate response was to put on one of his famous scenes. "The Germans are being treated like niggers," he screamed; "nobody dares to treat even Turkey this way. On October 1 I'll have Czechoslovakia where I want her." Wilson reported delicately to London that he and Hitler had had a "very violent hour," the führer applying epithets to Chamberlain and himself that "could not be repeated in a drawing room."

Hitler's substantive response, however, was reserved for a speech he gave in Berlin's Sportpalast the following evening. After a lengthy condemnation of Prague's rejection of his "practical" and "reasonable" terms, he shouted that his patience was at an end. The decision now lay in Beneš's hands: peace or war. If the decision was war, Czechoslovakia would find itself confronted by a united German nation, a nation much different from that of 1918. He concluded by appealing to his people to take their stand behind him, "man by man, and woman by woman."

Hitler was not bluffing. He was impatient to use force to solve the "Sudeten problem." However, he did not want a general European war at this moment. There were many reasons for this. Bluster as he might about German strength, Hitler realized that his Wehrmacht was not ready to face a major war in 1938. It lacked sufficient armor, heavy artillery, ammunition, and trained reservists. Hitler's generals realized this as well, and a few of them made their doubts known to him. Even some of Hitler's closest political cronies urged caution. Göring was especially concerned about possible Russian intervention. He pleaded with Hitler to avoid any actions that might pull Russia in on the side of the Western powers. Nor could Hitler be so sure that the German people were as bellicose as he claimed. On September 27, to heighten the populace's enthusiasm for war, he had ordered a motorized division to roll through Berlin on its way to the Czech border. According to the foreign correspondent William Shirer, not two hundred

---

*Officially Wilson was chief industrial adviser to the government. Like Chamberlain, he believed fervently in the necessity of Anglo-German cooperation. "The two leading white races on earth must not exterminate each other," he said. Later he became ambassador to Washington.

people lined the streets. A "grim and angry" Hitler canceled his plan to review the troops. Above all, the führer was sobered by France's and Britain's apparent willingness (despite the best efforts of Chamberlain) to intervene. As always, Britain concerned him more than France. He later told Göring that Britain's mobilization of the fleet had convinced him that he could not expect a limited war.

What Hitler did not know at this moment was that a few of his top officers, intelligence agents, and diplomats not only opposed going to war but even planned to try to topple his regime if he insisted upon doing so. After General Beck's resignation in August 1937, the anti-Hitler campaign in the military was taken up by Beck's successor, General Franz Halder, along with General Erwin von Witzleben and a few others. These men and their civilian confederates apparently planned to arrest Hitler and place him on trial the moment he plunged Germany into war. Of course, the execution of this plan was predicated upon the West's picking up Hitler's gauntlet and obliging him to fight.

Even had the Western powers satisfied this requirement, however, it is rather doubtful that the resisters could have successfully carried off their putsch. A considerable portion of the officer corps would have had to join the action to make it succeed, and there is no evidence that a majority of officers were prepared to challenge Hitler. Nevertheless, the claim that Hitler would have been overthrown from within had the West forced him into a military confrontation in 1938 has become one of the enduring myths of Munich. It has been of particular use to former German officers who like to assert that the West "saved" Hitler from his own army.

Meanwhile Neville Chamberlain was beginning to despair of a diplomatic solution to the Czech crisis—an impasse he blamed more on the Czechs than on the Germans. It struck him as positively obscene that a major war might be fought over this minor place. In a speech broadcast to the nation on September 27, he cried, "How horrible, fantastic, incredible it is that we should be digging trenches and trying on gas masks here because of a quarrel in a far-away country between people of whom we know nothing. It seems still more impossible that a quarrel which has already been settled in principle should be the subject of war. . . ."

Chamberlain's agonized reflections, however, now appeared unimportant; both his own government and Berlin seemed determined to let Czechoslovakia become another Bosnia. But as the prime minister waited helplessly for "the lights of Europe" to go out for a second time in the twentieth century, an urgent letter arrived from Hitler. In it the führer said that he did not want to attack Czechoslovakia, that Prague had distorted his intentions, and that he hoped Chamberlain would use his splendid diplomatic talents "to spoil [Czechoslovakia's] maneuvers and to bring the government in Prague to reason at the very last hour."

This was all Chamberlain needed to restart the sputtering engines of appeasement. He immediately wrote two letters—one to Hitler offering to come to Berlin to discuss anew the Czech crisis with representatives from Italy, France, and Prague; the other to Mussolini asking him to second this proposal with the führer. He chose the duce as an intermediary because he knew that Mussolini, for all his earlier bluster about wanting to help Hitler "wipe Czechoslovakia off the map," desperately wished to avoid a European war. At the same time Chamberlain apprised Paris of his initiative, which Daladier enthusiastically welcomed. Bonnet did even more: he instructed Ambassador François-Poncet in Berlin to tell Hitler that France would give him everything he wanted in Czechoslovakia. To the British historian John Wheeler-Bennett this action justified another Englishman's bitter judgment: "France, among a multitude of virtues, has one vice unpardonable to Northern men: she turns from a fallen friend." The northern men in London, however, had hardly encouraged their Latin ally to show more fortitude.

As Chamberlain had hoped, Mussolini proved willing to help. He had his ambassador in Berlin urge Hitler to accept Chamberlain's latest demarche. François-Poncet was making a similar appeal on behalf of France. Although still half wishing he could just crush Czechoslovakia and be done with it, Hitler now showed himself as the man of peace: he postponed his mobilization against Czechoslovakia and promised to give serious consideration to Chamberlain's call for a conference.

The prime minister did not know what Hitler's response would be when he began an address to the House of Commons the next afternoon. Toward the end of his speech, which began with a bleak reference to 1914 and then described his latest effort to forestall a new war, he was passed a note from the government benches. As he read it, a smile crossed his face. Then he announced, "I have now been informed by Herr Hitler that he invites me to meet him at Munich tomorrow morning. Signor Mussolini has accepted and I have no doubt M. Daladier will also accept. I need not say what my answer will be."

Pandemonium immediately broke out in the House. According to the *News Chronicle*, Chamberlain had to "stand silent for nearly five minutes while members, foreign ambassadors, press and public jumped to their feet and cheered uproariously. Tears came to the eyes of Queen Mary sitting in the public gallery. . . ." For the Opposition, Clement Attlee assured the prime minister that everyone in the House was "desirous of neglecting no chance of preserving peace without sacrificing principles." In the general euphoria, no one seemed to notice that Hitler had modified Chamberlain's proposal: Czechoslovakia was not to be represented at the conference. But one witness had noticed. Jan Masaryk, Prague's ambassador to Britain, said to Joseph Kennedy, "I hope this does not mean they are going to cut us up and sell us out."

The next morning, September 29, found Chamberlain flying to Germany for the third time in less than two weeks—an early example of exhausting shuttle diplomacy. Daladier was also in the air from Paris, while the Fascist partners, having met on the Austro-German border, were proceeding to Munich in Hitler's special train. It is significant that the two Fascist leaders were traveling together, coordinating their plans, while the democratic leaders took no pains to work out a common strategy.

In fact, however, the dictators' preparations amounted to little more than Hitler's telling Mussolini how the conference would proceed. The Germans had already prepared a draft of the agreement they wanted to emerge from the meeting. But rather than present this proposal himself, Hitler wanted Mussolini to offer it as an Italian initiative. No doubt this reflected both his lingering resentment at having to settle for peace and his intention to wash his hands of the whole affair if it went awry.

The Munich conference took place in Hitler's newly built Führerbau on the Königsplatz. A typical example of Nazi architecture, the long, low, neoclassical building boasted a large bronze eagle over the main entrance and a huge central hall lined in marble. On the occasion of the conference the place was aflutter with "flocks of spruce young S.S. subalterns in their black uniforms, haughty and punctilious," heel-clicking and saluting "as though life were a drill." Hermann Göring, his prodigious girth enveloped in a white uniform, paced about along the upper galleries, doing his best to charm the guests.

But there was nothing charming about the Munich conference: it was, observed Lord Strang, "a hugger-mugger affair." After a brief buffet snack, the conferees repaired to Hitler's study and began talking with no apparent order or agenda. There were no notepads or sharpened pencils. According to Chamberlain and Wilson, Hitler eventually delivered a statement on Czechoslovakia that was calm, moderate, and reasonable. Daladier remembered a wild diatribe, complete with fist clenching and table pounding. Since Count Ciano (the Italian foreign minister) and Paul Schmidt (Hitler's interpreter) also recalled that the führer became rather "excited," Daladier's version is probably closer to the truth. Daladier later claimed that he announced he would simply go home rather than participate in a dismemberment of Czechoslovakia. "The French Premier," wrote François-Poncet (who got his information from Daladier), "spoke in accents of a determination that moved his hearers." None of the other accounts of the meeting verify this moving performance. In any event, after some more desultory conversation, Mussolini produced "his" draft agreement and proposed it as a basis for further discussion. The meeting then adjourned so that the British and French could study the agreement.

During the recess, Hitler and Mussolini retired to the führer's apartment in the Prinzregentenstrasse. Here Hitler unburdened himself regarding Chamberlain and England. Once again, he said, Chamberlain had impressed him as "insignificant." How thoroughly unheroic he was with his stupid umbrella and his endless twaddle about fishing! (At Godesberg, Chamberlain had praised the delights of fishing to Hitler, bragging that there was hardly a weekend when he did not fish.) As for England, its time of playing "governess of Europe" must end: the age of the Fascist "revolutionaries" had dawned. Mussolini fully agreed. He grunted that England was a country of little old ladies, its low birth rate a sign of sapped virility.

When the formal talks resumed, it soon became apparent that Britain and France would accept the essence of the German-Italian draft, while objecting to some relatively minor points. By late evening the principals, who had been joined by several additional advisers, had an agreement in hand that required only a few technical refinements before it could be signed.

The document in question provided for the evacuation and military occupation of the ethnic-German territories in a series of stages between October 1 and October 10. An international commission composed of representatives from the four powers plus Czechoslovakia would monitor the evacuation, determine final boundaries, and establish which areas would hold plebiscites. France and Britain would guarantee the new territory of Czechoslovakia. Germany and Italy would join in this guarantee only after the territorial claims of the Hungarians and Poles had been considered.

François-Poncet later argued that this agreement represented a significant improvement over the Godesberg memorandum. This was not true. As with the Godesberg proposal, the Sudetenland was to be occupied in short order by the German Wehrmacht. Czechoslovakia would lose invaluable industries, fortifications, and military supplies. The Anglo-French "guarantee" of the new Czech borders carried little conviction, and by allowing Germany and Italy to defer their own guarantee until the Hungarians and Poles were satisfied, the agreement gave the Fascist powers ample leverage to pry apart what remained of the Czech state.

Hitler should have been pleased with this solution, but in fact he was disgruntled. Chamberlain and Daladier had handed over to him what he would have preferred to grab. During the Polish crisis a year later he would say, "My only fear is that at the last moment some *Schweinehund* will present me with a mediation plan." The führer scratched his name to the Munich agreement "as if he were being asked to sign away his birthright." Mussolini, on the other hand, was in the best of spirits. Throughout the conference he had laughed, scowled, and strutted about, leaving at least one participant (François-Poncet) with the mistaken impression that the duce dominated Hitler. On the Western side, Daladier, recognizing the shame of it all, shook his head and "cursed circumstances." Chamberlain, serene and collected, seemed as confident as ever that he was doing the Lord's work.

The Prague government had no part in working out the Munich agreement, but at the last moment it had sent an "observer" group, which the Germans confined to their hotel. At about 10:00 P.M. a British representative informed the Czechs of the main outline of the agreement, to which they understandably objected. They were then told that if they did not accept the plan, they "would have to settle [their] affairs with the Germans absolutely alone." After the final document was signed, at 2:00 A.M. on September 30, a copy was taken to the Czechs in their hotel. Vojtech Mastny, the Czech ambassador to Berlin, broke out in tears. François-Poncet tried to console him by saying that nothing was final—which certainly turned out to be true. Later the Frenchman was heard muttering, sotto voce, *"Voilà comme la France traite les seuls alliés qui lui étaient restés fidèles"* ("This is how France treats the only allies that have remained faithful to her").

The main work of the Munich conference was now completed, but Chamberlain had another item on his agenda. He wanted to use this propitious occasion to revive a pet project: an Anglo-German agreement forswearing war between the two countries. Accordingly, later on September 30 he presented Hitler with a statement he hoped the führer would sign. It read in part,

> We regard the agreement signed last night and the Anglo-German Naval Agreement as symbolic of the desire of our two peoples never to go to war with one another again.
>
> We are resolved that the method of consultation shall be the method adopted to deal with any other questions that may concern our two countries, and we are determined to continue our efforts to remove possible sources of differences and thus to contribute to assuring the peace of Europe.

Hitler saw this pious statement as a blank check that he could soon fill in and cash at the expense of eastern Europe. He promptly signed it. Chamberlain, however, believed that this little document was the key to the world's salvation. "I've got it!" he shouted, as he returned to his hotel. It was this "victory," rather than the four-power agreement itself, that Chamberlain had in mind when he told the people of Britain that he had brought them "peace for our time."

"PEACE FOR OUR TIME"

The principals at the Munich conference might have differed in their assessments of what they had accomplished, but in the immediate aftermath of their meeting they encountered little but praise from their respective peoples.

As Mussolini's special train rolled through northern Italy, people knelt beside the tracks and offered up hosannas to their duce. To King Victor Emmanuel III, who met him in Florence, Mussolini boasted that he had "saved Europe" and made Chamberlain "lick his boots." His only complaint was that the Italians were cheering him as a peacemaker rather than as a conqueror. Even at Bologna, the "stronghold of bellicose Fascism," the people clearly preferred "the olive branch to the laurel, the dove to the eagle."

Hitler encountered similar sentiments in Munich, the city in which Nazism had had its birth. As he drove Mussolini to the station people shouted *"Friede"* ("peace") as loudly as *"Führer."* Clearly the Germans would need a few sweet military victories to revive their legendary appetite for war. Hitler blamed the

British prime minister for making him defer giving his people a bracing taste of military glory. "That damned Chamberlain has spoiled my parade into Prague!" he grumbled.

For the time being, at least, Hitler would have to be content with an entry into the Sudetenland, which he duly accomplished on October 3. Amid thousands of swastika-waving Germans, Henlein congratulated him: "Our assurance that we will not perish but will be called upon, as the German guard in the East, to enter the victorious path of the future with the whole German nation, is all due to your work."

As he flew over Paris, Daladier saw enormous crowds gathering at Le Bourget airport. Still convinced that Munich had been a shameful (albeit necessary) surrender, he thought that the crowds had come to lynch him. But when he stepped from his plane he was engulfed in a tide of adulation. Women tried to kiss him, or have him kiss their babies. *"La paix! La paix!"* everyone shouted. Daladier's drive from Le Bourget to central Paris turned into a triumphal procession. Shopgirls waved tricolor flags and yelled, *"Vive la France!"* (The journalist Alexander Werth heard one workman shout, *"Vive la France malgré tout!"*—"Long live France in spite of everything!") Daladier himself had enough sense of irony to grumble, "The fools!" as he received his people's acclamation.

None of the men of Munich was cheered more loudly than Neville Chamberlain. Most British newspapers covered him in glowing encomiums. The *Daily Sketch* suggested that "only a man of fine-steel calibre and honesty could have plucked success from the smoking cauldrons." To the *Daily Express* the prime minister's mission meant "millions of happy homes and hearts relieved of their burden. To him the laurels!" The *Manchester Guardian* noted the "injustices" that Czechoslovakia would suffer under the Munich agreement, but it argued that these paled in comparison with the "horrors that might have extinguished not only Czecho-Slovakia, but the whole of Western civilization." The *Times*, chief oracle of British appeasement, had no reservations at all regarding Chamberlain's accomplishment: "No conqueror returning from victory on the battlefield had come adorned with nobler laurels," it gushed.

Upon his arrival at Heston airport, Chamberlain was handed a command invitation from King George VI instructing him to come straightaway to Buckingham Palace so that the king could personally convey his "most heartfelt congratulations" on the success of Chamberlain's visit to Munich. Apparently London's common folk were no less appreciative. Chamberlain could gloat to his sister,

Even the descriptions of the papers give no idea of the scenes in the streets as I drove from Heston to the Palace. They were lined from one end to the other with people of every class, shouting themselves hoarse, leaping on the running board, banging on the windows, and thrusting their hands into the car to be shaken.

In Chamberlain's case, though, it was not just his own nation that was appreciative. From America, FDR telegrammed, "Good Man!" A few days later the president added in a letter, "I wholly share your hope and your belief that today there is the greatest opportunity in recent times to establish a new order based on justice and right." In France *Paris-Soir,* the paper that had hired Georges Simenon to investigate the Prince case during the Stavisky era, announced that it was launching a public subscription for the purchase of a French villa for Chamberlain near some stream where he might fish to his heart's content. In the first twenty-four hours the subscription netted 100,000 francs.

Carried away with all this acclamation, Chamberlain could not resist uttering the lines for which he is best remembered: "My good friends," he told a cheering crowd outside 10 Downing Street, "this is the second time that there has come back from Germany to Downing Street, peace with honour."* He then held up his copy of the Anglo-German agreement. "I believe it is peace for our time," he shouted. "Good old Neville!" responded the crowd, breaking out into "For He's a Jolly Good Fellow."

But it did not take long for the ecstasy to cool and sobriety to set in. Alexander Werth noted a certain nervousness in Paris, a growing skepticism regarding the "triumph" of Munich. After a fast start the *Paris-Soir* subscription for Chamberlain lost momentum, and the prime minister did not get his fishing villa after all. In America people made jokes about "canceled Czechs" and editorialists wondered if Munich was not in reality "a shocking defeat for democracy." More significantly, anti-appeasement forces in Britain collected their wits and began to raise serious criticism of the Munich agreement. Duff Cooper, not convinced that Munich was much of an improvement over Godesberg, resigned from the government, for which action most of his fellow Tories denounced him. At a House of Commons session on October 4, Winston Churchill rose to his grandiloquent best in denouncing Chamberlain's diplomacy. Those who cheered the Munich agreement, he intoned,

> should know that we have sustained a defeat without a war, the consequences of which will travel far with us along our road; they should know that we have passed an awful milestone in our history, when the whole equilibrium of Europe has been deranged, and that the terrible words have for the time being been pronounced against the Western Democracies: "Thou art weighed in the balance and found wanting." And do not suppose that this is the end. This is only the beginning of the reckoning. This is only the first sip, the first foretaste of a bitter cup which will be preferred to us year by year unless, by a supreme recovery of moral health and martial vigor, we rise again and take our stand for freedom as in the olden time.

*He was referring to Disraeli's return from the congress of Berlin in 1878, when the British statesman said he had brought "peace with honour."

A month later Churchill confronted Chamberlain in the House and withered him with one (now famous) blast: "You were given the choice between war and dishonour. You chose dishonour and you shall have war."

Cassandras like Churchill were quickly proven right. The ink was hardly dry on the Munich agreement before Hitler was encouraging the Slovaks to declare their independence from Czechoslovakia; by October 6, Slovakia had its own cabinet and premier. Poland, meanwhile, was taking over Teschen, and the Hungarians were demanding sections of Ruthenia. Exploiting the weakness and confusion prevailing in what was now officially called Czecho-Slovakia, Hitler sent his troops into Prague in mid-March 1939. He established a protectorate of Bohemia and Moravia and made Slovakia an "independent" state under German control. In all these regions German police and their local collaborators immediately launched waves of terror against Jews, socialists, democrats, and indeed anyone who did not toe the Nazi line.

Sudeten German Social Democrats fled to England in search of asylum. But when they applied for visas through Lord Runciman, they were told that the best he could do was contribute to a relief fund the mayor of London was establishing. Visas were refused because the British government feared that providing them might irritate Hitler, and in any case London did not want to encourage Europe's refugees from fascism to regard England as a possible haven. (This policy applied also to German Jews fleeing Hitler's persecution.) "Democracies exist to swallow toads," observed Mussolini.

Germany, it seemed, existed to swallow countries, but when Hitler began to ingest Poland in September 1939 the West finally tried to stop him. This time the Western powers would not hand him what he preferred to take by force, though some people in the West, on both the far right and the far left, were prepared to do just that. Hitler's invasion of Poland signaled the beginning of World War II, a war that the Munich agreement, signed just eleven months before, was supposed to have rendered impossible "for our time."

THE "MIRACLE OF MUNICH"

Since World War II, historians and political commentators have never ceased debating the significance of the Munich agreement. Munich's obvious failure to ensure a lasting peace, combined with its sacrifice of a loyal ally on the altar of appeasement, have made this pact one of the most widely condemned acts of diplomacy in modern history.

But Munich has always had its defenders. The defense revolves around three interrelated propositions: (1) Munich offered a chance for peace, and since peace is preferable to war the chance had to be taken; (2) the Western leaders had no choice but to take this chance because their nations were neither militarily nor psychologically prepared for war; (3) even if Munich did not secure a lasting peace, it ended up postponing war for eleven months—an invaluable "breathing space" during which the West was able to remedy some of its weaknesses and thereby fight more effectively when war did come. In this view, although Chamberlain and Daladier could not have known it at the time, their agreement with the Fascist powers was a "miracle" that ultimately saved the West.

In 1938 the argument was made that Munich represented a chance for peace because the Germans were likely to be "satiated" once they had incorporated Central Europe's ethnic Germans into the Reich. In hindsight, we know that this was not so. Chamberlain's defenders have argued that one ought not employ the wisdom of hindsight to fault the prime minister: he could hardly have known in 1938 what the world learned only in 1939.

Fair enough, but one might point out that Chamberlain had plenty of information at his disposal that should have made him rethink his optimistic expectations. In his speeches and writings Hitler had called for lebensraum in the east, a goal that presupposed "wiping Czechoslovakia off the map." Many Western politicians, including Daladier, had few illusions that Munich would bring long-term stability. Some of Chamberlain's advisers believed that Munich might at best postpone war with Germany. Now and then even Chamberlain himself thought war inevitable, but he allowed himself at the time of the Munich conference to harbor illusions about lasting peace. That he could do so was primarily the result of his fundamental failure to understand Hitler or Nazi Germany. He simply had no sense for the radical, dynamic, unruly Nazi weltanschauung, no appreciation for what one historian has called the "Faustian scope of the Nazi thrust forward and vision of Empire." This failing in turn was perhaps a legacy of his "Victorian" faith in reason and order. But it should be said that a true Victorian like Cecil Rhodes or (for that matter) Joseph Chamberlain would probably have had a better feel for the Nazi dreams of limitless empire. It was Cecil Rhodes, after all, who said, "I'd annex the moon if I could."

As for the claim that the West was militarily unprepared to confront Germany in 1938, we must reiterate our earlier suggestion: the Germans were not so strong, or the West so weak, as the doomsayers seemed so eager to believe. As we have seen, the British chiefs of staff had submitted a more optimistic strategic appraisal of Britain's situation on the eve of the Munich conference. By way of assessing the "miracle" of Munich, however, more must be said regarding the strategic balance in 1938.

The most recent and authoritative study of the Germans' military and strategic posture at the time of Munich argues,

In nearly every respect, the Wehrmacht was not ready in 1938. It did not possess an armored force capable of winning decisive victories. It could not fight simultaneously in the east and west. Germany possessed neither trained reserves nor the industrial capacity to put substantial reserve forces in the field. Industry would have faced considerable difficulty in meeting wartime demands for fuel, ammunition, and weapons just for the regular army. Thus, it is hard to see exactly what major military operations the Germans could have mounted after the conquest of Bohemia.

German generals were particularly alarmed about their weaknesses on the western front, and rightly so. Germany's vaunted *Westwall* (western defensive line) was a "vast bluff" in 1938, when only 517 out of a planned 5,148 bunkers had been completed. The generals believed the *Wall* was too weak to prevent a French breakthrough.

The east also presented problems for Germany. Poland would undoubtedly remain neutral if Germany invaded Czechoslovakia, but if the Germans stumbled there, and the British and French intervened, Poland might strike at German Silesia, where the Reich had few defensive forces. Russia was not much of a threat, because, even if it wanted to, it could not get its land forces across Poland or Romania to help Czechoslovakia. But Stalin, like Poland's leaders, would certainly become restless if he smelled German blood, and he had an air force that, despite the purges, was capable of raising havoc in eastern Germany.

Apropos air power, the Luftwaffe, like Germany's land army, was not the formidable force in 1938 that it would be in 1939–40. A German military report in late 1938 admitted to a "lack of readiness in maintenance of flying equipment as well as in technical personnel." At this time Germany was still in the early stages of procuring the new aircraft it would use to fight the next war. The two bomber types then in mass production—the Dornier 17 and the Heinkel 111—lacked the range and capacity to act as strategic bombers. With all its deficiencies, the Luftwaffe would certainly not have been able to deliver the "knockout blow" to England that British statesmen feared.

The Reich was even weaker in naval power in 1938. It had no big battleships, heavy cruisers, or aircraft carriers. Its submarine force—soon to be the scourge of the Atantic—was still minuscule. In essence this meant that the Kriegsmarine would have been limited to defensive operations.

Military power, of course, is a matter not just of arms on hand but also of a nation's capacity to produce more arms quickly and efficiently. In 1938 Germany was in serious economic difficulty, its ambitious rearmament drive having overstrained industrial and financial resources. Göring's "four-year plan," designed to make Germany ready for "total war," was just getting under way. At the moment crucial raw materials, particularly petroleum, were in very short supply. There were also pressing shortages of iron, copper, and nickel. It was estimated that Germany's capacity for gunpowder production was only 40 percent of maximum production during World War I.

In 1938 Germany's only European ally was Mussolini's Italy. Whatever the duce might say about his country's military prowess, Italy was no great asset. The invasion of Ethiopia had cost Italy dearly without bringing significant economic or strategic gains. If Italy had in fact followed Germany into a war in 1938 (a duty it might well have evaded), it would have been a burden to the Reich, draining off resources while undoubtedly failing to hold the Mediterranean. Churchill's cruel quip during the war—that it was only fair that Germany take Italy as an ally in World War II because the Allies had had it on their side in World War I— summed up pretty well Rome's military value to the Axis.

As for that other Axis power, Japan, it was much stronger than Italy but in 1938 had its hands full with the Chinese. Japan had no intention of joining a general conflict at this time. (In fact, it waited until late 1941 to do so.) Spain was not a factor at all, because it was still embroiled in its civil war, and Franco had no inclination (then or later) to repay Hitler for his Condor Legion with Spanish intervention against the West.

The other side of the strategic picture in 1938 is equally revealing. Although France and Britain had their military weaknesses, in many crucial areas they were significantly stronger than the Germans at the time of Munich.

In 1938 France could mobilize 5.5 million men in one hundred divisions, fifty-six of which would face the ten (only five regular) divisions Germany could spare for the western front. In addition to their manpower superiority in the west, the French enjoyed a five-to-one margin in light artillery and a nine-to-one edge in heavy artillery. If despite these advantages General Gamelin and his colleagues were reluctant to engage the Germans, this was because the French general staff had little confidence that France could hold out against the Reich once Germany turned its full attention to the west. Events were later to show that this concern was not misplaced, but in 1938 Germany was in no position to mount an extensive attack on France.

The British land army was quite weak in 1938, but its navy was vastly superior to the Kriegsmarine, and the Royal Air Force, for all its shortcomings, was about on a par with the Luftwaffe at the time of Munich. Britain's great advantage lay in its ability to impose a strangulating blockade on Germany and thereby exacerbate its already precarious ecconomic-industrial situation. Germany's naval deficiencies would have prevented it from doing much to break the stranglehold. And if Britain were joined in this operation by Yugoslavia and Romania, Germany would be cut off from bauxite, grain, and oil supplies. Without access to oil Germany could no more have fought an extensive war in 1938 than Italy could have in 1935.

But Germany did not have to fight in October 1938; the West accepted Hitler's challenge only in September 1939. To Chamberlain and his defenders, this eleven-month interregnum benefited not Germany but the West. In retrospect, insisted Sir John Simon, Munich granted Britain "an invaluable twelve [sic] months in which to strengthen our preparations to wage [war]." Moreover, said Simon, Hitler's breach of his Munich promise in March 1939 "helped to secure, more than anything else could have done, that Britain went into war against Germany as an absolutely united nation, with a united Commonwealth at her side." On the eve of Dunkirk in May 1940, Chamberlain insisted, "Whatever the outcome, it is clear as daylight that, if we had to fight in 1938, the result would have been far worse." Though Chamberlain's (and Simon's) comments might be dismissed as self-justification, some historians have agreed with this position.

To assess this argument one must look closely at what happened in the eleven-month period between the Munich agreement and the outbreak of war. The first notable development was the loss of Czechoslovakia by the West. Defenders of the Munich agreement have argued that this did not mean much strategically, because Czechoslovakia was internally divided, its military untested, and its vaunted fortress system overrated. In fact, we will never know for certain how strong Czechoslovakia was, or how well it might have stood up to Germany had it been encouraged by the West to fight in 1938. Contemporary estimates by Allied military experts, as well as by German officers, suggest however that Czechoslovakia was stronger than its detractors believed and that a German invasion in 1938 would have been no *Spaziergang* (stroll). On the contrary, while the Germans would ultimately have prevailed, they would have undoubtedly suffered rather heavy losses in some battlefield sectors. It seems probable that Czechoslovakia would have caused the Wehrmacht more difficulty in 1938 than Poland did in 1939. In any event, Czechoslovakia's defensive potential was not only lost to the West but turned into additional offensive potential for the Third Reich. Shortly after the march into Prague, Göring told his staff that the incorporation of Bohemia and Moravia into the Reich had taken place "in order to increase German war potential by the exploitation of industry there." Germany also exploited Czechoslovakia's military capacity. In World War II Hitler's armies made excellent use of Czech tanks and weapons from the famous Skoda arms factory.

Another momentous development in the post-Munich era was the Soviet Union's decision to sign a nonaggression pact with Germany in August 1939. Although Stalin had already been secretly courting Germany, there can be no doubt that the Munich agreement, to which Russia was not a party, helped persuade the Soviet dictator that Russia was better off dealing with Hitler than with the West. But was Russia's defection a significant loss? We have seen that many Western military analysts downgraded the quality of the Red Army in light of Stalin's purges. Geographical factors also limited Russia's ability to aid Czechoslovakia. Russia's poor performance in the opening phases of World War II showed that there were good reasons to question its military capacity. Moscow may also have been a political liability, since the prospect of fighting alongside the Soviet Union was anathema to many in the West. And perhaps Stalin was urging a tough stance on the West only to derive "maximum profit" from a war—a view Vansittart came to hold. Still, when all these factors and possibilities are considered, Russia's defection must be rated extremely significant, for now its considerable natural resources (especially oil) benefited Germany rather than the West.

Germany went to war in 1939 fortified by Russian raw materials and foodstuffs, resources that made it much less vulnerable to Allied blockade tactics.

If the Munich agreement convinced Stalin that Britain and France were unwilling to stand up to Hitler, it sent a similar message to the United States. After initially misinterpreting it as a Western victory, the American press tended to see the agreement as a sellout, as another example of European perfidy. This appraisal reflected a growing American disillusionment with appeasement, though not necessarily a willingness to intervene militarily in Europe. In 1939 the influential American journalist Helen Kirkpatrick fumed,

They [Britain and France] have lost invaluable allies in Europe and the support of an American public opinion strong enough to have brought the moral and material resources of the United States to their aid. With the disappearance of Czechoslovakia, Britain has not only lost a vital strategic outpost of Empire in Europe [sic], but, in addition, the one cause for which the United States would in all probability have once again entered a European war.

In suggesting that the United States would probably have gone to war over Czechoslovakia in 1938, Kirkpatrick was surely wrong, but her appraisal of Munich's effect on American public opinion was accurate enough. Indeed, Britain's (and, to a lesser degree, France's) loss of moral prestige in America was a development with far-reaching consequences. As John Wheeler-Bennett argued,

France and Britain lost more friends in America, and the forces of Isolationism gained more recruits, by reason of the Munich Agreement than by almost any other event in the years between the wars. Though there was no great body of American opinion which would have favored intervention on the side of Britain had she gone to war in 1938, the fact remains that the hands of those who bitterly opposed the granting of American aid in 1939–41 were substantially strengthened by the suspicion and mistrust of British policy which was engendered by her surrender at Munich.

Of more immediate relevance to the "Miracle of Munich" debate is the development of public opinion in Britain and France between September 1938 and the outbreak of war. Chamberlain and his defenders insisted that the French and British people were unwilling to fight Germany in 1938 but solidly prepared to do so in 1939. Indeed, we have seen that pro-appeasement sentiment ran strong through much of the thirties, but also that in the wake of the Godesberg meeting a swing toward a tougher line became perceptible. This swing was also evident in the British Dominions, which traditionally had pushed appeasement even more wholeheartedly than London. Much of the public in the West, if not the leaders, seemed to be getting tired of swallowing Hitler's toads. Though few people would have welcomed war, the majority probably could have been made to understand its necessity. The western European public's celebration of the Munich agreement does not disprove this contention. The euphoria over Munich stemmed not just from an understandable relief at having escaped war but also from the mistaken belief that Chamberlain and Daladier really had brought "peace with honor." When the terms of the settlement became known, disillusionment replaced satisfaction in many quarters. In some circles this disillusionment increased over the next eleven months. After all, if appeasement had previously been "justified" because Germany was too strong, that nation was now stronger than ever; this was the vicious circle within which the logic of appeasement tragically operated. Moreover, those who had always believed in appeasement at any price retained that belief in 1939: they were no more prepared to die for "a bunch of Polacks" than for "those blasted Czechs." And now the Nazi-Soviet pact induced many French and some British Communists to declare their neutrality in an "imperialist" conflict. They joined the far Right in spreading defeatist sentiment at the outbreak of war. Finally, it should be observed that even if public opinion had been opposed to dying for Danzig or Prague, the duty of a political leader was not simply to kowtow before such sentiment but to enlighten the public on what was really at stake. In Chamberlain's case, however, one suspects that the prime minister simply used "the great oracle" (public opinion) to reinforce what his inner voices had already persuaded him to do.

Those who claim that the eleven months separating the Munich conference from the onset of war provided the West with a crucial "breathing space" stake this claim largely on Britain's and France's ability to repair grievous military deficiencies by the time war broke out. No doubt the Western powers did make some significant progress. Focusing on defensive air power, Britain added over twenty fighter squadrons equipped with modern Spitfire and Hurricane aircraft, the famous "crates" of the Battle of Britain. The British government also funded the construction of millions of "Anderson" air-raid shelters in city dwellers' backyards. On land Britain was able in 1939 to equip five divisions, whereas in October 1938 it could have fielded only two. It doubled the size of its territorial army and, in the wake of the Prague occupation, finally introduced conscription. The British fleet added a new destroyer flotilla. As for France, it focused mainly on pushing the British to rearm, but it did manage to augment its armor units by about one thousand light tanks and to strengthen its air force.

Important as these advances were, they by no means overcame some of the West's most pressing deficiencies, and the progress that was made could have been much more significant. In the first months after Munich, Chamberlain, still convinced Hitler did not want war (or that if he did, Mussolini could be trusted to hold him back), did his best to slow the pace of rearmament. He was instrumental in holding down bomber development and in curtailing funds for the land army. After the invasion of Prague he gave in to pressures for faster rearmament, but Simon's treasury did not: it fought most increases, still arguing that long-term financial strength was more important than guns and bombs. The result was that Britain was considerably less prepared for war in 1939 than it might have been: its land army was still relatively anemic, its fleet lacked a substantial submarine arm, and its air force had no strategic capacity.

France's "progress" was even more dubious. It did not repair glaring deficiencies in heavy armor or antiaircraft. Its army did not expand significantly in size. Most important, France did nothing to reform its antiquated and top-heavy officer corps—a military leadership determined to fight the next war according to the defensive tactics used at Verdun. This, more than any other military factor, would propel France to her "strange defeat" in the spring of 1940.

The crucial point, however, is that while the West may have made some military gains after Munich, Germany made a great many more. In the year before the war, Germany devoted 35 percent of its industrial production to armaments, compared with 7 percent for Britain and under 5 percent for France. By 1939 the Reich had two new heavy cruisers (the *Scharnhorst* and the *Gneisenau*), two additional pocket battle cruisers, five more light cruisers, and a total of twenty-six submarines ready for service in the Atlantic. Germany's standing army had not grown substantially, but its striking power was vastly enhanced by a doubling of its mobile armor force, the core of its blitzkrieg capacity. Germany's previous weaknesses in reserve forces were remedied by calling up twenty-nine divisions of combat-age men and twenty-two of older Landwehr (territorial) soldiers. This meant that Germany in 1939 had about as many divisions as France and that it could put twelve regular, ten reserve, and fifteen Landwehr divisions on the western front. The Luftwaffe had not greatly expanded, but its performance potential was much improved through the replacement of older planes with modern Messerschmitts, Stukas, and Heinkels. Moreover, in the spring of 1939 the seasoned Condor Legion returned from Spain, its pilots prepared to do to Polish (and, later, western European) cities what they had done to Guernica.

Taken together, these developments meant that the West was in a worse position to fight Germany in September 1939 than it had been in October 1938. In the famous "breathing space" Germany had breathed deeper. It was to use its enhanced resources to overrun first Poland and then most of western Europe between late 1939 and early 1940. In military terms, the historian Paul Kennedy has offered the appropriate epitaph for Chamberlain's "Miracle of Munich": "Whether or not the postponement of war for a year saved Britain, there is a strong case for arguing that it lost Europe."

There were "honorable" reasons for this tragedy. Chamberlain genuinely believed that his policy of appeasement was necessary to save Europe from a new cataclysm even worse than the one it had just suffered. But he believed so strongly in his own ability to avert this catastrophe that he refused to listen to criticism or to reexamine his assumptions when they were contradicted by painful experience.

His conviction that God guided his footsteps no doubt hardened his resolve to keep to the hazardous path he had chosen. But this path was not just hazardous; it was nearly fatal. Instead of quoting Hotspur on the morn of Munich, Chamberlain would have been better advised to remember Anthony's warning: "These quicksands . . . keep off them, for you sink."

Epilogue

On September 1, 1939, Germany invaded Poland, plunging Europe into its second major war in twenty-five years. This moment, wrote W. H. Auden, brought to an end the "clever hopes . . . of a low dishonest decade." But though some of the era's hopes for a "return to normalcy," domestic tranquillity, and international peace through appeasement died with the outbreak of war, others, such as territorial aggrandizement, racial "cleansing," economic pillage, and military glory, found in that new cataclysm their full realization, if only temporarily. Moreover, the sociopolitical problems and pressures that culminated in World War II did not simply vanish in 1945. Just as many of the troubles of the "dishonest decade" had their origins in the era before World War I, so most also left important legacies for the era after World War II.

* * *

As it prepared for a possible military confrontation with Germany in 1939, the Daladier government in Paris passed a series of anti-Semitic and antiforeign laws that recalled France's racist and xenophobic response to the Stavisky affair in 1934. Aliens, especially Jewish refugees fleeing from Nazi Germany, were considered by the government, and by much of the public, a threat to French security in this time of national peril. An immigration adviser to the government (and later to Vichy and to General de Gaulle) wrote that "physically inferior or ethnically heterogeneous elements might bastardize the race and introduce into it germs of diseases that it had managed to diminish." He found "no less pernicious . . . the moral delinquency of certain Levantine, Armenian, Greek, Jewish, and other *métèque* [alien] speculators." Jean Giraudoux, the famous dramatist and head of Daladier's newly created Commissariat of Public Information, complained that France was being inundated by waves of foreign "barbarians," particularly by "the bizarre and avid cohort of central and eastern Europe." To stem this threat to the "French artisan spirit of precision, trust, perfection," he advocated a new racial policy that would exclude all Jewish immigrants save "true Europeans"—like Freud. "We agree entirely with Hitler to proclaim that a policy reaches its highest form only if it is racial, for that was also the thought of Colbert or of Richelieu," declared Giraudoux.

The Vichy government, which was established in unoccupied southern France following that nation's humiliating defeat by the Germans in 1940, fulfilled Giraudoux's demand for a French racial policy of which Hitler might have been proud. In need of scapegoats for France's precipitous collapse, the Vichy leaders Philippe Pétain and Pierre Laval, who had first served together in the post-Stavisky government of Doumergue in 1934, established concentration camps for the internment of non-French citizens and "undesirable elements," including Jewish refugees. At first most native Jews were spared this fate, but new anti-Semitic legislation made all Jews subject to arrest and internment. In 1941 Vichy's first commissioner general for Jewish affairs, Xavier Vallat, helped the Germans in the unoccupied zone to strip Jews of their property in advance of their internment or deportation. Vallat, in fact, managed to outdo the Nazis by defining as "Jewish" certain ethnic groups, like the Karaite Russians, which the Germans did not place in this category. No less assiduous was Vallat's successor as commissioner general, Louis Darquier, who had begun his political career in the rightist riots of February 1934 and then gone on to found an anti-Semitic newspaper with German funds. Under Darquier the Vichy regime began (in 1942) to turn over foreign, and eventually French, Jews to the Nazis for deportation to the death camps in the east. By 1944 some 75,000 Jews had been sent from France to the eastern killing centers. About one-third of these were French Jews, and a little over 2,000 were children under six. A German official responsible for the Reich's "final solution" in France could say with justice, "We found no difficulty with the Vichy government in implementing Jewish policy."

The Action Française, which had whipped up racial hatred during the Stavisky affair, quite naturally felt at home in the Vichy era. Both Vallat and Darquier were members of the group. Its paper praised Vallat's *Statut des Juifs*, though it believed it should have been more draconian in excluding Jews from all aspects of French life.

Of course, there had always been some Frenchmen who opposed such racist bestiality, just as there were some Frenchmen who opposed collaboration with the Germans from the outset. As the war began to turn against the Germans, this latter group, if not necessarily the former, expanded substantially. The vaunted French resistance movement now became a force to be reckoned with, though it was never as "crucial" to the German expulsion from France as many Frenchmen liked to maintain. But the resistance was directed not just against the German occupiers but against the French collaborators as well. Indeed, the wartime resistance campaign should be seen as another episode in France's long-term "civil war," of which the Dreyfus and Stavisky affairs were both significant chapters. When Charles Maurras, leader of the Action Française, was condemned for treason in 1945, he said the verdict was "the revenge of Dreyfus." He might also have said it was the revenge of Stavisky.

Conservative Frenchmen's embrace of Vichy, like their reaction to the Stavisky affair six years before, was animated partly by a nostalgic longing for an allegedly simpler, purer, more harmonious past. Vichy promised a return to the soil, to the church, to large families and small businesses. In the end, however, Vichy turned out to have a strong "technocratic" side that triumphed over these traditionalist aspirations. And it was the Vichy modernizers, more than the Vichy traditionalists, who survived the liberation in 1944 to play an important role in France's postwar reconstruction.

The old hostilities, prejudices, and fears, however, lived on behind the streamlined facade of the "new France." Sometimes they came to the fore in outbursts of regressive protest. A notable example of this was the mid-1950s crusade of the demagogical shopkeeper Pierre Poujade, who, echoing the rightist leagues of the 1930s, denounced the ruling government as an "alien" cabal out to destroy traditional French values and institutions. More recently these themes were sounded by the National Front leader Jean-Marie Le Pen, a porcine demagogue whose impassioned tirades against "aliens" and immigrants recalled those of the Stavisky and the Vichy eras, except that Le Pen's primary targets were North Africans rather than eastern European Jews.

Though Le Pen's politics may have had a certain déjà vu quality for those Frenchmen who could recall the thirties and, more specifically, the Stavisky affair, for the vast majority of people that troubled era was increasingly "recalled" not through lived experience but through historical studies, literature, and film. In the early 1970s Alain Resnais made a film based on the Stavisky scandal that played to packed houses throughout France. This movie, starring Jean-Paul Belmondo as the Beau Sasha, glamorized Stavisky as a lovable rogue and played down his fundamental seediness. It also revealed little of the racism and antidemocratic sentiments that the case brought to the fore. This was unfortunate, because those tendencies in French political life hardly disappeared with the victory over fascism in 1944.

* * *

No feature film has been made about the Austrian civil war of February 1934, but this event, like the Stavisky affair for modern France, had important implications for the Austrian Second Republic, which emerged from the wreckage of Hitler's Greater German Reich in 1945. Austrians were well aware that internal divisions and a lack of consensus regarding the identity of the Austrian nation had left their country ripe for Hitler's plucking in 1938. At that moment the majority of Austrians enthusiastically welcomed the *Anschluss*, but rigid controls from Berlin, followed by the pressures and ultimate devastation of war, led many Austrians to rethink their identification with Germany (though many more, it should be said, retained their faith in the führer to the end). From their prewar and wartime experiences Austrians tended to draw two fundamental lessons: in foreign affairs they must stress their independence as a sovereign Austrian—as opposed to a "German-Austrian"—nation; and in domestic politics they must overcome or reduce those chronic divisions that had invited Italian and German manipulation in the 1930s and that might bring Soviet manipulation after 1945.

It is not surprising, then, that in foreign policy Austria's Second Republic promised strict neutrality as a price for its independence in the postwar era. On the home front Austria established a governmental system characterized by coalition rather than confrontation. Its two major parties, the conservative People's party and the Socialist party, divided ministerial posts and the top offices of chancellor and of president, so that when the chancellor was "Black," the president was usually "Red," and vice versa. This so-called proportional system extended to the federal bureaucracy, where some functions were actually shared by representatives from both parties (and, it was said, often by a third person, who did the work). The old dichotomy between Vienna and the western provinces lost some of its potency as the capital became less "Red," the provinces less "Black." The People's party increasingly courted better-off workers, while the Socialist party, like its counterpart in West Germany, assumed a "new look": efficient, technocratic, no longer at war with the church or tied exclusively to labor interests. In 1970 the Socialists won the chancellorship (the most influential office) with a candidate, Bruno Kreisky, who seemed to embody the nation's as well as the Socialist party's transformation. Kreisky was a skillful manager who had spent the war years in Sweden—and he was a Jew.

In one important sense, however, Austria's maturation as a modern, cosmopolitan nation was incomplete and perhaps even deceptive. The proportional system that governed Austrian politics, it turned out, had its counterpart in a kind of complicity of silence regarding the recent past. Through an unspoken agreement designed to preserve harmony and avoid mutual embarrassment, the Left said little about the Right's embrace of Nazism and complicity in the Holocaust, while the Right said little about the Left's enthusiasm for an *Anschluss* before 1933 or about its predilection for stale Marxist theory and revolutionary posturing. The result was that most Austrians either avoided examining the past altogether or adopted the convenient position that their country had simply been a "victim" of forces beyond its control. Austrian Nazism, they insisted, was an import from Germany and Austria's own contribution to the Third Reich minimal.

In this obfuscation, it should be added, Austria had considerable help from abroad. As early as 1943 the Allies decided to consider Austria a "victim" of German aggression and to treat it as a "liberated" rather than a conquered nation. Austria was not considered to have been a wartime belligerent when the former

Allies ended the occupation period in 1955, and a reference to Austrian "respon-sibility" for participation in the war was deleted from Austria's "State Treaty" of that year. A decade or so later, Hollywood produced a highly popular film, *The Sound of Music,* which seemed only to confirm what Austrians had long managed to make most of the world believe: that Beethoven was an Austrian and Hitler a German.

The Waldheim affair of the mid-1980s revised the image of Austria for many foreigners. Kurt Waldheim's successful bid for the presidency despite—indeed, perhaps partly because of—the international outcry over his previously hidden wartime past as a Wehrmacht officer in the Balkans, made many wonder whether the "new Austria" was precisely what the Austrians had said it was. Suddenly it seemed apparent not only that this tiny nation had some large skeletons in its closet but also that the skeletons still had some pretty pungent flesh on them. While some Austrians now called for a more open and thoroughgoing reckoning with their recent past, many more seemed determined to lock those closet doors and hold their noses against the stink. Yet perhaps one can still hope that the Waldheim affair will become what one Austrian historian pleaded it must: namely, "an Austrian Dreyfus affair leading to opposite results—to a political-intellectual clarification of the past and a victory of forward-looking democracy over the forces of restoration."

* * *

Just as many Austrians during the war developed second thoughts about following their führer to the bitter end, some Germans, especially in the Wehr-macht officer corps, did so as well. In the summer of 1944, when it became clear that Hitler was leading the nation to ruin, a group of conspirators, mainly military officers, tried unsuccessfully to kill him. Among their motives for this desperate act was the hope that it might help restore the army's "honor," which had been besmirched in the Blood Purge of 1934, then in the Fritsch and the Blomberg affairs, and finally through the military's complicity in Nazi crimes during the war. Even had the conspirators been successful, however, they could not thereby have washed away the sins of 1934, not to mention the countless atrocities that followed. In any event, the vast majority of officers did not participate in the anti-Hitler resistance; instead, they prided themselves on "doing their duty" re-gardless of the consequences. The Wehrmacht leadership, for its part, willingly provided the "honor court" that stripped the anti-Hitler conspirators of their rank before they were shot or hanged from meat hooks in Berlin's Plötzensee prison.

The SS, it can safely be said, watched this bloodletting in the military with grim satisfaction. As we recall, this organization began its rise to prominence through its brutal role in the Blood Purge. In the late 1930s and during the war, it went on to become a veritable state within the state, replete with its own police and intelligence branches, vast economic enterprises, and a heavily armed mili-tary wing. Not surprisingly, many Wehrmacht officers who had initially welcomed the SS as their ally against the hated SA, now bitterly resented the Black-shirts' expansion and usurpation of army functions. For the military leadership the only silver lining in this black cloud was the opportunity to claim after the war that responsibility for Hitler's crimes lay not with the army but solely with the SS and the Nazi party.

The former generals' postwar parade of innocence was part of a larger German failure, particularly in the first decade or so after the war, adequately to confront the painful past (though Germany—at least West Germany—did this more conscientiously than Austria from the outset). Eventually, indeed, German historians, journalists, writers, and artists embarked on an extensive exploration of the Nazi era and the historical factors that had produced it. *Vergangenheitsbewäl-tigung* (reckoning with the past) belatedly became a growth industry.

Yet the very prevalence of these investigations (particularly in films and on television) began to generate complaints in some circles that Germany was wallowing obsessively in the slimy dreck of its Nazi past and that this self-abasement or *Nestbeschmutzung* (soiling the nest) was thwarting a necessary recovery of national pride and assertiveness in world affairs. The late Franz Josef Strauss, former leader of Bavaria's Christian Social Union, told a German historians' conference in 1985 that Germany must develop the "power to forget," without which it "would be vulnerable to political extortion for generations to come."

Few historians agreed with this, but some tried to make the German past less burdensome by arguing that the Nazi crimes were neither unique nor self-inspired. Ernst Nolte, the most prominent of the revisionist historians, insisted that the Holocaust was a "copy" (except for the gassing technology) of Stalin's "liquidation of the bourgeoisie and the kulaks." He further argued that Hitler committed this "Asiatic act" in response to Stalin's original barbarism, which Hitler feared the Russians, with the help of the international Jewish community, would export to Germany. Nolte offered no concrete evidence for his bizarre assertions (in fact, there was none); he simply insisted that they demonstrated the need to place the Third Reich in proper historical context and to discontinue its "demonization."

Efforts like Nolte's to "relativize" the Nazi crimes, or like Strauss's to put them out of the national consciousness, generated considerable controversy in Germany* and much consternation abroad, especially among Germany's former victims. (Japan's recent efforts at apologetic historical revisionism had the same effect.) Yet there were also foreigners who agreed it was time to forget or forgive the sins of the past, especially since West Germany was such a loyal and valuable partner in the Western alliance. President Ronald Reagan was an influential

---

*The controversy became so acrimonious and embarrassingly well publicized that President Richard von Weizsäcker, regarded by many as chief custodian of the nation's moral conscience, sought to end it by declaring before the 1988 German Historical Conference, "Auschwitz remains unique. It was perpetrated by Germans in the name of Germany. The truth is immutable and will not be forgotten."

spokesman in this camp. In connection with the commemorations in May 1985 marking the fortieth anniversary of the end of World War II, he and West German Chancellor Helmut Kohl paid a now-infamous visit to the Bitburg military cemetery, where a number of *Waffen-SS* veterans are buried. The purpose of his gesture, Reagan said, was to help "put the past to rest." For the sake of the future, one can only hope that such efforts do not succeed.

* * *

Italy had an easier time with its Fascist legacy than Germany (or even Austria) because, though fascism was an Italian invention, Mussolini's regime had seemed increasingly "foreign" to the Italian people as it fell under heavy German influence in the late 1930s and during the Second World War. The duce, once "the most dangerous man in Europe," was more and more obliged to play a distant second fiddle to the führer, whose Nazi henchmen made no secret of their scorn for Italy's lack of Fascist zeal and martial vigor in the opening phases of the war. With the Allied invasion of Sicily in July 1943, the Fascist grand council itself rose up against Mussolini, whom it accused of selling out Italy to the Germans and opening it to destruction from the Allies. Soon the king and the military leadership took over the reins of government, arrested Mussolini, and made a separate peace with the Western powers, whose armies were steadily advancing up the Italian peninsula.

These momentous events prompted the Germans to occupy Rome and northern Italy, "liberate" the duce from Italian-military captivity, and install him on the shores of Lake Garda as their pathetic puppet. (Goebbels, reflecting the Nazi leadership's continued admiration for the duce but contempt for his people, now referred to Mussolini as "the last Roman," behind whose "massive figure a gypsy people had gone to rot.") When the Germans were forced to abandon Italy entirely in April 1945, Mussolini tried to leave with them, but Communist partisans intercepted the German column with which he was hiding (disguised, appropriately, as a German soldier). Along with his mistress, Clara Petacci, Mussolini was taken away, unceremoniously shot, then hanged upside down from the roof of an Esso station in Milan's Piazzale Loreto. The local citizens beat, spat on, and urinated on the duce's half-naked, bloated corpse. Ten years earlier, as he announced the conquest of Ethiopia, they had hailed him as Italy's new Caesar.

Four years before this inglorious end, Italy's short-lived rule in Addis Ababa had also collapsed. Mussolini's invasion of Ethiopia had estranged him from the West, so it was only appropriate that his dominion there was snuffed out largely by the British. Their war against Italy in Ethiopia had the support of Haile Selassie, whom they brought back to Africa to encourage native rebellions against the Italians.

Though grateful for this British support, Haile Selassie feared that Britain intended to liberate his country only to incorporate it into the British Empire and to keep him forever off his throne. Indeed, some British generals and politicians wanted to do just that, but Churchill, mindful of Haile Selassie's popularity in

England, insisted that he be allowed to return to Addis Ababa. The negus reentered his capital on May 5, 1941, five years to the day after the Italians had conquered the city. For the rest of the war, and for some time thereafter, Britain exerted considerable influence over Ethiopia, but Haile Selassie resisted outright control. His resistance was emblematic of the anticolonial "revolt against the West" that would gradually tear down the old European empires in Africa, and elsewhere around the world as well.

One of Haile Selassie's first steps in the postwar era was to enter Ethiopia in the United Nations. This move, too, was fraught with symbolism. As we recall, Haile Selassie had hoped for assistance from the League of Nations, the UN's predecessor, when Italy invaded his country in 1935. Now he put his trust in this new international organization, which was determined to avoid the mistakes of the League in the thirties. The UN charter provided for wider and less legalistic peacekeeping powers, including the option to intervene militarily in world crises. Though such intervention was subject to veto by any of the Security Council's five permanent members, this provision represented an improvement over the League covenant, which allowed any state to thwart substantive action by the League council.

The UN, of course, had its problems keeping the peace in a bipolar world whose two main antagonists were both permanent members of the Security Council. The UN General Assembly, for its part, increasingly gained the reputation in some circles as a tool of the Third World countries, which eventually constituted its majority. However, for many of these states, especially the newly independent black African states, the real problem was that their claims of "nonalignment" often masked extensive economic and military dependence on first or second world states. Ethiopia was a case in point. In the late forties it managed to stave off British control only to become an economic client of the United States, which also sent Ethiopia military aid to fight a war with its old enemy Somaliland, now a Russian client. But in 1974 a leftist military coup overthrew Haile Selassie and moved Ethiopia into the Russian camp. The United States immediately switched its support to Somaliland, and Ethiopia, increasingly cut off from the West, lapsed into chronic misadministration, civil war, and famine. In its brutal campaign to stamp out a rebellion in Eritrea, the Ethiopian government began bombing undefended villages—a grim emulation of Italian tactics fifty years before.

Italy, of course, has experienced a much less tortuous history since the fall of fascism. Its economic growth rate between the late forties and early sixties was so robust that people spoke of an "Italian miracle." Freedom from the burdens of empire and absurd Fascist economic policies clearly helped spur this growth. On the political front, Italy suffered from extensive corruption and "revolving-door" government, as one cabinet followed another in bewildering succession. These problems, however, were nothing new; they had characterized the Italian scene from unification to Mussolini's March on Rome.

The legacy of fascism found some ardent champions in postwar Italy despite the horrors and humiliations visited upon that nation during the duce's rule. Chief keeper of the flame was the MSI (Movimento Sociale Italiano), a neo-Fascist political party with about two million members in the sixties and seventies. Led by one Giorgio Almirante, an aging veteran of the Ethiopian war, and supported by Vittorio Mussolini, the duce's youngest son and a former bomber pilot in Ethiopia, the MSI spouted all the old imperialistic, militaristic, and macho slogans—without, however, gaining more than minimal influence. It was Italy's fourth-largest party, but, like the larger Communist party, it never formed part of a national governing coalition.

More threatening was the bloody campaign of the "Black Brigades," neo-Fascist terror groups with connections to the police and army. In 1969 a neo-Fascist group inaugurated postwar Italy's terrorist troubles by bombing the Piazza Fontana in Milan. Claiming that fascism was again on the rise, leftist extremists belonging to the "Red Brigades" responded with terror attacks of their own. Yet these attacks and counterattacks, which peaked with the Red Brigades' murder of Premier Aldo Moro in 1978 and the Black Brigades' bombing of the Bologna train station in 1980, did not prompt the Italian government to abandon constitutional rule or to return to the mailed fist of the twenties and thirties. Italy, it seemed, had learned something from its experiment in "total" government.

* * *

Italy's principal antagonist in World War II, Great Britain, emerged from the war as convinced as ever of its great-power status. And in some important respects Britain was a great power. In 1945 it had the largest European economy, a huge navy, and colonies and military garrisons around the world. But having just pushed Mussolini out of the imperial sun, Britain soon saw the sun finally set on its own, vast empire. Politically the country remained stable enough, but as it ceased to rule the waves it seemed to drift helplessly in the currents of world politics. The Suez crisis of 1956 showed that Britain could no longer act as it chose in its old Third World domain if the United States disapproved. In 1962 the former U.S. secretary of state Dean Acheson, an Anglophile, noted sadly, "Britain has lost an empire and not found a role."

Significant as this imperial eclipse was for postwar Britain's political psyche, that nation's decline as a great power over the next half century was rooted more in its economic failings than in its loss of colonies, which had become an expensive burden. Like that in World War I, victory in World War II militated against fundamental reforms of Britain's antiquated industrial infrastructure. Just as in the twenties and thirties, economic development in the industrial north languished even while the country as a whole enjoyed respectable growth. (Britain's growth rates, however, were significantly lower than West Germany's or Italy's.) And finally, just as in the thirties, shipbuilding stood out as one of the weakest branches of the British economy.

When the Second World War ended, much of the Tyneside's revived shipbuilding activity ended with it. The northeast quickly fell into a new slump, if this term can be used for a virtually permanent condition since the war. And Jarrow, that economic black hole of the thirties, again became the symbolic center of northeast Britain's new bad-old-times. During the fifties and sixties it led the country in unemployment. In 1980, forty-four years after the crusade, Jarrow's unemployment rate was still roughly twice the national average. In that year its employment office listed four openings for the four hundred high school graduates seeking work. Half a dozen old men who had marched in 1936 were still hanging around the street corners and the town's main pub, now fittingly rechristened the Jarrow Crusader. They were joined in their aimlessness by sons and grandsons who had never worked at all. When asked to comment on the crusade's legacy, one grizzled veteran said that the episode had subsequently split the participants: about half thought it had been a good thing; the other half was not so sure. A visiting reporter from the *Manchester Guardian,* looking around the town, had no doubts about the march's long-term meaning: "[The crusaders'] protest," he wrote in 1980, "freeze-framed the depression of a decade which seems set to re-run for their grandchildren."

Two years later the American novelist and travel writer Paul Theroux visited Jarrow in the course of his own rerun of Priestley's trip around England in 1933. The town, he reported, "had the poisoned and dispirited look of a place that had just lost a war. . . . It was like a sight of China—black factories and narrow, necessary gardens, and a kind of visible hopelessness. It was one of the dreariest landscapes I had ever seen."

But there was life and fight left in Jarrow after all. Four years after Theroux's visit, and fifty years after the 1936 crusade, the town decided to stage a reenactment of the great march. This reenactment would not only recall Jarrow's most famous moment but also show the world that conditions had not gotten much better there since the original march. Accordingly, some thirty people set out from Jarrow for London in October 1986, carrying the same banners and oak petition box that their fathers and grandfathers had carried in 1936. In a sad echo of that earlier occasion, one young participant said that their purpose was "to draw attention to the national plight of those out of work, their feeling of hopelessness and rejection by the rest of society." In fact, the marchers were well received along the way, just as their predecessors had been. But there were also significant differences. This march was paid for by the Labour party, which saw it as good electoral ammunition against Margaret Thatcher's Conservatives. There were women along this time, as well as three punks with purple hair and dead-rat necklaces—signs of the times. The march generated a good deal of publicity and attracted predictable appearances from Labour party politicians as diverse as Tony Benn and Neil Kinnock. But—just as predictably—Margaret Thatcher, like Stanley Baldwin fifty years before, refused to receive this delegation from the impoverished north.

* * *

Less than a year after Jarrow reenacted its famous crusade, the town of Guernica also staged a symbolic act. On April 26, 1987, a small biplane dipped low over the town's central square and dropped hundreds of flowers to the throngs below. No happy outburst of spring fever, this gesture was meant to commemorate a more lethal bombing fifty years earlier. It was also a lament for the fate of the Basque country in the Spanish civil war and during the nearly half a century since Franco's victory.

The brutal destruction of Guernica in 1937 served for a time to strengthen the Basques' defensive resolve, just as terror bombings in World War II would often harden the survivors' will to fight on. But the Spanish Nationalists and their Fascist allies' superiority in firepower slowly pushed the Basques back into their "Ring of Iron" around Bilbao. After weeks of systematic bombing, Bilbao fell on June 19, 1937. The victorious Nationalists immediately set about crushing Basque separatism. Schoolteachers were fired unless they could prove they had no connections to the separatist movement. El Arbol in Guernica was closed off from public view.

The Nationalists' final victory in March 1939 inaugurated thirty-six years of rule by General Franco. Shortly after assuming dictatorial power, Franco concluded that his *limpieza* in the Basque country should be combined with efforts to win the Basques over to his new regime. He thus officially "adopted" Guernica and ordered that a high priority be placed on its reconstruction. Ironically, the rebuilding was completed in the pretentious, heavy style favored by Hitler and Mussolini.

At the same time, Franco's censors prohibited any published mention of Guernica's destruction by Nationalist planes. The official version continued to insist on Red arson and dynamiting. In this respect, the Guernica story bore a striking similarity to the manner in which Franco's publicists "explained" Lorca's death in August 1936. The poet had not been killed by the Falangist militia, they said, but by "Red extremists." (Later they amended this to "unknown assassins," and still later they claimed he was killed by a jealous homosexual lover.)

By the middle to late 1960s the official line on Guernica had begun to change. Franco's government was increasingly aware that its interpretation was undermining its efforts to mend fences with the Basque community. Hardly a week passed when there was not a terrorist bombing or shooting carried out by the ETA (Euzkadi ta Askatasuna—Basque Homeland and Freedom), the Basque separatist organization. Thus the government gradually ceased emphasizing the arson theory and began placing all blame for the destruction of Guernica on the Germans. The regime's official historian of the civil war, Ricardo La Cierva, stated in an interview in 1970 that Guernica was bombed by a "special [Luftwaffe] testing group which came directly from Germany, destroyed Guernica and went back to Germany, without our knowing anything about it." A month later La Cierva retracted this nonsense about a "special testing group" and stated that the Condor Legion had done the bombing, but without any Spaniard's prior knowledge or agreement.

In the middle of the same year the respected journalist Vincente Talón published *Arde Guernica* (Guernica burns). Talón was not an official historian, but since his book passed Franco's censors, we can assume it was at least acceptable to the government. Talón's extensive study certainly discredited the arson theory, for it marshaled a great deal of evidence to show that Guernica was destroyed by Condor Legion planes. At the same time, however, Talón insisted that Franco and Mola knew nothing of the raid and in fact were shocked by its outcome. He quoted Franco as saying some time later, "Guernica! Even now I cannot explain how that could have happened." Talón, however, could explain it: the Germans were a beastly lot, and it was Spain's tragedy to have called on their assistance in the first place.

The Germans have made convincing and useful whipping boys in many contexts, but Spanish efforts to put the entire onus of Guernica on their shoulders, thereby exonerating the Nationalist command and perhaps helping improve relations between Madrid and the Basques, did not make the Guernica legacy any less troubling for modern Spain. Basque separatists continued, even after Franco's death in 1975, to interpret the Guernica bombing as proof of Spain's enduring hostility toward the Basque people and their ancient liberties. As that biplane dropped flowers over Guernica to mark the fiftieth anniversary of the bombing, one hundred demonstrators in the square below demanded amnesty for convicted ETA terrorists. Today young Basques make regular pilgrimages once again to the dead husk of El Arbol, which stands next to two smaller oaks, said to be the old tree's son and grandson. It appears that the Guernica legacy, with all its agonizing implications for modern Spain, will live on for some time to come.

* * *

Problematical as the Guernica legacy has been for modern Spain, it did not significantly harm Franco's cause or jeopardize the survival of his dictatorial regime. The same cannot be said of Stalin's purges, which threatened Russia's very existence as an independent state when Hitler elected to violate the Nazi-Soviet nonaggression pact and attack the USSR in June 1941. The Russian defenders—ill-prepared, poorly equipped, and under inexperienced leadership—surrendered by the thousands. As the German troops penetrated ever deeper into western Russia, they were often greeted as liberators rather than as conquerors. Ukrainian and Belorussian village streets were lined with peasants shouting and waving gleefully. When German planes shot down Soviet aircraft, the villagers cried, "Soon Stalin will be kaput!" Such sentiments were a legacy of Stalin's brutal collectivization policies and his assault on "bourgeois nationalism" during the purges. His purges not only had failed to eliminate a "fifth column" but had evidently helped create one.

Russia might well have disintegrated entirely under the German onslaught had not the invaders alienated the populace through their own barbarous inhumanity—Hitler reportedly described Russia as "our Africa" and the Russians as "our Negroes"—and had Stalin not suddenly reversed the misguided policies that had made his regime so vulnerable to German penetration. Advocates of partisan warfare who had earlier been purged were now authorized to gather volunteers, and partisan bands soon began wreaking havoc on the overextended German supply lines. Politically discredited officers were brought back from the Gulag and given new commands, while some of Stalin's inept cronies were removed from the field. Most important, Stalin's regime exploited age-old nationalistic sentiments by restoring imperial insignia and symbols, invoking the authority of the church, commissioning patriotic films and music—in short, rediscovering Mother Russia and rallying the people to her defense.

During the eight years between the end of the war and Stalin's death, the Soviet people had no opportunity to dwell critically on the prewar sins of their chief. The hot war segued quickly into the cold war, with its demands for renewed vigilance and political purity. During the war, the Communist party had expanded and become somewhat lax in its internal discipline; now it was again purged of suspect or apathetic members. In agriculture new stress was placed on collectivization. These policies did not lead to mass arrests, deportations, and killings, as they had in the thirties, but they showed clearly enough that the chief was not about to loosen his controls over the Russian people just because they had performed heroically in the war. Nor was he about to permit any reassessments of prewar repressions that might have challenged their necessity. At the Nineteenth Party Congress, in November 1952, Georgi Malenkov, Stalin's new right-hand man, insisted that if the purges had not taken place, "we would have found ourselves in time of war in the position of people under fire from front and back, and we would have lost the war."

Not long after the Nineteenth Party Congress, a new "plot," reminiscent of the "medical murders" trumpeted during the "bloc of Rights" trial, shook the Soviet Union. On January 13, 1953, *Pravda* announced that the agencies of state security had recently exposed a "terrorist group of doctors who had made it their aim to cut short the lives of active public figures of the Soviet Union through wrecking methods of medical treatment." The doctors were said to belong to two conspiratorial groups: one an international Zionist organization sponsored by the CIA, and the other an arm of the British Secret Service. No doubt the episode reflected Stalin's now full-blown anti-Semitic paranoia, his genuine belief that an international Jewish conspiracy was bent on destroying his regime. Equally probable is that he believed his personal rule was threatened by his closest aides, who had noted his growing physical frailty and were already positioning themselves to succeed him.

Some historians have suggested that Stalin's ultimate aim in this affair was a new full-scale purge of the party leadership, another cleansing fire designed to sweep away all those close enough to the dictator to know his weaknesses. But if this was Stalin's intention, he did not get the chance to realize it: on the night of March 1–2 he was felled by a massive stroke, and three days later he was dead. Within a month of his death Stalin's successors proclaimed the doctors' plot to be a hoax cooked up by a deputy minister of state security.

Three years after Stalin's death the new premier, Nikita Khrushchev, launched a biting attack on the former dictator in his famous "secret speech" at the Twentieth Party Congress, in 1956. Yet while Khrushchev faulted Stalin for all sorts of excesses, he did not condemn the show trial system per se or seek to rehabilitate its chief victims. One of the reasons for his reticence was that he himself had profited from the purges and applauded their results in the thirties.

During the Khrushchev era the military victims of Stalin's purges were rehabilitated, along with a few minor party officials. But Khrushchev's attack on the Stalinist legacy aroused opposition among influential party circles. In the wake of his 1956 speech old Stalinists like Voroshilov condemned him for undermining the "prestige" of the party and the country. He was accused of fostering a "negative attitude toward authority" and "spitting on the nation's history."

Leonid Brezhnev, Khrushchev's successor, undertook a partial rehabilitation of Stalin, who was hailed as a heroic and wise leader despite some "mistakes." Soviet publications even defended the purges of the thirties as a necessary "struggle against destructive and nihilistic elements." Brezhnev's successors, Yuri Andropov and Konstantin Chernenko, both also heirs of Stalin, continued along these lines.

It remained for Mikhail Gorbachev to reopen the critical investigation of the Stalinist era that Khrushchev's successors had closed. In preparation for the seventieth anniversary of the Bolshevik Revolution, in November 1987, Soviet historians were given permission to explore certain forbidden corners of the Stalinist past. At a historical conference in October 1987, several Soviet scholars attacked the purges. One of them, Yuri Polyakov, declared that most of the purge victims were innocent. Yuri Afanasyev, head of the Moscow Institute of Historical Archives, said that the purges were not simply an aberration but reflected systematic weaknesses of Stalin's regime—a point that Western historians had long been waiting for their Soviet colleagues to admit..

In his much-anticipated speech commemorating the revolution's seventieth anniversary, Gorbachev spoke of Stalin's "enormous and unforgivable crimes . . . for which our people paid a heavy price and which had grave consequences for the life of our society." At the same time, however, he said that "historical truth" required the recognition of Stalin's "incontestable contribution to the struggle for socialism, to the defense of its gains."

Tentative and cautious as it was, Gorbachev's speech was interpreted by some of his countrymen as an invitation to denounce the departed dictator and his accomplices in much clearer terms. A spate of new films, plays, and novels spoke openly of Stalin's reign of terror and his paranoid mentality. "Everyone is sick of silence," declares the narrator of the anti-Stalinist film *More Light.* "We are going to try to talk about the past with more honesty, more light." In January 1988 the semiofficial *Literaturnaya gazeta* shed a particularly unflattering light on Stalin's zealous public prosecutor, Vyshinsky. It branded him a "monster and a thug," alleging that in addition to hounding innocent men in the Moscow trials, he had also signed a warrant for Lenin's arrest as a German agent during the provisional-government period in 1917.

While Vyshinsky was being vilified, his principal victims were at last being officially rehabilitated. In February 1988 Bukharin and Rykov were cleared by the Soviet Supreme Court of the crimes for which they had been condemned in 1938. In June the court rescinded the guilty verdicts against Zinoviev, Kamenev, Pyatakov, and Radek. A month later, and exactly fifty years after he was executed, Bukharin's party membership was restored by the Politburo. One commentator suggested that it was as if the pope had reinstated Martin Luther in the Catholic church. (Actually, this analogy might have applied more accurately to a reinstatement of Trotsky, but this the Red pope did not attempt.) In addition to exonerating these central figures, Gorbachev's regime also rehabilitated over six hundred lesser victims of Stalin's purges. It even sponsored an exhibit on the injustices of the Stalin years and established a commission to look into the assassination of Kirov, the event that launched the first round of purges.

Gorbachev did not undertake his critique of the Stalinist legacy and his rehabilitation of its victims only to be truer to his nation's historical past. He hoped that a more critical confrontation with Stalin's closed, rigid, xenophobic system would expedite Russia's socioeconomic and political modernization. He identified with Bukharin's more flexible brand of socialism and with his belief in the need for cooperation with the West. In terms of future party politics, Gorbachev's rehabilitation of Stalin's victims suggested that the party leadership was "ready to accept open debate and not denounce Party members who have different ideas as heretics or enemies."

But it was precisely the connection between reappraising the past and moving forward in the future that turned some members of the Soviet establishment against Gorbachev's historical revisionism. Those who had made their careers in the Brezhnev era were reluctant to see Brezhnev's patron, Stalin, vilified as a betrayer of the Bolshevik Revolution. For such stalwarts of the old order, criticism of Stalin amounted to "playing into the hands of bourgeois historiography." The bold forays of the anti-Stalinist historians also generated a pro-Stalinist reaction from some of their colleagues. One antirevisionist insisted that Stalin was a true populist who did not let the bureaucratic managers lord it over the little people. "The popular reverence for Stalin," he said, "was genuine."

In some quarters it still exists. Every year on March 5, the anniversary of Stalin's death, thousands of vodka glasses are raised to the memory of "our great leader who made the motherland strong." In Georgia, truck drivers sport Stalin icons in the windows of their rigs. His birthplace in Gori, which has been turned into a small museum, stands as a shrine for the faithful.

Lingering reverence for Stalin, along with conservative resistance to Gorbachev's reforms, could endanger not only the new views of the past but also the new visions of the future. Although few expect a full-scale revival of Stalinist practices, caution is undoubtedly in order. As a Russian proverb has it, "A pessimist is an optimist with a sense of history."

* * *

Gorbachev and his supporters have often spoken of the lessons to be learned from Stalin's mistakes. Western historians, political commentators, and statesmen have often spoken of the lessons to be derived from the era of appeasement culminating in the Munich conference of 1938.

Writing ten years after Munich, the British historian Hugh Trevor-Roper suggested that the lesson we must all learn from this episode is that "an aggressor can never be appeased. Appeasement has never succeeded in history. . . . From the debris of [Chamberlain's] disaster we may extract some comfort only if we can be sure that Munich was the final end of appeasement." Twenty years after Munich another British historian, A. J. P. Taylor, asked, "Has the [Munich] story a moral? An obvious one: no deal with Hitler was ever possible. But he was a human phenomenon who occurs once in a thousand years. Appeasement was a sensible course, even though it was tried with the wrong man; and it remains the noblest word in the diplomatist's vocabulary."

Not in very many diplomatists' vocabulary! Since World War II, statesmen and diplomats have for the most part drawn the moral Trevor-Roper urged them to—they have derived from Munich a general principle of intransigence to be applied whenever an "aggressor" raises his ugly head. As early as 1948, Winston Churchill characterized the Soviet Union as analogous to Nazi Germany and warned against indulging Stalin in a "new Munich." In the same year President Harry Truman saw Soviet Russia's clampdown on Czechoslovakia as a repeat of Hitler's challenge to the West in 1938. "We are faced with exactly the same situation with which Britain and France were faced in 1938–9 with Hitler," he wrote his daughter. Anthony Eden, British prime minister during the Suez crisis of 1956, insisted that he had to pursue a hard line against the Egyptian strongman Gamal Nasser so that the dictator would not be "encouraged," as were Hitler and Mussolini at Munich. During the Korean conflict, Truman again saw analogies between Communist aggression there and Fascist expansionism in Manchuria, Ethiopia, Austria, and Czechoslovakia in the thirties. Truman's head of the Office for Far Eastern Affairs, Dean Rusk, was eager to show that America had learned the "lesson of Munich" by sending U.S. troops over the 38th parallel into North Korea. At the Geneva summit in 1955, Secretary of State John Foster Dulles worried that President Eisenhower would fall into the "Munich trap." He urged him not to give an inch to Khrushchev. Eisenhower apparently got the message, at least with respect to the symbolism of appeasement: though it was raining in Washington when he returned from Geneva, he refused to carry an umbrella. Avoiding umbrellas seemed to make good political sense: students at West Berlin's Free University sent John F. Kennedy one after the United States responded weakly to East Germany's construction of the Berlin Wall in 1961. Kennedy's successor, Lyndon Johnson, announced upon taking office that he would be "no Chamberlain umbrella man." He set out to prove this by escalating the American military engagement in Vietnam. His under secretary of state, George Ball (later a vocal opponent of the Vietnam War), justified this policy in 1965 by declaring,

> We have . . . come to realize from the experience of the [1930s] that aggression must be dealt with wherever it occurs and no matter what mask it might wear. . . . The central issue we face in South Vietnam . . . is whether a small state on the periphery of Communist power should be permitted to maintain its freedom.

In 1977 two prominent political commentators, Bayard Rustin and Carl Gershman, condemned America's failure to counter the Soviets in Angola as the clearest demonstration "since Munich [of] the impotence of the democratic world in the face of totalitarian aggression." Eight years later a former ambassador to the UN, Jeane Kirkpatrick, insisted that Munich—not Vietnam—was the "appropriate analogy" for understanding America's backing of the Nicaraguan contras. As recently as 1988, Senator Jesse Helms's Conservative Caucus campaigned against ratification of the Intermediate Nuclear Force (INF) agreement by running newspaper advertisements depicting Chamberlain, Hitler, Reagan, and Gorbachev together under un umbrella. "Appeasement is as unwise in 1988 as in 1938," said the caption.

Well before this latest travesty (all the more ironic since Munich was the responsibility of conservative politicians), some historians had begun asking whether a more useful lesson of Munich might be the need to avoid deriving ironclad rules of behavior from that event, or indeed from any historical event. According to one of Chamberlain's biographers, Larry Fuchser, the prime minister's main problem was that he had so thoroughly learned the alleged lessons of World War I that he was incapable of acting creatively or flexibly when the threat of war arose again. Santayana said that "those who do not remember the past are condemned to repeat its mistakes." But for Fuchser the "real 'lesson' of appeasement, if there is one, is that it is precisely those who most vividly remember the past who are condemned to repeat its mistakes." Another historian of Munich, Keith Robbins, applied this rule to Anthony Eden. Eden had learned the antiappeasement lesson of Munich so well that he precipitously applied military force in the Suez crisis, thereby alienating his most important ally, the United States. Robbins echoed Fuchser in concluding,

> Whatever contemporary practice, contemporary theory has erected "antiappeasement" into a general law of foreign policy. The stale legends of political polemic still serve as substitutes for serious thought. Yet the only great lesson of Munich, the most difficult to learn, is that there are no great lessons. Historians, useless in predicting the future, achieve something if they prevent others from doing so.

But are there really no lessons to be learned from history in general or from Munich in particular? Perhaps there are no "great lessons" in history, but there may well be some smaller ones. A few of these in the case of Munich were suggested by the eminent British diplomatic historian Sir Charles Webster in his Stevenson Memorial Lecture, at Chatham House (1960):

> [Munich] shows the folly of unilateralism and neutralism, the necessity of close co-operation between threatened States, the penalty of deserting faithful allies, the dangers of discussions at the highest level without careful preparation and adequate advice, and the special danger of negotiating under the threat of immediate war.

This having been said, however, sensible caution regarding the "use" of the Munich legacy—or any other historical legacy—seems definitely in order. The alleged great lessons of Munich have been used to discredit all sorts of bargains and compromises, intelligent or not. Munich has been turned into a rhetorical blunt instrument with which to pulverize political flexibility. Its primitive exploitation, indeed, illustrates the dangers of simplistic metaphorical and symbolic thinking, which is essentially nonrational and polemical. Is the situation in Nicaragua, for example, really illuminated by references to Munich? Does not this alleged analogy obscure the complexities of both cases? And if one has erred in the past, does one necessarily profit from taking the opposite action ever after? Must we behave like the proverbial cat that, having once sat on a hot oven, will never sit on an oven again, not even a cold one? To be more specific: most of us can agree that Chamberlain's policy in 1938 was misconceived, but can we afford simply to take the opposite tack in our present, nuclear era?

Notes ⟶

ATCT	*The Case of the Anti-Soviet Trotskyite Centre*
AZ	*Arbeiter Zeitung*
FRUS	*Foreign Relations of the United States*
MG	*Manchester Guardian*
NC	*Newcastle Chronicle*
NFP	*Neue freie Presse*
NYT	*New York Times*
SG	*Shields Gazette*
TZT	*The Case of the Trotskyite-Zinovievite Terrorist Centre*

CHAPTER 1
"Down with the Robbers!"

p. 24 *virtual French civil war:* Robert O. Paxton, *Vichy France: Old Guard and New Order* (New York, 1975), 243.

p. 24 *figure at 1,700,000: NYT,* Jan. 1, 1934.

p. 24 *"No deputies served here":* Quoted in Eugen Weber, *Action Française* (Stanford, 1962), 319.

p. 25 *"rotten in the Republic of France":* Alexander Werth, *France in Ferment* (Gloucester, Mass., 1968), 77.

p. 25 *"Another Republican Scandal": L'Action française,* Dec. 29, 1933.

p. 25 *"no justification":* J. E. C. Bodley, *France* (London, 1897), 2:273.

p. 26 *"perfect insignificance":* Quoted in Eugen Weber, *France: Fin de Siècle* (Cambridge, Mass., 1986), 113.

p. 26 *out of the way:* D. W. Brogan, *The Development of Modern France, 1870–1939* (New York, 1966), 1:279.

p. 26 *"before me":* Quoted in Theodore Zeldin, *France, 1848–1945: Politics and Anger* (Oxford, 1979–82), 219.

p. 26 *"righteousness or carelessness".* Ibid., 219–20.

p. 26 *"nothing about money":* Quoted in Alistaire Horne, *To Lose A Battle: France 1940* (Harmondsworth, Eng., 1979), 47.

p. 27 *"synonymous terms":* Simone de Beauvoir, *The Prime of Life* (Cleveland and New York, 1966), 45.

p. 27 *"business at first":* Ibid., 127.

p. 29 *"as French as croissants":* Weber, *France,* 130.

p. 29 *"he needs money":* Jean-Michael Charlier and Marcel Montarron, *Stavisky: Les Secrets du scandal* (Paris, 1974), 58. For other treatments of Stavisky's upbringing and early life of crime, see the French chamber's official inquiry into the Stavisky affair: Ernst Lafont, ed., *Rapport général, fait au nom de la commission d'enquête, chargée de rechercher toutes les responsabilités politiques et administratives encourues depuis l'origine des affaires Stavisky* (Paris, 1935), 40–144; Paul Lorenz, *Les Trois Vies de Stavisky* (Paris, 1974), 13–34; Rudolf Brock, *Stavisky: Der grösste Korruptions-Skandal Europas* (Berlin, 1934), 14–28.

p. 29   an *"illusionist"*: Lorenz, *Stavisky*, 8.

p. 29   *"blew over Paris"*: Charles Rearick, *Pleasures of the Belle Epoque: Entertainment and Festivity in Turn-of-the-Century France* (New Haven, 1985), 39, 61.

p. 30   *"mettre le prix"*: Lorenz, *Stavisky*, 16.

p. 30   *apt this was*: Lafont, *Rapport général*, 50–51; Charlier and Montarron, *Stavisky*, 65–66.

p. 31   *police files*: Charlier and Montarron, *Stavisky*, 71–72; Lafont, *Rapport général*, 51–56.

p. 31   *Sasha was bilked*: Charlier and Montarron, *Stavisky*, 103–5; Lafont, *Rapport général*, 96–112.

p. 33   *weak and ineffectual*: Joseph Kessel, *Stavisky: L'homme que j'ai connu* (Paris, 1934), 16.

p. 33   *"le grand financier international"*: Ibid., 102.

p. 36   *Arlette feared the worst*: Charlier and Montarron, *Stavisky*, 42.

p. 36   *a new identity*: Xavier Vallat, *Le Nez de Cléopâtre: Souvenirs d'un homme de droite, 1918–1945* (Paris, 1957), 111.

p. 37   *"see them dishonored"*: Charlier and Montarron, *Stavisky*, 42.

p. 37   *"a woman wouldn't understand"*: Lucette Almeras, *Ce que je sais . . . : Les Huit Derniers Jours de Stavisky* (Paris, 1934), 20–21.

p. 37   *"on the lam"*: Ibid., 113.

p. 38   *worth of bonds*: *Le Petit Parisien*, Jan. 3, 1934.

p. 38   *market his bonds*: Weber, *Action Française*, 321.

p. 39   *"be adversely affected"*: *Le Petit Parisien*, Jan. 4, 1934.

p. 39   *"chickens will grow teeth"*: *L'Action française*, Jan. 5, 1934.

p. 39   *The Bayonnaise has turned"*: Werth, *France in Ferment*, 30.

p. 39   *"Cher Ami"*: *Le Canard enchaîné*, Jan. 5, 1934. For a good account of the Paris press's orchestration of the Stavisky scandal, see Maurice Chavardès, *Une Campagne de presse: La Droite française et le 6 fevrier 1934* (Paris, 1970), 25–33.

p. 39   *"deal of explanation"*: *Times* (London), Jan. 9, 1934.

p. 39   *"in the usual way"*: *NYT*, Jan. 5, 1934.

p. 39   *"French Secret Service"*: Ibid., Jan. 6, 1934.

p. 39   *lay with his subordinates*: *Times* (London), Jan. 9, 1934.

p. 40   *"have taken him"*: *NYT*, Jan. 6, 1934.

p. 40   *"honesty and justice"*: Quoted in Weber, *Action Française*, 322.

p. 40   *"the rotten bastards"*: Almeras, *Ce que je sais*, 128.

p. 40   *"C'est la fin"*: Ibid., 178. For Stavisky's last days see also Charlier and Montarron, *Stavisky*, 137–82; and Lafont, *Rapport général*, 279–92.

p. 42   *"expedite matters"*: *Le Canard enchaîné*, Jan. 10, 1934.

p. 42   *"places were involved"*: Ilya Ehrenburg, *Memoirs, 1921–1941* (Cleveland, 1963), 251.

p. 43   *"suicide by persuasion"*: *Journal des debats*, Jan. 18, 1934.

p. 43   *"under lock and key"*: *Le Canard enchaîné*, Jan. 10, 1934.

p. 43   *make himself scarce*: Lorenz, *Stavisky*, 120.

p. 43   *rioting in years*: Weber, *Action Française*, 322; Chavardès, *Campagne*, 28–33.

p. 43   *troubled postwar era*: William Shirer, *The Collapse of the Third Republic* (New York, 1969), 199.

p. 44   *"get very far"*: Brogan, *Modern France*, 2:655.

p. 44   *corrupt politicians*: For a particularly biting attack against Chautemps by an old enemy, see André Tardieu, *Sur la pente* (Paris, 1935).

p. 44   *"attacks against [him]"*: Edouard Herriot, *Jadis* (Paris, 1948), 374.

p. 45   *"on leur cassera"*: Quoted in Weber, *Action Française*, 327.

p. 45   *"suffice to create a great mind"*: Pertinax (André Geraud), *The Grave Diggers of France* (Garden City, N.Y., 1944), 88.

p. 45   *something of a hothead*: On Frot's role see Geoffrey Warner, "The Stavisky Affair and the Riots of February 6th 1934," *History Today* 8 (June 1958): 380–81.

p. 46   "in the street": Ibid., 380; Weber, Action Française, 328–30.

p. 47   "Protestants, and Freemasons": For an "exposure" of the government's "Jewish-Masonic connections," see Vallat, "Nez de Cléopâtre," 118–19.

p. 47   Queen Marie Antoinette: NYT, Feb. 7, 1934. For my account of the riots I have relied mainly on Shirer, Collapse; Weber, Action Française; Chavardès, Campagne; Warner, "Stavisky Affair"; Serge Bernstein, Le 6 Février 1934 (Paris, 1975); René Rémond, "Explications du 6 Février," Politique: Revue internationale des doctrines et des institutions 2 (July–Dec. 1959): 218–30.

p. 49   "Ici il n'y a pas de Députés": Quoted in Werth, France in Ferment, 151.

p. 49   "lady from good society": Herriot, Jadis, 376–77.

p. 49   the republican system: Weygand's second in command, General Gamelin, suggests in his memoirs that his chief may have been involved in a "plot" against the government some six weeks before the February riots. But Gamelin was a bitter rival of Weygand's, and his charge should be judged accordingly. See Maurice Gamelin, Servir: Les Armées françaises de 1940 (Paris, 1946), 2:106. For a good argument against the "Fascist plot" theory, see Rémond, "Explications."

p. 50   royalists of the Action Française: On this see especially Raoul Girardet, "Notes sur l'esprit d'un fascisme français, 1934–1939," Revue française de science politique 5 (July–Sept. 1955): 529–46.

p. 50   mythology of the Third Republic: Max Beloff, "The Sixth of February," in James Joll, ed., The Decline of the Third Republic (London, 1959), 10–11.

p. 50   "the republican regime": Quoted in Shirer, Collapse, 220.

p. 51   "of the cabinet": Quoted ibid., 222.

p. 51   was necessary: Werth, France in Ferment, 169.

p. 52   "pas du sang Français": Quoted ibid., 180.

p. 52   "old men": Ibid., 186.

p. 53   "lease of death": Richard Cobb, A Second Identity: Essays on French History (London, 1969), 20.

p. 53   Conseiller Albert Prince: On the Prince affair see especially Werth, France in Ferment, 199–211; Charlier and Montarron, Stavisky, 232–80; Lorenz, Stavisky, 148–68; and Alfred Detrez, L'Affaire Prince: L'Etat secret demasqué (Paris, 1935). This last work, written by a friend of Prince's, insists that he was murdered by the Sûreté.

p. 54   "women agents": NYT, Feb. 22, 1934.

p. 54   political unrest in France: MG, Feb. 23, 26, 1934.

p. 54   "Send more cash": Quoted in Werth, France in Ferment, 203.

p. 54   conclusively like murder: Ibid., 206–11.

p. 55   even a national hero: L'Action française, Feb. 22, 1934.

p. 55   wake of the Prince affair: Werth, France in Ferment, 209.

p. 55   "have to have a murder": Quoted in Weber, Action Française, 349.

p. 55   republican leadership responsible: L'Action française, Feb. 22, 23, 1934; L'Humanité, Feb. 23, 1934.

p. 56   "suspect of major importance": Lafont, Rapport général, 287.

p. 56   Sûreté and the Parquet: Ibid., 271–88.

p. 56   "judgment of God": Werth, France in Ferment, 218–19.

p. 57   the British: Marc Bloch, Strange Defeat (New York, 1968), 25.

p. 57   by the Germans: Alexander Werth, The Twilight of France (New York, 1942), 365.

p. 57   "France against Herself": See the classic study by Herbert Luethy, France against Herself (New York, 1957).

Chapter 2
The Death of Red Vienna

p. 59   "routine—with cheers": George Clare, Last Waltz in Vienna (London, 1982), 128.

p. 60   "Vienna has fallen": Stephen Spender, World within World (New York, 1951), 199.

p. 60   *inflation figures:* Bruce F. Pauley, *Hitler and the Forgotten Nazis* (Chapel Hill, 1981), 6.

p. 61   *"caste and privilege":* G. E. R. Gedye, *Betrayal in Central Europe* (New York and London, 1939), 4.

p. 61   *"without a Communist revolution":* John Lehmann, *The Whispering Gallery* (London, 1955), 199.

p. 63   *revolutionary consensus:* Klemens von Klemperer, *Ignaz Seipel: Christian Statesman in a Time of Crisis* (Princeton, 1972), 74–124.

p. 63   *"mirror image":* Ibid., 231.

p. 64   *Heimwehren:* See David Clay Large, *The Politics of Law and Order: A History of the Bavarian Einwohnerwehr* (Philadelphia, 1980), 54–56; F. L. Carsten, *Fascist Movements in Austria* (London, 1977), 105–40.

p. 64   *Schutzbund:* See Ilona Duczynska, *Workers in Arms: The Austrian Schutzbund and the Civil War of 1934* (New York, 1978), 27–65; Karl Stadler, *Opfer verlorener Zeiten* (Vienna, 1974), 34–35; Rudolf Litschel, *1934—Das Jahr der Irrungen* (Linz, 1974), 42–45; Anson Rabinbach, *The Crisis of Austrian Socialism* (Chicago, 1983).

p. 64   *"terror and counter-terror":* NFP, July 6, 1927.

p. 65   *"has no Schutzbund, no Heimwehr":* Heinrich Drimmel, *Vom Justizpalastbrand zum Februaraufstand* (Vienna, 1986), 21.

p. 65   *confrontations in Burgenland:* Carsten, *Fascist Movements,* 110.

p. 65   *Schattendorf incident:* Gerhard Botz, *Gewalt in der Politik: Attentate, Zusammenstösse, Putschversuche, Unruhen in Österreich, 1918–1934* (Munich, 1976), 107–11; Charles A. Gulick, *Austria from Habsburg to Hitler* (Berkeley, 1948), 1:725–29.

p. 66   *Schattendorf trial:* Norbert Leser, *Zwischen Reformismus und Bolshevismus* (Vienna, 1968), 398–99; Douglas Alder, "Decision-Making amid Public Violence: The Vienna Riots, July 15, 1927," *Austrian History Yearbook,* 19–20, pt. 1 (1983–84): 242; Gulick, *Austria,* 1:730–31.

p. 66   *"all justice-loving people":* AZ, July 15, 1927.

p. 66   *"much excitement":* Ibid.

p. 67   *"justice of shame"; "murderers of workers"; "tough test":* NFP, July 15, 1927.

p. 67   *had hitherto lacked:* Gulick, *Austria,* 1:735–42.

p. 67   *"ran from the scene":* Heinz Roscher, *Die Februar Kämpfe in Floridsdorf* (Vienna, 1935), 9.

p. 68   *"raced around the square":* Ibid., 10.

p. 68   *burning of files:* NFP, July 18, 1927.

p. 68   *"smoke them out":* Botz, *Gewalt,* 149.

p. 69   *call for calm:* Roscher, *Februar Kämpfe,* 12; Gulick, *Austria,* 1:742.

p. 69   *"mass psychosis":* Quoted in Leser, *Zwischen Reformismus,* 406.

p. 69   *Seipel response:* Von Klemperer, *Seipel,* 265–68.

p. 69   *"tree by tree, house by house":* NFP, July 18, 1934.

p. 72   *"Greek temple":* Ibid., 4.

p. 72   *"heart of civilized Europe"; "Wozu":* Ibid., 4–5.

p. 72   *"bring about civil war":* Gulick, *Austria,* 1:747.

p. 72   *"economic weapons":* Ibid., 748.

p. 73   *destruction of Grundbücher:* NFP, July 18, 1934.

p. 73   *"when they return home":* Ibid.

p. 73   *"gains at jeopardy":* AZ, July 18, 1927,

p. 73   *"iron discipline":* Ibid.

p. 73   *conscious betrayal:* Roscher, *Februar Kämpfe,* 15.

p. 74   *"done their duty":* Gulick, *Austria,* 1:756.

p. 74   *"the wounded Republic":* Von Klemperer, *Seipel,* 266.

p. 74   *"Prelate without Mercy":* Ibid., 267.

p. 74   *"1934 inevitable":* Clare, *Last Waltz,* 100.

p. 74   *"four feet from the ground":* Lehmann, *Whispering Gallery,* 180.

p. 74   *Dollfuss's early "democratic" leanings and popularity:* Gordon Brook-Shepherd, *Dollfuss* (London, 1961), 83–84.

p. 75   *Dollfuss Bauer conflict:* Gedye, *Betrayal,* 53–54.

p. 75   *Dollfuss's first government:* Brook-Shepherd, *Dollfuss,* 87–90.

p. 76   *"my tin soldiers":* Ernst Rüdiger von Starhemberg, *Between Hitler and Mussolini* (London, 1942), 2.

p. 76   *"victory be ours":* Friedrich Scheu, *Der Weg ins Ungewisse: Österreichs Schicksalskurve, 1929–1938* (Vienna, 1972), 75.

p. 76   *"antiquated party system":* Starhemberg, *Between Hitler,* 86.

p. 76   *"tragedy of Dollfuss":* Gedye, *Betrayal,* 55.

p. 76   *"deep hatred for the Austrian state":* Adolf Hitler, *Mein Kampf* (Boston, 1943), 16.

p. 77   *Austrian Nazi party:* Pauley, *Hitler,* 36–51.

p. 77   *Mussolini's Austrian policy:* Denis Mack Smith, *Mussolini: A Biography* (New York, 1983), 182–83.

p. 78   *"full of homosexuals"; "fly-blown carrion":* Starhemberg, *Between Hitler,* 27, 73.

p. 79   *"Is he a Jew"; "left alone":* Ibid., 90, 93.

p. 79   *"understanding friend.":* Gulick, *Austria,* 2:1052.

p. 79   *the preceding decade:* Lajos Kerekes, *Abdämmerung einer Demokratie: Mussolini, Gömbös und die Heimwehr* (Vienna, 1966), 121–63.

p. 79   *"advantage for all":* Jens Peterson, "Das faschistische Italien und der 12. Februar 1934," *Der 12. Februar: Ursachen, Fakten, Folgen* (Vienna, 1984), 514.

p. 80   *"confusion and despair":* Mark Twain, *The Man Who Corrupted Hadleyburg and Other Stories* (London, 1901), 284.

p. 80   *"all our mistakes":* Stadler, *Opfer,* 24.

p. 81   *"weak bladder":* Gedye, *Betrayal,* 73.

p. 81   *"strong and courageous government":* Peterson, "Faschistische Italien," 514.

p. 81   *"speed and vigor":* Ibid., 515.

p. 81   *"would not return"; "Christian and German people":* *Wiener Zeitung,* May 16, 1933, quoted in Carsten, *Fascist Movements,* 231.

p. 81   *"strong, authoritarian leadership":* *Reichspost,* Sept. 12, 1933, quoted ibid., 231.

p. 82   *"speaker's dias":* Gedye, *Betrayal,* 80.

p. 82   *"mini-Nuremberg party rally":* Clare, *Last Waltz,* 126.

p. 82   *"reunions and patriotic rallies":* Ibid., 127.

p. 82   *"final reckoning with the Social Democrats":* Peterson, "Faschistische Italien," 517.

p. 82   *"clarify the situation":* Ibid., 518.

p. 82   *"into Hitler's jaws":* Ludwig Jedlicka, "Neue Forschungsergebnisse zum 12. Februar 1934," *Österreich in Geschichte und Literatur* 8, no. 2 (Feb. 1964): 70.

p. 83   *"clean sweep of it":* Gulick, *Austria,* 2:1270; Litschel, *Jahr der Irrungen,* 47.

p. 83   *"Austria from Marxism":* Starhemberg, *Between Hitler,* 123.

p. 83   *"shame and disgrace to them"; "postpone the undertaking":* Gulick, *Austria,* 2:1279.

p. 83   *"to the weapons":* Litschel, *Jahr der Irrungen,* 47.

p. 84   *hands in the air:* Ibid., 50.

p. 84   *other parts of the city; dismembered them:* Ibid., 50–60.

p. 85   *surrounding woods:* Ibid., 67–74.

p. 85   *escalation of the conflict:* Gulick, *Austria,* 2:1281–82.

p. 85   *municipal housing projects:* Ibid., 1283–84.

p. 86   *the desired result:* Ibid., 1283.

p. 86   *defenders had fled:* Ibid., 1284–85.

p. 86   *"twenty-four hours":* NFP, Feb. 15, 1934.

p. 86   *"humane" suppression of the uprising:* Brook-Shepherd, *Dollfuss,* 138.

p. 86   *"closed the eyes":* *Reichspost,* Feb. 15, 1934.

p. 87   *"of a barracks"; "attacks of the fascists":* Lehmann, *Whispering Gallery,* 208.

p. 87   *Karl-Marx-Hof fighting:* Gulick, *Austria,* 2:1285–89; *NYT,* Feb. 16–18, 1934; *NFP,* Feb. 15–18, 1934; *Reichspost,* Feb. 15–18, 1934.

p. 88   *"didn't see any of it":* Stefan Zweig, *Die Welt von Gestern* (Berlin and Frankfurt, 1968), 349–50.

p. 88   *contained women and children:* Clare, *Last Waltz,* 130.

p. 88   *"with the government":* NYT, Feb. 14, 1934.

p. 88   *government's dragnet:* Gulick, *Austria,* 2:1289–90.

p. 89   *"ruined the city"; "known many years":* NYT, Feb. 14, 1934.

p. 89   *"end of Red Vienna":* Reichspost, Feb. 14, 1934.

p. 89   *gallows on a stretcher:* Gulick, *Austria,* 2:1300; Stadler, *Opfer,* 44–45.

p. 89   *"fast work":* Reichspost, Feb. 21, 1934.

p. 89   *twelve minutes to die:* Scheu, *Weg,* 165.

p. 90   *"defenders of their homeland":* Reichspost, Feb. 23, 1934.

p. 90   *Louvre circle:* Scheu, *Weg,* 27–28.

p. 90   *"at all costs"; "hatred and international strife":* NYT, Feb. 14, 1934.

p. 90   *"Metternich Horrors":* Ibid., Feb. 15, 1934.

p. 91   *"in all history":* Quoted in Gulick, *Austria,* 2:1294.

p. 91   *"carefully controlled":* Times quoted ibid.

p. 91   *"soon be working overtime":* NYT, Feb. 13, 1934.

p. 91   *"power of Adolf Hitler":* NYT, Feb. 13, 1934.

p. 91   *"international situation":* Le Temps, Feb. 23, 1934.

p. 91   *Communists and the Soviet Union:* Stadler, *Opfer,* 176–77.

p. 91   *"avoid unnecessary casualties":* Quoted in Gulick, *Austria,* 2:1295.

p. 92   *"gas from Munich and Berlin":* NYT, Feb. 13, 1934.

p. 92   *"bad mistake":* Quoted in Peterson, "Faschistische Italien," 521.

p. 92   *"increasingly difficult":* Quoted in Jedlicka, "Forschungsergebnisse," 78.

p. 92   *"recent disturbances":* Quoted in Gulick, *Austria,* 2:1302.

p. 92   *"all possible mildness":* Stadler, *Opfer,* 46.

p. 93   *"trade unions and Socialists":* NYT, Feb. 15, 1934.

p. 93   *"takeover in Vienna":* Quoted in Peterson, "Faschistische Italien," 521.

p. 93   *"sorely needed":* FRUS, 1934, 2:11.

p. 93   *"dominated his view":* Ibid., 19.

p. 93   *"helping America":* Ibid., 20

p. 93   *"arrival last September":* Ibid., 22.

p. 94   *"for several years":* Quoted ibid., 15.

p. 94   *"independence of Austria":* Peterson, "Faschistische Italien," 521.

p. 94   *"met its deserved downfall":* Quoted in NYT, Feb. 13, 1934.

p. 95   *terrible catastrophe:* MG, Feb. 21, 1934.

p. 95   *returned with more:* Naomi Mitchinson, *Vienna Diary* (London, 1934), 185.

p. 95   *Socialist vigilante squad:* Gulick, *Austria,* 2:1304.

p. 95   *returned the parcels:* Mitchinson, *Vienna Diary,* 27, 95.

p. 95   *some successes:* Ibid., 148.

p. 96   *joined the underground Nazi movement:* Stadler, *Opfer,* 93–94.

p. 96   *death in his office:* See especially Pauley, *Hitler,* 122–37.

p. 96   *"pompous," yet "somehow moving":* Clare, *Last Waltz,* 132.

p. 96   *"horrible sexual degenerate":* Mack Smith, *Mussolini,* 185.

p. 97   *been so "foolish"; "march in step together":* Ibid., 218.

p. 97   *"Never, never, never":* Joachim Fest, *Hitler* (New York, 1974), 547–48.

p. 97   *"chased to the devil":* Gulick, *Austria,* 2:1291.

p. 98   *"revenge for February 1934":* Stadler, *Opfer,* 265.

p. 98   *straight to Dachau:* Ibid., 272.

p. 98   *"covering false pretenses":* Quoted in Pauley, *Hitler,* 120.

p. 98   *death warrant:* Kurt von Schuschnigg, *Austrian Requiem* (New York, 1946), 3–27.

p. 99   *"easier time":* Ibid., 27.

p. 99   *"not lift a finger":* Ibid., 17.

p. 100 *"even at this tragic hour":* Ibid., 51.

CHAPTER 3
The Night of the Long Knives

p. 101   *Karl Ernst:* Max Gallo, *Night of the Long Knives* (New York, 1972), 39, 251–52.

p. 102   *"dedicated fighting association":* Quoted in Wolfgang Sauer, "Die Mobilmachung der Gewalt," in Karl Dietrich Bracher, Wolfgang Sauer, and Gerhard Schulz, *Die nationalsozialistische Machtergreifung* (Cologne and Upladen, 1962), 831.

p. 102   *"thirst for blood":* Ernst Jünger, *In Stahlgewittern* (Berlin, 1934), x.

p. 103   *"threatening to become sober":* Quoted in Joachim C. Fest, *The Face of the Third Reich* (New York, 1970), 139.

p. 103   *Röhm's early career:* Ernst Röhm, *Geschichte eines Hochverraters* (Munich, 1934), 13–16.

p. 104   *"wrestling club with a political bias":* Fest, *Face*, 139.

p. 104   *Frontschweine:* Röhm, *Geschichte*, 123–27.

p. 105   *Hitler's differences with Röhm:* Sauer, "Mobilmachung," 836–37.

p. 106   *loyal "party tool":* Richard Bessel, *Political Violence and the Rise of Nazism: The Storm Troopers in Eastern Germany, 1925–1934* (New Haven, 1984), 57.

p. 106   *"common great ideal":* Quoted in Sauer, "Mobilmachung," 837.

p. 106   *Röhm in Bolivia:* Röhm, *Geschichte*, 357–64.

p. 107   *SA financial schemes:* Henry Ashby Turner, *German Big Business and the Rise of Hitler* (New York, 1985), 117.

p. 107   *"North Pole does from the South":* Winston Churchill, *The Gathering Storm* (New York, 1961), 54.

p. 107   *"in the public squares":* Quoted in Sauer, "Mobilmachung," 844.

p. 107   *SA revolts:* Bessel, *Political Violence*, 62–65.

p. 108   *"unlimited trust in Röhm":* Quoted in Henry Ashby Turner, ed., *Hitler—Memoirs of a Confidant* (New Haven, 1986), 103.

p. 109   *"filth of the lowest order":* Ibid., 104.

p. 109   *"aberrations [had] been overcome":* Ibid., 105.

p. 109   *"yelled at him for hours":* Ernst Hanfstaengl, *15 Jahre mit Hitler: Zwischen Weissem und Braunem Haus* (Munich, 1980), 342.

p. 110   *"National Socialist Reich":* Fest, *Hitler* (New York, 1974), 449–50.

p. 110   *"realization of its program":* Helmut Krausnick, "Der 30. Juni 1934," *Aus Politik und Zeitgeschichte* 25 (June 30, 1954): 318.

p. 110   *"repeated interventions":* Heinz Höhne, *Mordsache Röhm* (Hamburg, 1984), 42.

p. 111   *"evolutionary channels":* Ibid., 47.

p. 111   *"stupid and dangerous" entourage:* Ibid., 59.

p. 111   *"Adolf [was] rotten":* Fest, *Hitler*, 451.

p. 111   *stiff penalties:* Höhne, *Mordsache*, 61.

p. 112   *"most important assignment":* Fest, *Hitler*, 454.

p. 112   *"your most faithful followers":* Gallo, *Night*, 45.

p. 113   *"must be order":* Hanfstaengl, *Jahre*, 350.

p. 113   *"emperor ever possessed":* Franz von Papen, *Der Wahrheit eine Gasse* (Munich, 1952), 341.

p. 116   *"revolution from below":* Ibid., 342.

p. 116   *"future of their fatherland":* Ibid., 343.

p. 117   *"Better a zero than a Nero":* Churchill, *Gathering Storm*, 24–25.

p. 117   *"full sovereignty":* Andreas Dorpalen, *Hindenburg and the Weimar Republic* (Princeton, 1964), 451.

p. 117   *"restore some order":* Papen, *Wahrheit*, 348.

p. 117   *"grandeur has now been celebrated":* Gallo, *Night*, 73.

p. 118   *"defense of the Reich":* Ibid.

p. 118   *"brown flood":* Krausnick, "30. Juni 1934," 318.

p. 118   *"regular Prussian soldiers":* Hanfstaengl, *Jahre*, 305.

p. 118   *Hitler-army-SA meeting:* Krausnick, "30. Juni 1934," 319.

p. 119   *"long vacation":* Ibid., 319.

p. 119   "matter ripen": Ibid.

p. 119   "pile of shit": Höhne, Mordsache, 219.

p. 119   Sauhund: Hanfstaengl, Jahre, 340.

p. 120   "destiny of Germany": Höhne, Mordsache, 299.

p. 120   Papen's Marburg speech: Papen, Wahrheit, 346–48.

p. 121   "the Hitler autocracy": William E. Dodd and Martha Dodd, eds., Ambassador Dodd's Diary, 1933–1938 (London, 1941), 125.

p. 121   "possess all the brains": FRUS, 1934, 2:227. See also André François-Poncet, Als Botschafter in Berlin (Mainz, 1947), 188.

p. 121   "breach of trust": Papen, Wahrheit, 349.

p. 122   "dwarfs"; "little worms": Gallo, Night, 144.

p. 122   "severe breach of discipline": Dorpalen, Hindenburg, 479.

p. 122   "the smell of blood": Hans Bernd Gisevius, To the Bitter End (Boston, 1947), 143.

p. 123   "I've had enough": Klaus-Jürgen Müller, Das Heer und Hitler (Stuttgart, 1969), 125.

p. 124   "one of us": Quoted in Gallo, Night, 197.

p. 124   "darkest day of my life": Höhne, Mordsache, 266; Müller, Heer, 137.

p. 124   "with this treachery": Albert Speer, Inside the Third Reich (New York, 1970), 51.

p. 125   "a disgusting scene": Gallo, Night, 212; Gisevius, Bitter End, 169.

p. 125   "armed guards to use against us": Speer, Inside, 51.

p. 125   "two naked boys": Ibid.

p. 126   "Colibri": Gallo, Night, 220.

p. 126   "something cooking": Speer, Inside, 51.

p. 126   "Puss-in-Boots": Gisevius, Bitter End, 152.

p. 126   Papen's meeting with Göring: Papen, Wahrheit, 353–54.

p. 127   scene at vice-chancellery and Papen villa: Ibid., 354–55.

p. 127   Klausener assassination: Gallo, Night, 232; Höhne, Mordsache, 282.

p. 127   Schleicher assassination: Gisevius, Bitter End, 149; Gallo, Night, 235–37; Höhne, Mordsache, 288.

p. 128   Kahr murder: Gallo, Night, 238–39.

p. 128   "have those revolutionaries": Speer, Inside, 52.

p. 128   "past services rendered": Gallo, Night, 243.

p. 129   "abscess lanced and drained": Ibid., 247.

p. 129   SA purge in eastern Germany: Bessel, Political Violence, 130–46.

p. 130   Röhm's death: Höhne, Mordsache, 293–96; Gallo, Night, 269–70.

p. 131   SPD survey: Detlev Peukert, Inside Nazi Germany (New Haven, 1987), 71.

p. 131   Dodd's reports: FRUS, 1934, 2:230, 235.

p. 132   "have happened here": Dodd's Diary, 130–31.

p. 132   "leadership is so crazy": Ibid., 138.

p. 132   "Animals, I hope": Quoted in Ivone Kirkpatrick, The Inner Circle (London, 1959), 90.

p. 132   "passes comprehension": FRUS, 1934, 2:239.

p. 133   "misconstrued as official": Ibid., 240.

p. 133   "thank God you weren't here": Hanfstaengl, Jahre, 342.

p. 133   "civil war": Dodd's Diary, 131.

p. 133   "unity of the government": Gallo, Night, 281; Papen, Wahrheit, 361.

p. 133   "acts of state security": Höhne, Mordsache, 298.

p. 133   "legal recourse of the state": Karl Dietrich Bracher, Die deutsche Diktatur (Cologne, 1969), 263.

p. 134   "not be soft": Dorpalen, Hindenburg, 480.

p. 134   "profound thanks and recognition": Gallo, Night, 296.

p. 134   "snatched avidly at excuses": Speer, Inside, 53.

p. 134   "that were illegal": Hanfstaengl, Jahre, 249.

p. 134   "great future exploits": Gallo, Night, 282.

p. 134   "inwardly convinced: Fest, Hitler, 466.

p. 134   Hitler's Reichstag speech: Ibid., 467–69.

p. 135 *"young National Socialist movement"*: Ibid., 475.

p. 135 *"offended against paragraph 175"*: Bessel, *Political Violence*, 140.

p. 136 *"rid of these laws"*: Krausnick, "30. Juni 1934," 317.

p. 136 *"camps of the East"*: Fest, *Hitler*, 470.

p. 136 *"events of June 30"*: Ibid., 472.

p. 136 *"horrible sexual degenerate"*: Denis Mack Smith, *Mussolini: A Biography* (New York, 1982), 185.

p. 137 *"than a coward"*: Quoted in Sauer, "Mobilmachung," 831.

CHAPTER 4
"Revenge for Adowa"

p. 138 *"European colonial history"*: Anthony Mockler, *Haile Selassie's War* (New York, 1984), xxiii.

p. 140 *"scar of Adowa"*: Quoted in Samuel Hoare, *Nine Troubled Years* (Westport, Conn., 1976), 150.

p. 140 *"jingoist dream"*: Angelo Del Boca, *The Ethiopian War, 1935–1941* (Chicago, 1969), 9.

p. 140 *"really great war"*: Denis Mack Smith, *Mussolini: A Biography* (New York, 1983), 26.

p. 140 *"fierce gladiatorial pose"*: Ibid., 161.

p. 140 *"most moral city in the world"*: Ibid., 160.

p. 141 *"tears to [his] eyes"*: George Seldes, *Witness to a Century* (New York, 1987), 215.

p. 141 *"clothes fit better"*: Luigi Barzini, *The Italians* (New York, 1986), 147.

p. 142 *"ever will be"*: Ibid., 146.

p. 142 *"in the streets"*: Mack Smith, *Mussolini*, 148.

p. 142 *"burdens and dangers"*: Quoted in Christopher Hibbert, *Benito Mussolini: The Rise and Fall of Il Duce* (Harmondsworth, 1975), 96.

p. 142 *"greatest figure of our age"*: Ibid.

p. 142 *"without reserve"*: Quoted in Seldes, *Witness*, 168.

p. 142 *"right Dictator"*: Quoted in John P. Diggins, *Mussolini and Fascism: The View from America* (Princeton, 1972), 27.

p. 142 *"their spirits"*: Quoted in Hibbert, *Mussolini*, 96.

p. 143 *"soft cheese"*: Mack Smith, *Mussolini*, 130.

p. 144 *"more the honor"*: Ibid., 173.

p. 144 *"the inconvenience [of Ethiopian independence]"*: Emilio De Bono, *Anno XIII: The Conquest of an Empire* (London, 1937), 5.

p. 145 *"respected, and feared"*: Hibbert, *Mussolini*, 91.

p. 145 *"geographical boundaries"*: Peter Schwab, *Haile Selassie I: Ethiopia's Lion of Judah* (Chicago, 1979), 11.

p. 146 *"dignity entirely unassumed"*: Wilfrid Thesiger, *The Life of My Choice* (New York, 1988), 23.

p. 146 *"did you eat him"*: Mockler, *Selassie's War*, 3.

p. 147 *"electric installation trade"*: Evelyn Waugh, "A Coronation in 1930," *When the Going Was Good* (Harmondsworth, 1951), 76.

p. 147 *"public school O.T.C."*: Ibid., 84.

p. 148 *"fleas and lizzards"*: Leonard Mosley, *Haile Selassie* (London, 1964), 167.

p. 148 *"breasts in back"*: Ibid., 168.

p. 148 *"Ghiz"*; *"wide awake"*: Waugh, *Going*, 95, 96–97.

p. 149 *"oblivious of death"*: De Bono, *Anno XIII*, 34.

p. 149 *"perfect strangers"*: *Times* (London), quoted in Mosley, *Selassie*, 170.

p. 149 *"heard for miles"*: Quoted in Daniel Waley, *British Public Opinion and the Abyssinian War* (London, 1975), 46.

p. 149 *"four fullgrown men"*: G. B. Shaw, *What George Bernard Shaw Thinks of the Italo-Abyssinian Dispute and the Intervention of the League of Nations* (Harvard University Collection of Periodicals on the Ethiopian War), (n.p., n.d.), 2.

p. 149 *"barbarism"*: F. D. Laurens, *France and the Ethiopian Crisis, 1935–1936* (The Hague, 1967), 56–57.

p. 152 *incident at Walwal*: See especially Mockler, *Selassie's War*, 37–43.

p. 152 *"any beneficial results"*: De Bono, *Anno XIII*, 5; see also Renato Mori, *Mussolini e la conquista dell'Ethiopia* (Florence, 1978), 1–5; Mockler, *Selassie's War*, 37–43.

p. 152 *"total conquest of Ethiopia"*: Mori, *Mussolini*, 3.

p. 152 *"our own standpoint"*: De Bono, *Anno XIII*, 58.

p. 153 *"feared most"*: Mack Smith, *Mussolini*, 191; Renzo De Felice, *Mussolini il fascista: L'organizzazione dello stato fascista* (Turin, 1968), 614.

p. 153 *"crisis in Europe"*: Pierre Laval, *The Unpublished Diary* (London, 1948), 34.

p. 153 *"Franco-Italian amity"*: Laurens, *France*, 32.

p. 154 *"bad neighbors"; "medieval Africa"*: Hoare, *Nine Years*, 150.

p. 154 *"fame and sand"*: Robert Vansittart, *The Mist Procession* (London, 1948), 523.

p. 154 *"spirit of realism"*: George W. Baer, *Test Case: Italy, Ethiopia, and the League of Nations* (Stanford, 1976), 3.

p. 154 *"eighteen months—before Stresa"*: Vansittart, *Mist Procession*, 521.

p. 154 *"an Italian conquest"*: Quoted in Baer, *Test Case*, 4.

p. 154 *"conquest of Ethiopia"; "its torpor"*: Laurens, *France*, 56.

p. 155 *"ballot of blood"*: Waley, *British Public Opinion*, 21.

p. 155 *"international community"*: David Carlton, *Anthony Eden* (London, 1986), 60.

p. 155 *"Italian demands"*: Hoare, *Nine Years*, 155.

p. 155 *"age limit for bellicosity"*: Count Ciano, *Ciano Diary, 1937–1938* (London, 1952), 8.

p. 155 *"by a British statesman"*: A. J. P. Taylor, *The Origins of the Second World War* (Harmondsworth, 1964), 122.

p. 155 *"acts of unprovoked aggression"*: Hoare, *Nine Years*, 170.

p. 155 *"run by all"*: Ibid.

p. 156 *"Italian aggression in Ethiopia"*: FRUS, 1934, 2:769.

p. 156 *"of the Pact"*: Ibid.

p. 156 *"of the United States"*: Ibid., 770.

p. 156 *"psychology of the colored races"*: Quoted in Brice Harris, *The United States and the Italo-Ethiopian Crisis* (Stanford, 1964), 44.

p. 156 *"than any other people"*: Ibid., 52.

p. 156 *"humanitarian purposes"*: Diggins, *Mussolini*, 287.

p. 157 *"white men in Europe and America"*: Harris, *United States*, 46.

p. 157 *"great and important"*): Del Boca, *Ethiopian War*, 25.

p. 157 *"benevolent neutrality"*: Manfred Funke, *Sanktionen und Kanonen: Hitler, Mussolini und der internationale Abessinienkonflikt, 1934–1936* (Düsseldorf, 1970), 46–47.

p. 158 *clandestinely to Ethiopia*: Ibid., 45–46.

p. 158 *"sabotage it"*: Ibid., 45.

p. 158 *"sin of deficiency"*: De Bono, *Anno XIII*, 7.

p. 158 *"war of mass formations"*: Ibid., 33.

p. 159 *"inferior peoples"*: Ibid.

p. 159 *"steadfast to Ethiopia"*: Mockler, *Selassie's War*, 58.

p. 159 *"boys of the same age"*: Ibid., 51.

p. 159 *"where to run away"*: George Steer, *Caesar in Abyssinia* (Boston, 1937), 57.

p. 159 *"macaroni melted"*: Ibid., 56.

p. 160 *"Legion of Amazons"*: Del Boca, *Ethiopian War*, 40.

p. 160 *"live as slaves"*: Steer, *Caesar*, 46.

p. 160 *"Abyssinian culture"*: Evelyn Waugh, *Waugh in Abyssinia* (London, 1984), 49.

p. 160 *"climactic emergency"*: Ibid., 50.

p. 161 *Hubert Julian and John C. Robinson*: Diggins, *United States*, 308.

p. 161 *Graziani preparations*: Mockler, *Selassie's War*, 53.

p. 161 *"for a colonial campaign"*: Ibid., 54.

p. 161 *"consented to enrol themselves"*: De Bono, *Anno XIII*, 112.

p. 161 *"Duce is leading it"*: Ibid., 124.

p. 162 *"stupid act of aggression"*: Ibid., 92.

p. 162 *"early on [October] 3"*: Ibid., 219–20.

p. 162 *"place in the sun"*: Mockler, *Selassie's War*, 61.

p. 162 *"road to empire"*: Del Boca, *Ethiopian War*, 44.

p. 162 *"shall be pitiless"*: De Bono, *Anno XIII*, 232.

p. 162 *"had been observed"*: Ibid., 235.

p. 162 *"overwhelming odds"; "to a bomber"*: Vittorio Mussolini, *Bomber über Abessinien* (Munich, 1937), 21, 25.

p. 163 *"happen next"*: Theodore Konovaloff, *Con le armate del Negus* (Bologna, 1937), 55.

p. 163 *flying the red cross:* Anthony Eden, *Facing the Dictators* (London, 1962), 273.

p. 163 *"several cattle"*: De Bono, *Anno XIII*, 235.

p. 163 *"against Napoleon in 1812"*: Konovaloff, *Con le armate*, 28.

p. 163 *"intimidate him"*: Ibid., 56.

p. 164 *"black man's face"*: De Bono, *Anno XIII*, 263.

p. 164 *"be redressed"*: Ibid., 227.

p. 164 *"touching little ceremony"; "words to each"*: Muriel Currey, *A Woman at the Abyssinian War* (London, 1936), 115.

p. 164 *"of its sackcloth"*: Baer, *Test Case*, 19.

p. 164 *"there is liberty"*: De Bono, *Anno XIII*, 251.

p. 164 *"Who feeds [us] now"*: Ibid., 253.

p. 164 *"heated on the stove"*: Herbert Matthews, *Two Wars and More to Come* (New York, 1938), 27–28.

p. 165 *"thrill of a lifetime"*: Ibid., 74–75; see also Mockler, *Selassie's War*, 65–67.

p. 165 *for the moment:* ibid., 68–70.

p. 166 *"no strategical importance"*: Del Boca, *Ethiopian War*, 53.

p. 167 *"matter of arms"*: Eden, *Dictators*, 290.

p. 167 *"too late"*: Steer, *Caesar*, 85.

p. 167 *"austerity campaign"*: Del Boca, *Ethiopian War*, 67–68.

p. 167 *"vital national interest"*: Denis Mack Smith, *Italy: A Modern History* (Ann Arbor, 1959), 450.

p. 168 *" 'I told you so' "*: Daniele Vare, *British Foreign Policy through Italian Eyes* (Harvard University Collection of Periodicals on Italo-Ethiopian Conflict) (n.p., n.d.).

p. 168 *"all other nations"*: *A British Author's Impressions of Abyssinia* (Harvard Collection), (n.p., n.d.), 4.

p. 168 *"Vive l'Italie"*: Thomas Barman, *Diplomatic Correspondent* (New York, 1968), 80.

p. 168 *"not directly interested"*: Laurens, *France*, 173.

p. 169 *"sanctions meant war"*: Ibid.

p. 169 *"on the same footing"*: Eugen Weber, *Action Française* (Stanford, 1962), 289.

p. 169 *"Italian participation"*: Eden, *Facing the Dictators*, 275.

p. 169 *"reward the aggressor"; "had to be content"*: Ibid., 273, 286.

p. 170 *"land fit for Fiats"*: Quoted in Diggins, *United States*, 294–95.

p. 170 *"mother country"*: Ibid., 302–6; Harris, *United States*, 73–94.

p. 170 *"in a week"*: Pompeo Aloisi, *Journal 25 juillet 1932–14 juin 1936* (Paris, 1957), 324.

p. 170 *"minimum of risk"*: Winston Churchill, *The Gathering Storm* (New York, 1961), 159.

p. 171 *"phallus-hunting"*: Vansittart, *Mist Procession*, 540.

p. 171 *"acting under the League"*: Hoare, *Nine Years*, 180–81.

p. 171 *"off the map"*: Ibid., 182.

p. 171 *"an Englishman's honor"*: Waley, *British Public Opinion*, 57.

p. 172 *"My God"*: Harold Nicolson, *Letters and Diaries, 1930–1939* (New York, 1966), 232.

p. 172 *"preparations"*: Pietro Badoglio, *The War in Abyssinia* (London, 1937), 23–24.

p. 173 *"bare hands"*: Del Boca, *Ethiopian War*, 75.

p. 173 *"general situation"*: Badoglio, *War*, 37.

p. 173 *"burned and killed"*: Quoted in Del Boca, *Ethiopian War*, 78–79.

p. 174 *"apologies for eyes":* J. W. S. Macfie, *An Ethiopian Diary: A Record of the British Ambulance Service in Ethiopia* (London, 1936), 77.

p. 174 *"to be used":* John Spencer, *Ethiopia at Bay* (Algonac, Mich., 1984), 50.

p. 174 *"more or less badly":* Matthews, *Two Wars,* 119.

p. 174 *"petals of a flower":* Vittorio Mussolini, *Bomber,* 35, 33.

p. 174 *"valour of our soldiers":* Badoglio, *War,* 71.

p. 175 *Mulugueta himself:* Mockler, *Selassie's War,* 103–4.

p. 175 *"deadly work"* Matthews, *Two Wars,* 124.

p. 176 *"Empire depends is over":* Badoglio, *War,* 147.

p. 176 *rest of his life:* Spencer, *Ethiopia,* 63.

p. 176 *"dispel them":* Quoted in Mockler, *Selassie's War,* 142.

p. 177 *"Imperatore":* Ibid., 147.

p. 177 *Buckingham Palace:* Ibid., 151.

p. 177 *"confident cynicism":* Baer, *Test Case,* 248.

p. 177 *"ourselves in Europe":* Ibid., 288.

p. 177 *"That is too much":* Ibid., 282.

p. 178 *"bonds of vassalage":* Quoted in Spencer, *Ethiopia,* 75.

p. 178 *"worst of all worlds":* Vansittart, *Mist Procession,* 350.

p. 178 *"disintegrate civilization":* Ciano Diary, 9.

p. 178 *four "great powers":* Ibid.

p. 179 *"legitimate campaign":* Funke, *Sanktionen,* 163.

p. 179 *"never, never forget it":* Ibid., 164.

CHAPTER 5
"Red Ellen" Wilkinson and the Jarrow Crusade

p. 180 *"which they passed":* Daily Herald, Oct. 31, 1936.

p. 182 *"the wide world":* J. B. Priestley, *English Journey* (Harmondsworth, 1977), 23.

p. 182 *"good shape":* Ibid., 66.

p. 182 *"[in the] night":* Ibid., 71

p. 182 *"forlorn shanties":* Ibid., 273.

p. 182 *"come here":* Ibid., 292.

p. 183 *"miserable bankruptcy":* Ibid., 298–99.

p. 183 *"cigarette coupons":* Ibid., 375.

p. 183 *"whole inter-war period":* John Stevenson and Chris Cook, *The Slump: Society and Politics during the Depression* (London, 1979), 9.

p. 183 *"a baby human":* A. J. P. Taylor, *English History, 1914–1945* (Harmondsworth, 1970), 379.

p. 184 *in the evening:* Robert Graves and Alan Hodge, *The Long Week-end: A Social History of Great Britain, 1918–1939* (New York, 1963), 274–75.

p. 184 *"aprons respectively":* Ibid., 274.

p. 184 *"swimming baths":* Evelyn Waugh, *Vile Bodies* (Boston, 1977), 170.

p. 184 *"lesbian tarts and joyboys":* Michael Davie, ed., *The Diaries of Evelyn Waugh* (Boston, 1976), 315.

p. 185 *south to the markets:* For a good discussion of Britain's industrial decline in the late nineteenth century, see Paul Kennedy, *The Rise and Fall of the Great Powers* (New York, 1987), 224–32.

p. 186 *"disappointments of the present":* Robert Wohl, *The Generation of 1914* (Cambridge, Mass., 1979), 115.

p. 186 *34.4 percent in 1935:* Stevenson and Cook, *Slump,* 56–57.

p. 186 *personally owned wealth:* John Hilton, *Rich Man, Poor Man* (London, 1938), 28.

p. 186 *"adequate nutrition":* Ibid., 78–79.

p. 186 *"working capacity":* Ibid., 79.

p. 187 *"unemployment benefit"*: Quoted in E. Wright Bakke, *The Unemployed Man* (London, 1933), 63.

p. 187 *"western world"*: Priestley, *English Journey*, 288–89.

p. 187 *"extravagant and profligate"*: Jessica Mitford, *Hons and Rebels* (London, 1960), 56.

p. 187 *"took his meals"*: Graves and Hodge, *Long Week-end* 285.

p. 188 *"religion and science"* George Orwell, *The Road to Wigan Pier* (London, 1959), 10–11.

p. 188 *"to their support"*: Quoted in Stevenson and Cook, *Slump*, 68–69.

p. 189 *"flea-bite and a sop"*: Ibid., 64.

p. 189 *"Black Sabbath"*: Priestley, *English Journey*, 295–96.

p. 190 *Jarrow as mining center:* See Ellen Wilkinson, *The Town That Was Murdered: The Life Story of Jarrow* (London, 1939), 13–55.

p. 190 *"required lengths"*: Ibid., 35.

p. 191 *"Palmer's Town"*: Sidney Pollard and Paul Robertson, *The British Shipbuilding Industry, 1870–1914* (Cambridge, Eng., 1979), 53.

p. 191 *"smoke—smoky."*: Quoted in Wilkinson, *Town*, 72.

p. 194 *"back streets"*: Ibid., 76.

p. 194 *Jarrow population growth:* Frank Ennis, "The Jarrow March of 1936: The Symbolic Expression of Protest" (M.A. thesis, Univ. of Durham, 1982), 47–48.

p. 194 *early twentieth century:* Wilkinson, *Town*, 78.

p. 194 *"piece of urban civilization"*: Priestley, *English Journey*, 295.

p. 194 *gin houses:* Wilkinson, *Town*, 105.

p. 194 *blight and squalor:* Ennis, "Jarrow March," 77–86.

p. 195 *voted Labour:* Ibid., 78–88.

p. 195 *"specialist aides"*: Pollard and Robertson, *Shipbuilding Industry*, 75.

p. 195 *"limitless expansion"*: David Dougan, *The History of North East Shipbuilding* (London, 1968), 148.

p. 196 *"extremely depressing"*: Ibid., 141.

p. 196 *"black year for Jarrow"*: Wilkinson, *Town*, 138.

p. 196 *"deficit of £109,000"*: Dougan, *History*, 147.

p. 196 *grow in the berths:* Ibid., 161–62.

p. 197 *"last of the tycoons"*: J. M. Reid, *James Lithgow* (London, 1964), 11.

p. 197 *"activity of the country"*: Ibid., 99.

p. 197 *"reduction of costs"*: Ibid., 100.

p. 197 *"damaging bankruptcies"*: Ibid., 130.

p. 197 *"former position"*: Ibid., 131.

p. 198 *"chances of employment"*: Ibid., 133.

p. 198 *never produced ships again:* Wilkinson, *Town*, 155–59.

p. 198 *"shipping prices"*: Ibid., 172.

p. 199 *were occupied: NC,* Oct. 3, 1936.

p. 199 *"get fed"*: Quoted in Ennis, "Jarrow March," 66.

p. 199 *Pickwick Papers; teenage crime and wife beatings: SG,* April 7, 17, 1936.

p. 199 *"prosperous new industries"*: Quoted in Wilkinson, *Town*, 163

p. 199 *by the cartel:* D. L. Burn, *The Economic History of Steelmaking, 1867–1939* (Cambridge, Eng., 1940), 462.

p. 199 *"Jarrow steel works"*: *SG,* July 1, 1936.

p. 199 *"industrial opinion"*: *NC,* Oct. 3, 1936.

p. 200 *"parliament for"*: *SG,* July 1, 1936.

p. 200 *"not keep swine"*; *"not withdrawn"*: *SG,* April 1, 1936.

p. 200 *"all Party Districts"*: Stevenson and Cook, *Slump,* 137.

p. 200 *Jarrow election results:* F. W. S. Craig, *British Parliamentary Election Results, 1918–1949* (London, 1968), 345.

p. 200 *not a revolutionary one:* Ennis, "Jarrow March," 77–78.

p. 201 *"most important woman politician"*: Kenneth O. Morgan, *Labour People* (Oxford, 1987), 101.

p. 201   *"credible and effective"*: Ibid.

p. 201   *"Little Miss Perky"*: Betty Vernon, *Ellen Wilkinson* (London, 1982), 6.

p. 201   *"birds off trees"*: Ibid., 53.

p. 201   *"proletarian purple"; "house and person"*: Ibid., 1–2.

p. 201   *"early twenties"*: Ibid., 19.

p. 202   *"out of your head"*: Morgan, *Labour People*, 103.

p. 202   *"school years"*: Vernon, *Wilkinson*, 8.

p. 202   *"red-haired spitfire"*: Ibid., 32.

p. 202   *"she is a woman"*: Ibid., 48.

p. 203   *"or the British"*: Quoted ibid., 59–60.

p. 203   *"whoring with capitalist forces"*: Ibid., 59.

p. 203   *Wal Hannington and the NUWM:* See Wal Hannington, *Never on Our Knees* (London, 1967); Peter Kingsford, *The Hunger Marchers in Britain, 1920–1940* (London, 1982).

p. 204   *"illustrations to Karl Marx"*: Vernon, *Wilkinson*, 76.

p. 204   *"bright red hair"*: Ibid., 78–79.

p. 204   *"so neglected"*: Ibid., 80.

p. 205   *"thrust meeting bills"*: Ellen Wilkinson, *Clash* (London, 1929), 7.

p. 205   *"spirit of revolution"*: Ibid., 56.

p. 205   *"involved in the . . . struggle"*: Ellen Wilkinson, R. W. Postgate, and J. F. Horrabin, *A Workers' History of the Great Strike* (London, 1927), 101–3.

p. 206   *"golden age"*: Morgan, *Labour People*, 103.

p. 206   *"blueprint of the city"*: Vernon, *Wilkinson*, 112.

p. 206   *desert the Labour party:* Taylor, *English History*, 405.

p. 207   *"and postwar era"; "as in Italy"*: Ellen Wilkinson and Edward Conze, *Why Fascism?* (London, 1934), 14, 16.

p. 207   *"different type of fascism from Mosley's"*: Ibid., 65.

p. 207   *"pure and simple reaction"*: Ibid.

p. 207   *"don't do such things"*: Ibid., 23–33.

p. 208   *"increased unemployment"*: NC, Oct. 2, 1936.

p. 208   *"they to her"*: Vernon, *Wilkinson*, 139.

p. 209   *"various industrial interests"; "human life"*: Ibid.

p. 209   *"could still do it?"*: SG, July 3, 1936.

p. 209   *"maximum publicity"*: Ibid.

p. 209   *rejected this advice:* Vernon, *Wilkinson*, 142.

p. 209   *"good stout fellows"*: NC, Oct. 2, 1936.

p. 210   *by bus or train:* SG, Oct. 1, 1936.

p. 210   *"let us down badly"*: Ibid., Oct. 2, 1936.

p. 210   *"adopted by so many"*: Daily Herald, Oct. 5, 1936.

p. 210   *enterprise a grant:* NC, Oct. 2, 1936.

p. 210   *"as we go down"; "business very strictly"*: SG, Oct. 2, 1936.

p. 211   *men were away:* Ibid., Oct. 3, 1936.

p. 211   *"Special Areas"*: NC, Oct. 2, 1936.

p. 211   *"Jarrow industrially"; "hoping to achieve"*: NC, Oct. 5, 1936.

p. 212   *"Jarrow's good name"*: Ibid., Oct. 6, 1936.

p. 212   *"as may be met"*: Full text of petition printed in Ennis, "Jarrow March," 135, appendix 4.

p. 213   *"on its route"*: SG, Oct. 6, 1936.

p. 213   *"lost its cunning"*: Ibid.

p. 213   *"if possible, adventure"*: NC, Oct. 7, 1936.

p. 213   *"fit as fiddlers"*: SG, Oct. 7, 1936.

p. 214   *"been up to now"*: NC, Oct. 9, 1936.

p. 214   *"initiatives against unemployment"*: Ibid.

p. 214   *"pauperize our marchers"*: SG, Oct. 9, 1936.

p. 214   *"head of our land"*: Ibid., Oct. 14, 1936.

p. 214   *"bread and butter"*: Ibid., Oct. 17, 1936.

p. 214   "*effort to get work*": Ibid., Oct. 10, 1936.

p. 215   "*police action occurred*": Stevenson and Cook, *Slump*, 186.

p. 215   "*padre for the men*": *SG*, Oct. 9, 1936.

p. 215   "*confusion and danger*": Quoted in *SG*, Oct. 24, 1936.

p. 215   *meetings for Wal Hannington:* Tom Pickard, *Jarrow March* (London, 1982), 22.

p. 215   "*capital out of the Jarrow March*": *SG*, Oct. 19, 1936.

p. 215   "*Conservative or Labour banner*": Ibid., Oct. 13, 1936.

p. 215   *expelled one Communist:* Stevenson and Cook, *Slump*, 185.

p. 216   "*smartest body of men*": *SG*, Oct. 23, 1936.

p. 216   "*business-like air*": Ibid., Oct. 29, 1936.

p. 216   "*apparent on every side*": *MG*, Aug. 23, 1980.

p. 217   "*walking depressed area*": Wilkinson, *Town*, 208.

p. 217   "*briskly and cheerfully*": *Times* (London), Nov. 2, 1936.

p. 217   "*courage in their hearts*": *Daily Herald*, Oct. 31, 1936.

p. 217   "*along the busy streets*": *SG*, Oct. 31, 1936.

p. 217   "*good nature in the world*": *Times* (London), Nov. 2, 1936.

p. 217   "*severely from industrial depression*": ibid.

p. 218   "*cheered lustily*": Stevenson and Cook, *Slump*, 187.

p. 218   "*right to work*": *SG*, Nov. 4, 1936.

p. 218   *window dressing:* Wilkinson, *Town*, 211.

p. 218   "*cooperated with Sir John*": *SG*, Nov. 4, 1936.

p. 218   "*thousands*" *of new jobs:* Pickard, *Jarrow March*, 17.

p. 218   "*fairy godfather*": Ibid.

p. 218   "*chimney smoking*": Ibid., 17–18.

p. 218   "*speak afterwards*": Ibid., 18.

p. 219   "*members of Parliament*": Stevenson and Cook, *Slump*, 185–86.

p. 219   "*further delay*": Ibid., 187.

p. 219   "*to the galleries*": Pickard, *Jarrow March*, 19.

p. 219   "*has been solved*": Ibid., 20.

p. 219   "*this kind of thing*"; "*stay-in strike*"; "*see the Prime Minister*": Ibid.

p. 219   "*not to create a scene*": Stevenson and Cook, *Slump*, 187.

p. 220   "*this means nothing*": Pickard, *Jarrow March*, 20.

p. 220   "*you have endured unemployment*": Vernon, *Wilkinson*, 145.

p. 220   "*necessitating police action*": Stevenson and Cook, *Slump*, 187.

p. 220   "*good will*": Julian Symons, *The Thirties* (London, 1960), 51–52.

p. 221   *hearing as well:* Vernon, *Wilkinson*, 145.

p. 221   "*keep our self-respect*": Ibid., 146.

p. 222   *rich men's tables:* *MG*, Aug. 23, 1986.

p. 222   "*achievements of the Red Army*": Morgan, *Labour People*, 104.

p. 222   "*power from 1940 onwards*"; "*posthumous victory*": Ibid., 106.

Chapter 6
Death in the Afternoon

p. 227   "*revolutionary conquest of power*": Hugh Thomas, *The Spanish Civil War* (Harmondsworth, 1977), 109–10.

p. 227   "*Social Fascists*": Ibid., 119.

p. 228   "*only among themselves*": José Antonio de Aguirre, *Escape via Berlin* (New York, 1944), 43.

p. 229   "*the same tactics*": Thomas, *Spanish Civil War*, 153–54.

p. 229   *Spanish Communist intentions and weaknesses:* See David T. Cattell, *Communism and the Spanish Civil War* (Berkeley, 1955), 19–34.

p. 229   "*eternal destinies of Spain*": Thomas, *Spanish Civil War*, 155.

p. 230   "*is still green*": Ibid., 161.

p. 230   "immortal road": Paul Johnson, *Modern Times* (New York, 1983), 324.

p. 230   "we will save Spain": Juan Antonio Ansaldo, *¿Para que?* . . . *(De Alfonso XIII a Juan III)* (Buenos Aires, 1951), 42.

p. 231   "take a lie-down,": Thomas, *Spanish Civil War*, 204.

p. 232   "No pasarán": Dolores Ibarruri, *They Shall Not Pass* (New York, 1976), 195.

p. 233   "Everything, except surrender": Quoted in Raymond L. Proctor, *Hitler's Luftwaffe in the Spanish Civil War* (Westport, Conn., 1983), 13.

p. 233   "NO": John F. Coverdale, *Italian Intervention in the Spanish Civil War* (Princeton, 1975), 70.

p. 234   "Bolshevization of Europe": Ibid., 82.

p. 234   *Franco appeal to Germany:* See especially Manfred Merkes, *Die deutsche Politik gegenüber dem spanischen Bürgerkrieg, 1936–1939* (Bonn, 1969), 19–20.

p. 235   "with so little money": Peter Wyden, *The Passionate War* (New York, 1983), p. 81.

p. 235   "would endanger Germany": Ibid.

p. 235   *bloc on his western flank:* Hans-Henning Abendroth, *Hitler in der spanischen Arena* (Erlangen, 1970), 103.

p. 235   *even seen the führer:* Wyden, *Passionate War*, 82.

p. 235   *own, ongoing rearmament:* Abendroth, *Hitler*, 104–6; Merkes, *Politik*, 24–26.

p. 238   "Fraternally yours Giral": D. W. Pike, *Conjecture, Propaganda and Deceit and the Spanish Civil War* (Stanford, 1970), 19; see also Jean Lacouture, *Léon Blum* (New York, 1982), 306.

p. 238   "prudent": Lacouture, *Blum*, 308.

p. 238   "hell to pay": Douglas Little, *Malevolent Neutrality: The United States, Great Britain, and the Origins of the Spanish Civil War* (Ithaca, 1985), 196.

p. 238   *should assist:* David Carlton, *Anthony Eden* (London, 1986), 86–87.

p. 239   "my family and friends": Winston Churchill, *The Gathering Storm* (New York, 1961), 192.

p. 239   "internationalization of the war": Anthony Eden, *Facing the Dictators* (London, 1962), 451.

p. 239   "Bolshevists and anarchists": Pike, *Conjecture*, 26.

p. 239   "Byron of the Age": Thomas, *Spanish Civil War*, 351.

p. 239   "side of the Russians": Carlton, *Eden*, 86.

p. 240   *to provide it:* On the Soviet decision to intervene in Spain, see David T. Cattell, *Soviet Diplomacy and the Spanish Civil War* (Berkeley, 1957).

p. 240   *Spain as a "Communist Republic":* Adam Ulam, *Stalin* (Boston, 1987), 426.

p. 240   *pack their bags:* Proctor, *Hitler's Luftwaffe*, 20–21.

p. 241   *more aggressive fashion:* Ibid., 25–33.

p. 241   "Hitler and the new Germany": Werner Beumelberg, *Kampf um Spanien: Die Geschichte der Legion Condor* (Berlin, 1939), 50.

p. 242   "prefiguration of our future": Quoted in David Caute, *The Fellow Travellers* (New York, 1973), 170.

p. 242   "light and darkness"; "an 1848": Quoted in Humphrey Carpenter, *W. H. Auden* (London, 1983), 206.

p. 242   *enough to be killed:* On Cornford and Bell in the Spanish civil war, see Peter Stansky and William Abrahams, *Journey to the Frontier* (New York, 1970).

p. 242   "Republic had of us": Thomas, *Spanish Civil War*, 453.

p. 242   "domani in Italia": Ibid.

p. 242   *their own civil war:* Karl Stadler, *Opfer verlorener Zeiten* (Vienna, 1974), 265–72.

p. 243   "when there was no doubt": Quoted in Phillip Knightley, *The First Casualty* (New York, 1975), 192. For Hemingway in Spain see also Wyden, *Passionate War*, 321–38; and Aldo Garosci, *Los intelectuales y la guerra civil de España* (Madrid, 1981).

p. 243   "about the war" Quoted in Knightley, *First Casualty*, 195.

p. 243   *Badajoz atrocity:* Wyden, *Passionate War*, 132–39.

p. 243   *unknown even today:* Ian Gibson, *The Assassination of Federico García Lorca* (Harmondsworth, 1983).

p. 244   "seventeenth-century-minded Spanish people": Quoted in Little, *Neutrality*, 61.

p. 245   "with its terror": Ibid., 195.

p. 245   "strict neutrality": Ibid., 234.

p. 245   "The Intervention Committee": Wyden, Passionate War, 178.

p. 246   one-hundred-meter sprint: Ibid., 125.

p. 246   "barred the door for Moscow": Quoted in Klaus A. Maier, Guernica, 26.4.1937: Die deutsche Intervention in Spanien und der "Fall Guernica" (Freiburg, 1975), 27.

p. 246   "see one's own ears": Wyden, Passionate War, 155.

p. 246   "Hitler's entire Wehrmacht": "Freiherr von Richthofen," in Wulf Bley, ed., Das Buch der Spanienflieger (Leipzig, 1939), 7–8.

p. 247   "most brutal-looking general": Thomas, Spanish Civil War, 469.

p. 247   "at a diplomatic function": Wilfred von Oven, Hitler und der spanische Bürgerkrieg (Tübingen, 1978), 363.

p. 247   "führer and the volk": Bley, Buch, 8.

p. 247   bullet in his leg: Max von Hoyos, Pedros y Pablos: Fliegen, Erleben, Kämpfen in Spanien (Munich, 1939), 63–65.

p. 248   next to the squat Spaniards: Denis Mack Smith, Mussolini: A Biography (New York, 1983), 207.

p. 248   "quarrelsome and despotic bullies": Coverdale, Intervention, 255.

p. 248   "European Aldershot": Thomas, Spanish Civil War, 463.

p. 248   "dishonest farce": Claude Bowers, My Mission to Spain (New York, 1954), 325.

p. 248   "stop Franco from winning": Abendroth, Hitler, 428.

p. 248   "ammunition into Spain": Bowers, Mission, 328.

p. 249   "three danger points": Abendroth, Hitler, 426–27.

p. 249   "Italian defeat since Caporetto": Carlos Baker, Hemingway (New York, 1969), 303.

p. 249   "get the better of Italians": Coverdale, Intervention, 255.

p. 250   "before the autumn": Luis Bolín, Spain: The Vital Years (Philadelphia, 1967), 269.

p. 250   resources to the campaign: Maier, Guernica, 39–41.

p. 250   "charm and kindness": Bolín, Spain, 271.

p. 250   "industries of war": Thomas, Spanish Civil War, 616.

p. 250   "up to March 31, 1937": Bowers, Mission, 343.

p. 250   "want of energy": Proctor, Hitler's Luftwaffe, 122.

p. 250   "for the civilian population": Maier, Guernica, 46.

p. 251   "only social discontent": Ibid., 51.

p. 251   "soot and ashes": Ibid., 53.

p. 251   "a great deal": Ibid., 54.

p. 251   "Gernika is in flames": George Steer, The Tree of Gernika (London, 1938), 242.

p. 251   "dreamed of for centuries": Ibid., 243.

p. 252   with a sheet: Ibid., 243–44.

p. 252   "bombardment of Gernika": Ibid., 244.

p. 252   "with wings spread": Ibid., 245.

p. 252   "hurt [the Germans'] susceptibilities": The History of the Times (London, 1935–52), 4:907.

p. 253   "on top of their victims": NYT, April 28, 1937.

p. 253   "liberty and our democracy": Ibid.

p. 254   "eight meters deep" Quoted in Robert Payne, ed., The Civil War in Spain, 1936–1939 (New York, 1962), 195–97.

p. 254   "could hardly have bombed Guernica": Quoted in Herbert R. Southworth, Guernica! Guernica!: A Study of Journalism, Diplomacy, Propaganda, and History (Berkeley, 1977), 32.

p. 254   "piloted by foreigners"; "own criminal intentions": Ibid., 32.

p. 254   "attribute the crime to us": Ibid., 35.

p. 255   either side's version: Knightley, First Casualty, 205–6.

p. 255   "fires and dynamiting": Ibid.

p. 255   "experiment with incendiary bombs": Ibid.

p. 255   "objectives of military importance": Southworth, Guernica, 37.

p. 255   "towards other defenses": Ibid., 38.

p. 255   "justified a bombing": Ibid.

p. 255   "incendiary dynamiters": Ibid.

p. 256   "enemy around Marquina": Maier, Guernica, 55–56.

p. 256   "EC.B1s [firebombs]": Ibid., 56–57.

p. 256 *over the city center:* Ibid., 156.

p. 256 *"good effect":* Ibid., 57.

p. 257 *"hit anything at all":* Quoted in Gordon Thomas and Max Morgan Witts, *Guernica: The Crucible of World War II* (New York, 1975), 146.

p. 257 *Asturian dynamiters and arsonists:* Maier, *Guernica,* 62–63.

p. 258 *"significant influence" . . . operations in the north:* Ibid., 67.

p. 258 *"without reference to higher authority":* Thomas and Witts, *Guernica,* 198.

p. 258 *"made on [his] own people":* George Hills, *Franco: The Man and His Nation* (London, 1967), 277.

p. 259 *"to a table":* Thomas and Witts, *Guernica,* 41.

p. 259 *"bits and pieces everywhere":* Ibid., 228.

p. 260 *"for the slaughter":* Ibid., 247.

p. 261 *"attack on the Basques":* Quoted in Allen Guttmann, *The Wound in the Heart: America and the Spanish Civil War* (New York, 1962), 107.

p. 261 *"unless Bilbao surrenders" FRUS,* 1937, 1:290.

p. 261 *"Fascist strategy":* Quoted in Southworth, *Guernica,* 187.

p. 261 *"morality and civilization":* Guttmann, *Wound,* 107.

p. 261 *"and German pilots"; "Spanish invasion":* Southworth, *Guernica,* 187.

p. 262 *"misleading the public":* Ibid., 111.

p. 262 *"and departed":* Ibid., 111–12.

p. 262 *"anarchists in their retreat":* Ibid., 109–10.

p. 262 *"beaten all its records":* Pike, *Conjecture,* 111.

p. 262 *"as they say":* Southworth, *Guernica,* 141.

p. 262 *means of expediting victory:* Pike, *Conjecture,* 111.

p. 262 *"duty-bound to revolt":* Ibid., 118.

p. 262 *"persecuted in Barcelona":* Thomas, *Spanish Civil War,* 628.

p. 263 *"they burned Irún":* Pike, *Conjecture,* 113.

p. 263 *"Red lies":* L'Action française, May 6, 1937.

p. 263 *"fervent Catholic, General Franco":* Southworth, *Guernica,* 155.

p. 263 *"every big town in Europe":* William Laird Kleine-Ahlbrandt, *The Policy of Simmering: A Study of British Policy during the Spanish Civil War* (The Hague, 1962), 50.

p. 263 *"operations against Bilbao":* Southworth, *Guernica,* 96.

p. 263 *"German aircraft":* Eden, *Dictators,* 500.

p. 263 *"the Basque government":* Hansard, May 3, 1937, 767.

p. 264 *"re-currence of such happenings":* Ibid.

p. 264 *"definition of an 'open city' ":* Abendroth, *Hitler,* 447.

p. 264 *"Non-Intervention Committee":* Carlton, *Eden,* 106.

p. 265 *burned the town: Guernica: Being the Official Report of a Commission Appointed by the Spanish Nationalist Government to Investigate the Causes of the Destruction of Guernica on April 26–28, 1937* (London, 1938).

p. 265 *"if I were you":* Virginia Cowles, *Looking for Trouble* (London, 1941), 69.

p. 265 *"pain and death":* Quoted in Arianna Stassinopoulos Huffington, *Picasso* (New York, 1988), 232.

p. 265 *"horrors of human conflict":* Lord quoted ibid., 234.

p. 265 *"liberated Guernica":* Ellen C. Oppler, *Picasso's Guernica* (New York, 1988), 131.

p. 265 *"and I was right":* Ernst quoted in H. Reinhardt, *Das Selbstporträt* (Hamburg, 1967).

CHAPTER 7
"The Revolution Eats Its Children"

p. 267 *"history has known":* Adam Ulam, *Stalin* (Boston, 1987), 485.

p. 268 *"than anybody else":* Quoted in Robert Conquest, *The Great Terror* (New York, 1973), 99.

p. 268 *"kill such a nice man":* Roy A. Medvedev, *Let History Judge* (London, 1976), 159.

p. 268   *"forced me to do it"*: Ibid.

p. 269   *"fired at the Party"*; *"Take him away"*: Alexander Orlov, *The Secret History of Stalin's Crimes* (London, 1954), 22.

p. 269   *"officials of the Soviet government"*: Conquest, *Great Terror*, 84.

p. 270   *"that city's housing problem"*: Louis Fischer, *Men and Politics* (London, 1951), 495.

p. 270   *"degeneration of those criminals"*: Isaac Deutscher, *Stalin* (London, 1949), 357.

p. 271   death penalty for oppositionists: Orlov, *Secret History*, 15–20.

p. 271   giant *"frame-up"*: Ibid., 15–24.

p. 271   *"events of that night"*: Walter Krivitsky, *I Was Stalin's Agent* (London, 1940), 183.

p. 271   clear to him: See Ulam, *Stalin*, 383–88; J. Arch Getty, *Origins of the Great Purges* (Cambridge, Eng., 1985), 207–10.

p. 271   *"era of the confessions"*: Krivitsky, *Agent*, 184.

p. 272   *"rotten liberalism"*: Eugenia Ginzburg, *Into the Whirlwind* (New York, 1967), 11.

p. 272   drunkenness and hooliganism: Getty, *Origins*, 60–67.

p. 272   figures in the October Revolution: On Stalin's role in the revolution, see especially Robert M. Slusser, *Stalin in October* (Baltimore, 1987).

p. 272   *"third-rate provincial mind"*: Ulam, *Stalin*, 232.

p. 272   *"the Prophet Unarmed"*: See Isaac Deutscher, *The Prophet Unarmed* (London, 1959).

p. 273   starting point for Stalin's crimes: Bertram D. Wolfe, *Khrushchev and Stalin's Ghost* (London, 1957), 90.

p. 273   become obnoxious: Ulam, *Stalin*, 398.

p. 273   *"idyllic interlude"*: Conquest, *Great Terror*, 133.

p. 274   *"make a prince"*: Deutscher, *Prophet Unarmed*, 548.

p. 275   *"Communist Party of the Soviet Union"*: *Report of Court Proceedings: The Case of the Trotskyite-Zinovievite Terrorist Centre* (New York, 1967), 25 (hereafter *TZT*).

p. 275   into a real one: Orlov, *Secret History*, 61–64.

p. 275   Voroshilov, and Kagonovich: Ibid., 65–68.

p. 276   *"leadership and seizing power"*: *TZT*, 18.

p. 276   *"in prison for several years"*: Orlov, *Secret History*, 96.

p. 277   *"know it is a lie"*: Ibid., 113.

p. 277   *"pressure of the state"*; *"senses at once"*: Ibid., 118.

p. 277   *"primarily against Stalin"*: *TZT*, 14.

p. 277   military court and *"annihilated"*: Orlov, *Secret History*, 120.

p. 280   *"saw all this"*; *"against the Party"*: Ibid., 127–29.

p. 280   *"crowd and back again"*; *"golf at Sunningdale"*: Fitzroy Maclean, *Escape to Adventure* (Boston, 1950), 63.

p. 280   defend the men: Medvedev, *Let History Judge*, 169.

p. 280   execution for the entire group: Conquest, *Great Terror*, 154.

p. 281   *"Comrade S. M. Kirov"*: *TZT*, 10.

p. 281   *"as well"*; *"L. Trotsky"*; *"exploiting classes"*: Ibid., 11–12.

p. 281   *"dangerous knowledge"*: Ibid., 55.

p. 281   Ivan the Terrible: *NYT*, Aug. 20, 1936.

p. 281   *"terroristic activities with Marxism"*; *"present Party leadership"*; *"crawling on their belly"*: *TZT*, 55–56.

p. 282   *"openly in our country"*: Ibid., 170.

p. 282   *"lecturing his class"*: *NYT*, Aug. 21, 1936.

p. 282   *"movement impossible"*: Ibid.

p. 282   *"You have found it"*: *TZT*, 68.

p. 282   *"[politically necessary] one"*: Ulam, *Stalin*, 387.

p. 282   charges against him: *TZT*, 45–46.

p. 283   *"is always there"*: Orlov, *Secret History*, 57.

p. 283   *"taught us a lesson"*; *"follow Stalin"*: Ibid., 165–67.

p. 283   *"adopted a different decision"*: *TZT*, 72.

p. 283   *"Party mind"*; *" 'objectively' false"*: Conquest, *Great Terror*, 179.

p. 283   *"hide from the Party"*: Ginzburg, *Whirlwind,* 22.

p. 284   *"they accused themselves"*: Arthur Koestler, *Darkness at Noon* (New York, 1948), 180.

p. 284   *post-Christian form:* See Rudolph Binion, *After Christianity: Christian Survivals in Post-Christian Culture* (Durango, Colo., 1986), 73–74.

p. 284   *"unworthy attitude at the trial"*: Conquest, *Great Terror,* 170.

p. 284   *"rotten agents of the Gestapo"*: Medvedev, *Let History Judge,* 169.

p. 284   *"accusers the accused"*: *NYT,* Aug. 20, 1936.

p. 284   *"English jurist Pritt"*: Conquest, *Great Terror,* 174.

p. 285   *"coward he had always been"*: David Caute, *The Fellow Travellers* (New York, 1973), 118.

p. 285   *"indifference to death"*: *NYT,* Aug. 21, 1936.

p. 285   *"they must know"*: Caute, *Fellow Travellers,* 118.

p. 285   *"gone against the Party"*: Alfred Kazin, *Starting Out in the Thirties* (Boston, 1965), 97.

p. 285   *"too good for him"*: *NYT,* Aug. 20, 1936.

p. 286   *"just as [he] did"*: *TZT,* 68.

p. 286   *"has just begun"*: Orlov, *Secret History,* 169.

p. 286   *"members of the Politburo"*: Boris Nicolaevsky, "Letter of an Old Bolshevik," in Boris Nicolaevsky, ed., *Power and the Soviet Elite* (New York, 1965), 63.

p. 287   *"representatives of the NKVD"*: Quoted in Conquest, *Great Terror,* 218.

p. 287   *"God got in his way"*: Alexander Yanov, *The Origins of Autocracy: Ivan the Terrible in Russian History* (Berkeley, 1981), 293; Ulam, *Stalin,* 701.

p. 287   *"tobacco-stained teeth"*: Ruth Fischer, *Stalin and German Communism* (Cambridge, Mass., 1948), 205.

p. 288   *"(among the youngest) [in the party]"*: Wolfe, *Khrushchev,* 265.

p. 288   *Shakhty trial:* See Kendall Bailes, *Technology and Society under Lenin and Stalin* (Princeton, 1978), 69–94.

p. 289   *"interests of his employers"*: Ibid., 117–18.

p. 290   *"existing in the USSR"*: *Report of the Court Proceedings in the Case of the Anti-Soviet Trotskyite Centre, January 23–30, 1937* (New York 1967), 4–5 (hereafter *ATCT*).

p. 290   *"flecked with gray"*: *NYT,* Jan. 24, 1937.

p. 290   *"for socialist construction"*: *ATCT,* 60.

p. 290   *"resources it needs"*: Ibid., 64.

p. 290   *"helping fascism"*: Ibid., 67–68.

p. 290   *"German and Japanese concessionaires"*: Ibid., 56.

p. 290   *"contagious diseases"*: *NYT,* Jan. 24, 1937.

p. 291   *carte blanche in China: ATCT,* 114–16.

p. 291   *"and then disappear"*: Ibid., 101.

p. 291   *"Trotsky's beautiful eyes"*: Ibid., 124–25.

p. 291   *only from him, Radek:* Ibid., 129

p. 291   *worthy enemy of Trotsky: ATCT,* 302–33.

p. 291   *accidents between 1935 and 1936: NYT,* Jan. 28, 1937.

p. 291   *retarded coal production: ATCT,* 244–60.

p. 291   *"Trotskyite underground"*: Ibid., 462.

p. 292   *"really dealing"*: Ibid., 462–68.

p. 292   *"to which you sent them"*: Ibid., 516.

p. 292   *"lost his very self"*: Ibid., 541.

p. 292   *"the far winds"*: Edward Crankshaw, *Khrushchev: A Career* (New York, 1966), 112.

p. 292   *justifying the trials:* Elisabeth K. Poretsky, *Our Own People* (London, 1969), 198.

p. 293   *"crimes in world history"*: *NYT,* Jan. 24, 1937.

p. 293   *"richness of detail"*: Ulam, *Stalin,* 424.

p. 293   *"seeker after truth"*: *NYT,* Jan. 27, 1937.

p. 293   *"true as gold"*: Ibid., Jan. 26, 1937.

p. 293   *"not read Dostoevsky"*: Ibid., Jan. 25, 1937.

p. 294   *"fits the facts"*: Quoted in Conquest, *Great Terror,* 257.

p. 294   *"confessions of the accused"*: Ibid.

p. 294   *"put it over"*: *NYT,* Jan. 29, 1937.

p. 294   *"admirable moderation"; "normal physically"*: Joseph Davies, *Mission to Moscow* (New York, 1941), 37.

p. 294   *"Belasco in stage production"*: Ibid., 43.

p. 294   *charges brought against him*: Caute, *Fellow Travellers,* 120–21.

p. 294   *"with foreign powers"*: Ibid., 121.

p. 294   *"possession of the subterranean truth"*: Ibid., 119.

p. 295   *"know what truth is"*: Ibid., 121.

p. 295   *"artificial about the trial proceedings"*: Quoted in Paul Johnson, *Modern Times* (New York, 1983), 307.

p. 295   *"deny fascist intervention in Spain"*: Caute, *Fellow Travellers,* 118.

p. 295   *"enemies of the people"*: I. E. Gorbatov, *Years off My Life* (New York, 1966), 103.

p. 296   *a mixed blessing*: Krivitsky, *Agent,* 217.

p. 296   *"a few spies . . . could do"*: Conquest, *Great Terror,* 293.

p. 296   *Stalin promptly paid*: Walter Schellenburg, *The Schellenburg Memoirs* (London, 1956), 49.

p. 297   *subordinate status*: Ulam, *Stalin,* 449.

p. 297   *"Ils sont déjà invincibles"*: John Erickson, *The Soviet High Command* (London, 1962), 413.

p. 298   *lebensraum in the east*: Ibid., 450.

p. 298   *"with her Front Populaire"*: Krivitsky, *Agent,* 214–15.

p. 298   *alliance with France*: Hans von Herwarth, *Zwischen Hitler und Stalin* (Frankfurt, 1985), 59.

p. 298   *conquer Poland in 1920*: Ulam, *Stalin,* 189–90.

p. 298   *"Long live Stalin"*: Ibid., 462.

p. 299   *false sense of security*: F. Beck and W. Godin, *Russian Purge and Extraction of Confession* (New York, 1951), 105.

p. 299   *command of lieutenants*: Alexander Weissberg, *The Accused* (New York, 1951), 8.

p. 299   *suddenly vanished*: Memoir of A. T. Stuchenko, "In the Frunze Military Academy," in Seweryn Bialer, ed., *Stalin and His Generals* (New York, 1969), 80.

p. 300   *and promptly shot*: Erickson, *Soviet High Command,* 451–52; Conquest, *Great Terror,* 316.

p. 300   *"innocent people he wronged"*: Bialer, *Stalin and His Generals,* 74–75.

p. 300   *spitoon over his head*: Conquest, *Great Terror,* 311–12.

p. 300   *redoubled vengeance in 1938*: Erickson, *Soviet High Command,* 466–70.

p. 301   *navy purge*: Ibid., 475–77; Conquest, *Great Terror,* 317–18.

p. 301   *probably executed*: Erickson, *Soviet High Command,* 500.

p. 301   *secrets abroad*: Ibid., 500–501.

p. 301   *"parachutes too late"*: Bialer, *Stalin and His Generals,* 87.

p. 301   *no talk at all*: Erickson, *Soviet High Command,* 499.

p. 302   *executed in 1937–38*: Robert Conquest, *Inside Stalin's Secret Police* (London, 1985), 30.

p. 302   *purged or shot*: Bialer, ed., *Stalin,* 59.

p. 302   *experienced in peacetime*: See Ulam, *Stalin,* 447.

p. 302   *"worry about the hair"*: Ibid., 457.

p. 303   *"got mislaid"*: Boris Pasternak, *Doctor Zhivago* (New York, 1958), 508.

p. 303   *"barracks and government offices"*: Weissberg, *Accused,* 7.

p. 303   *"long arm of the Kremlin"*: Maclean, *Escape,* 23–24.

p. 303   *Central Committee memberships in 1937–38*: Roy Medvedev, *Faut-il rehabiliter Staline?* (Paris, 1969), 42.

p. 303   *Tartar Republic in prison*: Ginzburg, *Whirlwind,* 142.

p. 304   *"spoken to by him"*: Maclean, *Escape,* 15.

p. 304   *ordinary citizens went to prison*: Conquest, *Great Terror,* 375.

p. 304   *"remain among the living"*: Krivitsky, *Agent,* 249.

p. 304   *"they could think of"*: Ginzburg, *Whirlwind,* 134–35.

p. 304   *"arrested for nothing"*: Nadezhda Mandelstam, *Hope against Hope* (New York, 1970), 11.

p. 304   *"make a case"*: Ibid., 14.

p. 304   *"be found somewhere"*: Victor Serge, *Russia Twenty Years After* (New York, 1937), 61.

p. 305   *similarly incautious colleagues*: Conquest, *Great Terror,* 431–32.

p. 305   *"nothing but dung"*: Ibid., 436.

p. 305   *"broad-chested Ossete"*: Mandelstam, *Hope*, 13.

p. 305   *"rash, has he"*: Ibid., 22.

p. 305   *mentionable in public:* Ibid., 139.

p. 306   *"Hitler's agents abroad"*: Conquest, *Great Terror*, 578.

p. 306   *torn out by the NKVD:* Ginzburg, *Whirlwind*, 154.

p. 306   *after the war:* Ulam, *Stalin*, 471.

p. 307   *on the way:* Ibid., 472.

p. 307   *"fights and wins"*: Karl Stadler, *Opfer verlorener Zeiten* (Vienna, 1974), 289.

p. 307   *the February 1934 uprising:* Ibid., 280–82.

p. 307   *"world proletariat"; "of the Communist Party"*: Ibid., 290–92.

p. 307   *complain about Soviet actions:* Conquest, *Great Terror*, 580–81.

p. 307   *resident in the Soviet Union:* Ibid., 582–83.

p. 308   *"working class and of Socialism"*: Krivitsky, *Agent*, 255.

p. 308   *"NKVD has caught up with me"*: Sidney Hook, letter to editor, *New York Review of Books*, March 6, 1988.

p. 308   *"the Dachau of republican Spain"*: Hugh Thomas, *The Spanish Civil War* (Harmondsworth, 1977), 704–6.

p. 309   *"heap of human garbage"*: Stephen F. Cohen, *Bukharin and the Bolshevik Revolution* (New York, 1973), 374.

p. 310   *"on a beaky nose"*: Maclean, *Escape*, 65.

p. 310   *"German intelligence service"*: Robert C. Tucker and Stephen F. Cohen, eds., *The Great Purge Trial* (New York, 1965), 36.

p. 310   *"a single crime"*: Ibid.

p. 310   *"Party and the Government"*: Ibid., 53.

p. 310   *said in public before:* Ibid., 65.

p. 310   *"preliminary investigation"; "I have committed"*: Ibid., 157–58.

p. 310   *"well-learned lesson"*: Maclean, *Agent*, 65.

p. 311   *"policy of Moscow"*: *Great Purge Trial*, 91.

p. 311   *"members of our Right organization"*: Ibid., 103–4.

p. 311   *British Labour party:* Ibid., 289–90.

p. 312   *"hand in every plot"*: Maclean, *Agent*, 68.

p. 312   *"jesuitry and inhuman villainy"*: Ibid.

p. 312   *"shadow over the world"*: Cohen, *Bukharin*, 360–63.

p. 312   *"service of fascism"; "arrest, try, and shoot"*: Ibid., 370–71.

p. 312   *"in any particular act"*: *Great Purge Trial*, 328.

p. 313   *"tautology"; "counter-revolutionary organization"*: Cohen, *Bukharin*, 378–79.

p. 313   *"last hours of the trial"*: Harold Denny, of *NYT*, quoted ibid., 380.

p. 313   *"lined with despair"*: *NYT*, March 11, 1938.

p. 313   *"of his own play"*: Maclean, *Agent*, 70.

p. 313   *poisoned candle:* Ulam, *Stalin*, 483.

p. 313   *"answer that question"*: Conquest, *Great Terror*, 545.

p. 313   *"done their work well"*: Maclean, *Agent*, 71.

p. 314   *"towards Communism"*: Quoted in Conquest, *Great Terror*, 564–65.

p. 314   *more important charges:* Ulam, *Stalin*, 483–84.

p. 314   *"we had him shot"*: Ibid., 487.

p. 314   *"would be staged"*: Davies, *Mission*, 269–70.

p. 315   *why did they confess:* Maclean, *Agent*, 75–77.

p. 315   *"we needed the space"*: Quoted in Walter Isaacson and Evan Thomas, *The Wise Men* (New York, 1986), 173.

p. 315   *similar to that of the Zinoviev-Kamenev affair:* *NYT*, March 4, 1938.

p. 315   *"confessions as untrue"*: Quoted ibid.

p. 315   *"between the Soviet Union and Germany"*: *Great Purge Trial*, xxxix.

p. 315   *trusted most were being eliminated:* Herwarth, *Zwischen Hitler*, 118–19.

p. 316   *"reduced to impotence"*: Quoted in *Great Purge Trial,* xxxix.

p. 316   *magazine was called Spark:* James H. Billington, *The Icon and the Axe* (New York, 1970), 23–25.

CHAPTER 8
"Peace for Our Time"

p. 317   *"pluck this flower, safety"*: Quoted in Telford Taylor, *Munich: The Price of Peace* (New York, 1980), 15.

p. 319   *"affair of the heart"*: Martin Gilbert and Richard Gott, *The Appeasers* (Boston, 1963), 5.

p. 319   *"once launched, uncontrollable"*: Quoted in Larry William Fuchser, *Neville Chamberlain and Appeasement: A Study in the Politics of History* (New York, 1982), 7.

p. 319   *"will always get through"*: Keith Robbins, *Munich 1938* (London, 1968), 89–90.

p. 320   *"strength . . . in the air"*: Williamson Murray, *The Change in the European Balance of Power, 1938–1939* (Princeton, 1984), 198.

p. 320   *"I know it"*: George Orwell, *Coming Up for Air* (New York, 1950), 183. See also Willard C. Frank, Jr., "The Spanish Civil War and the Coming of the Second World War," *International History Review* 9 (Aug. 1984): 373–74.

p. 320   *"next ten years"*: Paul Kennedy, *The Realities behind Diplomacy* (London, 1981), 231.

p. 320   *British defense budgets:* Ibid., 231, 240.

p. 320   *"has to face"*: Ibid., 233.

p. 320   *"the Cossacks will rule Europe"*: Edouard Daladier quoted in Anthony Adamthwaite, "France and the Coming of War," in Wolfgang J. Mommsen and Lothar Kettenacker, eds., *The Fascist Challenge and the Policy of Appeasement* (London, 1983), 248.

p. 321   *"psychology of a defeated power"*: D. W. Brogan quoted in Taylor, *Munich,* 103.

p. 322   *"not a national state"*: A. J. P. Taylor, *The Origins of the Second World War* (Harmondsworth, 1964), 190.

p. 323   *"learn Czech"*: J. W. Bruegel, *Czechoslovakia before Munich: The German Minority Problem and British Appeasement Policy* (Cambridge, Eng., 1973), 25–26.

p. 323   *"nothing can separate us"*: Ibid., 79.

p. 324   *"Germans in Czechoslovakia"*: Ibid., 76.

p. 324   *"with that of Stresemann"*: Robbins, *Munich,* 145.

p. 324   *Czechs in Siberia:* Boris Celovsky, *Das Münchener Abkommen, 1938* (Stuttgart, 1958), 87.

p. 324   *Hossbach conference:* Text in Francis L. Loewenheim, *Peace or Appeasement? Hitler, Chamberlain, and the Munich Crisis* (Boston, 1965), 2–5.

p. 325   *"only road for us"*: Bruegel, *Czechoslovakia,* 107.

p. 325   *"path to freedom"*: Ibid., 113.

p. 326   *"upon the leader principle"*: Celovsky, *Abkommen,* 116.

p. 326   *"revision of [Czechoslovakia's] borders"; "of long standing"*: Ibid., 112, 121.

p. 327   *"local representative of Hitler"*: Ibid., 114.

p. 327   *"frontiers of the Reich"*: Robbins, *Munich,* 142.

p. 327   *"reasonable man"; "speedy settlement"*: Celovsky, *Abkommen,* 168.

p. 327   *"far-reaching settlement"*: Gilbert and Gott, *Appeasers,* 106–7.

p. 327   *"probably from France"*: Ibid., 107.

p. 327   *"unprovoked aggression", "by peaceful means"*: Ibid.

p. 327   *"exotic flower"; "thing as Czechoslovakia"*: Ibid., 106.

p. 328   *"friendly intentions"*: Celovsky, *Abkommen,* 152.

p. 328   *"improve Czech German relations"*: Nevile Henderson, *Failure of a Mission* (New York, 1940), 129–30.

p. 328   *"to the Czech government"; "nonintervention by Britain"*: Loewenheim, *Peace,* 10–11.

p. 328   *"shape its laws"*: Celovsky, *Abkommen,* 154.

p. 329   *"never to have a motherland"*: Quoted ibid., 169 n. 3.

p. 329   *"the least notion"*: Quoted in Eugen Weber, *Action Française* (Stanford, 1962), 423.

p. 332   *"pinhead"; "weaned on a pickle"*: Charles Loch Mowat, *Britain between the Wars* (London, 1968), 414.

p. 332   *passions in his policy*: Fuchser, *Chamberlain*, 11–12.

p. 332   *"continue my efforts"*: Ibid., 125–26.

p. 332   *"appeasement much more difficult"*: Ibid., 112.

p. 333   *"of the English people"*: Quoted in Gilbert and Gott, *Appeasers*, 128.

p. 333   *laissez-passer in Austria*: Alan Campbell Johnson, *Viscount Halifax* (New York, 1941), 439.

p. 333   *"maintain her in it"*: Gilbert and Gott, *Appeasers*, 111.

p. 333   *do so unaided*: Ibid.

p. 333   *"to that country"*: Ibid., 112.

p. 333   *"peace of the world"*: Henderson, *Failure*, 3.

p. 333   *"than Great Britain"*: Johnson, *Halifax*, 426.

p. 334   *"given by Mr. Newton"*: Henderson, *Failure*, 130.

p. 334   *"based on violence"*: Fuchser, *Chamberlain*, 116.

p. 334   *"attrition and starvation"*: John Dunbabin, "The British Military Establishment and the Policy of Appeasement," in Mommsen and Kettenacker, eds., *Fascist Challenge*, 185.

p. 334   *"business deal"*: C. A. MacDonald, *The United States, Britain and Appeasement, 1936–1939* (London, 1981), 76.

p. 334   *"demands for justice"*: Ibid., 87.

p. 335   *"fields of dead"*: Ibid.

p. 335   *"might as well say so"*: Duff Cooper, *Old Men Forget* (London, 1953), 218.

p. 335   *"only do harm"*: Text of Chamberlain's speech in Loewenheim, *Peace*, 7–10.

p. 336   *"as widely acclaimed"*: Fuchser, *Chamberlain*, 119.

p. 336   *"be the Bolshevists"*: Adamthwaite, "France," 248.

p. 336   *"hard-boiled and cynical"*: Alexander Werth, *France and Munich, 1939* (London, 1939), 137.

p. 336   *"the privileged class"*: Ibid.

p. 336   *"scale as in the Great War"*: Fuchser, *Chamberlain*, 123.

p. 336   *"demonstration of force"*: Ibid., 124.

p. 336   *"the peace of Europe"*: Gilbert and Gott, *Appeasers*, 116.

p. 337   *"become involved also"*: Fuchser, *Chamberlain*, 128.

p. 337   *"pigheaded of the lot"*: Gilbert and Gott, *Appeasers*, 135.

p. 337   *"matter of indifference"*: Ibid.

p. 337   *"in the near future"; "must be removed"*: Robbins, *Munich*, 227–28.

p. 338   *effective defiance*: Klaus-Jürgen Müller, *Armee, Politik und Gesellschaft in Deutschland, 1933–1945* (Paderborn, 1979), 97–100.

p. 338   *"haben unser'n Runciman"; "influence in Czechoslovakia"*: Gilbert and Gott, *Appeasers*, 130–31.

p. 338   *"pacification of the state"*: Taylor, *Munich*, 404.

p. 338   *"the other side"*: Ibid.

p. 339   *"irreconcilable enemy"*: Ibid., 408.

p. 339   *"note of that fact"*: Hitler quoted in David Dilks, ed., *The Diaries of Sir Alexander Cadogan, 1938–1945* (New York, 1975), 97.

p. 339   *"irritant effect"*: Ibid., 96.

p. 339   *"fate of hundreds of millions"*: Loewenheim, *Peace*, 19.

p. 339   *"given his word"*: Ibid., 133.

p. 339   *he was coming*: Fuschser, *Chamberlain*, 138.

p. 339   *"greatest living German"*: Gilbert and Gott, *Appeasers*, 36.

p. 339   *"did not want war"*: J. R. M. Butler, *Lord Lothian* (London, 1960), 203.

p. 340   *"security"; "were a woman"*: Gilbert and Gott, *Appeasers*, 22.

p. 340   *"a peaceful solution"*: Fuchser, *Chamberlain*, 140.

p. 340   *"lunatic at that"*: Loewenheim, *Peace*, 20.

p. 340   *"thunderstruck"*: Joachim Fest, *Hitler* (New York, 1974), 554.

p. 341   *"unprecedented a step"*: Fuchser, *Chamberlain*, 140.

p. 341 *"transfer of Czech territory"*: Ibid., 141.
p. 341 *"new Canossa"*: Vansittart quoted in Dilks, ed., *Cadogan Diaries,* 95.
p. 341 *"rendered impossible"*: Quoted in Werth, *France,* 259.
p. 341 *"towards Austria"*: Loewenheim, *Peace,* 132.
p. 341 *"extraordinary success"*: Chamberlain's record printed ibid., 21–27.
p. 342 *"alone prevented an invasion"*: Fuchser, *Chamberlain,* 144.
p. 342 *"commonest little dog"*: Cooper, *Old Men,* 229.
p. 342 *"meant what he said"*: Murray, *Change,* 200.
p. 342 *"undue predominance in Europe"*: Cooper, *Old Men,* 230.
p. 342 *bombs per day on Britain:* Murray, *Change,* 200.
p. 342 *"or—the U.S."*: Dilks, ed., *Cadogan Diaries,* 93.
p. 343 *"Germans in Czechoslovakia"*: Eduard Beneš, *Memoirs of Dr. Eduard Beneš* (Boston, 1953), 43.
p. 343 *"even being heard"*: Werth, *France,* 263.
p. 343 *"Sudeten Germans in Czechoslovakia"*: Beneš, *Memoirs,* 43.
p. 344 *"in variegated uniforms"*: Loewenheim, *Peace,* 76.
p. 344 *"Germanic heroic legend"*: Ibid., 135.
p. 344 *"das geht nicht mehr"*: Ibid., 77.
p. 344 *"claims be met"*: Ibid.
p. 344 *"by German troops"*: Ibid., 78.
p. 345 *"on its inhabitants"*: Ibid., 79.
p. 345 *"limit of concession"*: Murray, *Change,* 202–3.
p. 345 *"beloved Prime Minister"*: Harold Nicolson, *Diaries and Letters, 1930–1939* (New York, 1966), 364.
p. 345 *international commission:* Loewenheim, *Peace,* 43.
p. 346 *"ultimate outcome"*: Murray, *Change,* 209–10.
p. 346 *"in negotiations"*: Fuchser, *Chamberlain,* 151.
p. 346 *"war thereafter"*: Ibid.
p. 346 *"die for f—— Beneš"*: Weber, *Action Française,* 423.
p. 346 *"romance of modern warfare"*: Werth, *France,* 277.
p. 347 *"territory to be handed over"*: Text of Chamberlain letter in Loewenheim, *Peace,* 45–47.
p. 347 *"where I want her"*: Fest, *Hitler,* 556.
p. 347 *"repeated in a drawing room"*: Gilbert and Gott, *Appeasers,* 165.
p. 347 *"woman by woman"*: Text of Hitler's speech in Loewenheim, *Peace,* 47–52.
p. 347 *possible Russian intervention:* R. J. Overy, *Goering: The "Iron Man"* (London, 1984), 81.
p. 348 *review the troops:* William Shirer, *Berlin Diary* (New York, 1941), 142–43.
p. 348 *"subject of war"*: Fuchser, *Chamberlain,* 156.
p. 348 *"very last hour"*: John W. Wheeler-Bennett, *Munich: Prologue to Tragedy* (New York, 1964), 160.
p. 349 *"wipe Czechoslovakia off the map"*: Denis Mack Smith, *Mussolini: A Biography* (New York, 1983), 223.
p. 349 *"a fallen friend"*: Wheeler-Bennett, *Munich,* 166.
p. 349 *"answer will be"*: Fuchser, *Chamberlain,* 160.
p. 349 *"in the public gallery"*: Roy Douglas, *In the Year of Munich* (London 1977), 69.
p. 349 *"sacrificing principles"*: Ibid.
p. 349 *"sell us out"*: Taylor, *Munich,* 11.
p. 350 *"life were a drill"*: Lord Strang in Loewenheim, *Peace,* 139.
p. 350 *"hugger-mugger affair"*: Ibid., 138.
p. 350 *"moved his hearers"*: André François-Poncet, *The Fateful Years* (New York, 1949), 270.
p. 350 *"insignificant"; "governess of Europe"*: Taylor, *Munich,* 35.
p. 351 *"mediation plan"*: Fest, *Hitler,* 594.
p. 351 *"away his birthright"*: Kirkpatrick in Loewenheim, *Peace,* 86.
p. 351 *"cursed circumstances"*: François-Poncet, *Years,* 272.
p. 351 *Lord's work:* Taylor, *Munich,* 44.

p. 351 "absolutely alone": Ibid., 46.
p. 352 "restés fidèles": Quoted in Fest, Hitler, 565.
p. 352 "peace of Europe": Fuchser, Chamberlain, 162.
p. 352 "I've got it": Ibid., 163.
p. 352 "lick his boots": Mack Smith, Mussolini, 224.
p. 352 "dove to the eagle": Taylor, Munich, 59.
p. 353 "parade into Prague": Fest, Hitler, 566.
p. 353 "due to your work": Robbins, Munich, 321.
p. 353 "the fools": Werth, France, 320.
p. 353 newspaper celebration of Chamberlain: Robbins, Munich, 327.
p. 353 visit to Munich: Taylor, Munich, 64.
p. 353 "car to be shaken": Ibid.
p. 354 "justice and right": MacDonald, United States, 104–5.
p. 354 100,354 francs: Werth, France, 321.
p. 354 "peace for our time": Taylor, Munich, 65.
p. 354 "the olden time": Churchill, Gathering Storm, 293.
p. 354 "shall have war": Taylor, Munich, 978.
p. 355 "to swallow toads": Quoted in Fest, Hitler, 572.
p. 356 Chamberlain's defenders: Among the more important defenses of Chamberlain's policy are Roy Douglas, "Chamberlain and Appeasement," in Mommsen and Kettenacker, eds., Fascist Challenge, 79–88; Iain Macleod, "In Defense of Chamberlain," in Loewenstein, Peace, 161–73; Donald N. Lammers, Explaining Munich: The Search for Motive in British Policy (Stanford, 1966); Maurice Cowling, The Impact of Hitler (Chicago, 1975); Viscount Maugham, The Truth about the Munich Crisis (London, 1944); George E. Christ, The Myth of Munich (London, 1968).
p. 356 "vision of Empire": Ronald M. Smelser, "Nazi Dynamics, German Foreign Policy and Appeasement," in Mommsen and Kettenacker, eds., Fascist Challenge, 41.
p. 357 "conquest of Bohemia": Murray, Change, 222.
p. 357 bunkers had been completed: Ibid., 240.
p. 357 "technical personnel": Ibid., 246.
p. 357 production during World War I: Ibid., 257–58.
p. 358 nine-to-one edge in heavy artillery: Ibid., 240.
p. 358 "preparations to wage [war]": John Simon, Retrospect (London, 1952), 238.
p. 359 "at her side": Ibid., 239.
p. 359 "far worse": Taylor, Munich, 985.
p. 359 did in 1939: Murray, Change, 222; Taylor, Munich, 989–92.
p. 359 "exploitation of industry there": Overy, Goering, 82.
p. 360 "entered a European war": Helen Kirkpatrick, This Terrible Peace (London, 1939), 162.
p. 360 "surrender at Munich": Wheeler-Bennett, Munich, 434.
p. 361 "the great oracle": Kennedy, Realities, 297.
p. 362 "it lost Europe": Ibid., 293.

EPILOGUE

p. 364 "low dishonest decade": W. H. Auden, "September 1, 1939".
p. 365 "métèque [alien] speculators": Michael R. Marrus and Robert O. Paxton, Vichy France and the Jews (New York, 1983), 51.
p. 365 "Colbert or of Richelieu": Ibid., 53.
p. 365 "implementing Jewish policy": Ibid., 343.
p. 366 "the revenge of Dreyfus": Eugen Weber, Action Française (Stanford, 1962), 475.
p. 366 France's postwar reconstruction: On this see Robert O. Paxton, Vichy France (New York, 1972), 330–57.
p. 367 Soviet manipulation after 1945: On this see Fritz Fellner, "The Problem of the Austrian Nation after 1945," Journal of Modern History 60 (June 1988): 264–89.

p. 367   *exclusively to labor interests:* See Karl R. Stadler, *Austria* (London, 1971), 290.

p. 368   *"forces of restoration":* Gerhard Botz, "Österreich und die NS-Vergangenheit," in Dan Diner, ed., *Ist der Nationalsozialismus Geschichte?* (Frankfurt, 1987), 141.

p. 369   *the SS and the Nazi Party:* On this see especially Gotthart Breit, *Das Staats- und Gesellschaftsbild deutscher Generale beider Weltkriege im Spiegel ihrer Memoiren* (Boppard, 1973), 159–219.

p. 369   *"generations to come":* Die Zeit, Sept. 13, 1985.

p. 369   *"demonization":* For Nolte's views see especially his "Zwischen Geschichtslegende und Revisionismus?" and "Vergangenheit, die nicht vergehen will," both reprinted in *Historikerstreit* (Munich, 1987), 13–35, 39–47. For a perceptive critique of Nolte's comparison of Hitler's Holocaust to Stalin's attack on the kulaks, see Stefan Merl, " 'Ausrottung' der Bourgeoisie und der Kulaken in Sovjetrussland," *Geschichte und Gesellschaft* 13 (1987): 368–81.

p. 369   *"will not be forgotten":* Quoted in *NYT,* Oct. 28, 1988.

p. 370   *Bitburg:* On the Bitburg affair, see Geoffrey Hartman, ed., *Bitburg in Moral and Political Perspective* (Bloomington, 1986).

p. 370   *"had gone to rot":* F. W. Deakin, *The Brutal Friendship: Mussolini, Hitler, and the Fall of Italian Fascism* (London, 1962), 531.

p. 371   *by the League council:* James Barros, *The United Nations: Past, Present, and Future* (New York, 1972), 3.

p. 372   *if the United States disappeared:* Paul Kennedy, *The Rise and Fall of the Great Powers* (New York, 1987), 424.

p. 372   *"found a role":* Flora Lewis, *Europe* (New York, 1987), 34.

p. 373   *"re-run for their grandchildren":* MG, Aug. 23, 1980.

p. 373   *"I had ever seen":* Paul Theroux, *The Kingdom by the Sea* (Harmondsworth, 1984), 315–16.

p. 373   *"by the rest of society":* MG, Oct. 23, 1986.

p. 374   *placed on its reconstruction:* Manuel Leguineche, "A la sombra del arbol," *Geo* (Spanish edition), May 1987, 37.

p. 374   *homosexual lover:* Ian Gibson, *The Assassination of Federico García Lorca* (Harmondsworth, 1983), 183–210.

p. 374   *"anything about it":* Herbert Southworth, *Guernica! Guernica!* (Berkeley, 1977), 278–82.

p. 375   *"could have happened":* Vincente Talón, *Arde Guernica* (Madrid, 1970), 138.

p. 375   *"will be kaput":* Charles Thayer, *Hands across the Caviar* (Philadelphia, 1952), 190.

p. 375   *"our Negroes":* Gordon Craig, "The Other Russian Army," *New York Review of Books,* Nov. 24, 1988, 8.

p. 376   *"lost the war":* Zbigniew K. Brzezinski, *The Permanent Purge* (Cambridge, Mass., 1956), 155.

p. 376   *"medical treatment":* Adam Ulam, *Stalin* (Boston, 1987), 736.

p. 377   *"spitting on the nation's history":* Nikita Khrushchev, *Khrushchev Remembers* (Boston, 1970), 347.

p. 377   *"nihilistic elements":* International Herald Tribune, March 5–6, 1983.

p. 377   *along these lines:* Seweryn Bialer, *The Soviet Paradox* (New York, 1986), 98–99.

p. 377   *colleagues to admit:* NYT, Oct. 26, 1987.

p. 377   *"defense of its gains":* Ibid., Nov. 3, 1987.

p. 377   *"monster and a thug":* Ibid., Jan. 29, 1988.

p. 378   *Catholic church:* Jonathan Steele in *MG,* July 17, 1988.

p. 378   *cooperation with the West:* See Heinz Timmermann, "Gorbatschow—ein Bucharinist?" *Berichte des Bundesinstituts für ostwissenschaftliche und internationale Studien* 15 (1988):5.

p. 378   *"heretics or enemies":* MG, July 17, 1988.

p. 378   *"bourgeois historiography":* NYT, Oct. 26, 1987.

p. 378   *"was genuine":* International Herald Tribune, March 5–6, 1983.

p. 378   *"the motherland strong":* Ibid.

p. 379   *"final end of appeasement":* Quoted in Francis L. Loewenheim, *Peace or Appeasement? Hitler, Chamberlain, and the Munich Crisis* (Boston, 1965), 157.

p. 379   *"diplomatist's vocabulary":* Ibid., 160.

p. 379   *"in 1938–9 with Hitler":* Walter Isaacson and Evan Thomas, *The Wise Men* (New York, 1986), 439.

p. 379   *Czechoslovakia in the thirties:* Richard E. Neustadt and Ernest R. May, *Thinking in Time* (New York, 1986), 89.

p. 379   *carry an umbrella":* Michael R. Beschloss, *Mayday* (New York, 1986), 104.

p. 379   *"Chamberlain umbrella man":* Isaacson and Thomas, *Wise Men,* 642.

p. 380   *"maintain its freedom":* Quoted in Larry Fuchser, *Neville Chamberlain and Appeasement* (New York, 1982), 3.

p. 380   *"totalitarian aggression"; "appropriate analogy":* Time, Oct. 3, 1988, 37.

p. 380   *"repeat its mistakes":* Fuchser, *Chamberlain,* 4.

p. 380   *"from doing so":* Keith Robbins, *Munich 1938* (London, 1968), 4–5.

p. 381   *"immediate war":* Webster quoted in Loewenheim, *Peace,* 190.

Index

italicized page numbers refer to photographs